ALSO BY ALAN BRINKLEY

Voices of Protest:
Huey Long, Father Coughlin, and the Great Depression

The End of Reform:
New Deal Liberalism in Recession and War

The Unfinished Nation

Liberalism and Its Discontents

Franklin Delano Roosevelt

The Publisher

The Publisher

Henry Luce and
His American Century

ALAN BRINKLEY

ALFRED A. KNOPF   NEW YORK   2010

THIS IS A BORZOI BOOK
PUBLISHED BY ALFRED A. KNOPF

Published in the United States by Alfred A. Knopf,
a division of Random House, Inc., New York, and in Canada
by Random House of Canada Limited, Toronto.
www.aaknopf.com

Knopf, Borzoi Books, and the colophon are
registered trademarks of Random House, Inc.

A portion of this work originally appeared in *Vanity Fair*.

Library of Congress Cataloging-in-Publication Data
Brinkley, Alan.
The publisher : Henry Luce and his American century / by Alan Brinkley.—1st ed.
p.   cm.
Includes bibliographical references.
ISBN 978-0-679-41444-5
1. Luce, Henry Robinson, 1898–1967.   2. Journalists—United States—
Biography.   3. Publishers and publishing—United States—Biography.
4. Periodicals—Publishing—United States—History—20th century.   I. Title.
PN4874.L76B75 2010
070.5092—dc22
[B]   2009038834

Manufactured in the United States of America
First Edition

For Evangeline

CONTENTS

Preface

In May 1966 Henry R. Luce—cofounder of what became the largest and most influential magazine empire in America—agreed to participate in an exclusive television interview for the first time in his life. Luce was then sixty-eight years old and had retired as editor in chief of Time Inc. two years earlier. But he remained a figure of fascination to many Americans—all the more so because he was so seldom seen by the many people who were influenced, fascinated, and sometimes outraged by the contents of his magazines.

His interviewer was Eric Goldman, a Princeton historian who had recently worked in the Johnson White House and who now hosted an austere NBC program called *Open Mind.* Goldman was a courteous and respectful interviewer but not a tame one, and he pressed Luce on a number of controversial issues that had swirled around him through much of his life. Were the magazines Luce had launched—*Time, Fortune, Life,* and *Sports Illustrated*—"Republican magazines"? Was there an inherent "conservative outlook" in them? Did his "own attitudes and convictions shape the contents" of his magazines? Had he "stepped over the line" in promoting Republican candidates he had particularly admired and openly supported—Wendell Willkie, Dwight Eisenhower? And most of all, did Luce's many interventions in the debate over America's international policies represent "a kind of modern-day American imperialism"?

Luce sat slouched in his chair through most of the hour, his clothes slightly rumpled, his tie askew, his pants pulled up over his crossed legs.

He looked gaunt, and he had an alert, slightly restless demeanor. He rambled in conversation, often stopping in midsentence and starting over again, circling around questions before actually answering them, sometimes speaking so fast that he seemed to be trying to outrace the stammer that had troubled him in childhood and that occasionally revived in moments of stress. But he responded to Goldman's prodding without rancor. "One gets the feeling," Goldman said, "that you have a view of a kind of American mission in the world . . . to go out and to bring these nations into a type of civilization much like our own." Luce—whose famous 1941 essay "The American Century" had said exactly that—noted that his 1941 views had been shaped by the circumstances of World War II. But he did not refute Goldman's claim. Europe "would not be able to lead the world in the sense it had for a couple of centuries," he said. "The burden of leadership would fall more and more on the United States . . . and this burden of leadership necessarily would want to be in the direction of those ideals which we presume to acknowledge."

As the conversation moved to Asia, Luce's preoccupation through much of his life, his long-standing grievances became more apparent. He refuted Goldman's suggestion that other nations should "pursue their own, different paths" and that America should not be troubled by a Communist China. Although he admitted that there was little the United States could do in 1966 to topple the Communist regime, he continued to lament America's earlier failure to "save" China when, he insisted, it had still been possible to do so. "I think we [had] an obligation to restore Chiang Kai-shek to the position he had before the war," he said of the 1940s. "It was by no means inevitable that China had to go Communist." He still could not "excuse the American government."[1]

One could have imagined a very different interview with Henry Luce—one that would have focused on the extraordinary success of his magazines, the great power he had wielded as a result, the ideas for which he fought, the enormous wealth he had accumulated, the remarkable network of powerful people who had become part of his world, even his marriage to one of the most famous women in America. For decades he had been among the most influential men in America— courted by presidents, feared by rivals, capable of raising some people to prominence and pulling others down. It must have been frustrating to him that his first (and only) television interview was dominated by the criticisms he had heard through much of his career. For as he neared the end of his life, what meant most to him was his effort to make a difference in history—to embrace a mission that would somehow justify his work and his life.

Like many Americans of my generation, I grew up with the Luce magazines without knowing very much about them. My parents read *Time* for years with consistent interest and frequent irritation. *Life* was the first magazine to which I subscribed. And a bit later, like many boys of my generation, I was an enthusiastic reader of *Sports Illustrated*. As I began my life as a historian, I encountered Luce's "The American Century." In the grim, antiwar climate of the 1970s, the essay seemed to me an obsolete relic of an earlier, more muscular, and now repudiated American age. Little did I know how soon its sentiments would be popular again.[2]

Many years later, as I began thinking about writing a biography of Luce, I started reading a series of letters between the young Harry Luce and his father, a missionary in China. He and his family were seldom together after Harry began attending boarding school—first in China, then in the United States—starting when he was ten years old. His family was a close one, and he sustained his relationship with them through an extraordinary correspondence that continued for years and introduced me to a remarkable young man. Luce was an ambitious child, just as he became an ambitious adult. He was a striver from his earliest years, always aware of his own formidable intelligence, never satisfied with his achievements—in school as in the later periods of his life. He was often a lonely boy—feeling abandoned in a British boarding school in China when he was young, marginalized at times as a scholarship student at Hotchkiss, unskilled in developing deep friendships and sustained intimacy. But in his letters home, at least when he was young, he revealed another part of himself—a person who was unafraid to reveal his weaknesses and failures, a young man who struggled not only to be successful, but also, like his revered father, to be virtuous. That struggle would be a part of him throughout his life. It was from my immersion in his early, remarkably documented life that I began to understand the man he would later become.

Luce was not alone among missionary children who became important public figures later in life. Like young Harry, many others were influenced by the shining example of their ambitious, virtuous parents and the great sacrifices they chose to make for their faith and for the improvement of others. And many missionary children, like Luce, went on to distinguished public careers in diplomacy, politics, academia, literature, and other influential endeavors.

. . .

One of the first major biographies of Luce, W. A. Swanberg's *Luce and His Empire*—published in 1972, five years after Luce's death—reflected the strong opinions many of Luce's contemporaries had developed about him. It portrayed Luce as a relentless polemicist, whose magazines were more vehicles of propaganda and opinion than of reporting and journalism. In my copy of Swanberg's book—a used one I picked up years ago at the Strand in New York—some earlier reader had written in pencil on the flyleaf: "A great hatchet job, and 99 percent true."[3]

To Swanberg, to that anonymous defacer, and to many others who came to distrust and even despise Luce over the years, what seemed important about his career was his arrogance, his dogmatism, and his reactionary, highly opinionated politics—all of which found reflection in the contents of his magazines. Henry Luce was indeed arrogant. He was often dogmatic, particularly on issues he cared deeply about and thought he understood. He was famously opinionated, and he showed no hesitation about insisting that his opinions be reflected in the editorial content of his magazines. And on some issues—China, the Cold War, Communism, capitalism, the Republican Party—he developed deep and largely unshakable opinions that sometimes blinded him to the realities around him.

But Luce was other things as well. Those who worked for him often bridled at his interference and his orders; some left the company in frustration. But almost all of them considered him brilliant, creative, even magnetic. On many issues that were not part of his personal obsessions, he was tolerant and inquisitive, eager for new information and new ideas, even receptive to challenges and contradictions. Like Luce himself, his magazines had many dimensions. They were both polemical and fair-minded, both reactionary and progressive, both dogmatic and tolerant, both rigidly formulaic and highly creative. They were the great American magazines of their time: great in their flaws but also great in their breadth, originality, and creativity.

The construction of Luce's publishing empire is part of a much larger phenomenon of the middle years of the twentieth century: the birth of a national mass culture designed primarily to serve a new and rapidly expanding middle class. That new culture had many vehicles: newspaper chains, movies, radio, and eventually television. But those years were also the heyday of national magazines, and the Luce magazines were the most successful, popular, and influential of them all. More than most figures in American publishing, Luce gave his magazines a distinctive and reasonably consistent voice—to some degree his own voice. The magazines were in many ways very different from one another, but they all reflected a set of values and assumptions in which Luce believed and that he assumed were (or at least should be) universal. Part of his considerable achievement was his ability to provide an image of American life that helped a generation of readers believe in an alluring, consensual image of the nation's culture.

By the time of Luce's death in 1967, although he himself may not have realized it, his magazines were already on their way either to obsolescence or to a very different future. *Life* died in 1972. *Time*, *Fortune*, and even *Sports Illustrated* gradually ceased to be the assured voices of a common culture. They became by necessity the chroniclers of a much more fragmented and visibly conflicted world—a role that left them with much less influence and coherence (and, at least for a time, with much less profitability) than they had once enjoyed. But in the four decades of Luce's dominance, he never stopped believing that he could understand the changing world in which he lived, and that he could use his magazines to shape a better future.

The Publisher

I

Americans Abroad

In the beginning they were a tiny vanguard, clinging precariously to the rim of the great Chinese landmass—a few earnest, lonely, often frightened men and women engaged in an almost entirely futile enterprise. They lived among Western merchants but shared little with them. For their task was not to build trade. It was to save souls.

Generations later, China became a major target of Western capitalism—and a target as well of a much larger and more ambitious missionary project. The missionaries' task remained difficult and in the end mostly unsuccessful. But they were no longer lonely and less often frightened, and they promoted not just Christian faith, but Western progress. The legacy of these missionaries was not only their work, but also the work of their children who inherited their parents' ambition and their sense of duty to do good in the world. Henry R. Luce was one such person—a man whose great power and influence always reflected his childhood among what he considered modern saints, his father among them, and from whom he inherited his own missionary zeal, which he carried with him into the secular world.

The first Christian missionaries in China were Italian Jesuits, who arrived in the late sixteenth century, flourished for a time as favorites of the imperial court, lost that favor as a result of doctrinal controversies, and were mainly gone by the 1790s, having converted few and antagonized many. Early in the nineteenth century some American Catholic

priests traveled east from Turkey and Palestine and, like their Jesuit predecessors, entered China alone. They too confronted a complex, sophisticated, insular society whose language they could not speak and whose
culture they did not understand. Few stayed for very long.[1]

Starting in the 1830s, as scattered English and American trading
outposts grew up along the Chinese coast, another wave of missionaries
arrived, this time mostly Protestants. They attached themselves and
their families, somewhat uneasily, to the coastal merchant posts and seldom strayed far from them. They were large in ambition but small in
numbers. In the decades before the American Civil War, the American
Board of Commissioners for Foreign Missions—the principal recruiter
of missionaries in the United States—sent only forty-six ordained missionaries (and another fifty or so spouses, relatives, and assistants) into
all of East Asia, fewer than half of them to China. Perhaps that was
because those they did send were so singularly unsuccessful. Protestant
missionaries spent eighteen years in China before they won their first
native convert.[2]

The Chinese did not become very much more interested in Christianity in the latter decades of the nineteenth century than they had been
during the earlier ones. But missionaries became a great deal more interested in China. That was partly because of the expansion of the Western
presence in Asia, as American and European businessmen built railroads, created oil companies, and extended their reach inland from the
coast. Their growing presence helped open up new areas for missionary
activity. More important to the future of the missionary project, however, were events in England and America—several profound shifts in
both the theological and institutional foundations of Anglo-American
Protestantism.

The social upheavals of the industrial era and the great scientific
advances of the late nineteenth century—most notably the widespread
acceptance in England and America of Darwin's theory of evolution—
had produced a crisis of faith in many Protestant denominations. Most
Anglo-American Protestants responded by moving down one of two
new theological paths. One was the road that led, in many cases, to fundamentalism: a fervent defense of traditional theology and a rejection of
the new science that seemed to challenge it. But it was also an inspirational belief, because it suggested that preparation for the Second Coming of Christ, when only Christians would be saved and redeemed,
required strenuous efforts to expand the community of believers.[3]

Other Protestants—many of whom eventually came to call them-

selves modernists—chose to accept Darwinism and other scientific discoveries and to adapt their faith to them. Evolution, they argued, was an
even more inspirational story than the literal Creation, because it
described continuing progress and development through the ages—a
process to which they believed living men and women could usefully
contribute. It helped inspire the large, diverse movement among late-
nineteenth- and early-twentieth-century Protestants that became known
as the "Social Gospel," a commitment to combining faith with active
efforts to solve the social problems of the industrial world.[4]

These emerging Protestant factions were at odds with one another
on many issues, but they converged, even if somewhat uncomfortably at
times, on one of the great Christian projects of the late nineteenth century: the dispatching of thousands of missionaries out into the world.
One source of the new missionary fervor was a Bible conference in the
summer of 1886 in northern Massachusetts convened by Dwight
Moody, a Methodist layman who became one of the most influential
evangelists of his time. More than one hundred college students
emerged from Moody's conference having pledged themselves to
become missionaries. Their commitment was the beginning of a wave of
student interest that over the next two years attracted more than two
thousand additional volunteers and that inspired the creation, late in
1888, of the Student Volunteer Movement for Foreign Missions. It soon
became the largest and most influential student movement in the nation
and spread as well to Canada, Great Britain, Ireland, Australia, New
Zealand, and the European continent. By the end of World War I the
Student Volunteer Movement (SVM) had dispatched more than eight
thousand American missionaries from the United States to foreign
lands.[5]

For Moody himself and for many of the student converts, the inspiration for the volunteer movement was the desire to prepare the world
for, and thus hasten, the imminent coming of Christ. "The Evangelization of the World in this Generation" was the ambitious, urgent slogan
of the new movement. Its most important text was Arthur T. Pierson's
The Crisis of Missions, published in 1886. "The fullness of time has
come," Pierson wrote, "and the end seems at hand, which is also the
beginning of the last and greatest age. . . . Such facts mark and make the
crisis of the missions. Now or never! Tomorrow will be too late for work
that must be done today. . . . He who lags behind will be left behind."
For evangelists, he insisted, "the field is the world."[6]

But the Student Volunteer Movement also attracted modernists, to whom the end did not seem near and who considered missionary work not just a project of leading believers to Christ but also an effort to uplift the oppressed and improve the life of the world. The president of the Union Theological Seminary in New York argued that "the gospel for heathen lands is not alone a gospel of deliverance for a life to come, but a gospel of social renewal for the life that now is—a gospel that patiently and thoroughly renovates heathen life in its personal, domestic, civic, tribal, national practices and tendencies." The task of the missions, many volunteers came to believe, was to produce educated elites in "heathen" lands—"a thinking class, a class of leaders," one missionary wrote—who would be capable both of spreading the faith and of improving society.[7]

Although the Student Volunteer Movement sent missionaries to many parts of the world, some evangelists considered China their greatest and most important challenge: the world's most populous nation, most of whose hundreds of millions of souls had never been exposed to Christianity. "China for Christ" was their rallying cry, and it drew to the Chinese missions the most committed and indomitable of the young volunteers, a new generation, charged with an energy and zeal that transformed and expanded the missionary enterprise.[8]

Among the many energetic, idealistic students attracted to the Student Volunteer Movement in the 1880s was the Yale undergraduate Henry Winters Luce. He was born in 1868 into a moderately prosperous family in Scranton, Pennsylvania; his father owned a wholesale grocery business and was a member of the town's commercial gentry, a society Henry for many years expected to enter. As a young man he displayed what was for his time a more or less ordinary Christian faith. He participated in the youth activities of the Presbyterian Church and joined the Young People's Society of Christian Endeavor, commitments balanced against an active social life outside the church community. But he had something more than ordinary energy and ambition. His desire to attend Yale, and his father's willingness to send him there, was itself evidence of his own and his parents' exceptional expectations, for in the 1880s going to university—particularly to one as distinguished by its elitism as Yale—was unusual for Scranton, even for the son of a comfortably middle-class family.[9]

As a member of the Yale class of 1892, Harry Luce (as he was known to his classmates) at first followed a relatively conventional path. He pursued the prescribed, largely classical curriculum but also began preparing himself for a career in the law. He joined clubs, became editor of the *Yale Courant* (a weekly magazine that was the least prestigious of the four campus publications of its time), engaged in spirited arguments with his classmates (developing a reputation as a man of very firm opinions), and became active in the YMCA—for which he also worked in Scranton during the summers. But the most important thing that happened to him at Yale was almost certainly his friendship with Horace Pitkin, a mesmerizing young man of intimidating religiosity. Pitkin shunned liquor, cards, and dancing, and refused to attend events at which any of those things might occur. "He took a stronger stand than any man in the college," a classmate commented. When he and his friends gathered at night in their rooms at Yale, Pitkin led them in prayer before any ordinary conversation could begin.[10]

Pitkin decided very early that his life would be devoted to the ministry. He became the leader of the Student Volunteer Movement at Yale and committed himself both to joining a foreign mission himself and to persuading others to do so as well. Luce resisted for a time, but in his senior year he finally succumbed to Pitkin's daunting, inspiring example. According to his own later accounts he experienced an irresistible call to the faith while reading a devotional pamphlet, and he announced to his startled but ultimately supportive family that he would not return to Scranton to read law. He would instead attend divinity school and seek a posting abroad, perhaps in China (where Pitkin also hoped to go). "God willing," he wrote from college, using the language of his new religious fervor, ". . . I propose to go into the foreign field and witness for Him as best I may in the uttermost parts of the earth."[11]

Luce and Pitkin moved together from Yale to the Union Theological Seminary in New York, a nondenominational institution that gradually became a bastion of liberal theology. The two men, and another Yale friend, Sherwood Eddy, met every day (in Luce's words) "to pray over the things pertaining to 'our great purpose.'" After two semesters at Union, Luce, Pitkin, and Eddy all spent a year as traveling evangelists for the SVM. Luce worked mostly in the American South, where he apparently recruited many new volunteers with his now well-honed religious eloquence and where he also developed a lifelong commitment to racial equality. The following year he enrolled at Princeton Theological Seminary, earned ordination and a degree in 1896, and began traveling for the SVM once again, including another period in the South, where he raised funds for his own posting abroad. He had heard much about the revered missionary Calvin Mateer, who had established a small school in Shantung,* China, in the 1860s. By the 1890s it had grown to include a college for Chinese converts to Christianity. Mateer was an important spokesman for combining evangelism with efforts at education and social improvement, and his progressive image of missionary work matched Luce's own generally modernist sensibility. Luce requested assignment to work with Mateer in China.[12]

On a visit home to Scranton, he met Elisabeth Root, an attractive, well-educated, somewhat reserved young woman who had grown up in Utica, New York, in an unhappy middle-class family blighted by divorce. She was operating a hostel for factory girls run by the YWCA—a classic Social Gospel project. She met Harry at a weekday prayer service, and their mutual attraction was almost immediate. Although Elisabeth did not share Luce's exuberantly evangelistic temper, she was a woman of deep and active faith ("*very* religious," a daughter-in-law once recalled of her, not altogether kindly). In later years she often sent her children long letters consisting entirely of prayers copied from religious tracts. Her earnest charm attracted Luce; his energy and faith attracted her. They were married on June 1, 1897 (in the Presbyterian church Harry had attended through most of his life and in which he had been formally ordained less than two weeks before). Three months later, after the SVM persuaded James Linen, a Luce family friend in Scranton, to pledge one thousand dollars to support the young couple, Harry and Elisabeth sailed for China, having already conceived their first child.[13]

The opportunities for missionaries in China were a great deal more expansive when Harry and Elisabeth arrived there in 1897 than they had been a generation before. The Western imperial powers—particularly Britain, Germany, France, and the United States—had wrested new concessions from the feeble provincial governments and the even feebler imperial court in Beijing. They had built more railroads, established more businesses, and in some areas—especially Shanghai—created whole urban districts built and populated by Europeans. It was much easier, and seemingly much safer, for Westerners to move around China than it had been earlier in the century.

---

*I have chosen here not to use the modern transliteration of Chinese place-names. Instead (with the exception of Beijing and Shanghai), I have tried to use the Western place-names that Luce used in his own time. For the names of Chinese people known to Luce, I have used the traditional Wade-Giles form of Luce's time (for example, Chiang Kai-shek, Sun Yat-sen), but pinyin for other historical names.

But missionaries had made contributions of their own to the expansion of their enterprise. Discouraged by their inability to win converts through evangelization alone, they set out to build schools and colleges and to create missionary compounds, where Western clergy could find communities of like-minded people with whom to live. Shantung, in northeast China, was a particularly attractive destination for Western missionaries, with its long coastline and its important ports. It was one of China's most densely populated regions (even after the departure or death of four million people after floods and famines earlier in the nineteenth century). The growing presence of prosperous German and British businesses eased the lives of missionaries, but it did little to alleviate the great poverty of the vast majority of the Chinese population. The wretchedness of most of the province reinforced the Westerners' belief that they must work to lift China out of its backwardness and into their own modern world.[14]

The Luces joined Calvin Mateer in the small Christian college he had established at Tengchow, on the Shantung coast. (Their friend Horace Pitkin, now married and a father, was several hundred miles west in Paotingfu—separated from them by a slow and arduous journey that prevented regular visits, although they joined one another on a seaside vacation in the summer of 1898.) The Tengchow college was a modest place: a walled compound containing a little church, a small observatory, and a few red-brick buildings, among them some spartan homes shared by several missionary families. Both Luces set out quickly to learn the Chinese language, since Mateer himself had been something of a pioneer among missionaries both in learning Chinese and in translating the Bible into the language. Harry learned Mandarin without tremendous difficulty. But Elisabeth did not. Her letters to friends at home described days devoted almost entirely to prayer, Bible reading, and above all "Chinese study," often three times a day for a total of six to seven hours. For all her agonizing efforts, however, she never developed any real facility in the language, perhaps because of her partial deafness, the result of a childhood attack of scarlet fever. She finally gave up language study and focused her energies on her household. She was known to the other missionaries, according to friends, as "wickedly clean" and a "great house-keeper," which to Anglo-Americans in China—as in much of the Victorian middle class in America and England—generally meant managing the household staff effectively. Her Chinese servants (with whom she could barely converse) "always looked better than any of the rest. She had them keep their garments clean and no wrinkles." She was also a voracious reader, and as her enthusiasm for studying Chinese faded, she spent more and more time reading the Western literature that she and her neighbors had brought with them and shared with one another.[15]

Harry was a dynamo almost from the moment he arrived in Teng-chow. His reverence for Mateer, nurtured from afar, increased on exposure to him, a tall, imposing man with a great white beard, reminiscent of an Old Testament figure who both inspired and intimidated. But even more than Mateer, Luce exhorted the small missionary community to take education more seriously. Evangelization alone would win few converts to the faith, he argued. Only by demonstrating Christianity's capacity to improve the conditions of life could Westerners hope to draw larger numbers of Chinese into the faith. His own first assignment at the college was a course on physics—a subject he had never previously studied, and which he had to teach in a language he was only just learning. He plunged into the task with the same enthusiasm and commitment he brought to nearly everything he did.[16]

In these first months, as throughout Luce's long career in China, he met resistance from less enthusiastically progressive missionaries. Many of them believed that no reform was possible until *after* the triumph of Christianity, and saw little hope of improving conditions in China except through conversion. Such views had theological origins. They also had social roots—the discouragement of missionaries who found the Chinese elite almost wholly resistant to them, which left the Westerners little choice but to work with the poor and uneducated. It was no wonder, perhaps, that some began to develop a real contempt for the people they were trying to help. Such views found expression in the widely read book *Chinese Characteristics*, published in 1894 by the American missionary Arthur H. Smith. In building his argument that the Chinese were essentially irredeemable within their present culture, Smith presented a numbingly contemptuous portrait of them in chapters titled "The Disregard of Time," "The Disregard of Accuracy," "The Talent for Misunderstanding," "Contempt for Foreigners," "The Absence of Public Spirit," "The Absence of Sympathy," and "The Absence of Sincerity." But his most important critique was of China's spiritual weakness: "Its absolute indifference to the profoundest spiritual truths in the nature of man is the most melancholy characteristic of the Chinese mind," he concluded. "In order to reform China the springs of character must be reached and purified. . . . What China needs is righteousness," and that need "will be met permanently, completely, only by Christian civilization." Smith and others drew encouragement from the substantial increase in Chinese converts in the last decades of the nineteenth century: from a few hundred in 1850 to one hundred thousand in 1900, an increase that could not be explained by any significant improvement in social conditions. That remained a tiny percentage of China's nearly half-billion population, and it seemed likely that not even all the ostensible converts really understood what conversion to Christianity meant. Even so, some missionaries argued that if conversions continued to increase exponentially at the same rate by which they had grown since 1870, China would be a predominantly Christian nation within a generation or two. Luce did not share their optimism. Conditions in China were so bad, he said, that it was irresponsible to focus on conversion alone. He believed, rather, in respecting Chinese culture and religion while at the same time educating and elevating the Chinese to Western levels. If such efforts were successful, Luce's students might decide on their own to embrace Christianity.[17]

But even he did not fully understand the volatility of Chinese society and the precariousness of the missionary project. The Luce family's arrival in Shantung had roughly coincided not only with the crumbling of the Qing dynasty and the collapse of local political authority, but also with the rise in northern China of a large, secret, paramilitary society that (not without reason) blamed China's troubles on Westerners and pledged itself to purge the nation of "foreign devils." It called itself the Society of the Righteous and Harmonious Fists, but it was known to Westerners as the "Boxers" (because of its emphasis on martial arts). Its members were mostly poor peasants, coolies, and destitute former soldiers. They had no strong leaders, few weapons, and modest resources, but they did have a fervent commitment to their cause and a fanatical belief that they were invulnerable to bullets. In 1899, less than two years after the Luces arrived in Shantung, the Boxers staged a murderous rebellion. They rampaged through towns and cities, killing whatever Westerners they could find (mostly missionaries, about 135 in all) as well as a much larger number of Chinese converts to Christianity—perhaps as many as thirty thousand, nearly a third of the total. One of their victims was Horace Pitkin. In the absence of his family, who were visiting relatives in America, he had refused to flee from Paotingfu with other missionaries. "We must sit still, do our work—and then take whatever is sent us quietly," he wrote a friend. He was captured and killed by the Boxers, who then paraded his corpse through the streets.[18]

The Luces were more prudent, and also more fortunate, than Horace Pitkin, since Tengchow was on the Shantung coast. The family stole away from the missionary compound after dark one night. Guided by their Chinese nurse, they raced through nearby fields and arrived (still in darkness) at the docks, where a ship was waiting to take them and other refugees first to the Chinese port city Chefoo (now Yangtai) and then to Korea, where they stayed until after the rebellion was finally and brutally suppressed. In the summer of 1900 a combined force of European, American, and Japanese troops descended on Beijing to rescue a group of Western diplomats under siege in their walled compound, crushed the Boxers, and—in a rampage of their own—killed many other Chinese in the process. They then extracted reparations and further concessions from the now permanently crippled imperial government, which survived for only another twelve years with minimal authority.[19]

Some of the missionaries who had survived the Boxers were, for a while, consumed with vengeance and indeed seemed at times as bloodthirsty as the Boxers themselves. They exhorted the Western troops to punish the Chinese even more ferociously than they already had; a few actually joined the soldiers and led them to people they believed had been instrumental in fomenting the rebellion. There were even reports of missionaries looting Chinese homes to compensate themselves for their own lost property. Although such incidents were probably rare, the American press made much of them and, in the process, tarnished the image of the missionaries in the United States and Britain. At the same time, however, the martyrdom of the murdered Christians aroused many American evangelicals, and a large new wave of missionaries began flowing into China in the first years after the rebellion.[20]

Luce returned to China deeply shaken by Pitkin's death and chastened by the evidence the rebellion had given of the frailty of the missionary enterprise. But he was not one of those who called for vengeance. Instead he became more than ever determined to understand the Chinese and to help them improve their society. He began agitating immediately to move the college inland from its remote location on the coast to the provincial capital, Tsinan, where it could become a much more visible and important presence in the life of Shantung. Because of lack of funds and inadequate resolve among his colleagues, he was forced to compromise. The theological school and the primary and secondary schools remained in Tengchow. Only the medical college moved to Tsinan. But in 1904 the arts and sciences college, in which Luce taught, moved to Wei Hsien, a more central area in the interior, where it had access to a much larger local population. It could not have been lost on the members of the college that their new, well-fortified compound— which they shared with an English Baptist missionary community—was built near the site of an earlier mission station that had been destroyed by the Boxers.[21]

Luce had a compelling reason to flee the Boxers in 1900 and to concili- ate the Chinese on his return: He was now a father. His first child, a son, was born on April 3, 1898, and was baptized soon after by Mateer (in a Presbyterian ceremony conducted in Chinese) as Henry Robinson Luce. His middle name was chosen in honor of the Luce family's pastor in Scranton. Like his father, he was always known as Harry.[22]

Harry and Elisabeth were besotted by their new baby, and like many parents attributed to him from the beginning characteristics of bril- liance, even greatness. Elisabeth, in particular, focused almost constant attention on the infant. She kept a journal of his development ("Nov. 11 baby got up in crib—2 or 3 days before he was 8 mos old"); and she drew sketches of his room noting the position of furniture and the locations of his favorite toys. Her preoccupation with her son did not prevent her from hiring a Chinese nurse, or amah, to look after the child, who taught him his first words, in Chinese. (It was the amah who arranged for the family's escape to Korea during the Boxer Rebellion, at what must have been considerable danger to herself.)[23]

Back in Tengchow after their fearful months in exile, the Luces became even more preoccupied with young Harry and began educating him in the home (like most other missionary families) at the age of three. By the time he was five he was already writing simple letters (almost cer- tainly with his mother's help) to his frequently absent father ("I will be glad when you get home. . . . I think the new testament better than the old") and copying out prayers in his notebooks. The unsurprising ubiq- uity of religion in the home and the community shaped the child's early life. Just as young American children in other places might imitate base- ball players or cowboys, Harry mimicked the clergy, who were almost the only adult males he knew. Listening to sermons was one of the most eagerly anticipated activities in mission communities; and at the age of four Harry began delivering his own impromptu sermons occasionally while standing on a barrel in front of his house, no doubt borrowing from those he had heard in church.[24]

Young Harry was soon joined by two sisters, Emmavail, born in 1900 (just weeks before the family fled to Korea), and Elisabeth, born in

1904. Five years later the last of the Luce children, Sheldon, was born. Harry, however, remained the center of the family's world. He was the eldest child and (until he was eleven and away at school) the only boy. His father was often away, and during his absences, young Harry was the only male in a family of women, and the consistent focus of their attention.[25]

To a notable degree, family life in the missionary compound resembled that of middle-class Victorian America or England. When the family moved in 1904 to Wei Hsien, where the college built a more substantial but still relatively modest walled compound, the Luces lived in makeshift quarters—as they had in Tengchow—until they were finally able to move into a new, comfortable two-story house (financed for them by a patron in the United States) with broad, sloping roofs and wide verandas. They filled it with Western furniture, decorative items, and household goods—including the white damask tablecoths and napkins they invariably used for their meals and for the lavish afternoon teas Elisabeth liked to prepare. Their income was small but vastly greater than that of all but a few Chinese, so they were able to afford a substantial staff of servants—at times as many as six—who relieved both the children and their mother of household chores. Instead they spent their time in lessons. Elisabeth was their first teacher, and she continued to involve herself closely with the children's education until they went away to school. After a time, however, the Luces hired a severe German governess, a reflection of the turn-of-the-century conviction that German scholarship was the best in the world. Young Harry, who thought governesses were inappropriate for boys, rebelled, and so his mother took over much of his instruction again. When not engaged in lessons, the children prayed and studied the Bible with their parents, or gathered to hear their mother read to them from her growing library of English poetry and fiction.[26]

Despite the exotic surroundings it was an extraordinarily insular life. Outside the compound were the fetid villages and devastated landscapes of a desperately poor region. Harry's sister Elisabeth later recalled being able to look out her second-story window, over the walls (on the tops of which broken glass had been carefully scattered to discourage intruders), at a barren landscape stretching as far as she could see. Virtually all the trees had been cut down for firewood or building supplies. Only in the cemeteries—sacred places where trees could not be touched—was it possible to see any greenery. Inside the compound were the neatly tended homes and gardens of a middle-class Anglo-American community. There were even rows of trees, many of them planted and lovingly tended by the senior Harry Luce. The Luce children found friends among the sons and daughters of the other missionaries. There were about a dozen boys roughly the same age as Harry, with whom he often played tennis (on the college's one clay court) and other games.[27]

It was a world of greater social and intellectual homogeneity than anything its inhabitants could have experienced in America or England; a world of like-minded men and women, most of them well educated and from upper-middle-class backgrounds, engaged in common pursuits and focused on shared interests. The contrast between the ordered, harmonious world of the missionary compound and the harsh physical and social landscape outside it reinforced the assumptions driving the missionary project: the unquestioned belief in the moral superiority of Christianity and in the cultural superiority of Western culture; the commitment to showing the way to Christ, but also—for Henry W. Luce and many other missionaries—a commitment to creating in China a modern, scientific social order based on the American and European models.

Except for the servants who cleaned their houses and cooked their meals (preparing primarily Western food), the children had virtually no contact with the Chinese. Their occasional excursions outside the compound were carefully supervised sightseeing tours; and even when Harry was old enough to venture out alone or with his friends—on his own, prized donkey—he tended to ride through the countryside, not the town, exploring the landscape, not the people. Later, writing from school in America, he urged his parents to let his seven-year-old brother, Sheldon, see more of China than he himself had done. "I feel that I made a great mistake in not exploring Wei Hsien as thoroughly as I explored the meaningless wheat fields and grave mounds for miles around the compound," he confessed. "I don't know enough about Chinese mercantile life, and I know nothing about their social life aside from the formal feasts and holidays. For instance, what do Chinese talk about over their pipes?" He also knew little of the language. Whatever Chinese he had picked up from his amahs as a young child he had largely lost even before he left for America. He never retrieved very much of it despite his lifelong passion for the country.[28]

Members of the missionary community, even more than their counterparts in England and America, cherished the rituals of Western culture. The American families celebrated the Fourth of July with great exuberance, preparing large feasts (including big tubs of ice cream, a rarity in China) and accumulating large stores of Chinese firecrackers for the occasion. (Harry later expressed "utter contempt" when—away at school in another part of China—American students failed to celebrate the Fourth. "Has patriotism fallen to this degraded state?" he complained.) The British missionaries staged somewhat more sedate but similarly elaborate observances of the king's birthday. Throughout the year Harry and his father pored over the British newspaper from Shanghai, which usually arrived in Wei Hsien many weeks after publication; and they read avidly about the dynamic presidency of Theodore Roosevelt (almost the only American news the British editors chose to report). They developed an intense admiration for Roosevelt that neither ever wholly abandoned. He seemed to embody the same energy, enthusiasm, and progressive optimism that characterized Henry W. Luce and that he sought to instill in his son.[29]

Missionaries were avid consumers of Western goods, despite their Far Eastern location and their relatively spartan surroundings. The Luces were passionate readers of magazines. Harry commented years later on "the importance of *Ladies' Home Journal* to my mother, and the *Outlook* to my father, and *The World's Work*, and then *St. Nicholas* to me." They pored intently over the elephantine Montgomery Ward catalog when it arrived each year, spending days planning their annual order (which, because it would arrive nearly a year later, required estimating the children's clothing sizes many months in advance). When the shipment finally came the children took a day off from lessons to open the large cases and to revel in the luxury of their new possessions. There was also tremendous anticipation at Christmas, when large crates of gifts arrived from American relatives, often weeks before the holiday. Harry's sister Elisabeth remembered the lavish hats she sometimes received from America and the thrill she had as a little girl wearing them to Sunday services and on holidays. Harry recalled the tennis rackets and other sports equipment—and most of all the books.[30]

In the summers the family decamped to Tsingtao, on the Shantung coast, and vacationed in a small bungalow on a dramatic point, Iltus Huk, outside the city at the foot of sharply rising mountains looking out over the sea. Around them were other American and English vacationers, with whom the children swam on the broad, attractive beach and with whom Harry played enthusiastic tennis. Mostly, however, the family spent time with one another—reading English novels aloud, listening to the parents play music (she the piano, he the violin), and writing long letters to friends and relatives in America. Young Harry remembered these months as the happiest of his childhood, and after his return to America in 1912 daydreamed frequently about building for himself "a summer home out on the extreme end of Iltus Huk."[31]

After five years in China, Henry W. Luce had established himself as one of the most assertive and energetic members of the college faculty. And because he had been the principal force behind the move from Tengchow to Wei Hsien, it was not surprising, perhaps, that his colleagues looked to him to raise money to support the expensive new venture. And so in early 1906 the entire Luce family boarded a ship in Shanghai—the first large city young Harry had ever seen—and sailed, second class, to San Francisco, where they began an eighteen-month sojourn in the United States—a trip young Harry had been eagerly anticipating for over a year. "I come to America in one year from now," he wrote a family friend in Scranton, whom he had, of course never met. "Tell my other friends [whom he also knew only through correspondence] that I can hardly wait one year till I go to America and see them."[32]

They traveled first down the California coast, spending several weeks in the still-modest city of Los Angeles, where the young Harry suffered through bouts of, first, measles (which all his sisters contracted as well) and then malaria. When the children recovered, the family headed east, stopping in Chicago to rejoin Henry senior, who had already been traveling for weeks raising money. There they visited, among others, a woman who would play a significant role in the family's life: Nettie Fowler McCormick. She was the enormously wealthy and deeply religious widow of Cyrus McCormick, the creator of the great farm-machine company. She had long been active in the Presbyterian Church and was a significant donor to the missionary movement. She took an immediate liking to the Luces, and to young Harry in particular. At one point she proposed that he be left in Chicago with her, even (according to his parents' later accounts) that she be allowed to adopt him, a shocking suggestion that the senior Luces politely declined and did not reveal to their son until many years later. Apparently unoffended, she found other ways to assist the family. She established a trust fund to supplement their modest missionary society income, and she paid for the construction of the comfortable home they built in Wei Hsien. She retained an interest in the family, and in young Harry, for the rest of her life.[33]

Harry spent most of this first visit to the United States in Scranton, living with friends and relatives of his father and attending, for the only time in his life, an American public school. His adult memories of that early visit, which began when he was seven and ended when he was nine, were luminous if not detailed. Until his visit Harry had known relatively little about America other than the idealized image of it that his father and other missionaries created to justify their own work. America to him began not as a physical place, not as the diverse and contentious culture it actually was, but as a model and an ideal. And so when he finally arrived, he seemed to view the real America through the prism of his expectations. He was "overwhelmed," he later recalled, by the wealth and stability and comfort of the United States, by how much more "civilized" it seemed than China, by how much more educated and knowledgeable its people appeared to be. He was desperate to learn as much about his newfound homeland as he could. He began collecting and studying railway timetables, memorizing schedules and stops, even inventing new timetables of his own to get him to places he wanted to visit—part of an almost frantic effort to inhale the experience so that he could remember it all once he was back in China.[34]

The trip to America was the beginning of what became an increasingly important, and wholly unanticipated, part of Henry W. Luce's life: fund-raising for the Christian mission in China. While the family stayed in Scranton he traveled almost constantly, searching for donors and presenting his vision of a Christian educational community in Asia. He was very good at it, perhaps to his surprise, and soon became comfortable befriending wealthy patrons and persuading them of the importance of his work. It was the first of many such trips he would take over the next twenty years. His frequent absences contributed to his many disappointments in China—particularly his failure to win the presidency of the Shantung Christian College, whose growth he had done so much to enable. "He had to spend most of his life as a money-raiser . . . which is of all jobs the worst job," his son Harry recalled years later, "and so in this sense God was not kind to him." But that was the son's view, not necessarily the father's. The elder Harry's indomitable optimism seldom permitted regrets or self-pity.[35]

On his return to Wei Hsien in 1908, young Harry—eager to maintain his now-severed link with his homeland—sent a letter to *St. Nicholas*, the popular children's magazine to which he had become devoted in Scranton, describing his life as an American abroad. It was his first published work. "I am a boy born in China," he wrote. "I live in the country near

Weihsien (Way Shen) city, in a compound or big yard about two blocks large. There are eight dwelling houses, a boys' and girls' school, a college, a big church, and two hospitals. . . . I think you are fine." But Harry's comfortable life in China was about to change dramatically, for in the fall after the family's return he left home for boarding school.[36]

There were few educational options for Western children in Shantung, and Harry's parents had little choice but to send him to the China Inland Missionary School, known to its students by the name of the town in which it was located—Chefoo (the same port city from which the Luces had fled to Korea during the Boxer Rebellion). Chefoo was a British boarding school, and the combination of the limited amenities available in Shantung and the stern educational philosophy of Victorian English schools made it a harsh, unforgiving place—with terrible food, almost no heat, and stern masters who regularly caned students for not keeping up with their lessons.[37]

Harry loathed it. He was ten years old, separated from his family for the first time, and distanced from his classmates by his American-ness (80 percent of the students were British) and by a painful stammer, which he had recently (and perhaps traumatically) developed. He complained to his parents about the "downright detestable loathsome filthy clammy food," and he wrote yearningly to his mother with detailed descriptions of what he wanted her to cook for him when he came home ("1. Lintle [*sic*] soup 2. Roast chicken 3. Sort of a crisp potato that is served around the roast 4. Beans 5. Carrots or Beats [*sic*] 6. Rice (good home kind) 7. Chocolate Pudding, you know the kind I like"). He complained about the cold, about the mosquitoes, about the teachers, about the other students (his roommate, he said, was "selfish, saucy, bossy and more over ignorant").[38]

Most of all he complained of loneliness. Desperately homesick, he wrote his parents constantly begging them to let him come back to Wei Hsien. "I think I could learn much more in either a small school or by myself," he pleaded. "I would not fall behind in lessons at all," he promised, "and I don't think I would take up your time very much." "There are 63 more days which equals 9 weeks exactly," he wrote early in his second year. "How sweet twill be when there are 0 more days which equals 0 wks. It is then and only then that I will be at the least happy." He made strained efforts to reassure his parents even as he tried to alarm them: "Don't get worried about me, remember this chorus as I have: 'God will take care of you thro' every day. . . . He will take care of you, He will take care of you.' " Sometimes, however—as in a particularly anguished letter in 1910—his misery was so intense that he lost all restraint: "Everything is going as usual but not very well. It sort of seems to hang on not in spells of homesickness but a hanging torture, I well sympathise with prisoners wishing to commit suicide." Weeks later, apparently in response to worried letters from his parents or to rebukes from Chefoo faculty ("Mrs. Fitch asks why I write such blue letters home") he wrote again: "I can never forgive myself if I have in any way worried you." The faculty's apparent intrusion into students' personal mail was likely another of Harry's many grievances, and he combined the apology with bitter sarcasm: "I meant only to impress upon you how much I liked the school, its freedom, good diet, splendid and learned professors." In another letter, he proclaimed, "I am getting that hatred of which I will never get over even tho I was here hundreds of years." His parents naturally agonized over his unhappiness and at one point allowed him to leave school and return home for part of a term. But neither his mother nor anyone else in the compound was capable of teaching Harry at the level of Chefoo, and so he reluctantly returned.[39]

His willingness to go back to school was almost certainly driven by his ambition. The homesickness and the loneliness, in the end, did not paralyze him. On the contrary, they seemed to help spur the emergence of an extraordinary drive for achievement and success that would characterize the whole of his life. In his years at Chefoo he struggled constantly for distinction. He yearned to be first in his class. "I think I have again retained my place in form," he wrote, "though am almost positive that, excluding drawing, I would be 2nd. At least I have the satisfaction that there is only one better student in the Form than myself. . . . I know that I ought to be content with nothing less than first place but somehow I feel its [sic] different here." He became a stalwart debater, despite his stammer, which he was determined to conquer. "We took the side that was unanimously esteemed the worst and didn't prepare a thing," he boasted to his parents, "and won by a vote of 15–3. It must be remembered that we didn't prepare a bit, that two of the votes were lost because my friend Smith drew a comparison between Jews and Scotch!" He tried to excel at sports. ("My game is tennis, so I must practis and practis [sic] to become a good player. . . . I am the 2 best server in the school.") He sought positions of leadership. ("I am now permanent "leader-of-boys-to-Union-Chapel—quite a distinction is it not?")[40]

He did not just strive to succeed. He also analyzed his achievements in almost obsessive detail, comparing himself with other boys and reveling in his small competitive triumphs. ("My years [sic] ambition has been accomplished, that is to lick Hayes [in class rank]. . . . For this year I have made the form record in going up places, that is 8 places.") And he offered detailed explanations for his occasional failures, explanations that almost always absolved him of blame for them. "In my writing I am really 66%, not 54," he explained after one disappointing grade. "I was cheated out of 12%." Another low grade, he explained, was from a teacher who "gives everybody low marks." Toward the end of his years at Chefoo he wrote of his efforts and ambitions: "I have continued in work, literature, music, about as usual getting a rub off here and taking an edge off there, each moment making me nearer or farther from man's chief goal—perfection."[41]

In later years Harry sometimes spoke warmly of the "primitive little school," even saying at one point that "by far the most valuable education I ever got I got there." But at the time, while he learned to tolerate the place and even to excel there, he never ceased to despise it, never stopped counting the days until his vacations, and never stopped imploring his parents—to whom his letters home must have been a source of continuing anguish—to rescue him.[42]

Harry had no memory of huddling in Chefoo in 1900 with his family, waiting to be rescued from the Boxers. But he never forgot his exposure to the Chinese Revolution of 1911, which raged around him during his final year at school and transformed the nation's history.

The Qing imperial dynasty had governed China since 1644, but it had become increasingly enfeebled during the nineteenth century as European, Japanese, and American intruders seized control of more and more of China's land and trade and wrested increasing authority from the imperial court. The dynasty's fortunes worsened considerably beginning in 1898, when ministers eager to restore the moral authority of the court persuaded a new young emperor, Guangxu, to issue a series of reform decrees. He was quickly arrested and interned in a coup d'état orchestrated by his aunt, the powerful and devious empress dowager Cixi, who then executed six of the reform leaders. The following year Cixi encouraged the Boxers to attack the foreign legations in Beijing, and the disastrous aftermath of that rash decision—the invasion and looting of the city by Western forces—compelled her to flee the capital and to make devastating new concessions to the invaders. For the rest of her life she presided over a crippled and unstable government, rocked repeatedly by uprisings and challenged by increasingly assertive reformers. She died in 1908, having murdered her nephew, the still-imprisoned emperor, shortly before. She was succeeded by the three-year-old Xuan-tong (known later as Pu Yi) amid a growing clamor for a constitutional monarchy. Pu Yi's ministers responded with some transparently token reforms but did little to restore the power of the dynasty.

The weakness and continuing intransigence of the Qing court strengthened the appeal of the great Chinese revolutionary leader of the early twentieth century: Sun Yat-sen, who helped inspire a wave of uprisings in 1911 that soon spread through most of the country. By the beginning of 1912 revolutionary forces controlled fifteen of China's twenty-four provinces, and Sun had proclaimed himself president of a new Chinese republic. Within a few weeks the emperor abdicated—bringing to an end not only the Qing dynasty but two thousand years of Chinese imperial history.

To progressive Westerners in China like the Luces, the fall of the Qing dynasty and the triumph of Sun's revolutionary movement (now a political party—the Kuomintang) was a sign of the nation's emergence into the modern world. Harry watched it from Chefoo with a combination of anxiety, wide-eyed curiosity, and excitement. "How about the revolution?" he wrote his parents in October. "Don't things go like a streak! It is about Shanghai's turn now. I guess nothing of real seriousness will happen though." By February the uprising had spread to Shantung and was even visible in his own school. The Chinese servants demanded a twofold increase in their salaries and walked out when the headmaster refused. "The older boys [Harry among them] have had to do all the work," he reported home. Harry was more concerned, however, about reports of violence against missionaries in the North. He wrote his parents: "Isn't it terrible about the burning of the mission houses at Paotingfu" (a place of unhappy significance for the Luces, since it was where Horace Pitkin had died at the hands of the Boxers). "Of course nothing of that kind will happen at Wei Hsien," he added, probably to reassure himself as much as to comfort his family.[43]

But while Harry expressed fleeting concern about the "slightly belligerent tinge" of the atmosphere around him, he left no doubt as to where his sympathies lay. "The smoldering embers of this tremendous Revolution are still glowing in the obscure light of this port," he wrote to a family friend visiting his parents in Wei Hsien. "Please excuse this poor attempt at welcoming you to a great land, peopled by a great nation, endowed with a great past, overshadowed by a greater future." He told friends in Scranton: "This revolution sends a ray of hope down China's broadening future." Even three decades later he referred to the events of 1911–12 as one of the great moments in China's (and his own) life. In the aftermath of their "long and bloody revolution," he recalled, the Chinese did not "revolt against their civilization." Instead, "as I was privileged to see . . . they embarked upon a Reformation. It may turn out to be the greatest and most stupendous Reformation in all history."[44]

On the whole, however, Harry spent more time in 1912 thinking about his own future than thinking about China's. In August he left Chefoo for good—leaving behind the "drudgery and dissatisfaction" and celebrating the arrival of what he called "the first day of freedom's august star." Only three months later, after a last, treasured summer vacation at Iltus Huk, he was boarding a ship in Shanghai to begin a long journey back to America, alone.[45]

It was common for English and American boys in China to travel home at fourteen to begin boarding school, and virtually all of Harry's classmates at Chefoo spent much of their last year planning for the change. Harry had always expected to attend Yale, like his father, but there was no family tradition to dictate the choice of a boarding school. The senior Luce turned to one of his own former teachers for advice: Walter Buell, who had once headed the School of the Lackawanna in Scranton but by 1912 was a teacher at the Hotchkiss School in Lakeville, Connecticut. Almost all its graduates went on to Yale. Buell arranged for Harry to receive a scholarship, for the Luces' missionary income was far too small for the tuition at Hotchkiss. He was invited to enroll in the fall of 1913. Hotchkiss may also have been attractive to the avid Presbyterian Rev. Luce because, unlike many other elite prep schools, it was not tied to the Episcopal Church. In the meantime, the family decided, Harry would spend the better part of a year in Europe—much of it at a school in England whose headmaster was reputed to have had great success in helping boys overcome their stuttering.[46]

The months before his departure must have been as emotional a period as this reticent, prematurely self-possessed boy had ever experienced. Although he repeated all the rituals of family and vacation that he had treasured through his childhood, he was almost certainly aware that he was experiencing them all for the last time: the joyous welcome home at Wei Hsien, the donkey rides through the countryside, the idyllic holiday at Iltus Huk, the family evenings of reading aloud and listening to his parents play music, the long talks with his father. Late in October he said good-bye to his mother, his sisters, and his younger brother (who was only three and who would have virtually no childhood memories of

Harry: "Passing ships," he later described their relationship). He traveled by railroad to Shanghai to meet his father, who would escort him to his ship.[47]

Along the way he began what would soon become an almost ritualistic chronicling of his life for his distant family, composing letters describing his experiences and, in the process, practicing his skills as a writer. "Today we saw . . . great quantities of beans. They must have had a fine crop here though the people have a very disreputable look, I must say," he wrote in his first letter home, only a day after his departure. From Nanking, where he stopped for several days with a missionary family, he wrote excitedly of having seen the "various spots connected with the late Revolution—the place where Gen'l Dyang stood—the forts of the Shantung soldiers etc." He spoke even more excitedly of having met two American boys who were, like him, "planning to go to Hotchkiss on the scholarship plan (tho' from the appearance of their home I don't see how they can justify a plea for a scholarship) & of course eventually I suppose they will both land up in Yale." And from Shanghai he reported that his father had arranged for him to sail on November 9 on the *Prinz Eitel Friedrich*, a German steamer. He would be under the care of an English missionary family heading home, and he would arrive in Southampton "just in time to see a London Xmas."[48]

No record survives of Harry's last few days with his father in Shanghai, but it is not hard to imagine the intensity of their conversations as they prepared for this momentous parting. Already, during Harry's years at Chefoo, he and his father had established a pattern of long-distance intimacy that would characterize their relationship for many years. While young Harry was writing his meticulous and sometimes anguished descriptions of everyday life in school, his father was responding with detailed "advice letters" about how to study, which courses to take, how to deal with his friends, and even—as the boy approached puberty—how to handle his sexual maturity. (In one letter he urged Harry to discourage "your friends" from developing the "very bad habits" of "playing with their private parts." Such a habit, he warned, "inevitably ruins their physical and mental strength to say nothing of their spiritual life.") "I hope you won't think your father is preachy," he wrote shortly after his son's departure. "I hope you will always think of me as a dear companion to whom you may come freely with every problem or question. . . . It will not be easy for you to realize how I long to help you so that you will not make the mistakes that I did."[49]

Nothing loomed larger in Harry's childhood—and even through

much of his adult life—than the image of his father's moving determinedly through the world promoting good works and exhorting his son to do the same. In China the young boy had watched his father struggle, as he saw it, patiently and selflessly to improve the lives of his Chinese students and to persuade his missionary colleagues to pay more attention to the social conditions in Shantung. In America he had watched him travel constantly, exhaustingly, and uncomplainingly, raising money to support his great purpose. Even before he left China, Harry had begun to absorb his father's seriousness, his ceaseless search for self-improvement, his energy, his ambition, his certainty of purpose. But what he wanted most to absorb—and what he spent much of his life reproaching himself for failing to acquire—was what he considered his father's consistent virtuousness, his sheer "goodness." Harry learned from his father to think of life as a great mission, to be judged by its contribution to the betterment of the world. But unlike his father, he also developed a considerable appetite for wealth, power, and worldly success. The tension between his own secular ambitions and the image of his proud, committed, ever-encouraging father, sacrificing himself for the good of others, was both the great inspiration and the great agony of his life.[50]

"I am now almost on the verge of another precipice," he wrote his mother as he prepared to sail. "One was leaving home, another is the leaving of *a* homeland." He was clearly excited, describing the new clothes he had purchased in Shanghai, the "excellent food," the comfortable stateroom he would occupy in "what appears to be a fine part of second class," and "the very nice crowd" of Americans, English, and Dutch of which he soon became a part. But he could not disguise the difficulty of the parting. "Well I am off at last—off the China boundaries. Sailing on the river, the one that leads to the sea," he wrote as the docks on which he said his last farewells to his father slipped from his view. "I knew I would not be at home always & yet the parting that I know I want comes hard, it must be hard."[51]

II

The Striver

On his own at last, without serious adult supervision for the first time, the fourteen-year-old Harry set out to construct his mature self—to take the ordered, disciplined life that others had once imposed on him at home and at school and rebuild it as he began anew. He made a daily schedule: time for reading, time for writing letters, time for socializing with other Americans and Europeans, for meals, and for retiring. He chronicled his experiences in long and at times self-consciously literary letters to his family, searching for a writing style that would express his newfound maturity. Describing the ship's approach to Hong Kong, he wrote, "On the left an island rose to greet perhaps us, perhaps the luring dawn, and then as if in parlous rivalry a promontory stretched itself as if perhaps to wreck, perhaps to land our ship." After a stopover in Singapore, he described the beauty of "an essentially botanical city . . . while I see the beauty in Nature's products still I will not rave over a city where Botany is apparently first & Humanity second." In his account of a tour of Penang, he presented his emerging persona as an impassioned, intrepid sightseer. Having left a tour group from his ship, he wandered into a mosque without removing his shoes and "was almost slain (so I feared at the time) by the angry scowls and red fire glaring eyes of the Mosque Keepers. . . . I quite believed I was to be a martyr to the cause of sightseeing but somehow here I am!"[1]

There were spells of seasickness, homesickness, and sheer boredom: "It is too hot to play, let us read, & doze, read & doze, & doze & look or rather gaze into nothing, into everything—infinity of space," he once wrote. Later he confessed to his parents: "I am excelling in the art of loafing." But even at the end of the long, uncomfortable voyage, he continued to absorb new sights and new experiences with enthusiasm, if not always admiration. Port Said, Egypt, "was the rottenest port yet, and the vilest hole on earth . . . full of sin." Naples and Genoa, the first European cities he had ever seen, were, by contrast, almost indescribable. A church in Naples was, he said, "by far the most wonderfully beautiful building that I have ever seen. . . . Italy, even the little that I have seen of it, beats everything yet except the States & Wei Hsien."[2]

He arrived in England in mid-December. To his dismay (because it meant seeing nothing of London), the missionary family that had been looking out for him dispatched him immediately to the St. Albans School north of the city, to the tutor he hoped would cure him of his stammering—an affliction of which he later said that "nothing in the world could possibly be more painful." The lessons, which began with great optimism ("Mr. Cummings doesn't think I'll need more than a month"), turned out to be of little use. Cummings told him his problem was "absolutely imaginary" and an "evil habit" that he could easily break; their sessions turned into long, pleasant, but essentially purposeless discussions of politics and literature. Harry's father tried to encourage his son. Mr. Cummings "only seeks your good," he said, evidently in response to his son's disillusionment. But the real solution lay, he argued, in Harry's own efforts. "The whole question, of course, is of your getting *control* of your speech again," he wrote. Daily "practice in reading aloud and lip-movement . . . might facilitate your recovery." Luce ignored Cummings's advice but slowly improved his ability to control his stammer nevertheless.[3]

Not surprisingly Harry soon turned his attention to other things. Cummings offered him a place in his school, but Harry was uninterested in enrolling. Four years of English boarding school in China had undoubtedly been enough. He spent the time between lessons working on various self-improvement schemes. He experimented with a new handwriting (a "business hand," he called it); he sent for a mail-order course from the Pelham School of the Mind, which suggested how "one can train oneself to . . . a high pitch of brain perfection" simply through "concentration" and "observation." He studied Buddhism, read Caesar and Dickens, wrote poems, and "took German lessons twice a week . . . polishing up for Hotchkiss." He played tennis and chess with the boys from the school. But most of all he traveled. He bought a bicycle, taught himself to ride it, and cycled through the countryside around St. Albans the way he had once ridden his donkey around Shantung, visiting villages and churches and farms. He took frequent trips into London by train, where he resumed his now-habitual sightseeing (Saint Paul's, he said, was the "greatest Christian Temple I have ever seen"), observed a session of Parliament, and attended a Chefoo reunion.[4]

In January he learned that his mother, sisters, and brother would be relocating temporarily to Switzerland the following summer, where the girls would attend a French-speaking school. His father would be in England within a few weeks for a brief stopover en route from China to a fund-raising sojourn in America. "What news!" he wrote back excitedly, giving elaborate instructions on packing, tipping, and sightseeing, and outlining plans for showing his father the sights of England. When his father arrived in early February, Harry took him on tours of London, Oxford, and Stratford and on visits to several palaces and great country houses before seeing him off on a ship to New York. A few weeks later, after a last frantic round of sightseeing on his own in England, he left St. Albans and took the ferry to France alone.[5]

Harry's letters from Europe, where he spent the next six weeks traveling, reveal a young man who was already accustomed to being on his own— and who compensated for his loneliness with relentless, methodical sightseeing and disciplined efforts at self-education. They also reveal an increasingly visible characteristic of his personality: a voracious appetite for knowledge and experience, a consuming curiosity, a determination, it sometimes seemed, to see and know everything. During his few days in Paris, he crisscrossed the city on foot visiting sight after sight—the Louvre, the relatively new Eiffel Tower, Notre Dame, Montmartre— before leaving for Lausanne, where his mother and siblings were to arrive a few weeks later. But the pleasant, quiet city quickly made him restless. "The days are at times long without a companion," he wrote of his time in Switzerland. He adopted a regimen that he thought would help him deal with the tedium. "Now that my English lesson books have come the inter-eating hours will doubtless pass quickly enough," he assured his father. But his time in Lausanne was brief, because he had already planned (with his father's help) a monthlong trip through Italy, which he would take entirely on his own. "Guidebook in hand and camera on my little finger, I go out to make investigations," he wrote from Rome, which he visited with the same frugal efficiency he had displayed in London and Paris. He stayed in a small, inexpensive hotel and spent several days trying to move into a smaller, even less expensive room—partly to preserve his very limited budget but also because his lodgings were of so little interest to him. He was utterly preoccupied with sightseeing. He moved methodically through the city, as if checking off the obligatory attractions. "In the seven days I have been here," he boasted, "I have seen all the principle [*sic*] sites. The only things that are ever visited & that I will not have seen, are a few miscellaneous & uninteresting churches (comparatively) & a few galleries that are absolutely eclipsed by Florence's exhibition—& to Florence I am bound!"[6]

Harry traveled this way because he believed that systematic investigation was more likely to deepen his knowledge than casual or impulsive methods, and he apparently derived real satisfaction from his deliberate sightseeing style. "I believe that I have carried away with me some parts of Rome that can never be taken from me," he wrote happily as he prepared to leave the city. "Whether I wish or no the remembrances and impressions of that great city will always hold their place in my memory & that tenaciously." His father heartily approved. "Once one has arrived at a place," he advised, "it is worth while seeing it well." "Not many fathers," he added, would have permitted a son to travel alone at this age, but Harry "had never failed me yet."[7]

In Florence, Harry was befriended by a professor of German—"an exceedingly nice man"—from Wells College in Aurora, New York, whom he met while touring the Baptistery. "We have hit it off and have agreed to continue our wanderings as much in conjunction as possible. We leave for Venice Monday 6:20 a.m. & are deliciously indefinite how long we shall stay there," he wrote, adding that "my newfound friend . . . insisted on presenting me with tickets [to a film]." For whatever reason, the relationship does not appear to have lasted very long. A few weeks later, after a whirlwind tour (again alone) of Bologna, Milan, Turin, and Genoa, he was back in Lausanne, reunited with his mother, Emmavail, Elisabeth, and Sheldon—and already thinking ahead to his journey to America.[8]

As if to confirm his passage to maturity, he bought his first adult clothes in Switzerland—long trousers, cuffs, and stiff shirts, the standard uniform for young middle-class men in America. He complained about the "daily torture," but he wore the uncomfortable new outfit diligently until he got used to it. In the meantime he embarked on a new round of sightseeing in Switzerland and studied ferociously for the Hotchkiss admissions exams. In August, he joined Harold Burt, an English friend from Chefoo, for a two-week trip of "concentrated sightseeing" down the Rhine to Strasbourg and then to Brussels—before finally going to Hamburg to meet his father, who had returned to Europe a few weeks earlier. Several days later father and son boarded a ship for America.[9]

It must have been clear to his parents, and perhaps also to Harry himself, how profoundly their relationship to their son had already changed in the months since he had left China. Harry still loved his family and enjoyed his time with them; his relationships with his parents and siblings remained the most important in his life. With his father in particular he still had an unusually close and warm relationship. But his home—wherever it was—was clearly no longer with them. He was now a visitor in their lives, dropping in for a few days or weeks as they themselves moved restlessly around the world. Their time together was affectionate and intense. "You are 14, & I am 44," the older Harry wrote his son after they spent a few days together in Europe that summer. "I don't feel that difference, & I hope you don't. This is because motive and outlook are similar, & the fact is a great joy to me." But such times were almost always brief, with Harry or his parents leaving after a short while for other obligations or other adventures. During their months together in Europe, there had been few moments when the entire family was in one place. And there would be very few such moments at any subsequent point in Harry's life. "Of course, I long for a house, where I could gather you all, especially at the dear Christmas time," his mother wrote him from Germany, "but that seems to be withheld, and it is a hard thing for us all to bear." Emmavail once complained, "We seem not to belong *anywhere*," and her mother agreed that "it seems to be our fate to be in a continual state of uncertainty."[10]

But such laments were rare from any member of the family, and rarest of all from Harry. This was the common lot of missionary families, and their members learned to accept it as a necessary price of their unusual and, they believed, privileged lives. "I know that God will take care of it all, and will give us our hearts' desires in just so far as they are in harmony with His will for us," Elisabeth wrote her son. "It is a strange life we are leading," his father echoed, "but I do feel that God is leading us and blessing us." Harry simply forged ahead, spending time with his family when he could, but focusing intently on what he liked to call the "task at hand" when he could not. He adjusted to his new independent life with little apparent difficulty and with no evidence of the loneliness and homesickness about which he had so often complained at Chefoo, even though he was now far more alone than he had been then. Instead he eagerly embraced the "great adventure" of pursuing experience and knowledge. It was a willed replacement—in many ways, it turned out, a permanent one—for the intimate personal attachments that had once anchored his life.[11]

Harry arrived in New York in mid-September 1913 and got his first glimpse of "the great city" that would be the center of so much of his life. He was soon alone again, for his father was called away on fund-raising business shortly after their arrival. But Harry was undaunted. As he had done in Paris and Rome, he traveled from one end of Manhattan to another, trying to see as much as he could in the few days he had. On a bus trip up Fifth Avenue, he passed the city's already famous skyscrapers as well as the " 'big bugs' roosts"—the lavish hotels and mansions surrounding Central Park. A few days later he was in Lakeville, Connecticut, singing "My Country 'Tis of Thee" in front of a gymnasium filled with jeering boys who were initiating him into the life of the Hotchkiss School.[12]

Hotchkiss was founded in 1892 through the awkward intersection of two very different people. One was Timothy Dwight, the august president of Yale, who in the 1890s was busily trying to transform his institution—once a small, insular college—into an academically serious university. And like the presidents of other universities experiencing similar transformations, Dwight feared that the nation's public schools were failing to produce students that met Yale's newly heightened standards. As a result he had begun to consider founding a new private school that would prepare young men for Yale. As luck would have it, he discovered a wealthy and somewhat eccentric widow—Maria Hotchkiss—who was looking ineffectually for a way to memorialize her recently deceased husband (a successful industrialist and the inventor of the machine gun). Dwight persuaded her to finance the construction of a private high school for boys in her hometown, Lakeville, Connecticut. It became one of a wave of such institutions—known now as "preparatory" schools—that opened their doors around the same time and for the same purposes. Among them were Lawrenceville, Groton, Taft, Choate, Middlesex, Deerfield, and Kent, all created with the encouragement, and sometimes the active involvement, of Harvard, Yale, Princeton, Columbia, and other elite universities. Older private schools, such as Exeter, Andover, and St. Paul's, greatly expanded in these same years.

The creation of these schools served not only the needs of the universities that promoted them but also the desires of the newly wealthy families of the industrial age. Prep schools were among a broad range of developments—including the growth of affluent suburbs, country clubs, summer resorts, lavish Protestant churches, and elite men's clubs—that marked the emergence of a distinct, national upper class. Not all the boys at Hotchkiss, not even all the nonscholarship boys, came from the new aristocracy. But most were at least from prosperous, solidly middle-class backgrounds. The school represented, therefore, both the ideals and the social customs of the upper class and the aspirations of many middle-class families to rise in the world.[13]

That was one reason why relations between Mrs. Hotchkiss and the school that bore her family's name were tense from beginning to end. She wanted an institution that would serve the needs of poor children from the community; Yale wanted one that would train the sons of wealthy families for the university. They reached an uneasy compromise by setting tuition at six hundred dollars a year for the vast majority of boys—a sum far beyond the reach of all but the relatively affluent—while establishing a handful of scholarships for less wealthy students from the area. But Maria Hotchkiss remained unreconciled, and her support of the school ended at its founding. It flourished without her, since it soon was able to rely on the many enormously wealthy families whose sons it educated.[14]

Hotchkiss was twenty years old when Harry (now 15) arrived, and the school had by then significantly reduced its always scant interest in recruiting poor boys from Lakeville. But it retained its scholarships and parceled at least some of them out to students whose backgrounds, if not their finances, seemed compatible with the character of its socially eminent student body. Harry—the son of a Yale-educated missionary and a graduate of a British boarding school—fit the profile well. Even so, the distinction between scholarship boys and everyone else was carefully and very publicly maintained. Harry's early weeks at Hotchkiss became his first lessons in the American class system. He lived apart from the rest of the students, in a boardinghouse in the village, about a mile away from campus, where he shared a room with a nineteen-and-a-half-year-old farm boy from Kansas, who was also a scholarship student. The dormitories—complete with maid and laundry service—were reserved for the tuition-paying boys. He rose every morning at six and caught a ride on a delivery cart into campus, where he first cleaned and dusted the chapel before having to "scoot" into the dining hall for a rushed breakfast followed by waiting on the tables of the paying students.[15]

Even so, Harry had no doubt which side of the class divide he wished, and expected, to inhabit. He got along with the other scholarship boys, but he did not really identify with them. He was a far better student than most of them (and in fact spent considerable time tutoring his roommate and others). But he did not accept their sense of being outsiders. "I will like to get away from the round of serving on table and to eat once again, not as hog, but as human!" he wrote as his first Thanksgiving vacation approached. "These scholarship fellows here are all fundamentally fine, but they lack certain qualities—especially noticeable at table—that one misses!" The "greatest burden of the scholarship," he noted on another occasion, "is the school fellows I have to associate with. Many of them are still boorish, showing the trade of the farm or perhaps Brooklyn!" (The school apparently agreed. One teacher told him that "the Faculty was very dissatisfied with the calibre of the new scholarship boys—'Present company excepted,' he remarked!—and that therefore they were going to make an endeavour to advertise [Hotchkiss scholarships] . . . among a better grade of boys.") The other students, in contrast, were "are all fine, nice fellows," and he yearned to be one of them. In one letter to his family, he pondered his chances of being chosen to serve refreshments at an upper-class dance—an honor reserved for the popular and socially eminent people Harry called "pets." "I can only hope that they allow me in on that feed," he wrote, with a tinge of self-pity, "tho I might not add any lustre to the social glimmer of the evening & early morning!"[16]

But it was not only his ambiguous position in the school's rigid class structure that set him apart. It was also a certain social awkwardness, a product in part of his conspicuous foreignness. He dressed differently, wearing jackets and trousers made for him inexpensively in China and Europe that looked dated and slightly shabby compared with the elegant American wardrobes of some of his wealthy classmates. He spoke differently, not only because of his continuing (if somewhat improved) stammer, but also because of his unfamiliarity with American idiom. His speech sometimes seemed formal, even slightly stilted, not because he intended it to but because he had never learned the relaxed, slang-heavy diction of American adolescents. He had little knowledge of American popular culture; he did not understand his schoolmates' jokes; and perhaps most damaging of all in a boys' school, he knew little about American sports at an institution where (according to a Hotchkiss graduate writing to Harry) the "big men" were athletes, their "friendship coveted by anyone [they] care to associate with." ("I did not know a single rule of football when I came here," Harry wrote ruefully to his parents in Octo-

ber.) He went out briefly for the football team and later considered trying out for baseball, but he gave them both up quickly and chose instead
to play tennis and to inform himself about the sports he did not know by
covering games for the school newspaper. In addition to everything else
he and his fellow students were obliged to learn, Harry had the task of
learning how to be American.[17]

Despite all the ways in which Harry felt like an outsider at
Hotchkiss, he loved the school from the beginning—loved it with an
almost uncritical enthusiasm that was nearly as intense as his implacable
bitterness toward Chefoo had been. "Hotchkiss is fine!" he wrote his sisters after his first days in Lakeville. "I have been forced to pinch myself
several times to assure myself of normal senses." For a time at least he
forgave the school almost everything: the humiliating hazing of new
boys by the seniors ("they gave us real solid advice & warm welcome,"
he wrote, once the ritual was over); the harsh regimen of the scholarship
students (they held a "high position" in the school, he insisted, because
they had such important responsibilities); the demeaning rules for new
students (although they could not speak to seniors, or even look at them,
unless spoken to first, Harry simply anticipated the day when he would
be the beneficiary rather than the victim of the customs). He even tolerated his hated nickname, "Chink," attached to him in his first weeks at
Hotchkiss when the older boys learned he had listed his hometown as
Wei Hsien, China. (He "must have sneaked in thru Mexico or Canada,"
the Hotchkiss *Lit* wrote in a humorous retrospective on the class of
1916.) He expressed admiration for the school's stern and pompous
headmaster, Huber Gray Buehler, whom he would later come to loathe.
"Mr. Buehler is commonly called 'the King' & is a very fine man," he
wrote after their first meeting. "I met him first in the corridor, received
according to his manner a very formal & dignified welcome."[18]

What Harry lacked in social or athletic distinction, however, he
made up for in academic and literary achievement. He emerged almost
immediately as one of the most gifted students in the school—an especially impressive triumph since he had missed an entire year of formal
education during his prolonged journey from China to America, while
most of his classmates had spent a first year at Hotchkiss. But Chefoo
had prepared him well, he grudgingly admitted. "I find that the easiest
part of my life here will be my studies," he wrote a few weeks into his
first term, a view he never had occasion to change. He had no great difficulty excelling, and he ranked first in his class ("First Scholar") in all
but a few terms during his three years at the school. "I am awfully proud

of the way you have faced your first term's work in this land," his father wrote on hearing news of his marks. "It is a great joy and comfort to me to know that I have a son who can be trusted absolutely to do the right thing just so far as he has light." Such praise only increased Harry's determination to achieve and succeed.[19]

The curriculum at Hotchkiss was unusually narrow, even by the standards of its time. Harry took a scattering of courses in English, algebra, and Bible studies, but the vast majority of his academic work was in languages. Walter Buell, his father's old teacher from Scranton—a formal, aloof man with whom Harry never became close—kept a close eye on the new boy and decided early that he had great potential. He persuaded Harry to begin studying ancient Greek—one of the more demanding language courses in the school. Harry was soon immersed in the strange, beautiful language, taking two Greek courses a term (along with Latin, French, and German), and, characteristically, already looking ahead to the public distinctions his newfound talents could bring him. Yale offered a prize to the entering student who could demonstrate the greatest proficiency in Greek, and Harry determined early that he would try to win it.[20]

In the meantime he had his eye on prizes more immediately at hand. In addition to striving perpetually, and usually successfully, to be "First Scholar," he tried to excel in public speaking and debating—an unlikely ambition for a boy with a painful stammer, but one he embraced all the more intensely because of the obstacles he had to overcome. A few weeks after arriving at the school, he read a paper he had written—"Hannibal, a Leader of men"—before one of the Hotchkiss debating societies, as a kind of audition for membership. The next morning he wrote home excitedly: "I write principally this morning to tell you of the success of my essay. It was considered the best of the bunch—the first essay ever committed to memory in the Forum—And I am a member of that august society!"[21]

Since he could not become a "big man" at Hotchkiss as an athlete, Harry was determined to become an important literary figure on campus. In addition to debating, he began working for both the school newspaper (the *Record*) and the literary magazine (the *Hotchkiss Literary Monthly*, known to students as the *Lit*) in his first term. Both awarded places on the basis of strenuous and highly quantitative competition. Boys received points not just for the quality and quantity of their submissions but for selling ads and subscriptions, doing clerical chores, even cleaning up. Harry had great success in getting his stories and poems published, but he did not stop there. He took every opportunity he had to pile up points, so that by the end of the term he could boast that his contributions to the *Lit* "have evidently been well thought of as I lead the competition of the whole school." He was elected to the *Lit* in his first year. The path to distinction at the *Record* was longer and more difficult and therefore, to Harry, more desirable. "You ask why I want to make both papers," he wrote his father in April, after "heeling" (competing like a dog following its master) for the *Record* for months without securing a place. "Well, first & foremost, because it's quite some honor and quite something which very few if any others in my class will do. Secondly because it's up to me to make good in everything I can." Not until the middle of his second year—during which he worked almost maniacally for the newspaper to the slight (and temporary) detriment of his grades—did he finally win election. "My work on the Record has had quite a wonderful—not to say phenomenal—success," he reported. "2500 odd points in 2 weeks has not been won since I have been at Hotchkiss."[22]

Even though he was one of the poorest boys in the school, Harry managed to stay on a fairly equal footing with his fellow students while he was at Hotchkiss. During most vacations, however, he was conspicuously different from all but a few of them. His parents were usually far away—in China, in Europe, or traveling, with no fixed address except when they were in Shantung. ("I do not know where I shall be" at Christmas, his father wrote from Pittsburgh in mid-December, outlining an exceptionally complicated travel schedule, "but since I 'commit my way to the Lord' constantly, He surely 'directs my path.' So all is well.") There were no close relatives left in America from either side of the family, and no relatives at all with whom Harry had any more than a glancing acquaintance. So each holiday presented him with the challenge of finding, largely on his own, a place to go and something to do. It was, on the whole, a challenge he confronted eagerly, even joyously. He undoubtedly missed his family, but he faced a world of opportunities for experience and advancement.[23]

His first such opportunity came from the old friend and devoted patron of the Luce family, Nettie McCormick. Harry had not seen Mrs. McCormick since his childhood visit to Chicago in 1906. But the family had remained in close touch with her, and Harry's father had been a frequent visitor to her home on fund-raising trips to Chicago. Young Harry, whom she had once offered to adopt, was the member of the family she remembered most warmly. She began writing to him even before he returned to the United States: "I am addressing the little boy I loved so well long ago!" she wrote in the spring of 1913, when Harry was in Europe. "It is only yesterday—as ages count—and as my memory counts it I would say it was last night sunsetting when I took your little hand." She treasured the photographs of him that Harry's mother occasionally sent. "I recognize 'the boy of 1906' in the picture more readily than you will recognize me when you next come to Chicago," she observed. So perhaps it was not surprising that she invited Harry to spend his first Christmas vacation in the United States with her, an invitation Harry immediately and eagerly accepted, with his parents' approval. "It will give you an opportunity to come to know some of the best people in the land," his father wrote. His mother confided to her husband that she had decided to abandon a planned trip to New York and stay in Europe through Christmas so as not to interfere with Harry's plans to visit Mrs. McCormick in Chicago. (He had shown no such eagerness, to his mother's considerable chagrin, when relatives had invited him to spend Thanksgiving in Scranton a month earlier, and he had declined their invitation to stop in over Christmas as well. "Where do *we* come in?" his uncle wrote, only partly in jest, when hearing of Harry's holiday plans.)[24]

Mrs. McCormick lived in a towering brownstone mansion on Rush Street in downtown Chicago (when she was not in her "country" home in the affluent suburb of Lake Forest). She was surrounded by servants but otherwise alone, visited occasionally by her wealthy but, to her, disappointing children. She welcomed the polite, intelligent, earnest young man from Hotchkiss with warmth, and she dazzled him with generosity. Suddenly Harry found himself in a social whirl unlike anything he had ever experienced. He was invited to dinners and dances and debutante balls at wealthy homes and country clubs. He went to the opera on Christmas Eve with the younger McCormicks and spent Christmas day on Rush Street, opening expensive gifts from the "great lady," as the Luces always called her. (His modest gifts from his parents arrived at Hotchkiss by mail weeks later.) Mrs. McCormick's generosity was not, however, restricted to Christmas. She "had four prs of fine silk socks laid out in front of my door one morning," he wrote his mother. "Gave me $10 today for 'incidental expenses' and made me promise to take a taxi if ever caught in the rain—'no matter what the cost,' she said!"[25]

When he returned to Hotchkiss, she paid for his train tickets, gave him pocket money for the trip, and sent him gifts of cash periodically during the rest of the year. Almost immediately, she began planning for his next visit. "The glow has fled that radiated through these humble halls, where at Christmas time young voices were heard—and light footsteps on the stair!" she lamented a few days after he left. In the meantime Harry sent her copies of his speeches in the debating society and his articles in the *Lit*, and wrote her—as he did to his parents—recounting the great events of his struggle to succeed. For the rest of her life, he remained her "dear boy," the object of her continued attention, the recipient of her frequent largesse. Harry had no qualms about accepting her many gifts. Missionary families were accustomed to surviving through the generosity of others.[26]

The summer of 1914 was a rare opportunity for the Luce family to be together. Harry's mother and siblings had come over from Europe—his mother in February, leaving the girls behind in their German school until they hurriedly escaped Germany in midsummer on the eve of World War I. His father was committed to another full year of fundraising in the United States. So the family rented a house in Hartford (despite young Harry's preference for New York) and spent the summer months—as they had so often done at Iltus Huk—pursuing self-improving activities for themselves. Harry created a chart to encourage the family to take "healthy walks"—"Nothing less than a consecutive half mile may be counted," he announced—and made sure that he finished first in what he, at least, automatically considered a competition. In August he logged thirty and a half miles, more than twice as many as anyone else.[27]

His parents remained in the United States long enough for him to spend at least part of both the 1914 Christmas holiday and the 1915 summer vacation with them. But he rarely stayed for long. The day after Christmas, despite earlier protestations that he hoped to spend the entire holiday with his family, he left for two weeks with Mrs. McCormick in Chicago. During the summer of 1915, he worked for a time on a farm in Massachusetts (a job he found through a friend at school), but he also visited family friends near Scranton, where he was "forthwith shouted into a whirl of golf and tennis." Toward the end of the summer, he traveled west to San Francisco to see his family off as they finally returned to China—his sisters en route to Shanghai, where they would enroll in an American boarding school; his parents and Sheldon temporarily to Wei Hsien, pending the move of Shantung Christian University to a new campus in Tsinan, the provincial capital—built largely as a result of Rev. Luce's prodigious feats of fund-raising in the United States. Characteristically, Harry combined his emotional farewell with a bout of strenuous sightseeing, into the Yosemite Valley and through the Muir Woods ("all fine exercise . . . [and] a good tanning process"), and later into San Francisco to get a look at the celebrated evangelist Billy Sunday, whom Harry dismissed as "that loud-mouthed fellow . . . [who] could jump pretty well, and knew how to box the ears of the wind." He was much more impressed with a distinguished Presbyterian minister who was visiting a church for the New York City elite. He was "famous as Rockefeller's pastor," Harry noted, and spoke both more "intelligently" and more "beautifully" than Billy Sunday had. On his way back east he spent most of his time in the train's observation car, even though he was traveling on a second-class ticket that did not entitle him to sit there. "I went on the plan 'go, keep going till you're stopped,' " he unapologetically explained.[28]

He spent the last several weeks of the summer in Chicago with the McCormicks, where he found himself drawn into conversations about the long unfolding of the Chinese Revolution. "Ideals are a nation's greatest asset," he wrote his father after a spirited conversation with some conservative members of the Chicago business elite, whose views he seemed to have adopted. "But the ideal of democracy is not and never has been, in my mind, either understood or embraced by China as a nation." Perhaps, he said, the nation would be better off with "a monarchical form of government," which might "let China find that law and order & courage which is the foundation of liberty," outside the circle of America and Western Europe. Like his boyhood hero Theodore Roosevelt, he was coming to think of China as one of the "problem" nations for which the best course was "Order first, Liberty second."[29]

Harry was a junior when he returned to Hotchkiss in the fall of 1914 and was living now, he excitedly reported, in one of the school buildings, no longer in a rooming house in the village. He was also beginning the year in which the school's great prizes would be open to him: editorships, club presidencies, class offices, and the like, all of which were bestowed in the spring. Harry's competitive impulses, which had shaped much of his first year at Hotchkiss, now grew in intensity, and he spent much of his time scrambling for advancement in one organization after another—and writing to his parents with elaborate accounts of his achievements, along with detailed and self-exculpatory explanations of his occasional failures. His father warned him about his "nervous disposition," which he said ran in the family and which had, he claimed, physical as well as psychological risks. Harry should avoid his tendency to eat too quickly, which could cause stomach ailments and "distemper"; and he should also avoid rubbing his face nervously with his hands—which, his father insisted, contributed to Harry's mild acne problems. "I note that the people of best breeding I know never touch their faces, noses, or ears." But he did not discourage Harry from pursuing his ambitions. Perhaps he knew that such discouragement would be futile.[30]

Harry paid little attention to his father's advice. He continued to strive for and almost always attained academic distinction (with courses again narrowly concentrated in Latin, German, Greek, French, English, and the Bible); he remained first in his class through almost all of his junior year and was the only junior to make the High Honor Roll. As a result, as he somewhat smugly put it, he became "the object of a little more respect than here to fore." But his principal ambition was now not for grades but for office. To achieve a high position in the school, he explained to his occasionally skeptical parents (who urged him to give first priority to his academic work) would "mean that I have made good—slightly above the average—in at least one branch of school life." He added (somewhat disingenuously for the top scholar in his class) that "this is what scholarship boys are supposed to do and if I want to have my scholarship renewed it behooves me to push things as best I can."[31]

He continued to work hard at debating, hoping to become a major figure in the Debating Union, "one of the foremost school offices!" A highlight of the debating year was the contest between the school's two debating societies: the Forum and the Agora, for which Harry prepared with some trepidation, since his opponent was a senior widely regarded as the school's best debater. But he defeated the school star and won "the gold medal for myself" and critical points for the victorious team. "Thus another event in Life's circle goes round," he reported to his parents, "—'something accomplished, something done!' " Toward the end of the year, when the Debating Union chose its officers, Luce was named president of the Agora.[32]

He cast an occasional, hopeful eye at student government but did not pursue it, aware that social standing, not ability, played the principal role in the selection. He tried out for the drama society and secured a minor part (as "a new young missionary just going out to his field") in one of its productions. He became involved with the campus Christian organization, the Saint Luke's Society—although he did not see it as one of his principal commitments. His greatest hope, however, was to be president of the *Lit*, a goal he had set for himself during his first year and that he now single-mindedly pursued. He flooded the editors with poems, essays, and stories and kept meticulous notes on what was accepted (mostly poems, some essays, few stories). He assisted in the design of the magazine, helped with the sale of advertisements, and even came to the rescue of the business manager, who fell ill before a school play and asked Harry to accompany his date in his stead. His election as editor in chief in the early spring was anticlimactic: He had no serious rivals. Almost immediately he began looking ahead to his own time at the helm, determined to make a mark for himself in his new position. He organized a banquet for the outgoing board, "establishing a new precedent here at Hotchkiss . . . [and] putting the Lit on a distinctly respected and dignified basis." In the meantime he was laying plans "for the wonderful Lit that we hope to make next year. If our dreams come anywhere near true, we shall give those interested in School Publications an eye opener!"[33]

Harry's high ambitions for the *Lit* were at least in part a result of his realization that he would not be a major figure on the more prestigious campus publication, the *Record.* Even though he heeled successfully for the newspaper in the winter of his second year, and even though he worked hard and published many stories in the paper, he was never in contention for the editorship. That was, he explained to his mother, because another of his classmates already had the office virtually locked up—"a boy, Hadden, who is already on the Board." He did not know it at the time, but the "boy, Hadden," was to become—with the exception of his parents—the most important figure in Harry's young life.[34]

Briton Hadden was born in February 1898 into a prosperous Brooklyn Heights family. His maternal grandfather was a successful silk importer. His father's father was president of a Brooklyn savings bank. Brit's childhood was in most respects as conventionally American and middle class as Harry's was unusual. His father died when he was seven, but a close extended family and a doting mother softened the trauma of the loss. His mother eventually remarried, and Brit's new stepfather—a physician—became a devoted and affectionate parent.

As a child in Brooklyn, Brit was an exuberant, highly social boy, the leader of a circle of neighborhood friends, and—his mother later claimed—someone with strong opinions about everything. He had two passions: writing and baseball. He wrote poems, stories, and reports of the neighborhood, beginning even before he entered school—including a series of mostly violent tales about battles among rabbits, cats, and other usually more innocent creatures. As a student at Brooklyn Polytechnic Preparatory School, which he entered at the age of ten, he created an unofficial, handwritten newspaper, illustrated with his own cartoons. He called it the *Daily Glonk*, after a word used in the popular comic strip *Krazy Kat* to describe the noise made when someone hit Krazy on the head with a brickbat. The paper was lively and irreverent. "The 'Daily Glonk' wishes to apologize to its many subscribers for its tardyness," Brit wrote in one issue. "This was unavoidable, however, as the paper was twice destroyed by a rough politician who did not like to see his name in print." It was also at times both cruel and openly bigoted. Of a Jewish classmate with a lisp, the *Glonk* wrote that "Theo. Oswald Clarke thallied forth to thcool arrayed in a thplendid new thuit. Unhappily for Theo., however, he forgot to remove a Moe Levy price mark. . . . Take it off Theo. We know you." In a May 1913 issue he wrote of the "great success" of the "grand Yiddisher ball," at which the "Jew Theo. Clarke performed wonderfully as leader of the grand march." Under a crudely racist drawing of a local African American, the paper went on to note that "the niggers are jealous," and that in response the "champion Nigger Spitter of America . . . is promoting the 'Coon's Cake Walk.' " In the insular, white, Protestant middle-class world of the Hadden family, such sentiments offended almost no one.[35]

However much Brit liked writing and editing, he liked baseball more. Like many Brooklynites, he was a passionate Dodger fan, but his love for the game was actually almost indiscriminate. "I go and see either Brooklyn or the Giants play every day," he wrote a cousin in 1914, "and that's my idea of a good time." When he was unable to go to the stadium, he often stood outside the *Brooklyn Eagle* offices waiting for scores. In the summers he organized fiercely competitive baseball games almost every day near the family's summer home in Quogue. He dreamed of being a major-league player himself and spoke with contempt of friends and relatives who liked more sedentary or genteel sports like golf and tennis. When he entered Hotchkiss in the fall of 1913 (at the same time that Harry arrived), his principal ambition was to become a member of the school's baseball team, as his brother had been before him. But he had little talent for baseball or, for that matter, any other sport. "I'm still on the class squad but I might as well be a dummy for all the baseball I'm getting," he wrote his mother in despair. "Gee, my chances for making the big team before I get out of here are about as big as the Brooklyns' of winning the pennant." Unsurprisingly, perhaps, Brit soon turned his ambitions to student journalism instead, where he found himself before long in an unstated rivalry with another refugee from Hotchkiss team sports: Harry.[36]

In many ways it would be hard to imagine two boys more different from each other than Harry and Brit. Brit was gregarious, witty, and charismatic (his classmates named him "Mouth Hadden" in a graduation spoof), enormously popular with his classmates and a "great pet" (as Harry observed) of the faculty. He was a creature of American popular culture—attuned to its slang, its jokes, its entertainments, and its sports. He liked to affect the loping, swaggering walk of professional baseball players, to speak at times in an exaggerated Brooklyn accent, and to express emphatic opinions about almost everything. He was also a mediocre student, despite his considerable intelligence, and had trouble concentrating on subjects that did not interest him—which, in the very narrow Hotchkiss curriculum, was most subjects. Harry, of course, shared none of those characteristics.[37]

But perhaps the biggest difference between them, visible even in adolescence, was in their views of the world. Brit had what was in many ways an intensely parochial outlook, bounded by the limited experiences and inward-looking assumptions of his family, community, and class. The childish racism and anti-Semitism he displayed in the *Daily Glonk* was one example of this insularity. So was his breezy dismissal of people and ideas that departed from those he had absorbed in Brooklyn Heights and at Hotchkiss. And yet Brit was also an iconoclast—sassy, cynical, unimpressed with established authority and existing institutions, already showing signs of what would become the trademark social disenchantment of his generation of writers, artists, and intellectuals. One of his heroes and models as he grew older was H. L. Mencken, and one of his favorite magazines was the one on which Mencken got his start and that helped give voice to his time, the *Smart Set*. Like many of his contemporaries, Brit was in one sense a true snob, contemptuous of dull, ordinary people and of those he considered his social or intellectual inferiors. But he was also a rebel, always ready to ridicule the pretensions and affectations of his peers, always eager to defy authority (within reasonably safe bounds), never comfortable fitting into a conventional mold.[38]

Harry, by contrast, had a much more serious and in many ways more cosmopolitan approach to the world. He lacked Brit's natural ease with American popular culture, had difficulty forming casual relationships with his peers, and was in general less socially successful. But he had a much more comfortable relationship with the larger world, of which he had seen a great deal more than Brit (or almost any other of his classmates) ever would. Harry had absorbed the values of his father's sense of Christian mission—unshakable faith in the superiority of American and Western culture, to be sure, but also a tolerance of, and intense curiosity about, other cultures, other ideas, other peoples. He may not have been offended by displays of racism or anti-Semitism among his peers, but he rarely expressed such sentiments himself. Even as an adolescent Harry could be arrogant and aloof, but he was rarely—then or at any time in his life—cynical or conventionally snobbish. And because he did not take his American-ness for granted, because his view of his country had been shaped by his early separation from it and his eager idealization of it, he was much less inclined than was Brit to criticize or ridicule its mores.

And yet for all their differences, Harry and Brit did have some important things in common. They were both precociously intelligent, both drawn to literature, ideas, and writing, both attracted to journalism, and, perhaps most of all, both exceptionally ambitious and competitive. At Hotchkiss, at least, Harry was a slightly awkward outsider trying to fit in; and Brit was a consummate, supremely popular insider trying in some unfocused way to break out. Somehow, in their common efforts to transcend their designated roles, they met on common ground. But not right away.

Harry was not the only one determined to make his publication an "eye opener." Brit, too, set out to make the *Record* he edited into a campus sensation. The result was an intense but mostly friendly competition that both cemented their friendship and established a long-term rivalry. Each was eager to best the other, but both were committed to winning for their shared literary efforts the same respect and acclaim that the school had traditionally given to sports.

Harry spent several days toward the end of the summer visiting potential printers for the magazine in an effort to reduce costs. He also met with established journalists and editors (among them the editors of *Outlook* and *Scribner's*) to request advice and, it was surely not lost on him, to make connections. He watched the "October Scribner being run off the gigantic machine—but not one page of it could I carry to the outside world as a proof that I had seen it! I saw where the many beautiful color plates are made, and the foreman gave me a score or two of the beautiful pictures that had adorned Scribner's in the past. In short, I learned a good deal of the mechanical part of publishing, and had a most interesting afternoon."[39]

Back at Hotchkiss for his long-awaited senior year, he claimed not to "feel that elation or exultation which had been promised me." But he leaped nevertheless into his usual frantic schedule. "The pleasant days of summer have given way to the days of work," he wrote. "Which are more blessed, even to the schoolboy, I cannot say." Most of all he leaped into his new role as editor of the *Lit*. Recalling his memorable day watching *Scribner's Magazine* roll off the presses, he launched the magazine with an issue containing a special picture supplement ("First in the Prep School World," he boasted on the cover). The pictures were relatively simple black-and-white drawings and photographs, not the "beautiful color plates" he had admired in New York. Even so, they were an expensive innovation for a school publication, and they were made possible in part by his success in attracting an unusual amount of advertising through the parents of wealthy classmates and friends of the McCormicks. Harry managed as well to increase the number of pages in the *Lit*, expand the number of articles (including many of his own), and add more essays dealing with contemporary issues and events. Under his direction the *Lit* became not just a monthly literary magazine, but a journal of reportage and opinion. The response, he wrote his mother, was gratifying. "Such a stir over a mere magazine I never had in my life expected to see," he wrote after the first issue appeared. "I would, unnoticed, walk in a room, the Senior Room perhaps, and the comments I overheard positively prevented my keeping a straight face. In short, the school appears to approve of our new Lit, with all its obvious faults and shortcomings. . . . [W]e intend to proceed on the ever forward movement for a 'better' magazine." "The Better Magazine" became, in fact, the *Lit*'s masthead slogan.[40]

The implicit challenge from the *Lit* did not escape Brit, and he took a gentle swipe at Harry's pretensions with a review in the *Record* of the rival publication. "We are well aware that 'The Better Magazine' means a magazine which aims to be 'better' than itself in each successive issue. At the same time, however, we still fear that the slogan might readily be misinterpreted by an outsider as meaning better than any other magazine." Brit was making his own mark on the *Record* (with Harry's occasional help as an assistant managing editor). He transformed it from a weekly to a semiweekly, added coverage of national and international news, and received much the same enthusiastic reception from faculty and students that Harry was getting for the *Lit*. Over time their good-natured rivalry evolved into something like a mutual admiration society. "Luce's poem, entitled 'Stanzas,' is by far the best that has appeared in the *Lit* this year," Brit wrote in the *Record*. " 'Mediocrity in Scholarship' by the same author is an article which should receive the thoughtful and sincere attention of every fellow in the school. More articles by this writer would be desirable." Harry responded late in the year with an editorial, "The Literary Game," arguing that writers deserved as much respect as athletes, and paying a particular tribute to Brit: "To run a semi-weekly, six-page newspaper—outside of study hours—and to have not more than one typographical error a fortnight, and to have a keen, clear, pointed editorial to each issue . . . we say that there is no harder job in the entire Hotchkiss School—no football game that ever will demand more 'guts' than this." Naturally he did not exempt himself from such praise: "Casting the convention of modesty to the dust, we say that to publish a monthly magazine with 300 pages . . . and to pay for nearly 200 electrotypes . . . is no tea-parlor, silk-sock, poetically temperamental game."[41]

In his senior year Harry was well established as both an impressive scholar and an important campus leader, and he was well satisfied with his success. "I think, if I were to boast of my career here," he wrote, "it is that while I am not popular in the crowd, I have not an enemy in the class. And this is in spite of some harsh things I have said and some mistakes I have made." He still carried the stigma of a scholarship student, with his daily chores (now working in the library and serving as an usher in chapel) and his inferior accommodations (a garreted room in the attic of a teacher's home, which he shared with another scholarship student, "joined to Bissel Hall, wherein will live our classmates of better means"). But he seemed less conscious of this difference in status than he had once been—confident now that he had proven himself the equal of even the wealthiest and most socially prominent students. It was, perhaps, that eager confidence that made him react so bitterly to a falling-out with the school's imperious headmaster.[42]

Until his last term at Hotchkiss, Harry had what he considered a good relationship with "the King." "I flatter myself that I am decidedly in the good graces of Dr. Buehler," he wrote in his junior year. "Whereas most fellows go from one term's beginning to its end without conversing with him, he has already spoken to me half a dozen times—and not by way of reprimand." But something went badly wrong as he neared graduation. Buehler began to chastise him for neglecting his duties as a scholarship student, for neglecting his library work, for being careless in his chores. To Buehler the problem was that Harry now believed he had so risen in the world that scholarship work was beneath him. (He once referred in a school sermon to "the supercilious boy, the fellow who thinks he knows too much" as someone in "great danger.") Harry blamed the problem on Buehler's own determination to keep a poor boy in his place. Both of them were probably at least partly right. Whatever the reasons, Buehler appeared determined to slap Harry down—and he did so by humiliating him in the way he knew would hurt him the most, by doing so in the eyes of his father. In a letter to Shantung in March 1916, he wrote, "You should know that for sometime we have not been satisfied with Harry's attention to detail in connection with some of his duties." He was doing well academically and in his activities, Buehler conceded, but "he has seemed careless or indifferent in regard to things which he should consider equally important." His complaint seemed to rest on reports of Harry's entering the library too noisily and leaving his drawer of books "carelessly open." This fault, he insisted, "is more serious in its relations and bearing on his future than he seems to realize," particularly since he was "a scholarship boy and . . . expected to set the right example." As apparent punishment, Harry was reassigned from the library to the more menial task of taking care of the "Bissel Hall lights."[43]

Harry's furious and almost desperate reaction to Buehler's reprimand—a wounding but ultimately petty slight—suggests how fragile his new self-image as a mature, self-reliant young adult still was, and how painful it was to be reminded so bluntly of his social standing, which he thought he had transcended. To his father he wrote imploringly that he hoped "it will not shake what trust you have had in me, because that's a thing a fellow hates to lose most of all." But he could not help adding swipes at Buehler for his pettiness in reporting "highly magnified nothings." Rev. Luce urged him to be conciliatory and to accept the criticism "gracefully, without resentment," but Harry was in no mood to compromise. He would talk to "the King" about the problem, he assured his father, but he would not go "crawling" to him. Privately he was much angrier than he let his parents know. At the bottom of Buehler's letter reassigning him to Bissel Hall, Harry wrote a draft of a reply, which he clearly never sent: "Sir, My opinion of you is that you are a damned fool, and someday I'll prove it to you."[44]

Harry's conflict with Buehler even caused him momentarily to question his otherwise seldom-questioned ambition. In the light of this "aspersion on my general character," he said, he had begun to contemplate "the call of the road, outcast from convention and the etiquette of morality and manners." It would be wonderful, he mused, "to live near the heart of the highways and byways of life, to buy bread by any occasional pence I could get, to smile at men and the world, to help lame dogs over any sty's [*sic*] I can. . . . [T]he life of a fool is greater than the temporal power of some demagogue (Dr. Buehler or Napoleon)." But he knew, of course, that he would "never follow" such a path; and although he did not forgive Buehler and, indeed, spoke bitterly about him even forty years later, he neared the end of his years at the school still loyal to Hotchkiss and proud of his record there. "I have made a success," he said, "as few will ever appreciate or understand." His class, he claimed, "has done some big things at a critical time in the history of the school" in fighting the "dry-rot of self complacency" that had been "at the core of the place."

But it was time to look ahead. "I dread leaving my moorings and jumping into the race again," he wrote a few months before his graduation. "But unless we race we rot." As he looked ahead to the next chapter in his life—Yale, which, along with fifty-two out of his sixty-nine classmates, he would be entering in the fall—he saw only new challenges, new opportunities for achievement. "They say—and they are saying it pretty loudly—that Hotchkiss is not holding its own at Yale." It was up to his class to change that impression. Always calculating, always striving, Harry was leaving little room for spontaneity, even as he prepared to enter an institution he barely knew. "For one thing we must show that we have a man with enough ability and 'guts' to make the [Yale Daily] News," he wrote, clearly referring to himself. The News was " 'Yale's choicest prize' " and "a man who makes the news has a 99% chance of success everywhere in life." He would "hit the News hard in freshman year—then . . . go after Phi Beta K and the Lit Board in sophomore and junior years."[45]

Hotchkiss graduation was a difficult moment for Harry. Most of his classmates were surrounded by proud parents and siblings. He spent the day in the company of a distant cousin he barely knew. He had been named class poet and read a short ode at the Class Day ceremony, but the position of class orator, which he had particularly coveted, went to Brit instead. He finished his senior year not first in his class, as he had almost always been, but second, "beaten by a terrible greasy grind! I wish somebody had had the time or opportunity to beat him out." In a class poll he received no votes at all for "most likely to succeed"; he ranked high not only as "brightest" and "most energetic," but also in such categories as "most absent-minded" and "most eccentric." In the class yearbook, he was mildly ridiculed for having used "stolen" yearbook photographs in the *Lit*. He was, in short, confronted by his own hidden self-image and how he appeared to others. When it was over he expressed relief but little exaltation. "*It is done*," he wrote flatly in his first letter home after commencement. "For the last forty-eight hours I have been capable of no other thought than 'It is done.' My school boy life with all its many failures and few half-successes is over." He left Hotchkiss looking unsentimentally ahead, as always, to the next step, to a new life once again, "without illusions, romance, high flown talk or sentimental teas."[46]

III

Big Man

At eighteen years of age, dispatched from Hotchkiss and bound for Yale, Harry was at once remarkably mature and strikingly naive. He was more traveled and more knowledgeable of the world than almost any of his peers—a gifted student, an accomplished linguist, and at times an unusually sophisticated writer. Thousands of miles from his family, with no expectation of seeing any of them for months and sometimes years, he had learned to make his way alone in a country that not long ago had been almost entirely new to him; and he had learned to handle aspects of his own life—finances, travel plans, doctors, housing, vacations—that most adolescents of his background still left to their parents.

In other respects, however, Harry was still very much a boy. Even when dressed up in the formal suits that young prep-school men donned for portraits and formal occasions, his thatch of reddish brown hair always seemed slightly tousled, his clothes slightly wrinkled and ill fitting, his gaze somewhat too studied in its seriousness. Away from school he still sometimes wore the knickers he had grown up with in China. He was tall, nearing the six feet he would soon attain, but thin (usually just under 150 pounds) and slightly gawky. He had begun to smoke, but tentatively and self-consciously, insisting it was only to ease his discomfort in public and that it would never become a habit. (In fact it became a lifelong addiction that eventually helped to kill him.) And perhaps most painful to him of all, he was socially awkward and sexually inexperienced. His Hotchkiss classmates, in their senior poll, ranked him ninth in the class as "worst woman-hater." One of his friends, writing to him of the attractions of summer in Nantucket, noted that "the dancing is fine (but that doesn't interest you!), the girls—(but there again I forget who I'm writing to)." Both the maturity and the naïveté were visible in one of the most conspicuous aspects of Harry's personality at this turning point in his young life: his intense ambition. He had been a diligent striver for years, working desperately to prove himself to his father, his teachers, and his classmates. But his ambition to succeed in school was only a prelude to his much greater ambition to lead an important life. As he looked forward to Yale, he was planning once again an assault on the honors and privileges available to him as a student; but he was also beginning to look beyond—to a larger world he hoped to find some way to shape.[1]

Harry was an avid, if only modestly talented, poet at Hotchkiss. Many of his poems for the *Lit* were purely descriptive—for example, his sentimental account of life in Shantung, a poem he liked so much he tried in vain to have it published in a national literary magazine. Other poems expressed his emerging view of his place in the world. In one of them, "Mankind," he wrote of the tension between two human impulses: the "doubt and fear" that leads individuals into safe, small lives in "huddling valleys," and the drive to ascend to something greater, to "the billowy wind-swept hills" from which one can see the world more broadly. He left no doubt that he had resolved that tension for himself: "Ah! Let me climb my little hill, / And make achievement own my will. / Let all the lowland mark me high, / And praise me once before I die."[2]

Harry prefaced his poem with a quotation from "Henry W. Luce": "Too often we fear the greater vision." It was an appropriate inscription, because the shape of Harry's aspirations owed much to those of his father—a similarly driven man who had committed himself to a kind of life that, in his own youth, had attracted many ambitious men hoping for greatness and glory. The elder Harry was deeply spiritual. But he also coveted the worldly rewards associated with his missionary calling and agonized over his frequently thwarted ambitions. He never achieved his dream of being elected to the presidency of Shantung Christian University. Once it moved to the new campus at Tsinan that his fund-raising had made possible, his hopes were thwarted by rivalries between the British and American missionaries and between Presbyterians and Baptists. But his hopes were also dashed by the very intensity of his own ambition and the abrupt, confrontational style he sometimes adopted when his own plans and visions faced opposition. He recognized this flaw in himself ("I have been hyper-critical and antagonistic where it was not vitally necessary. . . . I have possibly 'felt' too deeply often more than the occasion called for"). And he was perceptive enough to see in his son some of the same tendencies and to warn him against them. ("It is the kind and unselfish man who attracts. . . . *People like to be agreed with*.") Rev. Luce's own ambitions did not subside, however, and for the rest of his own active life he strove for advancement within his world and suffered from the animosities his aggressive personality sometimes aroused.[3]

Harry agonized over his father's disappointments, but he gave no evidence of absorbing their cautionary lessons. The problems in Tsinan and Beijing, he always insisted, were a result of the pettiness and selfishness of others, not of any flaw in his father's own behavior. ("I fear me there is trouble in the State of Denmark," he wrote in response to his father's penitent description of his own flaws. "Perhaps the cause of Christian missions has enlisted more rotten eggs than its heroes can make up for!") For a time he at least claimed to want to follow the missionary path himself, perhaps to vindicate his father's struggles through his own future triumphs. "I know that [the missionary life] is the most honourable calling in the world," he wrote his father from Hotchkiss. And while he confessed to be pondering other paths for himself, he continued to insist that he was not "aiming at rather paltry ambition for the chances are 99 to 1 that I become a prof (!) in S.C.U. I have now no greater ambition than to be of use in the Foreign Field."[4]

But despite his very real admiration for the career his father had chosen, Harry was already charting another course for himself, one no less ambitious and, in his view at least, no less likely to provide him with an opportunity to add value to the world. "I am just about coming to that stage," he wrote shortly before leaving Hotchkiss, "when the world of fact and of ideas is intensely interesting. And I hope that I may attain one thing: 'to wear life as a mantle.' Until one can do that, I believe no man can really be said to live." The best route to "the world of facts and ideas," he was rapidly coming to believe, was journalism. He had already decided to enter the arduous competition for a place on the *Yale Daily News*. But even more significantly, he had arranged—entirely on his own—to spend the summer working for a small newspaper in central Massachusetts, the *Springfield Republican*, "perhaps the most famous paper in the country for its size." It had an impressive history, edited in the nineteenth century by Samuel Bowles, a founder of the Republican

Party, a strong antislavery advocate, and a leading liberal of his time. The twentieth-century *Republican*, small as it was, aspired to sustain its illustrious history. The paper had hired him to work in its business office, which would, he said, "offer limitless possibilities for experience, and that, as varied as possible, is what I'm after." But he hoped over time "to creep into the reportorial department somehow."[5]

The summer began poorly. Springfield was a place "where I really don't know any one," Harry lamented, and he was sometimes almost paralyzed by loneliness. He took a room in the YMCA and spent most evenings there by himself, reading, writing letters to his family, and fighting "severe attacks of the 'blues.' " At the *Republican* he was assigned to the subscription desk alongside two other young men who, unlike him, depended on the jobs for their livings and feared he would take their places. The work was menial and repetitive ("a great deal of entering, checking, noting, billing, etc. etc.,—which makes it quite overpoweringly complicated for a beginner"), precisely the kind of work on which Harry had always had difficulty concentrating, as his run-ins with Buehler at Hotchkiss had demonstrated. Even so, he tried to make a virtue out of the experience. "Now red-tape is all right for men like Dickens to harangue against," he wrote his parents, "but a certain amount of it is very necessary,—and woe betide the poor ass that so much as tangles the silken cord by one small strand." As the days and weeks wore on, however, his lack of fitness for clerical work became ever clearer. "I don't seem to be progressing at all well in my office work. I keep on making 'error' after 'error,' " he noted after his first six weeks on the job. The work was a "grind," he complained, "babyish" and "boring." And the indulgence of his supervisors, who consistently took responsibility for his mistakes, only deepened his unhappiness.[6]

Eventually, however, Harry found himself drawn into the larger work of the newspaper, and his spirits rose accordingly. He did no actual reporting, but he began accompanying reporters as they worked on their stories, and was recruited at times to help rewrite copy. "I am learning lots of things, that one takes for granted that everybody knows, but which, I guess, very few do know," he told his parents. "I never saw a cell before. I never spoke to a prisoner. I never saw a brave tear-stained mother come to bail out her son, held on sure charge of forgery. These things reveal the Christ who said, 'I came not to the righteous.' " He was awestruck by the reporters who befriended him, envious of their free-and-easy way with strangers (a talent he himself would never master), and mesmerized by their self-serving descriptions of their profession. He was particularly impressed by one of the *Republican*'s "star reporters," who had traveled with Roosevelt, Taft, and Wilson and who, Harry recounted, "broke away from his taciturn self the other day, and said 'Damn it all, anyway, even if I do say it, there's not a game on the face of the earth that requires more manhood of every kind than the reporting game. There's hardly a firm in this city, respectable or otherwise, that I don't know a good deal about. And not one of them takes the physical, intellectual or nervous energy that a man simply must put into the reporting business, if he doesn't want to quit at it.' " Once in a while Harry even managed to write small "notices" of his own and slip them by the city editor. He excitedly cut them out and sent them home to China.[7]

By the end of the summer he was filled with admiration for the people he had met at the *Republican*, and filled also with pride at his own performance there. "Have had fine experience," he reported as he prepared to leave Springfield. "Feel like I could run a paper!!!" And he was more than ever attracted now to the world of journalism. "I believe that I can be of greatest service in journalistic work," he wrote his parents late in August, "and can by that way come nearest to the heart of the world. . . . Having made this absolute statement at last—have I met with your approval?" By the time he received their guardedly positive response, he was a student at Yale.[8]

The Yale Harry encountered in the fall of 1916 was a very different place from the college his father had entered twenty-eight years earlier. For one thing it was more secular. The evangelical fervor that had inspired the Student Volunteer Movement and that had made conspicuous piety a common and respected characteristic of college life in the 1880s was now spent. Religion had become a routine but far from fervent part of student culture. Harry's own faith was almost certainly stronger than that of most of his classmates, but he usually gave scant evidence of it. "All this publicity of Christianity, this carrying Christ around in public like a circus side-show, is highly repulsive to me," he wrote after a first meeting at Dwight Hall, a campus religion center. "And young men that talk too much about the man Jesus—I wonder, do they know of what they talk, or are they only religiously drunk?" The "fervid Xianity [Christianity]" of the meeting, he added, "has completely alienated my friend Brit Hadden from its holy halls."[9]

Yale was also a very different place academically from what it had been a generation before. Like colleges and universities across the nation, it had transformed itself in response to the burgeoning of new scholarly interests, which were, in turn, arising out of the rapid social and economic development of the United States. No longer were American colleges simply finishing schools for gentlemen, educating them in the classics, theology, and languages. They were becoming training grounds for the professions and the new economy. They were offering instruction in the social sciences and the natural sciences alongside the traditional disciplines. Faculties were organizing into "departments," and many universities, Yale among them, were now offering graduate degrees. Although traditional requirements remained, there were now also many new choices open to undergraduates—including the choice of concentrating in an area of knowledge of particular interest or value to the individual student.

For all the changes, however, Yale remained a small and fairly provincial college, drawing students mainly from the social and economic elites of the Northeast and the industrial Midwest. And despite the modernity of much of its new curriculum, the character of student life was much as it had been in the 1880s. The great badges of achievement were not academic honors. As at Hotchkiss, success at Yale came from such things as playing varsity football, heeling the *Daily News*, winning election to the board of the literary magazine, and gaining admission to the prestigious clubs and senior societies that dominated the social life of the campus. Owen Johnson's classic novel, *Stover at Yale*, published in 1912, provided a mostly accurate picture of life in New Haven in 1916. From the moment they arrived, ambitious students were encouraged to succeed by "working for Yale" and striving for the distinctions that campus activities offered. "You may think the world begins outside of college," an upperclassman explained to Dink Stover his first night on campus. "It doesn't; it begins right here," in the struggle to get in with "the real crowd," to become "one of the big men in the class." "The immediate goal was to be regarded as a success by your friends . . . to be known as the big men," recalled Henry Seidel Canby, who had graduated from Yale a few years before Harry arrived and later served briefly as an instructor in English there before becoming a distinguished magazine editor. These were things Harry already knew, having come from a school almost all of whose graduates went on to Yale. He also knew what Stover had to be taught: that the most important badge of success at Yale was election to one of the elite senior societies—and above all to the most prestigious of them, Skull and Bones.[10]

Harry wanted to combine serious academic work with the many nonacademic temptations of the university. And as at Hotchkiss, he was determined to excel at everything. But the balance of his interests had subtly changed. His first priority—which he had articulated many months earlier while still in Lakeville—was to heel the *News* and win election to its board. But because heeling the *News* was an exceptionally intense and time-consuming experience (the heelers "slept never more than four hours a night . . . and were rusticated or sent to the infirmary by the dozens," Canby recalled), he worried about its possible impact on his academic work. "It certainly is very hard to decide just what one ought to do," he wrote his parents months before his arrival in New Haven. "Theoretically, if it came down to an issue between Phi Beta Kappa and the News, I would take the former." That was what he knew his parents wanted to hear. Even in writing them, however, he could not leave it at that. "But if, practically, a key and a News charm were laid before me now, I am afraid my hand would almost unconsciously grasp the latter." The "best policy," he decided, was to concentrate on the *News* in his freshman year, "then to go after Phi Beta K and the Lit Board in sophomore and junior years." He had elaborate rationalizations for his choice: "Success will mean prestige and chance for influence," he predicted, as well as money (since members of the *News* board shared in the paper's modest profits). And since his goal was a life in journalism, "I do not see how it can help helping me."[11]

By the time he got to New Haven the rationalizations and negotiations were behind him, and he was ready to jump into the fray. "Already the race is on," he wrote after his first few days on campus, before classes or any other activities had begun. "The goals must soon, or never, be chosen, and the quest begun." Almost single-mindedly he set out to conquer the *News*. Several of his friends from Hotchkiss were doing the same, but from the beginning he knew his greatest competition would come from Brit Hadden, both because of Hadden's prodigious talent and because Brit was at least as determined as Harry was. *News* heelers earned points for writing stories, offering story ideas, selling advertising, and doing chores around the paper. Harry and Brit (both of whom had experienced a similar heeling process at Hotchkiss, modeled on Yale's) spent almost every spare moment in the *News* building, as if fearful that any absence would give their competitors an edge. Brit often got out of bed in the middle of the night to put a reporting "scoop" in the *News* box, so that it would be the first thing the editors would find in the morning. Harry often stayed in the building until late at night helping with the writing and editing, even cleaning up.[12]

Harry was awed at times by the intensity of the *News* competition. He had entered it with extraordinary apprehension ("All I ask is strength and ability to stick out to the end!"), and he moved through it almost as if in a dream. His moods swung up and down with every minor achievement and every small setback. At one moment he despaired of making the paper at all, the next he predicted he would finish the competition in first place. In the fever of his ambition, he was already calculating not just what would happen in his freshman year but who would be elected chairman of the *News* almost three years later. Heeling, he said in a moment of optimism, "is a very holy and wonderful piece of complicated machinery," which "serves very well." In lower moments he complained that his competitors were taking unfair advantage of a fallible system. "This heeling business is awful," he wrote at one point, "and you can't imagine how depressing it is." Most of all he obsessively calculated where he stood in the competition—now fourth, then second, later third, from time to time first—all these predictions based on nothing but his own uninformed and subjective judgments.[13]

Finally, in March, the great announcement came: Harry was one of four first-year students elected to the *News*. He had come in third, behind Brit and one other Hotchkiss classmate. But for the moment, at least, he seemed not to care about anything but his appointment. "Successful," he wrote his parents in a one-word telegram to China, and they of course understood immediately what it meant. ("It is too splendid for words!" his mother wrote back.) For the next few weeks Harry basked in the glow of his triumph. "The bright sun and wind of a March afternoon sweep leisurely through my room," he wrote a few days after the election. "No more, as on other Mondays, the blind mad rush of heeling, not again as in that last Monday, the intolerable suspense; but now assurance, quiet leisure, duty and pleasure." He was, for once, almost smugly self-satisfied—the raging ambition that made him so chronically and methodically hyperactive through most of his life suddenly, if briefly, quelled: "My position in college, in so far as I can make it is made. I have come to Rome, and succeeded in the Roman circus. Now there is for me free rein to enjoy over three years of philosophy, history, and poetry. So I hope to be able to say at the end of this college course with Johnson: 'The days of thought were the goodly days.' "[14]

Harry had good reason to be pleased with himself. Only a little more than one semester into his life at Yale, he had not only achieved one of the most coveted positions in the college—a place on the *News*—but had placed first in his class academically, had a poem accepted by the literary magazine, and been awarded the Chamberlain Prize for the best performance by any Yale student on the university's comprehensive entrance examination in Greek, which he had coveted throughout his years at Hotchkiss. "This achievement will mean a holiday for the Hotchkiss school [a tradition when recent graduates achieved something notable], and a valuable reputation for myself," he wrote. Harry also found himself socially popular, something he had never quite been in the much more class-conscious environment of Hotchkiss. "Am meeting more fellows all the time, and, to be brief, am enjoying college," he boasted. He even joined a club for "foreign" students—which mostly consisted of young Americans, like Harry himself, who had lived abroad. One of its members was the future playwright Thornton Wilder, a missionary son from China who had spent a miserable year with Harry at Chefoo. Harry's roommate—a result of pressure from his parents—was Horace Pitkin, Jr., the son of his father's beloved, martyred college classmate. The younger Pitkin was a slightly troubled young man utterly without the restless ambition that drove Harry's life and whom Harry gradually came to view with some condescension and even contempt. Harry's relationship with Brit Hadden was close, friendly, and slightly tense, as it would always remain, reflecting their tacit acknowledgment of both powerful bonds and profound rivalry. His larger social circle—the young men with whom he had an easier intimacy—consisted, at least at first, almost entirely of other Hotchkiss graduates.[15]

At Yale, unlike at Hotchkiss, Harry was not a scholarship student. He paid his own way with his own earnings at college and in summers, with help from his parents, and with generous gifts from Nettie McCormick. That spared him the outward badges of inferiority he had experienced in prep school. There were no demeaning work assignments, no talk of "special responsibilities," no banishment to remote accommodations. Even so Harry remained one of the least affluent members of his class, a problem he seldom revealed to others but one he agonized over privately. He struggled to keep within his tight budget even as he yearned to join the expensive activities of his friends. His residence hall, he conceded, "is not the most desirable dormitory socially." He claimed not to mind, but he balked at eating in the college commons, at $5.00 to $6.00 a week the cheapest place on campus. Instead, Harry chose to join a dining club, which cost $7.50. He explained this "extravagance" to his parents by saying that "the food is excellent," and "the fellows are the nicest in our class." His father, always concerned about Harry's social status and—intrepid fund-raiser that he was—acutely aware of the advantages of connections with the wealthy, supported the decision.[16]

Yale was, in fact, a turning point in Harry's attitude toward wealth. An important part of the missionary ethos he had absorbed as a child was a kind of pride in having forsaken the material rewards of more lucrative professions, a belief that material self-denial was a sign of virtue and character. Although Harry had already decided not to become a missionary himself, he tried still to embrace the ethos and struggled (with scant success) to resist material temptations. Even years later, when he himself was enormously rich, he often seemed impatient with and even embarrassed by the opulence of his life and from time to time tried ineffectually to escape from it. But his experience at Yale also helped intensify his fascination with, and attraction to, wealth—an attraction that had begun in his first years in America during his frequent visits to Mrs. McCormick's palatial home in Chicago. His thirst grew stronger as he became exposed to the way his more affluent classmates lived.

During Yale's spring recess in 1917, in the aftermath of the exhausting competition for the *News*, Harry's Yale and Hotchkiss classmate Alger Shelden invited the newly elected board members to spend a week at his home in Detroit. Harry claimed to enjoy the visit most because it gave him a chance to take walks through the "soggy wood and muddy field" surrounding the Shelden estate. "My heart beat high in praise of 'the country again,—the country!' " he wrote at the time. But his accounts of the week in letters to his parents could not disguise his awe at the manner in which his friend's family lived. Alger's father, he wrote, was a high-ranking executive at the Ford Motor Company and "one of Detroit's richest of the rich." His home was "one of the largest and handsomest estates in Grosse Point." The young men from Yale were entertained lavishly, with visits to the Hunt Club, the country club, and other institutions serving the city's automobile aristocracy. They went riding and hunting on "splendid mounts." They were served a "sumptuous supper" after going to the theater one night. On another day they were taken on a tour of the Ford factory—young princes in suits and ties quietly watching what Harry described, without comment, as the "thousands of workers whose job consists of 'screwing one screw or hammering one nail, or turning one lever of a machine.' " The vacation, he wrote en route back to New Haven, "gave me about as much fun as I ever had in my life." It was the last such vacation he was to have for several years.[17]

Three years earlier, at the beginning of his second year at Hotchkiss, Harry had returned from the summer to find a large map of Europe on one of the school bulletin boards, with dozens of blue and red pins stuck

along a line running through Belgium and France: The First World War
had begun. Every day the teachers would move the pins to mark the
slow, inconclusive movement of troops back and forth across the swath
of France in which the torturous, stalemated struggle was being fought.
The war was naturally the subject of much conversation among Harry
and his classmates, but until 1917 their interest was essentially academic.
"I do not believe in the possibility of [America going to] war," Harry
wrote in March 1916, a few months before his Hotchkiss graduation.
The "heroes of Verdun"—British, French, and German—would never
"allow innocents like ourselves . . . [to] interfere much in the way they
settle things."[18]

But in April 1917, as he and his friends returned to Yale from their
lavish week in Detroit, the war was no longer an academic question. The
United States, after more than two years of hesitation, had finally
entered the conflict, and Harry knew that, in one way or another, he
would enter it too. Looking back a year or so later, as the war shuddered
to a close with Harry never having left America, he claimed to wish he
had chosen what his more adventurous classmates had done—left the
college and enlisted right away. "Had I done that I would probably be in
France now," he said wistfully. But Harry was not one to defy the norms
of his institutions, and so he did what the president of the university,
Arthur Hadley, urged all Yale students to do: stay in school, stick
together, join the Reserve Officers Training Corps Field Artillery Unit
that the army had established on campus, and prepare for war as "Yale
men." There were plenty of available troops, Hadley said; what the
nation needed was officers, and the university would provide them.[19]

As a result the next fourteen months produced relatively modest
changes in Harry's life and in the lives of most of his classmates. The
routines of the college, the academic and social rituals, continued. The
only major exception was a few hours a week when there was military
training by officers of the special Yale unit—ranks of college boys doing
calisthenics and marching up and down the New Haven Green dressed
in pressed khakis and carrying rifles they almost never fired. About two-
thirds of Yale's students enrolled in the program, which took the place of
one academic course. (The other third had already gone to war.) Harry
still talked occasionally of leaving college to join the army, to work in
military intelligence in Washington, or to do something else—anything
else—that might put him in closer touch with the war, including a fanci-
ful proposal that he go to China to help the United States recruit coolies
to help in the war effort (a proposal the American consular service in

Shanghai brusquely rejected). In the end, he convinced himself that his best option was to stay at Yale "unless something turns up in which I can serve with my brains as well as my heels and hence educate myself in the act of service."[20]

Once he made his decision, duty and ambition seamlessly merged. With the *News* competition over, he wrote, "another form of strenuous life is forced upon me." Harry would contribute to the war effort by writing exhortatory editorials for the *News* "pushing Yale to a more and more intensive war-training life." While doing so he could advance his fortunes on the paper by filling in for the older editors who were being "called away" to the war. In early June he was elected to the "emergency council" the *News* had established to run the paper in the absence of some of the more senior board members, and he predicted that his election as chairman for 1920 would soon be "railroaded through." The council would work to sell Liberty Bonds and "keep Yale together." Harry explained, perhaps slightly defensively, that "I may be of some service to my country here."[21]

So little did the war impinge on life at Yale that after a few weeks of ROTC camp in early June, the students scattered and began their normal summer vacations. Harry spent July and August working on the farm of family friends in western Pennsylvania, reading Homer, and making plans for "my conduct next year." His priorities, he said in a letter to his parents a few weeks before returning to Yale, were to "give more attention to personal affairs, economy, clothes, correspondence, reading, etc., . . . to discharge thoroughly my college obligations," and to tend to "the cultivation of 'myself' by all the cultural means that come in the course of the day's work, from religion to friendly chatter." He did not mention the war.[22]

By the time Harry returned to New Haven in September 1917, the war had become a somewhat more prominent part of life. "Here at college we are practically in government service. All members of the R.O.T.C. . . . are obliged to stay in uniform the entire time, except when they go out of town," he wrote in October. Seeing an opportunity in the new military frenzy, Harry spent his first few days on campus serving as an agent for a local tailor who was providing uniforms for students. For days he could be seen running up and down the stairs of the freshman dormitories taking orders. His profits financed most of his sophomore year.

On the whole, however, Yale's leisurely, gentlemanly approach to the conflict continued for a while longer. Students spent a few more hours in military training than they had the previous spring, but their principal concerns remained largely unchanged. For Harry that meant excelling in his language, literature, and history courses; continuing to advance at the *News* and in the many other activities to which he found himself drawn; and consolidating his social life. He ran for a position on the student council, survived the primaries to become a finalist, but came in fourth in a race in which only three men were chosen (Hadden finished first). "I am just as glad that I didn't get the election," he wrote in a characteristic effort to rationalize his disappointments, "because it would have meant that in spite of my determination to have a 'literatus' year, I would once more be deeply plunged by another route into the trifling turmoil of collegiateness." He won election to the Elizabethan Club, a literary organization for faculty and students that he called "a joy and delight." He had another poem accepted by the *Lit*, which almost assured him election to the board. He and Brit Hadden recruited a table for one of the Yale dining societies, attracting "a nucleus of the best men in the class, . . . the most desireable [*sic*] 'crowd' socially." In return, they received their own meals free "without scarcely turning my hand."[23]

Most of all, however, he was preoccupied with the impending selection of new members to the Yale fraternities. And as always he wrestled with himself over what to do. Psi U "is the socially best, so, of course, I should prefer to get in that," he said at the beginning of the process. But he was soon "soundly disappointed" to discover that there was no likelihood of his receiving an invitation there. The "social types," with whom he still had awkward relations, had "blackballed me," he explained, not just at Psi U, but at his second choice, DKE. That suddenly threw Luce's view of the whole process into a different light: "The Junior fraternities at Yale do not seem to mean much," he now wrote, and he had little "respect and regard" for them. Psi U, he decided, was no longer "the big fraternity," for "this year there was a general stampede from it, because it catered strongly to purely social elements." He finally joined Alpha Delta, which he now insisted had many of the "best men" in the class— among them, a year later, a recruit of whom Harry was particularly proud, "Frank Gould, who will be the richest of the third generation of Goulds." Adding to his poorly disguised disappointment was his usual guilt about devoting so much time to what he feared his father would consider trivial things. "The social side of life—which I suppose is a necessary evil—throws one so completely off one's trolley," he wrote shamefacedly to his parents. "My room is in a terrible state, as are also my finances and studies. In fact the first half of the first term ends to-day, and I shall have a ridiculously low average, and the only comfort I'll get will be that it is probably higher than any other fraternity man's." Even so his grades remained within Phi Beta Kappa range, and he consoled himself for his social disappointments by insisting that he was certain to achieve "the three things I wanted most to: News, Lit, & P.B.K."[24]

By the beginning of the spring term, military training had expanded to fill almost half the college curriculum, and there was talk of turning the campus over altogether to the military, of establishing a "West Point at Yale." More and more students were leaving the university to join the military, and Harry continued to consider doing the same. Although he was only in the middle of his second year, he took to referring wistfully to "my last year under the academic aegis," and to imagining himself a commissioned officer leading troops in France. "Well, so this college world gets along," he mused in March 1918. "And a very happy and pleasant place it is. How soon shall it be but a memory."[25]

One of the reasons Harry may have been looking beyond Yale so soon was a crushing disappointment he had suffered in January 1918. Because so many upperclassmen were away in the military, the *News* felt obliged to elect its 1920 board a year earlier than usual. Harry and Brit were clearly the two leading contenders for chairman. But by a single vote Hadden won. Publicly Harry dealt with the defeat calmly and graciously. He deflected a suggestion that the *News* create a special, unprecedented position for him—vice chairman—and agreed instead to serve as managing editor. He told everyone that Brit was an excellent and talented choice, which at one level he truly believed. But beneath his stoic surface was a profound sense of failure. "My fondest college ambition is unachieved," he wrote his parents in a letter suffused with disappointment. "It's been a hard pill to swallow. You can say such things are petty etc. etc., but just the same a man's heart's desire is his heart's desire whether it be President of the U.S. or Chairman of the News. Not a soul, I think, has seen what this all means to me."[26]

A few days later he began trying to convince himself that the decision might still be reversible. Hadden's election, so far ahead of schedule, had been a result of wartime disruptions. Luce briefly clung to the possibility that there might be a second vote at the normal time, which he might win. Harry wrote his parents that the "final vote" had not yet been taken, and one of Hadden's supporters told Harry that he was willing to switch and vote for him. But when the time came there was no reconsideration of the earlier vote, and Hadden's election was confirmed. Once again Harry was plunged into despair. "I could have been chairman of the News," he insisted, had he pressed his supporters to reconsider the vote. But "in the greatest sacrifice of my life I signed away the possibility." The whole story was too painful to recount, even to his parents, with whom he usually shared almost everything. "When a man fails, the less he had better talk of it," he wrote dejectedly (and again with more than a trace of self-pity). "However, I hope you won't think too harshly of me, nor believe that I have been irretrievably unworthy of you. . . . When I lie down tonight I shall be supremely glad that there are some that love me forever." His parents did not underestimate the severity of the blow to Harry's passionate ambition. From his mother he received an anguished letter of sympathy, praising him for his "great renunciation." From his father came a letter comparing his son's disappointment over the News election to his own disappointment in failing to gain the presidency of his college. "Usually the door opens to wider and richer experiences than if we had attained the idol of our hearts' desires; and wonderful is the way the heart forgets the past and presses on."[27]

More disappointment eventually followed. Harry was elected to the board of the Lit, on the basis of his fifth publication in the magazine, early in 1918. Several weeks later the Lit board met to choose its new leaders. At one point, according to Harry's own accounts, the other members of the board voted to choose him as chairman, despite what he claimed was his own stated reluctance to serve. But "then the row started." Several members of the board were enraged that someone who had never heeled the Lit and had played no previous role in its editorial processes should be chosen. In fact, during the entire previous year, Harry had done little more than submit an occasional piece to the magazine. "I decided that the Lit didn't mean enough to me to go through with a public scandal,—which was impending. I therefore resigned from the Board. Finally I was persuaded to return to the Board, and the Board against its will, but because I said so, elected Andrews," a more conventional choice—"typically 'literary' &—well, just a bit effeminate," as Harry described him.[28]

The story as Harry told it is revealing whether or not it is wholly accurate. It seems clear, first, that having lost the News competition, he had at least flirted with the compensatory idea of taking over another, if slightly less prestigious, campus publication—just as he had edited the Lit at Hotchkiss while Hadden edited the newspaper. It is also clear that, as with the News, it was important to him to be able to claim that he had in fact prevailed but had declined the position out of some combination of principle and self-interest. Most of all, however, the story demonstrates Harry's desire to portray himself as a person of stature and authority, admired by his peers if at times resented by them for his talents, able quietly to curb their own excesses and steer them in the right direction. He had quelled a rebellion against Hadden at the *News*, he claimed, to ensure a smooth transition. He had turned down the chairmanship at the *Lit* to avoid a damaging controversy, and had dictated the choice of a responsible alternative. In this way he turned his liabilities into strengths, his failures into triumphs.

In spite of the elements of self-deception that lurk in these descriptions, Harry was in many ways unsparing in his assessment of himself. He knew that despite his prodigious intellectual talents, despite his formidable abilities as a writer and editor, he was somehow lacking in social skills—able to attract the respect but not usually the genuine affection of those around him. It was a failing that was particularly visible to him because it stood in such contrast to the great strength of his friend and rival. Hadden was a much less gifted scholar than Harry and perhaps no more talented as a journalist, but he used his charismatic affability to win genuinely loyal friends and admirers. Harry was often intimidating in his unrelenting gravity. Brit, by contrast, was relaxed, even somewhat flippant, gently derisive of those who seemed to him too serious. "Watch out, Harry, or you'll drop the college," Hadden once shouted mockingly at Luce, who was walking with grim purpose across a Yale quad. Harry was aware of this difference and at times was almost morbid in his descriptions of his tangled relations with his peers. In the anguished aftermath of the *News* election, for example, he described his relationships with Hadden in painfully cautious language: "I have the greatest admiration and affection for Brit, which in some measure at least, is reciprocated."[29]

That these two close friends and colleagues were also very different from one another was not lost on their friends and classmates. They were almost constantly together, and they were also often at odds. "You never knew whether they were ready to fight or agree," one of their classmates later recalled. Dwight Macdonald, who observed Hadden and Luce as a young Time Inc. writer in the late 1920s, described in retrospect the contrasts in their great friendship and rivalry:

Luce/Hadden: moral/amoral, pious/worldly, respectable/raffish, bourgeois/bohemian, introvert/extrovert, somber/convivial, reliable/unpredictable, slow/quick, dog/cat, tame/wild, efficient/ brilliant, decent/charming, Puritanical/hedonistic, naive/cynical, Victorian/18th Century.

Almost all of these comparisons, in Macdonald's view at least, favored Hadden. Having been on the losing end of most of their competitions, and knowing how much more successful Brit was in making friends and securing allies, Harry almost surely sensed, but never admitted, that he was to some extent the junior partner of their collaborations. But no one could doubt the bond between them, a closeness greater than either man ever experienced with anyone else outside his own family.[30]

Harry sometimes gave himself less credit than he deserved in his own comparisons between himself and Hadden (and many of his other friends). He was especially different from them in his rejection of the cynicism and detachment that would become hallmarks of his generation's intellectual elite, which were already visible in the culture of the Yale of his time. Harry was unapologetically a man of conviction, principle, and faith; and while he understood the social cost of his seriousness and tried at times to mute it, he was far too preoccupied with the moral basis of his actions to disguise his real self for very long. Running through his own commentary on his triumphs and setbacks, his elation and his disappointments, is a consistent return to the question he had learned from his father always to ask himself: What "higher purpose" was he serving?

In the early months of 1918 that was a relatively easy question to answer—supporting and promoting the war. For by then, with the United States fully engaged in combat, it was no longer possible for Yale—or virtually any other institution in America—to sustain its casual, genteel approach to preparing for combat. War fervor was reaching a high pitch throughout the United States, driven in part by energetic government propaganda and in part by spontaneous popular commitment to the conflict. That many Americans—socialists, pacifists, members of various ethnic groups, and others—continued to oppose the nation's intervention in the war only drove supporters to greater levels of fervor. Seldom in American history had patriotism been so deliberately and effectively inflamed—and Harry, who had always been inclined to support the idea of an American mission in the world, eagerly embraced the passions of war.

A few months earlier he and Brit had been obscure sophomores, slogging away on the lower ranks of the *News* staff. Now, suddenly, they were in charge of the newspaper. And despite whatever tensions survived from their bruising battle for the chairmanship, they worked well together and turned the *News* into a powerful voice for intensifying the university's—and, they hoped, the nation's—engagement with the war. Among their innovations was a new section of the paper devoted to national and international news, which Hadden and Luce hoped would remind their readers of the great events of which they were a small part. But most of their stories and editorials were aimed at Yale matters. Harry, for example, exhorted Yale students to buy war bonds, not just as a way to contribute to the government's coffers but "as a vigorous test of a man's idealism." He challenged the campus to turn a "search-light" on all its activities "and confess just what of its parts is justified as 'war industry' and just which of its parts are not so justified." "We in college are attempting to our utmost capacity in our own lives," he wrote, "to put the military first." Yale, he insisted, was "at last ready to go to any extreme, ready to make any efficacious sacrifice in pursuit of our object." It was rebuilding itself "on the only foundation upon which we many now worthily build . . . intelligent and consecrated and intensive patriotism."[31]

Most of all he and Hadden defended and promoted the Yale officer-training units of which they and most of their classmates were a part. Outsiders might consider the all-Yale military unit—still training dutifully between classes in New Haven while so many others were already enlisted and in combat—a "pampered" or "effete" corps smacking of the "redolent plutocrat," Harry wrote defensively; but it was nothing of the sort. "We have committed ourselves to a definite course of action. We have set our faces in the light. We have undertaken the quest." When the navy offered some of the Yale trainees an opportunity to join a battleship cruise during Easter vacation, Harry cited it as "only one more illustration of the remarkable esteem in which the Yale Unit is held by the Navy Department."[32]

Despite the increased intensity of military training on campus, the academic calendar continued to govern. The Yale ROTC unit closed down for a month in June 1918, and its members, Harry among them, dispersed for vacation. Harry joined his family—temporarily back from China—in New Jersey. It was an anxious few weeks, because his sister Elisabeth—and eventually his mother and his other siblings—were stricken by the deadly influenza epidemic of 1918–19 that, before it was done, killed more Americans than died in World War I (and more

American soldiers than died in combat). The Luce family was fortunate. Everyone recovered, and Harry avoided the disease altogether. In mid-July he was back at Yale for more training. And a few weeks later he and seven other members of his ROTC troop (including Hadden) were shipped off to Camp Jackson, South Carolina—a mammoth army training base with a capacity for one hundred thousand men. The Yale trainees were now themselves assigned to train new recruits as artillerymen.[33]

As "student officers" charged with preparing fresh recruits for battle, Harry and Brit came into prolonged contact for the first time with Americans from outside their own relatively insular social world—young men with limited education from the rural backwaters of the South, many of them away from their home counties for the first time in their lives. These "hillbillies," as the Yale men called them, often knew nothing about the war. "All they knew," Harry recalled years later, "was that Uncle Sam had somehow been insulted." And so the officers, who were no older than their troops, not only had to train their men to operate artillery but also to give them lectures several times a week explaining the reasons for the war. "They were on the edge of their chairs," Harry liked to remember, and they displayed an impressive "eagerness to do the right thing." They did not even bridle when Harry explained to them the uses of a toothbrush, something many of them had never seen before.

The few months Harry and Brit spent at Camp Jackson occupy an important place in the considerable corporate mythology of Time Inc. Various official and quasi-official histories of the company claim that Luce and Hadden, struck by the eagerness of provincial people for knowledge of the world, decided at Camp Jackson to start a magazine or newspaper that would help educate the uninformed. They allegedly took long walks together during idle hours and began to imagine the new kind of journalism that would eventually transform the soldiers' lives. That Luce and Hadden talked about a magazine at Camp Jackson is almost certainly true, but nothing in Harry's writings at the time, or in his subsequent reminiscences, supports the claim that the people under their command had any impact on the way they thought about the venture. Nor did the subsequent history of his magazines, none of which targeted the kind of people he had encountered at Camp Jackson. Luce's own accounts at the time say nothing about the magazine but describe how he plunged wholeheartedly into the world of the army—viewing it as he had viewed school and college, as an opportunity for achievement and distinction.[34]

Harry reported to his parents on his performance on military tests—math, geometry, languages—as if he were describing a semester at Hotchkiss. He searched eagerly for signs that the Yale unit was excelling. "The seven Yale men assigned here, even if I do say it, do pretty well on their job," he wrote after his first weeks in camp. "Consequently we have little difficulty in making the best showing of any of the twelve batteries. . . . Several high officers have said that the progress made by this organization in the first twelve day period bests any they have seen. Consequently we are all very much elated." The great dream of all the Yale men was to receive formal commissions, a dream thwarted at first by the requirement that all officers had to be at least twenty-one; none of Harry's group was older than twenty. But a few weeks after their arrival in South Carolina the army lowered the age limit, and the Yale contingent was marched en masse (along with a great many other student officers) to a swearing-in ceremony. "You can scarcely [imagine what this] means to me and all the others," he told his parents shortly before the event. "It will be the consummation of a great deal of hitherto unrecognized work. We have been college boys training! People that didn't know probably laughed at our safe and sound uniforms. But, boy—if this goes through, and a third of the Yale R.O.T.C. is commissioned, it will make 'em sit up and take notice." Harry and his friends immediately went into town and ordered custom-made officers' uniforms from a local tailor.[35]

Harry complained occasionally about the rigors of camp life. When the officer trainees who had not received commissions were sent home, he described them as "lucky dogs." On the whole, though, he embraced the military ethic with uncritical enthusiasm and strove to adapt himself to its demands. "In the army," wrote the person who had spent a year and a half of the war living comfortably on the Yale campus when he was not away on vacation, "we thoroughly despise any young man who is able bodied, and who by his own choice gets into any kind of uniform but the line uniform. Even men who are doing the sine qua non jobs of the quartermaster department etc. etc. get a slant-eyed look. And as for any young man in a YMCA uniform,—well, of course, we are gentlemen enough not to smile." Nothing now was more important than the war, which Harry—like many others—considered a battle for the survival of civilization and the defeat of German barbarism. Colleges "no longer exist," he said, and "the one greatest thing to do now is to fight, with all the life one has, that the continuity of history toward the truth and the right of things shall be maintained. Everything else is subservient, or, if it does not serve this purpose, is simply to be annulled for the time being." His ambition now was "to have my next birthday in France, wearing silver (1st Lieutenant!)."[36]

But Harry and the other Yale men did not go to France. For the next month or so they were shuttled back and forth from one camp to another, undergoing additional training themselves or helping to train others. "Words cannot begin to picture my disgust with the idea," Luce complained. "Here's a case where one has to 'grin and bear it' without there being anything to bear it for,—no principles at stake, no glory to achieve!" His frustration was all the greater because it was becoming clear that "peace is unquestionably at hand." There was, he said, "not one of us that isn't sorry he hasn't seen France, not a one that wouldn't almost sell his soul to go there tomorrow." By late October, with the prospects of making it to the front becoming dimmer by the day, almost everyone in the Yale officer corps was becoming restless and bored, suddenly seeing the "infinitesimal details" of the artilleryman's life not as a prelude to glory but as the tedious, mechanical process it actually was.[37]

The armistice found Harry, Brit, and the others in Louisville, en route to another training assignment. They spent three days staying in a downtown hotel, eating in restaurants, smoking cigars, reading, idling, and thinking about the future. Harry found it difficult to disengage all at once from the new military ambitions the war had inspired in him. He thought about entering an officers' training program and winning a promotion before being discharged, and he even toyed briefly with becoming an officer in the regular army after the war. But in the end he left the military almost as quickly as he could ("I have absolutely lost all military ambitions," he wrote at the time), less than a month after the armistice.[38]

He went immediately to New York, where he spent much of the Christmas holidays planning feverishly for his return to Yale. The competition for most of the positions in campus organizations was now over, but Harry had other unfulfilled ambitions: to be elected to Phi Beta Kappa and, most of all, to be tapped for the most prestigious of the Yale senior societies, Skull and Bones. He set out to accomplish them both in the remaining semester of his junior year.[39]

The Yale to which he returned in January 1919 was, he once lamented, "a very poor place in which to get educated." That was in part because the university had not recovered from its wartime disruptions. Many faculty members had yet to return from military service; the campus was crowded with returning veterans, some of whom had been away for two, even three years, and others—like Harry—for only a few months. But Harry was also commenting on what he considered, despite Yale's many efforts at modernization, a narrow and inadequate curriculum. Henry Seidel Canby later described it as "the college of the catalogue. . . . One of the most irrational and confusing educational institutions the world has ever seen . . . [whose] handicap was the lack of a real education." "I suppose it is natural," Harry once commented, "that by junior year one begins to realize that the importance of American college life lies in its possibilities for friendship." He expressed high regard for the celebrated honors course he took with the historian Max Farrand. On the whole, however, he did his academic work dutifully, without great excitement, complaining occasionally about the "monotony" but determined to excel nevertheless. Late in the semester he was rewarded with election to Phi Beta Kappa.[40]

Nothing, however, was remotely as important to him by now as "going Bones," the one mark of success that almost everyone at Yale recognized—the one sure sign of having, in Owen Johnson's words, "won out at the end." The chairmanship of the *News* might have meant more to him a year before, but once he had failed to win that prize the possibility of Skull and Bones came to seem all the more important—and thus, as with all his other goals, a subject of almost obsessive contemplation and calculation. Everything he did, he assumed, would be watched by those who would judge his worthiness. When he flirted with taking the chairmanship of the literary magazine, he conferred with a member of the faculty about the possible implications of such a move on his prospects for Skull and Bones. His enthusiasm for the contest diminished considerably when the professor warned him that the *Lit* chairmanship would likely disqualify him from consideration, that the post was considered too remote from the "grand old Yale" of the senior societies to impress the Bones men.

At the Yale prom in February 1919, the great social event of the year, Harry—still without any significant experience with women—was accompanied by his sister Emmavail and preoccupied about the impression he would make. "The Prom affair, you know, is where social aristocracy does its best to rule," he wrote his mother, "and it's all an outsider can do to maintain his status quo." But even maintaining his status quo as a respected but not socially eminent member of his class required great vigilance. As a result he carefully scrutinized the invitations he received and the names on his dance card, trying to judge what they said about his standing and what they would convey about his taste. He was incensed when one of the campus fraternities failed to invite him to its preprom tea (even though all seven of the others did); and for the prom itself, he took care to see that he would be seen dancing only with prestigious guests. "My Prom dance card is absolutely 'O.K.,' " he tried to assure himself. "There are about three undesirables on the program, but I have secured the services of stags to 'cut in' before the undesirables get very far." His preoccupation with Skull and Bones seemed to have blinded him to his own unkindness.[41]

In the weeks leading up to Tap Day—the great spring event when the senior societies chose their new members—Harry alternated between hope and despair. At one point he concluded that "I shall not make 'Bones.' . . . I have felt all along that somehow I was not typical enough of Yale to 'come through' at that point." It surely did not help his spirits that Brit Hadden took him out for a walk one day—"Brit, my rival since early Hotchkiss days"—and proposed getting "ten of the sure Bones men together to make it known that none of them would go Bones without me." Harry was either deaf to or chose to ignore the condescension implicit in this implausible plan. It was, he said, "one of the greatest compliments I have ever received." He declined Brit's offer, however, arguing that "Bones meant everything for Yale, and that bucking it did no good for the college which means so much to us." As with the *News* and the *Lit*, he again chose to see himself as one who looked "beyond the interests of the individual" to protect a larger good. When the *New York Times*—which regularly devoted substantial space to the social world of the Ivy League—published a story speculating about those likely to be chosen for Bones, Harry suffered over being mentioned as a "possibility" who would likely fail. ("I'm sorry I didn't or rather won't, make the grade," he wrote miserably to his father. "With all the advantages I have had, it does not speak well for me not to come out on top.") But he also happily reported campus gossip that both he and Brit were certain of selection. And he comforted himself that "what I shall never have to admit,—in fact, what it would not be true to say is this:—that in my own class I was not counted on as a 'Bones' man!"[42]

Tap Day, May 15, was carefully orchestrated to create excitement and drama. Late in the afternoon much of the student body gathered on the lawn in front of the imposing, windowless buildings of the senior societies to watch the nervous juniors, who waited along a fence nearby. The windows of surrounding buildings were crowded with observers from the faculty and the town. At the tolling of the chapel bells at 5:00 p.m., the doors of the three societies flew open; and the senior members threaded through the crowd, pounding the chosen juniors on their backs and telling them to return to their rooms to be informed of their induction. Harry's apprehension grew as the Bones seniors plucked one after another of his classmates (Hadden among them) while passing him by. But at last, at 5:20, as he wrote the next day to his parents, "your elder son received a terrific smack across the shoulders, delivered him by Winter Mead, 1919, Captain of the Crew and President of Phi Beta Kappa, and a member of the so-called society of Skull and Bones. And you can easily imagine that said son upon being told to go to his room did so go, and did moreover vouch for his being Henry Robinson Luce, and did accept an election to the so-called society! . . . I am sure you understand what perfect satisfaction is mine." (One of his first tasks as a member was to choose a secret "club name." Luce chose "Baal," an ancient Hebrew name for "Lord" or "Master." Hadden chose "Caliban," the feral, half-human servant in Shakespeare's *The Tempest*. No one ever used Luce's somewhat pretentious club name outside of Skull and Bones, but "Caliban" seemed so appropriate for Hadden that it stuck— until it was gradually replaced by the nickname "Bratch.")[43]

Perhaps to compensate for the semester he had missed while in the army, Harry remained in New Haven during the summer after his junior year, enduring what he described as the "monotony" of courses at the law school. When the college reconvened in September, he stepped easily into his new role as one of the "big men" among the seniors. He continued to work hard at the *News*, both as an editor and editorial writer and as a supervisor of the newspaper's business affairs. He joined the debating team. He took more challenging and interesting courses than he had in the past. He was particularly drawn to the English political theorist Harold Laski, who was teaching for the moment at Yale, and he wrote a senior thesis under Laski's supervision titled "The Influence Exerted on the American People by Theodore Roosevelt During the Last Ten Years of his Life: A Study in Public Opinion." In the spring, when the national convention of collegiate Republicans met in New Haven, Harry served as the meeting's chairman—"the highest public honor of my college days," he wrote exuberantly at the time.[44]

But Harry was not through pursuing honors yet. In the spring he won the college's most distinguished public-speaking prize, the DeForest oratorical contest—an especially rewarding feat for a young man who had worked for years to conquer his childhood stammer. He did so with a Wilsonian speech calling for America "to do her share in the solution of every international difficulty, that she will be the great friend of the lame, the halt and the blind among nations, the comrade of all nations that struggle to rise to higher planes of social and political organization, and withal the implacable foe of whatever nation shall offer to disturb the peace of the world." A few weeks later he was voted a degree of "honors of the first rank," the equivalent of summa cum laude—although in a collegiate world that had relatively little respect for academic honors, he would probably have preferred the distinctions that Brit, a mediocre student, received. Hadden was voted by his class "most likely to succeed" and perhaps most important of all by Harry's standards, the person who had "done most for Yale." Harry took consolation when he was quietly chosen as the Skull and Bones member of a defunct sophomore society, Eta Phi, to which two seniors were appointed each year "so that the things would be handed down in perpetuity in case they should ever be revived." It was, he conceded, "in the eyes of the world a very insignificant matter—a pleasant bauble." But to Harry, still yearning for signs of social acceptance, it was "an honor which I treasure as only one other." (The other, it went without saying, was election to Skull and Bones, which he once described as a "religion.") He had assumed he "had taken in all I could of collegiate honors," he wrote, but now he was a member "of the most exclusive society in the world."[45]

If Harry had graduated from Hotchkiss still very much a boy, he graduated from Yale self-consciously an adult. He now looked and dressed like an older man than he was—his tall frame no longer gawky and adolescent; his hair oiled and parted in the middle; his clothes well tailored and conservative; his gaze studied and serious. Having succeeded so brilliantly at Yale—academically, organizationally, socially—he considered himself a man of substance and importance, someone to whom greatness was due. Unlike many of his classmates, he had little money of his own. But he managed nevertheless, even if precariously, to maintain a lifestyle compatible with his Yale contemporaries through his own modest earnings and the gifts he continued to receive from Nettie McCormick. He was still sexually inexperienced, but he interpreted even that as a sign of maturity. To friends in the throes of romance and contemplating marriage, Harry cited "Hannibal, Napoleon, Disraeli, & Company, dealers in careers, and discounters of domesticity!"[46]

His newfound manhood also altered his relationship with his family. The Luces remained a close and loving family, even though separated by vast distances. But their letters to one another—letters that for many years constituted virtually the entirety of their relationship—were changing. Harry no longer implored his parents to approve his activities, no longer apologized for doing things he feared might disappoint them. When they chided him, as they occasionally did, about being careless with money, he replied so sharply that his mother wrote an anguished letter back saying that "the only reasons I even wish for money is that I might pour it out to you." When his father—whose influence over him had always been profound—wrote him with some gentle advice about tempering the language in his *News* editorials, Harry patiently but unapologetically explained that Yale had changed since the senior Luce's time there. His father also advised him to prepare himself for a "trade" (journalism, the senior Luce warned, was a "dog's life"), even to see a "vocational specialist." Harry ignored that advice too. The entire Luce family with the exception of Harry senior returned from China in the spring of 1918 so that the girls could enter Abbot, a girls' secondary school associated with Andover. Harry—partly because of his military obligations but also because of his preferences for his own social life—visited them infrequently, despite his mother's frequent pleas to "come to us" and his father's request that he spend time with Sheldon, who "needs a 'big brother.' " He was drifting away from them, in the way adults almost always do.[47]

And yet for all his confidence in his own adulthood and for all his seeming certainty about his future, Harry was not quite ready to venture out into what college students would later call the "real world." Completing college in the early twentieth century, Henry Seidel Canby recalled, was "more painful than triumphant" as the graduate "stepped out into the world trailing clouds of memory behind him." Harry sought to postpone that painful day by spending a year at a university even more storied than the one he was leaving: Oxford. Although he had visited Oxford during his first trip to England in 1913, there is no evidence that he had ever thought about attending the university until his senior year, when Harold Laski began to encourage him and others to consider studying there and offered to help him gain admission to the most famous of the Oxford colleges, Christchurch. Harry applied for a Rhodes Scholarship—not surprisingly, given his propensity for pursuing badges of achievement—but did not seem perturbed when he did not receive one, even though his friend and classmate Bill Whitney did. ("We are all proud and delighted," he wrote, adding that his own failure to be chosen was a result of his "half-way method." If he had tried harder, he implied, he too might have been selected.) But the experience only increased his eagerness to attend Oxford, and he now went about arranging a year there with typical single-mindedness. He wrote to Nettie McCormick asking if she might provide him with the thousand dollars that he calculated the year would cost him, and she quickly agreed. Another fifteen hundred dollars he received as his share of the profits of the *Daily News* ensured that he would be financially comfortable for many months. He explained earnestly to his parents how a year at Oxford would prepare him for the "public life" he expected to live as an adult. But it seems likely that the idea of going to Oxford was most appealing because it would postpone the difficult decision of how to begin his professional life—and perhaps also because it would help confirm his acceptance into the upper levels of the Anglophilic American aristocracy.[48]

The social attractions of his new undertaking seemed foremost in his mind from the day he sailed for England in July, a few weeks after attending the Republican National Convention in Chicago, where he developed no enthusiasm for the party's nominee, Warren G. Harding. On board the SS *Olympia*, he found himself once again in the same second-class accommodations he had become accustomed to in his travels in 1912–13. But this time he was acutely conscious of his inferior surroundings. The bunks, he complained, were "precariously narrow," the food barely edible, and his companions "good natured boors." And so he and several other Yale friends similarly consigned to second class began a furtive shipboard life—sleeping in their modest staterooms, enduring tasteless meals, but spending virtually all the rest of their time in first class. "We tremble . . . lest the hand of the law be upon us," he conceded. "But so far all is fine; and . . . first class travel aboard this vessel is quite agreeable," particularly since it gave him a chance to socialize with people more to his liking, several of whom extended invitations for him to visit when he arrived in England.[49]

His first days in London were an uncharacteristic whirl of social activity, during which—for the first time—he wrote of his relationships with women. Perhaps now that he felt liberated from the closely scrutinized, all-male social world of Yale, he felt free to behave less cautiously. "Friday night I took Katherine Bissell out for a party," he wrote happily, "dinner, theatre, cabaret, usual stuff. She and I have (apparently!) hit it off very well." That was particularly fortunate, he added, because her sister was married to a wealthy Englishman, and Harry was invited to visit their country house in Worcestershire "for as long as I want to stay." After a week in London he and some Yale friends took a sightseeing trip through Devon, the Lake District, and Scotland—"a glorious trip, and we all enjoyed each other's company in every kind of weather." Back in London he resumed his glittering social life, dining with Goulds and Auchinclosses and Whitneys, meeting more young American women and escorting them about town. "London, you know, is rippingly cheap for bachelor bums," he reported, "but once you go swanking round with a lady on your arm it's quite as bad as New York!" Somewhat to his surprise, he found himself a sought-after guest—both for evenings in London and for weekends in the country, where his strong tennis game "managed to earn some kudos." "I suspect you're very provocative to women," his friend Thornton Wilder wrote him a few months later. "Your interestedness makes 'em sit up."[50]

The Oxford term did not begin until October, so late in August, Harry traveled to Paris, hoping to spend some time with Brit Hadden, who was expected in early September. Once again he found himself in demand, chaperoning the daughter of a Yale alumnus "for three entire days—which by the way is some job. . . . On Friday we tore all over town, seeing as much as we could, and went to the opera, Faust. Saturday the same, driving through the Bois in the evening. . . . Altogether we, or at least I, had a ripping time." A few days later, before Brit arrived, Harry left unexpectedly on a trip to Istanbul, which he, like many Anglo-Americans (and virtually all Greeks), still called Constantinople. His wealthy Yale friend Hugh Auchincloss had arranged the trip months before, only to find that his original traveling companion could not join him. He invited Harry to come along and offered to pay his expenses "over a certain amount," since he himself planned to travel in style. They rode first class on the Orient Express, in berths reserved for them by the American ambassador in Paris, an Auchincloss family friend; and they found themselves lavishly attended by embassy officials in almost all the cities they visited.[51]

Even so, Harry was appalled by eastern Europe—"another world, a world poorer, more animalistic, uncontrolled, dishonest, a people of geniuses and crooks, whose geniuses unfortunately are dead." Istanbul itself was a "dirty, filthy place," made tolerable to the young travelers through their "pull with the embassy," which gained them access to lavish dinners and even the chance for a monthlong trip around the Black Sea aboard an American destroyer—an invitation they had to decline. Next was a hurried trip back through Romania, whose capital, Bucharest, was a "beautiful city—the Paris of the Balkans," but whose people were "a lot of dirty crooks! That goes without saying." Returning finally to Paris, he felt as though he were "coming home."[52]

By the beginning of October he was ensconced at Oxford, living in modest "digs" near Christchurch with a Yale classmate and bemoaning the "Britannic shell" that made it difficult to make friends with English students. He arranged to read English history, beginning with the Tudor period. He joined the Oxford Union (although he had little hope of actually speaking before it). He played a great deal of bridge and tennis. And he energetically socialized with other Americans at Oxford, and with their families and friends in London. There was none of the methodical striving and frantic competitiveness that had characterized his time at Hotchkiss and Yale. The year at Oxford, he explained to his skeptical parents, was "a holiday I feel justified in taking. I think it will bring me back stronger and fresher and broader-gauged." To their suggestions that he was being frivolous and extravagant, he replied defensively: "I don't think I can be accused of having sought out rich friends. I have never tried to be ostentatious in the slightest. I have tried to get to know all the best men I could. Some of them are very rich, with an occasional exception they are all much wealthier than I. That comes of going to Yale." In any case, he argued slightly defiantly, it was too late to back out now, and "precious little opportunity for economizing." Still, after receiving their gentle reprimands, he was careful in future letters to write more often about his intellectual than about his social life.[53]

In reality, although Harry drew some excitement from his reading of British history and enjoyed his frequent encounters with Harold Laski (now back in England) and his "bolshevik crowd," he was not very interested in the intellectual life of Oxford. Instead he spent as much time as he could traveling and engaging with the upper ranks of expatriate society. Over Christmas he visited Geneva and used his Yale contacts to arrange a privileged visit to the inner workings of the League of Nations. He then spent time in Rome, guided by help from the American Embassy and his former Chefoo and Yale schoolmate Thornton Wilder, who was ensconced at the American Academy writing plays. "Next week," he wrote from Rome on Christmas Eve, "I attend a dance or two—a side of Rome I didn't see last time!" At one of those dances he met an attractive young American woman, Lila Hotz, to whom he was apparently immediately and powerfully drawn. ("For twenty-three years," he wrote her later, "I never considered marriage except with supercilious scorn. . . . Then one night in Rome, theories, attitudes, pronouncements were demolished by—well, by a mere fact.")[54]

Lila was from a wealthy, socially prominent Chicago family. She had attended the Spence School, in New York City, one of America's most prominent and most academically serious schools for young upper-class women. She was now spending a year in Europe, in the manner of many young women of her class, studying art and leading an active social life. She had rich, curly dark hair, pale skin, and large, dark, haunting eyes. Although she was not nearly as serious or intellectually curious as Harry, she was well read, well educated, and sophisticated enough to find him intriguing and to intrigue him in turn.

They soon began an extended if at first somewhat guarded correspondence, to which Harry was by far the more frequent contributor. Unaccustomed to the rituals of courtship, Harry apparently made various social blunders, for which he periodically wrote long, erudite apologies. He was frequently on the defensive against what he called Lila's "powers of psycho-analysis" and her complaints that he was not sufficiently open about his "inner feelings." He once sent her a cartoon from *Punch*, which he evidently considered appropriate to their relationship; titled "Psycho-Analysis, or The New Game of Laying Bare One's Inmost Soul," it portrayed a young couple in evening clothes sitting on a sofa—the woman looking searchingly at her partner waiting for some emotional revelation, the young man sitting rigid, his hands on his knees, his eyes wide with terror. At one point, in Paris, Harry left flowers for Lila at her hotel, with a penitent note: "In the hope that violets are sufficiently impersonal." But the petulance and the apologies were themselves something of a teasing ritual between two young people deeply attracted to each other without knowing each other very well. In the spring Lila—with her mother along as chaperone—came to Oxford as his guest for polo matches and a dance at Magdalen College. ("The shock of coming down to earth has been too exhausting," he wrote her in London a day or two after she left Oxford.) He made no mention of her in his letters home.[55]

Harry's year at Oxford—and more significantly the extensive European traveling he did during the course of it—made a very different impression on him than had his earlier European journey in 1913. Then, as a young boy traveling alone and living penuriously, he had marveled at the artistic splendor and rich history of the first Western countries he had seen since his childhood trip to America. Now, as a young man—traveling on the Continent as often as he could during the long vacations between the Oxford terms, moving portentously through embassies and aristocratic homes in the company of wealthy friends—he judged everything in comparison with the United States, and (except for England itself, for which he had developed a typical upper-class American admiration) found almost every place wanting in contrast. Rome, he noted, was still striking for its storied magnificence, but it was also notable for the squalor of its politics—wholly "bourgeois," having "nothing whatever to do with society, which consists of decayed nobility." Rome's splendor was in the past, he concluded, and "one realizes that magnificence is now of America. May it prove to be a moral and spiritual magnificence." For the rest of his life Harry was an avid overseas traveler, and his year abroad after Yale remained, in a way, a prototype for the kind of journeys he would later routinely make—in the careful planning for maximum comfort; in the expectation of lavish attention from diplomats and local elites; and in the energetic pursuit of new sights and experiences. He also displayed a newly dismissive contempt for the "filthy," "crooked," and "backward" cultures he encountered, which he judged by rigid Western standards as objects for improvement and elevation.[56]

Through it all he was pondering his future, in ways that revealed a wavering from his earlier firm resolve to enter journalism. He was, he insisted, still committed to entering "public life," perhaps as a journalist but also perhaps as a writer or a politician. (He was even then beginning to write essays designed for publication in such American magazines as *Harper's* and the *Atlantic* and was sending them timidly across the Atlantic under a pseudonym, so that rejections—which he consistently received—would not damage his reputation.) But having spent so much time with much more affluent friends and their families, he was naturally becoming more aware of the significance of wealth. To his parents he was apologetic about his growing interest in what he called, only half jokingly, "dirty sordid money," but he did not back away from his determination to make some. He would, he said, consider spending the next ten years working in business (most likely manufacturing) "until I can get to the point where money will mean nothing to me." And he was already in correspondence with Mrs. McCormick—old, ailing, but still very fond of Harry—about the possibility of a job in the family firm, International Harvester, when he returned from Europe—a possibility, given its source, that he came to consider a virtual certainty.[57]

His last weeks at Oxford—weeks when degree candidates were absorbed with exams but during which the departing Harry had no responsibilities—were a time of idyllic leisure, interspersed with attendance at crew races, polo matches, and other Oxonian social events. "Everything goes along monotonously happy. I am playing tennis every afternoon. . . . Doing practically no serious work but read as the spirit moves me." He might, he said, begin work at Harvester on August 1 or—if his social life in America replicated the life he had built in England—"loaf all of August" and begin in September. Brit Hadden, he reported as he prepared to sail, might move to Chicago as well, "which will be mighty lucky for me. We would share digs, etc. That lad is really quite tremendous."[58]

IV

"The Paper"

Brit Hadden did not move to Chicago that year. He returned to New York after a summer of traveling and went to work for the prestigious *New York World*, a job he got by marching into the editor's office and stating that he needed experience at a good newspaper to prepare himself for starting his own. But Luce was not really much interested in what Hadden was doing in any case. He had other plans, centered on the promise of a job and, perhaps more important, the promise of romance.

The job at International Harvester proved chimerical. Shortly after his arrival in Chicago, in the midst of the severe recession of 1921, he went to the office of Mrs. McCormick's son Harold, the president of the company. According to Luce's own later accounts, one of the McCormick executives told him that, given Mrs. McCormick's interest, he could have a job if he wanted one, but that someone currently on the payroll would have to be fired to make room for him. "Of course I don't want you to fire anyone," Harry remembered replying. The story is certainly plausible. But it is also consistent with Luce's earlier explanations of thwarted ambitions—most notably his failure to win the chairmanship of the *Yale Daily News*, which he also claimed to have selflessly abandoned in the interests of others.[1]

Luce soon found another, less lucrative job, on the *Chicago Daily News*. The *News* was, in the eyes of the city's prosperous middle class, the "respectable" paper in town—without the egomaniacal flamboyance of Col. Robert McCormick's *Tribune* or the Hearstian populism of the

Herald-Examiner. But the *Daily News* was hardly the sober guardian of standards that its defenders liked to believe—as Luce soon discovered when he was assigned to work as an assistant to the popular columnist Ben Hecht, who later became a successful playwright and screenwriter. He was perhaps best known for the play, and later film, *The Front Page*, which he wrote with Charles MacArthur—a classic, if romanticized, portrayal of life in a Chicago newsroom.

Hecht was only four years older than Luce, but he had already developed the crusty style of a grizzled newspaperman. His column, "A Thousand and One Afternoons," consisted of colorful and often sentimental stories about ordinary Chicagoans. And while Hecht did not invent the stories—there was always a real event at the core of his column—he had no inhibitions about embroidering and enhancing reality. Luce's job was to find a nugget of truth, an offbeat story or event, on which Hecht could base his flights of fancy. The relationship was apparently not a successful one, and it lasted little more than a month. Hecht was condescending toward his assistant. Luce was privately contemptuous of the column he was helping Hecht create. After a few weeks they parted ways.[2]

Years later Hecht claimed to have fired Luce for incompetence. But Luce did not leave the paper when he left the column, which casts some doubt on Hecht's self-serving account. Luce joined the general news staff (moving, he later claimed, because both Hecht and his editor decided he was too talented to be Hecht's legman). He worked for a while as a junior reporter, scouring police stations, the courts, and the streets for news. His occasional stories were not invented or embroidered, but they were sometimes as idiosyncratic as Hecht's column had been. Among his published pieces were an account of a millionaire tossing money to a crowd in front of his hotel, a description of a Russian pianist giving a concert from a rowboat in Lincoln Park, a story about a religious group that had declared playing baseball a crime. He remained frustrated by what he considered the triviality of his assignments and by his lack of greater progress at the paper. "I haven't shown any brilliance," he wrote desolately to his parents (describing what he called his "fatuous existence"), "yet apparently the work has been satisfactory." Even that did not last very long, however. The *Daily News* was no more immune to the postwar recession than was International Harvester, and it began laying off employees in the fall of 1921. Luce, among the most recently hired, was one of the first to go. "It was a pretty bad blow," he confessed to his mother, but he took some comfort from the assurances he received from his editors that his work had been "thoroughly satisfactory" and that they would gladly hire him again if they could. "I don't suppose it really means I have failed," he concluded, "but just that I haven't been anything out of the ordinary."[3]

Once more without a job, he "went back to the conclusion I had come to in England"—that he should find a position in business and ensure his financial security. But the bleak recession winter was not a good time to be looking for work anywhere. He wrote Harold McCormick again asking about the possibility of a place at International Harvester, but there were still no jobs. He made the rounds of other Chicago businesses but found only more discouragement. As he always did when he sensed defeat, he tried to distance himself from his failure and took refuge in "philosophy." He was, he insisted, not really interested in "worldly things," and he was determined to wait before committing himself to any specific future. He expressed pity for Harold McCormick, whose path in life had been predetermined and who thus had "never had a chance." And he insisted, perhaps somewhat too emphatically, that "I regret nothing." He also took comfort in what he considered his great achievements at Yale. "What has been can never be destroyed. It is treasure laid up in heaven, and perhaps all I shall ever be able to claim there. And I am determined that no action of mine in the future shall cast a shadow upon the brightness of the past." By the end of the year he was considering moving back to Manhattan, where his parents were living temporarily. But there was, he told his mother, "something that may keep me away from New York": That "something" was Lila Hotz.[4]

Harry and Lila's infatuation with each other had been sustained primarily by letters until they found themselves together in Chicago. In the nine months between their first meeting in Rome and their reunion in Chicago, they had spent a total of little more than a week in each other's company. Now that they were in the same city, they had their first chance to spend extended time together—although it was carefully bounded by the proprieties of Chicago society and the strict chaperonage to which, even at age twenty, Lila was still mostly subject. For Harry the relationship was dazzling not just because of his feelings for Lila, but because of the glamorous social world to which it gave him entrée. Lila's family was wealthy, well connected, and socially prominent, and Harry found himself drawn into a swirl of parties, balls, dinners, and other events in the busy Chicago and Lake Forest social scenes. Modestly subsidized by the now-ailing Mrs. McCormick, he acquired some expensive clothes, hats, and even a slightly foppish walking stick. For a short time he sported a fashionable mustache. (Returning once to the *Daily News* building in the evening to retrieve a book he had left behind—dressed for Lake Forest, walking stick in hand—he entered an elevator with the editor in chief, Henry Justin Smith, who looked him over and said sardonically, "Ah, Luce, a journalist I see.")[5]

Sometime in October, having previously said almost nothing to his parents about Lila, he wrote his mother a "personal line" on a subject he thought would be "of some interest to you." He was seeing "the young woman," he said, "about every other day, with the result that I am in no condition to have the custody of my own person and am totally irresponsible for any of my actions." This was his first serious relationship, and he did not yet trust himself to succeed at it, particularly given his own penury and his fear (which turned out to be justified) that Lila's mother would oppose their relationship because she believed Harry to have inadequate social or financial standing. And so he tried to prepare himself, as he often did, for disappointment. "I don't dare look ahead," he told his mother (after cautioning her not to say anything about Lila to his father, whose disapproval he still feared above all else). "I suppose the crash is bound to come, but it's just too awful to think of. At present, everything is ok, in fact, magnificent, because, as I say, I just don't think."[6]

As their relationship deepened, Harry and Lila managed to find more time to themselves—on weekends, when they spent afternoons alone in the garden or in a sitting room at Lila's home, or occasionally in the evenings, when they went alone to a restaurant or club for dinner. At some point that fall they proclaimed their love for each other, and Harry asked Lila to marry him. She was not ready to accept. She still had some "reservations" about their relationship, she told him, but had "great trust" in his ability to "work things out." Harry claimed to be puzzled. "I did not absorb a very accurate understanding of these reservations," he wrote her. "I hope you will explain them more formally." But he almost certainly sensed that they were related to his straitened economic circumstances, which still made him seem an inappropriate match to Lila's socially ambitious family (and perhaps to Lila herself). Speculating in a letter to Lila about the continuing uncertainty in their relationship, he suggested coldly that perhaps "it was unfortunate that I should have allowed myself to become interested in you since you would never marry such an impecunious nobody, even if I should succeed in making myself fairly agreeable, which apparently I have not altogether done." But at other moments he expressed real pain. "Do you think I wanted to fall in love with you or anybody?" he asked, recalling his earlier and now abandoned determination to lead a single life. "Don't you know how I tried to kid myself out of it? . . . Can't you imagine how . . . I almost cheered when first it occurred to me that perhaps $1,000,000 stood between us, and how I almost praised God for such a thoroughly practical, sensible world? And—don't you *see*?"[7]

One reason being laid off at the *News* came as such a blow to him was the threat it posed to his hopes of marrying Lila. It was also because the sense of professional failure it produced in him was in such contrast to the intoxicating social world he was simultaneously inhabiting. He yearned for the wealth that he saw around him. "How I should love to have an ancestral home where I could bring you," he confessed. "I have never wanted this kind of thing before." He even began to regret, even slightly to resent, his father's choice in going to China and "giving up all that America offered." This was, he said, "the only bitterness my heart has felt, that I have not the things I should love to give you."[8]

At this dark moment, with Luce wrestling with his desire for Lila and his fear of failure, lifelines suddenly appeared. He accepted a verbal offer of a job with a machine-manufacturing firm in New York, despite Lila's unhappiness about his leaving Chicago. He no doubt concluded that he would have a better chance of winning her if he was employed in New York than unemployed in Chicago. But before he could begin the new job, Brit Hadden wrote him to relay an offer to the two of them to go to work on the *Baltimore News*, part of a chain of newspapers owned by the legendary Frank Munsey, the longtime publisher of the popular *Munsey's Magazine*. The jobs had been arranged for them by their Yale classmate and fellow Skull and Bones member Walter Millis, who was already working there. They would be paid forty dollars a week (far more than either of them had made at their previous newspapers), he wrote excitedly to Lila, and they would "circulate in all departments of the newspaper, with practically a guarantee that inside of a year we will be minor officers at $4,000 a year. They are crazy to get us." They would also have a chance, Hadden reminded Luce, to work on what they both were now calling "the paper," the magazine they still dreamed of starting. Luce wavered at first about taking the Baltimore job, but Hadden— "furious at me" for not being as enthusiastic as Brit was—finally persuaded him that it was a "good gamble," and he accepted the position. Hadden had already quit his dreary job at the *World*, where he had been toiling on such stories as "Sugar Bowl Made Lump on Her

Head," and "Cuts Wife Silk Hose for Use as Socks." He had spent pre-vious months working on a tramp steamer. Like Luce, he was ready for a challenge.[9]

Suddenly filled again with self-confidence, Luce wrote his former editor at the *Daily News* that he was leaving "the grand army of the unemployed" for a job he made clear was considerably better than the one he had lost. He was, he said with mock regret, ignoring Smith's advice to "get out of newspapers." "What makes it worse," he cockily added, "is that two of us are showing signs of pernicious insanity and will probably undertake a new publishing venture in a few months." In a ten-tative postscript, however, he revealed his lingering professional anxiety: "I suppose I am not under any obligation to explain to Mr. F. Munsey's representatives that I was 'fired' from the News. If you think I am, will you please let me know?"[10]

Luce spent no longer in Baltimore than he had in Chicago. Except for his separation from Lila, however, it was a much happier experience. The work at the *Baltimore News* was in fact not very challenging. He and Hadden were the junior reporters on the staff, and they were again cov-ering the least-appealing stories. But because he was once again working with friends, and because the Baltimore paper, unlike the Chicago one, was proud to have "college men" on the staff, he was much better treated and felt much more confident than he had been at the *Daily News*. "I did a totally unique story, rather impossible, but elicited favorable com-ment," he wrote shortly after his arrival. "Interest shown in us is the main point." A few days later he reported, "Nothing that either of us has written has been rejected. . . . We seem to be quite the pets of the office." Luce and Hadden quickly developed a reputation as "star men" in writing features and (ironically, given Harry's experience in Chicago) were asked to "try our hand at working up a 'Ben Hecht' series."[11]

But the newspaper job, despite the chances for rapid advancement— his salary, he reminded Lila, "will be about as much as any class-mate is making (with a year's start on me)"—was only an expedient. He and Brit were quietly planning what Harry called "the gamble of our lives on which everything depends, everything . . . the crazy half-romantic thing that has ruined thousands before us." They were, he told Lila, going to start

a weekly called "Facts." It will contain all the news on every sphere of human interest, and the news organized. There will be articles on politics, books, sport, scandal, science, society, and no article will be longer than 200 words. Nothing will be too obvious. We assume nothing—e.g. that our readers know what 5-5-3* means, or who is John Masefield or Babe Ruth. . . . [It would] serve the illiterate upper classes, the busy business man, the tired debutante, to prepare them at least once a week for a table conversation.[12]

Luce and Hadden usually finished their work at the paper at 3 o'clock (the *News* was an evening paper). They then returned promptly to the apartment they shared with Millis on the shabby top floor of a Baltimore mansion (rented out by "nice people" who were in financial difficulty) to plan strategy and experiment with formats. "We were groping toward . . . the practice," Luce later recalled, "by actually chopping up the *New York Times*, and reorganizing [it] on a weekly basis, and then trying to put these stories together." Stopping only for dinner, which they took with another " 'society' family, slightly impoverished," they worked for hours every night. They typed out sample stories, experimenting with different styles and formats. Millis, who had the greatest literary talent of the three, actually did most of the writing; but Hadden and Luce were clearly in charge. They were trying to find the fatal flaw in their idea and, they claimed, failing to find it. But their ideas about timing, location, and business plans changed constantly. They would start publishing almost immediately; they would wait six months; they would wait a year, or more. They would stay in Baltimore; they would move to Washington; they would establish themselves in Detroit or Cleveland or New York. Hadden and Luce would be the sole stock owners; they would distribute stock among investors; they would attract people to work on the magazine by giving them stock as well. Almost everything was in flux. But the core idea—what the magazine would be and what purpose it would serve—remained fairly constant. "The thing is very largely Hadden's idea," Luce privately confessed to Lila, "but he swears that without me he cannot put it over. Personally I think I am dashed lucky to be teaming up with him again."[13]

After a few intense weeks they began to interrupt their work occasionally to participate in the Baltimore social world—a world far more staid and conservative than the New York and Chicago scenes with

*The ratio established by the 1922 Washington Naval Treaty that reduced the armaments of the Great Powers.

which Luce and Hadden were familiar. "Before I forget it, please send dress suit and white vest and cut-a-way [*sic*] and old heavy shoes," Harry wrote his mother. "Baltimore is very old-fashioned." Making use of their Skull and Bones connections, they found themselves "adopted for the nonce" by several families of the Baltimore elite, who secured them invitations to the city's major social events. Luce viewed these social leaders with the same envy and awe he had felt in Detroit and Chicago when in the presence of wealth.[14]

Left to himself, the security-conscious Luce might have settled in at the *Baltimore News*, at least for a while, and tried to build a life for himself (and Lila) in the city. But Hadden never let him get too comfortable. He goaded and exhorted Harry to move their joint project—"the gamble of our lives"—forward more rapidly. Even while still working for the *News*, both Hadden and Luce began traveling intermittently to New York, to solicit advice from, among others, their former Yale English teacher Henry Seidel Canby, and to court potential investors through their Yale (and Skull and Bones) connections. In Baltimore they continued to refine their plans for what they were not yet calling a "magazine," but rather a "weekly newspaper," still tentatively titled *Facts*. By the beginning of February 1922, they decided they were ready to take what Luce called the "great leap into the unknown." Although they had as yet raised very little money and had still not hired any staff, they negotiated a seven-week leave from the *Baltimore News* and moved to New York to begin bringing "the paper" to life. "I am confident," Hadden wrote his mother, "that in the seven weeks prior to April 1, we shall be able to determine whether or not the paper, *Facts*, is going to be brought into existence."[15]

They were nothing if not presumptuous—two twenty-four-year-olds, with almost no money and less than two years of professional journalism experience between them, setting out to start a magazine at the tail end of a severe recession. But their youth and relative inexperience were in many ways advantages in the task they had embraced. If they had not still been cocky young Yale prodigies, if their outlook had been more tempered by the realities of the world, they might not have dared to imagine so bold a project. And because they were determined to create something, as Luce wrote, "totally different from anything now being given to the American public," it was not entirely a disadvantage to have had relatively scant training.[16]

From their earliest conversations about "the paper"—at Yale, at Fort

Jackson, South Carolina, during the war, and most recently in their apartment in Baltimore—their vision of their magazine was shaped by their sense of the inadequacy of existing sources of news, which were thus not models for their own task. Both men were critical of the daily newspapers of the 1920s—the impassioned Brit far more outspokenly than the methodical Harry. Hadden was particularly contemptuous of the Hearst and Pulitzer papers, whose sensationalism, he said, pandered to the ignorance of their working-class readers, whom he disdained as "gum-chewers." But he and Luce were almost equally contemptuous of the "serious" newspapers—what they considered their leaden formulaic prose, their slavish adherence to the mechanical style of the Associated Press, and their excessive length. Anyone interested in lively or imaginative writing, a professor at the Columbia School of Journalism wrote in 1922, "makes a nuisance of himself in the newspaper." An eye for "objective facts" and "clean copy" were what editors should want. "People have to think too hard to read [the newspapers]," Luce observed of the dry, fact-laden broadsheets. Hadden, never afraid to attack sacred cows, was particularly contemptuous of the most respected newspaper of the day, the *New York Times*. It was, he liked to say—throwing the paper dismissively onto a table—"unreadable."[17]

The modern *Times* was the creation of Adolph Ochs, the publisher of the *Chattanooga Times*, who had moved to New York City just before the turn of the century to make his mark in the newspaper capital of the nation. He bought the floundering *New York Times* for $75,000 in 1896 and announced that he would transform it into a paper that would "give the news, all the news, in concise and attractive form, in language that is parliamentary in good society . . . impartially, without fear or favor, regardless of any party, sect, or interest involved." By 1922 the *Times* had long since established itself as the most serious and important paper in New York, and indeed the nation. "Taking" the *Times* was for many New Yorkers a symbol of membership in the educated elite, something close to a social obligation. But few people read the *Times* for pleasure. Its dense eight columns of small type, only occasionally relieved by pictures or illustrations, was daunting enough. But the sober language, the statesmanlike nonpartisan conservatism, the dutiful reporting of obscure political and diplomatic events, the vast transcripts of speeches and press conferences, the dry public documents, the scrupulous resistance to analysis or overt expressions of opinion—all contributed to the *Times*'s other, less-welcome reputation. It was not just the "newspaper of record," it was also the "great gray lady," or, as the legendary journalist

A. J. Liebling described it, "the colorless, odorless, and especially taste-less *Times* . . . a political hermaphrodite capable of intercourse with conservatives of both parties at the same time."[18]

Luce and Hadden found only a little more inspiration in the magazines of their time than they did from newspapers. There had in fact been something of a revolution in American magazines beginning in the late nineteenth century. The dominant journals of earlier decades—among them *Harper's Monthly*, the *Atlantic Monthly*, and *Century*—were written explicitly for educated Protestant social elites and usually expressed their readers' provincial literary tastes and their class and ethnic prejudices. But the new magazines sought, as one publisher put it, to convey the "whirlpool of real life," and to do so in a livelier, more vivid way than had the staid, genteel publications of the past. The result was a dramatic increase in magazine circulation, which more than doubled between 1890 and 1905. (Newspaper readership increased by only about 50 percent in those same years.)[19]

The new magazines achieved this impressive growth by charging less, by broadening the range of their stories, and by encouraging livelier and more accessible writing. As a result they reached beyond the narrow, elite audiences of their older competitors and engaged the interest of an emerging new, urban middle class, increasingly diverse in both background and interests. The highest-circulating genteel magazine of the late nineteenth century had been *Century*, with a readership of roughly 250,000. By the early twentieth century, *Munsey's*—having transformed itself from a weekly to a heavily illustrated and slightly racy monthly, and having lowered its price from a quarter to a dime—was regularly selling seven hundred thousand issues a month, more than the circulation of *Century*, *Harper's*, and the *Atlantic* combined. *McClure's Magazine*, another low-price illustrated monthly, which specialized in heroic biographies and history before it turned gradually into the leading journal of the "muckrakers," was selling nearly three hundred thousand copies an issue by the turn of the century. *Collier's*, long a publisher of popular and prestigious fiction, added commentary on public affairs, war reporting by the famous Richard Harding Davis, muckraking investigative work by Samuel Hopkins Adams and others, and a heavy dose of controversial social gossip. Later it flourished by publishing lengthy excerpts from important books. Its circulation, about half a million in 1912, approached a million in the mid-1920s. The *Saturday Evening Post*, purchased and saved from bankruptcy in 1893 by Cyrus Curtis, became the largest-selling magazine in the country (its circulation

passed a million in 1908 and reached two million by the early 1920s)
with its mix of Horatio Alger–like business stories, romantic fiction,
Norman Rockwell covers, and conservative anti-immigrant politics
laced with a vague anti-Semitism (one of its most popular features in the
early twentieth century was a series of "funny stories about Jews"). Many
other periodicals were also searching for an audience within the expanding middle class: Hearst's *Cosmopolitan*, a lively mélange of high and low
culture and popular fiction, which had well over a million subscribers by
1920; *Vanity Fair*, reinvented by Condé Nast and Frank Crowninshield
in 1913 as a sleek monthly "which covers the things people talk about at
parties—the arts, sports, humor, and so forth," and which acquired a relatively small but devoted readership among what was soon to be known
as the "smart set"; and most important of all to Hadden and Luce, the
Literary Digest, the only popular magazine that attempted to present real
news.[20]

The *Digest*, which was to be *Time*'s principal competitor, was already
a publishing legend by the early 1920s. Launched in 1890 by Isaac Funk
and Adam Wagnalls—two Lutheran ministers-turned-publishers, best
known in later years for encyclopedias and dictionaries bearing their
names—it was modeled on several earlier efforts, in both Britain and
America, among them the London-based *Review of Reviews*. Such magazines aspired to present readers with a wide selection of writing from
other publications, which in an age before strict international (or even
national) copyright laws was both cheap and easy to assemble. The
Digest's editors called it "a repository of contemporaneous thought and
research as presented in the periodical literature of the world." The
Digest did not really synthesize the material it collected. It usually simply
reprinted it (mostly unsigned and unattributed), often at great and
redundant length. When it published straight news, it often chose the
most detailed and extensive stories. A 1928 article entitled "A Free Hand
for Coolidge in Nicaragua," for example, sprawled over three densely
printed (and densely written) pages: "A signal victory for sound principles and common sense is seen . . . in the vote of Republicans and
Democrats in the United States Senate, fifty-two to twenty-two, in favor
of keeping American marines in Nicaragua." When it ran editorials
from other publications, it tried to pair opposing views—an argument
against the United States joining the League of Nations paired with one
in favor of it, for example. It also cannibalized other periodicals for
humor and advice columns, poetry, society items, and cartoons. It did no
reporting, and very little writing, of its own—other than its eclectic

weekly quizzes on the contents of the issue ("What great European power has accepted the Kellogg plan to renounce war?" "What will take the pucker out of persimmons?") and a gossipy feature called "Personal Glimpses."[21]

By 1920, its circulation well over a million, the *Digest* launched the first of its celebrated straw polls by sending out sixteen million postcard ballots to readers (and many others) all over the country, asking them to name their choice in the upcoming presidential election. The sample, although dramatically larger than that of any modern public opinion survey, had no real scientific basis; it simply reflected the *Digest's* own subscriber list (largely middle class) and other lists it was able to acquire. Even so the *Digest* polls accurately predicted the outcomes (although not the margins) of four successive presidential elections starting in 1920, giving the magazine enormous publicity. The surveys also helped the *Digest* pick up subscribers—seventy thousand as a result of a 1932 straw poll on Prohibition alone.[22]

The success of the *Literary Digest* was both an inspiration and a challenge to Luce and Hadden as they contemplated a newsmagazine of their own. It proved that there was a large appetite for a "digest" of the news—that they were right in thinking that many Americans found most newspapers an inadequate or unsatisfying vehicle for learning about the world. It also suggested that they would face stiff competition. They themselves, however, were not intimidated by the *Digest*. It was, they believed, a staid relic of an earlier age—with its Christian earnestness (a legacy of its founding by theologians, who had envisioned it as a high-minded tool for "educators and ministers"), its essential humorlessness, and its dreary design. Their "paper" would be better.[23]

Back in New York, without salaries or any immediate prospects of them, they moved in with their families. Hadden went back to his mother's home in Brooklyn, and Luce settled on the Upper West Side, near Columbia University, where his family was living during one of his father's arduous fund-raising sojourns in the United States. At the same time that they were boldly launching new careers, they were also returning to the familiar rituals of family life—rushing home for dinner, going to family birthday parties and anniversaries, celebrating holidays. Both men also led active social lives in the circles to which their Yale experiences had given them entry, although they often had to make strained excuses to avoid events that would cost them money. But in many ways Luce's and Hadden's social lives were very different from each other.

Hadden preferred late-night excursions with colleagues and college friends to restaurants and bars. Luce was more likely to attend lunches and teas, to go to the theater or the opera, or to meet friends for dinner at the Yale Club (events mainly paid for by others).[24]

Mostly, however, they worked on their "paper." Luce wrote confidently of their prospects a few days after arriving in New York: "This next month . . . will probably be pretty crucial. The first 10 days we spend marching from expert to expert, until we have convinced ourselves that there is no obvious, potent, reason why *Facts* cannot succeed. We then spend a week or 10 days amassing the necessary capital, and having done that, we hold our breath and jump!" But things did not go as smoothly as they expected. Days turned into weeks, weeks into months, and still they had failed to raise the money they needed. They alternated between periods of great optimism, even elation, and other periods in which they seemed almost to recognize the folly of trying to start a new national magazine at the age of twenty-four with no money and no reputations. "We were never surer of our idea than at this moment," Luce wrote in March, one of many times when the project seemed stalled. "The only question is whether we are old enough, etc. etc., to put it over." The fear of failure—of ceasing to be the dazzling golden boys they had been since Hotchkiss, or as Hadden once put it, of losing the "respect of my friends and acquaintances"—drove them forward almost as much as the dream of success.[25]

Even in their moments of greatest discouragement, however, Luce and Hadden stuck meticulously to their plan. The first step was drawing powerful and influential people into the orbit of their venture—asking advice from editors, publishers, and potential investors, and soliciting endorsements from the famous. It never occurred to Luce and Hadden that such people would refuse to see two unknown young men with no money or experience. For they understood instinctively how their social connections could ease their task. Their paths radiated outward from their fellow "Bones" alumni to the parents of their Yale friends, to other Yale alumni who remained loyal to the university, to a wider circle of eminent people to whom their Yale acquaintances provided access. They fanned out across New York—and up and down the East Coast—presenting their idea to prominent men, asking for advice, and, when the advice was encouraging, requesting a public endorsement. Not everyone was impressed. The well-known advertising executive Bruce Barton dismissed their plan as unfeasible: The *Literary Digest*, he said, already had a monopoly on magazine news—a warning they heard frequently from others as well. The former president of Harvard,

Charles W. Eliot (himself the ostensible editor of the *Harvard Classics*, a popular condensation of great books), huffily dismissed the idea of condensing the news as "disgusting and disgraceful."[26]

Others were encouraging and at least generous enough to lend their names to two earnest young men trying to get started, although they too could sometimes shake Luce's and Hadden's confidence. They paid a frustrating visit to Robert Underwood Johnson, former U.S. ambassador to Italy, whom Luce described as insufferably pompous, talking interminably about himself, unwilling to listen to their plans for the magazine, but ultimately agreeing to endorse the project nevertheless. Luce visited Cyrus Curtis—the famously successful publisher of the *Saturday Evening Post*. Curtis was aloof and condescending, unwilling to lend his name to the magazine, but he ultimately offered vaguely encouraging advice. Such were the perils of courting the rich and famous. Privately annoyed, Hadden and Luce were publicly polite and deferential. And they eventually won over a remarkable group of people. They attracted endorsements from academics: the presidents of Yale, Princeton, Williams, and Johns Hopkins, and the dean of Columbia College; the editor of the *Literary Review* (their old Yale instructor Henry Seidel Canby), the editor of the *Springfield Republican* (where Harry had worked during the summer after Hotchkiss), the editor of the *New York World* (where Brit had worked for a year after college), and Edward Bok, publisher of the *Ladies' Home Journal* and other magazines, author of a renowned autobiography, now retired from business and "posing as the Medici of Philadelphia." The editors of the *Hartford Courant*, the *Century Magazine*, and *Harper's* also provided endorsements—but not, significantly, anyone at the *New York Times*, and not their former boss Frank Munsey. Walter Lippmann lent his support ("No American," Luce said at the time, "has written more brilliantly during the last ten years on politics and government"). There were theologians (among them the Catholic archbishop of Baltimore, the dean of Riverside Church in New York, the Episcopal bishop of Massachusetts, the Presbyterian minister and diplomat Henry Van Dyke); financiers, secondary government officials, and a few people who were simply generically eminent—among them Theodore Roosevelt, Jr., son of the former president. The list of names was a centerpiece of the magazine's first advertising circular, sent to five hundred thousand people in the spring of 1922.[27]

Raising the money was far more difficult. Luce and Hadden drew up a budget that required them to find one hundred thousand dollars in order to put out their first issue, after which, they believed, circulation

and advertising revenue (and additional investors attracted by their presumed success) would keep them going. They started with nothing.
Renting a tiny office in a converted town house on East Seventeenth
Street with money borrowed from Hadden's parents, living abstemi-
ously at home, deferring salaries for themselves and for most of their
tiny staff, they began by seeking funds from friends and their friends'
families, confident that they could quickly find ten wealthy acquaintances, each of whom would invest ten thousand dollars. But it was a
frustratingly slow process, and the confidence Luce had expressed at the
beginning ("we will . . . spend a week or 10 days amassing the necessary
capital") quickly evaporated. "Every day," Luce wrote in May 1922, "we
see one or more 'rich young men' with the idea of getting them to come
in with us on a proposition in which we expect to give them a pittance
and take all the rest ourselves." (Their plan was to offer investors "preferred" stock, while retaining for themselves almost all the "common"
stock, the only stock that conferred voting rights.) "On the face of it," he
confessed, "this is not the easiest job imaginable." His mood was not
helped by a meeting with a "smart young vice president down at Bankers
Trust," who "as much as called us a bunch of crooks" and insisted that
their entire financial plan was unrealistic, verging on fraudulent. (In fact,
their financial plan, although slightly unorthodox, was in no way illegal.)
"This is an awful month," he moaned. "If we fail, our name is simple
M-u-d mud."[28]

The frustrating process fueled Harry's envy, bordering on resentment, of his contemporaries who had inherited great wealth—and particularly of those who refused to part with any of it to help his own
cause. He took sardonic note of the lavish homes, the expensive cars, the
polo matches, the smug self-satisfaction of the rich young men he visited. (He made the mistake of expressing his disdain in one of his late-
night letters to Lila, a young woman entirely committed to the world of
wealth, only to receive a sharp rebuke from her. Harry quickly back-
tracked: "Far from being opposed to ancestors and aristocracy, I am
heartily in favor of them. . . . Far from looking askance at inherited
wealth, I only wish to heaven that I had nothing to do on earth but to
inherit wealth.") And working so closely with Hadden, he also
occasionally—and uncharacteristically—echoed some of Brit's class-
bound prejudices as well. "Bratch and I are going to Philly to-morrow to
see Gimbel (Jew store)," he wrote in early June. A few days later he
reported a "raid upon 'Charlie' Rosenbloom—the Jewboy we missed,
stupidly, at Pittsburg [sic]."[29]

At meeting after meeting they encountered friendly but guarded receptions, which usually ended with expressions of goodwill but no willingness to invest. Even those who did agree to buy shares usually did so in small increments—five hundred dollars here, a thousand there. ("Of course, any loose change I have is yours," one of their wealthy Yale friends said, somewhat condescendingly, when they asked him for support.) "It's an awful strain on the nerves," Luce wrote, "because one has to believe and believe and believe." In reality the fund-raising was going badly only when measured by their own unrealistically optimistic projections. By early June, only a few weeks after they had begun searching in earnest for investors, they had raised twenty thousand dollars. "Not bad," Harry confessed in a hopeful moment. In mid-June they received a five-thousand-dollar pledge—one of their largest so far—from their Yale friend Shorty Knox, a wealthy, polo-playing "S-v-g-" ("Savage," the Skull and Bones epithet for a member of a rival Yale senior society). A few days later another Yale friend invited Harry to lunch and, unsolicited, offered one thousand dollars. Even so it was hard to maintain their confidence and optimism in the face of the "terrible grind and slow results." "People are naturally very scarey," he admitted, "about entrusting their hard earned cash to youngsters." It was not, he confessed, "the easiest thing ever attempted by three unknown musketeers." It was harder still because he could not turn to his most reliable supporter, Nettie McCormick, who was now gravely ill. Harry, in desperation, wrote to his father, who was himself traveling the country in search of money, asking (in vain) for five hundred dollars for the magazine and for help in identifying other investors. He even guiltily hinted that he would not be displeased if his father asked Mrs. McCormick for help on his behalf. (There is no evidence to suggest that his father did any of these things.) "If I had only $1,000, I would put it all in," he said. "So much so, that right now, at least, I wish I hadn't gone to Oxford—although fundamentally, I suppose, the Oxford year is indirectly invested in the paper as it is." Even decades later Luce looked back on "that business of raising the money" as "about the toughest, hardest, most discouraging work that I've experienced."[30]

In the midst of this grueling process they received a surprising inquiry from the *Independent*—a once-distinguished journal of opinion, closely associated with Woodrow Wilson and the League of Nations, which was now floundering. The owners proposed that Luce and Hadden abandon their plans for a new magazine and take over the *Independent* instead. It would, they argued, be easier to raise money for an established publication than for a new one. "Of course, it is hard to resist the chance of stepping at our age into control of what has been a pretty famous and powerful publication," Luce conceded. But after considering the *Independent*'s grim financial circumstances, they declined the offer. (The magazine declared bankruptcy a little over a year later.) Their own prospects did not seem much brighter than the *Independent*'s, but, Harry explained, "the best thing seems to be to keep lugging until we're licked and we can stand a lot of licking yet. So carry on in hope is our motto." By late July they had made modest progress—"38,000 in hand"; but that was still far from the one hundred thousand dollars they believed they needed. They were, Harry said, "laying many traps, wires, and fences, and are not without hope of achieving our purpose." But "not without hope" was far from the confidence they had once expressed, and both Hadden and Luce were spending many long nights worrying about failure.[31]

Suddenly, in August, their fortunes changed. At the suggestion of a friend, Harry rode up to the Yale Club for a meeting with a recent graduate, William Hale Harkness, class of 1922, and his wealthy mother, Mrs. William L. Harkness, hoping at best for a $5,000 investment. To his astonishment Mrs. Harkness pledged $20,000 to the magazine, and her son $5,000 more, which—when combined with other small investments they had recently accumulated—brought their total up to $65,000. Another $10,000 came quickly from two other members of the Harkness family. "That means," an exultant Luce wrote, "that by the end of September at latest we will be capitalized. So the end of a very long and arduous and trying job is now at least within crying distance." And while the last $25,000 proved even more difficult to raise than the first, they managed to push their total up to nearly $87,000 by late October, at which point they decided to move ahead. A few weeks later—as carpenters banged away in the new and larger offices they had rented at Eighth Avenue and Thirty-third Street—they filed the papers that would create their new company.[32]

It had been hard during the long months of collecting endorsements and money to focus on the magazine itself. But Luce and Hadden did work steadily, amid all their other efforts, at building a staff, refining and elaborating their plans, and—not least—finding a name.

Hadden and Luce always claimed that they had never intended to stick with "Facts," the working title for many months of what they were half-mockingly calling between themselves "the world's greatest magazine." In the spring of 1922 they began to experiment with alternatives. For a while, they were attracted to "What's What," and they briefly considered such others as "Destiny," "Chance," and the "Synthetic Review." But one spring morning Luce came into the office to propose another name. He had, he later said, been riding home on the subway the night before, exhausted and glassy eyed, mindlessly reading the advertising cards above the car windows. For some reason he focused on an announcement—"Time for a Change," or something like it, he later recalled—and he became convinced that "Time" was the right title. Hadden immediately agreed, and they never reconsidered. "Time" was attractive to them because it captured something of the dual purpose of their enterprise—to chronicle the passage of time and to save readers precious time. "Take Time—It's Brief," was one of the early slogans they attached to their announcements of the new publication; "Time Will Tell" and "Time Is Valuable" were others. They also attached a pretentious Latin phrase (*De omni re scibili et quibusdam aliis*—"About all things knowable and some others"). "Time" was not a particularly original title. Newspapers all over the world called themselves the *Times*, and there had been an English magazine in the late nineteenth century named "Time," which Luce and Hadden soon discovered and whose logo they used as the basis of the distinctive lettering in the title of their own magazine. They experimented with various subtitles, using such words as "chronicle" and "digest" and "weekly newspaper"; but they finally settled on a term of their own invention: "news-magazine." (The hyphen disappeared in the late 1920s.) It reflected Hadden's delight in creating new compound words and phrases.[33]

At first they worked virtually alone. Culbert Sudler, their Yale classmate and close friend, joined the staff early on and seemed briefly to be a third and almost equal partner. (He even lived for a time with the Luce family in Morningside Heights.) He was energetic, enthusiastic, and good at using his contacts to identify potential investors. But he was never able fully to commit himself to the venture, partly because of pressure from his family to find a more secure job, and partly because he simply could not keep up with Harry and Brit. "Cully is unfortunately not equal to the 'present crisis,' as has been shown during the past two weeks," Harry wrote during one of the many discouraging moments of their first months in New York. In August, Sudler left to take a publishing job with Doubleday Page. Later, Luce and Hadden tried to recruit their friend Walter Millis, who had remained behind at the *Baltimore News* when they moved to New York. Millis, Luce believed, "had the best mind in Yale 1920" and was destined to be their "star writer." But he, too, wavered at the prospect of committing himself to so uncertain a venture; and after changing his mind several times, decided finally to stay in Baltimore after the newspaper offered him a raise—"an affair doing him very little credit," Harry complained angrily. "His defection simply means that more still depends upon the Bratch & me."[34]

Gradually they moved beyond the circle of their Yale contemporaries—but not far beyond. The early staff of the magazine was drawn entirely from their own generation; almost none of their significant colleagues was older than they were. And it was also drawn almost entirely from their own social world—recent graduates of Yale, Harvard, Princeton, Oxford, and Columbia, all of them, unsurprisingly, white male Protestants. "We didn't hardly know anybody else," Luce plaintively explained years later. For the most part Hadden and Luce did not question, or even really notice, what was in fact one of the most distinctive characteristics of their enterprise—its striking homogeneity. It seemed even less remarkable to them that the staff was virtually all male. They hired a few young women as secretaries ("stenos," they called them), and Luce, at least, flirted at times with bringing in talented social acquaintances to do substantive work on the magazine—on the assumption that such women were likely bored and in need of something interesting to do. He wrote Lila at one point to see if one of her Chicago friends, then living in New York, might be interested in writing the music column for the magazine. And he once asked Lila herself if she would like to help with the religion section. Nothing came of either idea. Hadden and Luce had lived virtually their entire previous lives in all-male institutions—Chefoo (for Harry), Hotchkiss, Yale, the army, newspaper staffs. It rarely occurred to them, or to most other male professionals of their time, to question the absence of women from their offices.[35]

Their first important recruit after Sudler was Manfred Gottfried, an aspiring novelist, who had heard about the Luce-Hadden venture through the rumor mill at Yale, where he was a senior. He showed up one day in February at the office on East Seventeenth Street to find Harry and Brit alone in the room, sitting at matching, end-to-end desks under the window, an iron kettle between them to catch cigarette butts. Luce spoke energetically about their plans and grilled Gottfried about his modest experiences. Hadden, who was oddly shy with strangers, remained unsettlingly silent. A few days later Harry traveled up to New Haven to offer Gottfried the job, even if in a typically distracted way. He asked Gottfried to accompany him to see a tailor. Talking all the way, Luce finally made his proposal standing pantless in a shop stall while his trousers were being pressed. Gottfried (who soon became known within the office as "Gott" and who remained with the magazine for decades) immediately accepted and began work in October, several weeks before his salary was scheduled to begin. Eager and capable, he did everything from writing copy to fetching coffee. He even persuaded his father to invest one thousand dollars in the magazine.[36]

Not long after that they met Roy Larsen, a 1921 Harvard graduate and former business manager of the university's literary magazine, the *Advocate*. He was trying to find a place in publishing in New York. Predictably his youth and limited experience did not open up very many important positions for him. His Harvard classmate John Cowles, son of the publisher of the *Des Moines Register*, offered him an attractive, low-level job in his father's company. But before he could take it, *Time* stepped in. Luce and Hadden could provide far more senior positions within their nascent organization than someone of Larsen's age could have expected anywhere else, and they took his undergraduate achievements more seriously than other employers would have done. They pursued Larsen aggressively, perhaps because they recognized something in him they badly needed. He was competent, certainly, but he also exuded an air of solidity, maturity, and competitive tenacity ("a grim but smiling terrier," a colleague once described him) that, for all their self-confidence, they feared they still partly lacked. In a company staffed entirely by people in their early twenties, Larsen (although a year younger than Luce and Hadden) seemed the most securely adult. He turned down the job of advertising manager, but Harry and Brit went back to him and finally persuaded him to take charge of circulation, a job more to his liking. They even offered him a salary of forty dollars a week, more than they were paying themselves. In return they got a talented and energetic partner, who struggled to build a subscription base for a magazine no one had heard of and few understood, and who—next to Luce and his successors as editor in chief—would become the most important figure in the company until his death in 1979. Using multiple mailing lists and enthusiastically written circulars, Larsen managed to build up a base of about eight thousand subscribers before the first issue appeared—a disappointingly small number to Luce and Hadden, although even they occasionally had to confess that it was "not so bad for a group of whippersnappers."[37]

As they moved closer to publication, they expanded the staff further, still drawing from friends, acquaintances, and people suggested by their Yale contemporaries. On the basis of a suggestion from a friend, they hired a young Oxford student, Thomas J. C. Martyn, by cable, without ever meeting him, because they had heard he was an experienced journalist. They discovered when he arrived in New York that he had no experience at all. "It was a stupid thing for us to do," Luce later conceded. But Martyn turned out to be a talented writer of exactly the kind of stories Harry and Brit wanted. Thomas Rinehart, the son of a well-known novelist and a recent Harvard graduate (who, Luce believed, hid a "quick intelligence" behind a "simple" facade), and John A. Thomas, another recent Yale graduate, also joined the writing staff.[38]

In the meantime Hadden and Luce strove to shape the magazine itself. To some degree the concept remained remarkably unchanged from the idea they had developed in Baltimore, and even earlier—as the prospectus they prepared early in 1922 to present to potential investors made clear. "No publication has adapted itself to the time which busy men are able to spend on simply keeping informed," they stated in bold letters on the first page of the document. They followed quickly with a claim of "COMPLETE ORGANIZATION"—six departments (National Public Affairs, Foreign News, The Arts, Sports, and People) and twenty-four "sections" (among them Books, Theater, Music, Education, Religion, Business, Law, and The Professions). There would be approximately one hundred short articles each week, "none of which are over 400 words in length," each placed "in its logical place in the magazine, according to a "FIXED METHOD OF ARRANGEMENT."[39]

Into this rigid structure they would pour the results of what they described as a comprehensive search through "every magazine and newspaper of note in the world." The cover of their first advertising circular was framed by a list of almost ninety periodicals, which they promised to read every week and use as sources. Unlike the *Literary Digest*, they pointedly claimed, they would cover "EVERY HAPPENING OF IMPORTANCE." And while they would not have an editorial page and would not write "to prove any special case," neither would they strive for "complete neutrality on public questions." They even presented a slightly fussy "catalogue" of their own largely conservative "prejudices"—which included "a belief that the world is round," "a general distrust of the present tendency toward increasing interference by government," and a "respect for the old, particularly in manners." In this, Larsen later remembered, they were drawing from Mencken, whom Hadden (far more than Luce) greatly admired.[40]

Only in November 1922, after they had raised enough money to start publishing, did they begin the serious work of turning these plans into an actual magazine. In their larger (but still modest) offices on Eighth Avenue, the slowly growing staff began squeezing into newly built cages and cubicles. The few walls were paper thin, so no one, including Luce and Hadden, could easily have a private conversation. Desktops were piled high with magazines and newspapers, and the floor was littered with the scraps of periodicals from which useful stories had been cut. Neophyte writers wrestled to condense complex news stories into a few hundred lively words, while Hadden and Luce sat at their desks reading the results, marking them up with pencil, and sending them back. (On weekends there was so little heat in the building that they sometimes retreated to the card room of the Yale Club and spread their stacks of papers out on tables there.) Hadden, in particular, was a tough critic, snarling and growling at prose he considered dull or obscure, penciling in adjectives and phrases that he thought would enliven the story, intimidating the writers, none of whom was much younger than he was. As they produced prototypes of the various sections of the magazine, they took them to the established editors and writers with whom they had been consulting from the beginning. "First section to get into form is 'Books,'" Luce wrote, now that "Wells (Harpers) & Canby (Evening Post) have given OK." But mostly they were on their own.[41]

It was slow going. "We publish the first issue of *Time* the last week of January or the first of February," Luce wrote in November 1922, acknowledging that the date of the inaugural issue had slipped from December into 1923. "But first we have to make *Time* good enough to publish and that means eight weeks of writing, editing, and printing 'practice issues.' The writing of the practice issues will be carried on by a full staff just as if we were publishing. We shall be just as busy and rushed (if not more so) as we will when the thing is actually being published. . . . If they do not meet with our expectations, we will stop, having failed to produce what we said we would produce. If they meet our expectations, then the only thing that stands between us and certain success is that unknown quantity 'luck,' absolutely unguessable."[42]

But while Luce and Hadden had often worried about the financing and marketing of the magazine, they rarely expressed real doubts about their capacity to write it successfully. "TIME is doing very well," Luce wrote Lila early in December. "In fact a most unusual spirit of optimism seems to pervade the ranks." A few weeks later, with the first "fairly good complete [sample] issue of TIME" in hand, he claimed to be in "a sort of soggy pleasant frame of mind." There were, to be sure, moments of concern. "Things are going very badly," Luce wrote after the second "specimen issue" appeared. "We have yet to find the ideal assistants." Hadden once returned deeply discouraged from a meeting with Walter Lippmann, who had been harshly critical of another sample issue. They postponed publication three times as they tried to improve. But little by little, the magazine began to approach their image of it. The later specimens already contained some of the magazine's most enduring features. There was the distinctive lettering of the title; the cover portrait of a significant individual (the first complete dummy carried a black-and-white drawing of the financier Bernard Baruch); the brief, punchy news items ("Who will be the Republican presidential nominee in 1924? Senator James E. Watson answered this question on the floor of the Senate with an emphatic: 'President Harding is the only possible choice!' At once political tongues began to wag"). There was also the casual insertion of opinions into the most straightforward stories ("President Harding, in a speech before Congress, placed a constructive program before the people"; "The great Senator John T. Morgan of Alabama advocated [a second Isthmian canal] in 1897").[43]

For Harry the last weeks of 1922 were doubly stressful. Not only was he working with Hadden to shape the content of the magazine, he was also working more or less alone to ensure that *Time* would be able to function as a business. This was an area of the enterprise in which Hadden took almost no interest and for which he had little talent. Luce, however, proved to be a very good businessman, somewhat to his dismay—since, like Brit, his original interest in "the paper" had been primarily editorial. ("Now the Bratch is really the editor of TIME," he wrote, "and I, alas, alas, alas, am business manager. . . . Of course no one but Brit and I know this!") He negotiated contracts with paper suppliers and printers. He contracted out the advertising. He supervised the budget. He set salaries and terms for employees. He supervised the setting up of the office. And whenever he could, he sat with Brit and marked up copy or discussed plans for the next issue. In the meantime he continued to have obligations to his family, to lead at least a modest social life, and of course to write to Lila in whatever spare minutes he could find. Even for someone in his twenties, the days were long and difficult. He described one of them in December:

> . . . my new steno arrived. Put her to work on 78 letters. . . .
> Then conference with paper-man. . . . Then down town to
> [bank] to open up our second account. Back to the office,

advised . . . as to employing new man. . . . Then dashed to the
Lotos Club where a disappointed printer gave me a drink and
lunch. . . . Saw Hadden for a second and then began series of
interviews with artists (commercial). Threw them out in time to
dictate a few belated letters and then rushed out in pursuit of taxi
and Helen [one of Lila's friends from Chicago]. Arrived at
Helen's at 5:45, made *profuse* apologies . . . and then sat down to
tea. . . . Skidded under the 7 o-clock wire at home for dinner. . . . After dinner back to work.[44]

"The whole staff felt the pressure," Gottfried remembered years
later. "For a couple of months nobody had any regular days off, and now
[in January 1923] nobody had any days off whatsoever." One by one staff
members succumbed to the stress and exhaustion. Gottfried "was the
first to weaken" and announced that he was going to take every Wednes-
day off. Nancy Ford, whose job as fact-checker for every article was one
of the most difficult and time-consuming jobs on the magazine, seemed
constantly to be battling exhaustion. (She left the magazine altogether a
few months after it began publishing, unable to take the strain.) Luce,
too, complained of the stress. "I've a splitting headache," he wrote in the
midst of one of those frantic days, and "never seem able to get as much
done as seems positively *necessary*. If there were only 20 Bratches and 20
'me's, we might have a chance of making good." But for the most part
these young pioneers—as they sometimes saw themselves—persevered;
and as the release of the first real issue approached, they grew increasingly excited. "After this week," Luce wrote as the publication day
approached, "it's head-on either to glory or perdition!"[45]

The intensity was partly a result of the smallness of the staff in relation to the size of the task it was managing. In addition to Hadden and
Luce, there were four writers (Gottfried, Martyn, Rinehart, and
Thomas), a circulation manager (Larsen), a fact-checker (Nancy Ford
for a short time), and a few secretaries and part-time workers. Advertising sales (almost nonexistent) were handled by an outside contractor.
Some copy came in from "contributing editors," mostly recruited from
friends and acquaintances, many of whom never appeared in the office;
and much of what they wrote had to be heavily edited or entirely rewrit-
ten. In the end the tiny full-time staff did the vast majority of the writing. Although the magazine itself was neatly subdivided by topic, there
were no clear divisions among the responsibilities of the writers and editors. Everyone did a little of almost everything.[46]

In mid-February they decided they were ready to publish, and they began aiming for the last week of the month. Their already frenzied lives grew more frantic still as they aimed to meet their self-imposed deadline. But finally they delivered the last of their copy to the printer. Virtually the entire staff, launching a tradition that would continue through the first year of the magazine, crowded into taxis for the trip to the presses—to proofread copy once it was set and to write new stories as the morning papers arrived. After a few hours they sent out for fried-egg sandwiches and coffee. People stretched out on the long tables at the back of the shop and slept. Everything—sandwiches, copy, clothes— became covered with printers' ink. Finally, in the early morning hours, they stumbled out and headed for home, crossing paths with Wall Street workers on their way downtown.[47]

The first issue of *Time* appeared on late February 27, 1923 (with an official publication date of March 3). It was twenty-seven pages long, entirely in black-and-white, printed in small type. It had scant advertising, confined to the inside and back covers and the last few pages; most of the eleven advertisements were from banks and book publishers. But for now Luce and Hadden were concerned above all with the editorial content. And even in the first issue, readers could see the curious mixture of innovations that the two young men had been planning for years—rigid organization, concise news summaries, lively language, whimsical diversions, and casual, even at times sophomoric, expressions of opinion—that would characterize the magazine through much of its early history.

The cover was a black-and-white drawing of the retiring Speaker of the House of Representatives, Joseph Cannon. "Uncle Joe," as he was known, had been a strict, even tyrannical, leader of the House for decades, and the editors of *Time* made no secret of their disdain for the "old guard" he represented. "Never did a man employ the office of Speaker with less regard for its theoretical impartiality," they wrote. He was, they said, "no mere voice crying in the wilderness, but a voice that forbade anybody else to cry out—out of turn." What was most striking about the inaugural issue, however, was how disciplined it was. No story was longer than four hundred words, and most were two hundred or fewer. There was no deviation from the "FIXED METHOD OF ARRANGEMENT" they had promised subscribers months before: a "National Affairs" section with eleven subsections; "Foreign Affairs" with sixteen subsections, each representing a particular area of the world; and another twenty sections covering the arts, professions, sports, finance, crime, the press, and other topics. A section titled "Milestones" presented news of significant marriages, divorces, and deaths. There was a strange (and deservedly short-lived) feature—"Imaginary Interviews"—that presented clever statements that the editors thought eminent people could or should have made. Perhaps most illustrative of Luce and Hadden's commitment to sharing even their most trivial opinions with their readers was a pair of features at the end of the magazine—"Point with Pride" and "View with Alarm"—which gave them license to reveal their own passions and prejudices. In the first issue, for example, they "pointed with pride" to an effort by Yale faculty members to retain the requirement that all students study classics, and "viewed with alarm" the literary regard given to T. S. Eliot's great, despairing poem *The Waste Land* and the high proportion of "Orientals" in the population of Hawaii. Over the next several years many of the frivolities and excesses of the first issue disappeared (sometimes to be replaced by others). But the enduring core of the idea for the magazine—organization, brevity, comprehensiveness, and partiality—was visible from the start.[48]

With the first issue finally in print, most of the staff went home to sleep. Luce, however, returned to his office, where he found Larsen on his knees on the floor, frantically burrowing through a chaotic pile of papers. They were the mailing wrappers for subscription copies. Larsen had hired a group of young women—"debutantes," as he called them—to write the addresses on the wrappers and prepare them for the arrival of the actual magazine. Now he discovered that nothing was in order, that many of the addresses were wrong, and that some of the wrappers were too small to contain the magazine. Some of the subscription copies of the first issue did not get into the mail until after the third issue had been published.

Luce uncharacteristically ignored Larsen's panic and went to his desk in the back of the office. Putting his feet on the table, he picked up the newly printed magazine—his already ink-stained fingers getting blacker still as he held it—and read it cover to cover. He had seen everything before, three or four times. But, as he recalled years later, "I had this sort of surprising feeling that it was pretty good."[49]

V

"Time: The Weekly News-Magazine"

I can only say," Luce wrote late in March 1923, "that Vol 1 No 4 will be published and that Vol 1 No 5 may or *may not* be published."[1]

For a moment following the publication of the first issue, optimism ran high. Grasping at the compliments they received from friends and colleagues, seizing on the rapid sale of the inaugural issue in a few Manhattan locations, Luce, Hadden, Larsen, and their colleagues began to believe that *Time* might indeed be an overnight success. But those illusions vanished quickly. In the end the first issue sold nine thousand copies, a little more than a third of their projections. This was partly a result of the staff's inexperience, as illustrated by the incompetent mailing of subscription copies of the first issue. But half of the five thousand newsstand copies were returned unsold as well. Nor was the critical reception encouraging. "The first issue of TIME," Luce wrote disconsolately, "has received extraordinarily little praise." For the next weeks and months the *Time* staffers worked simply to stay alive, "watching the mail-bag with maternal care" to see if enough subscription income would arrive each week to allow them to keep going, and praying "for courage to face the daily—in fact hourly disappointment." In the meantime their initial capitalization—just short of one hundred thousand dollars—was dwindling fast, and everyone recognized that substantial additional investments were unlikely until the magazine began to prove itself.[2]

At one point Luce and Larsen sat down "to see what was the worst we could expect in the next three weeks," and they concluded that there was "no limit to the extent of the immediate catastrophe!—Not when people are already writing in at the rate of over *100* per day, telling us to cancel their trial subscriptions." As he usually did when faced with difficulties, Luce shrouded himself in gloom and self-reproach. He was, he wrote to Lila, doomed to be a "second-rater." And he claimed that he was resigned to the failure. "I really don't believe I care what happens in April," he wrote at the end of March. "I shall be more than happy to be April's fool." Worst of all "a lot of people who have bought the thing think it is the most terrible of all terrors." But as in other times of anxiety, he also strove to maintain hope. "We have not begun to realize our aspirations in the making of our paper," he wrote Nettie McCormick, with more optimism than he actually felt. "But the testimony of thousands of readers every week & in every state of the Union seems to indicate that we are on the right track." After Condé Nast, the famously successful publisher of *Vanity Fair* and *Vogue*, invited Luce and Hadden to meet with them, Luce wrote brightly that the invitation—designed, they assumed, to satisfy the publisher's curiosity—meant that the "big fellows are beginning to realize we exist." He was grasping at straws.[3]

All the members of the staff braced themselves for the daily struggle—the struggle to write, edit, and produce the magazine; to keep up with the bills despite minimal funds; to wrest payment from their charter subscribers. "It was just like pulling teeth to get the $5 bills in," Luce later recalled. In March they received slightly over eleven thousand dollars in subscription income, and in April more than seventeen thousand dollars. But whatever optimism this healthy increase produced was shattered in May, when income dropped to just over ten thousand dollars. "With any luck," Luce noted sardonically, "one day we will have $5,000 on deposit." Advertising income was also minimal. "From the advertising world as a whole," their first annual report frankly observed, "*Time* has met with a cold reception. . . . Advertisers are human. It was years before evolution was generally accepted as a theory." Inside the office they were less philosophical. Luce and his new (and first) advertising director, E. R. Crowe, were battling constantly—Crowe calling Luce amateurish, Luce accusing Crowe of extravagance. Crowe left angrily after only a few weeks of publication, returning his shares of TIME Inc. stock and, as Luce later recalled, saying "the hell with you." There were other casualties as well. Hadden was unhappy with John Franklin Carter, one of the new writers, and dismissed him after a few weeks, leaving the editorial operations seriously undermanned. Luce, who was already fully occupied with the magazine's precarious business operations, had to pitch in. (Carter went on to become a successful columnist, writing as "the Unofficial Observer.")[4]

Little by little, however, *Time*'s fortunes improved—not so much as to erase the anxiety, but enough to create some realistic hope. Word of mouth was drawing new subscribers to the magazine, slowly increasing circulation. "I *think*," Luce wrote in May, "that two weeks from now I will be saying with some light degree of definiteness that TIME will in all probability at least outlive the summer, and that if it can do that there may be hope for it." His spirits brightened considerably in June, when he was invited to give a short speech at the Yale commencement as a representative of recent distinguished alumni. "Feeling fit as fiddle and 'morale' is very high," he wrote after the event. "The speech is of absolutely no importance . . . except as a soothing reassurance that our classmates cannot point the finger of scorn at us."[5]

Having resisted paying to publicize the magazine in the early months, Luce and Hadden now decided to use some of their precious dwindling capital to take out advertisements in prestigious but relatively inexpensive magazines such as *Harper's*, the *Atlantic, Century*, and *Literary Digest*. They seemed to help. Circulation began a slow but steady rise and averaged 18,500 over the second half of the year—more than twice where they had started, even if little more than half of their projections. They ended the year with a little over $36,000 in the bank and another $9,500 still owed them by subscribers and advertisers. They had spent more than half their initial capitalization to stay afloat, but they had feared much worse. *Time*, Hadden wrote optimistically at the end of 1923, "has grown from an idea into an established institution" and "has gradually been accepted by an increasing number of people as part of their weekly reading." But the boasting was, they realized, to some degree premature. The charter subscriptions were set to expire in February, and they knew that to survive they needed a healthy renewal rate. Once again they waited nervously each day for the mail to gauge their success. In fact renewals were strong, and new subscribers were continuing to sign up as well.[6]

According to their initial agreement, Luce and Hadden were scheduled to trade jobs each year, alternating between running the business and editing the magazine. Early 1924 was Luce's turn to be editor. But the switch did not occur. Both men realized that Hadden had little interest in or talent for business matters, and Luce—who in other circumstances might have insisted on the trade anyway—decided that the time was not right. Despite the improvement in *Time*'s health by 1924, Luce remained appropriately worried about survival. "Oh, we were in too much trouble . . . too much trouble," he later recalled of his decision to stay where he was.[7]

By mid-1924 they were becoming more confident. Over the next nine months they raised an additional fifty thousand dollars from the original stockholders, "quite easily" according to Luce, in return for more stock. They were even willing to consider expansion. Henry Seidel Canby, their onetime Yale instructor, was now the editor of the struggling *Saturday Review of Literature*. He approached *Time* and proposed a partnership, which Luce and Hadden were, as Luce later put it, "nervy enough" to accept. *Saturday Review* moved into offices in *Time*'s inelegant building, contributed to the rent, and shared other expenses. Larsen in return helped them more than double their subscription base. The editorial life of the *Review* remained largely autonomous, but the partnership gave *Time* more visibility and, perhaps as well, an entry point into the *Review*'s small but elite readership. *Time*'s circulation grew even more rapidly in the second half of the year, so much so (to seventy thousand a week) that the magazine registered its first profit at the end of 1924 (a modest $674, but a tremendous advance from the heavy losses in 1923).[8]

Launching *Time* and tending it during its perilous early months was an enervating job. Luce worked constantly, maintaining only the most minimal social life and even seeing very little of his family when they were still in New York. Often he returned home after everyone else was asleep and left in the morning before anyone was awake. In the summer of 1923 the family moved out of Manhattan to a summer house (which Harry never visited) in upstate New York for a few weeks, after which his mother and Sheldon returned to Beijing (joining Emmavail, who was working at the YWCA there). Later that fall his sister Elisabeth returned to Wellesley, and his father embarked on another arduous round of fund-raising in the Midwest. Harry remained in the city, so busy that he seemed almost oblivious to his family's dispersal. With the family apartment in Morningside Heights now gone, he lived for a time in a room at the Yale Club and then moved downtown to a spartan and less expensive room ("four walls and a door, and a very fine desk," as he described it) on Stuyvesant Street, to be nearer the office. He was accustomed to a frenzied life, and the pace of work—exhausting as it must have been—did not often seem to bother him. Quite the contrary, in fact, for despite his frequent complaints about the grim fortunes of his enterprise, he loved the battle. "Doing something, getting something done, . . . finding a way out of a difficulty, . . . just the 'game' of it,— that . . . is the 'kick' I get out of it all—whatever it is, now, or in the future." And yet this period of intense preoccupation with the magazine coincided with a period in which he was desperately attempting to sustain what at times seemed to him a hopeless romance.[9]

The struggle for *Time* was, in fact, crucially connected—in Luce's mind at least—to his struggle for, and sometimes with, Lila. Harry remained infatuated with her and was constantly fearful that she might give up on him. At the same time he worried that the woman he loved might not be wholly compatible with the life he envisioned for himself. By now he and Lila had known each other for more than three years and had developed a very serious relationship. They had quietly and informally agreed to marry. But the marriage, at least in Harry's mind, remained far from certain, since Lila's family—in particular her somewhat imperious stepfather, Frederick Haskell, a prominent Chicago banker—remained skeptical. Haskell questioned the suitability of a young man with little money and an uncertain career: "a person of no importance," as he put it. His views were no secret to Harry, who wrote Mrs. McCormick that his prospective stepfather-in-law was "apparently convinced that I am thoroughly worthless."[10]

The relationship, with the exception of the few months Harry had spent working in Chicago, had been—and remained—mostly epistolary. Harry wrote long impassioned letters to Lila every two or three days, often rushing to Penn Station late at night to get them onto the last train to Chicago. Lila wrote frequently in return, less often than Harry but with equal affection. They had pet names for each other: Lila was "Tod," and Harry was "Chuck." More often they used gushing terms of endearment—"Beloved," "Dearest," "Carissima," "Angel," "Beautifulest," "Totally adored." And yet they rarely saw each other. Lila traveled occasionally to New York with Mrs. Haskell, but even then Harry found it hard to see her, both because he was busy at work and because, when he was free, Lila's vaguely hostile mother had often made plans that excluded him. For a while they took to meeting in Washington, where Lila went occasionally to see friends. But even these infrequent, furtive visits came to a sudden halt in late June when Lila sailed with her mother for a summerlong sojourn in Europe—a trip perhaps designed to encourage her to forget about Harry.[11]

Despite her constant reassurances Harry could not help but fear that

Lila's love was incomplete and unreliable, and he rarely hesitated to share his anxiety with her. He believed, or at least claimed, that his love had begun earlier, and was deeper than hers. He insisted, for example, that he had fallen in love with Lila in Rome in 1920 "at first sight," but that Lila did not then reciprocate. Even three years later he continued to search for reassurance. "I am desperate to find out whether or not you love me," he wrote her in Europe in July, not long after reading Lila's own impassioned assurances that she did. He could not help worrying about how Lila's mother might be turning her daughter against him, and he wrote—perhaps preemptively—of the financial uncertainty about which he felt certain Mrs. Haskell was warning her daughter. He begged her to "reconcile yourself to the fact that for a little while you have got a lover who cannot play that role [the successful provider] as it ought to be played." When Lila wrote that he should be satisfied with knowing she loved him, Harry continued to fret. "When it's this job and that job, and get up and rush to the office, and hear this bad news and that bad news, . . . and get a bad lunch, and find this gone wrong and 'must do that,' and catch the subway and be late for dinner, and this *must* be done tonight, and now let's get to bed, and start all over again tomorrow— Well, Tod, it's not in me to maintain through all that drab and wretched business the calm and philosophical confidence of the idealist whose feet are planted upon the bases of the universe and whose right hand upholds the footstool of the throne of God." The grandiose rhetoric could not disguise his terrible mundane anxiety.[12]

His relationship with Lila was almost certainly the first serious romance of his life, and at times he seemed—at least in writing—utterly besotted, writing page after page of impassioned statements and restatements of his love. But as the level of commitment grew, Harry also began trying, in effect, to "improve" Lila. This was visible at times in small and inconsequential ways: his graceless references to her misspellings ("By the way, you might spell the great man's name [Sam Insull] correctly!"); his blunt corrections of minor factual mistakes ("Tuchuns [Chinese military governors] have nothing to do with bandits . . . either etymologically or socially"); and his complaints about the brevity, superficiality, or, as he saw it, condescension of her messages. ("Don't treat me like a pitiable dachshund with one leg shot off, but like a live animal!")[13]

But his criticisms were also visible in larger ways. He chided her for her frivolousness, and for a while lectured her about spending too much time playing bridge. He balked at times at Lila's aristocratic prejudices, sometimes by mildly ridiculing her ("We are having turkey hash. It's very unByronic & besides I know you despise anything so plebeian"), and sometimes by challenging her, as if to test her loyalty. "Some time ago you spoke scornfully of the 'flats' your young married friends inhabit," he wrote almost tauntingly at one point. "Well, you shall see, as soon as we can afford anything even as good as that—pop! We shall be in it." In fact the relative claims of status and achievement were a frequent source of discussion between them. "Some people," he wrote pointedly, "do attach great importance to comfort, to eminent respectability, etc. . . . Other people believe that these things, while *very* desirable, are not to be compared in value to other things. The corollary of the former belief is that there is no immortality and that therefore no one will even know whether it was not just as important to attend the right party and have a 'good time' as it was to attend the right church and love 'justice.' " On another occasion he accused Lila of not valuing his work. "I think you care a great deal more for the kudos (fame etc) or the general results which personally accrue to me out of it than for the actual doing of it, and I care just the other way around."[14]

Harry was right about Lila, at least in part. She was a vivacious, even flirtatious young woman who was immersed in the whirl of society and who—as Harry perceptively noted—lived "for the entire crowd." She was preoccupied with the trappings of the upper class: its social conventions, its material expectations, its style, its values. She loved things— furniture, clothes, houses, jewelry—and continued to do so throughout her very long life. She cared a great deal about appearances and looked to Harry not just to be successful but also to be socially presentable, which at times he still was not. He often dressed badly ("dashed in and bought a suit, all ready made so that it probably fit about as well as a pair of pajamas," he once wrote her); he had almost no awareness of his physical surroundings (he once described his residence to her as "two beds, four chairs, and a table"); and he was not yet wholly comfortable—and perhaps never fully became so—in Lila's elite social world because he did not like, and was not good at, small talk and gossip. In some ways it was hard to see how someone as serious and intense as Harry had found himself drawn to Lila—and vice versa.[15]

And yet a large part of Lila's appeal to Harry had always been that she provided things he himself did not have. Despite his protestations, he shared her aristocratic aspirations, coveted her social position, and envied her family's wealth. These were not his only ambitions, of course, but they were far from the least important. His own social life, limited as it was, was securely rooted in the world of his wealthy friends from Hotchkiss and Yale. He spent weekends in the summer of 1923, a summer in which he never visited his family in their own modest summer quarters, playing tennis and attending dinners at the country homes of people in his "circle." As much as he tried at times to resist the values and prejudices of the world of the wealthy, he found himself drawn to them—to their assumptions of entitlement, to their camaraderie, to their willingness to express and even defend positions that might shock people outside the circle. For Luce, at least, this was still a predominantly male world; and through his late-night conversations with his upper-class friends, he labored to find a social philosophy of his own— one that seemed to change almost weekly but was always at least to some degree in opposition to his understanding of Lila's worldview. When she wrote him about the value of the aristocracy, he subtly chided her by hinting that she did not understand what the aristocracy really meant. He parroted for a time the views of his English colleague, Thomas Martyn, citing Martyn's pompous statement that if the Duchess of Devonshire thought him ill-mannered, "I shouldn't care twopence." But if "the man who sells newspapers in front of my club should fail to respond heartily to my 'Good morning,' I should be upset for a week." This was evidence, Harry claimed, of the "undeveloped" American sense of "what it is to be aristocratic." And yet on another occasion, apparently after an evening of conversation with his Skull and Bones colleagues, he wrote to Lila very differently, but again implicitly chidingly, about her modest charitable work in Chicago: "Don't kid yourself into believing that you really sympathize or 'feel for' the poor people. . . . I make no pretense about the poor. . . . My claim to virtue is that at least I don't pretend to sympathize with them." And even though he rarely expressed, and often fiercely criticized, racial and religious prejudice, he continued occasionally to fall unthinkingly into the casual bigotry of the upper class of his time, referring, for example, to his physician as "the Jewboy doctor" who lived in a "swank Jew apartment on Riverside."[16]

The summer of 1923 was a hard one for Luce, despite the slowly rising fortunes of *Time*. His family had left the city. Lila was in Europe. He was living in a depressing room. And he was beset by bad news. One of his friends from Yale, Harry Davison, had been diagnosed with tuberculosis and had been rushed off to the West, where the dry climate was supposed to help with recovery; Luce was aware that tuberculosis was often fatal and was distraught—in part, no doubt, because Davison was an important *Time* supporter and a member of its board of directors.

(Davison eventually recovered fully.) He learned that one of his Chefoo friends, the Englishman Harold Burt, with whom he had traveled in Europe in 1920, had committed suicide. He reproached himself bitterly for not having contacted him recently: "Suppose he had received a cheerio letter from his nursery companion," he lamented. But the greatest blow was probably the death of Nettie McCormick, Harry's unwavering patron and surrogate parent since his childhood. Only days before her death he had written her warmly about his relationship with Lila and his hopes that she would attend the wedding (not mentioning that he was still not entirely confident that it would occur). The letter never reached her and was returned unopened. Days later he was in Chicago serving as a pallbearer at her funeral.[17]

These worries and losses, combined with his lonely stressful life in New York, made him even more obsessive in the way he thought and wrote about his relationship with Lila. His own anxiety contributed to his complaints about her behavior and values, his efforts to improve her, and to his fears that he would lose her. It also brought to the surface a clearly harbored but seldom expressed darkness in his understanding of his life. In an uncharacteristic letter to Lila in the fall of 1923 he described himself as "sick at heart" and laid out for her an "egoistic parade of my troubles"—a litany of resentment, ambition, envy, and insecurity. He described life in America, from his earliest days at Hotchkiss, as a grim "struggle for existence," made all the more difficult because of a series of injustices: "the disgrace [a family divorce] which disrupted my mother's family" and cut him off from his distinguished (distant) cousin Elihu Root; his paternal grandfather's financial setbacks and failures; his own father's demeaning existence as a fund-raiser ("begging for money for which he got no credit"); and his realization that the McCormick family—and even his beloved patroness, Nettie McCormick—had, as he put it, "played me for a sucker," making him think he was in effect a member of their family when he was in fact "the poor well-deserving protégé" who had become not a family member but a family project. (He was not mentioned in Mrs. McCormick's will. Unsurprisingly, the estate passed on to her own sons.)[18]

The great, redeeming event in this dark narrative of his life was, as he saw it, his election to Skull and Bones, a "trifle," he conceded, but an "honor that I probably took in with absurdly ludicrous seriousness," not because of the friends he made or the connections he acquired, but because of its validation of him as a man of importance. Receiving an honor so coveted by so many others—"nice boys with nice families . . . wanting that so badly" and not getting it "for one reason—because *I* got it"—was "as evil and human a delight as probably even Mr. Satan had, but I had it and I couldn't but have it." But Skull and Bones was far from enough. Harry needed to achieve it all—the wealth, the fame, the influence that others had been handed by birth but that he would have to acquire by sheer effort. "The main thing is to win and nothing is justified except in that perspective. . . . I have got to rise to the ordinary level of the ordinary upper-class bourgeois. Then and only then can I begin the great march, the great knight-erranthood, of achieving my knighthood, my rank among the good and faithful." A few days later he wrote again—perhaps afraid that he had revealed too much—and asked Lila not to take the letter seriously. "Don't think about it much. I don't think about it. If I did, I would have been beaten long ago."[19]

All of this—the ambition, the resentment, the fear of failure—made his still-uncertain marriage into a kind of lifeline. He loved Lila, to be sure, but he also needed her both as validation of his rise to respectability and as an entrée into the social world he coveted. As her return from Europe approached, his letters became more ardent. "You can think of this pilgrimage to the boat [to mail a letter to Lila] as a pentecostial [*sic*] march to the shrine of you, there to confess——everything!" And to his great delight, Lila too—despite having spent months with her mother away from Harry—became more impassioned as their reunion drew near. "Paris looked so appealing," she wrote of her last days before returning to America, "and [the city] reproached me sadly for being so anxious and glad to leave her." Later she wrote emotionally, "I cannot understand why Heaven rewards one of its most impractical miserable sinners with a husband who is among the most capable men of his generation on this continent. May Heaven make up the deficiency on my side and thus reward you." Lila's arrival in New York, and her obvious joy at being reunited with Harry, seemed to dispel his remaining doubts. Having kept an almost morbid secrecy about their relationship for over three years, he now began to talk openly about it. Lila, in turn, started spending more time in New York, and more unchaperoned time with Harry. Her family even seemed to warm up to the prospect of their marriage, perhaps in part because of the signs of *Time's* progress and because Harry began paying himself, at Frederick Haskell's insistence, more than five thousand dollars a year. Early in the fall they announced their engagement, and for the next several months—until the wedding day, December 22, 1923—they were awash in the details of planning the event, the honeymoon, and their home together after they were married.[20]

The wedding itself reflected none of the doubts that Lila's family had once expressed about the marriage. It was a lavish Chicago social event, painstakingly orchestrated by Lila's mother. The ceremony was conducted jointly by the Haskells' parish minister and Harry's father. It took place in the same enormous church that Harry had often attended with Nettie McCormick. His sister Beth was there as well, but the rest of his family—his mother, Sheldon, Emmavail—were far away in Beijing. The distance from his family was not only geographical. The pious Emmavail had ceased communicating with Harry months before and was talking sternly to her parents and siblings about her disapproval both of the marriage and of the values that she believed lay behind it. Harry was saddened but resigned. "Write me about Vail if you want to," he said dismissively in a letter from the Homestead resort in Virginia, where he and Lila spent a brief honeymoon. His mother seized on this cool reference as an excuse to forward the letter to Emmavail, noting plaintively in the margin that "in his real heart, Harry *does* care about you and he *wants* your welfare and happiness. This is the 2d time he has asked about you. . . . Harry knows the real from the false in life—& I do believe he and Lila will not become like the idle rich."[21]

Back in New York, Harry and Lila settled in an apartment on Fifth Avenue, a place considerably better than the dreary "flats" that Lila had claimed her newly married friends occupied. They could afford to do so, and to hire a maid to help them, because of financial assistance from Lila's family. Harry valued the home because it made Lila happy and because it served as a sign of his own ascent. But he paid little attention to the organization and running of the household, for within less than a week after his marriage he was again working almost unceasingly— making his absence from family life an enduring part of their marriage. ("I do wish you would come home in time for dinner these days & at least stay till after breakfast," Lila pleaded resignedly three years after their wedding.)[22]

The improvement in *Time*'s performance in 1924 dispelled much of the panic that had characterized the magazine's first year, but the business was not yet on sound footing. As circulation grew, problems of production and distribution became more serious. Luce and Larsen were particularly frustrated by the New York City post office, through which all issues of the magazine were mailed to subscribers. "In New York," one member of the staff recalled, "we were nothing but a pamphlet, and we got put on a train when they didn't have anything else to do with the space." The hope was that all readers would get the magazine on the same day; but given the delivery problems, many *Time* subscribers received one issue after the next issue had already been printed. Luce soon came to believe that the only solution was to move operations out of New York.[23]

He and Hadden had been considering moves almost since the first days of the magazine. Throughout 1923 they seriously explored a move to Washington, D.C., in part because of the reportorial advantages of being in the nation's capital (although for a magazine that as yet did no reporting, this was hardly a decisive factor); in part because Luce liked the city and knew that Lila did too; and partly because they recognized that there were significant financial advantages to being outside New York. The Washington idea quietly died in late 1923, Luce and Hadden finally agreeing that "our organization was still too rickety to move." A year later, however, the idea of moving seemed to Luce a way to rescue, not threaten, the business.[24]

Early in 1925 Hadden and Larsen, to Luce's considerable chagrin, took six weeks off for a trip to Europe. During (although not necessarily because of) their absence Luce redoubled efforts to find an alternative site for the magazine and soon settled on Cleveland, Ohio, in part because it was a major industrial city and cultural center, one of the most important cities in the Midwest. But it was also because of the Penton Press, located in Cleveland, which offered to print the magazine at a significantly reduced cost. Penton also offered office space in its building for a modest rent. The move, Luce claimed, would save the company twenty thousand dollars a year and would, in effect, give everyone a raise by placing them in a city with much lower living costs than New York. It would also give *Time* better access to its subscribers, both because of its location closer to the center of their circulation base and because the local post office was much more hospitable to the magazine than was the Manhattan one. By the time Hadden and Larsen returned, the decision to move was almost irrevocable. Larsen did not protest, but Hadden balked, although Luce always insisted he had kept him informed of the plans by mail during his absence. Hadden's reluctance was almost wholly personal. His family, his friends, indeed his life, were deeply tied to the city. Unlike the newly domesticated Luce, he thrived on New York's late-night social world and its tolerance of iconoclasts. At times Hadden seemed to regard moving to what he considered a provincial city in what he called "the sticks" as a kind of death. He argued so strenuously with Luce that they eventually adjourned to a nearby hotel to continue their heated debate away from the rest of the staff. But Hadden had no answer to Luce's case for the financial advantages of moving and finally, if grudgingly, agreed.[25]

For a company later known as a place that treated staff unusually well, the move to Cleveland was harsh, even brutal, to the small community of *Time* employees. Luce and Hadden announced the move with little advance notice, terminated all employees, and then gave them two days to move to Cleveland. Once there they were rehired, but in most cases with no help in financing the move—except for the young women of the research team, who were provided with chaperones and hotel rooms until they could find more permanent lodging. Despite the difficulties—dictated by the magazine's still-parlous financial condition—the vast majority of editorial employees followed the magazine to Ohio. (A significant exception was Thomas Martyn, the English "aristocrat" whom Luce so admired. Martyn resigned in anger when told that the company would not reimburse him for the costs of moving. In 1933 he became the founding editor of *Newsweek*.) The advertising staff stayed behind in New York, as did the *Saturday Review*, which—disgruntled at what it considered the poor service it was receiving from its distant partners—soon severed its ties with *Time*. (Luce later considered the loss of the *Saturday Review* a serious mistake.)[26]

For Luce, relocating to Cleveland was part of the process of building the kind of family life that—never having had such a life himself—he imagined was the American norm. He and Lila rented a comfortable apartment in the affluent suburbs, bought a car, hired a servant, joined the country club, and happily entered the social world of the local gentry. Their first son, Henry III (named for Harry's father but always called Hank), was born in April 1925, shortly before the move. Both parents believed that this "more friendly," "hometown-like" city would be a good place to raise a child and to improve their own social standing. In New York, *Time* was still a small, obscure operation. But in Cleveland it was considered a significant institution, and it made Luce a prominent figure in the community.[27]

Hadden, however, hated Cleveland. Reluctant to move there in the first place, he began unhappy and became progressively more so. Separated from family and friends, he lived in a room in a downtown club and developed an awkward social life with the unmarried male members of the magazine staff, conducted mostly late at night in downtown speakeasies. When sober, Hadden was usually able to hide his contempt for the city. But late at night, after hours of drinking, he would often ride around town in his used Chevrolet shouting, "Babbitt!" at Clevelanders he passed on the street. He traveled to New York almost every week as soon as the magazine went to press, then returned a few days later to edit the next issue. "I have been here 44 weeks," he said after his first ten months in Cleveland, "and made 36 trips back to New York." After a little more than a year in Cleveland, he finally agreed to switch jobs with Luce—Harry to serve as editor and Brit to manage the business. Hadden made no secret of his motives. He knew that the business affairs of the magazine would allow him to spend even more time in New York.[28]

For the sake of the magazine, however, Hadden did make some efforts to ingratiate himself with Cleveland. He published an article in the *Clevelander*, a local Chamber of Commerce magazine, in which he praised the resources of the city, thanked the local newspaper staffs for their help to the magazine, and even insisted, somewhat hypocritically, that Cleveland did not have the "blatant, back-slapping, 'booster' style of city salesmanship that makes one blench [*sic*] as he reads the Babbitt books." And he accurately cited the principal attraction of the city to *Time*—its location at the geographical center of the magazine's subscriber base. "Time is here to stay," he said, as he continued to maneuver to get out. "We like Cleveland."[29]

Hadden and Luce tried to raise their profiles in the community by introducing a *Time* quiz to local Chamber of Commerce audiences. The exercise was, Harry said at one such event, an antidote to the ennui that many people felt about their "specialized selves," a way of reintroducing them to the "multiple selves" they remembered from their youths. The quiz tested the audience's knowledge of current news as reported in *Time*. The tests were well received, and Luce and Hadden repeated them for a while in other Midwestern cities (as well as printing them in the magazine and using them as radio promotions). But they tired of the device quickly and dropped them after a few months.[30]

Whatever the tensions and conflicts created by the move to Cleveland, it played a critical role in the evolution of *Time*. In a period in which the magazine's finances remained precarious, the relocation saved the company substantial costs and facilitated much more effective distribution to their growing subscriber base. Far more important, being in Cleveland enabled *Time* to achieve something seemingly mundane that was in fact essential to its survival: a second-class mail permit, which would allow the magazine to get first-class mail treatment at reduced rates. In the past only newspapers had received this service. Luce had tried in vain to secure the permit in New York, arguing that *Time* was a "weekly newspaper." But without a proven track record, and without influential supporters, he had been unable to make progress. In Cleveland, however, *Time* became a project behind which the entire commercial community rallied. (It was, Hadden ungraciously explained later, because "there was nothing else going on in that town.") The city government, the Chamber of Commerce, the local post office, individual businessmen, and several Ohio congressmen were all eager to help what they saw, correctly, as an institution that could bring luster and profits to Cleveland. With their help, both in Cleveland and in Washington, *Time* received the permit in early 1927. "It was," Luce wrote his directors, "the single greatest piece of good fortune that has ever come *Time's* way." Even years later he continued to believe that this one event "made all the difference." By mid-1927, less than two years after the move to Cleveland, circulation had risen to more than 130,000, and advertising income was also increasing. *Time* was now making a modest but growing profit.[31]

As the business grew stronger, however, the attractions of Cleveland grew fainter—despite the enormous boost the community had given to *Time's* growth. In June 1927 Harry and Lila left on a long-promised monthlong trip to Europe, in some ways, a deferred honeymoon. When they returned in July they discovered that Hadden had persuaded almost the entire staff and the members of the board of directors to support moving back to Manhattan. It would, he argued, allow *Time* to become "the authoritative, up-to-the-minute, all-seeing newsmagazine that it has never been." It cannot have been lost on either of them that this sudden reversal paralleled almost exactly the decision to move to Cleveland in the first place, taken by Luce while Hadden had been traveling in Europe two years earlier. Luce was not as enthusiastic about leaving as Hadden was. He and Lila had grown comfortable in Cleveland, although they too sometimes showed signs of boredom with the city. Lila was often in Chicago, leaving Harry alone at times for several weeks; and Harry was often in New York—less often than Brit was, but enough to suggest at least a measure of restiveness. He occasionally complained about their isolation. "Are we lost in the Midwest?" he half-jokingly asked at one point on noticing that they had received fewer Christmas cards than they had gotten in New York. In the end, though, this move was a business decision, just as it had been in 1925, and there was no longer a compelling business reason to stay where they were—particularly once Luce struck a deal with R. R. Donnelley, a reputable Chicago printing company that offered to produce the magazine, thus preserving the geographical advantage of sending *Time* out from the Midwest. Luce may also have been at least partially persuaded by Hadden's argument that being in Cleveland robbed *Time* of energy, of direct access to news, and of the stimulus of competition. And he may have felt, as Hadden certainly did, that *Time* was beginning to outgrow Cleveland. In any case, Luce said later, "Hadden was so determined to get back to New York that there was no use arguing." The move occurred abruptly within just a few weeks of Luce's return from Europe. In late July Hadden threw a party at the Rowfant Club, where he had been living, to celebrate *Time*'s departure, a party so rowdy that he was asked to resign from the club the next day. By August 1 the circulation staff (with the exception of Larsen) had moved to Chicago, and everyone else was back in New York.[32]

Returning to New York far more prosperous than they had been when they left, both Hadden and Luce traded up. Brit, who had lived in Brooklyn Heights with his parents before moving to Cleveland, now moved into a large apartment on East Tenth Street, which he shared with two friends. Harry and Lila leased a spacious town house on East Forty-ninth Street in Turtle Bay.

By the end of 1927 *Time* had finally become what Hadden had somewhat presumptuously called it at the end of 1923: "an established institution." The magazine was not yet the great national, and even international, phenomenon it would eventually become, but it was stable, profitable, and increasingly popular. The company started the year with more than $154,000 in cash, twice the amount of a year before. Advertising revenue, which had been almost negligible in the first year or so, now exceeded subscription revenue, which itself had increased dramatically as circulation rose above 170,000.[33]

The magazine itself had changed less profoundly than had its finances, but it too had evolved in a number of ways. The look of the magazine was only slightly different from what it had been in 1923. Photographs, rare in the first few issues, became common by 1924, although their tiny size tended to limit them to portraits. In 1926, after the move to Cleveland, the familiar red border appeared on the cover—made possible by the use of coated stock, which also permitted the printing of color advertisements on the inside and back covers. Issues became fatter, less because of an increase in editorial content, which the editors determinedly kept more or less steady, than because of the growth in advertising. *Time* was a reasonably attractive magazine by the standards of its era, but somewhat staid. Its three narrow columns and its unvarying typeface—a layout that changed relatively little for more than forty years—made it look more like the serious newspapers that Luce and Hadden sometimes scorned than like the youthful, somewhat sassy magazine it aspired to be.[34]

The basic structure of *Time* remained largely unchanged as well. The relentless "departmental" organization, the disciplined brevity, the reliance on borrowed sources, and the commitment to giving readers a comprehensive view of the week's news that could be read in less than an hour all survived the transition from precariousness to success. Not everything stayed the same, of course. Some of the sillier features of the first years gradually fell away: the "imaginary interviews" with historical figures, the "Comings and Goings" of celebrities, the pompously opinionated "Point with Pride" and "View with Alarm" columns, the news "quizzes" that had begun in Cleveland. So did some of the rote reporting dictated by the magazine's format. News of state governments and foreign nations, for example, became more selective and more reflective of the importance of events and less dutifully in response to the need to fill up all of the magazine's "departments."

The more significant changes were a result less of shifts in philosophy than in the character of the editorial process. From a magazine written by a small group of young, like-minded, Ivy League men working inhumanly long hours under tremendous pressure, *Time* slowly became a publication produced by a large staff of professional writers, few of them any longer friends and classmates of Hadden and Luce, trained in what were becoming the settled conventions of the magazine. *Time* was not yet dispatching reporters out into the world to gather news and did not begin to do so until the 1930s. It did have a research department, which had begun with the hiring of Nancy Ford in the first months of the magazine and grew to become a large and very active part of the editorial process. (It was the only nonclerical area of the magazine to hire women, whom Hadden called "young lady assistants," and for many years it hired only women.) On the whole, however, *Time* continued to rely on newspapers (above all the *New York Times*) and other magazines as the source of its stories—to the increasing dismay of the journalistic community, which had ignored the borrowing when *Time* was obscure and unknown but which sometimes complained loudly once the magazine was a success. Writing, not reporting, was the most highly valued aspect of *Time's* internal culture. Partly because the stories were distillations rather than reportage, no story carried a byline, and only the most knowledgeable or observant reader could distinguish clearly among the styles of different writers.[35]

The emerging organizational culture actually cemented and standardized the style and tone that Hadden, in particular, had imposed upon the magazine through sheer force of will in the magazine's early days. Most of the writers emulated his tastes—both because they feared his wrath and because they admired his brilliance and wished to absorb it. Indeed, by institutionalizing the style and tone of the early *Time*, the staff was also in some ways expanding and exaggerating the magazine's peculiarities.[36]

The most visible and famous idiosyncrasy of *Time* was its language—sometimes admired, often ridiculed, never as pervasively distinctive as its critics claimed, but a defining element of the magazine nevertheless. In setting out to challenge the norms of journalism, Hadden and Luce wanted, among other things, to confront the sober and, in their view, drab language that was the lingua franca of the newspapers of their time. *Time*, they believed, should be not only concise but also lively, irreverent, and entertaining. Developing a distinctive literary style for the magazine was the first important step toward that goal—and a feature promoted heavily from the start in the company's own promotional literature. "TIME has given such attention to the development of the best narrative English," Larsen wrote grandiosely in a letter to potential subscribers, "that hundreds of editors and journalists have declared it to be the greatest creative force in modern journalism."[37]

As with most other editorial innovations in the early years, Hadden took the lead—although Luce was an active partner in the effort. Both had studied Greek at Hotchkiss and at Yale; but while Luce was by far the more serious Greek scholar, it was Hadden who proposed the *Iliad* as a model for the language the magazine should use. He carried a tattered, heavily annotated translation with him to the office and kept a notebook filled with lists of words and phrases that would, he believed, replicate the energy and poetry of Homer. The *Iliad** used such phrases as "much-enduring Odysseus," "wine-dark sea," "fleet-footed Achilles," "far-

---

*Hadden likely used a translation by Samuel Butler, the most commonly used English text of the early twentieth century.

darting Apollo." *Time* created its own compound adjectives to describe people in the news: "flabby-chinned," "snaggle-toothed," "coffee-colored," "bandy-legged," and "trim-figured." While the *Iliad* referred to "many-fountained Ida," *Time* wrote of "many-towered Danzig." In the *Iliad* were inverted sentences such as, "Up to his side he dashed and flanked Great Ajax tight." *Time* countered with: "Up to the White House portico rolled a borrowed automobile," or the especially clumsy: "As impossible of fair historical evaluation is [Hoover's] two-year record as was the battle of Gettysburg at noon of the second day." And at times the magazine provided long, irrelevant passages that directly (and inelegantly) mimicked the *Iliad's* lofty language: "The pens and tongues of contumely were arrested. Mocking mouths were shut. Even righteous protestation hushed its clamor, as when, having striven manfully in single combat, a high-helmed champion is stricken by Jove's bolt and the two snarling armies stand at sudden gaze, astonished and bereft a moment of their rancor" (an introduction to a story on the 1925 Scopes trial).[38]

But Hadden did not stop with the *Iliad*. He made exhaustive lists of other techniques that he proposed for the magazine. Occupations, origins, and personality types became titles: "Teacher Scopes," "Governess Ross," "Editor Mencken," "England's Baldwin," "Demagog Hitler." Middle names sprouted everywhere, whether or not the subjects in question (or anyone else) ever used them: "Herbert Clark Hoover," "Samuel Morgan Shortridge," "Alfred Emanuel Smith." In 1930 a Smith College professor wrote an article in *Philological Quarterly* about what Lewis Carroll had once called "portmanteau words," combinations of two distinct terms. Among his most prominent examples were words from *Time:* "cinemactor" and "cinemactress," "primogenial" (to describe a pleasant young man who had inherited his father's congressional seat). Hadden's crudely handwritten style sheet for *Time* writers used other examples of this kind of vivid wordsmithing: "Broadwayfarer," "eccentrician." In writing about Alabama senator Tom Heflin, Hadden created a verb, "to heffle," which he defined as "to talk loud and long without saying much." He also liked heavy-handed metaphors: "eyes big as baseballs," "ruddy as a round full moon." Hadden encouraged *Time* writers to use vivid words, whether newly invented or not. People in *Time* were "famed," not "famous"; "potent," not "powerful"; "blatant," not "obvious." They "whacked" rather than "struck," "ogled" rather than "looked," "strode" rather than "walked," and "smirked" rather than "smiled." They "irked," "bumbled," "vexed," and "ousted."

Rhyming and alliteration were popular devices, too, as in the frequent use of "late, great" to describe recently deceased people, or the euphemism "great and good friend" to describe someone's unmarried lover. Obituaries did not simply report but banally philosophized, with the frequent introduction: "Death, as it must to all men, came last week" to the subject of the notice.[39]

At times, particularly in its first years, the magazine's language was often flip and even sophomoric. *Time* often began a story with an irrelevant cliché or a banal truism. In writing about the divided views of Alaskans, *Time* began: "Some like it hot, some like cold, and some like it in the pot nine days old." Or, in describing a meeting between the president and a senator, "When a sharp tongue takes to soft words, good nature prospers." On other occasions stories were introduced with what can only be called pedantry: "There is no more tragic phenomenon in this vale of tears than the deliberate perversion of an idea or philosophy out of its original meaning in order to serve the base purpose of its enemies." But even as the magazine matured and shed some of its more egregious excesses, writers—in their effort to avoid conventionally informative leads—forced readers to wade through considerable imagery before encountering any real information. "Winter tramped prematurely out of the Northwest last week," a 1927 story on a Labor Department unemployment report began. "A Montana stockman died in a blizzard. Minnesota lakes were skimmed with ice. Michigan had icicles. . . . Car radiators froze in Illinois."

And yet *Time* frequently used these same techniques to real effect, successfully drawing readers into subjects they might otherwise have overlooked, and making people and events more vivid than a more conventional story could have done. A story on the Treasury Department's woes in 1931, for example, began: "For ten years, Secretary of the Treasury Andrew William Mellon has had fair fiscal weather. Ample taxes from a busy, thriving nation piled up whacking surpluses for him to administer. Under the sun of Prosperity, the public debt melted like a snowman in May. A happy man devoted to his job, Secretary Mellon was kept awake at night by no great problems of government finance." *Time* could be pompous, irritating, pedantic, even ridiculous. But if that was all it was, it would never have succeeded. To most of *Time*'s large and rapidly expanding readership, even many who were annoyed occasionally by its idiosyncrasies, the magazine was also lively, witty, entertaining, and informative. Perhaps most important, *Time*'s language, however idiosyncratic, was consistent and homogeneous. It presented readers with a familiar and predictable experience. *Time* boasted often of its "cover-to-cover readers," of whom there were many, and the magazine's language was almost certainly an important part of the reason.[40]

Throughout the 1920s Hadden drilled his writers in the literary formulas he had created for *Time*, using his oversize pencils and his gruff, booming voice to browbeat the staff into meeting his demands. T. S. Matthews, a *Time* writer and editor for many years, described his own early days at the magazine as a period when "all 'neophytes' [*Time*'s word for cub writers] were expected to memorize Hadden's invented words and phrases and to use them at every opportunity." But many writers later recalled adopting the style less because of pressure from above than because it was so much a part of the culture of the magazine that it was almost impossible to resist. Even decades later, after years of efforts to wean reporters from some of the excesses of the original Hadden style, Matthews recalled that "the iron had so far entered our souls that the attempt at reform was never successful." The standardization of style was sometimes stifling to serious writers. John O'Hara, the soon-to-be-famous novelist, spent a few months writing about sports for *Time* in the early 1920s and then fled to *The New Yorker.* Such defections, although usually after longer periods of service than O'Hara's, were common for many decades. But other writers settled comfortably into the *Time* system, came to value its distinctive kind of writing, and remained for many years.[41]

"Timese" or "Timestyle"—as the magazine's writing was often called, sometimes mockingly, sometimes affectionately—was, if nothing else, contagious, and not just within the magazine itself. Words that *Time* invented, retrieved from obscurity, or borrowed from foreign languages became enduring parts of modern English: "tycoon," "pundit," "socialite," "kudos." For years schools and universities reveled in producing parody issues of *Time* and took special delight in their mastery of Timese. "White-sweatered, good-looking friend of beauty-queen Virginia Clark, James Graham ('Cheerleader') Woodford strode into a . . . meeting breathing fire," a University of Washington lampoon wrote in 1931. "To the stacccato blast of forty machine guns Hizzoner Pedro de Miguel took office," a Foreign News story announced in a Naval Academy satirization of *Time.* Hotchkiss, Luce and Hadden's alma mater, produced an issue of the student magazine, the *Index*, in Timese. *Time* itself encouraged some such parodies. In 1934 the White Company, a manufacturer of trucks and buses, enlisted some of the editors to help them produce a mock issue promoting the company, with a cover story on "Truck of the Year." Even mainstream newspapers and magazines reporting on the progress of *Time* or on the activities of Luce and Hadden could not resist mimicking aspects of Timese in their own stories. "Birth of a new species of man of power, the tycoon, was predicted this noon by quick-speaking successful young Henry R. Luce," a Rochester reporter noted in 1929. An Edmonton, Alberta, newspaper wrote of a Luce appearance in Banff, "No speaker for publication is pleasant, personable, energetic, ex-cub Henry Luce." Even Harry's own mother could not resist a gentle poke at Timese in September 1926 when she wrote him about her imminent departure from China: "As *Time* would say, America looms."[42]

As distinctive as *Time*'s language, and closely related to it, were the magazine's opinions and attitudes. Luce and Hadden had promised from the start that *Time* would not be a "digest of opinion," that it would have "no axe to grind," that it would be "objective" and "unbiased." And in many respects, at least in the beginning, they kept that promise. *Time* did not clearly favor any political party, and Luce, at least, was himself unsure in the 1920s of whether he preferred Democrats or Republicans. (He and Hadden voted for Calvin Coolidge in 1924; Hadden voted for Hoover in 1928, but Luce supported Al Smith.) Unlike in later years, when Luce's own strong views on certain issues reliably shaped—and at times distorted—reporting, *Time* in the 1920s and much of the 1930s only rarely took clear or sustained positions. But the magazine was nevertheless filled with opinions, even if not consistent ones. Indeed, its insistence on expressing its own views on almost everything it reported, however random and varying those views may have been, was a fundamental part of its character.[43]

To some degree the opinionated tone of *Time* was simply a literary device, much like the magazine's eccentric language. It reflected in part the generational irreverence of those who, like Luce and Hadden, had grown up during and after World War I and had been shaped by the skepticism and impatience with pretense of their time. Hadden, in particular, continued to emulate H. L. Mencken's talent at ridiculing almost everyone of importance. The attitudes of *Time*, although not its literary style, had at least some things in common with Mencken's the *Smart Set*, which he edited with George Jean Nathan and called "a magazine of cleverness."

But *Time*'s outlook reflected more than a generalized irreverence. It conveyed as well the elitist cultural conservatism of its principal editors and writers. On the one hand *Time* shared the contempt of Sinclair Lewis and others for the tastes and values of the lower bourgeoisie (or what Hadden, borrowing a term from Mencken, privately called on occasion the "booboisie"). The magazine only hinted at this contempt in its pages, knowing that its targets were, or could become, an important constituency for the magazine. But in the early years at least, there were many signs of condescension—the demeaning descriptions and nick-names assigned to people the editors considered crass and boorish, the sly anecdotes and dismissive phrases that made those they considered dull look pompous and ridiculous. ("It is the conviction of stupid peo-ple," a *Time* review of an irreverent play stated, "that only that which is solemn may be profound and that to seem satirical is to be unsym-pathetic.")[44]

Time was similarly contemptuous of the iconclasts of its own gener-ation who sought to overturn many of the canons of traditional high cul-ture. Hadden and Luce were as hostile to artistic revolution as they were to dull conformity. In the very first issue of *Time*, the editors wrote with-eringly of what they considered incomprehensible books. "Lucidity is no part of the auctorial task," the editors wrote censoriously of mod-ernist writers. *Time* was particularly contemptuous of what are now con-sidered two of the great masterpieces of the twentieth century. "To the uninitiated," the magazine described James Joyce's *Ulysses*, "it appeared that Mr. Joyce had taken some half a million assorted words—many such as are not heard in reputable circles—shaken them in a colossal hat, and laid them end to end." Of T. S. Eliot's *The Waste Land*, the writers dis-missively noted, "It was rumored to be written as a hoax." (The article was cryptically titled "Shantih Shantih Shantih,"* after the obscure last line of the poem.) Even less radical intellectuals attracted *Time's* scorn. The witty, self-consciously "clever" writers and intellectuals who popu-lated the Algonquin Round Table were, the magazine gratuitously com-mented, "the supposedly elect," "log rollers and back-scratchers," and really little more than "clever gossips." Modern art attracted skepticism, too. Cubism, the magazine claimed, "is in danger of itself becoming a mere convention." In the same issue *Time* ran a strong defense of classi-cal education, because "Greek and Roman thinking is the core of our culture."[45]

Time was also distinctive for its fascination with powerful men and women. "People just aren't interesting in the mass," Luce once said. "It's

---

*From a Hindu prayer for peace.

only individuals who are exciting." For decades, beginning with the first issue, virtually every cover of *Time* carried a portrait of an important man or, on rare occasions, woman (and once, in 1928, a basset hound, to draw attention to the Annual Dog Show of the Westminster Kennel Club in New York). The magazine chose a "Man of the Year" every January beginning with Charles Lindbergh in 1927. (There were only two "Women of the Year" in *Time*'s first fifty years—Wallis Simpson in 1937 and Queen Elizabeth II in 1953). Cover portraits—black-and-white drawings and photographs at first, gradually replaced by color images starting in 1929—became a signature feature of the magazine. For decades being selected for the cover of *Time* came to seem to many readers (and increasingly to the editors themselves) a very high honor. The magazine in fact attracted considerable criticism when on occasion it chose controversial or reviled people for the cover—for example, Al Capone in 1930 (smiling and elegantly dressed), which one reader called "an outrage to public decency"—as if the selection was by itself a sign of approval. But cover subjects were overwhelmingly people of relatively conventional distinction and respectability. Major public figures—statesmen, business leaders, generals, and the royalty of the worlds of art, entertainment, and sport—were the staples. Although most subjects were American, the Anglophilic Hadden and Luce included a heavy representation of English figures and a scattering of people from other nations. The profiles of cover subjects could be breathlessly admiring or, on occasion, bitingly critical, but they almost always had a heightened level of judgment and descriptive detail. (*Time*'s distinctive language could burnish a reputation as easily as it could tarnish one.) Cover stories were usually preoccupied with power, and so it was not surprising that the magazine focused on the world's most powerful men. In the magazine's first half century Stalin appeared on the cover twelve times, Roosevelt, Churchill, Franco, and Mussolini eight each, Hitler seven, and Chiang Kai-shek ten.[46]

The covers themselves were only symbols of *Time*'s deeper commitment to the role of powerful people in history. The opening passage of every issue was an account of the president's week, no matter how trivial his activities. Receiving tickets to a World Series game that the president had no intention of attending was as newsworthy as signing legislation. Accepting the honorary presidency of the Camp Fire Girls attracted as much attention as his consideration of American membership in the World Court. The trivia of a president's vacation—leasing a country house, getting "caught in a sodden, drenching shower" during a walk, celebrating a son's birthday—could occupy columns of text. Presidents were also, almost by definition, men of great virtue. Warren Harding, although "not a superman" like Theodore Roosevelt or Woodrow Wilson, was "important and successful as the embodiment of the American ideal of humility exalted by homely virtues into the highest eminence." Coolidge, too, was a man of "genuine humility" and "flinty integrity," who had developed a deep "kinship with his people." Herbert Hoover, even at his lowest moments, was "a high-minded, able, industrious, conscientious individual who is devoted to his country, to the art of Government, to children," with "unbounded faith in himself." Only when Franklin Roosevelt entered the White House did *Time* begin to abandon its reverential tone.[47]

Like many Americans the *Time* editors were fascinated by Mussolini and by his apparent success in bringing order and stability to the usually chaotic politics of Italy. He was, the magazine noted, the "all-powerful," "virile, vigorous" "autocrat of all the Italians," a "miniature Napoleon." The fascination was often indistinguishable from admiration— something *Time* also shared with many Americans, including many fellow journalists, in the 1920s. Mussolini, *Time* wrote, was a man with "remarkable self control, rare judgement, and an efficient application of his ideas to the solving of existing problems." He was a person "of high moral integrity with a magnetic personality." Looking back over 1925, *Time* concluded that there was "no doubt" that Mussolini had "worked wonders for Italy in the last year," and that he deserved "unstinted praise and congratulations." *Time* was, however, far from the most admiring journalistic chronicler of Mussolini. The Hearst papers were highly sympathetic ("He is a marvelous man," Hearst himself said after being flattered by Mussolini in an interview). The long-serving *New York Times* Rome correspondent, Anne O'Hare McCormick, consistently idealized him. The *Saturday Evening Post* ran idolatrous stories throughout the 1920s. *Time* gradually darkened its view of Mussolini in the late 1920s and beyond, as his regime grew more brutal and militaristic, but the magazine was never as appropriately critical in those years as were at least a few other journals, among them Hadden's former employer the *New York World*.[48]

While Mussolini frequently seduced the editors of *Time*, Stalin had no such effect. To be sure, Stalin was of great interest to *Time*, as all great and powerful men were. But in most cases the magazine had great difficulty concealing its contempt. *Time*'s view of the Soviet Union itself— unencumbered by almost anyone's firsthand experience of Russia—was clouded in orientalist mystery. It was a "weird and mystic land, whose soul is steeped in the mysterious, the fire of whose eyes is sometimes fanatical, and whose life breath has been impregnated with flesh-creeping legends." Stalin himself was a reflection of the darkness and mystery that characterized his nation: a man shrouded by a "taciturnity without beginning, without end." The editors of *Time*, again like most Americans, understood him as the principal exponent of a radicalism they both detested and feared. Although the great "red scare" of 1919–20 was a largely discredited memory by the mid-1920s, hatred of bolshevism (as opposed to exaggerated fears of internal subversion) remained intense, even feverish. Soviet Russia was, *Time* noted, the self-proclaimed "graveyard of capitalism." It was the enemy of Christianity, conducting an "anti-Religion crusade." And it was a revolutionary power, whose "frankly avowed purpose is to foment in every land 'The World Revolution of the World Proletariat.' " "Dictator Stalin," as *Time* routinely called him, was a "coldblooded man of deeds" with a "mask of oriental ruthlessness."[49]

The tenor of *Time*'s coverage of the world outside the United States was reasonably consistent with the attitudes of Luce and Hadden. But it reflected even more the views of one man: Laird Goldsborough, the talented and controversial Foreign News editor from 1925 to 1938. Goldsborough—five years younger than Luce and Hadden—came to *Time* almost immediately after his graduation from Yale, and he quickly solidified his power within the editorial staff through his virtuosity in writing the Foreign News section—almost entirely by himself—punctually and cleanly every week. In the pressurized world of the *Time* newsroom, causing no problems was a tremendous asset. Very early in his tenure, he became one of the few members of the staff whose copy Hadden, Luce, and later managing editors rarely edited in more than minor ways. And if Goldsborough frequently expressed views that were more vigorous or extreme than Hadden and Luce might have liked, they usually accepted that as the price of his skill and efficiency. (In any case Goldsborough's views were infrequently very far from their own.)

Goldsborough was a strange, almost romantic figure. Partially disabled from childhood as a result of an accident, he walked with an elegant, gold-headed cane that was almost a part of his personality. His partial deafness added to his image of intimidating aloofness. He was an ardent admirer of Europe—its traditions, its culture, its aristocracy. He was skeptical of the modernist trends of his time. He was supremely confident in his own strongly held attitudes and opinions. He had a taste for luxury, and in later years, during his extensive travels in Europe, he strained even *Time*'s legendarily generous expense accounts.[50]

His deep conservatism, both cultural and political, intensified his loathing of bolshevism, which shaped almost everything he wrote. His admiration for Mussolini, sometimes lavish, sometimes grudging, was primarily a result of his hatred of communism and Stalin, to which Italian fascism and Mussolini seemed a preferable if perhaps flawed alternatives. In the 1930s few American journalists were more hostile to the Republican cause in the Spanish civil war than was Goldsborough, who, not entirely inaccurately, associated it with communism. And few were more friendly to Franco, whom—like Mussolini—he viewed as a bulwark against bolshevism. Although Goldsborough expressed only contempt for Hitler, he failed to recognize the extent to which the Nazi regime endangered the world, and never showed much concern about the deteriorating condition of German Jews. He was not usually overtly anti-Semitic, but he clearly shared the belief of many Americans and Europeans that there was a special connection between Jews and radicals. In the mid-1930s he gave particularly virulent voice to this assumption in his attacks on French premier Léon Blum, who headed the nation's first Popular Front government. Blum was a man of the Left but not himself a communist. According to Goldsborough, however, Blum's "emphatic Jewishness makes the No. 1 French socialist thoroughly at home in Moscow." He consistently referred to him as "Jew Blum" and claimed that he was "fired with religious fanaticism" (by which Goldsborough meant the combination of what he claimed was Blum's ardent Jewishness and his hatred of fascism).[51]

On at least one issue, however, *Time* was well ahead of many contemporaries: its interest in the question of race. *Time* was not a crusader for racial equality, to be sure, and it had its share of offhanded racial slurs. (Among the many absurd new words Hadden invented, and probably the most offensive, was "blackamoron," to describe an African American criminal or villain.) But frequently during the 1920s, and indeed throughout most of its long history, *Time* used its opinionated style to draw attention to racial injustice. In an era in which African Americans were routinely described demeaningly and condescendingly, *Time* self-consciously chose to treat them with respect. They often used the title "Mr." and "Mrs." when referring to black men and women, a practice rare in most American newspapers and virtually unknown in the South. This did not escape the notice of many white Southern readers, who protested angrily to no avail. ("Would Mr. Henderson himself care to be styled plain 'Henderson,' " Hadden replied curtly to a letter from a white Southerner complaining about the "glorification of the Negro." In fact *Time* rarely used the title "Mr." for white subjects either, which led Luce to comment years later that Hadden was being "a little devilish.") With uncharacteristic sobriety, *Time* reported in its first issue on a demonstration in Washington: "In dignified and quiet language, two thousand Negro women of the Phillis Wheatley Y. W. C. A. protested against a proposal to erect at the Capitol a statue to 'The Black Mammy of the South.' "[52]

In *Time*'s early years, the most compelling racial issue for black Americans was lynching, frequent in the 1920s and into the 1930s, but largely ignored by many of the major organs of journalism. *Time* consistently reported lynchings in harsh and telling detail. "James Scott is dead," the magazine noted at the end of a lurid account of a lynching in Missouri. "He was put to death by the premeditated violence of yokels who believe in their gross way that they were maintaining the honor of the race that bred them. What they did, some people call murder; others, lynching." For many years *Time* was among the very few white publications that kept a running tally of lynchings each year.[53]

Hadden, a man of many prejudices, may have focused on lynchings and other egregious acts of racism more because of his contempt for the white "yokels" responsible for them than because of any real identification with the cause of racial justice. Luce, although himself no crusader on this issue, was somewhat more cosmopolitan both in background (given his youth in China) and his outlook, and his record over many decades of reporting and commenting on race was evidence that his commitment to this issue, although limited in many ways, was nevertheless sincere.[54]

More important than *Time*'s many idiosyncrasies—its language, its opinions, its attitudes, its youthful impetuosity—was its format: Because above all else *Time* was, and wanted to be, a practical digest of the news. From its first imaginings in the dreams of Hadden and Luce at Yale, to the choice of its name as a symbol of its purpose, to its founding as an institution that synthesized reporting done by others, the magazine considered its principal purpose to give busy people an efficient and thorough account of the world's news in a brief, readable, and organized way. *Time* advertised itself in many forms, but nothing was more consistent than its promise to save people valuable time while keeping them well informed. One striking example was a foldout postcard distributed to potential subscribers in 1925 that presented what it called a "play in three acts." It featured a character named "Busy Man," sitting disconsolately in his living room surrounded by discarded newspapers: "I bought this mass of printed matter to find out what is going on in the world," he complains, "but it's no use! I am not abreast of the news in anything outside of my business." His wife, "Busy Woman," agrees. A knock on the door signals the arrival of a third character, "TIME," who presents to them "a new idea in journalism. In my twenty-six pages is every fact of significance in all those newspapers and periodicals on your floor."[55]

Hadden and Luce came to the conclusion that saving busy people time could be a successful and lucrative enterprise almost instinctively—without market research (which remained a very primitive science in the 1920s) or any other kind of systematic evidence. But even had they been able to use the more sophisticated marketing tools of a later era, they would likely have reached the same conclusion; for *Time* magazine was almost perfectly designed to respond to several of the most important social changes of its era. Among those changes were the increasing pace of modern life, the growing nationalization of commerce, and the need of middle-class people to know much more about the nation and the world. At the same time there was growing pressure on many professional people to devote more hours to their jobs. Finding opportunities to educate themselves even minimally about what was happening outside their own communities was becoming difficult, particularly since the volume of information that people believed they needed to know—and the vast variety of publications that attempted to convey that information to them—had become nearly overwhelming. The success of *Time* was, to a large extent, a result of its editors' understanding of how eager many Americans were for something that would identify and organize for them the important information of their day.[56]

Time was not alone in recognizing the growing demand for digests of information and knowledge aimed at the new middle class. Harvard University had helped launch this trend shortly before World War I with its successful "Harvard Classics," which claimed to provide readers with an efficient condensation of great literature and thought throughout history. Purportedly assembled by Harvard president Charles W. Eliot himself, the "five-foot shelf of books" promised a "reading course unparalleled in comprehensiveness and authority." A supplementary volume guided readers through the volumes in a way that the editors claimed would allow them to educate themselves in fifteen minutes a day. In 1922, only a year before the first issue of *Time* appeared, DeWitt and Lila Wallace launched the *Reader's Digest*, which offered condensed information from many sources—books, newspapers, and other magazines, carefully edited and packaged for readers who did not have the time or inclination to read widely or thoroughly. (Unlike *Time* the *Reader's Digest* paid most of the publications from which it drew its material and usually attributed its stories to their original sources. Also unlike *Time*, it did not synthesize from multiple sources and made no claim to originality in what it published.) By the mid-1930s the *Digest's* circulation was over one million, still well over *Time's*.

Time was also a response to the nationalization of American culture—and eventually a contributor to that nationalization. The era following World War I saw a rapid standardization in the way many Americans lived, worked, and understood the world. In Sinclair Lewis's famous 1922 novel *Babbitt*, the central character, George F. Babbitt, points to this change in a speech to the Real Estate Board of Zenith (the mythical city, apparently modeled on Cincinnati, in which the novel takes place):

> I tell you Zenith and her sister-cities are producing a new type of civilization. There are many resemblances between Zenith and these other burgs, and I'm darn glad of it! The extraordinary, growing, and sane standardization of stores, offices, streets, hotels, clothes, and newspapers throughout the United States shows how strong and enduring a type is ours.

To Babbitt this was the great accomplishment of middle-class culture (and to Lewis, one of its great failures). It represented the creation of a common, national, middle-class worldview; a reorientation of interest among middle-class people away from their local communities and toward national issues, events, and institutions. It represented as well a new kind of consumerism, born of prosperity and urbanization, reflecting the more secular, pleasure-seeking culture of the modern middle class—what a *Time* advertising circular called "a younger generation accustomed to things of beauty and convenience." The standardization of culture for such people was a result of many things, among them commercial radio (born in 1920) and movies (elevated in importance in the 1920s by the great urban movie palaces and, beginning in 1927, sound). But *Time* played a modest role as well. With the exception of the national wire services, whose stories were filtered through local newspaper editors with their own interests and tastes, *Time*—which even in its early, frail years had subscribers in every state—was for a while the only genuinely national news organ. No newspaper had a reach very far beyond its own city. Radio news in the 1920s consisted of an announcer reading headlines a few times a day. Newsreels were not yet prominent. Even with its relatively modest circulation in the 1920s, *Time* established itself as an important force in journalism if for no other reason than that it reached men and women in all parts of the country and promised to rescue them from isolation and provincialism and prepare them for the cosmopolitan world. "Can you afford to be *labelled* as a man from Main Street?" an early advertising leaflet asked potential *Time* subscribers. "Can you afford to *be* a man from Main Street? Civilization moves forward on a thousand fronts,—business, art, politics, science, religion. You have only to ignore it, and you slip back again centuries in time. But can you afford to live in the dark ages?"[57]

Luce, Hadden, and the other founders of *Time* did not expect (and in the beginning did not particularly want) a vast circulation. They were, they believed, creating a "quality" magazine, aimed at a relatively elite readership—the busy professional people who had largely inspired them to imagine their great project. Their target audience was wealthy, educated men and women, "modern-minded by environment and education." They solicited subscriptions at first from the alumni of Ivy League universities, from the members of elite men's clubs and country clubs, from directories of corporate board members, from buyers of the *Harvard Classics*, and from people listed in social registers and in *Who's Who*. *Time* boasted of the eminent bankers, industrialists, and politicians (among them Franklin D. Roosevelt) who were early subscribers to the magazine. But the more important characteristic of its readership, at least for advertisers, was its relative youth ("70% of TIME's subscribers are under 46," the company boasted) and its wealth. "Our subscribers," they claimed, "are overwhelmingly classifiable as . . . potent business & professional leaders, . . . younger business and professional men, already influential but still climbing the ladder—definitely en route for greater fortune and influence . . . [and] Wives of Business & Professional men." In a nation characterized by "a hundred temperaments and a hundred degrees of wealth and class," one *Time* advertisement argued, "our success is the result of hitting the fancy and imagination of America's most important and interesting class—the Younger Business Executive—young in years—young in spirit and young in outlook."[58]

During its early struggles the *Time* staff drew a perverse satisfaction from what they considered the "exclusiveness" of their circulation. It was, they believed, a kind of club: a group of like-minded people in tune with the sensibilities and opinions of the editors. ("One reader on a train would see someone else reading *Time*," Luce once said, "and that would be enough to serve as an introduction.") *Time* readers, they claimed, constituted a "colony" filled with "men and women who have in common a desire to *know* and *comprehend the news* . . . a distinctive unit . . . set apart from all other magazine readerships." This profile was a useful advertising device. But the leaders of *Time* genuinely believed it to be true, and they based that belief in part on the extensive, if unscientific, surveys they frequently did of their readers. In 1928, shortly after the return of the company to New York from Cleveland, *Time* mailed out a questionnaire, whimsically titled "Do You Own a Horse?", to ten thousand subscribers and received more than four thousand responses, which constituted about 3 percent of the readership. It reinforced all the assumptions the circulation and advertising departments had been claiming. Ninety percent of the respondents were under sixty-five years old. More than 80 percent were "plainly of the *executive and professional* class," 27 percent were officers and directors of "companies other than their own," and 62 percent owned stocks and bonds. More than half of *Time*'s surveyed subscribers had servants, and a quarter had more than one. More than 40 percent were members of country clubs. A third had traveled to Europe, and another quarter planned to do so. And nearly 11 percent of respondents actually did "own a horse." For several years in the 1920s and early 1930s—before circulation grew so large that the economic base of readers could not easily be characterized—*Time* was ranked in some surveys first among magazines in the wealth of its subscribers, a position later occupied for many decades by *The New Yorker*. *Time*, a 1928 advertisement grandly claimed, "has built up the greatest, the largest, the soundest quality circulation in the history of U.S. publishing."[59]

Hadden liked the idea of *Time* readers as a distinctive, elite "club," and he came to believe that circulation should not rise much above 250,000. Anything more might dilute the quality of the subscriber base. Luce imagined a much larger readership. Shortly after the publication of the first issue, Luce wrote desperately to Lila asking her what her distinguished stepfather thought of the magazine. "His approbation [would be] a very valuable piece of evidence," he said, because of his wealth, his stature, and his "maturity and stability." If *Time* could "get by" men like that, "we can later broaden down and catch the rabble of George F. Babbitts etc." (Frederick Haskell apparently did not respond.)[60]

. . .

The return to New York, for which Hadden had fought so strenuously, did not for long relieve the boredom and restlessness that had plagued him in Cleveland. Friends and colleagues commented frequently on his apparent unhappiness, his almost frantic search for stimulation and excitement, and his erratic and sometimes self-defeating behavior. Shortly after the move, Hadden ceded the editorship of *Time* to Luce. Rotating jobs had been part of their plan from the beginning, but— except for Hadden's brief absence from editing in 1926, to allow him to spend more time in New York—neither man had really pushed to keep their initial agreement. To Hadden editing *Time* had been a kind of passion, and no other activity related to the magazine had been remotely as satisfying to him. That he agreed to give it up in 1928 was almost certainly a sign of boredom, a search for a new and different challenge. "He wasn't only losing his interest in *Time*," Luce claimed years later. "There didn't seem to be any other interest that was absorbing him."[61]

Although Hadden was ostensibly taking over the business side of the company, he spent relatively little energy dealing with the routine tasks that Luce had overseen for so long—circulation, advertising, production, staff management. Instead, he often came into the editorial offices late at night and reedited copy that Luce had already approved. He also began searching for other creative projects that might relieve what he quickly came to consider the tedium of his new job. In 1927 *Time* had begun producing a small house organ that it somewhat whimsically called *Tide* and that mimicked *Time*'s format and style. It was distributed free to potential advertisers as a kind of promotional brochure. Soon after leaving the *Time* editorship, Hadden decided—despite considerable skepticism from Luce and other colleagues—to transform *Tide* into a real magazine about advertising for paid subscribers. It quickly grew from a small pamphlet into a substantial-looking magazine, with a cover almost identical to *Time*'s (although with a blue, not a red, border) and with "departments" not unlike those in the newsmagazine. *Tide* rarely received letters, so Hadden and his fellow editors wrote them themselves, attributing them to invented people (a practice Hadden had occasionally employed in the early years of *Time*). For a while Hadden devoted himself to *Tide* with something like the same energy and enthusiasm that he had given to the launch of *Time*. But he was not content for long. *Tide* did not flourish in the way Hadden had hoped. In its first two years, its circulation never reached five thousand and it had only fifteen hundred paid subscribers. (The company sold it in 1930, and it became a modestly successful independent enterprise of the advertising industry that survived until 1959.) In any case a small advertising journal was not enough to satisfy Hadden, and he indicated his frustration by starting to run articles in *Tide* gratuitously attacking the very advertisers—including important *Time* clients—to whom the magazine was appealing. ("When a preacher turns commercial writer and applies the smug platitudes of his old calling to his new job," he wrote of a prominent automobile-advertising executive, "he should be hailed with raucous laughter.") In his restlessness Hadden also began thinking of new projects for the company. He devoted a page in his notebook to his ideas for expansion: "bus mag, spt mag, aviation mag, secy mag, letter mag, TIME monthly, women's mag, daily newspaper," and many others.[62]

In the meantime Luce threw himself into the editing of *Time*. He was a more efficient and organized editor than Hadden. He created a schedule for writers and editors, held regular meetings, had an organized staff critique of each issue every week. ("Don't hesitate to *flay* a fellow-worker's work. Occasionally submit an idea," he wrote.) He was also calmer and less erratic. Despite the intense loyalty Hadden inspired among members of his staff, some editors and writers apparently preferred Luce to his explosive partner; others missed the energy and inspiration that Hadden had brought to the newsroom. In any case the magazine itself—whose staff was so firmly molded by Hadden's style and tastes—was not noticeably different under Luce's editorship than it had been under Hadden's. And just as Hadden, the publisher, moonlighted as an editor, so Luce, now the editor, found himself moonlighting as publisher, both because he was so invested in the business operations of the company that he could not easily give them up, and also because he felt it necessary to compensate for Hadden's inattention.[63]

Outside the office the hard, wild life that Hadden had been leading for years grew harder and wilder. Friends began to note a change in him—he was, one friend later recalled, "increasingly nervous and irritable and hard to get along with. He wanted desperately to have a good time, and yet nothing seemed to give him pleasure." He complained frequently of boredom and drove those around him to join his frantic search for diversions. Always a heavy drinker, he gradually became a self-destructive alcoholic. He stayed up late, gave or searched for parties almost every night. He began to participate in, or provoke, brawls for which he was periodically arrested and spent nights in jail. He seemed to dread returning to his apartment to sleep alone, which suggested that his boredom and wildness was in part a result of loneliness. He would arrive at work many mornings bleary-eyed, having gotten only a few hours of sleep—and sometimes none. Hadden had many friends but few intimates. His "ferocious" temperament, one of his longtime colleagues later wrote, hid an uneasiness with normal personal relations, a profound shyness. He had few serious relationships with women and sometimes appeared to be a misogynist. (In 1926, when a member of *Time's* board proposed appointing a woman director, Hadden replied dismissively that "women are notorious for their inability to see things in perspective, their tendency to exaggerate, their desire to live in a fool's paradise.... They are conspicuously deficient in such fundamentals as sense of humor, fairmindedness, good sportsmanship and sense of responsibility.") He seemed to many people to be having trouble in general adjusting to adulthood. (A lifelong passionate baseball fan, he began participating in a youth baseball league in Central Park, even though it was restricted to players under eighteen. He tried to hide his mustache whenever park officials walked by.) According to a later (and unverifiable) account by one of his friends, Hadden began to disappear periodically for days and even weeks, once traveling to a farm in Indiana, on another occasion working on a tugboat, prompting Luce to send staff members out to find him and bring him home.[64]

Luce had little contact with Hadden any longer outside the office. He spent evenings with his family (his second son, Peter, was born in 1928) or at the kind of establishment social functions that Hadden scorned. At work the relationship between the two partners was rapidly deteriorating. Their friendship had always been a complicated and competitive one, and there had been many periods of tension between them over the years, but the problems had rarely lasted very long. By the late 1920s, however, their ability to recover from disagreements appeared to be eroding. Hadden seemed both contemptuous and envious of Luce—scornful of his bourgeois lifestyle at the same time that he yearned for some kind of stability of his own. In 1926 Yale awarded Luce an honorary M.A. degree—a significant honor for so young a man—for "distinguished accomplishments in a novel and worthy field of journalism." Luce, of course, was thrilled, although he recognized the effect this would have on Hadden, who might rightly have considered himself an equally plausible candidate. Harry happily attended the Yale commencement with members of his family, in-laws, and friends. But he did not invite Hadden and did not even tell him that he was receiving the degree. Hadden learned of it through reports from others and deeply resented the fact of the award and Luce's failure to inform him of it.[65]

Left: Henry Winters Luce, an aspiring missionary, and Elisabeth Root, a YMCA worker, marry in Scranton, Pennsylvania, in 1897. Less than a year later, they were en route to China.

Bottom: The Luces occupied this home in Tengchow through the first years of Harry's life. Elisabeth Luce sits on the porch with Harry, Emmavail, and a Chinese nurse. They shared the house with another missionary family.

Henry W. Luce and his four children posed for this portrait in the family's second home in Wei Hsien, approximately 1912. *From left to right:* Rev. Luce, Harry, Sheldon, Elisabeth, and Emmavail.

Henry R. Luce in China at three or four, posing imperiously in a chair that his father had used as a child.

Young Harry in 1914, on a farm in Colebrook, New Hampshire, during a summer vacation from Hotchkiss.

Luce (*left*) and Brit Hadden (*right*) at Hotchkiss in 1916, inseparable friends and rivals.

Left: Luce in uniform in 1917, a cadet at Yale. A few months later, he and Hadden were transferred to Fort Jackson, South Carolina, where they spent the rest of the war training infantry.

Bottom: Lila Hotz, the alluring Chicago socialite whom Luce met in Rome on New Year's Eve 1920 and who became Luce's first love and first wife. Luce was attracted to her both because of her warmth and energetic charm and because of her social distinction and family wealth. She is pictured with the couple's boys Hank (*right*) and Peter Paul.

The first offices of Time Inc. were above a retail store in a building on East Seventeeth Street in New York City. It was the first in a series of constantly moving and expanding headquarters for the magazine. This picture was taken some years later by Margaret Bourke-White, the first staff photographer for the company.

Brit Hadden was only twenty-five when this photograph of him was taken shortly after the publication of the first issue of *Time* magazine. Despite his sober pose, he was a lively, engaging, volatile young man of great brilliance, whose relationship with Luce was both extremely close and extremely competitive.

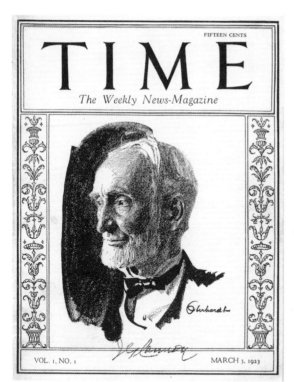

The first issue of *Time* magazine, in March 1923. The line drawing of the powerful Speaker of the U.S. House of Representatives Joseph Cannon was the first in a long tradition of portraying people on the cover. Soon after the magazine's debut, it acquired its trademark red border, and a few years later it began using color portraits created by a group of artists commissioned by the magazine.

Luce promised that *Fortune* would be the most beautiful magazine ever published. Whether or not it achieved that goal, its design was undeniably impressive—and expensive—as was the magazine itself. The first cover, in February 1930, designed by Thomas Cleland—who had also chosen the typefaces and other design elements—showed a "wheel of fortune," a symbol of the magazine itself and of the precariousness of fortune in the first year of the Great Depression.

Some of the successful early editors and writers of *Fortune* in the 1930s: *Clockwise from top left:* Ralph Ingersoll, managing editor; Archibald MacLeish, Luce's most admired writer; Dwight Macdonald, a talented young reporter who claimed to loathe his job; and James Agee, also unhappy at *Fortune* but reluctant to give up the salary. By the end of the 1930s, all of them had left. None of them had any previous experience in business writing, but Luce considered that an advantage—as in many ways it was until the group began to disband.

Top: Margaret Bourke-White was the first woman to be hired full-time at Time Inc. as a photographer—and for that matter, the first woman to serve outside the clerical and research staffs at the company. She was intrepid, and eager for the world to know it—as this dramatic photograph of her perched with camera on a parapet of the Chrysler Building far above Manhattan illustrates.

Left: Laird Goldsborough was Foreign News editor of *Time* from the late 1920s to the late 1930s. He was a brilliant and efficient writer with a big personality, and he towered over his colleagues even while writing often and favorably of Mussolini and bitterly criticizing the antifascist forces in the Spanish Civil War. Luce began easing him out shortly before the beginning of the war.

But the unhappiness was not all on one side. Harry, too, was growing resentful of Brit—of his erratic behavior, of his impatience with organization and detail, and of what Luce sensed was his greater charisma and influence within the organization. "This Hadden-Luce yoke is certainly galling," he wrote Lila late in 1927. "The differences between us are so great—However I don't see any way out which seem better than struggling through with it. . . . This letter should be torn up pronto." Most of all, he resented Hadden's contemptuous dismissal of Luce's ideas. Harry disliked *Tide*, thought it a serious mistake, but did not try to obstruct it. Beginning in mid-1928, however, Luce began developing a plan of his own for a business magazine. He encountered firm opposition from Hadden (even though "bus mag" was the first item on Brit's own expansion list). *Time* was still too fragile, Hadden argued, to launch another magazine—a concern that apparently had not occurred to him when he himself launched *Tide*. Luce might well have concluded that Hadden was balking because he wanted to block Harry from developing a magazine that Brit had not initiated.[66]

Before the move to Cleveland, when Hadden had been living at home with his parents, there had been at least some structure to his life. On his own, first in Cleveland and now back in New York, his behavior began to spin out of control. Given his boredom, his restlessness, his apparent depression, and his deep exhaustion, it was not a great surprise to anyone that by late 1928 he was beginning to flag. In December he complained to a friend who had come by to visit, "I'm not well. I don't know what's the matter. . . . I just don't seem to have any ambition and I feel weak." He was, one of his colleagues recalled, "just dragging himself to the office. He would come in for most of the week, then phone and say he wasn't well." An office assistant warned Luce, "You'd better look after Hadden, or he'll be dead. He must be really sick." One day he left the office early claiming he needed rest. He never returned.[67]

Unable to recover from a flu, very likely because of his exhaustion, he also developed a strep infection and was hospitalized in Brooklyn. A few years later he could easily have been cured. But in the absence of sulfa drugs and antibiotics, doctors had a limited range of treatment— which mostly consisted of blood transfusions. Luce and others on the *Time* staff donated blood several times, and Harry visited Brit as often as he could, although doctors, worried about Hadden's "nervous condition," barred visitors for many days at a time. Luce sent regular bulletins to the *Time* staff with reports from the doctors, none of them encouraging. By mid-January, Hadden had grown so weak that he could no longer even write (and had to dictate a will, which he then signed feebly with an *X*). When Harry talked with him about what was happening at *Time*, Brit became confused, unable to recall anything about the magazine's recent successes, and was surprised to learn that Herbert Hoover was now president. He was beginning to tell visitors, Luce among them, that "I won't get well." Harry had come to fear that too, and in late January, he wrote Manfred Gottfried and implored him to return to the magazine and take over as editor, explaining, as Gottfried wrote in his diary, that "Brit is ill unto death with streptococcus." On February 27, 1929, in the middle of the night, six years to the day from the publication of the first issue of *Time*, Hadden died.[68]

Despite the rift that had developed between them, Luce was stunned and distraught. "I don't know how I'll get along without him," he said to colleagues. And how could he have felt otherwise? He and Brit had been friends, rivals, allies, antagonists—but whatever else they were, they had been inseparable and essential partners since they had met at Hotchkiss in 1913. Luce certainly realized that his life would never be the same again.[69]

Time marked Hadden's death with a black-bordered notice in the magazine's Milestones department—after abandoning an overwrought effort by Hadden's cousin and *Time* editor, John S. Martin, to write a major obituary. "Death came last week to Briton Hadden," the notice began, in classic Hadden style. "Creation of his genius and heir to his qualities, *Time* attempts neither biography nor eulogy.... To Briton Hadden, success came steadily, satisfaction never." A week later the magazine departed from its usual format and ran a full page of letters on the back page containing tributes to Hadden. There was another change in format as well. At the top of the *Time* masthead, there was now only one name: Henry R. Luce.[70]

VI

Empire Building

What Luce called the "harrowing tragedy" of Brit Hadden's death may have been the most important event in Harry's life. It robbed him of a partner and friend with whom he had been inextricably entwined for more than fifteen years, and without whom he would almost certainly not have found himself at the head of a thriving company. It also left him in virtually sole control of Time Inc. Luce had at times yearned for such independence during the last, difficult years of his relationship with Hadden. But now he was frightened that he might not be able to hold the company together. His first concern, therefore, was to keep things as they were—to preserve the system and the editorial product that Hadden had mainly created. He asked John S. Martin, Hadden's cousin, to take over as managing editor of *Time*. Martin idolized Brit. Luce certainly knew that in giving him control of the magazine he was committing himself to Hadden's philosophy and style as the model for at least the immediate future. He confided occasionally to his wife, his sister, his father, and even to his board of directors that he was not certain he could sustain the company alone, that he had relied on Hadden's energy and imagination even more than he had realized, and that without it he feared the company would flounder. But for the most part Luce kept his anxiety to himself and tried publicly to reassure his colleagues and staff that he could maintain stability and continued success.[1]

It did not take long before he began to believe in the image he was struggling to create. The occasionally timorous Luce of the 1920s, who—although never openly admitting it—often saw himself as the slightly junior partner to Hadden and who exuded practical efficiency more than broad vision, slowly became the proud and even imperious leader whose powerful ideas and convictions became his own, and his company's, missions. Although he returned, in effect, to his customary position as business manager of the company, he never again conceded full editorial control to anyone else. He had many titles at different periods of his career: president, publisher, chairman of the board. But the one title Luce consistently held was Editor-in-Chief.

In the decades after Hadden's death, Luce rarely spoke of his former partner. At first, no doubt, he felt the need to establish himself without Brit, to create confidence among his colleagues that he was a worthy leader of Time Inc. His strategy worked. Over time, fewer and fewer people in the company had ever heard of Hadden, and those who remembered him learned to act as if they had forgotten. Luce paid modest tribute to Hadden from time to time. He contributed to the construction of a new building for the *Yale Daily News* in New Haven, which was named for Brit. He supported Hadden's cousin, Noel Busch, in the writing of a short biography of Hadden. But mostly, he simply moved on, seeing nothing to gain from dwelling on his former dependence on his longtime friend.

But what if Hadden had lived? One could imagine several scenarios, none of them remotely similar to Time Inc.'s subsequent history. Harry and Brit, having reached an impasse in their troubled relationship, might have gone their own ways—with Brit most likely retaining *Time* and Harry breaking away; or with the bored and restless Hadden leaving the company to Luce, who—with Hadden still in the background—would likely have had a much more difficult task in establishing his own authority (given Hadden's stockholdings). Or they might have stayed together, with Hadden still the editorial leader of the company and Luce still the manager of its business affairs. Had that been the outcome, much would have depended on Brit's ability to adjust to changing times. His death in 1929 came just before the end of the great prosperity of the 1920s and, for Harry and Brit's generation, the fading of the age of cynicism and irreverence. Could Hadden have left behind his exuberant iconoclasm? Could Time Inc. have flourished during the Great Depression with Hadden's raffish, Mencken-like outlook at the helm? Brit represented the disillusioned, skeptical, flippant culture of the "Jazz age." Luce, on the other hand, was a serious, earnest, questing exception to his generation's style; and his sense of purpose, even of mission, may have been better suited to the more sober 1930s than Hadden's ironic temperament might have been. The only certainty, however, was that the history of the company—and of Luce's life—would have been profoundly different had Hadden survived.

Among Luce's first acts as the solitary leader of the company was to acquire Hadden's stock. Hadden's hastily composed will left his entire estate to his half brother, Crowell Hadden, with instructions that he use the income to support his mother and stepfather throughout their lifetimes. He also directed that Crowell should "hold my stock in Time Inc. and not sell the same until after the expiration of forty-nine years after my death."[2]

Neither Luce nor Crowell Hadden seemed to take this last command very seriously. No record survives of the negotiations between Luce and the Hadden estate, but there is little to suggest that they were in any way hostile. In hindsight the Hadden family would have done better to keep the stock, which appreciated dramatically over the following decade and more. But no one at the time could have predicted the magnitude of the company's future success. And so selling seemed to make sense for both parties. Crowell wanted to diversify the estate to provide more security for his family, while at the same time retaining a healthy share of Time stock. Luce wanted to give himself more control over the company and to launch a stock-purchase plan for his employees. Brit had owned a total of 3,361 shares of Time stock, about the same as Luce. In September 1929 the estate sold just over 2,800 of them to a syndicate Luce had created, which consisted of the executive officers of the company. The stock had never traded on the open market, so Luce consulted with several investment bankers for advice on its value. They valued the stock at the astonishing price of $360 a share. (Two years later it passed $1,000 a share.) Luce himself, already the largest stockholder, took out a loan and bought more than 600 additional shares for himself. Roy Larsen bought 550 shares and became—as he remained for many years—the second largest stockholder. The rest went to nine other officers and directors of the company. The Hadden estate received more than a million dollars in return.[3]

The importance of the purchase was not so much that Luce increased his own holdings, which were already substantial. The real value to him was that the deal eliminated the Hadden family's ability to exercise control over the company or to transfer it to someone else.

With much of Hadden's very large share of the stock now dispersed, Luce now stood alone as the controlling stockholder. It was also important to him that ownership of so much of the stock lay within Time Inc.—not just because it reduced the circle of outside investors who might intervene in the company's affairs but also because it tied his colleagues more firmly to the company and thus gave them an additional incentive to work for its success and profitability. In short, the settlement gave Luce almost unlimited power to shape the future of the company as he wished—a power he used almost immediately to launch a new project that Hadden had tried to thwart.

Late in 1928, well before Hadden's death, Luce began planning for a new business magazine. He did so slowly and somewhat secretly because of Hadden's conspicuous lack of enthusiasm for the idea. *Time* was at a crucial point of development, Hadden argued, and should not yet have to compete for attention with a new project. Luce privately called Hadden's objections "specious" and bemoaned the "great spirit of stalling" that enveloped his proposal. But he did not give up. Work on the project took place within a new Experimental Department. Luce created it in part to insulate what he was doing from his censorious partner. He assigned the *Time* business writer Parker Lloyd-Smith—whom Luce described later as "brilliant" and someone with whom he had recently become "very simpatico"—and a talented researcher, Florence Horn, to work on the new magazine. He placed them in a small, remote room (almost as if he were trying to hide them). Luce's relations with Hadden were by now so tense that the two partners often communicated with each other through proxies. Hadden told Harry Davison that he thought Luce's project "should be abandoned." Luce replied, also through the board of directors, asking them to postpone a decision until he could explore the possibility further.

After Hadden's death Luce put off the project again while he worked to stabilize the shaken company. But the planning continued, and Luce finally brought a formal proposal to the board in May 1929, now claiming that Hadden would have approved of it had he lived. The venture was a gamble, Luce conceded, with perhaps a "50-50 chance" of success. But *Time* was enjoying "remarkable and unexpected prosperity" and "it would seem querulous to worry." The board approved, although not without reservations, and Luce began moving toward a late-1929 publication.[4]

Hadden and Luce had launched *Time* by describing it as the world's first newsmagazine; and while that title was open to dispute (the rival *Literary Digest* could make some claim to it), their boast was certainly plausible. In its format, style, and outlook, *Time* was—and for many years remained—a singular magazine. Not until *Newsweek* began publication in 1930 was there anything like it. Luce and the new business magazine's other founders insisted that it, too, was a pathbreaking publication—the first to examine business in real depth and with real detachment. "Publishers," they claimed in a prospectus, "have almost entirely overlooked the Vogue of Business." It would be the first real "record of Modern Industrial Civilization."[5]

But it was not the first American business magazine—not even the first effort to look at business in a broad social context. For several decades publishers had been trying to serve the world of business with a broad array of magazines. Most of them were specialized, industry-specific publications largely unknown to the general reading public. But there were also a few business-oriented journals that aspired to be more than trade magazines. One of them was *World's Work*—a monthly magazine with a 1930 circulation of about one hundred thousand—which had been chronicling American business since the 1870s. With its broad-ranging inquiries into the culture of the business world, it could make a fair claim to being not only a precursor to, but also a model for what became, *Fortune*. In a single issue in 1929, for example, *World's Work* examined the economics of managing the White House; the arcane field of book collecting; controversies over chain stores; and the character of the Harvard Business School. *World's Work* was also, like *Fortune*, a magazine with literary aspirations. It attempted to attract talented journalists and writers and sought to make its stories broadly interesting to a wide readership. But *World's Work* was also an unapologetic cheerleader for business. It expressed unqualified admiration for big corporations and the "captains of finance and industry." And it trumpeted undiminished optimism about the state of the economy—including the "Greatest of Bull Markets"—that made it highly vulnerable to the crashing fortunes and reputations of corporations and their leaders once the Great Depression began. It failed rapidly in the early 1930s. It was absorbed in 1932 by another magazine and was merged a few years later with *Time*'s former rival, the floundering *Literary Digest*, which itself ceased publication in 1937.[6]

The heady economic climate of the late 1920s inspired other publishers to launch new business magazines, including the short-lived *Magazine of Business*, which, like *Fortune*, claimed to be committed to a broad portrayal of the capitalist world aimed at a wide readership. In many ways, however, it epitomized the kind of business journalism for which Luce and the other founders of *Fortune* often expressed contempt. Luce's colleague Eric Hodgins might well have had the *Magazine of Business* in mind when he once described business reporting in the 1920s as "simply pap. . . . If they weren't written from handouts [from corporation publicists], they might just as well have been." The *Magazine of Business* was, indeed, a willing promoter of its corporate constituency. Launched in 1927, it was clearly failing by mid-1929, even before the stock market crash. In August it was absorbed by a new and more important periodical published by McGraw-Hill: *Business Week*—a magazine inspired in part by *Time* and once proposed to Luce, who rejected it in favor of *Fortune*.[7]

Luce's idea for what became *Fortune* had come in part out of his own longtime and growing curiosity about the world of business and the people who led it—an unsurprising interest for someone who was himself a young businessman working in the booming economic climate of the late 1920s. Seldom in American history had there been more interest in and enthusiasm for the corporate world and its leaders, an enthusiasm epitomized by the laconic Calvin Coolidge's claim that "the business of America is business." Luce echoed Coolidge's view. "Business is essentially our civilization. . . . Business is our life," he said in a March 1929 speech.[8]

But Luce's interest in business was also partly anthropological. Because corporations now exercised so much power in the world, Luce argued, it was important for Americans to understand how they worked. Corporate leaders in the past had tended to hide from public view, aided by what Luce called the "Stygian ignorance of business which has almost universally characterized the press." Corporations, he said, needed to be held up to honest scrutiny. Luce denounced the common belief in the 1920s that "anything faintly resembling an honest analysis of business was regarded as vulgar or Communistic or both," that "something called private business as then organized was the God-given order of the universe." He worried that most writing about business was uncritical, even adulatory. This slavish adulation of the "tycoons," as *Time* had famously named corporate titans, could not continue, in part because of a fundamental change in the nature of business management. Corporate leaders, Luce insisted, were no longer mainly the visionary founders of their companies; the "tycoon" was becoming "less and less the owner and more and more the semi-detached or, at any rate, detachable manager."

That meant that corporate leaders were more likely to play multiple roles in society, at times using their generalized expertise as strategists and managers in areas outside business altogether. "Many more tycoons . . . will emerge as public characters," Luce accurately predicted. "Being well-known they will be repositories of public trust . . . they will constantly be called upon for advice and even for positions in local and national government." They would, in short, be even more influential than the single-minded founders of great companies in the late nineteenth century had been. And so the press would now have to watch. Given the dramatic collapse of the American economy, and of the stature of business that began just as the new magazine was being launched, this idea of looking at business from the outside proved to be especially critical to the magazine's success.[9]

Most of all, however, the creation of a new magazine gave Luce a vehicle to establish a voice for himself within the company. He was proud of *Time*, to be sure, but it it had never really been his magazine— not only because Hadden had dominated its early years but also because its rigid format and inflexible system limited the ability of any one person, even its owner, to shape its content. The new business magazine, by contrast, would allow Luce to design a publication for his own boundless curiosity and ambition. Providing news to busy, uninformed people— the principal goal of *Time*—was a worthy but no longer a wholly satisfying purpose. Luce wanted as well to communicate big ideas, to tackle important questions, and to establish great goals for the world of business and for the nation. At first, he considered calling the new magazine "Power." But in the end, that seemed to him an inadequate name for what he envisioned. He settled instead—partly in response to a suggestion from Lila—on the title *Fortune*, which Luce liked because the name referred not just to wealth, but also to such ideas as "chance," "fate," and "destiny."[10]

Luce's almost passionate commitment to *Fortune*—his "real love among his magazines," Peter Drucker, briefly a Time Inc. writer, once observed—began to pour out of him once he threw himself into the planning. Among his first decisions was to emphasize design—to make *Fortune* "a beautiful magazine, if possible the most beautiful in the world." It was certainly among the most elaborately and lavishly designed publications of its time. Luce hired "one of the finest typographers and art directors in the country," Thomas Maitland Cleland, who revived an elegant eighteenth-century typeface, Baskerville, for the magazine. Luce also chose unusually expensive paper that would not have the shiny look of conventional coated stock but could still accommodate high-quality photographs. He commissioned eminent artists and designers—among them Rockwell Kent, Diego Rivera, Charles Sheeler, and Fernand Léger—to create elegant, complex covers. (The first issue bore a striking black-and-bronze image by Cleland of an almost abstract "wheel of fortune," symbolizing not just the magazine's title but industry and progress more broadly.) *Fortune*'s aesthetic represented, among other things, Luce's own new attraction to modern art and design. Only one printer in the country could handle *Fortune*'s exacting demands, the Osborne Chromatic Gravure Company in New Jersey. It was necessary to print each side of each page in a separate run. Covers sometimes had to go through seven different print runs to handle the complex coloring. *Fortune* was not only expensive to print. It was also, unsurprisingly, expensive to buy—one dollar an issue, an astonishing price in an era when most magazines sold for five or ten cents, but one that Luce correctly predicted would give *Fortune* a kind of status that would attract the affluent readership he was targeting—"those active, intelligent and influential individuals who have a relatively large stake in U.S. Industry and Commerce."[11]

"And now the question," Luce wrote in a crude early prospectus. "What's going to be *in* this magazine?" Luce, Lloyd-Smith, and the few others who worked on the creation of *Fortune* spent days, even months, proposing and testing story ideas. Luce himself used his few idle hours—sitting in hotel lobbies, riding on trains—listing potential topics on scraps of borrowed stationery: "the Rothschilds," "Inheritance—the Family Business," the "Biggest Farmers in the World," "Total value of art works in the U.S.," "Sleep—how many hours," the "Power Trust," "Sewage," "Why Jews in clothing business?" According to another early prospectus *Fortune* would be "not simply a magazine to look at or through." Like *Time* it would be "a magazine to read from cover-to-cover."[12]

Fortune did not set out to be a cheerleader for businessmen. But it did intend to elevate the importance of business in the minds of its readers. "Accurately, vividly and concretely to describe Modern Business is the greatest journalistic assignment in history," Luce's prospectus announced. Even years later *Fortune* described itself as "a magazine with a mission. That mission is to assist in the successful development of American Business Enterprise at home and abroad." But the real story of business, Luce insisted, was not simply industry and financial markets. It was "the daily activity of millions of men throughout the country and throughout the world." *Fortune* would look beyond the obvious stories of great corporations and their leaders and search for opportunities to illuminate the workings of economic life. In a sense, therefore, *Fortune*'s charge was nearly without limits. It would be "the log-book, the critical history, the . . . record of Twentieth Century industrial civilization." It would also, Luce insisted, be without ideological boundaries. "Not always flattering will be these descriptions," the prospectus announced (in high *Time* style), for *Fortune* "is neither puffer or booster. Both of ships and of men, *Fortune* will attempt to write critically, appraisingly . . . with unbridled curiosity." Reading *Fortune*, moreover, "may be one of the keenest pleasures in the life of every subscriber."[13]

As the publication date approached in late 1929, there was something close to euphoria about the rapid progress *Fortune* was making toward profitability, even before a single issue had been printed. Larsen reported to Luce in early November that there were now thirty thousand subscribers and that nearly eight hundred pages of advertising had been sold, with more than eighty pages already committed to the first issue alone. The magazine, he accurately predicted, would "break even for the year 1930." The rapid deterioration of the American economy after the October 1929 stock market crash only slightly dampened Luce's optimism. "We will go ahead and publish," he told the board, "but we shall be realistic. . . . We shall recognize that this slump may last as long as one year." Luce never wavered in his commitment to proceed, and he even persuaded himself that the emerging Depression might be a good thing for the magazine, whose first issue was published in February 1930. "We didn't want *Fortune* thought of as stock market fluff," he later recalled. "In starting out in a slump we had a more solid base."[14]

Fortune was indeed not stock market fluff. Although it went through several distinct phases in its first decade, it remained true to many of its initial goals. It was almost certainly, as Luce had hoped, the most beautiful broad-circulation magazine in America. It was also a true writer's magazine. Although its language sometimes mimicked *Time*'s, there was no consistent effort to impose a single literary style on *Fortune*. That was one reason that it attracted so many distinguished staff writers in its first years: James Agee, Archibald MacLeish, Dwight Macdonald, among many others. Another reason was the relatively high salaries Luce offered in the midst of an economic crisis. ("We have absolutely nothing now but what I earn here," MacLeish, who missed his poetry but on the whole rather liked writing for the magazine, wrote his family in a low moment, "and . . . it has meant that I have written nothing [except for

Fortune] for a year. Which I cannot endure.") *Fortune* was also distinguished by its commitment to photography, so much so that in its early years it promoted itself to a large degree by showcasing a woman who would become its most famous staff photographer, Margaret Bourke-White.[15]

Bourke-White came to the attention of *Fortune* by chance. She had been among the first American photographers to show an interest in industrial design. A series of striking pictures she took in Cleveland between 1928 and 1930—including a particularly impressive set of images of the Otis Steel Company—established her reputation as, in Luce's words, the "greatest of industrial photographers." ("It seems to me," Bourke-White wrote at the time, "that huge machinery, steel girders, locomotives, etc., are so extremely beautiful because they were never meant to be beautiful. They are an expression of something that has come about in a perfectly natural way.") Luce wired her in Cleveland and invited her to come to see him. Within a few weeks *Fortune* had hired her on unusual terms. She would work half-time for the magazine at the substantial salary of one thousand dollars a month and would have the remaining weeks to work on her own. Few photographers had achieved widespread fame by 1929; Bourke-White herself was still largely unknown. But Luce saw in her an opportunity to provide a new kind of star power to *Fortune*, and he began publicizing her association with the magazine as if she were already famous. Promotional literature in the months before publication contained full-page photographs—such as a picture of a steel mill that "imprisons the glow of molten metal"—credited to "The Photographer: Margaret Bourke-White of *Fortune*'s staff, now touring the U.S." She was, she later said, impressed by Luce's sophisticated understanding of what photographs could do and his curiosity about "what the average man is interested in. As though he was a sort of super-average man." She remembered Luce telling her that "the camera would be as an interpreter, recording what modern industrial civilization is, how it looks, how it meshes." It was almost "miraculous," she later said, that a magazine could so perfectly capture her own ambitious hopes—"I with my dream of portraying industry in photographs, and they with their new magazine designed to hold just such photographs."[16]

Time Inc. was not accustomed to hiring women for high-profile positions. Talented women abounded in the company, but almost never did they emerge from the virtually all-female research and clerical staffs, which—while indispensable to the magazines—were rarely considered pools from which to draw writers and editors. Bourke-White was among the first women to break that mold, and she was able to do so only because the company had never before hired professional photographers and could, despite her growing fame, consider her in some way outside the core editorial activities of the magazines. Perhaps as a result of her anomalous position, she and her editors were almost always in conflict—about money, about the quality of her photographs, about her "inappropriate" work for other publications. Her reputation with the editorial staff was, one editor wrote, someone who caused "troubles and headaches wherever she operates." And yet through the early years of *Fortune* (and later *Life*), she provided some of the most memorable and important images the magazines ever published, and she became in many ways more renowned (and more marketable) than any other editorial employee.[17]

Among the qualities that made Bourke-White so valuable to *Fortune* was that her own photographic aesthetic coincided with—and also helped to shape—an important aspect of the magazine: Luce's own fascination with and admiration for what was coming to be known as the "machine age." Just as Bourke-White had found herself drawn to the physical structures of modernity in Cleveland, so Luce, and his *Fortune* staff, were enthralled by the new social aesthetic that the modern industrial world was creating. Their enthusiasm for the beauty and power of technology was visible in the first issue of *Fortune*, in which Bourke-White provided photographs of the Swift Meatpacking Plant in Chicago. A factory that was, in essence, a slaughterhouse would seem an unlikely example of the new machine age. But Bourke-White's pictures revealed the state-of-the-art technology of the slaughterhouses with few glimpses of the carnage. Her opening photograph—accompanying an elaborate and clinical diagram of a hog's various cuts of meat—provided an almost abstract image of a vast herd of hog backs, nearly unrecognizable as living animals. Even the more conventional photographs of pigs moving through the plant emphasized the orderly, almost mechanical process. The text of the article, by Parker Lloyd-Smith, was similarly dispassionate in its description of the efficiency, and even the beauty, of the grisly process. The hogs that arrived at the Swift plant were, Lloyd-Smith wrote, "beautifully assembled mechanisms. . . . By countless individual acts of destruction, Swift & Company paradoxically increases the value of products which are the result of countless individual acts of creation."[18]

Fortune's admiring portrait of Swift had a special meaning, because Swift was the meatpacking giant that twenty-four years earlier had been a target of Upton Sinclair's sensational novel *The Jungle*. Sinclair had used the meatpacking industry as a symbol of the greedy, rapacious, and chaotic character of American industry. He was particularly effective in providing revolting depictions of the slaughterhouses, and especially accounts of how sausages were made:

> There would be meat that had tumbled out on the floor, in the dirt and sawdust, where the workers had tramped and spit uncounted billions of consumption germs. There would be meat stored in great piles in rooms; and the water from leaky roofs would drip over it, and thousands of rats would race about on it . . . a man could run his hand over these piles of meat and sweep off handfuls of the dried dung of rats. . . . the packers would put poisoned bread out for them; they would die, and then rats, bread, and meat would go into the hoppers together.

The book created a popular sensation and led directly to the passage of the Federal Meat Inspection Act of 1906, which imposed new sanitary standards on the industry.

Fortune's very different portrait of Swift deliberately reflected the broad, "modern" changes in meatpacking that Sinclair had helped create. The choice of Swift as the first article in the first issue of *Fortune* was also designed more broadly to contrast the character of modern industries from the unregulated, inefficient factories of a generation earlier. And it was also a deliberate effort to draw a contrast between the hostile muckraking of the Progressive Era and the more professionalized journalism of Luce's world. *Fortune*'s Swift was no longer a "jungle" but a model of modern, progressive technology:

> Here is a mechanical saw which grinds through the shoulder; there is a draw knife like a curved adz which scoops out the loin. Hundreds of white-sleeved arms swing back and forth. Hundreds of funnels gulp the morsels the knives flip aside. Some gulp lean trimmings; these will make sausage. Some gulp fats; these will make lard. Down one chute go the hams . . . down another go the shoulders.

In its clean, modern, clinical language, Lloyd-Smith seemed purposely to contrast his description with the censorious, emotional language of *The Jungle*.[19]

Fortune continued to feature striking examples of industrial design and productive efficiency throughout the 1930s: a story about the creation of an "ideal factory . . . in which the employees would work under optimum conditions as regards their five senses"; an article on the industrial designer Norman Bel Geddes, praising "this new, artistic generation . . . fixed not on the past . . . but strictly on the present. . . . modern aestheticism must embrace the machine with all its innuendos"; a utopian essay on functionalism in home design ("Machines for Living") by Lewis Mumford; a dramatic full-page Margaret Bourke-White photograph of the Chrysler Building under construction as it awaited its "sheathing in Nirosta Steel." In an unsigned editorial in May 1933, *Fortune* attacked the antimodern claims of H. L. Mencken that the machine age was destroying the "sense of the continent" and its literature. In an era of aviation and industrial transformation, the *Fortune* editorial replied, "the sense of America, the sense of the continent revives. And as always in the civilization of industrialism it revives not by a return to an earlier and simpler life but by a further complication."

Fortune's enthusiasm for the machine-age aesthetic was also visible in its fascination with serious artists who chose modern industrialism as their subjects. One example was a full-page painting by Charles Sheeler of the Ford Plant in Dearborn, Michigan. Sheeler was renowned for his use of industrial scenes as timeless art, and the magazine embraced the ideology behind his style. "An artist, observing a factory, usually finds in it some symbol of industrial grandeur, oppression, or monotony," the caption explained. "Charles Sheeler, whose calm and meticulous Fordscape appears on this page, has another approach. He looks at the Ford plant as it is; enjoys its patterns, shades, and movements; and its careless deductions." Another was a 1931 article on a lesser-known artist, the sculptor Max Kalish, who came to *Fortune*'s attention because of his focus on "linemen and steel workers and iron forgers and electric workers." His sculpture was a "reproach" to much American art. For it proved "that there exists in America the material for a primary and unspoiled [industrial] art." *Fortune*, in short, was part of the broad effort of its age (and now of Luce) to legitimize modernism, to reward those who contributed to the rationalization of industry and commerce, and to celebrate the sleek new aesthetic that accompanied it.[20]

One of the few stories Luce himself actually reported and wrote in the first year of the magazine was an especially powerful example of his fascination with the machine age. He had accompanied Bourke-White to South Bend, Indiana, in early 1930 to chronicle the life of an important industrial city. A year earlier the sociologists Robert and Helen

Merrell Lynd had published *Middletown*—a classic study of the supposedly typical community of Muncie, Indiana, in the 1920s. It was almost
certainly a model for Luce's story of neighboring South Bend. "We shall
seek to discover," Luce wrote in language similar to that of the Lynds,

> both how much and what kind of industrial productivity is
> required these days for the human reproductivity of South
> Bend. To understand the life which calls forth the babies in
> South Bend is to understand why all the babies in all the United
> States are born. For South Bend is the perfect microcosm, the
> living example, the photographable average.

But Luce's real purpose was not dispassionate investigation. The article
was, rather, a celebration of the power of the machine age, enhanced by
Bourke-White's muscular photographs. "Cosmic, titanic, great, majes-
tic. . . . Enter now the clang of steel, the roar of furnaces, the toots of
financiers, and the honks of salesmen, the great Modern or Automotive
Age," Luce wrote almost breathlessly. "What now is South Bend, what
now is the perfect microcosm of the golden age of the Industrial Era?"[21]

Fortune's approach to business fluctuated over time, reflecting the
changing character of the economy, the shifting ideas of the staff, the
new politics of the Depression years, and the inclinations of Luce himself (whose views were ultimately decisive). He was, of course, himself a
successful businessman, but his admiration for his peers was not unqualified. Time Inc. had succeeded, Luce believed, because it was innovative,
flexible, and as self-consciously modern as the gleaming Chrysler Building in New York City into which it would soon move. The companies
and corporate executives Luce admired were those similarly committed
to a modern, progressive approach to business. The industrial world, he
believed, was moving into a new era—no longer the province of ruthless
and reckless robber barons, but increasingly a world dominated by rational, well-educated executives who were transforming modern corporations. *Fortune* would reveal and celebrate this new world. Herbert
Hoover had once typified the kind of progressive leader Luce generally
admired. Luce became disillusioned with him because of the president's
apparent abandonment of the progressive spirit of the "new age." Evidence of his disdain was a harsh essay in *Fortune* in September 1932,
whose title was drawn from an infamous statement by Hoover—"No
One Has Starved"—with the scathing subtitle, "which isn't true."[22]

The Swift story was the first of a genre that would come to characterize almost every issue of *Fortune:* portraits of corporations and industries. Such articles were not always admiring. The editors sometimes chose companies they considered "behind the times" and compared them unfavorably with the modern model that Luce admired. A June 1930 article on the notoriously unstable cotton textile industry, for example, was unsparing in its description of the industry's failings: "The country's fourth largest industry is at the mercy of two forces—labor and a woman's vanity. Together they keep it without leadership and without stability." But far more often in *Fortune*'s first years, the stories focused on the progressive power of American capitalism. The great General Motors Corporation, famous for the efficient new organization that its president, Alfred P. Sloan, had imposed on it in the early 1920s, was a *Fortune* favorite: "Having ambition where the ordinary man has discontent," the magazine wrote in April 1930, "their only common characteristic is energy. Not bigger wheels but faster." In profiling AT&T, the world's largest corporation, *Fortune* noted that "its primary allegiance belongs to the people who buy its service instead of the people who buy its stock." (The company's CEO, much revered by *Fortune*, was fond of saying that the "captains of industry" must now be replaced by "statesmen of industry.") Luce was especially impressed with the companies that were moving aggressively to restructure themselves to survive the Great Depression, for example, the financial company Transamerica, which recognized that "the era of easy trading profits had come to its end" and had instead "reorganized itself with an eye to the new world." To Luce such stories of American innovation and success were a challenge to the eroding reputation of business in the first years of the Great Depression.[23]

Fortune's modestly restrained enthusiasm for corporations and business leaders did not protect it from the scorn of those who believed that the Depression had torn away the mask of capitalism and destroyed the credibility of the corporate world. "*Fortune* says, Long live the tycoon!" the *Nation* wrote dismissively in 1931, charging that "glorified success stories about tycoons and their profit-producing enterprises are consciously designed to encourage the purchase of securities in these undertakings." But Luce was far from a cheerleader for "tycoons." He believed that business leaders, and those who celebrated the business world, were woefully ignorant of the new shape of industry. They had an obligation to accept "the radical principle . . . that all business is invested in the public interest." Looking back on the early years of *Fortune* more than a decade later, Luce recalled his sense that there was "something particularly improper in people strutting around on the basis of their (or their husband's) business status, yet refusing to admit a drawing-room bowing acquaintance with the *realities* of industry and commerce." *Fortune*'s "crusading point," he bluntly insisted, 'was in effect this: 'God damn you, Mrs. Richbitch, we won't have you chittering archly and snobbishly about Bethlehem Common [stock] unless you damn well have a look at the open hearths and slagpiles—yes, and the workers' houses of Bethlehem, Pa.' "[24]

The undercurrent of skepticism about capitalism among many of his editors and writers, and at times in Luce himself, was only scarcely visible in the first few years of *Fortune*'s life. But it gradually became more pronounced through a combination of chance and circumstance. By the summer of 1930, Luce had become concerned that Parker Lloyd-Smith—whose creative and literary brilliance he continued to admire—was not succeeding at the day-to-day management of the magazine, which had become erratic, even at times chaotic. *Fortune*, Luce concluded, needed a reliable associate editor. He settled on Ralph Ingersoll, the managing editor of *The New Yorker*, who was renowned for his organized efficiency. Lloyd-Smith was offended at first, but he soon found Ingersoll a cooperative and even indispensable partner. A little over a year after Ingersoll's arrival, however, Lloyd-Smith jumped naked to his death from the small hotel room where he lived alone. The startling and unexplained suicide thrust Ingersoll into the managing editorship of the magazine. He was less charismatic and less likable than Lloyd-Smith had been, but far more efficient; and with Luce's support he set out to reorganize the staff so as to deepen the magazine's engagement with the economy generally.

By the end of 1931 hope for a quick recovery from the Depression was fading. And beginning in 1933 the presidency of Franklin Roosevelt and the energy and occasional radicalism of the New Deal—combined with the increasing influence of the Left generally in American culture—made criticism of business, and of capitalism itself, far more pervasive than in all but a few periods of American life. It also became a part of the character of *Fortune*. Ingersoll was certainly not a radical, and he was far too protective of his own career to put very much distance between himself and Luce. But Ingersoll tolerated and at times even actively encouraged the left-leaning inclinations of much of his staff. Luce inadvertently hastened the move to the left by urging Ingersoll to reorganize the editorial process in 1933 in a way that gave writers even more control over their work than they had in the past. Ingersoll, who considered *Fortune* as much a "writer's" magazine as *The New Yorker*, eagerly agreed. He was especially deferential to the poet and essayist Archibald MacLeish, who was trying to make *Fortune* into both a more intellectual and a more critical magazine than it had been at first. "Where the old *Fortune* . . . was to have concerned itself with business for business' sake," MacLeish later wrote, "the new *Fortune* would report the world of business as an expression—a peculiarly enlightening expression—of the Republic, of the changing world." The magazine was never as overtly partisan as journals of opinion such as the *Nation* or *The New Republic*, but in the mid-1930s it was often strikingly iconoclastic in its approach to the capitalist world it had set out at first to celebrate.[25]

The *Fortune* writer Eric Hodgins (who later became managing editor of the magazine) described it as "the most brilliant magazine staff ever to exist in America." Whether or not that was true, it was certainly one of the most adventurous. Few of the writers had any previous experience in either business or journalism. (It was, Luce said, "easier to turn poets into business journalists than to turn bookkeepers into writers.") They were hired for their literary skills, their intelligence, and their connections to one another, just as the original *Time* writers had generally come not from journalism but from successful academic lives in universities like Harvard and Yale. Luce hired Dwight Macdonald because another Time Inc. writer, Wilder Hobson, had known him at Yale. MacLeish had a previous relationship with Luce, also in part through their shared ties to Yale and Hotchkiss. James Agee came to *Fortune* through the efforts of his friend Macdonald. Russell Davenport, an aspiring poet who began his long career at Time Inc. as a *Fortune* writer, knew Luce through Skull and Bones, and his presence also opened the door for his brother, John. They were a close-knit group, and they chose to interpret "business" as anything related to the economy, which opened up most of the world to them—especially in light of the freedom Luce seemed to have given them. Not many writers embraced what the *Fortune* writer John Chamberlain later called his own "antibusiness radicalism," but there was a political affinity among many of the *Fortune* staff (not least among the female researchers, whose influence was profound if largely unacknowledged) for some of the great causes of the Left. They joined together to raise money for the antifascist forces in the Spanish civil war. Many of them were "ardent liberals," Macdonald later wrote, and identified openly with the most progressive initiatives of the New Deal. "Almost invariably," Ingersoll recalled, "wherever we touched on labor problems, we came out more sympathetic with labor than with management."[26]

Unsurprisingly these political inclinations found their way into the magazine—not consistently, but often enough to alarm some of *Fortune*'s powerful advertisers, subscribers, and friends. Eric Hodgins's 1934 article "Arms and the Men" created a sensation with its strident indictment of European arms merchants, whose "axioms," he wrote, are "(a) prolong war, (b) disturb peace. . . . Every time a burst shell fragment finds it way into the brain, the heart, or the intestines of a man in the front line . . . much of the profit, finds its way into the pocket of the armament maker." (Ingersoll boasted to Luce that the story "will make FORTUNE internationally famous for the rest of its life.") MacLeish published a devastating three-part portrait of the notorious industrialist Ivar Kreuger, who committed suicide amid revelations of—to use the title of MacLeish's third article—"A $250,000,000 swindle." MacLeish also wrote a powerful essay (later republished by Time Inc. as a book) on "Jews in America," linking the Nazi persecution of Jews in Germany to anti-Semitism in America. Particularly startling was a September 1934 article, unsigned but written by Dwight Macdonald, on the American Communist Party, which, without defending or endorsing Communism, challenged the deep antipathy most Americans felt toward it:

> The Reds may be "trouble makers," and "fomenters of rebellion," but they can make trouble and riots only when the capitalist system has done gross injustice to some social group. By leading the oppressed classes and making their grievances articulate, the Communists force the capitalist system to adjust its more glaring inequalities.

And despite Luce's own early and growing doubts about the New Deal, *Fortune* openly celebrated Roosevelt's apparent success, including a ringing endorsement of the ultimately failed National Recovery Administration:

> If it is [NRA director Hugh Johnson's] purpose to transplant the practice of democracy from the political field . . . to the industrial field . . . the result may be not only the salvation of American industry but the rejuvenation of the now decayed and outmoded ideal of democracy itself.[27]

Even one of the magazine's most ostensibly neutral features—Luce's idea for what became the much-heralded "*Fortune* Survey," which mobilized the new techniques of public-opinion research and presented a portrait of popular views of economic and other issues—often seemed to skew its questions to support the New Deal and other progressive causes. The first surveys, for example, asked for opinions about wealth distribution, public services versus taxation, income and estate taxes, the dignity of labor, and the responsibility of government to assure every man a job. The polling sample—gathered by the pioneering pollster Elmo Roper—was not *Fortune* readers but the general public. The results, predictably, reflected the left-leaning attitudes of the electorate in this highly charged time of upheaval.[28]

But it was not always easy to hold liberal or radical views while writing for a business magazine that, for all its flirtations with the Left, remained committed to the ethos of the capitalist world. They soon began to run up against the limits of radicalism Luce was willing to tolerate. Two of the most talented writers at *Fortune* were also the most disaffected. Both Agee and Macdonald had come to *Fortune* because they needed the money. Like almost everyone on the editorial staff, they wrote the standard company and industry stories. But they were always a poor fit with the magazine's culture, even in its most iconoclastic years. Agee described the spectrum of his feelings about *Fortune* as ranging from "a hard masochistic liking to direct nausea." Macdonald later claimed that he wrote for *Fortune* "with no special interest in the subject" or in his published stories, which were "impossible for me to reread or even remember writing, a month later. . . . Never did I think of myself as a member of the team, a loyal, dedicated Fortunian." Both began to chafe at what they considered the increasingly formulaic culture of the magazine.

Agee, taking advantage of *Fortune*'s growing interest in dysfunctional industries and regions, proposed a study of Southern sharecroppers, and in 1936 traveled to Alabama with the photographer Walker Evans to chronicle the lives of three families of white tenant farmers. The result was a remarkable series of photographs by Evans and a massive text by Agee—a sprawling, discursive expression of his own emotional response to the lives of the families he had visited. It reflected his simultaneously radical and antiprogressive belief in the "divinity of man," and it argued that neither journalism nor politics could adequately convey the richness of individual lives. *Fortune* unsurprisingly declined to publish the enormous, idiosyncratic manuscript, and Agee spent the next four years trying to find a publisher for it. (It finally came out in 1940 as *Let Us Now Praise Famous Men* and received scant, unenthusiastic critical attention. It sold about six hundred copies before being remaindered and forgotten—only to be revived in the 1960s and proclaimed a literary classic.)[29]

Agee's disaffection was no secret to anyone. Macdonald's restiveness remained mostly hidden. He argued with Luce occasionally, once accusing him of not having "enough social consciousness." But mostly he kept his opinions to himself until he finally decided to rebel openly. He was assigned in 1936 to coauthor a four-part series on U.S. Steel with his fellow *Fortune* writer Robert Cantwell. The story sharply denounced the company's harsh labor policy, "the most severely criticized and most uncompromisingly defended position ever taken by the Corporation." And it concluded sourly that "three great social groups are affected by the Corporation: its stockholders, its customers, its employees. . . . It has in the past pleased no one of them." But Macdonald was not content with criticism of the company's performance alone. In the course of his work on the project, he had taken a strong dislike to Myron Taylor, U.S. Steel's president; and he wrote scathingly in the last of the four articles that Taylor had come to head the giant corporation only because he "looked like a movie director's idea of a big corporation CEO." (Even years later, looking back on the story, he described Taylor as "that great ham character actor.") He also, as he himself later claimed, included a deliberate provocation to Luce: an epigraph that read " 'Monopoly is the final stage of capitalism.' V. I. Lenin." Luce demanded that Macdonald rewrite the article. Macdonald refused—apparently no longer able to suppress his loathing of his work at *Fortune*—which he later expressed openly in an acerbic article about Luce and his magazine in the *Nation*.[30]

Luce had been mostly tolerant of the critical tone of *Fortune* despite his frequent grumbling about the complaints he received from his friends and colleagues in the business world. But his intervention in the U.S. Steel piece was a clear sign of change. In 1936 Luce began to harden the tone of *Fortune*—partly in response to the passions raised within the company by the Spanish civil war, which was, Luce later wrote, "fought in the *Time-Life* Building with some bitter consequences." Many of the more left-leaning writers and editors departed. Macdonald resigned, openly defiant. His departure was the most wounding to Luce, who later recalled spending "more time trying to educate that young man than any other writer I've ever dealt with." Agee moved out of *Fortune* at about the same time and became a book reviewer for *Time*. A few years later he left the company to write novels. MacLeish resigned in 1938 to accept a position at Harvard, unhappy with the direction the magazine was taking and disappointed in Luce.

The growing restiveness among the *Fortune* staff was driven as much by their unhappiness with *Time* as by the changing character of their own magazine. Macdonald wrote Luce not long before his resignation that "the chief difference between *Time* and the [liberal journal of opinion] *Nation* seems to be that the *Nation* is consciously left-wing . . . whereas *Time* is ostensibly impartial but actually (perhaps unconsciously) right-wing." MacLeish, in his own last year with the company, frequently sent Luce tough if courteous criticisms of *Time*. He was particularly contemptuous of Laird Goldsborough, whom MacLeish, like many others, still accused of fascist inclinations. "I don't think anyone here has ever thought *Time* was fascist in intention," MacLeish wrote in 1936. But the magazine did have "a strong unconscious bias, particularly in labor stories and in foreign news relating to revolutionary developments." MacLeish engaged in an increasingly acrimonious exchange with Goldsborough himself about *Time*'s coverage of the Spanish civil war and its often-unsubtle admiration for fascism, Franco, and Mussolini. Goldsborough, in turn, accused MacLeish of being in league with communists. Luce stood largely apart from the fray, which MacLeish correctly interpreted as his siding with Goldsborough. "I wish some things had gone differently with you," he wrote Luce ruefully in a farewell letter. "You were meant to be a progressive—a pusher-over—a pryer-up. You were meant to make common cause with the people—all the people. You would have been very happy I think if you could have felt that the New Deal was your affair. Because it was your affair."

The angst within *Fortune* was, in short, a fear that it would become more like *Time*. That concern grew when Ingersoll moved out of *Fortune* and into a management position in 1936. The shift created anxiety about his successor and also doubts about Ingersoll's ability (or willingness) to resist Luce's influence. (Ingersoll later left the company entirely to start his own short-lived newspaper, *P.M.*) Ingersoll's departure from *Fortune* hastened the changing culture of the magazine. His immediate successor was Eric Hodgins, whose views were not unlike Ingersoll's but who was weaker and more deferential to Luce. He was replaced less than a year later by Russell Davenport, who was considerably more conservative than either Ingersoll or Hodgins had been and who set out enthusiastically to change the magazine's tone.[31]

The changes at *Fortune* were in part a result of Luce's loss of patience with what he had come to consider the increasingly anticapitalist and pro–New Deal tone of the magazine. As early as 1933 Luce had told MacLeish that he "ought not to resent the millionaires in the audi-

ence, and should cheerfully remember that *that* happens to be the audience to which they were invited to lecture." By late 1936 Luce was
becoming concerned by the rising level of complaints from advertisers
and by what he called the "considerable change in [*Fortune's*] philosophy." The trouble with *Fortune*, Luce once said, "is that it often forgets
it is a Journalist and imagines itself like the Oxford Union . . . (Socialist
these days, of course)."

He was also developing a "growing antipathy to Mr. Roosevelt and
the New Deal," despite some initial enthusiasm. Luce had arranged a
meeting with the president in 1933, and he brought MacLeish—who
was writing a *Fortune* profile of Roosevelt—along with him. As they left
the White House, MacLeish later recalled, Luce said excitedly, "My
God, what a man!" But by 1934 Luce was regularly criticizing the
administration—both in speeches and in print. And by the end of 1935
he was becoming exasperated by the great enthusiasm for the New Deal
among *Fortune* writers. He became determined to "get *Fortune* a little bit
straightened out ideologically." The magazine was, he later recalled,
"going more and more socialistic in its attitude. And the question was
how could we honestly ask businessmen to advertise in *Fortune* if our
editorial policy had diverged so far from the general business community's sentiment." The result was what Luce called a "Respectus" in mid-
1937, in which Luce charted a revised course for the magazine.
"*Fortune*," he announced, "can be either a great Communist magazine or
a great Capitalist magazine," and there was no doubt which choice Luce
was making: *Fortune* would "have a platform with two planks." One
would be the "free and fearless journalism of inquiry." The other would
be "a bias in favor of private enterprise" and against "State-control. . . .
Fortune views with alarm the weakness in private capitalism which
invokes collectivism; and points with pride to those merits in private
capitalism which argue against collectivism."[32]

The new direction for *Fortune* was not just a result of Luce's disagreements with his writers about capitalism. It was also a reflection of
Luce's own growing determination to impose a coherent ideology on
the magazine—and on the company as a whole. *Fortune* had, in fact,
never been an anticapitalist magazine. Most of its content always fit
comfortably into Luce's own sympathetic, if slightly skeptical, view of
the business world; the iconoclastic stories from some of his more left-
leaning writers were the exception. What Luce found increasingly
troubling about *Fortune* was less its politics than its diversity of opinion.

He had tolerated such diversity into the mid-1930s, but gradually, he had ceased to tolerate the wide range of views reflected in his magazines. Instead he had come to believe that the Time Inc. publications needed to reflect a shared sense of purpose—a purpose defined largely by him.

It was not easy to impose his own beliefs on a large and growing institution. For the rest of his life, Luce railed frequently about his inability to control the contents of the magazines, about the ways in which his writers and editors appeared to ignore his wishes. But he continued to try, and he succeeded often enough to ensure that the Time Inc. magazines would be distinctive in the world of journalism, that they would present not just the news, but the editor in chief's own sense of what it meant.

The battle for control began almost immediately upon Luce's presentation of his "Respectus." Several staff members protested vehemently against it, not because it marked a turn away from the "socialist inclinations" of the past, but because of the very idea that the magazine should have a more-or-less official "purpose" at all. *Fortune*, they argued, should "not stoop to a profession of faith . . . we do not need a platform." Seventeen female researchers signed a statement denouncing the "total disregard of facts" and the "deliberate bias" that was creeping into the magazine; the principle underlying *Fortune*, they insisted, had always been the honest pursuit of truth without "a pre-established editorial bias." Davenport and Luce emphatically disagreed with them. Davenport had, in fact, accepted the managing editorship in 1937 precisely because, as he later wrote, it was necessary "to develop a policy that business men could accept . . . if *Fortune*'s reputation in the business world was to be saved." Luce had a larger goal. He believed that the magazine should take a stand on the great issues of the day—a stand that would reflect Luce's own political and ideological progress.[33]

Although Luce would eventually become best known, and most controversial, for his opinions on international affairs—and for his passionate views on China—his first active political interventions focused on the role of government in the economy. He was unhappy with the New Deal and what he considered its arrogant and dismissive attitude toward business. But he was not a reactionary. He was impatient with the rigidity and conservatism of many corporations and their leaders. Beginning tentatively in 1935, and with greater emphasis in the later years of the decade, he helped craft an economic policy for himself and for his magazines—a set of ideas similar to what some years later would come to be known as "corporate liberalism." He began increasingly to argue that the dangerous path to "collectivism" could be averted only by a change in the character of private enterprise. He also came to believe that one of *Fortune*'s missions must be to explain and promote his views.

Corporate liberalism as Luce understood it had roots in the efforts of some corporations in the 1920s to create a benevolent environment for their workers, a system known at the time as "welfare capitalism." The relatively few industries that embraced this concept had provided employees with previously rare benefits such as pension contributions, paid vacations, and most of all higher wages. Luce was a quiet champion of welfare capitalism in the late 1920s. But more than that, he was a harsh critic of what he considered the "defensive, suspicious, false" conservatism of many business leaders. "Toryism resists change," he had said in 1928. "But business is the great innovator. Business discards the good for the better, the best for the once impossible. . . . And with business came liberalism. It remodeled thrones, rewrote constitutions, altered, adapted, renovated, recreated. And what could not be renovated, it removed."

Although Luce disliked many New Deal policies, his principal complaints against Roosevelt were more personal. The president, he believed, was governing outside the rule of law; he had become an authoritarian leader who exercised power almost arbitrarily, and had used his position to make demagogic attacks on rival institutions, most notably business. As early as 1935, in an article titled "The Case Against Roosevelt" (which Luce, somewhat capriciously, assigned to the very pro-Roosevelt MacLeish), *Fortune* noted the "personal character" of New Deal regulation, its apparent vindictiveness, its "feel of the human interferer." The president, MacLeish wrote, "has opened a door through which a dictator could easily pass." Such criticisms grew steadily over the next several years—in commissioned pieces in *Fortune* from such anti-Roosevelt figures as Senator Arthur Vandenberg of Michigan ("This either is, or it is not, a government of laws rather than of men," Vandenberg wrote, citing the New Deal's "disregard for the spirit as well as the letter of the Constitution"), and in Luce's own public statements ("It is now Franklin Roosevelt's task without delay to restore the long-term conditions of confidence which private capitalism requires," he told a group of Ohio businessmen).[34]

Corporate liberalism, therefore, was simultaneously a plea for government to respect the "rule of law" and the prerogatives of business, and a call for the private sector to embrace an enlightened policy of social responsibility. As early as 1934, despite his unhappiness with the New Deal, Luce was—through *Fortune*—exhorting business to accept a series of progressive principles: "that a livelihood should be guaranteed to every man, ... that there must be a dwelling for every man, woman and child, and that it must conform to some minimum standard of decency," and that "there must be developed a widely understood pattern for the reward of talent" because the "greatest practical test of a nation's devotion to liberty is the extent to which it maintains the open door of opportunity."[35]

Luce's commitment to enlightened business leadership as the key to a successful society was clearly at odds with the belief of many liberals, and virtually all socialists, that capitalism was a less reliable provider of justice than was the state. But Luce was not entirely hostile to government. Were the New Deal to fail, he predicted, the result would not (and should not) be "a return to laissez-faire capitalism." The nation's economy "can be established only by Business working with Government and Government working with Business, over a long period of years, toward a progressively higher standard of living derived from the incentives of private enterprise."[36]

By 1939 *Fortune*'s idea of a rapprochement between government and business was far from that of the left-leaning liberals who had written for the magazine in the mid-1930s. By the end of the decade, *Fortune* reflected instead the emerging moderate Republican position of accepting some of the New Deal and rejecting a great deal more. Through a series of *Fortune* "Round Tables," the first published in March 1939, the magazine presented the views of a carefully selected group of business leaders brought together to discuss important political issues, beginning with federal fiscal policy. "In general," the panel agreed, "the social and labor reforms so far established should be retained ... [and] public spending should indeed be used to counterbalance the business cycle." But while government spending was not inevitably bad, it should be used to "increase productive opportunity rather than merely *spend* to create purchasing power." *Fortune*'s editors summed up the Round Tables with considerable pride: "We have the satisfaction of having done a small bit in the herculean job of bringing business and government points of view into alignment." A year later they boasted further about the new, progressive business spirit, which had changed not only political economy but culture.

In "The Culture of Democracy," an essay in a special 1940 issue of *Fortune* on America, the editors argued that literature and art were no longer the property of Popular Front critics of capitalism. They were, rather, moving into a "dialectic" with the world of enlightened business, helping to create a stronger, more abundant, and more pluralistic America. The essay concluded with a passage from Walt Whitman, which expressed—in a way certainly unintended by Whitman himself—*Fortune*'s own optimistic vision of the new, enlightened capitalist age:

Fresh come, to a new world indeed, yet long prepared,
I see the genius of the modern, the child of the real and the ideal,
Clearing the ground for a broad humanity, the true America, heir of the past
  so grand,
To build a grander future.

Fortune had not given up its commitment to elevated language, as Whitman's florid poem made clear. But it had made a decision about what the magazine stood for: no longer a broad, pluralistic look at the strengths and weaknesses of capitalism, but a vehicle for expressing the ideas and convictions that Luce had come to believe must be *Fortune*'s new mission.[37]

VII

"Time Marches On"

B y the mid-1930s Luce had become—as he would remain for the rest of his life—a famous publishing titan, admired by some, reviled by others, but to almost everyone in his orbit an object of curiosity and fascination. "How could you work for Luce?" was a question serious writers such as Dwight Macdonald often encountered from friends and literary colleagues. And yet many important writers did flock to Time Inc. Some of them stayed for decades, attracted in part by the good pay but also in part by Luce's own magnetism and energy.

He was still a very young man. (He turned thirty-seven in 1935.) He had good reason to feel satisfied with what he had achieved. *Time* itself was healthy, robust, and consistently profitable even during a deep Depression. The erratic performance of its managing editor, John Martin, who was dogged by alcoholism and apparent depression, troubled Luce. But the rise of the talented and reliable John Shaw Billings, who now edited National Affairs, and the continued if controversial competency of Foreign Affairs editor Laird Goldsborough kept *Time* on a stable track. *Fortune* was admired, popular, and financially stable. In September 1931, Luce leased two floors in the prestigious Chrysler Building as if to announce Time Inc.'s transition from a presumptuous fledgling company to a publishing giant. "This was an extravagance," he said of the move in a memo to the staff. "I believe we will not regret it because of the satisfaction to be derived from such a unique place to work." Within a few years the company had expanded to all or part of eight floors.[1]

But success, however gratifying, did not create satisfaction. Luce was always searching for new challenges and new purposes. Early in 1932 he decided, almost abruptly, to change course, at least for a while. He made plans for a three-month trip around the world.

Luce had been an enthusiastic traveler as a boy and a young man. But since his return in 1921 from his year in England and Europe, he had done relatively little traveling and had left the country only twice—in 1927 and 1931—for brief trips to France with Lila. Now travel became again a central part of his life. To his father, who was "mystified as to the purposes of my trip," Luce explained that it would be a "vacation—sheer idleness! . . . I'm going to leave behind an awful pile of mental baggage." But Luce was as incapable of "sheer idleness" as he was of leaving behind his "mental baggage." The trip was a product both of his own insatiable curiosity and his belief that he must educate himself to guide the future of his magazines and to play a larger role in the world.[2]

He did not want to travel alone, but he apparently never considered asking Lila to join him. The trip would likely be too arduous and too dangerous, he explained to her, and he had no intention of traveling with his two young boys, Hank and Peter, in tow. Instead he asked Leslie Severinghaus—the husband of his sister Emmavail and now a high-school English teacher in suburban Philadelphia—to accompany him. ("I'd rather have you with me than anyone else," Severinghaus later recalled Harry saying.) The two men were not close, and Les was surprised—even if pleased—by the invitation to join his brother-in-law. Harry never explained his choice, but it is reasonable to assume that Les's modest, self-effacing manner and his fluency in Chinese were among his attractions. (The earlier tension with Emmavail had eased, and she was now friendly with Lila—perhaps another reason for his choice.)[3]

After a cross-country trip by train and two hectic days of sightseeing in Seattle and Victoria, they boarded the Canadian Pacific steamship *Empress of China* on May 7 for the long voyage across the Pacific. Except for a short interlude in Hawaii, during which Luce raced frantically from one meeting with local dignitaries to another, they were at sea for just over two weeks. There were relatively few passengers in first class, and it did not take long for boredom to set in. Luce spent much of his time reading, exercised every day in the gym and the saltwater pool, and tried—not always successfully—to avoid the bridge games and idle social conversations with which most passengers filled the day. It was, he wrote Lila, "the dullest trip I have *ever* made," leavened only by the presence on board of the missionary Leighton Stuart, president of Yenching University and a close associate of Harry's father. Although Harry brought most shipboard conversations to an abrupt end as soon as he became bored (which was generally very quickly), he often sat up late into the night talking with Stuart and reconnecting himself with China.[4]

He spent six crowded days sightseeing in Japan—"very drab" with an "occasional bit of loveliness," he described it. But he was already preoccupied with his impending return to China, which was the real purpose of the trip. In "a few lazy hours," he said, he had formed a "workable notion of the simple (though, of course, fascinating) history of the Island Empire. But China! . . . Here we have to deal with the complete gigantic and elaborate symphonies of the human heart, its incomprehensible discords and its resolutions of breath-taking sublimity. Oh brave new world! . . . Oh China!" (Aldous Huxley's newly published novel had been part of his shipboard reading.)[5]

Harry and Les rose before dawn—both of them too excited to sleep—to watch the Chinese shoreline come into view. Their first glimpse of the country was a nightmarish landscape of physical devastation, the product of recent Japanese air and gunboat attacks, which were among the first battles of a war that would continue for more than a decade. But once on shore they were whisked through customs and taken quickly to Shanghai, where Luce almost immediately began a busy series of meetings, visits, and social events—most of them carefully arranged in advance by the network of family friends and business acquaintances who had been paving the way for his arrival. Throughout his monthlong journey through China, Harry was at once reserved (rarely talking about himself) and almost aggressively inquisitive with guides, dinner companions, fellow journalists, and almost everyone else he met. ("The curiosity appetite of Harry is insatiable," Severinghaus noted in the extensive journal he kept of their trip. "You should have heard him fire questions at the guide!") Luce was tireless in exploring Beijing, a city he had not known during his childhood, and he organized sightseeing trips to shrines and mountains outside the city—on one of which he encountered an international commission that included U.S. Secretary of State Henry Stimson. He also visited Yenching University, for which his father had worked tirelessly for many years. It was, he wrote his parents, one of the "climaxes of the trip," although in fact he found the campus drab and disappointing.[6]

But to Harry the most rewarding part of his time in China was visiting the sites of his childhood. At the mission compound in Wei Hsien, where his family had lived for most of his youth, he talked so rapidly and excitedly that Les could hardly understand him. But Luce could not help feeling downcast after a while as he discovered that almost everyone he had known there twenty years before was now gone. "The shell of our house and our compound hasn't changed," he wrote, "but the spirit is gone out of it." He had a similar if fainter sense of loss when he visited the "sadly bedraggled" missionary compound in Tengchow, where he had been born (and from which his family had fled the Boxer Rebellion in 1900). Oddly enough, one of his warmest experiences was his return to the British boarding school at Chefoo, which he had so hated as a student. The real highlight of his trip, however, was a week at Iltus Huk, the seaside resort at which he had spent most of his childhood summers. "To be here is indescribable delight," he wrote Lila. "Mountains, hills, ocean, sand (*real* silky sand), rocks, woods, grass—I think there never was such a place. . . . Such a satisfaction to know that all these years I haven't been harboring a false illusion of first-love." He spent his days swimming in the ocean, hiking, reading, and driving around the region in a car he had leased—"an idyllic holiday within a holiday. . . . Along with the tan, health seems to be zooming in every department. A tremendous appetite."[7]

During the almost twenty years since he had left China, Luce had been only intermittently interested in what was happening there. He paid more attention to China than did most of his American contemporaries, to be sure. But his sense of connection had grown faint, beginning at Hotchkiss, where he struggled to escape the image of "foreign-ness" that had earned him the unwelcome nickname "Chink"; continuing at Yale, where he wanted nothing so much as to fit in to its powerful and wholly conventional culture of achievement; and persisting through the early years of *Time*, when he had relatively little influence over the contents of the magazine and struggled mostly to make it a financial success. Among the results of Hadden's death had been a new freedom for Luce to embrace and advance causes of his own, and during his 1932 trip he revived and strengthened his identification with China.

Reacquainting himself with the important places of his own childhood was only the beginning of this new commitment. A more enduring result of his visit was his discovery of a "new China," a China Luce believed to be struggling to its feet after centuries of oppression and backwardness and now joining the modern world. He had left China in 1912, in the midst of a revolution that had brought to an end four thousand years of empire. He returned in 1932 in the midst of a war with Japan and an emerging civil war between the Chinese Communists and the Kuomintang—the nationalist party created in 1936 by Sun Yat-sen and now led by the fiercely anti-Communist Chiang Kai-shek. Among the many Chinese leaders Luce met during his travels, perhaps the most important to him was T. V. Soong, the former minister of finance and a powerful banker of great wealth and even greater political connections. One Western journalist called him the "Pierpont Morgan of China." Luce was strongly attracted to Soong, a sophisticated, worldly, Harvard-educated man only slightly older than Harry. Soong was also a Christian—the son of a Chinese Methodist missionary and Bible sales-man. (One of his famous sisters had married Chiang Kai-shek and had been responsible for Chiang's conversion to Christianity.) Privately Soong himself was deeply worried about the future of his nation, but he kept his pessimism to himself. Instead he excited Luce with alluring pre-dictions of great economic and political progress in a united, democratic China. Luce had always believed in the power of great leaders to trans-form societies. Now the discovery of this new political and financial elite seemed to him to promise the fulfillment of his father's dreams of draw-ing China into the modern, Western, Christian world.[8]

That Luce could leave China in 1932 with such confidence in the nation's future was a measure of how selectively he processed his own experiences. Although he saw many signs of apparent progress and sta-bility during his travels, he also saw areas devastated by the expanding conflict with Japan, the growing civil war, widespread poverty and famine, and a governing elite that, however urbane and Christian, was awash in corruption and incompetence—and itself deeply divided. (Soong, for example, saw Chiang's preoccupation with fighting the Chi-nese Communists as a dangerous distraction from the more important conflict with Japan.) All this, Luce chose to believe, was simply the nec-essary price of China's wrenching transition to modernity—a transition the United States should support whatever the cost.[9]

The next leg of Luce's journey took him across the Soviet Union on the famous Trans-Siberian Railroad. He had traveled through China focusing on whatever buttressed his affection for the country, but his trip through Russia evoked what he described as a "violent dislike," much of which had preceded his actual arrival in the country. Russia was, he said, a "100% proletarian" society, whose people were "sloppy and boorish," with "an atrocious body odor." Indeed, the "stink" of Russia was perhaps his single most vivid impression of the country—perhaps understandably, given that he spent six days in a crowded, unventilated train filled mostly with Russian farmers and workers. He and Les had booked "first-class" accommodations, but there was little deference to such distinctions on the Trans-Siberian. As the train filled up, passengers squeezed into every available space, including Harry's supposedly private compartment (which he had refused to share with Les and which instead attracted a Russian woman and her five-year-old son, who used the compartment's small washbasin as a urinal). "Everybody on the train is getting somewhat on everybody else's nerves," Severinghaus wrote in his diary. Suffering from a head cold, revolted by the heavy food served in a dining car crowded with "barefooted Russians, dirty, bearded, and smelling of toil," so overpowered by the "stink and sourness" that he sometimes spent the night standing in the corridor to escape his fellow travelers, Luce began to think of Russia as a place outside the civilized world. The Russians, he wrote in a memo to his editors in New York, were "neither Oriental nor Occidental," a people without "an indigenous civilization." He referred to the Russians he encountered on the train and in Moscow as "natives," and the Americans and Western Europeans as "whites."

They spent a week in Moscow, doing a great deal of sightseeing and meeting with journalists and a few low-level Soviet officials. To the horror of his Intourist guide, they even visited a randomly chosen "typical Moscow apartment" identified for him by a fellow journalist. Moscow did little to change Luce's grim views of the Russian people, but it did much to increase his alarm about Stalin's regime. "The belt is being tightened," he wrote from Moscow, "by the screws of Terror." The journalists he met were "practically unanimous" in their loathing of the Soviet regime—and united as well in their contempt for the few Western journalists there, most notably Walter Duranty of the *New York Times*, who shamelessly continued to write optimistically about Stalin's policies. "Duranty—you take him seriously in America?" a hardened French reporter dismissively asked Luce.

Approaching the border with Poland after two weeks in the Soviet Union, Luce sourly watched the last miles of the "scrabbly," "drab" Russian landscape from another "stinky and dirty" train. Crossing into Poland was, he wrote, like entering "Paradise." He was dazzled by the contrast—"a beautiful sunny day," "the most beautiful railroad car in the world. Clean, glistening, all-steel, immaculate." Waiters came by offering ice cream and cake, while Luce admired the "perfectly cylindrical haystacks" in the fields outside, the "contented cows," the "buxom hausfraus positively stylish in black dresses trimmed with white lace. . . . Never in all my tens of thousands of miles of travel has a border seemed to signify so much." Looking back on his time in Russia, he wrote, "I don't think I learned or heard a single basic fact" that he did not already know from a recent *Fortune* article he had helped edit months before. And so Luce, the veteran traveler, came to the end of his long journey of education having absorbed many new images and many powerful impressions, but having interpreted them all through the lens of his already settled beliefs.[10]

Before returning home, Luce spent a few days in Western Europe with Lila and the boys, but he was already impatient to return to his company. The Great Depression (as it was now coming to be known) was heading toward its nadir. A critical presidential election was only months away. For now, at least, one of the biggest stories in the world was happening in the United States, and Luce was eager to be part of it. Time Inc. itself had so far largely escaped the impact of the Depression. Advertising dropped significantly in 1932, but far less than it did for most other publishers. And in 1933, both advertising and profits resumed their upward momentum. Luce was certainly aware of the momentousness of the crisis, and he periodically raised alarms within the company about "economic conditions," at one point proposing—but never enacting—a salary freeze for all employees. From time to time he examined expense accounts for waste. But the reality of the Depression had very little impact on his personal life or on his company's fortunes at the same time that the crisis became a powerful story that shaped the future of his magazines.[11]

Even without serious financial worries, Luce remained restless, tense, and unpredictable—"very fidgety . . . harassed and hard-hearted," one of his editors noticed. To a large degree this took the form of what Billings called "nervous, strange . . . high pressure" intrusion into the writing and editing of the magazines. Luce was, of course, editor in chief of all Time Inc. publications, but the managing editors of *Time* and *Fortune* were mainly responsible for the contents of the magazines. Luce's engagement was frequent enough to unsettle the routine of the editors and their staffs but not consistent enough to give him real control. In the fall of 1932, for example, Luce urged editors to highlight the accomplishments of the beleaguered Herbert Hoover, hoping to improve the president's chances of reelection. Most of his editors, however, wanted Roosevelt to win, and they quietly ignored his suggestions. When Luce pushed to have Hoover on the cover of *Time* shortly before the election, Larsen took him aside and talked him out of it. More often Luce simply dabbled. He gave after-the-fact notes to editors and picked up individual pieces almost randomly and rewrote them. Sometimes he tore a story apart, then—unable to concentrate long enough to fix it—dumped the ruins on an editor's desk and departed. Once he spent a morning cutting a few lines out of a small piece and then writing a memo to the staff about it, as if to make clear that he remained in charge. "I got fussing with it," he wrote. "Fuss. Fuss. Fuss. I fussed for an hour. At the hour's end, I had in 30 lines every single fact which was in the 50 lines." Because he was so unpredictable his staff was often on edge. "Luce rarely expresses satisfaction," Billings complained in his diary, " . . . a devil to please. . . . He never has any praise for anybody."[12]

And yet Luce could also be encouraging and generous. His editors generally hung on his approval, however infrequently expressed, and reveled in his occasional compliments. "Luce was rather critical," Billings noted in 1933. "I must get used to that. . . . But I am devoted to him—and would work my heart out for him." Luce was a shrewd judge of quality and, however hard-driving he might be, moved gently when he had to change or dismiss struggling personnel. In the early 1930s he found himself with real competition for the first time when *News-week**

began publication. No one at *Time* was much impressed with the new magazine. ("Dull and stodgy," Billings wrote. "This first issue doesn't frighten us. Most of its writers . . . were fired from *Time* for incompetence.") But Luce understood the potential danger and moved quickly to shake up his own editorial staff. John S. Martin's deteriorating behavior had become increasingly disturbing, and, Luce believed, threatened the future of *Time*. He had always deplored but tolerated Martin's conspicuous womanizing. But what made him finally lose patience was Martin's increased drinking and frequent absences. ("He gets drunk and says the most outrageous things about Luce . . . a horrible mess," Billings confided to his diary.) Luce finally eased Martin out as managing editor of *Time* in October 1933. He replaced him with Billings, who had already proved himself a brilliant if unflamboyant editor—perhaps the most talented ever to serve under Luce. Billings was from an aristocratic southern family, and maintained a large, historic (and expensive) family plantation—Redcliffe, in Aiken, South Carolina. He privately yearned at times for fame and visibility of his own. He longed to travel. He looked

*The hyphen disappeared in 1937.

enviously at the glittering social world that Luce (and a few of his other Time Inc. colleagues) inhabited. But he rarely achieved, or even spoke of, any of these ambitions, and seemed slowly to abandon them (especially after the traumatic death in infancy of his only child). He gradually became what, at first, he had only appeared to be: a sober, somewhat reclusive man, deeply devoted to his wife and content to provide sure and steady editorial guidance to *Time*.[13]

Once Billings took over, Luce's intrusions into the editorial life of *Time* became less frequent (although, to Billings, more unnerving when they did occur). Luce continued to take an active hand in *Fortune*, especially during its ideological tumult in the mid-1930s. But little by little he began thinking of new ventures. In March 1932, to the surprise of some of his colleagues, Luce bought an obscure magazine, *Architectural Forum*, which (having begun its life in the nineteenth century with the prosaic title *Brickbuilder*) had become a glossy but specialized trade journal for architects. Luce had recently developed an interest in architecture on his own and, as was often the case, assumed that anything that interested him would likely interest others. He had even toyed for a time with launching a new architectural magazine himself and had hired a recent Princeton graduate, C. D. Jackson (who was eventually to become a major figure in Time Inc.), to help him develop the idea. They produced a dummy issue, under the title *Skyline*, but never had enough confidence in it to proceed. *Architectural Forum* took its place. The magazine would, Luce wrote in his announcement of the purchase, chronicle "the several elements of the building world—architects, engineers, contractors, workmen, investors"—that were "at last integrating a great single industry."

There could hardly have been a less promising moment to invest in a magazine devoted to the construction industry, which was hit harder than most economic sectors by the Great Depression. Time Inc's own research—quoted in the dummy of *Skyline*—found the president of the American Institute of Architects warning architects to avoid New York City. Another architect asked, "We wonder if there will ever be a building again." But Luce's real interest was less in the economics of architecture than in its aesthetics and innovations, an outgrowth, perhaps, of *Fortune*'s interest in design. "We do not know when business will turn," he wrote to some of his investors and employees. "We do know that great changes in the building art lie ahead. . . . We believe that the architect, as he has been in days past, will again be the decisive factor in the rate and character of building progress." Luce liked the *Forum*

because its longtime editor, Howard Myers, used it to showcase important young American and European designers. It was also unusual
among trade journals in giving significant attention to the architecture
and design of private homes. That gave the *Forum* a small but significant
audience outside the professional world, among readers interested in
home design, and made it a precursor of the soon-to-be robust market
for what became known as shelter magazines. (Twenty years later *Architectural Forum* spun off its housing coverage into a second magazine
directed at a wider audience, *House and Home.*)

Architectural Forum never became a fully integrated part of Time
Inc. Myers stayed on as editor, and the magazine remained a largely
autonomous organization, in its own building with its own staff and its
own culture—although the merger helped the magazine's circulation,
which grew from under six thousand at the time of the purchase to forty
thousand, still modest, by the end of the decade. Although it was never
profitable, Luce resisted proposals to sell it, partly because it was a prestigious journal in a field he cared about, partly because he liked its content (the magazine once prudently ran a major story about one of Luce's
own homes, designed by Edward Durell Stone), and partly because he
continued to hope, in vain, that it would erase its small losses and generate real income. It remained part of the company until 1963, when Luce
finally closed down *Architectural Forum* and sold *House and Home* to
McGraw-Hill.[14]

Luce also authorized a new publication developed by the Experimental Department (an office created originally by Luce himself to help
him develop *Fortune*, but now a landing place for Martin after his
removal from *Time*). Martin argued that the correspondence *Time*
received from its readers could itself be the basis of a magazine, and in
January 1934 he launched *Letters*—a slim publication distributed free at
first to interested *Time* subscribers and later sold for a dollar a year. It
attracted a modest 35,000 readers at its peak, had relatively little success
with advertisers, and ceased publication in 1937.[15]

The company's greatest new commitment of the early 1930s after *Fortune* was its excursion into broadcasting and film. *Time* had made a brief
and tentative entry into radio in the mid-1920s, taking the news quizzes
that Hadden and Luce had developed to entertain business groups and
turning them into short promotional broadcasts. Later, Larsen launched
a weekly ten-minute broadcast that summarized the contents of the
most recent issue of *Time*. For it he coined the word "newscasting,"

which also became the show's title. The program appeared on a few dozen local stations and was sold to them much like other forms of advertising. But a much more significant experiment began in 1932 with the creation of *The March of Time*, a half-hour weekly radio news show that was broadcast over the CBS network.[16]

Both the idea for and the implementation of *The March of Time* radio show came largely from Larsen. What had begun for him as simply another way of publicizing the magazine gradually became something close to a creative passion—a belief that he was part of the invention of a new form of journalism. Luce never shared Larsen's faith in the importance of nontextual journalism and remained skeptical both of the radio *March of Time* and the newsreel version that followed it. But he grudgingly supported the projects, both because of his confidence in Larsen and because he understood the publicity value of these efforts even if he failed to grasp their potential as powerful news media on their own.[17]

The March of Time broadcasts aptly conveyed their divided mission: to promote the magazine on the one hand, and to present news in the style of *Time* on the other. No listener could miss the connection between the radio show and magazine. "Whatever happens," the show's narrators concluded at the end of most broadcasts, "you can depend on one magazine to summarize for you at the end of the week *all* the news of *all* the world. . . . That publication is *Time*—the weekly news-magazine. A new issue goes on all newsstands every Friday."

The source of the program's news was, of course, *Time* magazine itself, with all its strengths and all its idiosyncrasies—the distinctive language, the sometimes-overwrought dramatization, the heavy emphasis on personality and physical description. But *The March of Time* went well beyond the magazine in dramatizing the news by hiring actors to re-create real events in the world. Indeed, the broadcasts often consisted almost entirely of dramatized re-creations, without very much concern about literal accuracy. In one early episode, for example, the program offered a preposterous reenactment of an imagined conversation in New Delhi between the "nut-brown little Mahatma Gandhi" and some American women on tour. "Oh Mahatma," one of the Americans gushed, "when are you coming to America? They'll go wild about you there . . . simply wild." The more serious re-creations portrayed meetings between heads of state or statements of President Hoover and later President Roosevelt (until the White House protested and the practice stopped). They had a stagy quality that seemed contrived even by the normal, somewhat stilted standards of 1930s radio drama. A twenty-three-piece orchestra added to the dramatic quality of the program, as did the narrators themselves (who were identified to listeners as the "Voice of Time")—experienced announcers with grave, stentorian voices who concluded each segment of the program with the portentous trademark phrase: "Time marches on!" (a phrase borrowed from a Harold Arlen song that also served as theme music for the program).[18]

The radio *March of Time* was never profitable, but it gave a significant boost to the image and success of *Time* magazine. There are no reliable figures on the size of the program's audience, but no one involved with it—its producers, Luce, the radio networks that broadcast it—doubted its broad appeal to listeners. When Time Inc. announced the cancellation of the show in 1932, an avalanche of letters demanding its continuation (combined with Larsen's ardent support of the show) persuaded the unenthusiastic Luce to change his mind—and, perhaps more significantly, CBS to provide financial support to keep the program going. It remained on the air, with a short suspension at the end of the 1930s, until 1945.[19]

Although Luce never took much interest in radio, he was, at least briefly, more attracted to the idea of producing a newsreel, an idea first proposed to him by Larsen. The *March of Time* newsreel, Luce believed, could provide a more serious account of world events than did such existing newsreels as Fox Movietone News, Pathé, and Hearst—all of them weekly, all of them, in Luce's view, "juvenile—and stupid juvenile," providing nothing (as the *Christian Science Monitor* described them in 1935) but the "bare bones 'This happened here' kind of thing." Time Inc.'s newsreels would be monthly, would "get behind the news," would show "what has led up to a given event," and would have a "dramatic coherence," Luce wrote as the newsreel venture gathered steam. While radio was important, he told his staff in an internal memo, "the greatest supplement to the invention of language itself for the purpose of communication of news-fact is the photograph. And the most potent development of the photograph is the so-called moving pictures." The cinematic *March of Time*, therefore, would be "an instrument of significant journalism," in effect a newsmagazine on film.[20]

Despite Luce's initial enthusiasm for newsreels, he played only a slightly larger role in their production than he had with the radio broadcasts. *The March of Time* was largely Larsen's project, and he in turn recruited a talented young filmmaker, Louis de Rochemont, who became and remained the principal creator of the newsreels for nearly a decade. De Rochemont had begun making films as a high-school student in Worcester, Massachusetts, served as an unofficial wartime cameraman during World War I, and then did stints with the Hearst, Pathé, and Fox Movietone newsreels. Frustrated with what he considered the stale, formulaic content of commercial films, he left in 1933 to work independently, making unorthodox films of his own that relied heavily on dramatic re-creations of events. He noted the similarity between his films and the radio *March of Time*, and he approached Larsen in the spring of 1934 with a proposal to join forces with Time Inc. "It was love at first sight," Larsen recalled decades later. De Rochemont was not only skilled at making films, but also adept at uncovering existing film footage (from the Fox film library, among other places) that might be useful for the new series. After eight months of experimentation, the first *March of Time* newsreel opened in theaters across the country on February 1, 1935, after an intensive publicity campaign. It was an almost immediate success. Critics were, with a few exceptions, enthusiastic. "It has been left to *Time*," Alistair Cooke, then the BBC film critic, wrote, "and now 'The March of Time,' to combine for the first time in journalism, intelligence, energy, and aloofness." More important, *The March of Time* was, as *Variety* put it, "box office." Within a few weeks, it was being screened in more than four hundred theaters in 168 cities. At the end of its first year, it was in five thousand American theaters and in more than seven hundred in Great Britain. The crude audience estimates of the time claimed that within a year more than twenty million Americans saw each edition of *The March of Time* every month. "The *March of Time* is now established in the world," the company boasted in an in-house book celebrating the films' success. "It is a chapter in the history of pictorial journalism . . . a new gallery of American faces . . . the faces of the U.S." Time Inc.'s competitors likewise recognized this new format as a revolution in newsreel production. After "the *March of Time* came along" a Paramount filmmaker wrote, "the entire industry hunted around for the real purpose and medium of the newsreel," and there were soon dozens of imitators, both in the United States and abroad, attempting to capture the energy and popularity of the Time Inc. Films. The newsreel even received a special Academy Award in 1936, through the intervention of Luce's friend, the Hollywood producer David O. Selznick.[21]

"Harry and I were agreed," Larsen wrote at the launch of the project, "that before we even consider it, we must be sure that there is a lot of money to be made in it." But by the time *The March of Time* premiered, it was already clear to everyone that there was, as Luce told his directors in 1934, "little assurance as to its financial success." In fact, like the radio shows, the films never made a profit. But also like the radio shows, Luce and Larsen came to believe, the publicity the newsreels provided boosted sales of the magazines enough to justify the expense. It undoubtedly helped that Luce was more intrigued with the newsreels— "the most daring venture we ever made," he once said—than he had been with the radio show. In part this may have reflected his unspoken rivalry with William Randolph Hearst, the controversial newspaper magnate whom Luce regarded with a combination of envy, contempt, and awe. Luce considered Hearst's newsreels to be his principal competition, even though his Time Inc. colleagues denounced them for "the most stultifying self-imposed censorship ever known to journalism." Unlike Fox and Pathé, the Hearst films expressed strong political beliefs—most significantly Hearst's own militant anticommunism and anti-Stalinism. *The March of Time* was never as overtly polemical as the Hearst films (and never provoked the clamor and organized boycotts from the Popular Front that Hearst encountered), but Luce wanted his newsreels, like his magazines, to have a distinct point of view.[22]

There were tensions with Hearst, and even some initial efforts by his company to block the distribution of *The March of Time*. But relations between the two companies improved in early 1935, especially after *Fortune* ran a prudent and disingenuous story on the Hearst empire that deliberately understated the serious financial problems it was facing. ("Hearst . . . means $220,000,000: 28 newspapers, 13 magazines, 8 radio stations, 2 cinema companies, $41,000,000 worth of New York real estate, 14,000 shares of Homestake [a legendary gold mine in South Dakota], and 2,000,000 acres of land," the *Fortune* writers wrote admiringly, overlooking the mountains of debt that shadowed the Hearst empire.)[23]

Luce occasionally appeared in the editing room toward the end of initial production, prodding, criticizing, offering suggestions. "Why do you like it? Just what do you like about it?" he challenged his colleagues time and again. But for the most part he left the project to Larsen and de Rochemont. He attended the glittering premiere at the Capitol Theater in New York in February 1935, and for some months after that arranged dinner parties for friends and colleagues, interrupted by chauffeur-driven trips to a local theater to view the latest *March of Time* (but not the feature films that it accompanied), with the party returning to Luce's home for dessert. Little by little, however, he also came somehow to resent the newsreels. They were, he believed, superficial providers of news, and yet their enormous reach and reputation far exceeded that of the magazines themselves. He complained of encounters with strangers, in the United States and abroad, who associated Time Inc. more with *The March of Time* than with the magazines. (His lack of enthusiasm for his own newsreels may have contributed to his relative indifference toward television decades later.)[24]

Despite its high level of autonomy within the Time Inc. organization—even Larsen drifted away from daily contact with the films after the first few months—*The March of Time* reflected the culture of the company in many ways: in the stylized language of its superheated narration (deeply identified with the clipped, oratorical voice of the announcer Westbrook Van Voorhis); in its broad and somewhat unorthodox choice of topics; and perhaps most of all in its cultural and political attitudes.

The March of Time proudly announced in its opening credits that it was "a new kind of pictorial journalism," and in fact it did set out to differentiate itself from other newsreels both in its format and in its choice of material. Most other newsreels consisted of many short clips of visually interesting material: world crises, sports events, ship launchings, beauty pageants—"a series of catastrophes followed by a fashion show," one humorist quipped. *The March of Time* presented only a few stories in each of its monthly episodes, few of them shorter than five minutes, some as long as fifteen or twenty. De Rochemont was exceptionally talented at acquiring film footage from other companies, both in the United States and abroad, and from the growing number of independent photographers who were shooting film all over the world; so the newsreels, in fact, had more "real" material than did the radio show. But de Rochemont did not shy away from reenactments. Some of them were literal reenactments of actual events by the very people who had been involved in them (senators, governors, movie stars, and others doing on camera what they had previously done in other settings). Others were true dramatizations, using professional actors, sets, and extras. Everything in *The March of Time*, original or reenacted, reached its audience shaped not only through visual images, but also by the powerful narration and the almost unceasing musical sound track that self-consciously imposed an emotional tone on every scene. The pictures rarely spoke for themselves.

The films had their share of fluff: a breathlessly admiring feature on summer theater in New England featuring "the coming stars of stage and screen"; a worried story about hunting and the need to restrict shooting to allow the duck population to replenish; a piece on the sale of dogs filled with images of children cuddling small puppies; and an ominous account of the spread of Dutch Elm disease and other insect-borne plagues, with a militarylike description of "the nation's crucial battle against bugs." But *The March of Time* also dealt with more serious subjects, and as early as its first episodes in 1935 paid particular attention to the growing threats of war in Europe and Asia.[25]

The films, like the magazines, had one cultural standard that they used consistently to interpret and explain events: the progressive outlook of the Anglo-American world, reflecting Luce's own consistent views. Almost everything carried in *The March of Time* either displayed that world or made invidious comparisons with it. One example was an otherwise pointless piece about Lake Tana in Ethiopia, the source of the Blue Nile. "High in the mountains of northeast Africa," the narration boomed over shots of the landscape, "fed in the rainy season by the drainage of a vast plateau, lies a lake seldom visited by white men but of vital importance to one great white nation." The importance of the lake, in short, was that it irrigated cotton fields that were important to the British textile industry. An enthusiastic 1936 story on Palestine celebrated the "thriving Jewish settlements" that refugees from Europe were building there—"a miracle in the desert" that yesterday (in the hands of the Arabs) had been nothing but "a world of sand and cactus where jackals roamed." Not surprisingly given Luce's well-known interests, the films gave particular attention to China. It was a difficult subject, because China in the mid-1930s was simultaneously in the midst of an aggressive effort to "modernize" the nation while facing a growing invasion from the Japanese. Luce's preference, unsurprisingly, was to emphasize progress. As a result, the films offered a relentlessly optimistic picture of Chiang Kai-shek's success in bringing the once-backward nation into the modern, progressive, Western world. Over upbeat scenes of new buildings, museums, schools, and swimming pools, the film's announcer declared that "a new generation acquires a deepening sense of national unity, and a newborn happiness spreads through the land . . . and in mid-summer 1937, China's transition to a progressive, reorganized nation is in full swing." The Japanese, in contrast, were the backward alternative to the people of China—a combination of mindless automatons slavishly committed to the state, and smirking savages bent on violence and destruction. It was a portrait that augured the harshly racist American demonization of Japan during World War II.[26]

Among the most ambitious stories of the early *March of Time*—and the one most revealing of its techniques and standards—was a January 1938 film titled "Inside Nazi Germany." The film was not, in the beginning, a reflection of any strong interest in Germany by the filmmakers. Prior to 1938 de Rochemont had paid relatively little attention to the Nazis, except to display those Americans who were promoting measures to keep the United States out of any future war. The German story was, rather, the result of the availability of rare film from within Nazi Germany itself, shot by a freelance photographer, Julien Bryan. On assignment from *The March of Time*, he shot twenty thousand feet of what he claimed was "uncensored material." In fact Bryan's film was largely unremarkable. Whether because of restrictions on what he could shoot, or because he was himself cautious about what he filmed, he brought back footage that was of high photographic quality but of little real interest: images of middle-class Germans living ordinary, prosperous lives; footage of German youth groups and public-works laborers that were almost indistinguishable from American images of Civilian Conservation Corps camps or Works Progress Administration projects.

De Rochemont and his staff were undeterred. Determined to present a shocking image of a brutal state, they used Bryan's idyllic images as a kind of foil to set up their real message. The "air of prosperity" in Berlin, the "plain cheerful people" moving through cities or working on farms, portrayed what was, in fact, a Potemkin village hiding an evil regime. Germans were living normal lives on the surface but in fact they were part of a society "with one mind, one will, one goal—expansion," a nation in which, "for the good Nazi, not even God stands above Hitler." The upbeat music of the opening scenes quickly turned dark and ominous. The narration acquired a doomsday tone, with descriptions that were hyperbolic even for a regime whose crimes would seem almost impossible to exaggerate. "From the time the German child is old enough to understand anything," the announcer proclaimed, "he ceases to be an individual and is taught that he was born to die for the fatherland. Scarcely out of kindergarten, the child must take the place allotted to him in the great Nazi scheme and from then on think and act as he is told." To supplement the banal live footage, de Rochemont staged dramatizations—thugs painting anti-Semitic graffiti on buildings, police rounding up Jews, loyal Nazis saluting one another in their kitchens— creating the ominous visual images that Bryan had failed to provide. Much of the dramatized footage was shot in Hoboken, New Jersey, because its large German neighborhoods had a credible visual similarity to bourgeois Germany. John Martin, the former *Time* editor now (briefly) assigned to the newsreels, wrote the film's final words: "Nazi Germany faces her destiny with one of the great war machines in history. And the inevitable destiny of the great war machines of the past has been to destroy the peace of the world, its people, and the governments of their time."[27]

The film was predictably controversial—with German officials in the United States and small groups of German Americans attacking it as biased and inaccurate propaganda, and with anti-Nazi critics arguing that the film had not been anti-Nazi enough. Some distributors complained the film was simply too controversial, that it would alienate movie audiences. Jack Warner, the head of the Warner Brothers studio, argued that the film was "pro-Nazi" and refused to distribute it in his theaters. (Warner dismissed the anti-Nazi narration and argued that viewers were influenced only by what they saw, not by what they heard—an argument Luce disdainfully countered with a sarcastic reference to Warner's role in creating the first sound movies.) A few more thoughtful critics, drawn to comment on the film by the strong response it received, expressed concern that the manipulation of images and words to express an opinion—however justified—was a dangerous exercise of a power that could easily be misused.

The most ardent critics of the film, and of *The March of Time* generally, were the intellectuals and critics of the Popular Front—the broad coalition of the antifascist Left launched in 1935 by the American Communist Party. They did not object to the criticism of Nazi Germany. Their critique was more fundamental: that *The March of Time*, with its "chromium-bright polish," was, like the rest of Time Inc., simply doing the work of Wall Street and the capitalist world of which it was a part. The films displayed a "trend toward militarism and reaction" and were "doing exactly what Hollywood is doing: avoiding or distorting reality." The power of *The March of Time* was, however, unmistakable, and Popular Front filmmakers responded not just with criticism, but by creating a newsreel of their own, *The World Today*, which in its brief life adopted many of Time Inc.'s editorial and filmmaking techniques to present what they considered newsworthy events: most notably a sympathetic portrayal of a rent strike in Queens.[28]

"Inside Nazi Germany," despite its occasional critics, was one of the most successful and most watched of all Time Inc.'s films. Theaters that did not normally show *The March of Time* leaped at the opportunity to screen it when Warner and other theaters banned it. It was also, on the whole, one of the most highly praised of all Time Inc. productions.

"March of Time," a British critic wrote, had "won the field for the elementary principles of public discussion," and had strengthened the possibility of "a revitalized citizenship and of a democracy at long last in contact with itself." The *New Republic,* a frequent critic of Luce publications, grudgingly admitted that "it is heartening to see good young blood making a field-day of the creaky superstitions of the movie trade."[29]

"Inside Nazi Germany" was not an artistic or technical breakthrough. *The March of Time* had long ago learned how to shape material to convey a powerful message, whatever the visual images at its disposal, even if on less explosive topics. But this particular story was significant in other ways, for it marked a decisive step by *The March of Time* (a step paralleled by the rest of the growing Luce empire) away from its earlier vaguely pacifist and isolationist leanings and toward a more aggressive effort to mobilize the nation in opposition to the rise of fascism. For much of the rest of its relatively short life, *The March of Time* was increasingly, and ultimately almost exclusively, a chronicler of aggression and war, and a champion of America's growing leadership in the world.[30]

Luce's restlessness in the mid-1930s ultimately extended to his family life. He had a stable, comfortable, but increasingly conventional marriage, dominated by the demands of running a household and raising two young boys to whom he was only erratically attentive. Luce was endlessly immersed in the affairs of his company, working late into the evening and on weekends. Lila—who had tried to show an interest in the magazines early in their marriage—became increasingly remote from Harry's work. She and the boys decamped frequently to rented houses in Connecticut or New Jersey, or to nearby resorts. Harry as often as not failed to join them or arrived trailing business associates with whom he spent much of his time working. In New York, Harry was out almost every night, often without Lila, even though she liked social events more than he did. Real bonds of affection remained between them. Lila was devoted to Harry, but she was also somewhat in awe of him. (Friends occasionally commented on how much more animated and interesting she was when she was not with her husband—"most pleasant," Billings once noted, "bubbling and bouncing around rather ecstatically.") Harry, for his part, was tolerant of but generally bored with her preoccupation with decorating and fashion, and with the frequent presence of her wealthy mother, who reinforced Lila's more triv-

ial interests. The passion of their courtship and their early years of marriage had obscured some of the profound differences between them. But
now that the passion had faded, their relationship was driven more and
more by routine. In 1934 Harry and Lila agreed to move the family to
New Jersey so that the boys could enter a country day school. (Lila, who
had attended school in New York as a girl, was favorably disposed
toward city schools, but Harry clung to an image—largely unrelated to
his own peripatetic experience as a child—of his sons growing up in a
small, stable, sylvan community.) They found an imposing property in
Gladstone and began to build a large house (designed to resemble the
French châteaus that Lila loved) on a hill overlooking the pristine New
Jersey countryside. There was nothing to suggest that the marriage was
in jeopardy. Indeed, it might have survived indefinitely had it not been
for Harry's unplanned meeting with a woman who would change his,
and his family's, life: Clare Boothe Brokaw.[31]

Clare Boothe was born in New York City on March 10, 1903, into a
family clinging precariously—and not wholly successfully—to middle-
class respectability. Her mother, Ann Clare Snyder, was the daughter of
an immigrant butcher whom she later described, falsely, as the son of an
impoverished Austrian nobleman. As a young woman Ann Snyder was
an unsuccessful actress and dancer, and she never wholly lost her taste
for the fast, itinerant life of the show-business world. Clare's father,
William Boothe, was an off-and-on businessman and a professional
musician who periodically changed his name to escape his creditors.
William was already married to the first of his three legal wives when his
relationship with Ann began in 1901; he never married her. They lived
together in Tennessee for several years (then using the name "Murphy")
while Boothe embarked on a failed career as a violin teacher. Ann left
him in 1912 and returned to New York with Clare and Clare's younger
brother, David, and she sustained herself for several years through relationships with wealthy (and sometimes married) men. Joel Jacobs, a successful, unmarried businessman, took a special interest in the family and
provided them with enough financial support to allow Ann to send her
children to a series of elite boarding schools, which Clare mostly hated.
"I never drew a happy breath in my entire childhood," Clare later wrote
in a fragment of an unfinished and unpublished memoir.[32]

Shortly after World War I Ann began a relationship with Elmer
Austin, a successful and sophisticated surgeon whom she married in
1921, after vacillating for more than a year between the wealthier Jacobs

and the more "respectable" (non-Jewish) Austin. The marriage secured Clare's access to the world of wealth and privilege in New York, where she stood out for her beauty, her glamour, and her seemingly self-confident charm. In 1923 Clare married George Tuttle Brokaw, a socially prominent heir to a clothing fortune who was twenty-three years her senior. Their daughter, Ann, was born the following year. But the marriage was a disaster from the start. Brokaw was a boorish drunk with few interests beyond riding, golf, and gambling. Clare was a restless, ambitious young woman who felt stifled by her husband's dull, self-indulgent routine. They divorced in 1929, after a settlement that left Clare and her daughter financially secure. No longer content simply to seek a good marriage, Clare began looking for a career.[33]

For four years she did editorial work on several magazines, most notably Condé Nast's glamorous *Vanity Fair*, where Clare became managing editor in 1933. But a year later, bridling at the anonymity of editorial work, she left the magazine to become a playwright, an ambition shaped in part by her brief career as a child actress years before. Just as Joel Jacobs had smoothed her mother's path to stability during Clare's childhood, so she herself relied on Bernard Baruch—with whom she had a long-term and not wholly discreet affair—to help Clare along the path to her own career.[34]

Luce was certainly aware of Clare Brokaw for several years before he met her, both because of her social prominence and her somewhat anomalous success as a woman in publishing. Lila was aware of her too. ("Who should appear in our very hotel here—much to my amusement," she wrote Harry's mother and sisters from Salzburg in 1932, "—but one C. Brokaw! And what a stupid face she has got!") Clare, of course, was very aware of Harry—as everyone in publishing was by then—and had even written a short tribute to him in *Vanity Fair* several years earlier, despite her private belief that he sounded like a "dreary man." They met for the first time at a dinner party in 1934, when Luce sat down with her abruptly, talked shop briefly, and then stood up brusquely and left. They had a similarly brief encounter a few months later, which ended equally brusquely. Clare considered him "extremely rude." "He picked my brains and left me flat," she later recalled. But their third meeting was different.[35]

On December 9, 1934, the prominent hostess Elsa Maxwell invited Harry and Lila to a "Turkish ball" at the Waldorf-Astoria's Starlight Roof Garden. It was in honor of the opening of Cole Porter's Broadway musical *Anything Goes* and included a performance of songs from the show. At one point in the evening, Clare noticed Harry walking across the room carrying two glasses of champagne back to his table. "Oh Mr. Luce," she said flirtatiously as he passed, "you're no doubt bringing me that champagne." As the lights dimmed Harry sat down and began an intense conversation with Clare. When the lights came up, they were still talking. After a while he rejoined Lila briefly, told her cryptically that he had "been asked to stay," and suggested that she go home without him. Always obliging, Lila agreed. He and Clare continued talking. When the party ended Harry asked her to come with him to the hotel lobby. According to Clare's possibly embellished later accounts, he said to her: "I've read about it happening. But it has just happened to me. The French call it a *coup de foudre*. I think I must tell you—you are the one woman in my life." Clare was stunned and somewhat incredulous (but also, certainly, intrigued), and they ended the evening by agreeing to meet at her apartment several days later—a meeting Clare must have imagined might never take place. But Harry remained besotted, and when he called on Clare again, he was if anything even more insistent in his declarations of love.[36]

Thus began the most agonizing period in Luce's life. Since childhood he had struggled with the competing demands of ambition and virtue, a struggle rooted in his family, his education, and his faith. At every juncture—succeeding as a prep-school student, becoming a university leader, founding a company that in his view helped enlighten and enrich society—he believed he was reconciling these two goals. His passion for Clare was certainly compatible with ambition; she was, he realized, one of the most famous, glamorous, and accomplished women in New York and someone who would dramatically enhance his own celebrity. But leaving his wife and children was utterly incompatible with everything he had understood to be virtue throughout his life. At the same time that he was trying to persuade Clare to commit herself to him, a relatively easy task as it turned out, he was torturing himself with questions about the morality of his actions. Did he have the "Christian right" to take this step? What would his parents and his sisters think? How would this affect Lila and the boys? He took friends and colleagues aside and, uncharacteristically, poured out his anguish. "Harry . . . couldn't work, had to walk around the block," Billings commented. He had "been through hell for weeks." Archibald MacLeish (one of his confidants) said that Luce was "shaken, overwhelmed, infatuated." But in the end he returned to what he convinced himself was the decisive factor: his own sudden and largely unfamiliar passion. "Love is all there is," MacLeish recalled his saying. "I haven't any choice . . . because I *love* Clare." Or as

Ralph Ingersoll more cynically observed years later, "Any other course was beyond his capacity. Thinking, as Harry always did, in the most grandiose of terms, his new emotion was one of the Great Loves of All Time—possibly *The* Greatest."[37]

In the year between their fateful encounter at the Turkish ball and their quiet yet controversial wedding, Luce sought both to assure Clare of his all-encompassing love and to persuade Lila not to think ill of him. During their many separations, he wrote love letters to Clare that were almost uncannily similar in language and tone to the letters he had written to Lila during their courtship of more than a decade before. He created a pet name for Clare ("Mike") just as he had for Lila ("Tod"). He revived the exaggerated language of love he had developed during his earlier courtship, perhaps because in both cases he was unable to express his emotions except by relying on conventional, and sometimes banal, description. "Enchantress of our Twenty Thousand Days," he called Clare. "After so many years the big really incredible dream came true," he wrote. He was "hopelessly in love." He seemed in many of his letters more struck by her beauty than by anything else: "Darling, darling, I love you. . . . And no matter how often I may observe your face, I shall never catch the lighting trick by which it shifts from brilliant theatrical beauty to the heart-shattering beauty of tender and companionable affection."

Clare, in contrast, wrote more provocatively, and presciently:

> I, you see, have everything to gain by having you—I lose what? A tedious liberty? . . . The burden of independence, the loneliness of self sufficiency, that is all I lose. Precious little in exchange for love (with all its rigors) and companionship, with its joys. . . . But you—my little minister, you will lose a whole peaceful agreeable way of life.

And unlike Harry, she was willing to analyze herself with at least some honesty:

> I am capricious, deceitful, moody, impetuous, and utterly relentless in demanding patience and perfection in others. . . . Altogether you might say that I am a fine subject for a psychological novelist but a very trying creature for a wife.

While Harry was writing Clare, he was also writing to Lila insisting that she would remain an important, if absent, part of his life. "Darlingest," he wrote early in 1935, "(Because that word meant you and only you for so many years, let me keep it for you only.) They were years, too, which, in the short arc of life were, will always be, so important to us both. . . . Someday I shall try to put in writing what I have tried to tell you these weeks—my love and, weak though the work, my deep, my very deep appreciation for all that you have been willing to go through." A few weeks later he wrote again:

> A good many years ago I undertook the responsibility of being, in a way, the gardener of your heart's estate. . . . If it seems unthinkable to you that I could "walk out" on so important an undertaking, it is also true that I cannot construct any "defense" or "justification" for an action that is so unkind. . . . I can only pray that, if I did not turn out to be the magic that might have made roses blossom even in a desert—that anyway, somehow, I need not be only your blight and your unhappiness.

At the same time he was trying to explain to his family the reasons for what he feared would be, to them, an unthinkable decision. As expected, his mother and sisters responded with shock and some horror to the news, not only because of the divorce itself but also because of their sense of Clare as an ambitious and immoral woman. They rallied around Lila and listened to her own embittered descriptions of Clare ("an opportunistic woman . . . hateful. . . . She blinded him with her glamor"). His sister Beth was similarly alarmed, disdainful of Clare ("a coarse and dishonest woman"). She even wrote Clare to warn of the "tragic" impact of a divorce on the family. His father, as usual, was more understanding, concerned primarily about what would happen if his son's second marriage failed as well (something that Harry's mother considered highly likely). "At times I'd find him listless or blue as if he were sick," Billings wrote. He considered Clare "a yellow-headed bitch who is spending his money like water," and he viewed the divorce as "a disgusting piece of business." Harry continued bleakly on his chosen course, absorbing the blows, making no effort to counter them, and consoling himself with ever-increasing expectations of the happiness he would find with Clare.[38]

As they awaited his divorce and remarriage, both Harry and Clare alternated between striving to stay apart and contriving to find ways to meet. After Harry's declaration of love, Clare began traveling frantically in an effort to avoid scandal and gossip: to Florida, Bermuda, Cuba, South Carolina, France, Germany. Harry—sometimes discreetly, sometimes brazenly—followed her almost everywhere but stayed, usually, for only a few days. He was, of course, a busy man. But his reluctance to remain with Clare (and perhaps her reluctance to remain with him as well) was also a product of his guilt. Perhaps that was why his first sexual efforts with her were unsuccessful. (Clare, with characteristic indiscretion, told others of Harry's insistence that he had rarely had a similar problem with Lila, that, as Clare described it, "he simply did it and then rolled over and thought about *Time*.") During a brief, prewedding "honeymoon" in Charleston, South Carolina, in August 1935, they finally had their first successful sexual experience, and when they left Luce wrote her a somewhat stilted and slightly dolorous letter about their parting at the Washington, D.C., airport, from which they took separate planes back to New York:

> They tramp across a street, her arm in his, to a bleak cafeteria. They tramp back. He watches her go up the gang-plank into the Douglass.... She looks out of the little window. He stands beneath the wing. They signal goodbye ... the goodbye of those who know they are forever committed. But it was their first and they were strange to the possibility of being separate.[39]

After months of negotiations with Lila, alternately friendly and hostile, Luce finally agreed to a substantial settlement. Lila received the newly completed home in Gladstone, New Jersey; the contents of their rented home in New York; and two million dollars, roughly a third of Luce's net wealth. Lila traveled to Reno, Nevada, to finalize the divorce. During those same weeks Clare hid away on the South Carolina estate of her former lover, Bernard Baruch, and wrote her first play. It was a devastating, perhaps even vindictive, portrait of a dysfunctional marriage, clearly based on her own years with George Brokaw. *Abide With Me*, as she titled it, opened on Broadway on November 21, 1935, received almost uniformly savage reviews (including a tortuously edited one in *Time* that managed only to be somewhat less hostile than the others), and closed after thirty-six performances. Harry and Clare were married, seemingly unpropitiously, two days after the disastrous opening, in a private service at the First Congregational Church in Old Greenwich, Connecticut. It was attended only by Clare's immediate family and Harry's younger brother, Sheldon.[40]

Luce's marriage to Clare changed his life in many ways, but among the most important was a greatly increased visibility. After years of professional fame but relatively personal obscurity, Luce became a bona fide celebrity—a man of certifiable power married to a woman of enormous public interest. Everywhere they went they were noticed and watched. Newspapers and magazines chronicled their social lives, their travels, their public statements, their homes, their clothes. ("Ma came down for me in the car and saw Henry and Clare Luce on 43d St," Billings wrote about his mother-in-law in the spring of 1936, "a sight that thoroughly excited her.") And now that Luce was a focus of public scrutiny, his chroniclers felt free to publicize their grievances toward him as well. Nowhere were the costs of celebrity more visible to Luce than in a famously withering profile of him in *The New Yorker* less than a year after his second marriage—a profile that emerged out of, and greatly inflamed, a long-running feud between the two publishing organizations.[41]

Time Inc. and *The New Yorker* were in many ways fundamentally different. *Time* and *Fortune* were newsmagazines; *The New Yorker*'s sensibility was largely literary. *Time* aspired to reach a broad national audience; *The New Yorker* was self-consciously elite—not, it claimed, "for the old lady from Dubuque." Luce prided himself on his magazines' recognition of the importance, and even the virtues, of commerce ("Business is the focus of our national energies," he had written in the prospectus for *Fortune*). The *New Yorker* staff was equally proud of its supposed isolation from the world of commerce, leaving business matters to professional managers whom the writers claimed to despise. But there were also striking similarities, which very likely accounted for much of the rivalry between the two organizations. Both were the products of the generation that came of age after World War I, and both were the creation of bright and ambitious young men (Hadden and Luce at Time Inc., Harold Ross at *The New Yorker*). Both magazines reflected the skeptical culture of the young writers and intellectuals of the 1920s and their Mencken-influenced iconoclasm. ("Everyone was in [the Mencken group's] spell," Roy Larsen later recalled of the early *Time*; the same was true of many *New Yorker* writers and editors.)

Time, and to a lesser degree *Fortune*, reveled in skewering public figures with tart (and often invented) language. *The New Yorker* was no less censorious, and in fact built much of its reputation on its famous profiles, which were also often condescending and deflating. Both magazines were brash and opinionated in their early years, and both were largely apolitical but culturally conservative. And while *The New Yorker* prided itself on the quality of its writing and scorned the formulaic

"Timese" of its rival, its own language—although less consistent than *Time's*—displayed some of the same self-conscious cleverness. It had its own affinity for inverted sentence structure ("Particularly dire are the equinoctial storms that sweep the open-air gardens of Greenwich Village tea rooms this season"); its own use of vivid physical descriptions designed to deflate the pompous and powerful ("a rather heavy-set reddish person . . . a young face, despite two very long white fronds of mustachios, blue at the ends on account of having been inadvertently dipped into the inkwell so often"). Dwight Macdonald, the former *Fortune* editor whose disdain for the Luce publications was no secret, had a similar aversion to *The New Yorker.* In their different ways, he believed, both were creatures of the world of wealth and privilege, without any serious convictions. *Fortune,* he had long argued, was simply a tool of the capitalist elite. *The New Yorker,* in turn, was the "humor magazine of 'our ruling class.' " The renowned Columbia historian Jacques Barzun—a frequent contributor to *Life,* who once appeared on the cover of *Time*—expressed his own exasperation with the two magazines. A case could be made, he said, that "the liberal *New Yorker*" was a "match" for "the conservative *Time,*" both exhibiting "the same attitude—derisive, suspicious, faintly hostile." Ingersoll later wrote of *The New Yorker* in the *Partisan Review,* which he then edited, "Its editors confine their attention to trivia. Interlarded with the advertisements are various 'departments,' devoted to practical advice on the great problem of upper-class life: how to get through the day without dying of boredom."[42]

The 1936 *New Yorker* profile of Luce was an indirect result of the inherent competition between these two organizations, but it was more directly a result of the personal rivalry created by Ralph Ingersoll's movement from managing editor of *The New Yorker* to managing editor of *Fortune.* Harold Ross, the brilliant but disorganized founding editor of *The New Yorker,* had discovered Ingersoll in the first months of the magazine's life and had soon come to see him as indispensable—an obsessively hardworking dynamo who brought order to the once-chaotic office during the day and became a hard-drinking companion of the rest of the staff at their favorite bars late into the night. But Ingersoll's relationship with Ross soon deteriorated, a result of what *New Yorker* writer James Thurber described as Ross's "almost pathological cycle of admiration and disillusionment." The once-intimate friends gradually became embittered enemies. Ross was the self-educated, upwardly mobile son of a Utah grocer with a deep-seated resentment of the wealthy and well born, the very people to whom his magazine so effectively catered. He had particular contempt for the owners of his magazine, but he came as well to resent Ingersoll's own aristocratic, Hotchkiss and Yale background, which Ingersoll displayed every week in his lightly regarded pieces on what later would be known as Ivy League football. (Ingersoll "talked to people like Cornelius Vanderbilt," Ross once complained.) Ingersoll in turn came to despise Ross as an erratic and malicious man who treated him, and others, shabbily. Both were people of large egos who did not overlook or forget slights.[43]

Although Ingersoll left *The New Yorker* behind when he moved to *Fortune* in 1929, his simultaneous fascination with and resentment of his former magazine lingered for years. In 1934 he proposed a profile of *The New Yorker* for *Fortune*, and even toyed briefly with doing it collaboratively with the *New Yorker* writers themselves (who declined the invitation, despite Ingersoll's assurances that the piece would be "a labor of love"). The profile, which appeared in August 1934 and which Ingersoll wrote himself, was superficially friendly but—as Ingersoll certainly knew—certain to infuriate the *New Yorker* staff.[44]

"Harold Ross's father was not a Mormon," it began, with a barbed reminder of the editor's far-from-cosmopolitan childhood. "But his uncle joined the Church to get trade for his Salt Lake City grocery store. When Harold was fourteen he went to work in this store and, before he became sensitive about his eccentricities, he used to talk about his career there." And so it continued through seventeen pages of text, photographs, and *New Yorker* cartoons. Ingersoll knew the sensitivities and vulnerabilities of his former colleagues well, and skillfully assaulted them all. Ross, he wrote, was "furious" and "mad" and "had neither the wit nor the ability to write himself." James Thurber was a "blotter-and-telephone book scribbler." The cartoonist Peter Arno was "tall, handsome, arrogant . . . disagreeable," and "his wit has lost its tang." Wolcott Gibbs, he observed, "hates everybody and everything, takes an adolescent pride in it." As Ingersoll well knew, the *New Yorker* writers disdained business and took pride in their purely literary commitment to the magazine. He slyly described the magazine as "a good publishing property," whose "fundamental success is based on the simple mathematics that a merchant can, at $550 a *New Yorker* page, call his advertisement to the attention of some 62,000 active and literate inhabitants of the metropolitan area." Although he wrote positively, if somewhat condescendingly, of the literary quality of the magazine, he was mostly interested in puncturing its writers' pretense that they were engaged in an intellectual enterprise rather than a business. "*The New Yorker* is fifteen cents' worth of commercialized temperate, distillate of bitter wit and frustrated humor," he wrote. "It has nothing to apologize for as a money-maker. It ran more pages of advertising than—hold your breath—the *Saturday Evening Post* itself." He calculatedly infuriated the most prominent members of the staff by publishing their salaries—forty thousand dollars for Ross, eleven to twelve thousand for his most eminent writers. (They all claimed that they were paid much less than reported. Shortly after the *Fortune* piece appeared, E. B. White wrote sarcastically in *The New Yorker*'s "Talk of the Town," "The editor of *Fortune* makes $30-a-week and carfare.")

Although the profile was Ingersoll's project, Luce paid the consequences. Ross decided almost immediately that *The New Yorker* should take revenge, but he bided his time. Two years later he published a savage profile of Luce by the wickedly clever Wolcott Gibbs. In many ways it paralleled Ingersoll's portrait of *The New Yorker*—offering the same barbed profiles of *Time* writers and executives, the same indiscreet publication of the salaries of editors and writers, the same condescending praise for the magazine's success combined with barely disguised contempt for the content of the magazine. Gibbs described "strange, inverted Timestyle" as "gibbersish," the product of "Hadden's impish contempt for his readers, his impatience with the English language." To prove his point Gibbs wrote the entire article in a hyperactive version of *Time*'s own language, as in his brilliant quip, "Backward ran sentences until reeled the mind." Luce was an "ambitious, gimlet-eyed Baby Tycoon. . . . Prone he to wave aside pleasantries, social preliminaries, to get at once to the matter in hand." Of Luce's relationship with Hadden, Gibbs wrote invidiously:

> Strongly contrasted from the outset of their venture were Hadden, Luce. Hadden, handsome, black-haired, eccentric, irritated his partner by playing baseball with the office boys, by making jokes, by lack of respect for autocratic business. Conformist Luce disapproved of heavy drinking, played a hard, sensible game of tennis, said once "I have no use for a man who lies in bed after nine o'clock in the morning."

And of Luce's future:

> Certainly to be taken with seriousness is Luce at thirty-eight, his fellowman already informed up to his ears, the shadow of his

enterprise long across the land, his future plans impossible to contemplate. Where it all will end, knows God![45]

The Gibbs profile of Luce was mostly accurate and far from wholly negative. Just as the *Fortune* piece greatly boosted the visibility of *The New Yorker*, so the profile of Luce certified him as a major public figure and a man of extraordinary power and achievement. It probably did the company, and Luce himself, more good than harm. A man of less intensity and seriousness might have treated it as the brilliant joke it partly was, but Luce—who read the piece in galleys several weeks before it appeared—viewed it only as a savage attack. Perhaps unwisely he asked to meet with Ross and Gibbs and St. Clair McKelway (another *New Yorker* writer, who had worked on the profile with Gibbs) before publication—a decision he later bitterly regretted. Gibbs lost his nerve and failed to attend, but Luce, Ingersoll, Ross, and McKelway met for dinner, followed by a long night of drinking that ended at 3 in the morning. ("Oh, that terrible night," he recalled years later. "I should never have gone over. Ingersoll dragged me there.") Accounts differ as to who was drunk and who, if anyone, remained sober. But it is clear that Ingersoll and McKelway drank heavily and had to be separated at least once to avoid fisticuffs. Luce and Ross talked at length, neither giving an inch to the other. Luce complained of inaccuracies. Ross replied that getting the facts wrong "is part of the parody of *Time*." "God damn it Ross," Ingersoll remembered Luce saying, with the residual stammer that still reappeared at moments of stress or excitement, "this whole God damn piece is ma- ma - *malicious*." Ross replied: "You've put your finger on it, Luce. I believe in malice." A few days later Ross followed up with a five-page letter, which greatly intensified the feud. "I was astonished to realize the other night," he wrote,

> that you are apparently unconscious of the notorious reputation Time and Fortune have for crassness in description, for cruelty and scandal-mongering and insult. I say frankly but really in a not unfriendly spirit, that you are in a hell of a position to ask anything. . . . You are generally regarded as being mean as hell and frequently scurrilous.

He signed it with a bitter reference to the description of him in the *Fortune* profile two years earlier: "Harold Wallace Ross—Small man . . . furious . . . mad . . . no taste." Luce wrote back curtly and coldly,

I only regret that Mr. Gibbs did not publish all he knew so that I might learn at once how mean and poisonous a person I am. . . . Having located a poison more or less at large in society, he may perhaps like to help mitigate it. And this, I assure you, he can do if he will take any current copy of TIME and red-pencil every example of "cruelty, scandal-mongering and insult"—and send it to me.[46]

It is hard not to see in this feud something more than a rivalry between two magazines. It also appears to have been very personal, even if neither of the parties fully realized it. There was something about Luce that irritated people like Ross and Gibbs. Perhaps it was Luce's image of stolid, humorless propriety (an image his passionate relationship with Clare may have belied, but that did not change how he was perceived by the public). Perhaps it was his grim seriousness as he wrestled with the "great questions of the world," the kinds of questions that Ross (and most other *New Yorker* writers of the time) largely ignored. There was also something in this rivalry that resembled Luce's tortured relationship with Hadden (whose personality Gibbs mischievously compared, unflatteringly, to Luce's in the *New Yorker* profile). Ross, like Hadden, was iconoclastic, charismatic, brilliant, slightly crazy, and—at least on the surface—rarely serious, the kind of person Luce found discomfiting. Ross, like Hadden, fought against becoming an august and worldly figure. Luce, in contrast, embraced and carefully nurtured his fame and his power. The battle with Ross, transitory and frivolous as it may have been, provided a snapshot of the kind of person Luce was, and was not, as he entered a new period in his life.

VIII

"Life Begins"

The beginning of Harry's new life with Clare coincided with the creation of *Life* magazine, perhaps the most popular periodical in American publishing history. Together these momentous events—one personal, one professional—changed the trajectory of his career and his sense of his place in the world.

Luce's interest in a "picture magazine" had many sources. Clare, while serving as managing editor of *Vanity Fair* in 1932, had written a memo to Condé Nast urging him to create a magazine for photographs that she proposed naming "Life." Her first two social conversations with Harry, according to Clare's later accounts, were about the challenges and prospects of such a publication. Throughout their courtship and even during the first months of their marriage, the idea for a new magazine was part of the bond between them—a shared professional interest that intensified their physical and emotional attraction to each other. Early in their relationship, again according to Clare, Harry promised to make her managing editor of his new publication.[1]

But while the prospect of *Life* helped bring them together, it failed to avert a rift in their marriage that began within weeks of their wedding. Their relationship had begun as a product of passion and ambition. The passion ebbed fairly quickly, but the ambition survived. It did not take long for their love affair to turn into something like a marriage of state—enduring, but at the same time competitive and largely unromantic.

. . .

Days after their quiet wedding, Harry and Clare left for a two-month honeymoon in Cuba, where they had borrowed a villa from a friend. For the first several weeks the trip was marred by almost constant rain, which kept the newlyweds indoors and restless. Later a cruise on a friend's yacht was again spoiled by rough weather and Clare's seasickness. When the skies finally cleared, they tried playing golf, until Harry discovered that Clare was much better at the game than he was. (They never played together again.) Even the ocean sparked Harry's intensely competitive instincts when he realized that his was no match for Clare's strong swimming. In many small ways the long honeymoon introduced each of them to aspects of the other's personality that their whirlwind courtship had obscured. They were both intensely self-centered and exceptionally ambitious, and they saw each other in part as vehicles for their own aspirations, a belief that helped keep their marriage together for more than thirty years. But each also came to see the other in some ways as a rival, which contributed over time to an increasing coolness and distance in their relationship. Among the prices of this tense relationship, as Clare later wrote, was Harry's recurring difficulty in maintaining a sexual relationship with her, a problem that began before their honeymoon and gradually became permanent. (Both had subsequent multiple extramarital affairs—hers frequent, his more intermittent.) Equally damaging to the marriage were their preoccupations with their own careers— relatively unusual among affluent married couples in the 1930s and a situation that Harry, at least, found daunting and intimidating.[2]

One thing that did keep their intimacy alive for a time was the idea of the picture magazine that absorbed them both. During their honeymoon Harry gathered issues of European picture magazines. He and Clare cut them up and arranged the photographs together to try various layouts. In this exercise as in others, Clare was at least as skilled as Harry, which probably annoyed him as much as her skill at golf and swimming did. His alleged early promises of appointing Clare managing editor of the new magazine were not repeated, but Clare continued to believe that she would be involved in the project. She was not alone in that belief. During Luce's absence, Billings described in his diary a visit from John Martin, drunk as usual, during which Martin "indicated that Clare Luce was the real boss of the new magazine." Others in the organization, including Billings himself, undoubtedly shared such fears. The issue came to an inevitable head when Harry and Clare were invited to dinner not long after their return to New York by Ralph Ingersoll and Daniel Longwell, recently hired as picture editor for *Time*, who had previously edited picture books at Doubleday.[3]

According to Clare's later (and perhaps not wholly accurate) claims, Harry predicted to her that the purpose of the evening was to offer her a position on *Life*. But whatever her expectations, the dinner was, in fact, an organized effort—led by the aggressive Ingersoll—to "gang up on Harry" and persuade him to recommit himself to the company and to the creation of the new magazine. Accounts of the evening differ, but all versions agree that both men spoke harshly to Harry about his focus on Clare. Clare recalled that Longwell said, "Harry, you have got to make up your mind whether you are going to go on being a great editor, or whether you are going to be on a perpetual honeymoon with one hand tied behind Clare's back." Understandably offended, Clare lashed back, telling them, "Harry can publish a better magazine with one hand tied behind his back than you can publish with both of yours free." According to Ingersoll she said, "Harry, has it ever occurred to you that you have surrounded yourself with incompetents?" All accounts agree that Clare stormed out alone. She claimed later that after regaining her composure she told Harry that it would be best for her to have no connection with Time Inc., that she would instead return to playwriting. Escaping on her own to the Greenbrier Resort in West Virginia, she started work on what would be her most successful play, *The Women*.[4]

That *The Women* was written so soon after this humiliating episode may have reflected in part Clare's own sense of betrayal at the hands of men. ("I would be ashamed to have a wife who wrote so autobiographically," the privately caustic Billings wrote after attending a performance.) The play itself—a Broadway hit and later a successful 1939 film with a luminous cast—was a purely domestic drama. Mary Haines, a loyal and loving wife, is abandoned by her husband, who divorces her in order to marry a scheming temptress. Once alone, Mary navigates through a world of gossip and intrigue while retaining her own dignity. But eventually she decides to "sharpen her claws" and win her husband back. "Haven't you any pride?" one of her female friends asks as she prepares to return to her inconstant husband. "No, no pride," she answers. "That's a luxury a woman in love can't afford." In both the play and the film, only women are visible, revealing Clare Luce's sense of the separateness and vulnerability of the female world.[5]

Clare must certainly have realized by then that her own marriage—which tied her both to her husband and his company—was also embedded in a world in which men and women inhabited largely separate and highly unequal spheres. Harry's world, the world of Time Inc., was one in which only men served as editors, writers, and publishers, while the women occupied clearly subordinate positions as researchers and "reporters." The two groups lived together in a culture that discouraged even such modest interactions as shared business lunches—a taboo reflected in the exclusion and humiliation of Clare at the infamous dinner with Ingersoll and Longwell. Unlike Lila, who had always kept her distance from the company, Clare, an experienced magazine writer and editor herself, was a palpable threat to the all-male culture of Time Inc.—a culture very different from that of the Condé Nast empire, in which Clare had risen to the post of managing editor of *Vanity Fair*, and where women were in many positions of authority. Whether or not Clare's resentment of the Time Inc. culture shaped her play, she was almost certainly right in thinking that the evening with Ingersoll and Longwell was more about their resentment of her talent and apparent influence than it was about Harry's inattention to the magazines. Very likely, Harry's failure to defend her against the offensive behavior of his male colleagues became another factor in the changing character of their marriage.

Her return to playwriting did not, however, entirely end her interest in Time Inc. For years she continued—often with Harry's encouragement and support—to propose projects for the magazines. Billings complained frequently of the pressure from Luce to publish his wife's material, even when he believed it was "tripe . . . unprintable." Although he was honest enough to admit that Clare was "a good writer," and although he ran a number of her articles without complaint, his general view of her was contemptuous. He gleefully recorded in his diary criticism of Clare that other colleagues shared with him in office gossip: "a really shallow-minded [woman], with little native wit—but has a desperate drive which forces her on and on"; "a bitch" who exercised "an evil influence" on Luce; a woman of "intense ambition" who was making Harry miserable and causing him to have "lost all his old friends." Billings himself complained that "Clare and her petty-politicking give me a royal pain!"[6]

The gradual erosion of the passion that had driven Harry and Clare together was the result of many things. Harry never fully overcame his guilt at his abandonment of Lila, and he reproached himself for having allowed passion to overcome duty. They were also a childless couple, even though both had children from their respective first marriages. Harry's sons remained with Lila and visited their father only intermittently; Clare's adolescent daughter, Ann, was mostly away in boarding school at Foxcroft. Harry was opposed to having more children, and Clare did not push the issue, although she later resented it. But most of all the marriage cooled because their romance was always of secondary importance to their competing thirsts for power and fame. Time Inc. was the first site of their rivalry, but only one of many. Harry agonized over the competing desires of his wife and his colleagues and often made efforts, sometimes at considerable cost to himself, to facilitate Clare's aspirations. "I *have* tried and *do try*," he wrote her painfully, "a) not to let my career interfere with yours or with my greater career as your husband and b) at the same time to maintain a friendly diplomatic relation between them." A few days later he wrote again: "The only thing I *want* to say is that I'll promise to be good—but it seems fitting to withhold this promise until the time when my words may once again claim your faith." Clare, in the meantime, never ceased trying to create a public life of her own as important as her husband's, both inside the company and without.[7]

A compensation for their increasingly cool relationship—part of what kept the marriage mostly amicable even if decreasingly romantic— was the glittering public life they were able to build together. Harry provided the means. Clare provided the glamour—a glamour, to be sure, much enhanced by her marriage to a powerful man, but one that the socially awkward Harry could not have acquired alone. They may have realized that their marriage was not the "great romance" that both had once hoped for, but they continued to aspire to a great life. They would be, as Harry wrote plaintively to Clare on New Year's Day 1937 (which Clare spent away from him), "the Luces the Magnificents."

They began their search for magnificence with their homes. Shortly after their marriage they moved into a palatial eleven-room residence in River House, a fashionable building overlooking the East River. It was the first of several opulent apartments they occupied in the city. At the same time they established their official residence in Connecticut (largely to escape higher taxes in New York), renting for a while in Stamford, then buying a larger estate in Greenwich, and finally in 1947 settling in Ridgefield. Perhaps their most ambitious acquisition was a 7,200-acre former plantation named Mepkin, near Charleston, South Carolina—not far from the Baruch estate where Clare had spent much time before her marriage to Harry. The property had been neglected for years, but the Luces poured money into landscaping while at the same time tearing down most of the existing dilapidated structures and constructing a complex of new buildings designed by the young modernist

Edward Durell Stone, soon to be one of the architects of the Museum of Modern Art. A large white-brick main house overlooked a cluster of guest cottages, all furnished in austere but elegant International Style. Clare spent considerable time at Mepkin, writing and entertaining guests, usually without Harry, who came only occasionally on weekends.

Harry was slightly uncomfortable with the opulence and occasionally insisted that they should not live so ostentatiously, but he did little to stop Clare, who had more ambitious plans, from spending whatever she liked. In all their homes they displayed their many collections: Chinese art and pottery, important Impressionist and Postimpressionist paintings, photographs of themselves with statesmen and celebrities. There were lavish displays of flowers at all times. Clare loved monograms and put her initials on almost everything she could—towels, sheets, cigarette boxes, cocktail napkins, stationery. She loved the glass-and-mirrored style of the 1930s and even installed a circular glass staircase in her Greenwich home. They relied on servants for almost everything they did—ten or so in Greenwich and later even more in their even grander twenty-eight-room Ridgefield estate. They were rarely without guests, who sometimes stayed for days, and on occasions months, at a time, playing tennis, swimming in the pool, riding horses—whether Harry or Clare was there or not.

Buying and furnishing homes was only the beginning of the conspicuous luxury in which the Luces now lived. Always fashionably dressed, the oft-photographed Clare now spent much more on clothes than she had in the past, and she insisted on upgrading Harry's own often shabby wardrobe. She collected art and antiques. She commissioned a bust of Harry by the fashionable sculptor Jo Davidson and a portrait of herself by the famous Mexican artist Frida Kahlo. (Harry disliked the bust, and Clare disliked the portrait.)[8]

Clare traveled widely and expensively (often without her husband); spent time in Hollywood, where she briefly flirted with becoming an actress and screenwriter; then moved on to Hawaii, which she came to love and where she learned to surf. Harry watched nervously as Clare moved nomadically around the world, worried by her growing distance from him. He responded by spending even more money in an effort to please her, including an aborted effort to buy her a house in Hawaii. "Oh darling, we have got it—the chance to ride to glory," he wrote desperately in an effort to repair the rift that was opening between them. "I want to start all over again—first with the avowals, and then with the sweet reconnoitering through all the labyrinths of personality, and reconnecting, too, into the limits of space and time and human destiny and then, comfortably, nothing denied us, I want to start all over again with our plans." But the passion seemed to fade quickly when they were together. He suffered from the biting sarcasm with which she often responded to his opinions. ("You have really been too cruel," he once wrote. And "I am sorry," he wrote after another "unhappy" conversation. "Sorry for what? Well, I don't know *exactly*.") At one point he told colleagues at Time Inc. that he might abandon the company to save his marriage. But it was a threat that he never seriously considered implementing. However much he wanted to make his marriage work, he wanted professional success even more. And beginning in the spring of 1936, despite (or perhaps partly because of) his marital difficulties, he focused his ambition squarely on the new picture magazine.[9]

The idea for what became *Life* magazine came from many sources—so many, in fact, that it would have been surprising had Luce not considered the idea. A picture magazine had been one of Brit Hadden's many proposals in 1929 for diversifying the company—one he preferred to Luce's plan for *Fortune* but never pursued. Clare had been imagining a similar project for years, and Harry's friend John Cowles, publisher of the *Des Moines Register*, discussed with him his own ideas about a picture magazine (which eventually became *Life*'s principal rival, *Look*). By 1935, when plans for the new periodical began in earnest, there were already examples of successful picture magazines both in America and in Europe. *Fortune* itself had helped pioneer the use of serious photography as an integral part of its stories, and it had employed some of the same talented photographers who would later become important to *Life*. *The March of Time* had also increased enthusiasm within the organization for the use of visual images. (A lavishly illustrated 1936 book celebrating the newsreel—*Four Hours a Year*—became one of the models for the new magazine.) Many American newspapers, including the *New York Times*, had been experimenting since the early twentieth century with "rotogravure" sections that presented dense collections of photographs, usually in Sunday editions. *Vogue*, *Vanity Fair*, the *Saturday Evening Post*, the *Literary Digest*, and other mass-circulation magazines were making extensive use of photographs by the early 1930s. But using photographs to illustrate a periodical was not the same as making photographs the principal subject of a magazine. Luce and his colleagues had to look to Europe to find successful examples of that.[10]

The most direct influence on the creation of *Life* was probably the

Berliner Illustrierte Zeitung (known to most of its readers as "BIZ"). This was not because BIZ was a true picture magazine. For the most part it used photographs to illustrate text, which dominated its pages. But it was a pioneer in laying out multiple photographs—varying the size, shape, and positioning of pictures to enliven the page. And its most influential editor, Kurt Korff, spent some time consulting on *Life* after he fled the Nazi regime in the early 1930s. The Hungarian-born photographer Endre Friedmann, who later changed his name to Robert Capa, was also on the staff of BIZ before he, like Korff, fled the Nazis. He, too, moved to the United States, and became a staple of *Life*. But BIZ was only one of many European models. The Anglophiles on the Time Inc. staff, Luce among them, were also familiar with the *Illustrated London News*, whose format was much closer to *Life*'s than was the layout of the *Berliner Illustrierte*. In the London magazine, pictures dominated text. It was more adventurous than BIZ in its layouts, in its use of captions to turn pictures into stories, and in the wide range of subjects, some serious and some frivolous, it chose to attract readers. The most artistically interesting magazine of its time was the Parisian *Vu*, with striking modern typefaces, dazzling cover designs (not unlike those of *Fortune*), and ambitious "photo essays" that told such important stories as the return of the Saar to Germany, the Spanish civil war, and crises in Russia, along with elegant presentations of art, theater, and dance. Clare had cited *Vu* as the model for the photo magazine she proposed to Condé Nast in 1931; and one of the earliest efforts in the planning of *Life* was a largely unsuccessful attempt to lure some of the *Vu* photographers and editors to New York.[11]

The idea of picture magazines in the 1930s was not without its critics in Europe. To the socialist Left, the magazines were tools of the bourgeoisie, reinforcing a middle-class view of the world and luring the proletariat into its culture. To intellectual critics of popular culture (among them the philosopher Martin Heidegger, who wrote pessimistically in 1938 that "the fundamental event of the modern age is the conquest of the world as picture"), the photo magazines were vehicles by which "readers" became "lookers," and "understanding" became simply "seeing." That BIZ and other German picture magazines became tools of Nazi propaganda not long after 1932 without losing their popularity further persuaded many critics—in Europe and America—that mass-produced images were dangerously powerful manipulators of culture and society. (Such criticisms augured, and helped shape, the later emergence of a broad critique of "mass culture" in the United States—among whose leaders was the Time Inc. veteran Dwight Macdonald.) But the appetite for photographs overwhelmed the critics. To publishers, they were becoming irresistible.[12]

"The talk—everybody in '21' and everywhere else—was saying there ought to be a picture magazine," Luce recalled of the early 1930s. But despite broad enthusiasm for the idea, the actual creation of *Life* was a slow and difficult process that he almost abandoned at several points. As he had done with *Fortune* in 1929, Luce created an Experimental Department late in 1933 to consider "a new magazine—a weekly or fortnightly current events magazine for large circulation, heavily illustrated." He moved Martin out of his post as managing editor of *Time* to direct the project. Dwight Macdonald, the restive *Fortune* writer, served as Martin's "junior colleague." A few months later, Luce asked Daniel Longwell, the only editor in the company with extensive experience with pictures, to help plan the contents and look of the magazine, as his design of *Four Hours a Year* had made clear. Unlike the slow, relatively quiet planning for *Fortune*, which Luce had undertaken over the objections of Hadden and had tried to hide from him, the preparations for what became *Life* were intense, frantic, and visible to everyone in the organization. Within a few months of the creation of the Experimental Department, the first dummies appeared, using the then-preferred title "Parade." Reactions were mixed, and Luce began feeling uneasy with the project. "We were being completely fuzzed up by all this arty talk. . . . a lot of theoretical stuff," he later recalled. A little more than six months into the planning, he abruptly terminated the project. "No plans have been developed by TIME INC. for any new publication of any sort," he announced in June.[13]

For a time it appeared that the project might be abandoned permanently. "Even now they don't know if they are going to publish it," Billings wrote, worried that Martin might return to *Time* and displace him as managing editor. Luce himself told colleagues that he was not yet sure they were capable of producing the kind of magazine he was imagining. But in fact work on the project resumed after only a slight pause, largely because of the energy and commitment of Longwell—a passionate supporter of the magazine, who fought to keep the idea alive when many others seemed ready to give up. "A picture magazine is long overdue in this country," he wrote Luce in September 1935. "A war, any sort of war is going to be natural promotion for a picture magazine." Having invited Kurt Korff to consult, he found his advice rather obvious: choosing "a good title—a short one"; avoiding "brown color for printing. . . . Brown is not a gay color"; and saving "no money on editorial material. Get the best you can." But his presence and example helped legitimize Longwell's efforts, and he taught Longwell and others to look carefully at photographs, to choose pictures that were interesting and arresting, whatever the subject.

By early 1936 momentum was once again growing behind the project, driven in part by Luce's own revived enthusiasm for the idea, which was no doubt attributable in part to Clare and their honeymoon conversations about the project. "Luce was all for the picture magazine," Larsen observed at the time. "He's got it in his blood bad." The growing inevitability of the project was also evident to Ralph Ingersoll, who had opposed the idea during the first round of planning, fearing that it would compete with *Fortune*, but who now prudently changed course and became one of its champions. Ingersoll drew in Archibald MacLeish (who wired back that he was "too enthusiastic about the whole project to make any sense by telegraph"), solicited ideas from members of the *Time* staff, and attempted (ultimately unsuccessfully) to make the project his own.* Martin (when he was sober) and Longwell also began laboring again on designing the magazine.[14]

In the meantime Luce and others began working on the practical underpinnings of the project: production and finance, both of which presented at least as many challenges as did the editorial planning. Everyone at Time Inc. expected a successful picture magazine to attract a much larger audience than anything they had ever created before. But publishing the mass-circulation periodical Luce envisioned required a kind of printing for which there was as yet no capacity. High-quality photography needed expensive coated paper, which at the time was available only in single sheets, impractical for a circulation that Luce and others imagined reaching and perhaps exceeding a million copies a week. Using existing photographic printing techniques on rolled paper, of whatever quality, was also impractical because photographic images needed time

---

*Ingersoll—and his biographer, Roy Hoopes—make a strong claim that he was the principal creative force driving *Life* forward. There is no evidence to support this view. Although Ingersoll certainly played a significant role in *Life*'s creation once the decision to publish was made, he was never wholly behind the magazine and even two years after its launch continued to complain about how it had damaged the other magazines. "It might have been sounder *business* for *Time*'s proprietors to have minded their knitting and used their wits to move *Time* forward to an unquestioned Number One position in the magazine world," he said grumpily a few years later.

to dry and a rotary press would smudge them. But R. R. Donnelley, *Time*'s longtime printer in Chicago, was already experimenting with "heatset printing," which combined fast-drying ink with a gas-heated printing press capable of producing rapid, clean photographic images. At the same time the Mead Corporation, which had been supplying paper to *Time* for years, developed a new kind of paper—"Emmeline"— which was relatively inexpensive, capable of reproducing photographs well, and adaptable to the large rolls required by high-volume printing. We "presented these to Harry," a Donnelley executive recounted, "and explained to him what we thought were the speed possibilities. . . . Harry said, 'I think this is it. I think this will let me start an entirely new type of publication.' "[15]

The prospective size of the circulation was not only a production challenge but a financial one as well. By the spring of 1936 a consensus had developed within the company that circulation would start out at around 250,000 and gradually grow over the course of several years to a much larger number. The company offered prospective advertisers relatively low rates, consistent with the projected initial circulation, and promised them no cost increases for at least a year. There were tentative predictions of a modest profit of about four hundred thousand dollars in the first year. But everyone understood that their calculations were unreliable and that a circulation significantly above the guarantee would demolish their estimates. The magazine would be priced at 10 cents per issue on newsstands, and less for subscribers—well below the cost of production. Advertising would close the gap, but only barely, and only if circulation remained below 250,000; every copy sold above the guaranteed circulation would be sold at a loss. Luce was aware of the risk, and he considered suggestions for mitigating it—reducing the page count, cutting down the page size, using cheaper paper. But other colleagues opposed these changes. "Never in our history," one of his colleagues wrote him, "have we come out of any tight spot by a choice of conservatism or economy *in the usual sense of those words*, but always by expenditure of more money and more effort to gain greater income at greater expense." In the end Luce's own preference for quality trumped his concern about profit, and he made no significant compromises, betting that moderate circulation growth would protect the company from large initial losses. In the short term, at least, it proved to be a bad bet.[16]

To Luce, however, finding a way to make a profit was a less important and less interesting challenge than working on the content and design of the magazine, and he threw himself into the planning process with an enthusiasm comparable to his early involvement with *Fortune*. To the occasional dismay of his editors, he spent hours each day in the Experimental Department offices reviewing copy, marking up dummies, and flipping through photographs. Even when he was physically absent, his colleagues felt his presence through the frequent arrival of lengthy memos outlining a new feature or department that he wanted the staff to develop. Like everyone else Luce was struggling to develop a structure for *Life*. "He was constantly changing—tossing things out and putting things in—trying to arrive at the right formula," one of his colleagues noted. But there was a certain consistency in how he envisioned the project. It would be as broad as possible in its scope, attempting to embrace the totality of the world, not just prominent people and events. Its signature element would be the photographic essay, an extended examination of an event or topic driven by what Luce liked to call "beautiful pictures" with relatively minimal text. And while the magazine would take on some of the most serious issues of its time, it would not shy away from the frivolous, the fashionable, and even occasionally the salacious. If *Time* had been conceived as a digest of the news for busy, literate people, and *Fortune* had been created to serve the interests of businessmen, *Life* was promoted from the beginning as a magazine for everyone. It would, Luce insisted, cut across class, ethnicity, race, region, and political preference and become an irresistible magnet for men and women of all backgrounds. Unsurprisingly *Life* never really attained this lofty goal. "*Life* means more to the educated than to the illiterate," one of the company's early advertising executives conceded. But the aspiration to create a democratic periodical was real, and its creators genuinely wanted it to have "mass appeal." They believed that a broad readership was capable of understanding serious material and was not interested only in what Luce called "grue, sex, nonsense, and mugs." Those beliefs helped ensure that *Life*, even though it would never appeal to everyone, would eventually reach a much broader audience than all but a few magazines in American history.[17]

Many people, Luce among them, had attempted to write a prospectus for the new project, beginning as early as 1933. Most of these initial efforts presented detailed and often technical descriptions of what the magazine would look like and what it would examine. But in June 1936 Luce decided on a different approach—an essentially literary portrait of the magazine that would convey his own ambitions and aspirations and that would excite both potential readers and potential advertisers. To a considerable degree, the prospectus achieved this goal, especially in its opening paragraphs, which became a minor classic of journalistic writing:

> To see life; to see the world; to eyewitness great events; to watch the faces of the poor and the gestures of the proud; to see strange things—machines, armies, multitudes, shadows in the jungle and on the moon; to see man's work—his paintings, towers and discoveries; to see things thousands of miles away, things hidden behind walls and within rooms; things dangerous to come to; the women that men love and many children; to see and to take pleasure in the seeing; to see and be amazed; to see and be instructed. [. . .]
>
> Thus to see, and to be shown, is now the will and new expectancy of half mankind.
>
> To see, and to show, is the mission now undertaken by a new kind of publication.

Luce consulted with many people about the prospectus, most importantly Archibald MacLeish, whose poetic sensibility Luce wanted to incorporate into the document. In late June, MacLeish had sent him a draft that included a key phrase that appeared in the final product: "things thousands of miles away, things hidden behind walls and within rooms, things dangerous to come to." Luce adopted those lines, but little else from MacLeish's draft. MacLeish, in turn, made some important changes in the new draft that Luce created. The version Luce sent back to MacLeish began: "To see life, to see the world, the cockeyed world; to eye-witness the great events in the human comedy of error." MacLeish persuaded him to simplify the opening phrase and slim down the document, added a few short phrases, but did not substantially change the language. The prospectus itself had an unusually large audience: advertisers, journalists, editors, and current Time Inc. subscribers.[18]

Choosing a title for the magazine was itself a major undertaking. After abandoning the initial choice of "Parade" in 1934—a name rejected in part because of the difficulty of buying the title from an existing periodical—Luce and his colleagues spent almost two years trying to settle on another title. For surprisingly long they toyed with "Dime," which was the proposed cover price (and which, of course, rhymed with *Time*), but eventually almost everyone acknowledged that the price would likely change at some point and that publishing both *Time* and "Dime" would be confusing, if not ridiculous. Another early favorite was "Show Book of the World," which accurately described the goals of the magazine, but which many of the editors came to believe was too wordy and clumsy. There were many, many others: "Frame," "Sight," "Picture," "Wide World," "Earth," "Eye Witness," "Look," "See," "Scope," "Clicks," "Camorama," "Snaps," and "Eyes of Time." Roy Larsen made what Ingersoll at one point called "a pretty air tight case" for calling the magazine "The March of Time," which would capitalize on the name recognition (and large advertising budget) for the company's newsreels. Luce balked at them all.[19]

In retrospect it seems puzzling that the name "Life" came to the fore so late in the process. Luce himself was certainly aware of Clare's preference for the title, which stretched back to her 1931 proposal to Nast. "Life" appeared on almost all the lists that the editors considered in 1935 and 1936, and it received support here and there from many of the participants in the process, including Luce's family friend James Linen (who later joined the company and eventually became its president). It seems likely that the prospectus itself, and particularly its powerful opening phrase, "To see life," played a role in the final choice. The prospectus was still using "Show Book of the World" as a title, but even before its release, Luce was confiding to friends that he wanted the name "Life"—then the title of a once-popular humor magazine that had fallen on hard times. Luce asked Larsen to inquire about buying it out so that he could use the name, and the struggling *Life* publishers accepted with surprising alacrity, asking only for jobs for some of their employees and the relatively modest sum of $92,000 (much less than Larsen had been prepared to offer). Within a little more than a month, the deal was complete, and by early October the company had committed itself irrevocably, and publicly, both to the name *Life* and to the publication of the magazine.[20]

The biggest challenge, of course, was finding the right look, style, and content for the magazine they envisioned. Despite all the models of photographic journalism at their disposal, the creators of *Life* felt they were moving in uncharted waters, determined to create something that would be entirely new. Their initial efforts were discouraging. An early dummy was pieced together at the beginning of 1936 as an experiment in "articulating a language of pictures." It was widely viewed as a disaster: a jumbled mélange of celebrity portraits and underworld scandal with little coherence and even less sophistication. An offensive story about a police hunt for a black suspect, culminating in the suspect's murder, was entitled "Nigger Hunt." Several pages were devoted to a group of nudists in San Diego—a salacious appeal to an unsophisticated audience. But at the same time, it included a five-page spread on the tennis star Don Budge, which seemed to cater to the mostly affluent fans of the game. The second try—a "published" dummy, designed in May 1936 and printed in August—was more respectable in its contents, with striking photographs by Alfred Eisenstaedt and Bourke-White, color reproductions of early Christian art, and stories on Katharine Hepburn and the cosmetics titan Elizabeth Arden. But it, too, seemed to most of those who read it to be a drab and lifeless effort. Paul Hollister, the director of advertising at Macy's and a widely admired graphic designer, was appalled. "It is inconceivable," he wrote, "that even a dress-rehearsal just for 'fun' should have turned out so far short even of where you intended it should turn out as a teaser." At Luce's request he took the dummy home, spent a few days cutting and pasting, and sent back a version with the same content but with a design that Luce and others greatly preferred.[21]

The final trial run, titled "Rehearsal" and printed in September, was better. It included a multipage, vaguely Uncle Remus–like story on "cotton pickin' " that described black workers as "Pappy" and "Cap'n." But it also included a photo array of the U.S. Open golf tournament, inundated by rain; a gallery of pictures of world events; striking and reasonably tasteful photographs by the well-known commercial photographer Paul Outerbridge of a female nude, which nevertheless caused such a barrage of criticism that real nudity rarely appeared in the actual magazine; a story on a Nuremberg rally in Germany; and the first of many *Life* articles on Chiang Kai-shek. Its design was clean and reasonably handsome, although not particularly lively. Some pages looked like dull filmstrips; others—including one laid out by Luce himself—chaotically random in design. There were sharp criticisms from Ingersoll ("so much worse than the first dummy"), a view likely driven in part by his feeling that Luce was ignoring his advice; and from the prominent journalist Dorothy Thompson ("I don't think it's good enough. . . . unmodern"). Longwell himself conceded that it "is no good yet," but he believed nevertheless that it was "beginning to be a picture Book . . . one hell of an invention." Luce was critical too, but like Longwell he was encouraged, and he decided the time had come for the launch. "We won't experiment any more," he said. "We'll learn to do this in actual publication."[22]

In mid-October 1936, only a few weeks before the publication date, Luce decided that the existing *Life* staff was inadequate to the task before them. Martin's alcoholism and depression were becoming worse, making him more and more unreliable. He was increasingly abusive toward his colleagues (and especially toward Longwell, a creative if somewhat disorganized editor with limited managerial skills). A few months earlier Luce had named himself managing editor for an "unstated term of months or years," hoping he could compensate for Martin's weaknesses. But he quickly realized that this was not a long-term solution to the problem. In late October, after a disastrous lunch during which Martin drunkenly abused Luce in front of other editors, Luce abruptly moved Martin out of *Life* and back to his old job as managing editor of *Time*. He described Martin as "a most able editor and an equally difficult collaborator," and he evidently hoped—overlooking the addictive and abusive behavior that lay at the heart of Martin's problems—that once again alone at the head of *Time*, Martin would regain his old form. (Luce refused to do what Larsen and others recommended—fire Martin altogether. That was probably in part because Luce was sensitive about removing Brit Hadden's cousin and one of the few remaining reminders of Hadden's once-formidable presence, which in most respects Harry had already allowed to fade.) At the same time he moved Billings out of *Time*, with two days' notice, into a position he called "collaborator-in-chief" and "alternate managing editor" of *Life*, all the while preserving his own claim to be the real managing editor. Billings, the ablest editor in the organization, moved smoothly and successfully into the work-in-progress that was about to become *Life*—although not without reservations.[23]

"At 5 o'clock," Billings wrote in his diary on October 23,

> Luce called me to his office, shut the door, and proceeded to tell me that a great crisis had arisen on *Life*—a crisis due to Martin's behavior. . . . . He thinks he and I could work well together, and so on. I was surprised and startled at this proposal. I know nothing of the philosophy of *Life* and am devoted to *Time*, which is clicking along well. . . . Yet *Life* is a new job with fresh excitement—and much harder work, I suppose. My answer to Luce was: I am ready to do whatever he thought best for the organization.

A few days later, as Billings began his new job, Luce gave him his first and most important order: "We've been fussing around for six months with theory and philosophy. From now on, to hell with theory and philosophy—you've got to get out a magazine." The first issue, he said, would go to press in two weeks.[24]

The creation of *Life*'s first issue took place in the midst of so much haste and confusion that the many accounts of the effort seldom coincide. To Luce the last weeks were a time of consolidation, in which departments were organized, policies implemented, visual and literary style guidelines created. To Billings "everything was rush and confusion . . . and nothing was really accomplished." To other staffers it was a period of exhilaration combined with exhaustion. To outsiders—including editors and writers from the other Time Inc. magazines accustomed to their relatively tidy editorial systems—what was happening in the *Life* offices looked like pure chaos. Even so, a great many important decisions were made in these weeks that would shape the character of the magazine for decades. The logo—a simple red rectangle in the upper left-hand corner of the cover with "LIFE" spelled out in austere white letters—replaced earlier experiments that involved a floating logo with a more elaborate typeface. The cover design called for a single black-and-white picture covering the entire page, interrupted only by the logo on the top left and a red band at the bottom providing the date and price—again, a much simpler layout than earlier efforts had displayed. The trim size of the magazine was expanded, to make it slightly bigger than the *Saturday Evening Post, Vogue*, and other large-format magazines—both to increase the space for photographs and to ensure that *Life* would stand out from its competitors when lined up on the newsstands. Departments were established, as they had been during the creation of *Time*: a roundup of national and world events (*Life* on the American [or World] Newsfront); a regular feature on a new Broadway play or a new film or film star (later called Spectacle of the Week and then Movie of the Week); a short-lived President's Album, chronicling Franklin Roosevelt's activities; sports; science; and the popular feature Life Goes to a Party. Beginning in the second issue, a long-lasting feature—Speaking of Pictures, named after a casual comment Billings had made to Luce—became the opening piece in every issue, devoted to whatever photographs the editors found especially arresting. Thanks in large part to Billings's calm and unruffled demeanor, the frantic process of invention finally evolved into the careful assemblage of a first issue, which went to press on November 13 and appeared on the newsstands a few days before the official publication date of November 23, 1936. It was far from perfect, without the consistently crisp and often dazzling visual impact that *Life* would achieve in later years. But it was striking, varied, and entertaining.[25]

The first cover was an extraordinary Margaret Bourke-White photograph of the Fort Peck Dam in Montana—then the largest public-works project ever undertaken in the United States. Its monumental, turreted facade, wreathed in shadows, was almost abstract in its simplicity—an image that evoked both ancient and modern aesthetics. It gave the first issue a gravity that helped announce that *Life* would be something important. The cover was tied to the magazine's first major "photo-essay," a portrait (with text by MacLeish) of the community of workers and speculators in the small boomtown of Fort Peck that had grown up around the construction of the dam—men and women drawn to Montana by a New Deal project, but living and working in a setting that represented the on-the-make freedom of the imagined American frontier. It was typical of what became a staple of *Life*—a brief but suggestive image of a place far from the urban, cosmopolitan world in which most *Life* readers lived. Also in the first issue was a lively if condescending portrait of Brazil and its "charming" but "incurably lazy" people; a portfolio of color images of work by the then-popular regional painter John Steuart Curry; a worshipful story (carried over from the final dummy) on the hit Broadway play *Victoria Regina*, starring the "Greatest Living Actress," Helen Hayes; an equally gushing portrait of the rising movie star Robert Taylor; an Eisentaedt portrait of a San Francisco Catholic school for Chinese immigrants who, "slant-eyed and shy," were learning "to say *very* instead of *velly*"; an account of a French hunting party (the precursor of the Life Goes to a Party feature, which debuted in the second issue); a two-page set of images (also carried over from the dummy) of black widow spiders, the first in a long line of *Life* nature stories; and an interview with the cuckolded former husband of Wallis Warfield Simpson in the aftermath of his divorce. But perhaps the most memorable image of the first issue was a full-page photograph at the front of the magazine. It showed a doctor, wearing a surgical mask, standing in a delivery room, and holding a newborn baby. Its caption: "Life Begins."[26]

Even before the first issue appeared, it was becoming clear that *Life* would be an enormous popular success—a result of effective advertising, extensive press coverage, the reputation of the company, and the popular hunger for pictures that Luce had cited as a reason to create *Life*. "It is at once dumbfounding and deeply gratifying," Luce wrote in a letter to potential subscribers months before publication,

> to learn the response to our earlier letter inviting encouragement and support for the picture magazine we have been planning so long—

26,151 answers in one day—
72,955 within a week—
162,450 to date, with still more pouring in—

And saying
"You can count on me as a Charter Subscriber."

There were 235,000 subscribers by the time the first issue appeared—almost the entire guaranteed circulation before any newsstand sales, for which requests were also growing fast. Shortly before publication, the circulation manager announced that because of the frenzied, anticipatory interest "every dealer is to receive the same number of copies of *Life* that he receives of *Time*." "One dealer in New York who sells two copies of *Time* a week placed an order for 250 copies of *Life*," Pierre Prentice, the circulation manager, wrote. "All the dealers are . . . mad that we were not able to supply them with more copies of *Life*."[27]

Nothing, however, truly prepared Luce and his colleagues for the public response to *Life* when it finally went on sale. Some images collected by the editors at the time suggest the character of the magazine's first weeks: a used-book shop with a sign pasted in the window—"Life Wanted, Good Prices Paid"; a classified ad in the *San Francisco Examiner* in December 1936—"LIFE magazine, 1st edition; 2; $3.50 each. Phone VA1. 5927. afternoons"; a drugstore in Detroit with a copy of *Life* in the window below a sign—"Sold Out *But* Read It *Here;* heavily marked up distribution lists from newsstands in La Crosse, Wisconsin, and Keyport, New Jersey, from dealers who were saving copies of *Life* for regular customers (the Keyport dealer rationed copies by selling the magazine to each customer only on alternating weeks); and a cartoon in an advertising magazine showing a group of businessmen around a table, one of them sputtering, "W-w-what's that! You say you saw an unsold copy of this week's 'Life' at a newsstand on 42nd Street?" A Los Angeles dealer wired Time Inc.: "First issue of LIFE caused heaviest demand . . . of any publication ever known. Clean sell-out. We lost thousands of sales, and still a heavy demand." It was not an idiosyncratic response. All two hundred thousand newsstand copies sold out the first day, some of them in the first hour. Dealers from around the country wired their distributors that they could sell five hundred more copies (Cincinnati), one thousand more (Lansing, Michigan), fifteen hundred more (Worcester, Massachusetts), five thousand more (Cleveland). "The demand for LIFE is completely without precedent in publishing history," the overwhelmed Prentice wrote. "If we could supply the copies, the dollar volume of our newsstand sales of LIFE this month [December 1936] would be greater than the dollar volume of sales of any other magazine in the world. There was no way we could anticipate a bigger newsstand business the first month than magazines like Collier's and Satevepost have built up in thirty years."[28]

But popularity in this case did not mean success. Time Inc. paid a significant price for the overwhelming demand for *Life*. Part of the price was ill will—the anger of customers at the shortages. There were conspiracy theories that the scarcity was artificial to force prices up; that tying the distribution of *Life* to *Time* was a "racket" to lift *Time*'s circulation; that the company was favoring some newsstands unfairly over others; and more broadly, a belief that only incompetence could account for the vast shortages, which continued for many months. Prentice quickly abandoned the practice of tying *Life* allotments to copies of *Time* sold, and he deliberately underserved some of the news dealers whom critics had charged (falsely, Prentice insisted) that the company was favoring. But the more important problem of *Life*'s fantastic popularity was a financial one. Production of the first issue of *Life*, projected originally at 250,000, grew to nearly twice that by the time of publication—demolishing the careful financial estimates that had allowed the company to project a modest profit. With subscription and newsstand prices fixed more or less indefinitely, and with advertising prices fixed for a year, every copy sold above the projected 250,000 contributed to what soon became an enormous deficit. Losses quickly rose to fifty thousand dollars a week, and Luce predicted a $3.5 million loss in 1937.[29]

Within the company a debate emerged over how to deal with this seemingly catastrophic triumph. Luce himself appeared for a time to prefer limiting circulation, perhaps to reduce the deficits, perhaps because he was uncomfortable with the rapidity with which his "work-in-progress" was becoming a national phenomenon. But most of his colleagues urged him to swallow the losses in what Charles Stillman, a Time Inc. financial officer, called "an atmosphere of *complete and serene confidence*" and to grasp "the chance of a lifetime." Larsen backed Stillman; and Luce soon gave in and agreed to increase production as fast as possible, and to raise advertising rates as high as possible. By the end of 1937, a year after *Life*'s birth, circulation had reached 1.5 million—more than triple the first-year circulation of any magazine in American (and likely world) history—while the losses continued to grow.[30]

Increasing supply to keep up with demand required an almost Herculean effort. The production of *Life* was constrained by a serious shortage of paper, an inadequate number of presses, and serious fire hazards in the gas-heated presses already in use, which were running danger-ously almost twenty-four hours a day, seven days a week. The challenge was complicated by the uncertainty, laced with incredulity, about how high the demand for *Life* would rise. Every increase in production was overmatched by the increase in demand. Could *Life*'s popularity be sus-tained? How far would the demand extend? In an effort to answer those questions, *Life* staged an experiment in Worcester, Massachusetts, where the initial supply of 475 copies had sold out rapidly on the first day. A few weeks later, Worcester received 2,000 copies, which also sold out immediately, then in subsequent weeks 3,000, 4,000, 9,000, and finally 11,000. In every case the entire run sold out in a few hours. Extrapolat-ing from these numbers, the circulation staff began to believe that *Life* might reach a circulation of up to 6 million. That prediction proved unrealistic in the magazine's first decade; some of the demand for *Life* in its first months was surely a result of a short-term consumer frenzy driven by the scarcity itself. But it was clear nevertheless that the appetite for the magazine was not even close to being satisfied.[31]

In the end *Life* ran a deficit of three million dollars in 1937—driven in part by the company's almost ten million dollars of investments in production capacity and more than five hundred new employees in New York and Chicago. Time Inc. quickly outgrew its once-lavish quarters in the Chrysler Building as soon as *Life* began, and the company soon moved into its own building in the new Rockefeller Center. The result of this rapid and dramatic growth in expenses was that Time Inc. as a whole—accustomed to robust profits—cleared less than two hundred thousand dollars that year. "We are poor again," Luce wrote to his col-leagues in mid-1937. "We are no longer a rich company. . . . So what's to be done about it? What's to be done about it is, obviously, to get rich again." One way to do that was to continue to raise *Life*'s advertising rates for new customers, which the company had done repeatedly since the first months of publication. By the end of 1938 the rates were the highest of any magazine in the country—almost 20 percent higher than those of their closest competitor, the *Saturday Evening Post*.[32]

Many advertisers balked at the high rates, still uncertain about *Life*'s potency as an advertising medium. Luce was concerned that readers did not give serious enough attention to the magazine and thus to the adver-tisements, that they did little more than simply flip through the pho-tographs. Larsen believed that the problem was *Life*'s unconventional audience—a readership that had no distinctive characteristics (income group, gender, special interests)—and that advertisers were not certain whom they were reaching. To help the company and its advertisers understand the magazine's readership, Luce recruited a group of prominent survey researchers and statisticians, George Gallup and Elmo Roper among them, to measure the impact of *Life* and, most of all, to determine how many people were actually reading it. This "Continuing Study of Magazine Audiences" (CSMA)—funded by *Life* but technically independent—concluded in early 1938 that *Life's* impact was far larger than its circulation suggested; that there were as many as fourteen readers on average for every issue published; that the total readership of *Life*, therefore, was not the 1.8 million people who actually bought the magazine, but more than 17 million people—the "pass-along" readers—who actually saw each issue. Although rivals disputed the CSMA findings, *Life* used them vigorously to persuade advertisers that the magazine was an unparalleled advertising venue. Over time the notion that *Life's* readership went far beyond its formal circulation became a powerful assumption not just at Time Inc. but through much of the publishing world.[33]

By early 1938 *Life's* circulation growth seemed to have lost momentum. "We're having trouble selling 2,000,000 copies a week," Billings wrote in his diary. "Hence, we have to pick material that will sell that last 100,000 copies [to get circulation up to the two million guarantee to advertisers]." Luce worried that *Life* might be losing its novelty, that it was already growing tired and predictable. As always when he sensed editorial weakness, he made his presence felt. "We have to get more and more remarkable pictures," he complained. "We have got to have sound reading matter. . . . LIFE lacks humor." To Billings such periods were agonizing, not just because he found Luce's presence intimidating but also because Luce's interventions rarely provided useful advice. "Luce came in, sat down, looked at layouts over for 30 minutes," Billings wrote of a meeting with Luce to discuss "the form and patterns" of *Life*. "Then he got up and said, 'I can't help you—you'll have to work it out for yourself.' " Luce's intrusions were particularly unsettling to Longwell, whom Billings described as "a bundle of nerves and tall talk" and who, when Luce expressed his concerns, "yowled and yammered and swore and shouted—and plainly showed his frustration."[34]

Early in 1938 Joseph Thorndike, the *Life* editor responsible for coverage of the movies, learned of a controversial documentary titled *The Birth of a Baby*, which included an actual childbirth. Even by the prim standards of its time, the film was deliberately unsensational. It was intended to be instructive to new mothers, and it was sponsored by the U.S. Children's Bureau, the American Association of Obstetricians,

Gynecologists, and Abdominal Surgeons, and other medical and social service organizations. Despite its impeccable credentials and the mostly good reviews it received, the film faced strong attacks and extensive local efforts to ban viewings. Thorndike proposed that *Life* publish images from the film as a "public service" and as a challenge to narrow-minded censorship. Luce deferred to Larsen and Billings, who together decided to proceed, and they publicized the event heavily. At the same time they tried to cushion themselves from criticism. They wrote to all subscribers shortly before publication assuring readers that the story would be "wholly and sincerely frank" and "something which the public, and all the public, ought to see." The story as it appeared in the April 10, 1938, issue was understated to a fault, accompanied by lifelessly unimpeachable text—or, as the advertisers put it, "an altogether wholesome spirit." The layout was "a long series of small pictures," Billings wrote, "so as not to sensationalize the birth scenes." The mother giving birth was so shrouded in fabric that she was virtually invisible in the photographs. The entire story was bound loosely in the middle of the magazine so offended readers could remove and discard it, or hide it from their children. Despite all these precautions the story created a modest firestorm of criticism; and even though the U.S. Post Office had approved its distribution through the mails, publicity-seeking local prosecutors in dozens of cities, including New York, tried to ban the issue from the newsstands (largely in response to pressure from Catholic organizations). Larsen decided to exploit the controversy and arranged to have himself arrested by publicly selling one of the banned issues to a detective in the Bronx. The charges were quickly dismissed, but not before generating valuable press coverage for *Life*. A Gallup Poll revealed that 76 percent of the public approved of the article, and the April 10 issue sold out immediately. But the more important result of the controversy was to make *Life* once again a center of national attention. It brought to an end the brief lull in circulation growth. Beginning within weeks of the "Birth of a Baby" issue, subscriptions and newsstand sales were rising again. Circulation passed 2 million by midyear and continued to grow. A year later it was more than 2.5 million and finally making a profit ($950,000 in the first half of 1939). "*Life* has definitely turned the corner," Larsen wrote in late April 1938: "Now is the time to snowball its success trend."[35]

Life's sensational ascent in its first two years occurred despite the widely shared view among much of the editorial staff that the magazine was not yet very good. There were, of course, dazzling pictures and powerful individual stories and essays of which everyone was rightly proud. But most of the editors remained unhappy with the totality of the magazine—with what they considered its frequent blandness, its unevenness, its incoherence. "We all feel that the issues aren't as good as they should be," Billings confided to his diary in one of his many private expressions of dismay. "Are we slipping again?" he asked in February 1938, as circulation stagnated. "Are we getting routine?" "A lousy issue," he wrote in April. "A bad week—and a bad issue—and home with a bad taste in my mouth about the whole mag." Billings was not alone. The volatile Longwell erupted frequently with complaints about the mediocrity of the layouts and the poor photographic choices. Larsen intermittently looked over issues and complained about their dullness and predictability. Andrew Heiskell, then a young staff member, recalled "the feeling on many weeks that this phenomenally popular magazine was not up to our standards—and was sometimes really quite bad."[36]

No one was more chronically dissatisfied with *Life* than Luce himself. Although he spent less time editing once Billings was in charge, he continued to drop in, usually without notice, to take a hand in the process. Luce's arbitrary intrusiveness was driven by the same concerns that had bothered him during their work on the dummies. Like other editors he thought that the magazine was not yet right. "The text doesn't *look* inviting," he wrote in one of his frequent memos to the *Life* staff. The magazine "lacks humor." The pictures, even when beautiful, "don't always *look* beautiful." There was not enough "personality stuff." There was too much attention to people *"Life's* readers never heard of and never will again." But most of all Luce worried that the magazine did not have "a plan" or "a formula"—a consistent and coherent sense of what it should present. He tried at times to achieve this by fiddling with the structure of the magazine: changing departments, reordering stories, trying new kinds of layouts. More often than not these efforts simply produced disarray. "Luce is a disturbing influence," Billings complained. "He hurts rather than helps the smooth progress of getting out an issue. . . . He tosses everything up in the air like a juggler—and then ducks out and leaves it to us to catch the pieces as they come down." Equally often, Luce tried to energize *Life* by reshuffling the responsibilities of the editors—something else Billings and others found disruptive, even when they agreed with the principles behind the changes. Whatever Luce's tactics, his underlying concern was always the same: that "we wonder whether there's something wrong with the editing of the magazine." Even years later he described the issues in the first years of *Life* as "dull and pedestrian."[37]

Life benefited greatly from this concern about quality—and from the pressure it placed on everyone to do better. But in fact *Life* in its first two years was never as bad as its creators sometimes thought, and it was steadily improving. "*Life*," Longwell later said, "was not a magazine until two years after its publication." But during those first years Luce and his editors made considerable progress. They developed a writing style for the magazine, self-consciously different from "Timese," a simple and almost self-deprecating prose that tried to avoid competing with the photographs. They also developed a tradition of respecting the integrity of their photographs. Unlike many other publications, newspapers and magazines alike, that cropped, retouched, and otherwise altered photographs at will, *Life* treated its photographs as finished works, and quickly abandoned the random shapes and size (circles, ovals, and others) that most periodicals used to create visual interest. The editors learned quickly that buying photographs from the Associated Press and other suppliers would not be enough to meet their needs, and so they built a staff of photographers of their own, whose work soon dominated the magazine. The *Life* photographers were men and women of extraordinary talent to begin with, but their association with *Life*—now the nation's, and perhaps the world's, premier publication for serious photography—greatly enhanced their stature and helped make them famous. The editors also very quickly understood that *Life* had to have a structure—that readers needed to feel that they were not simply flipping through a randomly assembled album of photographs. From the beginning the editors had been committed to using photographs to create "essays" on important or interesting subjects, and they refined this technique until they felt confident they were creating powerful works of visual journalism. They were less successful in producing coherent departments within the magazine. *Life* was never organized clearly and predictably in the way *Time* had always been; nor, with its almost unlimited scope, did it ever develop the sense of editorial focus that *Fortune* had from the start. Over time the editors made progress in creating "balance" within the magazine and learning how to "sequence" different kinds of stories, but they also came to recognize *Life*'s unpredictability as one of its strengths. Most of all, perhaps, *Life* gradually became a mostly serious magazine, committed to presenting the most important issues of its time to a public hungry not just for textual information but for images of great events. This was in one sense simply a good marketing strategy, a way of differentiating *Life* from such lower-quality competitors as the early *Look* and the *Saturday Evening Post*. But it also reflected

Luce's own inherent preferences—particularly his belief that any publication he created had to serve an important purpose. *Life* continued, of course, to publish its share of light and even frivolous amusement, but the steady movement of the magazine was away from an emphasis on superficial entertainment and toward a serious engagement with an increasingly troubled world.[38]

Almost everyone who had been at Time Inc. for more than a few years recognized the enormous change that *Life* created in both the image and the internal culture of the company, which many people, including Luce himself, felt had reached a low point in 1936. C. D. Jackson, Luce's special assistant, wrote at the time about what he considered the precarious condition of Time Inc. There had, he claimed, been two periods in the company's history—first, the "enfant terrible" period when "no matter what we could do no wrong." In the early years "we could be guilty of practically anything and get away with it, because when we committed the uncommittable, there always were sufficient apologists to jump up and utter their particular version of, 'Okay, he killed his sister, but ain't he cute, he's only six'—and no more rational explanation was necessary." But by 1936, he argued, the company had long ago entered a second period, during which "the aura of success—the story—the two Yale boys and everything—was beginning to wear thin a little bit." There was "a touch of envy" emerging around the great success of the still-young and still-brash company, and increasing annoyance at what many observers considered its cocky, arrogant, and at times sophomoric style. "We became a storm center in the public eye," Jackson continued.

> Congressmen and Senators discussed what we wrote—President Roosevelt requested that we no longer imitate his voice on the air—Communists called us Fascists and Fascists called us Communists. . . . And all this time our manners did not improve because in the early days we had been too busy to develop manners, and in lieu of manners we developed brusqueness. . . . So people began to take an unholy glee in calling us names and whispering and sneering at our journalistic and business mannerisms. I think this second stage reached its peak and its end the day Wolcott Gibbs's story was published in *The New Yorker.*[39]

Luce, like Jackson, also came to believe that 1936 was a turning point, the beginning of a "golden age" in the company's history. It began with Ingersoll's effort to change the tone and style of *Time* magazine itself—to weed out the excesses of its language, to dampen its polemicism, to tone down its sarcasm. (He tried in vain to get rid of Laird Goldsborough as well.) But if Time Inc. was indeed entering a new era, it was doing so mostly because of *Life*. Luce made that point both privately and publicly as *Life* began its spectacular, if still unprofitable, rise. The success of the magazine, he said, "would repay us more than in dollars by restoring Time Incorporated," by bringing to it "a good will and . . . popularity." People may have respected *Time* and *Fortune*, he declared. But *Life* was different. "It wasn't a love-hate relation," he later said.

> It was a very likable relation . . . "I like *Life*," whereas *Time*—
> well, you know, "I love it" or "I'll fight it." . . . I'd done something which hit the whole big American public . . . whether they were archbishops or truck drivers—they all seemed to go for it. This popularity of *Life*—it meant a lot to me sort of personally . . . wide popularity. But it was also good for the corporation, I thought, in making Time Inc. a likable proposition, having taken some of the curse of hostility off it.[40]

Luce's pride in the popularity of *Life* was on full display in a speech he made in 1937 to the American Association of Advertising Agencies—a group whose opinion of the magazine was of crucial importance to its future. "A year ago," he said,

> . . . we chose to create a magazine called *Life*. . . . It has been an enormous success. Evidently it is what the public wants more than it has ever wanted any product of ink and paper. Nevertheless, I confront you with a question. . . . Should we publish *Life*? And this is not a question only for my partners to decide. We have decided. We like *Life*. . . . I stand before you as a court. Your court is also the Appropriations Committee of the American Press. . . . I ask that you shall appropriate over the next ten critical years no less than one hundred million dollars for the publication of a magazine called *Life*. . . . You will either give it to us, or you will not. If you do, there will be *Life*. If you do not, there will be no *Life*.

Luce had few doubts as to the answer he would receive. Over the following decade advertisers invested far more in *Life* than one hundred million dollars, making it one of the most lucrative advertising vehicles in the United States. But to Luce the endorsement of the idea—that *Life* was a product that people greeted with affection—was almost as important as its financial returns.[41]

Making *Life* into the enormously popular, enormously likable magazine it became—"the most successful weekly the world has ever known," an enthusiastic former editor once said—was a project not only of the people who created it and the advertisers who supported it but also of the millions of men and women who read it. Why did so many people "like *Life*"? In part, certainly, the interest was exactly what Luce and Longwell had predicted from the beginning: People wanted to see pictures. But *Life* was only one of many vehicles for displaying photographs. The enormity and durability of *Life*'s popularity was mostly a product of its concept, its look, its message. For many Americans, over many years, *Life* provided a vision of the nation and the world—a vision mediated by the magazine's photographers, its writers, its editors, and to a significant degree its owner and creator.[42]

Life usually published more than two hundred pictures a week (supplemented by photographs and images in the magazine's many glossy advertisements). Not every photograph was memorable, and not every layout was interesting. The magazine published more than its share of ordinary pictures of public figures and public events. Some were laid out in neat columns, numbered, to guide readers through a series of linked pictures, suggesting a preference for coherence and accessibility over design. The opening pages of the magazine routinely offered pictures of events around the nation and the world, similarly laid out in an almost mechanically symmetrical style. In later years *Life* became known for its slick and often dazzling presentation of photographs, but in the 1930s the magazine's design was often prosaic. And yet the impact of *Life*, even in its earlier years, was far greater than the sum of its sometimes drab layouts. That was largely because of the extraordinary talent of the magazines's photographers, and the editors' exceptional reverence for photographs. Wilson Hicks, the magazine's picture editor for many years, a man loathed by many of the photographers for his cold, autocratic, and sometimes abusive style, was nevertheless a tireless champion of great photography and a skilled judge of talent. Above all he was a true believer in the power and importance of photographs, which, he once said, constituted "the body of beliefs and convictions upon which the magazine was founded. . . . *Life* looked at what people thought and did in a particular way. It stood for certain things, it entered at once the world-wide battle for men's minds."[43]

One of the inspirations for *Life*'s early presentation of photographs—unacknowledged by the editors—was the rapid growth of documentary photography in the United States in the 1930s. Among the most famous examples of this new style were some of the products of the Farm Security Administration's photography division—which at times rivaled *Life* in the quality of its photographers. Dorothea Lange, Ben Shahn, Arthur Rothstein, and many other participants in the FSA project saw photography as a polemical vehicle for prodding social change. By documenting the social realities and injustices of their time, by using their pictures as political weapons, by publishing them in newspapers and political magazines and allowing them to be cropped and altered to emphasize their political power, they hoped to contribute to the projects of the New Deal and the larger task of pursuing social justice. They understood the power of photographs to convey an image of unassailable "truth" at the same time that they manipulated images to convey the messages they wanted to deliver. Many of the documentary photographs of the FSA, among others, were efforts to reveal difference, to portray oppression, suffering, or—in the work of Walker Evans and some others—noble endurance. Such photographs could be grim, even shocking, or they could be respectful and admiring. But they were almost always designed to reveal the "other," outsiders excluded from what was coming in the 1930s to be called "the American Way of Life." Perhaps the most famous example of this ethos was a photograph Margaret Bourke-White took in 1937 (not intended for *Life*) of a breadline populated by displaced African-American victims of a flood in Louisville, Kentucky, whom Bourke-White recruited to pose below a billboard showing a happy, well-dressed, white, middle-class family driving in a spacious automobile. It included the promotional text: "World's Highest Standard of Living . . . There's No Way Like the American Way." Such photographs—ironic, caustic, designed to produce outrage—virtually never appeared in *Life*.[44]

Instead *Life* used the techniques of documentary photography for a very different purpose. It rejected the critical view of social reality that characterized FSA photography and aspired instead to be "likable," affirming, enjoyable. "I think *Life*, like the United States, was not . . . chauvinistic," Longwell said. "It liked people, it liked the United States. . . . [I]f it was against something it was against it in a forthright manner. But it was a huge and amiable magazine. It—well, we liked dogs, we liked mountains, we liked scenery, we liked history, . . . we liked education, we thought art was fine." To *Life*, as to Luce, the United

States was not a nation dominated by difference, division, and exclusion. It was a single society that, however diverse, constituted a distinctively American community of shared values and hopes. That image was visible both in the tone and the look of the magazine, and in the topics it chose to explore. In the post–World War II era *Life* became, among other things, the celebratory face of the great middle class and its new suburban civilization. In its first years, however, the magazine focused more often on the extremes of society—the rich and powerful on the one hand, and some of the same people of modest means that the FSA photographers recorded. It did so, however, not to suggest difference but to affirm the essential cultural unity of the American people.[45]

The power of *Life*'s affirmative, inclusive vision could be seen in the magazine's very first issue—in its cover story about workers on the Fort Peck Dam in Montana. Its subjects were people so poor that they could not even afford the modest rents in the tidy new settlement that the government had built to accommodate them. Many workers had moved instead into a series of makeshift shantytowns, which filled up quickly, MacLeish wrote, with "barkeeps, quack doctors, hash dispensers, radio mechanics, filling station operators, and light-roving ladies"—an army of the unemployed moving to the empty plains for New Deal jobs. The men and women who lived there were, of course, more prosperous than the truly down-and-out denizens of much documentary photography. They had jobs, places to live (however crude and temporary), and at least some money to spend. But they were fragile in their security—employed on a public-works program of limited duration, living far from their homes and often separated from families that many of them were struggling to support from afar. Nevertheless the *Life* portrait of this rough-and-tumble community of the marginal was entirely friendly and lighthearted. "Franklin Roosevelt Has a Wild West," the peppy title to the feature announced. The opening photograph of a shantytown was taken from the air, blurring the shabbiness and squalor that a closer look would provide. Residents were photographed in restaurants and bars, laughing, drinking, flirting. Workers were presented amid the massive technological wonders of the dam, beginning with the tiny human figures at the bottom of the monumental cover picture. "Life in Montana's No. 1 relief project is one long jamboree slightly joggled by pay day," MacLeish cheerfully wrote. "College boys mingle with bums in the crowd." One, a University of Texas student working as a bouncer in a bar, "hopes to be a football coach when he graduates but he is studying history just in case." The *Life* story was, to be sure, a tribute to the New

Deal, but it was also a celebration of the survival of the "American dream."[46]

Life's determined amiability was visible as well in a 1937 photo essay on Muncie, Indiana—the small Midwestern city made mildly famous by the sociologists Robert and Helen Merrell Lynd in their classic 1929 work, *Middletown*, which compared the culture of Muncie in the 1920s with what it had been thirty years earlier. Despite the dispassionate, academic tone of their book, it was, in fact, a lament for a community they believed was being slowly transformed and debased by the corrosive impact of the modern consumer culture. *Life*'s interest in Muncie in the late 1930s was a result of the Lynds' return to the city to examine the impact of the Depression on the city's culture. Muncie, they wrote in their 1937 study, *Middletown in Transition*, "had been shaken for nearly six years by a catastrophe involving not only people's values but, in the case of many, their very existence," while its residents simultaneously struggled (often unsuccessfully) to retain their pre-Depression hopes. *Life*'s essay on Muncie referred to the *Middletown* volumes, and even timed the story's appearance to coincide roughly with the publication of the Lynds' new book. But the magazine's portrait of Muncie was considerably brighter than the Lynds'. It portrayed something close to a small-town idyll—a smiling barber shaving a customer, a tidy neighborhood of middle-class homes, a leafy boulevard showing the elegant houses of the "generous" Ball family, who controlled the principal industry (Ball's canning jars) as well as the city's banks, newspapers, and politicians. *Life*'s Middletown was a place of stable nuclear families living in comfortable middle- and upper-class homes, surrounded by books, glass collections, pets, and children. Even a photograph of a family at "the bottom" presented a picturesque elderly couple stroking their dog and tending to the chickens "fer eatin' " they were raising in their shabby kitchen. Muncie "at play" was the site of foxhunting, costumed lodge members gathering for meetings, community dinners, and a women's "conversation club" that had been active for forty years. Despite the Depression, *Life* wrote, "these earnest midland folk still steer their customary middle course, still cling to their old American dream."[47]

The range of *Life*'s efforts to portray American life and culture was vast and varied, but the great majority reflected the hearty, affirmative, inclusive tone that characterized the Fort Peck and Muncie stories. In *Life* rich people were not very different from everyone else, just more comfortable. But also in *Life* poor people, minorities, and even freaks and misfits were very much like other Americans—goodhearted, sharing a common dream, and doing the best they could. This made the magazine seem at times complacent: a friend of, rather than a prod to, the existing social order. But it also helped make *Life* a mostly generous and tolerant publication (at least in its portrayal of Americans) that at times gently challenged class and racial prejudice.

The popular feature Life Goes to a Party, which appeared in most issues, was notable for its broad and cheerful view of how Americans entertained themselves. Many of the parties it portrayed were events for social elites—an "Oilmen's Banquet" given by the American Petroleum Institute; a debutante ball in Philadelphia for some of the most eminent families of the city's Main Line; a lavish costume ball in the country house of the Earl of Jersey and his American-born wife; a luncheon for a deer hunt in the "oldest and best preserved" plantation in South Carolina; a Hollywood costume party given by Basil Rathbone and Marlene Dietrich. But *Life*'s parties ranged widely across the social and geographical landscape and offered an inclusive and affirmative vision of Americans "at play," a vision that tried to obscure the differences between the ways in which the wealthy and famous entertained themselves and the way more ordinary people did. *Life*'s parties included a high-school prom in the small town of Antigo, Wisconsin; a picnic in Los Angeles for forty thousand men and women, mostly working class, who had migrated to California from Iowa; a night at New York's Roseland, a dance hall where single men could buy dances with female employees for ten cents; an evening at the Savoy, a dance hall for "the boys and girls of Harlem . . . scorned by the black elite . . . home of the happy feet"; even a Ku Klux Klan rally on Stone Mountain in Georgia, which presented the Klansmen nonjudgmentally as people "who sometimes behave destructively but usually are not up to much more than a primitive form of transvestitism." Among the most unusual "social events" included in the series was a sit-down strike in a Woolworth's in Detroit staged by female employees demanding higher wages. To *Life* the political and economic meaning of the event was far less interesting than the quirky fun the "girls" were having. *Life* portrayed them sliding down banisters, curling their hair, "feeding the store's canaries cheerfully and efficiently," and enjoying the sorority-like atmosphere of this "newest type of camping excursion."[48]

The magazine was particularly interested in parties that themselves blurred class lines—people of modest means dressing in formal clothes, gathering in lodge halls or high-school gyms and mimicking the lavish balls of the wealthy; and similarly people of great wealth attending par-

ties in which slumming guests dressed up as farmers or domestic servants. *Life* boasted of the range of the parties it portrayed: "college
houseparties, quilting bees, military balls, church suppers, fashion
shows, football rallies, Indian festivals . . . a brewers' convention, a
meeting of Negro masons . . . a science fiction fans' jamboree." But this
diversity was consistent with *Life*'s more important mission: portraying
the essential unity and the shared values of the American people. The
parties *Life* "attended," no matter where they were or who participated,
were all "great good fun," "great entertainment," "plenty of fun," "a
wonderful frolic." According to *Life* all Americans, no matter what their
circumstances or background, knew how to have "a jolly good time."[49]

Life was hardly a pioneer in promoting tolerance and diversity. It was
most comfortable crossing class boundaries but less comfortable with
racial and gender differences. In the 1930s *Life* paid virtually no attention to Mexican Americans, Asian Americans, Native Americans, and
other minorities. Its relatively infrequent portrayals of African Americans were never hostile or openly racist, but the editors accepted many
of the existing stereotypes of their time. Black subjects were often exotic
entertainers (the musician "Lead Belly"—described in a story titled
"Bad Nigger Makes Good Minstrel"—who had been convicted of murder twice as a young man; Harlem dancers demonstrating the newly
popular "Lindy Hop" with "a native gusto and grace that no white couple can hope to duplicate"); or they were servants, visible in the backgrounds of social and official events in which affluent white people were
the prime attraction.[50]

   Life's most ambitious portrait of African American life was a major
1938 feature: "Negroes: The U.S. Also Has a Minority Problem," with
powerful photographs by, among others, Alfred Eisenstaedt. It conveyed
the real dismay with which Luce and his editors viewed racial prejudice,
and at the same time revealed how different, and even foreign, the black
community still appeared to them despite their claims of American universality. Racial prejudice, *Life* proclaimed, was the "most glaring refuta-
tion of the American fetish that all men are created free and equal." But
the material accompanying these lofty sentiments often contradicted
them. Photography of burly black men working on the Mississippi River
were captioned "Tote dat barge. Lift dat bale." "Baby needs new shoes"
was the label accompanying a picture of men shooting dice. "It must be
remembered," the editors noted cheerfully and condescendingly, "that
the Negro is probably the most social and gregarious person in America.

Nothing delights him more than a big lodge, with many a gold-braided official and many a high-sounding title."[51]

Images of women, of course, were omnipresent in *Life*, and on occasion they represented power, achievement, and talent. But except for actresses and other artists, *Life* rarely portrayed women at work. The magazine's interest in powerful women was largely restricted to royalty. *Life's* first issues coincided with the death of King George V, the abdication of Edward VIII (and his marriage to Wallis Simpson), and the accession to the throne of George VI. *Time* and *Life* covered the succession and coronation intensively. (Both magazines had considerable circulation in England, and were in fact among the principal sources of news in Britain about Edward VIII's romance—a subject the British papers were forbidden to report.) But throughout its extensive coverage, *Life* paid relatively little attention to the three kings who reigned during the magazine's first two years. At first Queen Mary, the widow of George V, was the principal subject of attention and adulation as she led the nation in mourning her husband and guiding the royal family through the abdication crisis. Gradually attention shifted to Queen Elizabeth, the consort of George VI, who was on two *Life* covers in the first year after Edward's abdication. (Not only did the king not appear on these covers, but he barely appeared in *Life's* pictures of his own coronation. *Life* gave virtually all its attention to the new queen.) Queen Wilhelmina of the Netherlands was another *Life* favorite.[52]

The most common images of women in the early years of *Life*, however, were connected to society, fashion, and sex. *Life* was very deliberately not a "girly magazine," and its editors looked with disdain on what they considered their lower-class rivals, such as *Photoplay* and even *Look*, which relied heavily on "cheesecake" to market themselves. But *Life* itself rarely missed an opportunity to display mildly erotic photographs when they could be presented as part of a supposedly more serious feature. "Camisoles Are Back," a 1938 cover announced, when the fashion industry introduced new lacy undergarments and gave *Life* an excuse to photograph "full-bosomed young women" wearing them. In a preview of the future *Sports Illustrated* swimsuit issues, *Life* offered a special feature on women's bathing suits to launch the 1941 "beach season" in Florida—a parade of attractive models displaying what were, for their time, provocative two-piece outfits. The Gilbert School for Undressing, whose principal clients were burlesque houses, became a pretext for what became a widely discussed story on how a woman should and should not undress. The decidedly unacademic-looking "Professor"

Connie Fonzlau demonstrated the "wrong" way to undress, while another member of the "faculty" demonstrated "attractive undressing technique." (A later feature offered similar advice for men.) A lesson in correct posture, a demonstration of how Hollywood taught actors to kiss, and frequent demonstrations of revealing new fashions all provided additional opportunities to portray women's bodies in the service of supposed news or instruction. (Men's bodies made occasional appearances as well, notably in a full-page photograph of the backfield of the University of Washington football team frolicking naked together in the shower.)[53]

Life's portrayal of women, and the uncertain appeal of *Life* to women, was of some concern to the editors themselves, who diligently gathered data on their audience that showed that more men than women read *Life*. "I do not feel that women and womanhood are well represented in *Life*," Luce complained in 1944. He later delegated the most senior woman on the research staff, Mary Fraser, to answer the question "Why are women losing interest in *Life*?" Perhaps, she concluded, it was "all those girls on the cover—women readers resent the constant parade of debutantes and publicity seeking starlets." Her solution to the problem was to move away from sex and toward domesticity. "What about a piece on Diet?" she proposed. "I'd like to see a story on Kitchens, with floor plans. . . . The kitchen is first in importance to women."[54]

This prescription for attracting women was entirely consistent with what *Life* was already doing. The occasional prurient images of women in *Life* were always far outweighed by efforts to celebrate their distinctive contributions to family and community (and only rarely to such male domains as work or government). When women in *Life* were not fashion models or actresses, they were most often wives, mothers, daughters, girlfriends, socialites, college girls, and consumers. Stories about prominent men almost always contained photographs and descriptions of the loyal women who supported them—Albert Einstein's stepdaughter cuddling a kitten; the composer Jean Sibelius's wife entertaining visiting singers from Yale; U.S. senator Arthur Vandenberg's wife pasting newspaper clippings into a scrapbook for her husband; Henry Ford's matronly wife (who "shares her husband's interests in antiques") accompanying him to a social event. In one Picture of the Week, Eleanor Roosevelt sits in a movie theater talking earnestly with the producer Samuel Goldwyn about how pleased she was that her son Jimmy "is getting along so nicely in Hollywood." College women were usually portrayed not as students but as fresh-faced sorority girls who (as in a feature on Kansas University) "cook and clean to save expenses," attend classes that teach them how to dress a baby, and "hope to find a husband on 'the Hill,' " as the main campus was known.[55]

Little changed in the magazine's first decade. "I'd like to see a round-up on the subject of GIRLS," Luce proposed in the last months of World War II, "the girls who are the sisters, wives, sweethearts and potential sweethearts of our soldiers and sailors." Perhaps the most famous picture in the history of *Life*—and one consistent with *Life*'s prevailing attitudes toward women—was the Eisentaedt photograph of VJ Day in Times Square showing a uniformed sailor embracing a passing young woman whom he did not know and passionately kissing her—as if to symbolize how returning men were preparing to seize back the women they loved, or at least wanted.[56]

In *Life*, the Depression was only occasionally visible—and usually through affirmative stories about the New Deal's or the private sector's ameliorative projects. Instead the magazine fixed its eyes squarely on the future. Like *Fortune*, it was in love with modernity, and with the idea of progress that modernity represented. Rockefeller Center—the dramatic complex of bold modern structures that arose in midtown Manhattan during, and despite, the Great Depression—was a favorite of the magazine, as reflected in Luce's decision to move his company into one of its buildings shortly after they were completed. Like *Fortune*, *Life* also celebrated technological progress: steam turbines that delivered power more efficiently; dams and hydroelectric plants that transformed landscapes and economies; technological innovations such as Polaroid ("the new wonder"), consumer innovations that improved, or at least changed, the lives of individuals. And *Life* conducted as well a long love affair with the way in which middle-class American families lived and the homes they inhabited—always emphasizing progress and improvement. In 1937 *Life* celebrated the "$5,000 Dream House" that the New Deal was helping middle-class families to buy through favorable lending policies. "Four out of five middle-class Americans would like to have homes of their own," *Life* noted, and then illustrated a range of suburban houses of various, but familiarly suburban, designs that were now within reach of many American families. The magazine itself in fact became a participant in the wheels of domestic progress a year later when *Life* commissioned "famous American architects" to design eight new homes for families earning two thousand to ten thousand dollars a year— incomes that encompassed a large part of the middle class. (The company also hired a Swedish designer to create simple, attractive furniture to complete *Life's* vision of middle-class comfort.) *Life* helped facilitate the construction of examples of each of the home designs—one a starkly modern structure by Edward Durell Stone but most of them traditional colonials and capes. The plans and models for the "*Life* Houses" were distributed at modest cost to thousands of families, and within months nineteen houses based on them were under construction. "In homes throughout the U.S.," *Life* reported, "youngsters and oldsters are using the models to help them project their dream house."[57]

Despite the claims of Luce and his colleagues that *Life* was of almost universal appeal—that people from all classes, regions, religions, races, and backgrounds were drawn to the magazine—they always understood that their readership was largely middle class. If they had any doubts, their own research confirmed it. In fact, the larger the circulation became, the more dominant the middle class was within it. A survey in 1950 (one of the first serious and reliable analyses of the readership conducted by Alfred Politz Research) revealed that more than a third of *Life's* readers were in the wealthiest 20 percent of the population, and that well under 10 percent were in the lowest. Readership declined on each step down the economic ladder. There was a similar correlation between education and interest in *Life*. Nearly 40 percent of *Life's* readers had at least some college education (at a time when few Americans had ever attended college), while only 7 percent of readers came from the large population cohort that had no more than a fourth-grade education. *Life's* readers were far more urban than rural, far more Northern than Southern, and considerably more young than old. (The second largest age group of *Life* readers consisted of ten- to nineteen-year-olds.) Politz was an independent survey researcher who conducted his "Audience" studies on commission from Time Inc., which published them internally. Further such studies later in the decade showed no significant change in the profile of the readership.[58]

"*Life* for me was like the American flag," the photographer John Loengard wrote after many years of work on the magazine. It was, the novelist William Brinkley wrote in 1961, "one of the most important elements in The American Civilization." Carl Mydans, in his memoir of his own career taking photographs for *Life*, recalled: "We had an insatiable desire to search out every facet of American life, photograph it and hold it up proudly, to a pleased and astonished readership. . . . America had an impact on us each week we made an impact on America." But not everyone, not even everyone who worked on the magazine, believed that

Life was in fact presenting a true picture of the world it portrayed. There was a slow but steady exodus of photographers and writers who felt stifled by *Life*'s amiable positiveness. (Among the founders of the important photography agency, Magnum, created in 1947, were many disillusioned refugees from *Life*.) "I didn't have to spend long at *Life* to face the facts," the photographer John Morris recalled of his early, alienating days at the magazine. "We were entertainers as much as journalists. Photographers worked from 'scripts,' and stories were 'acts.'" Whether they liked it or not, however, few doubted that *Life* exercised considerable cultural authority. It aspired to create a persuasive portrait of the nation's life as the American people experienced it; it succeeded in producing a powerful image of the middle class, an image that fit the assumptions of the magazine's creators and that affirmed and enriched the way in which most of its readership already understood their world. Large elements of society were either missing from the pages of *Life* or were portrayed in ways that made them compatible with the magazine's (and most of the readership's) outlook. In an era blighted by Depression, prejudice, social turmoil, and the shadow of war, *Life* offered the comforting image of a nation united behind a shared, if contrived, vision of the "American dream."[59]

IX

Man of the World

By the time of Luce's fortieth birthday in April 1938, he had been a wealthy and powerful man for nearly a decade. He was no longer the anxious striver, the brash young man who, against all odds, had—with Brit Hadden—created the brilliant and precocious success of *Time*. He now more often appeared to be a reserved, aloof figure, fully aware of his importance and unafraid to assert it. His relationships within his company were becoming increasingly distant. His colleagues noted that he socialized with them far less than he once had; that he even began to ride up to his office in an otherwise empty elevator—not something he ever ordered or acknowledged but a kind of isolation that everyone in the company understood and observed. His contact with his staff consisted largely of sudden and often unwelcome interventions in their work and long, abstract memos about the purpose of his magazines. "He is no longer the shy simple fellow I first knew," Billings observed. He had become "the great philosopher. . . . My complaint is that Luce is so busy being a Great Personage that he has forgotten the source of his greatness—the magazines we put out for him." Luce had not forgotten about his magazines, as Billings soon learned. But they were no longer the only, and sometimes not even the principal, focus of his attention.[1]

The change in Luce—his gradual transformation from hardworking editor to self-conscious "great man"—was the subject of much speculation among his colleagues and friends. Some argued that it was a result of the enormous success of *Life* magazine, which had pushed him clearly into the forefront of the publishing world. Others were certain that it was his marriage to Clare, whose thirst for fame and glamour (not to mention her competitive relationship with her husband) drove Harry to adopt a new persona compatible with her sense of entitlement and power. But by far the biggest influence on Luce in the late 1930s and 1940s was the advent of World War II, which drew him into the world of politics and statesmanship and significantly transformed his sense of his own importance. He was no longer just a successful editor and publisher. He was a man of the world, a person of influence and, perhaps most of all, a person of ideas—ideas that he believed were important to the future.

Prior to 1939 Luce's interest in politics and world affairs had been generally fleeting. He seldom made overt political statements in public, and he was reticent about expressing his own views openly in his magazines. In fact he tolerated, at times almost encouraged, views that he himself did not share. For years he permitted *Time's* foreign editor, Laird Goldsborough, to cover the European crises of the 1930s by lionizing Mussolini and shrugging off the threat of Hitler. Goldsborough was a good writer and an efficient editor, and that was enough for Luce. Similarly, for several years, he had not much interfered with the Popular Front sensibilities that Ralph Ingersoll and others helped bring to *Fortune*. The approach of war, however, strengthened and redirected the powerful sense of mission that had defined his life since childhood. Never fully content with personal and professional success alone, he saw in the great world conflict a defining moment in history—and also in his own life.[2]

Luce was not immediately committed to American participation in the war in Europe when it began in September 1939, but he was wholly committed to the destruction of the Axis and to an important American role in achieving that goal. "The American refusal to be 'drawn in,' " he wrote to a friend in Paris, "is a kind of failure to realize how deeply we are in, whatever we say or do." The Sino-Japanese War, the threat to France and Britain, the looming enigma of the Soviet Union—all pushed him for the first time into an active role in trying to shape American foreign policy. Gone was his laissez-faire attitude toward the contents of his magazines. They, like him, were now soldiers in a cause, and Luce set out to train them in the proper presentation of the crisis. That required regaining control of his magazines.[3]

The departure of Ralph Ingersoll in 1939 was one step in that effort. Ingersoll, who had acquired considerable authority over the editorial policies of the company, left of his own accord to start the newspaper

P.M., but he must have been aware of his deteriorating position within Time Inc., a position confirmed by the relief with which Luce, and many of his colleagues, greeted his decision to leave. The disillusionment with Ingersoll was partly because his arrogance and abrasiveness had made him unpopular with virtually all his colleagues. ("What a conceited egoist!" Billings noted after a farewell conversation with Ingersoll. "He's been a snake-in-the-grass in the organization for years.") But to Luce and Billings both, the main problem was that Ingersoll's politics were too often at odds with their own. "The old *Time* is now gone forever," Billings had lamented shortly before the shake-up. "Ingersoll has revolutionized and sovietized things."[4]

More significant than Ingersoll's departure was the fall of Goldsborough. Throughout the 1930s he had written about European fascism as if it were at worst a minor irritant that did not much threaten the United States. (In 1935, in the midst of Italy's invasion of Ethiopia, Goldsborough wrote about a modest Mussolini overture to improve relations with France, and insisted it made him a "prime candidate" for the Nobel Peace Prize.) Where once Luce had tolerated Goldsborough's essentially isolationist views, he now found them unacceptable. Goldsborough "has just has not grown up with the times," he confided to Billings, "and he sees Europe as it was in 1930." By mid-1939 Luce had begun to marginalize Goldsborough, sending him on long trips overseas and assigning the editorship of Foreign Affairs to others. By late 1940 Goldsborough was gone—exiled briefly to a new and meaningless job as "assistant" to Luce before a forced if lucrative retirement in 1941. "His fall will be a hard one," Billings accurately predicted. (After ten years of lonely obscurity Goldsborough jumped to his death in 1950—carrying his omnipresent gold-headed cane with him—from a window in the Rockefeller Center offices where he had once been a titan.)[5]

The weakness of Time Inc.'s global vision in the 1930s had been a product of both attitude and uncertainty. The magazines' cultural and literary style had remained rooted in *Time*'s early, slightly cynical brashness and its tendency to take nothing too seriously. These traits were increasingly incompatible with the serious and ominous state of the world of the late 1930s. Luce and his colleagues were also, for a time, uncertain about their position on the rise of dictatorships and the advent of war. Torn between the extremes of Goldsborough's quasi-fascist leanings and the Popular Front inclinations of others, the magazines struggled, and generally failed, to produce a coherent position on the looming crisis. But by the end of 1939, with Ingersoll gone and Goldsborough shunted aside, and with fighting under way in Europe and widening in China, Time Inc. had begun to recast itself as the chronicler of the great global catastrophe—a recasting launched through a series of dinners Luce held with his senior editors in 1939 in an effort to "reintroduce" himself to his own staff. The *Fortune* writer Charles Wertenbaker later described those dinners in his novel *The Death of Kings*, which included a thinly disguised profile of Luce. His employees sat mesmerized, Wertenbaker wrote of the only slightly fictionalized publisher portrayed in the book, awed by "the purity of his belief." Others who attended the dinners noticed a new tone of authoritativeness, rooted in Luce's increasing certainty about his own positions. "Is TIME utterly unbiased, impartial, objective?" he asked. "No, TIME is prejudiced" in favor of "individual liberty" and American leadership in the world. At the dinners and elsewhere he laid out his new vision for the magazines: "*Time* cannot escape the fact that it is the bellwether of the most successful journalistic group in the world," he wrote in one of several memos outlining the company's future course. "At last it is clear to me what FORTUNE's No. 1 Job in this crisis is," he announced a few months later. "The No. 1 Job is to straighten out U. S. Businessmen (*and* "Liberals") on the great matter of appeasement." He had similar conversations with his colleagues on *Time* and *Life*, advocating a new goal: a "journalism of information *with a purpose*." Having thought about the "great changes in the world," he wrote in November 1939, he had acquired "a deeper conviction that . . . in our execution of The Newsmagazine Idea we shall indeed 'justify journalism' in our time."[6]

Luce's sudden and deep conviction in 1939 was a departure from his and his magazine's outlook even a year before. Through much of the 1930s, the Time Inc. editors and writers eagerly covered the Japanese conquest of Manchuria, the Italian invasion of Ethiopia, the Spanish civil war, the growing arsenal of the German military, and the halting American steps toward rearmament. But covering war was not the same as taking a position in the emerging global conflict. During most of the decade, Luce and his magazines were largely indifferent to who was winning or losing the conflicts in Europe and Asia. Time Inc.'s coverage was clinical and detached, expressing little sense that the conflicts had very much to do with the United States.[7]

Time, for example, chronicled the Japanese invasion of China through much of the 1930s as a dispute between two tyrannies: Japanese warlords fighting Chinese dictators. The magazine routinely referred to

Chiang Kai-shek, later one of Luce's—and thus *Time's*—great heroes, as "Dictator Chiang," and even treated the brief kidnapping of Chiang by a militant Chinese nationalist in 1937 not as a crime or a tragedy, but as an example of China's disarray. The magazine took a similarly detached view of Mussolini. "The years have dignified and tempered Benito Mussolini," the magazine declared in 1936 in the aftermath of Italy's conquest of Ethiopia, "and he has dignified and tempered the Italian people" while speaking with "Augustan calm." Even Hitler, whom the magazines generally scorned, received gentle treatment on occasion. *Time* described the 1936 Nuremberg rallies benignly as "the greatest show and heartiest picnic on earth," admired Hitler's "magnetism," and uncritically reported the good news about Germany's economy that the führer had touted in his speeches. In August 1938 *Time* greeted Hitler's mobilization of a million soldiers with sunny indifference: "Last week Europe was in a mood to let Adolf Hitler exercise his boys and put on a show." And a few weeks later the magazine responded to the September 1938 Munich accord in which Britain and France ceded part of Czechoslovakia to Hitler, as a welcome example of settling a major conflict "by talking instead of shooting first." Indeed, the enforced surrender of Czechoslovakia, *Time* claimed, may have "set a precedent which might flower into a great influence for peace."[8]

In *Life* a story on a 1938 Hitler visit to Rome noted that "democratic observers relaxed" in the face of evidence that neither Germany nor Italy were likely to cooperate in any future wars. The magazine's grim 1938 reports of the Spanish civil war and the Sino-Japanese war made no judgments about the justice of anyone's cause and instead cited the fighting as a reason for the United States to insulate itself from the global crisis. "The love of peace has no meaning or no stamina unless it is based on a knowledge of war's terrors," *Life* wrote in a caption below a Robert Capa picture of corpses on a plain near Teruel in Spain. *Fortune*, in the meantime, treated the growing crisis only glancingly and with exceptional detachment—worrying about the impact of global instability on business, expressing more contempt for Britain's democratic weakness than for German tyranny, and displaying a cheerful confidence that war would be averted. In its September 1939 issue, published only days before the beginning of World War II, *Fortune's* only mention of international news was a brief upbeat story about the improvement in France's finances.[9]

The events of 1939 abruptly changed the attitude of Luce himself and of his magazines. The once-benign interpretation of Munich quickly turned into a savage attack on appeasement. Hitler's occupation of Czechoslovakia, which *Time* had largely shrugged off in September 1938, now became the conclusive evidence of Hitler's incorrigible ambitions. "The treaty-breaking, lie-telling German Dictator . . . threw away all pretence of being anything but a Conqueror," the magazine noted in March 1939. A month later, when Mussolini invaded Albania, the editors responded furiously both to the Italian aggression and to the spinelessness of Britain and France: "There are in Europe two madmen who are disturbing the entire world—Hitler and Mussolini. There are in Europe two damn fools who sleep—Chamberlain and Daladier." At about the same time the magazines began their (and Luce's) long love affair with Winston Churchill, who became "a symbol of British democracy . . . of the kind that totalitarian governments cannot endure." One of the decisive moments in Luce's full commitment to war was the August 1939 Nazi-Soviet pact, a "nightmare" that created "a mighty cordon of non-democracy stretching one-third around the world from the Atlantic to the Pacific" and that united the world's two leading "revolutionary tyrannies." By the time Germany invaded Poland in September 1939, formally beginning what *Time* had already labeled World War II (thus cementing the conflict's enduring name), the magazines were already mobilizing themselves for a full-throated defense of democracy and a determination to defeat tyranny.[10]

Nowhere was the new attitude more visible than in *Life*—as Longwell had predicted in 1935 and as Luce now mandated in 1939—which became one of the nation's most important chroniclers of war and the great champion of the Allied cause. A special issue of *Life* shortly after the invasion of Poland was devoted entirely to the war and not only portrayed the anguish of the Polish people as "German bombers rain death and destruction on Warsaw" but outlined in terrifying detail the ominous power and terrible ambitions of the Nazi empire. Among its many warnings were the first of many hypothetical scenarios showing the catastrophic possibilities of a German victory, including the total destruction of British and French industry through airpower. But it also began what would become an earnest celebration of the courage and resourcefulness of Britain. (The issue included the results of a new *Fortune* survey that showed 83 percent of Americans in favor of the Western Allies' winning the war—and only 1 percent hoping for a German victory.)[11]

For the next two years *Life* was the adoring chronicler of the British war effort and of the plucky courage of the British people. "The R. A. F. Fliers Are Young and Brave," the magazine announced as it presented portraits of "smiling, keen, and confident" British "heroes." Stories about the German bombing of London were accompanied by photographs of beaming, "unruffled" "Thumbs Up" young women singing, "We're going to show the world who's who." Despite the blitz, *Life* assured its readers, "the life of London continues with calm, incongruous persistence." The devastating British retreat from France at Dunkirk was an opportunity to salute the "unshaken, unbroken, unbeaten" British military.

Time and *Life* both became as well the indomitable foes of America's "appeasers" and isolationists. "Rather than risk involving U.S. troops in the War," *Life* wrote contemptuously (and not wholly inaccurately), the "appeasers" were "prepared to see Great Britain defeated and Hitler's power extended to the very sea gates of America." Unflattering photographs of aviation hero Charles Lindbergh, U.S. ambassador to Britain Joseph Kennedy, and U.S. senator Burton K. Wheeler accompanied a portrait of Lawrence Dennis, "America's No. 1 intellectual Fascist." *Time* was particularly hard on Lindbergh, "who to many Americans represents the narrowest isolationism, the broadest appeasement." Uncharacteristically dense essays explained to *Life* readers the great dangers of a German victory—among them a five-page article by Walter Lippmann describing the terrifying economic consequences of Axis control of Europe and the likelihood that Germany would then dominate and devastate the United States. "The small American businessman has long complained about how difficult it is for him to survive in the competition with the large American corporation," Lippmann warned. "What will he do when he has to face the competition of totalitarian monopoly organized on a continental scale?" At the same time a newly energized *March of Time* issued one of its most ambitious films: "The Ramparts We Watched," an unapologetic call for American military preparedness. And *Fortune* began to mobilize its readership for the struggle as well. "The people of the U.S. must now choose among retreat, isolation, and international leadership," the magazine wrote late in 1939.[12]

The rapid and dramatic movement of the Time Inc. magazines from ironic detachment to committed advocates of the Allied cause did not escape the notice of the editors of *The New Yorker,* Luce's most persistently biting (and wittiest) satirists. Harold Ross, always eager to tweak what he considered the pomposity of Luce and his magazines, took note of *Life*'s simultaneous fascination with "pretty women" and its doomsday fantasies as it attempted to prepare its readers for war. Shortly before Pearl Harbor, *The New Yorker* ran a satirical cartoon version of *Life* Goes to a Party titled "Life Goes to the Collapse of Western Civilization." It was most likely based on a trivial 1941 *Life* story about "twin sisters from Flint," Lois and Lucille, arriving in New York hoping to break into show business and meet "successful, cultured and refined people." *The New Yorker* parody told the story of two "pretty New York models"—Meenie and Babs—who move smiling and wide-eyed through a war-torn New York, always dressed in the latest and most provocative outfits. In one frame the girls dress in "scanty sport clothes for the task of lugging $3,450,000 in inflated United States currency to famed Elizabeth Arden's to buy a tube of vanishing cream." In another Babs and Meenie "buoyantly participate in a bread riot for a lark." "Goodness gracious," Babs exclaims, "if I ate even one slice of bread I'd have to stop wearing tailored suits."[13]

Luce had reacted to *The New Yorker*'s satirical 1936 profile of him with almost violent fury. But by 1941 he was so deeply immersed in the cause of the Allies that he gave *The New Yorker*, and his other critics, virtually no notice at all. His newly powerful sense of mission kept his gaze squarely on the global crisis, and on the important role he believed he must play in it. His frustration with America's slow path to intervention grew steadily, but no more than his frustration with his own inability to change the nation's course. Roosevelt, he charged, was guilty of "ape-like fumbling"; but in fact, he somewhat narcissistically insisted, "it is all, all our fault . . . that all this monkey-business happens when *we* are 'the most potent editorial force' in America." The intensity of his commitment even led him to propose transforming *Fortune* from a magazine of business to the "Magazine of America as a World Power." His staff talked him out of this radical notion, but not out of the sentiments that it reflected.[14]

Luce's view of the impending war, and of America's role in the global crisis, was not as clear or consistent as he later liked to claim. He had repudiated isolationism and had aligned himself with the growing circle of influential Americans who insisted that the United States must lead the world. But like many internationalists of the late 1930s, he had moved erratically from one strategy to another—wavering on how likely he believed the outbreak of war to be and wondering how deeply engaged with the conflict the United States should become. At some moments he was convinced that American military engagement was inevitable; at others he continued to argue that preparedness and aid to Britain would be enough. He sometimes admired Franklin Roosevelt's halting, cagey movement away from isolationism. ("How to express one's admiration and gratitude," he wrote the president in mid-1940. "I'd like to say it this way—that your speech at Charlottesville is the most important human utterance since Lincoln's at Gettysburg.") He sometimes railed against what he considered the president's timidity and fecklessness. (The administration, he wrote a few months later, "has contributed, blunder-ingly and unwittingly, to the conditions which have led to war.") In the last months before the outbreak of war in Europe, he became an excited advocate of a quixotic proposal by the journalist Clarence Streit for a federation of the Atlantic democracies—a new form of global gover-nance that would strengthen the ability of anti-fascist nations to resist aggression. Streit promoted this idea in a briefly influential 1939 book, *Union Now*:

> I believe there is a way through these dangers, and out of the dilemma, a way to do what we all want, to keep both peace and freedom, and keep them securely and be done with this night-mare. . . . The way through is Union now of the democracies that the North Atlantic and a thousand other things already unite . . . a great federal republic built on and for the thing they share most, their common democratic principle of government for the sake of individual freedom.

In later years Luce would look with something close to contempt on such notions of global governance—a plan that would have brought the United States into a federation that would reduce its sovereignty and embed it into something like the European Union of a half century later. But at the time he was looking for any answer he could find; and in the ominous summer of 1939 he saw "Union Now" as "the only way to begin the re-liberation of human energy and imagination and hope and will."[15]

Luce was excited, frightened, hopeful, angry. The war brought out the best of his missionary temperament—commitment, energy, moral inquiry, and high purpose; and it brought out the worst as well—arrogance, impatience, didacticism, and occasional dogmatism. His rest-lessness was visible in his almost obsessive writing in the early months of the war, memo after memo, outlining more and more ideas and beliefs. "Danger," he wrote in July 1940 in a message to his staff. "The country is in Danger. Danger. Danger. The country is in Danger. . . . Alas you have only to look about you to know that the country does not *feel* as we do." As he often did when restless and frustrated, he turned to travel, which brought him into direct contact with the reality of the crisis and helped clarify his own views of how to respond to it.[16]

For more than a year before the outbreak of war, Luce traveled periodically through Europe, meeting with important people, conveying his impressions to his staff, and supervising stories reflecting his views. If he had not already been convinced of the unsavoriness of the Nazi regime, he made his disillusionment clear during a visit in spring 1938. Just as Luce's impression of the Soviet Union had been profoundly shaped by the physical discomforts he had experienced while traveling across Russia in 1932, he was struck as well by what he considered the general shabbiness of life in Nazi Germany—the terrible food, the shortage of toilet paper, "the worst [conditions] I have encountered in years. . . . There is no luxury in Germany." But he was even more appalled by the "intensity" of anti-Semitism, a "brand of hatred" about which, he said, "there has been no exaggeration." And yet he remained optimistic about the prospects for peace and continued to hope that the Nazi regime might still evolve into a responsible state. A few days later he met President Edvard Beneš during a visit to Czechoslovakia, and described him as "an able idealist, great leader of a brave people" likely to defend his country successfully against Hitler's threats. It was characteristic of Luce that he became absorbed with whatever country he had most recently visited, and he often pressured the magazines to pay attention to anything that had struck his interest there. His excitement about Beneš led to an admiring cover story on him, only months before the nation's demise at the hands of Germany.[17]

A year later, in the spring of 1939, the writer John Gunther encountered Luce on a ship en route to Europe. The two men, who barely knew each other, struck up a shipboard friendship. Gunther later wrote to his wife about Luce's revealing account of himself. "He's aloof and sensitive at first, then bursts out in long, semi-articulate, highly intelligent talk." Gunther took note as well of Luce's apparent frustration and uncertainty. Luce was "ashamed to say I'm 41," an age at which he felt he should know more than he did and wanted to "go to school again." Luce spoke ruefully as well of how much of his life had become defined by his wealth and power, how too often he found himself in the company of rich reactionaries ("French semi-Fascists and 'Après nous le déluge—let them eat cake millionaires,'" Gunther described some of their shipboard companions, whom Luce chose to avoid). But Luce expressed as well his continuing uncertainty about the crisis that he knew would soon define his life and that of the world. "If he had to choose between Fascism & Communism," Gunther wrote, "(awful choice) he would choose communism because it meant more for 'the people as a whole.'" Despite Luce's great power, Gunther noted, "one almost senses a feeling of inferiority, or at least disatisfication [*sic*] with himself in spite of all he has accomplished."[18]

Once in Europe, Luce quickly abandoned his plans for "a very good rest" and plunged instead into frantic travel and interviewing. During a trip to Poland in late July (a month before Germany invaded), he continued to believe that "the chances of war this year are rather *less* than 50–50" in part because of his admiration for "the strength of Polish policy vis-à-vis Germany." After the announcement of the Nazi-Soviet pact in August he described the agreement as evidence of German weakness—and of Hitler's fear of the strength of the Allied front. "The Allies are winning," he wrote. "Americans have not realized how strong was the resistance-determination in England and France." And yet only days later, at lunch in Paris with Gertrude Stein and Alice B. Toklas, he spoke animatedly about the likelihood of catastrophic war. He returned to New York and wrote of a "war of words and nerves," of "rolling barrages of slander timed to the minute . . . whispering campaigns, mystification, currency raids, posters, mass meetings, blackouts—weapons against which military men can only point their guns in vain." In early September, with German tanks rolling into Poland, he was reproaching himself for not seeing the danger more clearly and not having advocated more effectively for preparedness and defense. "It is my fault for not having insisted harder," he lamented, and he promptly told his editors "that we didn't blame Hitler enough for starting the war, that we were too hard on Britain." Billings—an isolationist at heart—complained in his diary: "They want *Life* to go overboard for the Allies. 'I had tried to keep the issue fair and objective.'" But always the good soldier, he quickly fell into line.[19]

In the spring of 1940 Clare began an extended tour of Europe, this time to assess for *Life* the impact of the still relatively quiet war. (A year later she published her observations in a successful book, *Europe in the Spring.*) In April, as German forces began their great offensive, Luce raced to Paris to join her and to assess the changing situation for himself. (It was a classic example of Luce's practice of journalism—serial visits with heads of state and other dignitaries.) After a whirlwind round of interviews with French officials and a short visit to London, he wrote back perceptively to his editors that the "stand-out fact" of the war was "plain and simple aviation." England, France, and the United States, he argued, were in many ways better prepared for a long war than was Germany. But in a short war they were in great danger because of the enormous German advantage in airpower. If the "Allies had two or three thousand additional airplanes," he insisted, "the war would be shortened . . . the lives of hundreds of thousands of young men on both sides would be saved." The United States should not only increase airplane production but should also release to the Allies "every single airplane which they are willing to pay cash for." His editors accused him of oversimplification and kept the intensity of his feeling on this issue out of the magazines, but Luce did not back down. "Airplanes, airplanes, is the cry you hear from the land and . . . from the sea," he replied. The course of the war in the following months proved him to be mostly right.[20]

A few days later, on May 8, he and Clare were in Holland, which, like most of Europe, was awaiting the beginning of the German blitzkrieg that everyone by now knew was imminent. "Where will [Hitler] strike?" Luce wrote. "Anywhere"—except the already obsolete Maginot Line in western France. In fact German troops began flowing across the Dutch border almost as soon as the Luces arrived, and they quickly decamped to the American Embassy in Brussels. Early the next morning, a maid woke them with the news that "The Germans are coming again." They rushed to the window and looked out across the square, "when we heard a tremendous explosion. . . . The house across the street collapsed. The sirens began to blow . . . Red Cross ambulances appeared." Everyone in the embassy was frightened, particularly as the sound of German artillery began to be heard to the north. "But after that," Luce observed, "they got used to the war and were very mad." With the building vibrating from the noise of bombing, shelling, and air-raid sirens, the embassy staff made breakfast "because not eating would not keep the Germans away." Clare ignored the warnings of the embassy staff and strolled across downtown Brussels, watching Belgians read the grim news in their papers, noting women and children on their normal shopping rounds, and observing soldiers assembling with "great calm." Failing to find a taxi (they had all been commandeered by the army), she uncharacteristically rode a streetcar back to the embassy. Because the city was "in a state of siege," she and Harry stayed in the embassy and had "a very good luncheon in the mirrored gallery . . . the Ambassador served his best wine." Clare noted that they heard "three more alarms between the eggs mornay and the dessert course." As darkness fell "on the first day of the big show," Harry and Clare looked from the embassy balcony again to see "the green square where the glass from the bombhouse lies like jagged hail" and where two children had died. The next morning, shortly after Clare cabled to *Life* her own "eyewitness account of the first day of the Germans' grand attack on the western world," they were driven back to Paris in a car provided by the embassy. As always his thoughts turned immediately to what these events meant for the United States. "Don't ever doubt Hitler keeps a close eye on American opinion," Luce wrote as he departed from Brussels. Concern about the American reaction, he claimed, was the reason the German bombing of Belgium was relatively restrained. Hitler is "well pleased with the impotence of American opinion up to date, but the possibility of engaging America is the only thing which would really scare him." A few weeks later, back in New York, Luce responded to a friend's request for a conversation "when your desk is clear" with a blunt retort: "Desk won't be clear until Hitler either gives or receives the peace of death."[21]

"Our great job from now on is not to create power but to use it," Luce wrote Larsen from Europe in the spring of 1940. On his return to New York he gave two national radio addresses warning Americans that their way of life was threatened by "mighty and ruthless nations. . . . What can we do now?" he asked. "We can strip off the false cloak of neutrality and announce to the world—that we stand for . . . democracy." Luce was in effect announcing a new phase of his career in which he would use his magazines, and his personal influence, to shape public policy and national opinion. His first step in doing so was to become deeply engaged, for the first time in his life, with a presidential campaign.[22]

Luce had confronted earlier campaigns with relative indifference. He had cast a hopeful vote for Al Smith in 1928; and he had supported Hoover in 1932, only because he thought there was no difference between the two candidates and that continuity was preferable to change. He voted for Alf Landon in 1936, but with no enthusiasm, and he approached the 1940 political season without a strong preference. Through much of 1939 he spoke generally favorably of Robert Taft, the acknowledged front-runner for the Republican nomination. But by mid-1940 Taft's continuing isolationism had turned Luce away not only from the candidate but from the party. "The remarks of Roosevelt . . . sound wonderful here," he wrote from Europe in May. "I am practically prepared to become . . . a Third Termer unless the opposition offers some small degree of competition." The only ray of hope for the Republicans, he predicted, was "Davenport's man."[23]

"Davenport's man" was Wendell Willkie, a prominent utilities executive who had left his company early in 1939 after reaching a lucrative settlement with the government in a legal dispute with the Tennessee Valley Authority. Once a Democrat and a Roosevelt supporter, he turned against both the president and the party in the aftermath of his lawsuit, became a Republican, and began to emerge as a public figure through his frequent speeches and writings. In the summer of 1939 he agreed to participate in a *Fortune* round table, where he met Russell Davenport, the magazine's managing editor. Davenport returned home that evening and reported to his family, "I've just met the man who ought to be President of the United States." For the next several months the two men—soon close friends—met often, first at Davenport's weekend home on Long Island, later in Davenport's Manhattan apartment. (Willkie, too, lived in New York with his family in an apartment on Fifth Avenue, although by 1940 he was spending much of his time—only moderately discreetly—with Irita Van Doren, the book editor of the *New York Herald Tribune*.) Together Willkie and Davenport (with help from Van Doren) produced a "manifesto," published under Willkie's name and titled "We the People." It appeared in *Fortune* in April 1940 with an effusive preface by Davenport introducing Willkie: "The principles he stands for are American principles. . . . They are progressive, liberal and expansive. One cannot dare to doubt that they will eventually prevail. . . . For taking up this position . . . Mr. Willkie certainly deserves the respect and attention of his countrymen." In the document that followed, Willkie lashed out at Roosevelt: "You have usurped our sovereign power by curtailing the Bill of Rights . . . and by placing in the hands of a few men in executive commissions all the powers requisite to tyranny. . . . You have muddled our foreign affairs with politics . . . with wild fears and inconsistent acts. . . . We do not want a New Deal any more. We want a New World." But Willkie was actually less interested in attacking Roosevelt than in standing up against the isolationist right and steering the Republican Party toward a responsibly internationalist position on the war. When congressional Republicans tried to block proposed loans to threatened countries in Europe, he wrote: "There can be no question which is right and which is wrong. . . . We are opposed to war. But we do not intend to relinquish our right to sell whatever we want to those defending themselves from aggression."[24]

Davenport was not the first person to imagine Willkie as a presidential candidate. Low-level speculation about his political future had begun early in 1939 and had continued through the year. By the beginning of 1940, however, he remained the darkest of dark horses, with so little support (or even recognition) in the polls that almost no one had yet taken him seriously. But the publication of "We the People" in *Fortune* intersected with a growing popular boom—launched by Oren Root, a young lawyer (and relative of former secretary of state Elihu Root). Root, almost alone, implausibly but effectively organized a grassroots mail and advertising campaign that produced a remarkable response. Hundreds of "Willkie Clubs" sprang up around the country, and more than three million people signed petitions supporting his candidacy. To Root and Davenport both, what made Willkie so attractive was that he did not appear to be a conventional politician. He seemed to them an honest, uncalculating "clear thinker" whose views were not his party's or his handlers' but his own. Both men were also ardent internationalists and admired Willkie's opposition to the isolationist sentiments of many of their fellow Republicans. By early May the boom had grown so promising that Davenport resigned from *Fortune* to become one of Willkie's campaign managers. "I believe," he explained to Larsen, "that the principles that he has been expressing have a national, indeed an historical significance."[25]

Prior to his return from Europe, Luce had only a relatively vague notion of who Willkie was and what he represented. But the combination of Davenport's enthusiasm and Luce's own strengthened commitment to a major American role in the war drew him quickly into Willkie's orbit. Willkie and Luce began to meet frequently in Luce's office in Rockefeller Center, talking and drinking with their feet up on Luce's desk, sometimes until late into the night. A pragmatic friendship emerged, and with it Luce's deepening commitment to Willkie's candidacy. Indeed, for the first time in his life, Luce felt truly passionate about a political figure. For the next several months he seemed almost entirely to abandon any detachment from politics and became an open and unapologetic champion of (and frequent campaign adviser to) Willkie. "I know of no one in public life in our time who had greater magnetism than Wendell Willkie," Nicholas Roosevelt, the president's cousin, once wrote. Luce, consciously or not, seemed to have come to the same conclusion.[26]

Although Luce's commitment to Willkie was rooted in an extraordinary personal attraction that he never explained and perhaps never fully understood, he was also drawn to Willkie because of two growing convictions: that Franklin Roosevelt was incapable of leading the nation through the world crisis, and that Willkie was a bulwark against a dangerous Right, which in the absence of credible leadership might so obstruct support for the Allies that the great crusade for democracy could be lost. The two impulses—the passion for Willkie and the growing despair about the alternatives—reinforced each other.

Luce's intensifying hatred for Roosevelt was only partly a result of his frustration with the president's halting course toward support for the Allies. He had, after all, actually supported the administration's foreign policy only a few months before. He seemed more afraid of what he considered Roosevelt's autocratic leadership and his apparent radicalism, and the likelihood that they would destabilize the nation. "Franklin Roosevelt has done more than any President in the history of our Republic to destroy and undermine the spirit of American enterprise" and "the spirit of cooperation between all the various groups of which our society is composed." The administration, he charged, "has failed in its domestic objectives . . . and brought America to the verge of bankruptcy." It has created "vast and corrupt political machines." "If people want state socialism," he wrote Willkie in October, "let them vote for it with their eyes open. Indeed let there be summoned a constitutional convention to scrap the present dear old Constitution."[27]

But Luce was at least equally concerned about the Republican Right, and he saw in Willkie the only protection against what he saw as the bigotry and isolationism of much of the party. "I urge that Willkie make a speech specifically giving hell to the Tories and Reactionaries in his camp," he wrote Davenport in the summer of 1940. "Willkie has disavowed anti-Semitism, he has shown himself to be a true economic and social liberal. But . . . he has not specially disavowed the stupid, idle-rich, backward-looking economic royalists—all the people whom I really hate worse than Roosevelt." He was as persistent in pressing these concerns as he was in pressing any others. "Please reconsider desirability of repudiation of reactionaries, tories, snots, old dealers, and idle rich in your camp," he wrote again after his earlier entreaties went unanswered. "Reaffirm true progressive liberalism in contrast and treat all old dealers as pitiful anachronisms." The hatred of Roosevelt and the hatred of the Right combined to drive him to a third concern: an embrace of the rumored and already discredited notion—originally circulated by New Dealers themselves—that business leaders were planning a "capital strike" against the New Deal. His colleague C. D. Jackson warned that corporate leaders would "go on a much more dangerous sit-down strike than after the '36 election. . . . I don't think it is an exaggeration to say that within the next twelve months these people as a class may very well fall for some Fascistic putsch, simply for the sake of throwing a monkey-wrench into Roosevelt." Luce agreed, and warned that the uprising might be "infinitely vaster than Wall Street or La Salle Street [the banking center of Chicago] or all such streets." That was yet another reason, he insisted, for the importance of a Willkie victory.[28]

Time and Life had been touting Willkie even before Luce began to pressure his editors to do so. Life ran a glowing portrait of the candidate in mid-May 1940, while Luce was still in Europe, calling Willkie "by far the ablest man the Republicans could nominate for President at Philadelphia next month." Time consistently debunked the other leading Republican candidates—Robert Taft, Thomas E. Dewey, Arthur Vandenberg—while noting every sign that Willkie, still a long shot, was gaining ground. "Up and coming Willkie," the magazine wrote in early May, "upped himself several notches" in a speech to newspaper publishers, who went home "wondering if there was still time to convince his public that Mr. Willkie would make a top-notch Republican nominee." Once Luce returned from Europe and began making his support for Willkie clear, the magazines increased their efforts on his behalf, and gradually crossed the line separating analysis from advocacy. His followers had "a hopeful gleam in their eyes," Time noted in early June. His nomination, "which was believed impossible a few weeks ago, is decidedly within the realm of a possibility today." By mid-June, with Willkie still trailing all his major opponents, Time was ebulliently describing him as "the most rambunctious dark horse, getting more rambunctious daily." And little more than a week before the Republican convention convened, Time ran a cover piece ("The Story of Wendell Willkie") that could only be described, given its timing, as a campaign document. It included a heroic account of the grassroots effort to build support for Willkie, a mocking description of the bloated campaign efforts of his opponents compared with Willkie's humble simplicity, and a lengthy pro-Willkie statement by the columnist Raymond Clapper, unchallenged by any other voices. The only issue in the campaign, Clapper wrote, "is whether Mr. Roosevelt or a Republican could do a faster, better job of obtaining the industrial production for defense. . . . They must look ahead and offer a man who can make the country believe he would do a better job. . . . On that point Mr. Willkie is the only man the Republicans have who stands a chance of making an effective case."[29]

By the time Willkie won the Republican nomination in dramatic fashion on the sixth ballot in Philadelphia, the Luce publications were in full cry. The convention, *Life* claimed, was the site of "a political drama unique in [the party's] history." The other candidates "looked and sounded pretty much as they had at any political convention in the last 20 or 40 years—except more confused and dispirited. . . . The familiar pattern was broken only in six small rooms on the top floor of the Benjamin Franklin Hotel, where delegates, reporters, and visitors were crowding in . . . to see and hear a new kind of leader." "Dreary," "dull," "depressing," "desperate," "hopeless" were the adjectives describing Willkie's opponents. But the nomination itself was "the happy and inspiring ending," the result of "a tidal wave of popular demand" that "crumbled the opposition" and "swept the old bosses out." *Time* described Willkie's gallant supporters in Philadelphia: "Unbossed, unled . . . Willkiemen and Willkiewomen surged around Philadelphia . . . carrying the torches of their faith." Willkie himself, *Time* insisted, was "not a leader in any sense that was politically recognizable." In the end "the people had won. . . . For the first time since Teddy Roosevelt, the Republicans had a man they could yell for and mean it."[30]

Willkie's remarkable rise, and his stunning victory in Philadelphia, only deepened Luce's commitment to his candidacy. In the four months between the convention and the election he worked ceaselessly and almost obsessively to promote Willkie's election. The magazines continued to give Willkie warm treatment, but there remained some resistance from pro-Roosevelt editors, who complained bitterly about the bias in coverage and tried occasionally to balance it. Luce reacted with fury to this suggestion of evenhandedness. "I am deeply disappointed," he wrote to his editors in September. "Here we come to a Presidential election which I think is vitally important. And *Time* evidently doesn't think so. . . . Anyone who does not think this campaign is important should have nothing to do with the reporting and editing of the campaign—and should report to me accordingly now." And what made the campaign so important? Luce listed the issues that he considered "critical to the nation's future," all of them favorable to Willkie: the third term, Roosevelt's disgraceful record on foreign policy, the New Deal's corrupt appointees. "If an Administration was a failure," he asked his editors bitterly, "should it be excused its failure and given new power because the threat of War arises?" Most important was the bold alternative that Willkie provided and the growing endorsements he was receiving. "Last week a lot of people came out for Willkie," Luce snapped. "You mentioned none of them."[31]

But Luce could be critical of Willkie, too. The more emotionally committed he became, the more impatient he was with the campaign's shortcomings. After the convention Willkie relocated to Indiana, his onetime home state, and spent several weeks sitting on the front porch of a rented house talking with reporters (a reference to an earlier, simpler era of presidential campaigns and an effort to emphasize his own small-town background). Luce was furious. Willkie should stop "this cracker-barrel dawdling," he barked to Davenport. "Running for President might be fun for Mr. Willkie. . . . But it's a God damn serious thing for 130,000,000 Americans and maybe for the world." Willkie was "fast becoming just another Daily Columnist" at a moment when he needed "to begin to govern *now*." But it was one thing for Luce to criticize Willkie privately; it was another for such concerns to become public. Luce was deeply pained when concerns about Willkie's "lassitude" and disorganization started to appear in the press. Raymond Clapper wrote that "seldom has there been more chaos in a presidential campaign." Criticism even appeared in Luce's own magazines. *Time* reported in September that Republicans were beginning to believe that "the holy-rolling campaign of Wendell Willkie has gone sour," that "Amateur Willkie" had lost control of his own organization. Luce was torn between fury with the reporters and despair that the charges were largely true.[32]

For the two months of the formal fall campaign, Luce veered from periods of elation at evidence of Willkie's rising fortunes to something close to panic when his chances seemed to ebb. But whatever his mood, he never let up his effort to insert his views into the campaign and to persuade others of the importance of a Willkie victory. Almost every day, often several times a day, he deluged Davenport with letters, memos, telegrams, and telephone calls offering ideas and information, and frequently drafts of full speeches (a few of which Willkie actually gave). He agonized over the wording of what he believed Willkie should say, as if a turn of phrase might transform the race. "Let your indictment be completed before you turn to statement of positive principles. Or, if you like, group principles under negatives and positives . . . 'I will not do this . . . I will do this.' " "Continue to be specific," he wrote Willkie in late September. "Attack the New Deal, rather than Roosevelt." The president "is somewhat akin to our flag," but the New Deal as a concept is more vulnerable.[33]

In advising Willkie, Luce was also struggling to articulate his own rapidly changing views of the state of the nation and the world. He was searching for a philosophy that would shape his—and, he hoped,

America's—future course. More and more he focused that search on a definition of individual freedom. "The error of the New Deal is its effort to take all the responsibility for fixing everything. It has undermined individual responsibility." Americans should extend their aid to "peoples who are striving . . . toward the attainment and fulfillment of the democratic and Christian ideals." Willkie should emphasize "*Democracy* as a concept . . . the religion of democracy," a "renewed commitment to human freedom." And, repeatedly, "The campaign must be a Crusade for Free Men in a Free Land." To others these phrases must have seemed purely rhetorical, even platitudinous. To Luce, however, they were filled with meanings, even if he could not yet fully articulate them.[34]

As time went on and Willkie's poll numbers began to decline,* Luce became harsher and more partisan than ever. When Willkie spoke in or around New York, Luce was almost always in the audience (although he retained just enough awareness of his supposed impartiality as a journalist to decline invitations to sit on the podium with the candidate). Ten days before the election, Luce spewed out to Davenport a shorthand list of Roosevelt's crimes: "communist influence," "recession," "Japanese aggression largely financed by the United States," "partisan appointments to the Supreme Court," "Munich," "Scandal," "All Members of the Roosevelt family continue to make money!" By then it was clear to him that Willkie would not use this kind of invective in his campaign. Luce was just venting his own frustration, but he was also looking ahead. As the end of the campaign approached and the inevitability of a Roosevelt victory began to become apparent, he mounted an effort—which extended well beyond election day—to create a case for the importance of Willkie's candidacy despite his defeat. "If the story then is a story of repudiation, it is a story of one of the great repudiations of American history," he implausibly claimed to his editors (having already called the 1940 contest "the most important election since 1860"), "and we should land on it with both feet." In late October he wrote Manfred Gottfried (now managing editor of *Time*), "the day after Mr. Roosevelt's election the psychological face of this country will be strange and not very happy."

In early November, after Roosevelt was easily elected to his third term (albeit by a significantly smaller margin than in his previous two

*The 1940 election was the first in which scientific polling played a significant role in a presidential race, and the first in which the public (and Luce) took them seriously.

elections), Luce rationalized that "the real news . . . is the size of the minority vote. . . . Comments should show what tiny fraction changes in New York, Ohio, Illinois, and what other few states would have elected Willkie." And "the chief thing to speculate about," he added, "is the future of Willkie. This is really much more interesting than whether Whoosis is going to get what job in Washington. . . . Willkie is as unprecedented as the Third Term." In a letter sent out to many correspondents a few days after the voting, he still had nothing good to say about Roosevelt and argued instead that "the man you ought to thank God for more than for any other American . . . is a fellow you don't know anything about: Wendell Willkie. Any candidate could have, and perhaps any other candidate unwittingly might have, torn this country apart instead of uniting it in a passionate fervor pro-democracy."[35]

Luce's ardor for Willkie began to fade almost as soon as the election was over, but it did not vanish altogether. Willkie visited Luce at Mepkin in December en route to a Florida vacation, and they continued to correspond, to meet, and to work together on shared causes—although at a less intensive pace—over the following years. His admiration for Willkie survived, but his enthusiasm did not, especially once Willkie began cooperating openly with Roosevelt.[36]

At the same time that Luce was immersed in the Willkie campaign, he was also working quietly to persuade Roosevelt to take a more aggressive stance toward the war. The awkwardness of this situation was not lost on either man. While Luce was excoriating the president in his magazines, working actively against his reelection, and accusing Roosevelt of incompetence and something close to tyranny, Roosevelt was privately condemning Luce's "bias" and "propaganda" and making vague threats (rarely implemented) to challenge Luce's power. "There are some things in life that one should not let certain people get away with," Roosevelt wrote in 1940 after a petty dispute with *Time* about some inconsequential reporting errors. Luce, he complained, was "slippery." George Washington "had the courage to admit a lie," he wrote (crossing out the word "lie" and replacing it with "sin"), but "Henry Luce lacks that ability." And yet both men were pragmatic enough to know when to put their mutual dislike aside, and both sought ways to use each other to advance their own ends, which in reality had more in common than either was willing to admit.[37]

In the summer of 1940, as the military situation in Europe deterioriated and as Luce immersed himself in the Willkie campaign, he joined a nonpartisan group of influential men who were trying to pave the way for more active American support for Britain. The renowned Kansas editor William Allen White had just created the highly public Committee to Defend America by Aiding the Allies, which worked actively to combat isolationism through public exhortation. The group Luce joined, by contrast, relied on quiet and mostly secret diplomacy. They first convened in July 1940 at the midtown Columbia University Club and agreed to create a formal organization, which they later named the Century Group, after the elite New York men's club in which they held most of their subsequent meetings. Its director was Francis Pickens Miller, a Virginia congressman with ties both to the Council on Foreign Relations and to the Committee to Defend America by Aiding the Allies; and its members included other political figures (Lewis Douglas, Roosevelt's former budget director, now a Willkie Republican; Robert E. Sherwood, a playwright and Roosevelt speechwriter; Will Clayton, an official in the State Department); theologians (Henry Sloane Coffin, the renowned president of Union Theological Seminary and Henry Van Dusen, who later succeeded him); academics (among them Ernest Hopkins, the president of Dartmouth College); and the publishers of the *Louisville Courier-Journal*, the *St. Louis Post-Dispatch*, and the *New York Herald Tribune*. But there was probably no one in the thirty-member group more influential than Luce; and although he at times expressed discomfort at being a member of what was essentially a lobbying organization (a discomfort that rarely inhibited his participation in the Willkie campaign), he gradually became one of its most active members. He helped pay for the office and staff that the group opened on Forty-second Street, and he made himself increasingly central to their efforts to change American policy.[38]

The group often disagreed about tactics, but they were united from the start on one large issue: "that the survival of the British Commonwealth . . . is an important factor in the preservation of the American way of life," and that "the survival of the British Fleet . . . is a factor of critical importance in the defense of the United States." Very quickly these concerns coalesced around a specific proposal: sending some recently decommissioned American destroyers to the Royal Navy, an action that "would probably make the difference between defeat, and victory." But the committee was stymied at first by the legal and political obstacles that they knew would stand in the way. America's neutrality laws required that any nation receiving military supplies from the United States must pay for them, and Britain had no capacity to finance a purchase of this magnitude. And because the issue was arising in the year of a presidential campaign, everyone realized as well that Roosevelt would need political cover for anything he might do. "If saving western civilization hinges on these boats," Miller wrote Luce, "then a way through the technicalities must be found." Luce consulted the columnist Joseph Alsop for advice on how to influence Roosevelt, and he took to heart Alsop's blunt advice: "Suppress Lew Douglas's name . . . a red flag to the Presidential bull. . . . If possible, a courtier-like approach. . . . The President is very tired, and when tired is seemingly best dealt with from the position of the kow-tow." At the next meeting Luce argued that Roosevelt would need a "quid pro quo" from the British to justify the transfer of the ships, and he proposed that "these destroyers should be offered to Britain in exchange for immediate naval and air concessions in British possessions in the Western Hemisphere." Luce had not been the first person to embrace this idea. It had been circulating in elite conversations, and even in the press, for at least several weeks. But Luce was largely responsible for directing the Century Group toward the proposal.[39]

Having agreed on strategy, the group quickly turned to tactics. Who should see whom? they asked themselves. What should be "the method to cut through the technicalities"? How was the country "to be aroused"? The members responded in the way that powerful people usually do—by contacting other powerful people. Luce and Coffin visited Secretary of State Cordell Hull. They were pleased by Hull's approval of their idea, Luce wrote, but discouraged by his demeanor, "bordering on fatalistic despair. . . . The noble old soldier has been working so long in an atmosphere of frustration and defeat that he has perhaps lost the necessary faith in the possible victory of his cause." A few days later he called first on Frank Knox, the former Republican newspaper editor (and 1936 Republican vice presidential candidate) whom Roosevelt had recently named secretary of the navy; and then Lord Lothian, the British ambassador. He urged them both to support the destroyers-for-bases plan. Knox and Lothian surprised him with welcome but unexplained optimism—an optimism Luce did not at that moment share, because the day before he and Clare had spent the night at the White House.[40]

It was ostensibly a social event, organized around a screening for the president of the new *March of Time* film, "The Ramparts We Watch." On their arrival the Luces were shown to a White House bedroom— "utterly without charm," Harry wrote—and then proceeded to the pres-

ident's private study on the second floor. Roosevelt was sitting behind
his desk gleefully mixing what Luce considered "excellent martinis."
(The president drank two.) The party included some of Luce's
colleagues—Roy Larsen and Louis de Rochemont and their wives—as
well as such usual companions of the president as Missy LeHand, his
secretary, and Harry Hopkins, his most trusted aide. After dinner the
group convened in the "stifling hot" upstairs corridor to watch the film,
which the president seemed to like; and shortly after that Luce met privately with the president in his study.[41]

Luce found the conversation disappointing. He moved immediately
to what he later called "my big question . . . has he or has he not made
up his mind about sending destroyers to Great Britain." Roosevelt
equivocated, dismissing the idea as politically impossible at one
moment, then describing the congressional lobbying he would have to
do to enhance the proposal's chances. He was struck by the president's
"air of great confidence. . . . He feels a sort of reincarnation." Years later,
after Harry's death, Clare described the evening and claimed that Roosevelt had pressured Harry to support the destroyers-for-bases deal in
his magazines, that only with such backing could he hope to persuade
Congress to agree to the plan. Harry's own contemporary memoir of the
event mentions no such proposal, but he did indeed begin immediately
to promote the idea in *Time*, with a lengthy essay pointing out the
importance to the United States of bases in the Caribbean, "the first
outpost of U.S.'s maritime frontier." What had once been an
afterthought—using the acquisition of bases in the Caribbean to facilitate the much more important need to send destroyers to Britain—now
cleverly became, in public at least, *Time*'s principal goal. It was exactly
the kind of support Roosevelt needed to give him the cover to pursue the
deal. At the same time Luce, along with others, worked to persuade
Willkie not to oppose the destroyers-for-bases deal in the campaign.
Willkie agreed, even though he must certainly have known that such a
decision could strengthen Roosevelt's chances for reelection. On September 3, after a month of intricate negotiations with the British government, Roosevelt announced that he was issuing an executive order
(not reviewable by Congress) to acquire British bases in the Caribbean
"in exchange for fifty of our over-age destroyers"—a deal almost identical to the one Luce had proposed to him in July. The president's "bold
stroke," *Time* exultantly if slightly grudgingly reported, "was received
with cheers that drowned out criticism of the secret and questionable
method by which it was carried out."[42]

In November, only days after the presidential election, Luce quietly resigned from the Century Group, explaining that "happily, we are well embarked on armament and military production; we are pretty generally agreed on aid-to-Britain, etc." The committee's job was far from over, he conceded, but its task had shifted from influencing the president to influencing the public. "I think that as an editor I should not be an active member of a policy promoting group. . . . I doubt whether I should be in a position of being busily engaged in trying to influence myself!" Coming so soon after the end of the campaign, it is likely that Luce was also aware of the danger he had created for himself and his company by becoming such an obvious and partisan supporter of Willkie. It was time, he seemed to be signaling, for him to stop being a political activist and to focus again on his company and his magazines.[43]

But Luce could not contain himself for long. In December 1940 he found himself embroiled in a secret effort, spearheaded by a shadowy pacifist, Malcolm Lovell, to explore the possibility of a settlement of the war. Lovell arranged a meeting with an attaché in the German consulate in New York, Hans Thomsen; and Luce, perhaps out of curiosity and perhaps out of his continuing hope that he would somehow transform the course of world events, unwisely agreed to attend. Nothing came of the flirtation except to create another reason for the White House, which learned of the meeting, to distrust him. In the meantime, he continued an active correspondence with the members of the Century Group, who continued to fear that "our present scale of help will only achieve that miserable result . . . of just keeping England going until we get strong enough not to care." Luce warned them of allying with the "extreme Anglophiles" but agreed that the government's policy remained inadequate. Early in the new year he briefly involved himself in an Illinois Senate race, in an effort to ensure that a "non-isolationist candidate" would be nominated by the state Republicans. And by late January he was back in the thick of the effort—again orchestrated by many of the same establishment leaders with whom he had collaborated in 1940—to promote what became Lend-Lease, the much more expansive system of aid to Britain (and later other Allies, including the Soviet Union) that Roosevelt proposed and Congress approved in March 1941. Luce wrote an editorial for *Life* in January, "We Americans," which advocated the bill, but he sullenly backed away from it when confronted with objections from his editors to running an explicit editorial. He embarked instead on a speaking tour, in which he actively promoted Lend-Lease, and he began to speak more openly than ever before about direct American participation in the war. "I say that we are already *in* the war," he pronounced dramatically to an audience in Pittsburgh. "The irony is that Hitler knows it—and most of the American people don't." But he was also exploring larger themes: the nature of America's power and wealth, its capacity to reshape the world, its moral obligations. "Ours is the power, ours is the opportunity," he proclaimed to a group of oilmen in Tulsa, "and ours will be the responsibility whether we like it or not." On his return to New York he began contemplating a more systematic statement of his ideas on the war, a manifesto that would, he hoped, both confront the momentous issues facing the nation and thrust Luce himself into the center of the great debate.[44]

Luce never underestimated his own intelligence. Billings uncharitably called him a "thinking machine," lost in "the clouds of theory." Harry himself once said to Clare—according to her own perhaps apocryphal but not wholly implausible later account—that he could think of no one who was his intellectual superior. What about Einstein? Clare asked. Einstein, Harry replied, was a "specialist," without his own range. But despite his formidable intelligence he rarely took a strong public position without borrowing from the ideas of others and without validating his work through people he admired. And so, as he set out to write an important statement about his own dangerous times, he searched widely for inspiration and advice.[45]

He turned first to Walter Lippmann and Archibald MacLeish, both of whom had often influenced him in the past. Lippmann had been a regular contributor to *Life* for months, publishing articles that were more aggressively interventionist than anything Luce had yet written. Through the second half of 1940 Lippmann called consistently for Americans to recognize their responsibility as world leaders. "Either we shall fulfill that destiny or the world we have lived in will perish beyond hope of an early or an easy resurrection," he wrote in June. If totalitarian states came to control the great industrial capacity of Europe and Russia, he warned, the American economy would face "unprecedented difficulties. . . . A free economy, such as Americans have known, cannot survive in a world that is elsewhere a regime of military socialism." The defeat of democratic powers in Europe, he warned in October, would mean that "we and our children would stand on the unending defensive waiting for the blow to fall." But to Luce, Lippmann's most persuasive argument came even before the European war began, in an essay titled "The American Destiny," published in *Life* in June 1939. In it Lippmann talked less of the external threats to the nation than of its internal doubt and confusion. "In the generation to which we belong," Lippmann had argued, "unlike any that went before, the American people have no vision of their own future." They were fearful of their own wealth and power, convinced somehow that "their incomparable assets are in fact their most dangerous liability." The American failure, in short, was its unwillingness to accept its own greatness and its responsibilities to the world. "What Rome was to the ancient world, what Great Britain has been to the modern world, America is to be to the world of tomorrow," he proclaimed. "When the destiny of a nation is revealed to it, there is no choice but to accept that destiny and to make ready in order to be equal to it."[46]

If Lippmann helped Luce embrace the idea of an American destiny, MacLeish helped him express at least a part of the moral underpinning with which he would justify the nation's mission in the world. MacLeish wrote a series of drafts for him of a "Statement of Belief" that would, he hoped, capture the urgent mission of his time. It was an argument for the importance of freedom, and for the special role the United States had always played in exemplifying and defending freedom. "Freedom is still the greatest of human causes," MacLeish wrote, and "it is in the United States that the cause of freedom has its highest hope." If freedom was to become the normal condition of humanity in the world, he insisted, then

> the people of the United States, with their tradition of political responsibility, their mastery of the skills of industry and agriculture, their ownership of the wealth of the richest of all lands, have a better right to hope for its realization than any other nation has ever had.

Luce, as always, admired MacLeish's literary power (so much so that he borrowed passages from MacLeish in his own later essay), but he also worried that the statements were too narrow. "Why is it so hard?" he wrote in response to an early draft. "Not because we lack faith, but because what is included in our faith is such a multitude of things seen and unseen." His hope was to combine something of Lippmann's muscularity of purpose with MacLeish's moral temper. But he also sought to reshape some of his own earlier ideas and statements, which he had been developing throughout his adult life.[47]

His effort to articulate the meaning of America had begun in China, when, as a young boy, he attempted to construct an image of a nation he had passionately embraced but had never seen, a nation he associated with the good that he believed his own father was doing in the world. It continued in his first years in America as a student, nowhere more clearly than in his senior-year oration at Yale in 1920:

> When we say "America" twenty years from now, may it be that that great name will signify throughout the world . . . that America may be counted upon to do her share in the solution of every international difficulty, that she will be the great comrade of all nations that struggle to rise to higher planes of social and political organization, and withal the implacable and the *immediate* foe of whatever nation shall offer to disturb the peace of the world.[48]

In the crowded years during which he had worked tirelessly to create first a magazine and then a publishing empire, he spent relatively little time thinking or writing about the great missions he had embraced in his youth. But after the enormous success of his company, and in the face of the great world crisis of the late 1930s, he turned again to the task of articulating an "idea worth fighting for." His impassioned, sometimes reckless, and often frustrating involvement with the Willkie campaign was a first step. After the 1940 election, freed of his efforts to speak through Willkie, he began to express his own views, in the aborted article, "We Americans"; in his speeches across the country in 1941; and finally in a new essay for *Life*—this time urged on by his editors, who advocated a "modern Federalist Papers for this world A.D. 1941." The essay would become the most influential article he would ever publish.[49]

It appeared in the February 17, 1941, issue of *Life* under the title "The American Century," a phrase first used decades earlier by H. G. Wells, but one that Luce now made a part of American, and global, language. To a large degree it was a commentary on the current "confused" state of American life and the nation's uncertain relationship with the war. "We Americans are unhappy," he began (echoing Lippman in 1939). "We are nervous—or gloomy—or apathetic. . . . We are filled with foreboding." Luce then set out to explain, and dispel, the pessimism and confusion that he saw around him. Most of the essay consisted of a careful, guarded, and often prosaic analysis of the steps America had taken so far toward greater engagement in the war. "America is in the war," he wrote, "but are we in it? . . . We say we don't want to be in the war. We also say we want England to win. We want Hitler stopped—more than we want to stay out of the war. So at the moment, we're in." But being "in" was not enough. *Wanting* to be "in" is what Luce asked of the American people. And why should Americans want to be fully engaged in what promised to be the most terrible of all wars? Partly because staying out of the war, he argued (in a reflection of his continuing dislike and distrust of Roosevelt), could lead to tyranny at home:

> The President of the United States has continually reached for more and more power, and he owes his continuation in office to the coming of the war. Thus, the fear that the United States will be driven to national socialism, as a result of cataclysmic circumstances and contrary to the free will of the American people, is an entirely justifiable fear.

But also because Britain could not possibly win the war without American help. The United States was "the most powerful and the most vital nation in the world," and Americans were failing "to play their part as a world power—a failure which has had disastrous consequences for themselves and for all mankind." America had squandered "an opportunity unprecedented in all history, to assume the leadership of the world" in 1919. It had failed again in the 1920s, and again in the 1930s. It could not do so again. The twentieth century, he insisted, must at last become what it should have been a generation earlier: "an American Century."

"What can we say and foresee about an American Century?" he asked. His answer was bold, ambitious, idealistic—and filled with the missionary zeal that had shaped his life. "It must be a sharing with all peoples of our Bill of Rights, our Declaration of Independence, our Constitution, our magnificent industrial products, our technical skills. It must be an internationalism of the people, by the people, and for the people." America was already the "intellectual, scientific and artistic capital of the world," he claimed, and Americans were "the least provincial people in the world." But more important than that the United States now had "that indefinable unmistakable sign of leadership: prestige. And unlike the prestige of Rome or Genghis Khan or 19th Century England, American prestige throughout the world is faith in the good intentions as well as the ultimate intelligence and ultimate strength of the whole of the American people." The creation of an American century would require great vision. It would mean a commitment to "an economic order compatible with freedom and progress." It would mean a willingness to "send out through the world [America's] technical and artistic skills. Engineers, scientists, doctors, movie men, makers of entertainment, developers of airlines, builders of roads, teachers, educators." It would mean becoming "the Good Samaritan of the entire world," with a duty "to feed all the people of the world who . . . are hungry and destitute."

Most of all, the American Century as Luce envisioned it would require:

> a passionate devotion to great American ideals . . . a love of freedom, a feeling for the equality of opportunity, a tradition of self-reliance and independence and also of co-operation. . . . [W]e are the inheritors of all the great principles of Western civilization—above all Justice, the love of Truth, the ideal of Charity. . . . It now becomes our time to be the powerhouse from which the ideals spread throughout the world and do their mysterious work of lifting the life of mankind from the level of the beasts to what the Psalmist called a little lower than the angels.

From these elements, he concluded, "surely can be fashioned a vision of the 20th Century to which we can and will devote ourselves in joy and gladness and vigor and enthusiasm. . . . It is in this spirit that all of us are called, each to his own measure of capacity, and each in the widest horizon of his vision, to create the first great American Century."[50]

It should not be surprising that this strangely powerful essay—which never explicitly advocated an American declaration of war but called instead for an almost evangelical commitment to righting the wrongs of the world—evoked a set of highly disparate responses. The thousands of letters sent to *Life* in response to "The American Century"—far more than the magazine normally received for other articles—contained a predictable number of protests from people still strongly opposed to entering the war. "Let America be the 'Good Samaritan' to *United States Citizens*," a woman from Toledo wrote. "You are turning your magazine . . . into a war monger's tool," wrote a Pennsylvania woman. "You privileged entrenched cowards rant and rave to stir up this gory, godless thing called WAR," a Maryland man charged, "and then drink champagne in safety and ease while the sons of the common people are slain and their children cry for bread." Others, however, expressed great enthusiasm for Luce's vision: "BIG STUFF!

And I like it!," one reader wrote. "Henry R. Luce is showing the way to the American people towards their future," said another. "GRAND WRITING GRANDER THINKING," a New York man declared. "I hope this morning one BEAM of its GLORIOUS VISION will REACH the MYOPIC FRINGE of what was once the GRAND OLD PARTY!" More than one writer referred to him as "the Tom Paine of this generation."[51]

While most readers focused on what they interpreted as a call to war, many journalists and critics responded more energetically to Luce's vision of America's future role in the world. Walter Lippmann—whose own writings had helped shape Luce's views—was unsurprisingly enthusiastic, as was Robert Sherwood, the former Roosevelt speechwriter, who called it "magnificent," and the columnist Dorothy Thompson, who wrote (in a more aggressively imperialist tone than had Luce himself), "To Americanize enough of the *world* so that we shall have a climate favorable to our growth is indeed a call to destiny." Other less charitable critics, mostly on the Left, took a far more hostile view of what they considered Luce's imperialist ambitions. "A new brand of imperialism is fast gaining favor in this country," Freda Kirchwey, the editor of the *Nation*, wrote disdainfully. "Mr. Luce in a very large advertisement in his magazine *Life* calls it 'the American Century.' " The columnist Max Lerner, who shared Luce's belief that the United States should enter the war, nevertheless sneered at what he considered his proposals "to establish . . . hegemony in the world, control the world sea lanes and world," a vision that represented "a new capitalist-conscious group . . . who do not fear war but regard it as an opportunity." Norman Thomas, the Socialist Party leader, criticized Luce's "nakedness of imperial ambition."[52]

The wide range of responses to "The American Century" was in part a result of the bitter divisions over the war in early 1941. But it was also a result of the character of the essay itself. Luce's purpose in writing the essay, he later claimed, was "to help clear away the fogs of ambiguity" around the issue of the war "so that we could get on more vigorously." But in fact there was considerable ambiguity in the way Luce addressed his central issues. (Should America enter the war? What role should the United States play in the remainder of the twentieth century?) Luce had written elliptically about both these issues, leaving it largely to his readers to decide what concrete steps he was recommending. His language was most forceful and unguarded in the final, climactic passages, in which he presented an almost evangelical portrait of

America's virtues and destiny, language so florid that it invited interpretations well beyond what Luce may have intended. He was surprised by the accusations of imperialism, and surprised too when critics lambasted him for suggesting that (as Senator Robert Taft of Ohio charged) he was proposing "that a victorious all-powerful United States dominate the 20th Century world as England did the 19th." Luce's essay was not incompatible with such a view, but it did not embrace it either. "My basic premise," he wrote defensively in 1943, "was simply that America ought to assume in world affairs a responsibility corresponding to its strength. That surely is axiomatic—isn't it?" Indeed, for much of the rest of his life he continued to try to explain to curious readers, both hostile and friendly, what he had really meant.[53]

And yet, despite the lack of precision and despite the many misconceptions it helped to create, "The American Century" did have something significant to say about both the present and the future. For the world of 1941 the essay was a powerful work of propaganda, published first in the most popular magazine in America, and then republished and circulated widely throughout the United States, and the world, over the following months. It was designed to rouse Americans out of what Luce considered their slothful indifference and inspire them to undertake a great mission on behalf of what he considered the nation's core values. Despite Luce's demurral on the crucial question of military intervention in the war, the essay made a powerful case in accessible (and in some ways populist) language for the enormous stake the United States had in the outcome of the conflict. No one reading "the American Century" could miss Luce's warning that a totalitarian world would doom the nation's hopes for the future. And for those looking beyond the war, the essay was unequivocal in its belief in the extraordinary role the United States could and must play in the world, and the extraordinary power and virtue America would bring to its tasks, despite Luce's strenuous insistence that "you can't extract imperialism from the American Century."[54]

A little more than a year after Luce's essay appeared in *Life*, in the first months of America's formal entry into the war, Vice President Henry A. Wallace wrote what was in some respects the most important response to "The American Century"—a speech delivered on May 8, 1942, widely known as "The Century of the Common Man" (although its actual title was "The Price of Free World Victory"). Wallace would later become a controversial, even reviled, figure for his leadership of dissenting leftists in the early years of the Cold War, his bitter criticisms of what he considered America's excessive militarism and aggression, and for his perhaps unwitting alliance with communists in his 1948 presidential campaign as the candidate of the short-lived Progressive Party. But he gave his 1942 speech at a high-water mark in his political career. A little over a year into his vice presidency, he had a reputation—soon to be shattered—as the second most important figure in government, as the "assistant president," as Roosevelt's likely heir. He spoke in 1942 as a prominent, mainstream Democrat—an important and influential figure in the Roosevelt administration—attempting to rouse the public to more fervent support of a war that the nation was not yet clearly winning.[55]

Wallace was implicitly critical of what he, like others, considered the imperialistic rhetoric of Luce's 1941 essay, and he was careful to distance himself from any notion that the United States could, or should, unilaterally impose its values and institutions on the world. But he too presented a vision of the future that included a central role for the United States in both inspiring and shaping a new age of democracy. "This is a fight between a slave world and a free world," he said. "Just as the United States in 1862 could not remain half slave and half free, so in 1942 the world must make its decision for a complete victory one way or the other." Naturally Wallace expected all "freedom-loving people"—who were not Americans alone but among whom Americans stood preeminent—to answer that question and to shape the postwar world. Their answer, he said, was embodied in the Four Freedoms Franklin Roosevelt had proclaimed in January 1941, freedoms that "are at the very core of the revolution for which the United Nations have taken their stand." And just as Luce's vision of an American century included a vision of exporting Western industrial abundance to the world, so Wallace insisted that "the peace must mean a better standard of living for the common man, not merely in the United States and England, but also in India, Russia, China, and Latin America—not merely in the United Nations [as the Western Alliance then called itself], but also in Germany and Italy and Japan."[56]

"Some have spoken of the 'American Century,' " Wallace added, in an obvious effort to differentiate himself from Luce. "I say the century on which we are entering . . . can be and must be the century of the common man." In the years to come, as Wallace's own vision (and political fortunes) changed, he came increasingly to see his speech as a full-throated rejoinder to what he considered Luce's more imperialist vision. At the time, however, both Wallace and Luce spoke warmly about each other's remarks and seemed to agree that they were on the whole fighting the same battle. ("I do not happen to remember anything that you have written descriptive of your concepts of 'the American Century' of which I disapprove," Wallace wrote Luce shortly after he delivered his speech. Luce's essay, he added, "is almost precisely parallel to what I was trying to say in my talk." Luce in turn congratulated Wallace on the speech and even argued later that he was, if anything, overreaching. "Not every mission is appropriate to the political state," he said pointedly in a 1943 speech. "To claim for it an unlimited mission to do good is to invite infinite confusion, ugly strife, and ultimately disaster.")[57]

But whatever differences Wallace may have had with Luce, his vision of a world modeled on American notions of freedom, his commitment to spreading the fruits of economic growth to the world, his insistence that "older nations will have the privilege to help younger nations get started on the path to industrialization," and perhaps most of all the extravagant rhetoric with which he presented these ideas—all made his speech less an alternative to Luce's essay than a variation on it. "There are no half measures," Wallace concluded (with language no less evangelical than the language Luce had used to end his own essay). "No compromise with Satan is possible. . . . We shall fight for a complete peace and a complete victory. The people's revolution is on the march, and the devil and all his angels cannot prevail against it. They cannot prevail for on the side of the people is the Lord."[58]

"The American Century" and "The Price of Free World Victory" were important documents of their time, but not because their influence on the contemporary public conversation was profound. They were significant primarily because they were highly visible symbols of a growing movement among American leaders, and eventually among many others, to redefine the nation's relationship to the world and, in the process, to redefine America's sense of itself. Luce and Wallace were unlikely, and perhaps to some degree unwitting, partners, but together they helped launch an idea that survived well beyond the dark days in which they wrote—an idea that could not accurately be described as imperialism but that did outline a mission for the United States in the world that would when implemented (as it largely was) profoundly change the shape of the nation and the globe.

Given the intensity of Luce's engagement with the global crisis, it is surprising that until mid-1941 he had focused relatively little attention on China. He had visited Asia only once since his departure from his parents' home in 1914; and even that 1932 visit only briefly renewed his active interest in Asia. Nor had his magazines in the 1930s given more than ordinary coverage of the Japanese invasion of Manchuria and the expansion of the war into other regions of China. Through the first months of 1941, Luce was principally concerned with Europe, and with the survival of Britain in the face of the German threat. But in the spring of that year he accepted an invitation from the Chinese government to visit Chungking, an event that helped renew a passion for China that would continue for the rest of his life.

Luce's wartime involvement with China began modestly in the late 1930s with a philanthropic project—an effort initiated by Ida Pruitt, a teacher at Peking University and the daughter of Chinese missionaries, and the writer Edgar Snow, who had already become famous for his reportage on the Chinese Communist Party and his celebrated book *Red Star Over China*. Together Pruitt and Snow began promoting an effort to produce industrial cooperatives to help poor Chinese villagers manufacture modest goods for sale. Luce was responsive to their appeal, and in 1939 he began mobilizing wealthy friends and acquaintances to help support it. But he soon turned to a larger effort. Early in 1941 a group of eminent public figures—among them John D. Rockefeller III, Paul Hoffman (the president of the Studebaker car company), Thomas W. Lamont of the Morgan bank, David Selznick, Wendell Willkie, and Luce himself—began to coalesce around a much more ambitious goal: the creation of a broad effort to raise private money "for the relief of the Chinese—both soldiers and civilians," which became known as United China Relief (UCR). Luce had strongly encouraged the formation of the organization, but he declined invitations to chair it and for a time expressed considerable pessimism about its likely success. (In its first two months it raised only forty thousand dollars, not enough even to cover its expenses.) Nevertheless he allied himself with the effort and actively assisted it. "This is probably the most important letter I have ever tried to write," he began a letter to wealthy friends requesting support. "We have now undertaken to raise $5,000,000. . . . If we are successful in this effort, it will help to confirm, perhaps for years to come, the wide-spread belief in China that America feels kindly toward China." To help advance the project, he said, he would himself travel to China to provide "a first-hand report on the situation" and to try to enlist Mme. Chiang Kai-shek to support the initiative.[59]

Harry and Clare flew together on the still relatively new Pan Am Clipper service to Hong Kong and arrived at the end of April 1941 in a nation at war. By then China and Japan had been fighting for more than a decade, beginning with the Japanese conquest of Manchuria in 1931, and escalating sharply in 1937 when the Japanese army swept through eastern China. Chiang Kai-shek, China's leader since 1928, moved with his army far inland to Chungking, where the government regrouped. The war with Japan was not the only conflict Chiang faced. Civil strife had plagued China since the early twentieth century—conflicts between warlords and the Kuomintang (the Nationalist revolutionary party Sun Yat-sen had created in 1912), and later a conflict within the Kuomintang itself, between Communists and Chiang's Nationalists. In 1928 the Communists—under the leadership of Mao Zedong—left the Kuomintang and formed a government and an army of their own, which Chiang considered as dangerous an enemy as the Japanese invaders. Despite appeals from many sides that the factions unite to fight Japan together, Chiang was never able (and perhaps never willing) to cooperate with the Communists, a failure that would have momentous consequences throughout the war and beyond.

After arriving in Hong Kong, the Luces flew in the dead of night to Chungking on what Harry called "the most dangerous [airline] in the world"—a five-hour journey in a darkened plane, most of it over Japanese-occupied territory. They landed in a dry riverbed outside the city, and the passengers were carried up the steep bank in sedan chairs. That same day Luce watched a Japanese air raid from the terrace of the American Embassy and was struck less by the violence than by the efficiency with which the residents took cover. A similar optimism colored virtually everything he encountered during his weeks in China, finding silver linings in almost every cloud. The government's desperate escape to Chungking, he wrote, "has now brought modern ideas and methods to the vast agricultural hinterland . . . and has also served to give all the Chinese people an idea of what their total nation is. . . . The Chinese are discovering, in these years of bitter suffering, their own potentialities." Shortly after his arrival he observed that while "China is seething with political factions," it was also "accomplishing miracles in their defense of the country." The Nationalist army, he wrote, "is the best thing in China, morale is magnificent against appalling difficulties."[60]

But nothing contributed more to his optimism than his first encounter with Chiang Kai-shek, whom he was already describing as "the greatest ruler Asia has seen since Emperor Kyan Hsi [Kangxi] 200 years ago." He and Clare had received an invitation to visit Madame Chiang to discuss United China Relief. She was, Harry wrote, "an even more exciting personality than all the glamorous descriptions of her. . . .

What instantly convinced me of her greatness was her delivery of the most direct and unrestrained compliment to my wife's beauty I have ever heard." Sometime during their conversation, Luce sensed a door opening, and moments later he saw "a slim wraith-like figure in khaki [moving] through the shadow": the Generalissimo joining him for tea. Harry presented him with "a portfolio of photographs of himself and Madame," and Chiang "grinned from ear to ear . . . as pleased as a boy." They left after an hour of conversation "knowing that we had made the acquaintance of two people, a man and a woman, who, out of all the millions living, will be remembered for centuries and centuries."[61]

A few days later the Luces boarded a tiny Beechcraft and flew to the headquarters of a Chinese army division on the northern front, across the Yellow River from a Japanese encampment. It was a harrowing flight, traversing three steep mountain ranges while buffeted by high winds. There was no active combat under way during their brief visit, but they trekked through the encampments and entrenchments to the riverbank and looked across at the Japanese forces. Despite the terrible damage inflicted on the towns and villages near the front, Luce was again impressed by what he considered "as fine a morale, as strict discipline and as intent an expression as ever characterized any army in history." Clare took pictures to illustrate a story on the war she would later publish in *Life*. Harry took notes to send back to his editors. And even in the midst of the disarray of an active front, Chinese officers managed to organize teas and dinners to cement their relationship with a man they knew only as a powerful American in a position to help their cause.[62]

Luce's trip to China had a profound effect on his view of the war—and of the world. It renewed and intensified his love of the country and his faith in its ability to join the family of successful nations. Every place he went, no matter how damaged or desperate the surroundings, he took note of signs of progress: bankers demonstrating knowledge and sophistication in the management of the currency; soldiers in trenches working on primers as they tried to learn to read; officers helping them study "the doctrine of democracy with the teaching of Sun Yatsen and the American constitution as text books"; generals reading Clausewitz and other Western classics of military strategy; and many members of the Kuomintang elite—including Chiang Kai-shek and Mme. Chiang—converting to Christianity. "What strikes me about these far inland cities," he wrote of a brief stop in Sian, a large provincial capital, "is how modernized they have become . . . I see America and the 20th century stamped all over them." On his return to New York he began working furiously to raise money for United China Relief, which very rapidly met and exceeded its initial goals. UCR raised over four million dollars in 1941, most of it in the last four months of the year, the beginning of an impressive multiyear total of nearly fifty million dollars. But his most important task, he now believed, was to heighten American consciousness about the crisis in China and make the war in the Pacific as important to Americans as the war in Europe. "As long as the Army of the Republic of China remains in being," he said in one of a series of speeches he made shortly after his return to the United States, "Japan is doomed to defeat and disaster no matter what policy she tries." It was "absolutely certain that without China we cannot achieve a victory." In his discussions with his colleagues at Time Inc. he was even blunter: "I'm still convinced as I always have been that we must win the war in Asia first. . . . I wonder whether we have taken China seriously enough. . . . What about a full-out consideration of full-out aid to China? . . . When is the time to put Chiang Kai-shek on the cover again?"[63]

Luce's 1941 visit to China launched another important relationship. Waiting for him as he descended from his plane to the dry Chungking riverbed was a young man wearing khaki shorts and a sun helmet: Theodore H. White, known to everyone as "Teddy."

Only relatively recently had *Time* abandoned its tradition of simply rewriting news borrowed from other organizations. But by the late 1930s the magazine was posting correspondents in numerous areas of the United States and the world. The war rapidly expanded that effort. By the time World War II had begun, the staff of correspondents was already large and growing rapidly. White, then *Time*'s principal China correspondent, was someone about whom Luce was already curious. White was then twenty-six, short, wiry haired, round faced with oversize glasses and an infectious smile. He had grown up in what he later called the "Jewish ghetto" in the Dorchester area of Boston and had graduated from the famed Boston Latin School, open to the brightest of the city's children and an avenue of social mobility for the lower middle class. In the fall of 1934 he entered Harvard on a scholarship and almost by chance took up the study of Chinese, which soon led him to John King Fairbank, a faculty member only three years White's senior and soon to be the most influential historian of Chinese-American relations of the twentieth century. He became White's longtime mentor and friend.

White graduated summa cum laude and was awarded two Harvard traveling fellowships, which he used to finance a trip to China. Shortly after he arrived he accepted a position in the China Information Office, the Kuomintang's propaganda agency in Chungking. A few months later he encountered John Hersey, then a *Time* editor visiting the city in search of correspondents. He hired White more or less on the spot, offered him ten dollars a dispatch, and allowed him to continue his work for the Chinese government at the same time. White's lengthy, copious memos quickly attracted attention in New York, and soon he was on the Time Inc. payroll full-time.[64]

White was Luce's kind of correspondent, despite the great social differences between them. Like Luce, White loved China with an almost romantic passion. Also like Luce, he loved to talk, to argue, and to push the intellectual boundaries of conversation. Perhaps even more important, he had no qualms about using his dispatches to convey his own opinions and sentiments. "The chief fault that you are liable to find with my production is a pro-Chinese bias and a Chinese enthusiasm," he wrote to his editor in New York. As if to prove his point he wrote in one of his first dispatches, published in *Time* almost unaltered, that the "present Chinese Army has spirit. It glows. The men are willing to die. They mix and tangle with the Japanese with a burning hate that is good." He was for a time an ardent admirer of Chiang Kai-shek and his government. Chiang's "personal record," he wrote, "is one of the most positive and virile of any government leader today." Under Chiang's leadership, he observed, "China made such magic strides toward self-consciousness." And while White was observant enough to see the many flaws in Chiang and the Kuomintang regime, he kept his reservations mostly to himself. He had an obligation, he believed, "to say nothing at all that might help the Japanese . . . and to say nothing that might hurt the cause of China in American eyes," a position that he conceded "made impossible the telling of the rank corruption, inefficiency and stupidity that exists in high places in Chungking today." Little wonder that Luce found him so appealing. The two men spent much time together and formed an unusual friendship. White showed little of the timid deference that characterized Luce's relations with most Time Inc. employees. They were "Harry" and "Teddy," a mismatched pair who interacted—at least in Chungking—almost as equals. When it came time for Luce to return to New York, he brought White with him and appointed him the Far East editor of *Time*, a post he held for only a few months before returning to China to cover the war. Luce viewed him as an indispensable asset in the effort to generate support for the Chinese government, someone who shared his own view that, as White wrote shortly after his return to America, "If the United States must face the Axis on two fronts, it can do so for just one reason: that a Free China is fighting the Battle of the Pacific."[65]

Luce's publication of "The American Century" and his reengagement with China greatly increased his commitment to driving public debate over intervention in the war. His magazines attacked the "isolationists" and "appeasers" with almost gleeful vigor, and they continued to lambaste the Roosevelt administration for what Luce considered its timid and erratic path to war. *Time* even criticized the legendary Henry Stimson, Roosevelt's secretary of war, for being too old and feeble to run the military. "The whole civilian defense machinery," the magazine wrote, was "running without any responsible head" and was pursuing "uncertain policies . . . fresh confusions piled on stale confusions." *Time* referred so often to the "fog" in Washington that the *Harvard Lampoon* ran a parody: "Fog settled down over Washington last week. Coming by way of Chesapeake Bay at a mean rate of 10 m.p.h."[66]

Luce's simmering feud with Roosevelt burst into the open once again in November 1941 over what was, in fact, a trivial issue. *Time* had run a short notice about Chilean president Pedro Aguirre Cerda, who was encountering political troubles. "While the Popular Front swayed," *Time* wrote, "bushy-mustached President Aguirre felt more and more like a man who does not govern but merely presides. He spent more and more time with the red wine he cultivates." A few days later Aguirre died. The Chilean consul general in New York protested, and Roosevelt seized on the issue to do something he had long talked about but had never done: go after Luce. "The Government of the United States has been forced to apologize to the Government of Chile for an article written in *Time* magazine,—a disgusting lie," he wrote. "This article was a notable illustration of how some American papers and writers are stocking the arsenals of propaganda of the Nazis to be used against us." Luce seemed mildly shell-shocked by the ferocity of the attack and responded meekly and defensively that "no one had [previously] said anything in *Time*'s report was untrue."[67]

By the beginning of December, after a series of failed American efforts to thwart Japanese expansion, Luce—and many others—came to believe that war in the Pacific was imminent, perhaps inevitable. "Everything was ready," *Time* proclaimed in the December 8 issue (published on December 1):

> From Rangoon to Honolulu, every man was at battle sta-
> tions. . . . A vast array of armies, of navies, of air fleets were
> stretched now in the position of track runners, in the tension of
> the moment before the starter's gun. . . . A bare chance of peace
> remained. This bare chance was that the Japanese would remain
> immobile on all fronts but the Chinese. Very few men who were
> in a position to know thought much of this chance.[68]

On December 7 the Luces hosted a luncheon for twenty-two people at their home in Greenwich—an event typical of their lives ever since Harry's marriage to Clare. Among the guests were diplomats, theologians, business leaders, and some of Luce's colleagues from Time Inc. It was a crisp, clear day, and the guests were in good spirits, avoiding too much talk of war and enjoying the meal, the august company, and the lavish surroundings. Shortly after dessert was served, the butler— violating a strict rule never to interrupt a meal—handed Clare a folded piece of paper on a small tray. She glanced at it, tapped her glass, and said, with a tone of mockery perhaps unsuited for the occasion, "All iso- lationists and appeasers, please listen. The Japanese have bombed Pearl Harbor." Most of the guests rushed to the radio or the telephone. Harry raced to his car and within an hour was back in his office in Manhattan. Both *Time* and *Life* were already in production for the following week. Luce interrupted the press runs and helped remake the issues. For *Time*, he created a new department on the spot: The U.S. at War, and oversaw a lead story that called the attack "premeditated murder with a toothy smile." He added that "the war came as a great relief, like a reverse earthquake, that in one terrible jerk shook everything disjointed, dis- torted, askew back into place. Japanese bombs had finally brought national unity to the U.S." Luce and Billings completely remade *Life* as well, with a new lead cover story on Pearl Harbor—although forced to use photographs taken well before the attack. Louis de Rochemont and his staff hurried to recut the December *March of Time*.[69]

Sometime late that day Luce called his father in Pennsylvania to talk about their shared relief that the war had finally begun. "We will now all see what we mean to China and China means to us," Rev. Luce told his son. After hanging up, Harry, Sr., told his wife how reassuring it had been to hear from their son. Not long after the conversation he retired for the evening and died quietly in the course of the night. Harry left no record of how he viewed the symbolism of these two enormous events— one global and one personal—occurring on the same day. "My father was profoundly shocked by Japan's attack on Pearl Harbor," he later wrote a friend. To others he noted only that "it was wonderful that he lived long enough to see America and China as allies."[70]

A few days later Luce wrote to Roosevelt, offering something short of an apology for his earlier criticisms but a modest effort at conciliation. "We wished to do every last thing in our power, to strain every nerve, to assist our country to face the ordeal and triumph of it," he wrote of the months preceding Pearl Harbor. "We have made mistakes and fallen short of our best intentions. But . . . no company of men and women . . . have ever worked harder . . . to do their duty as they saw it." Time Inc. would, he promised, not only comply with wartime regulations but would "think of no greater happiness than to be of service. . . . For the dearest wish of all of us is to tell the story of absolute victory under your leadership." In a handwritten note attached to the letter, he was more frank. Referring to the president's attack on *Time*'s recent coverage of Chile, he wrote: "The drubbing you handed out to TIME— before December 7—was as tough a wallop as I ever had to take. If it will help you any to win the war I can take worse ones. Go to it! And God bless you." Roosevelt wrote back that he liked the letter, that it "combines honest patriotism with genuine sportsmanship. . . . The waters of Pearl Harbor have closed over many differences which formerly bulked big." But this warm truce in their long and sometimes bitter feud did not last for very long.[71]

X

Time Inc. Goes to War

The most terrible war in human history was in many ways very good to Time Inc. Its magazines had never been more popular. *Time*'s circulation exceeded a million copies a week by the end of 1942, and *Life*'s was approaching four million, making the company, according to Eric Hodgins, "the largest publisher of news on a national scale." And despite paper shortages that limited the size of the magazines, advertising revenue remained strong. The *March of Time* newsreels were shown in more than eleven thousand theaters, and the weekly *March of Time* radio broadcasts had an audience of nearly eight million. Time Inc.'s profits were the highest in the company's history—over ten million dollars a year even after steep wartime taxes. Its expenses were growing as well. The company's News Bureau, modest until the late 1930s, now maintained bureaus in almost every major city in the United States. Where it was possible to do so, it opened bureaus around the globe as well: London, Buenos Aires, Rio de Janeiro, Moscow, India, Turkey, Egypt, South Africa, Switzerland, and China. The reporting staff—more than a hundred full-time correspondents and many more part-time employees and stringers—was one of the largest of any news organization in the world, and the comprehensiveness of war coverage in the magazines was one of the reasons for their great success. The company generated additional goodwill through its distribution of 750,000 copies of *Time* and 650,000 copies of *Life* free to American troops abroad through a special "Air Express Edition," copies that were passed around to so many servicemen, according to one *Time* correspondent, that they literally fell apart. More than 60 percent of soldiers and sailors named *Life* their favorite magazine. Time Inc., through its March of Time division, also produced training films and publications for the military and worked hard in other ways to show its commitment to the war effort.[1]

The war also had personal benefits for Luce. His own profile and influence, and even his own popularity, rose significantly. A poll commissioned by the company early in the war found that more than 80 percent of those who had an opinion viewed him favorably. Perhaps more important, the war gave Luce a new sense of purpose. He was, of course, committed to chronicling the conflict and contributing to what he considered America's inevitable victory. But his larger mission was now to envision a postwar world that would remedy the failures that followed World War I. This war, he believed, must lead the world toward a stable and lasting peace and guide the nation into a position of global leadership. By early 1943 he had already created a Post War Committee within his company, with a full staff of editors and researchers committed to examining "the foreign and domestic post-war problems of the U.S. . . . post-war relations with Britain and the post-war problems of the Far East."[2]

The key to the great success of Luce's magazines in wartime was their almost total commitment to chronicling and, when appropriate, celebrating the war. *Time*, of course, covered the war week by week, battle by battle, and controversy by controversy in its usual disciplined, cocksure manner. *Life*, on the other hand, turned the war into a great visual story and significantly expanded its pool of photographers and graphic artists to make that possible. It was, it seemed, fulfilling at last its mission as a picture magazine—flooding its pages with powerful images of what was arguably the most important event in history.

Life's remarkable popularity in wartime was also a result of the great interest Americans had in the progress of the war, the magazine's sure-footed presentation of exceptional photography, and its effectiveness in tapping into the complicated interests and emotions of its readers. *Life*'s first issue after Pearl Harbor featured a large, black "WAR" in four-inch letters at the top of the first page, in effect announcing the momentousness of the event. Its 1945 VJ Day coda was the famous Eisentaedt photograph of a sailor embracing a young woman in Times Square, evoking the unrestrained joy of the return of peace. *Life* sought throughout to convey the "human feel and reality" of the war, and to promote its own view of its importance. *Life* was also determinedly optimistic. The Japanese attack on Pearl Harbor was a "desperate gamble" by Tokyo, the magazine insisted. Finding itself in a "hopeless corner," Japan was saying in effect: "If this be hara-kiri, make the most of it." Americans, on the other hand, "took the news, good and bad, with admirable serenity. . . . Ideologically the nation was united as it had never been at any other military crisis in all history." *Life* was simultaneously the scourge of the Axis, the champion of the armed forces, and the cheerleader of the American people. It was also a guide to America's future. The magazine's photography, Luce predicted, would help "make the activities of normal life more interesting and dramatic" and would after the war help the nation "overcome a general aspect of cynicism and distrust. . . . We must show how we rebuild a Western Civilization."[3]

For *Time* too the war was a transformative event. The magazine more than doubled its circulation between the invasion of Poland in 1939 and the end of the war in 1945. If *Life* was consistently named America's most "popular" magazine, opinion surveys almost always named *Time* the nation's most "important." It was, the editors boasted, "the magazine to which something like half the important people in America are turning for help in understanding the promise and the problems of our time."

Even its critics appeared to agree, if not about its wisdom then at least about its power. "The moral we draw [from reading *Time*] is that we had better be acutely aware of what goes on in its pages," a highly skeptical article in the liberal Catholic magazine *America* warned in 1944. Otherwise readers might inadvertently find themselves influenced by the "higher sophistry" of the Luce organization. Edmund Wilson offered an ominous warning that the "considerable value" of *Time*'s summaries of the news masked "the ineptitude and the cynicism of the mentality" behind the reportage. He urged Luce and his colleagues "to try to give some value and point" to what he considered the magazine's banal opinions. Paul Herzog, chair of the New York State Labor Relations Board, worried about "the power [the Luce] magazines could wield in influencing public opinion for [their] own selfish ends."

Luce, of course, strenuously and consistently denied any such intention. But he did not deny the presence of opinions—often strong ones—in his magazines. *Time*, he once argued, should be "a continuing seminar in how to develop the Good Society in the U.S.," because America's success in that effort, "morally and in every other way, is involved, favorably and unfavorably, with man's fate everywhere." In presenting the news, he noted in 1944, "there should be well-chosen villains and (much harder) well-chosen heroes." There was, in short, a narrative running through *Time* during the war—the obvious narrative of the course of battle and the more subtle one of "how America should or should not seek to influence its world environment."[4]

As much as he was preoccupied by the war, and as much as he feared its possible outcomes, Luce also saw the conflict as a great opportunity to reimagine America and the world, and to use his magazines to chart a glorious future. He bombarded his editors with expressions of high purpose. He complained about the "spotty and haphazard" editing of the magazines and pushed for consistent "brilliance." He continually reorganized his editorial staffs and, in the spring of 1944, moved Billings from his longtime position as editor of *Life* to a new position: "Editorial Director of all TIME INC. Publications." Billings wielded considerable power in his new position, particularly during the long periods in which Luce was away. But Luce was careful to make clear that he retained final authority over all editorial decisions, and his stream of memos to editors continued unabated throughout the war. (So did Billings's private complaints of Luce's constant interference.) "Our publications have been outstanding, and often pioneers, in showing to Americans what American life is like," Luce told his editors in 1943. "We must continue this job . . . [and] we must seek a somewhat greater degree of self-conscious criticism and appreciation of life as we find it. And some accent of enthusiasm must be put on what we find *right* in American mores." That meant attention to "the family as an institution" and "education . . . to instill moral notions into the young." Should "little boys and girls," he asked, "be taught to be patriotic?" What would be the "technological possibilities of the Future"? How could the magazines do a "much more vigorous job of pointing to the importance of the beautiful"? The war might be the principal task facing the nation, but the war also created an opportunity to reject the "iconoclasm" of the 1920s and the pessimism and despair of the 1930s and instead to embrace remaking America as a nobler and more admirable society. The great story of America in the war years, Luce believed, was not the battlefield but the story of individuals—"of human chances and mischances, of man's mores, prejudices, foibles, failings, of his extraordinary behavior which completes the picture of man as a living creature."[5]

Luce's hopeful and slightly sentimental assessment of the nation, and his optimistic view of the war and its aftermath, could not disguise a significant and deliberate change in his magazines. They were becoming ever more opinionated and partisan. Strong views were not new to the Luce publications, of course. But for nearly twenty years the expressions of "prejudice" in the magazines had mostly taken the form of what might be called "attitude." Although there had been no shortage of opinion in *Time* in earlier years, there had also rarely been a clear or consistent political message. Luce had been reasonably content with being both outspoken and largely apolitical until the Willkie campaign of 1940, which drew him for the first time deeply into a political cause. In the aftermath of Willkie's defeat, he worried that he had become inappropriately partisan and insisted that he would draw back. But his resolve did not last for long.

Luce's insistence that he, and he alone, must shape the positions of his magazines grew stronger during the months before Pearl Harbor. And once the United States entered the war, his determination to control content reached a new level. "Time Inc. does have policies and is not at all ashamed of having them or of what they are," he wrote testily after hearing that one of his bureau chiefs had said that there was no "central policy-maker" in the company. "The chief editorial policymaker for Time Inc. is Henry R. Luce—and that is no secret which we attempt to conceal from the outside world." The reality, of course, was not quite consistent with Luce's lofty claim. At the same time that he was asserting his dominance, his company was becoming larger and more decentralized; and he was becoming more and more remote from the actual writing and editing of his magazines. Much of his staff disagreed with Luce on many issues; most of them made no effort to shape their stories to match the views of the editor in chief. Luce was often unaware—at least until after publication—of what was going into his magazines.

His growing inability to control the content of his publications only increased his frustration, and his insistence on the centrality of his own role. There were periodic eruptions, as when Luce gave the managing editor of *Time* "blistering hell" for an editorial comment with which he disagreed. The editors did not have the right, he insisted, to present "an interpretation at variance with the views of the Editor-in-Chief." When the publisher of *Time* reported in 1944 that the magazine's coverage of the presidential campaign had not revealed a preference for either candidate, Luce responded caustically that "his verdict will be a real comfort to those who think the political convictions of TIME's Editor should be completely obscured in TIME." He complained repeatedly of "the embarrassment of continually finding myself to be the little man who wasn't there." At other times he strutted his views across memos and letters, railing at "our goddamned neutrality" and insisting that "there is no longer in TIME INC., I trust, even any lingering hangover for the nonsense that TIME became (sometime after its birth) immaculately immune from prejudice and innocent of conviction."[6]

Luce's growing insistence on turning the magazines into ideologically reliable vehicles led to a series of controversies both within the company and with the larger world. In October 1942 Russell Davenport—whom Luce had asked to write editorials for *Life*—published what he called an "Open Letter" in which he criticized the British government for its failure to move more quickly to launch a cross-Channel invasion. The reaction in London was savage, not only because of Davenport's blunt and undiplomatic language but also because some officials in London believed it to be part of an orchestrated effort to affect American strategy. Davenport, of course, was closely associated with both Willkie and Luce, and such an editorial in *Life* seemed to many English readers to be an attempted power play by these three influential men and their many allies. Some believed, inaccurately, that it was the beginning of an effort by Luce to position himself to run for president.

Because Franklin Roosevelt also sharply criticized the editorial, the furor in Washington and England became so intense so quickly that within days Luce (who in fact agreed with Davenport and had charged him with writing exactly the kind of opinionated essays that this editorial represented) felt he had to write a kind of "open letter" of his own to mollify his British critics. He distanced himself from the Davenport editorial, which, he insisted, "I did not write, did not cause to be written," and which he criticized for "not having said what we meant as clearly as we should have." (The disclaimer was the beginning of a deep and ultimately permanent rift between Luce and Davenport, who had done no more than what Luce had asked of him.) Luce penitently recommitted himself to "Anglo-American cooperation" and insisted that he had no intention of calling for "the break up" of the British Empire (a cause that the British government and press correctly suspected Luce privately supported). His statement cooled the controversy but did not eliminate suspicions about his real motives in running the piece. Nor did it represent any significant retreat from the increasingly polemical quality of his publications.[7]

A much greater series of controversies emerged over *Time*'s coverage of Stalin and the Soviet Union during the war. The Nazi-Soviet pact of 1939 generated strong criticism of Stalin in the United States and Western Europe, and the Luce magazines were far from alone in denouncing the Soviet regime. In June 1941, however, Germany invaded Russia, making the Soviet Union suddenly an ally of Britain, France, China, and—after December 7—the United States. The attitude of Americans toward Stalin and the USSR quickly and dramatically changed. To many Americans, including many correspondents and editors at Time Inc., Russia was no longer a dark and menacing tyranny but a gallant and courageous ally. For some people Stalin the despot evolved into the genial "Uncle Joe," a transformation much facilitated by the American media, which played a large role in smoothing over the rough edges of the Soviet Union. A 1943 Hollywood film, *Mission to Moscow*, portrayed U.S. ambassador to Russia, Joseph Davies, working to strengthen the USSR-U.S. alliance, while minimizing and rationalizing Stalin's murderous purges. But it was only one of the many efforts to transform a brutal dictatorship into a democratic ally. Even the Luce magazines were remarkably calm about the U.S.-Soviet alliance in the first years of the war—until a brilliant, troubled, eccentric man entered Luce's life and helped change his own, and his magazines', view of the world.

Whittaker Chambers joined the staff of Time Inc. in 1939 as a book reviewer for one hundred dollars a week. "It was the first real job I had ever held," he wrote in his memoir. "I have always insisted that I was hired because I began a review of a war book with the line: 'One bomby day in June.' " Except for his uncanny affinity for *Time* style, he could hardly have been more incompatible with the slick, confident, Ivy League culture of Luce's company. The son of a graphic artist for the *New York World*, he grew up in a slovenly house in a modest Long Island suburb and attended public schools, wearing his father's ill-fitting cast-off clothes. In the fall of 1920 he entered Columbia College, where he enjoyed a brief success as an undergraduate literary celebrity and became friendly with some of the most brilliant undergraduates of his time (among them the future literary critic Lionel Trilling and the future art critic Meyer Schapiro). But he soon wearied of the college and left without graduating. In 1924 he joined the Communist Party of the United States. Through most of the next fourteen years, he served the Party first as a writer and editor on the *Daily Worker* and the *New Masses*, and then, beginning in 1932, as an agent of Soviet military intelligence. For five years he lived in the murky underground of espionage, using assumed names, moving constantly from one address to another, and learning to trust almost no one. In 1937 he left the party—a dangerous step for a former agent. Chambers feared (not without reason) that his former Communist colleagues might assassinate him as they had other defectors, and he took elaborate precautions to obscure his whereabouts and his movements. He also developed a ferocious hatred of Communism and the Soviet Union, a true passion that drove almost everything he said and wrote. Communism, he believed, was a form of fascism—just as repugnant and just as dangerous as Nazism.[8]

Chambers had been writing in *Time* for almost a year before Luce noticed him. But in February 1940 he read Chambers's review of the John Ford film *The Grapes of Wrath*. Chambers had hated the Steinbeck novel on which the movie was based. He considered it crude left-wing "agitprop." But he praised Ford for creating "perhaps the best movie ever made from a so-so book." The film had, he wrote,

> purged the picture of the editorial rash that blotched the Steinbeck book. Cleared of excrescences, the residue is the great human story which made thousands of people, who damned the novel's phony conclusions, read it. It is the saga of an authentic U.S. farming family who lose their land. They wander, they suffer, but they endure. They are never quite defeated, and their survival is itself a triumph.

Luce read it, walked into a staff meeting, and asked who had written what he called "the best cinema review ever in *Time*." From then on he paid close attention to what this shambling, disheveled, and strangely secretive man wrote and said.[9]

The result was a period in Time Inc.'s history that became known within the company as the "Chambers War." It began slowly with complaints from colleagues about his reviews—reviews that were intelligent, well written, and savagely anti-Communist. Chambers was particularly vicious in writing about the work of left-leaning intellectuals. A year after Luce's first encounter with Chambers, he put him in charge of the entire "back of the book"—the culture section of *Time* that covered books, film, theater, and the arts. The obsessive, hardworking Chambers soon found himself, in effect, writing the entire section alone, sometimes spending the night on the couch in his office. As his influence grew, so did the anger among many of his colleagues about what they considered his ideological rigidity and polemicism. In a January 1941 *Time* essay, "The Revolt of the Intellectuals," he took on Communists and left-leaning intellectuals, without drawing any significant distinction between them. Former Communist Party member and literary critic Granville Hicks and the sentimental liberal Archibald MacLeish received the same withering portrayals as arrogant elitists contemptuous of the ordinary people they claimed to champion. "Dolefully they clumped together in circles like the *New Republic* and the *Nation*," Chambers wrote. "Substituting a good deal of intellectual inbreeding for organic contact with U.S. life, they developed a curious provincialism. . . . From this it was but a step to supporting the Communist Party." He had a special animus toward the literary critic Malcolm Cowley, a former but not particularly repentant Communist, and seldom missed an opportunity to denounce him. In early 1942 he launched an especially damaging attack on Cowley—who had recently joined the wartime government propaganda agency, the Office of Facts and Figures—with a scathing review of Cowley's new book of poetry, *The Dry Season*. (Oddly, the review appeared not in the Book section but in National Affairs.) Chambers combined dismissive condescension ("a sound, minor poetic talent") with ridicule of Cowley's romantic allusions to workers and activists. And he noted, maliciously, that "Congressman Martin Dies recently charged Cowley with having had 'seventy-two connections . . . with the Communist Party and its front organizations.' " Shortly afterward Cowley was forced to resign from the government.[10]

Chambers's real ambition, however, was to write for the Foreign News section of *Time*—to have an opportunity to explain the world to what he considered to be an uninformed and naive readership. He had auditioned for a position in Foreign News shortly after he arrived at *Time*, but his heavy-handed anti-Communism soured Manfred Gottfried, who urged him to be more moderate in his judgments. Chambers, Gottfried recalled, looked at him with wry contempt, as if to suggest that Gottfried and his colleagues were "innocents." Through much of the war *Time*'s coverage of the Soviet Union was—to Chambers's considerable dismay—consistently restrained and at times admiring. But Luce's view of the Soviet Union, never warm, cooled considerably as the war neared its end and Soviet intentions in Eastern Europe began to seem more ominous. Two other editors—John Chamberlain at *Life* and the Austrian refugee Willi Schlamm at *Fortune*—also complained frequently to him about *Time*'s sunny coverage of Russia. But it was Chambers who was the most consistent and persuasive critic. And when John Osborne, the Foreign News editor for the previous several years, decided to spend several months in Europe covering the war, Luce—to the surprise of almost all his colleagues—named Chambers the interim editor. Chambers wasted no time in establishing a new tone in foreign reporting: harshly anti-Communist and filled with forebodings about the future of Eastern Europe, which he believed (correctly) would become part of the Soviet empire. But what made his articles both powerful and, to his critics, infuriating, was the disdainful wit with which he presented his views. "Russia needed freedom from the fear of invasion," he wrote caustically in August, suggesting the thinking of Stalin himself,

> a *cordon sanitaire*, in reverse, on its western frontiers. Henceforth, from the Arctic Ocean to the Adriatic Sea, there must be a chain of governments friendly to Russia. Why not? That was the short-range goal. The long view? In ten, in 20 years—the powerful, prosperous U.S.S.R. might convert the whole world by its example. That was cheaper than revolution or conquest. Time and power would tell.[11]

The furor within the *Time* staff at Chambers's appointment as foreign editor only grew as the content of Foreign News became more and more intensely anti-Communist. "My views were well known and detested with a ferocity that I did not believe possible until I was at grips with it," he wrote in his memoir. One of his critics on the editorial staff wrote Luce to complain that "I read the incoming cables and I am amazed to see how they are either misinterpreted, left unprinted or weaseled around to one man's way of thinking." Chambers's bias, he added, "confuses, irritates, frustrates our correspondents." John Hersey later described a Chambers article as "written with bias and . . . filled with unjustified implications." But Chambers stood his ground. It was "self-evident," he argued, that the Soviet Union "was a calculating enemy making use of World War II to prepare for World War III." His battle within *Time*, he insisted, was "a struggle to decide whether a million Americans more or less were going to be given the facts about Soviet aggression, or whether those facts were going to be suppressed, distorted, sugared or perverted into the exact opposite of their true meaning." The controversy grew much fiercer when Luce asked Osborne to remain in Europe and named Chambers his permanent successor.

By the end of 1944 the hostility toward Chambers had become so intense and so widespread that Luce ordered Billings to survey the views of the magazine's foreign correspondents—all of whom responded with lacerating criticism of Chambers's "editorial bias." But Luce was by now a true believer, and he ignored the opinions that he himself had solicited. "The posture of events in January 1945," he wrote in a memo to his staff, "seems to have confirmed Editor Chambers about as fully as a news-editor is ever confirmed." A few days later, breezily dismissing the con-tinuing furor, he wrote Chambers that "Foreign News is, once again, by far the best reading in the issue. And it's *all* good."[12]

As if to flaunt his newly confirmed power, Chambers set out to write one of the most unusual—and controversial—articles ever to appear in *Time*. It was, unsurprisingly, a discourse on Communism, designed to challenge and even ridicule what he considered the naive optimism among many Americans about Stalin's intentions. But the article was not a work of reportage or even a conventional essay. He described it as a "political fairy tale," and he overcame substantial resistance from his colleagues before T. S. Matthews finally agreed to run it (with Luce's reluctant consent, and on the condition that Chambers eliminate a few particularly inflammatory passages). Published shortly after the conclu-sion of the meetings of Stalin, Churchill, and Roosevelt at Yalta in early 1945, it described an eerie visit to the conference by the ghosts of Czar Nicholas II and his family, who landed ("with the softness of bats") on the roof of the former imperial palace in which the meetings were taking place. They had come, Chambers suggested, because far from being appalled by Stalin (whose predecessors had ordered their deaths), they were fascinated by his ambition and his accomplishments. "What states-manship! What vision! What power!" the czar exclaimed. "We have known nothing like it since my ancestor, Peter the Great. . . . Stalin has made Russia great again!" That was why "the greatest statesmen in the world" had come to Yalta to meet with him. "Greater than Rurik [a ninth-century imperialistic Russian chieftain], greater than Peter! . . . Stalin embodies the international social revolution. That is the mighty, new device of power politics which he has developed for blowing up other countries from within." Chambers, the disillusioned Communist, portrayed Stalin not as an ideologue or a revolutionary but as the same kind of cynical power seeker who had created most of the tyrannies in human history. Nicholas, he imagined, admired Stalin because Stalin had succeeded at accumulating the great power that Nicholas had only aspired to achieve.[13]

"To most of my colleagues," Chambers later wrote, " 'The Ghosts on the Roof' was a culminating shocker. Feeling ran so high against it, the general malevolence swelled into my office so fiercely, that again I closed my door," as protection from an office hubbub that sounded "like the night of a lynching bee." Although he liked to describe himself as a kind of stoic in the face of criticism, the hostility Chambers encountered took its toll, particularly on his already precarious health. In the fall of 1945 he began to suffer severe chest pains. Once, he later recorded, "I blacked out on the train." Chambers himself blamed his frailty on the pressures of the job. The animus of his colleagues had, he believed, forced him to write virtually the entire Foreign News section himself. "I had no choice," he insisted: "Once more, a working day without sleep became my standard practice." (He did not mention that amid the pressures of work, he also became hugely overweight and addicted to coffee.)

Chambers knew he had to leave the office to recover, and he offered to resign from *Time*. Matthews suggested that he stay on the payroll but return to writing book reviews—from home, at least during his convalescence. John Osborne returned to edit Foreign News, but only on the condition that Chambers not succeed him again. Luce, who did not think Chambers would ever regain his health, agreed. When Chambers did rebound a few weeks later, he discovered that the door to the Foreign News editorship was now closed. "I should like to come back at once," he wrote plaintively to Luce. "I do not want to come back to *Time* to edit Books. . . . I want to edit FN." But in the end Chambers had no choice. For the rest of his years at *Time*, he wrote for the Culture section and took on special projects, including a number of important cover stories Luce sent his way. He worked mostly from home. He remained to Luce one of the best editors and writers he had ever employed.[14]

Luce's mounting concern about the Soviet Union (significantly intensified by Chambers) paled in comparison with his concern about China. His 1941 visit had reawakened a passion for his birthplace that had been largely dormant for many years and had introduced him to a leader—Chiang Kai-shek—whom he passionately admired. Still, he retained at least some skepticism about the viability of the Kuomintang and its military effort for several years after Pearl Harbor.

That skepticism was occasionally visible in the magazines themselves, which for a while after Pearl Harbor continued to report reasonably accurately on the travails of the Chinese military and the failings of the Chiang regime. That was largely because of the success of Teddy White in maintaining a warm relationship with Luce while slowly and cautiously building a case against Chiang Kai-shek. White's stature within the New York offices was such that his dispatches—although despised and ignored by Chambers—shaped the views of many other editors well into 1944, especially in the new International section, which allowed dispatches unacceptable to Chambers to appear in the magazine. *Time* ran one of those dispatches more or less verbatim in March 1943 and even gave White an almost unprecedented byline. It provided a harrowing description of a famine in Honan Province and an oblique but unmistakable condemnation of the failings and "tremendous miscalculations" of the government. He closed with a harsh description of a banquet given for him by local political officials, juxtaposed against a cannibalism trial in progress against a woman who had allegedly "eaten her little girl" after she had died of hunger. On his return to Chungking, White sent to New York an account of his subsequent visit to Chiang Kai-shek, who refused to believe his description of Honan until presented with photographs of the famine. "The Generalissimo has one simple remedy for that sort of graft," White noted, ". . . stand them against the wall." The country, he concluded, "is dying before my eyes." He was even more pessimistic when he returned briefly to New York in the spring of 1944. "Evidently China is going to pieces politically—and trying to suppress the news," Billings wrote in his diary after a lunch with White. "The Soong family is crooked." Luce himself talked with his staff about China's "terrible internal condition and the possibility of its collapse."[15]

Not long after White's piece appeared, Luce reluctantly agreed to publish a major article in *Life* by the novelist Pearl Buck. Like Luce a child of Chinese missionaries, Buck had a lifelong attachment to the country and its future. She was an ardent anti-Communist and a longtime admirer of Chiang. But she too was beginning to despair of the ability of the Kuomintang either to win the war or to create a stable China. "I do not want to be found guilty of misleading the American people," Luce wrote his colleagues when he agreed to let the piece run. Buck warned that the Chiang regime was riddled with corruption, was suppressing free speech, and was marginalizing officials who recognized the problems. "We are in the process of throwing away a nation of people who could and would save democracy with us but who if we do not help them will be compelled to lose it because they are being lost themselves." A year later Luce agreed to let *Life* run another major Teddy White story that provided one of the harshest indictments of the Chiang regime yet published anywhere. Chiang, White argued, "was doomed unless he could be shocked into reform by America." His government, White claimed, combined "the worst features of Tammany Hall and the Spanish Inquisition." White was elated when the article actually appeared mostly intact. Luce wrote to him shortly afterward that "You have written undoubtedly the most important article about China in many years—perhaps ever." White wrote back: "I was told you would never let anyone publish anything like the things I wanted to say," he wrote Luce. "I was scared as Hell, Harry, at what I thought would be an inevitable clash between my convictions and your policy." Only weeks later, when White was back in China, he would discover that these fears were more than justified.[16]

As early as the summer of 1943, Luce had been gently chiding White for his increasing pessimism. "Last winter there was some feeling here that, on balance, we were giving a too favorable view of China." But after the publication of some of White's more controversial pieces and of Pearl Buck's story in *Life*, he said, "we have pretty thoroughly discharged our obligations to print the bad with the good about China. . . . The plain fact, the great fact, the glorious fact is that China stands. . . . I think you can justifiably be more concerned to look for the facts which explain China's strength than to look for the elements of weakness." The *Life* story on Chiang clearly did not meet that standard. And while Luce had agreed to publish the piece, and had even praised it, he also wrote at length about White's failure to recognize the obstacles to Chiang's success and the remarkable fact of his survival. "I guess the hard tack I want to get down to is that we Americans are not in a very good position to tell China how she should integrate herself in a manner agreeable to us until we have integrated a little of our own 'democratic' might and majesty in a manner somewhat more beneficial to China." White's response—an impassioned nine-page letter about conditions in Chungking—expressed none of the optimism that Luce was advocating. To White the "great political fact" of China was not what Luce saw as its glorious survival but its growing internal chaos. "The Chinese peasantry turned on their own army and fought against it on the side of the invader!" he wrote. The people had developed "great contempt" for the army and for the government it served. "Even within the Kuomintang there is a bitterness that is completely new." He had, he added, "been chided many times by Lt. General Stilwell for the lush and unrealistic tone of all American public writing on China and its war effort."[17]

Joseph Stilwell, the American military commander in China, was a harsh critic of Chiang Kai-shek and his government. Known to many as "Vinegar Joe" for his tart, blunt manner, he had developed a great love for China over several decades and had fought gallantly in the first years of the American war in the Pacific to open up a supply route from India to China—known as the Burma Road—after the Japanese had cut China off from the sea. By 1944, however, he had become appalled by what he considered the incompetence and corruption of the Kuomintang. He was particularly critical of the government's apparent unwillingness actually to fight the Japanese. Chiang—whom the dyspeptic Stilwell called the "Peanut" in conversation and in some of his official dispatches—was, the general believed, more interested in holding on to power and isolating his Chinese Communist rivals than in winning the war. Stilwell's contempt for Chiang was no secret to the American military or to White, who came to rely on the general for information about the war that the Chungking government was often reluctant to provide. As the feud between Stilwell and Chiang grew increasingly bitter, White found himself siding more often than not with Stilwell. He was shattered in the fall of 1944 when Franklin Roosevelt recalled the general from China after Chiang had balked at the American demand that Stilwell take command of Chinese forces. (From the day of Pearl Harbor, Stilwell told White at the time of his dismissal, "this ignorant son of a bitch has never wanted to fight Japan.") At Luce's request White prepared material for a cover story on Stilwell's recall for *Time*. In it he made clear that he shared Stilwell's contempt for Chiang (whom he was now describing as a "man of almost appalling ignorance"). "Stilwell was relieved," he wrote in his memo to Luce, "because of Chiang's embittered opposition to him; Chiang's opposition sprang from the fact that he could no longer tolerate within his own country a group of men whose standards of honesty, efficiency and responsibility were so strikingly at variance with his own apparatus. . . . Chiang has outlived his historical usefulness." Nothing White might have written could have been more certain to enrage Luce, and the cover story on Stilwell that actually appeared in *Time* on November 13, 1944, made clear how great the rift between them had become.[18]

The article, written mostly by Whittaker Chambers, was relatively kind to Stilwell himself. It blamed the Roosevelt administration, not the general, for giving Chiang an ultimatum that "no self-respecting head of state could countenance." But Chambers made little reference to White's dispatches (which Chambers boasted he routinely dropped in the wastebasket without reading). The story as published was not about the war against Japan but about what Chambers considered the much more important war against the Chinese Communists. "Stripped to the bare facts," *Time* proclaimed, the "situation was that Chungking, a dicta-torship ruling high-handedly in order to safeguard the last vestiges of democratic principles in China, was engaged in an undeclared war with Yenan [the headquarters of the Communist forces], a dictatorship whose purpose was the spread of totalitarian Communism in China." The piece continued with a gratuitous attack on "the tone long taken by left-ists and echoed by liberals" in supporting Stilwell. And it concluded with a dark warning:

> If Chiang Kai-shek were compelled to collaborate with Yenan on Yenan's terms, or if he were forced to lift his military block-ade of the Chinese Communist area, a Communist China might soon replace Chungking. And unlike Chungking, a Communist China (with its 450 million people) would turn to Russia (with its 200 million people) rather than to the U.S. (with its 130 mil-lion) as an international collaborator.[19]

White heard nothing about the Stilwell piece until well after it had appeared in *Time*, and then only through scattered quotations from it that were broadcast over several Chinese (and Japanese) radio stations. But what he heard alarmed him, and he cabled Luce desperately. If the radio reports were true, he wrote, "I shall probably have to resign as I have no other way of preserving my integrity." "Keep your shirt on until you have full text of Stilwell cover story," Luce wired back dismissively. "Then roll up your sleeves and cable us what you regard as specific inac-curacies." But by now it was already too late for agreement between them on the Stilwell piece—or on almost anything else related to China. Both men had moved too far from their earlier, more compatible stances.

Luce continued to believe that Chiang "may have greater influence than any other single human being of our age," and he was determined to defend him on almost all points regardless of circumstances. His enthusiasm was stoked further by the sensational visit of Mme. Chiang Kai-shek to the United States in 1943, a visit Luce helped organize (with the help of David Selznick) to raise money for United China Relief. (Her public appearances across the country, *Time* wrote gushingly, had created "more effect than anything which has yet happened, in giving one great people the kind of understanding of another great people that is the first need of a shrinking, hopeful world.") White—unimpressed by the Generalissimo and Mme. Chiang both—was convinced that Chiang was a hopeless failure and an insuperable obstacle to victory.

The outcome of this disagreement was, of course, foreordained. "I do not think it becomes you to get angry if for once your editor does not instantly follow your instructions," Luce wrote coldly. His colleagues attempted to soften the tone of Luce's cables to White, but Luce was in no mood for conciliation. "Having for many years been *for* Chiang," he wrote to one of his colleagues, "White is now against him. Suppose our London correspondent was actually *against* Churchill or Moscow *against* Stalin." White responded with a thirty-page critique of the Stilwell piece, repeating his threat to resign from *Time*, to which Luce responded vaguely that "you will receive a statement of China policy as clear as cable discretion permits."

At about the same time, in what was perhaps a reckless effort to challenge Luce (and Chambers) directly, he sent a long dispatch reporting on the Communists in Yenan in mostly glowing terms. Where Chiang was corrupt and inept, the Communists, he claimed, were disciplined and committed. They had "an empirical wisdom that comes of ten years of civil war and seven years of anti-Japanese war. Within themselves they are trying to weed out the sins of intellectual dogmatism . . . [they] proclaim their friendship with America. . . . [T]hey are sincere and if reciprocated the friendship can become lasting." *Time* editors ignored his memos. White, now almost frantic, wrote Tom Matthews: "Our columns on China ever since the publication of the Stilwell cover, have been indistinguishable from the official propaganda of the Kuomintang party."[20]

White was far from alone in finding fault with *Time*'s uncritical view of Chiang. "You glorify Chiang Kai-shek," one of many outraged readers wrote. "All competent observers seem to agree that Chiang has about as much respect for democracy as Hitler or Mussolini." The journalist Richard Watts, stationed in China during the war, wrote in the *New Republic* that Time Inc., in its "policy toward the Kuomintang Party . . . abandons its lofty scorn for wide-eyed admiration." In February 1945 Luce—aware of the growing controversy—asked one of his researchers in China to explore reactions to the magazine's recent coverage. "Although the Stillwell [*sic*] cover on TIME . . . did not lack for readers," she wrote, "they certainly lacked for defenders. . . . A very large segment of the U.S. Army stationed from Delhi to Chungking operate on the theory that the Chinese government is composed of thieves and cutthroats." And the reporters in Chungking, she noted, "feel Teddy was sold down the river, should have made his resignation stick." Luce circulated the memo among his colleagues in New York—and entirely rejected its findings. "For myself," he wrote them, "I have not the slightest doubt that our policy has been right."[21]

Through the remaining months of World War II, Luce never wavered in his steadfast support of Chiang. He rarely allowed even faint criticisms of the Kuomintang to appear in his magazines. His 1943 comment on Pearl Buck's *Life* article—that there was "a very real question whether Pearl's article would not do much more harm than good"—suggested even then how far he was moving toward using the news for his own purposes. Reporting the truth was taking a backseat to doing "good" for the causes he believed in, and it was not long before this stance shattered his relationship with White. "Luce in a dither about Teddy White's 'partisanship' against Chiang," Billings wrote in his diary in August 1945, "—and he wrote him a stern cable." It was stern indeed. "I suggest you make supreme personal effort to give us nonpartisan news of Chiang in what we hope will be week of victory," Luce wrote caustically as *Time* prepared another cover story on Chiang Kai-shek (which White opposed). "We realize this might be an unreasonable request in view [of] your avowed partisanship."[22]

White hung on in Chungking through the end of the war, unable to get any material into the magazine that even hinted at the weakness of the Kuomintang. He began to focus instead on local-color stories and the fighting itself, and he remained in China to cover the Japanese surrender in August 1945. A few weeks later he was back in New York, hoping for a rapprochement with Luce. ("I would have done anything I could to keep or regain his affection," he recalled in his memoir.) He took a leave of several months to write a book—*Thunder Out of China*, coauthored with his colleague and friend Annalee Jacoby. In the spring of 1946 he sent a copy of the manuscript to Luce "as a courtesy," still hoping for some sign of approval. But the book, as White himself described it, was the story of "the inevitable collapse of Chiang Kai-shek." Neither friendship nor persuasion could have prevented Luce from feeling angry about, and even betrayed by, its contents. A few weeks later White presented himself at Time Inc. to request a new assignment. Luce was "terribly angry," called him an "ingrate," and lumped him together with another of his "disloyal" star writers, John Hersey, whose remarkable account of the bombing of Hiroshima had recently appeared not in the Luce publications but in *The New Yorker*. Luce gave White an ultimatum: Remain at Time Inc. with a willingness to accept any job assigned to him, no matter how menial, or leave the company. White protested that he would be of no value to Luce except as a foreign correspondent. He wanted to go to Moscow. But to Luce the issue was loyalty, not utility. ("We must resist the tendency to think of Time Inc. as a plum pudding from which everyone is concerned only to extract the plums of his choice," he wrote in a bitter memo shortly after the confrontation.) On July 12, 1946, White informed Luce's deputy, Charles Wertenbaker, that he "could not continue on Luce's terms." Unknown to White, Luce had already told Wertenbaker that "the bases of a satisfactory deal do not exist" (a euphemism for dismissal). White left the building no longer an employee of Time Inc.

The friendship between Luce and White, and its bitter unraveling, was the product less of their differences than of their similarities. Both men were somewhat disingenuous during their disputes in 1944 and 1945, because neither really aspired to "objective" or "nonpartisan" reporting. They saw journalism as a form of advocacy; and as their opinions diverged, their relationship inevitably frayed and ultimately collapsed precisely because they both had passionate views that they believed needed to be expressed. For White the termination of his job at Time Inc. was simply a small interruption in a brilliant career. A few days after leaving the company, he learned that his book was a selection of the then-mighty Book-of-the-Month Club. He was, for the time being, financially secure. And for the next four decades he successfully continued to combine brilliant reportage with his own deeply held opinions. For Luce the breach with White not only destroyed an important friendship but marked another significant step away from his willingness to tolerate a diversity of views within his organization.[23]

It was not only Russia and China that drew Luce more deeply into battle. His concerns extended to American politics and the state of the world. The nation's entry into the war, far from calming Luce's fears, had launched him into a period of ideological and political crusading far more fervent and dogmatic than during any earlier period of his life. The hard certainty of his own views—about how to fight the war, about how to plan for peace, and about who should lead the nation—made him increasingly vocal, both in his own public statements and in what he demanded of his magazines.

Among other things the war years intensified Luce's already strong dislike of Franklin Roosevelt. His contempt for the president was based in part on Luce's assessment of Roosevelt as a man without conviction or principle, unreliable and frequently dishonest, unfit for the great moral project that Luce believed the war demanded. He was not alone in finding Roosevelt frustratingly evasive. Even the president's own aides and allies understood that he confided fully in no one and that he was a fundamentally political man despite his occasional flights of idealism. But most of those who knew Roosevelt well recognized the great strengths of his political nature and believed that he was moving the nation in the right direction, even if not always boldly. Luce had no such faith in the president's aims, and he was constantly incensed by what he considered the administration's failure to move forcefully and clearly enough into the fray. At least equally important was his deep personal dislike of Roosevelt—a dislike that was clearly mutual.

The feud between Roosevelt and Time Inc. picked up in January 1942 almost exactly where it had left off the previous December, with a new dispute over the coverage of Latin America. A story in *Life*, published shortly after Pearl Harbor, made an erroneous reference to a "U.S. [Air] Field" in Brazil. A few weeks later a *Time* article entitled a story on a Pan-American Congress in Rio de Janeiro as a "Big Roundup" and referred to "corralling the 21 American republics into a homogeneous herd." The Brazilian and Chilean governments both protested, and Roosevelt once again lashed out. "Honestly I think that something has got to be done about Luce and his papers. . . . What to do about this attitude, which is definitely unpatriotic in that it is harmful to the U.S. to a very great degree." Even some of Roosevelt's aides were surprised at the strength of the president's anger, and they worked to calm him down. Stephen Early, the president's press secretary, told him that, "in all fairness," Luce had received approval from both the American and the Brazilian governments for the material in question. The editors at *Time* also argued about how to respond. Eric Hodgins urged his colleagues to use more "sedate language" in describing South American affairs, but Manfred Gottfried, *Time*'s managing editor, snapped back that they should "tell F.D.R. to go jump in the Potomac . . . the hell with sedate language!"[24]

Days later George C. Marshall, Army Chief of Staff, summoned Luce to Washington and (as Billings recorded Luce's account) "gave him and the company the devil, just on general principles. . . . Marshall raked up all the past grievances—and warned that the Luce papers must behave themselves." Everyone assumed that it was Roosevelt who had ordered up the "verbal caning." Several weeks later the president continued to fume about the "Luce papers" and ordered Undersecretary of State Sumner Welles to file a "formal protest with Mr. Luce" on all articles "which in any way hurt the Good Neighbor policy with Latin America or tend to promote disunity among any of the United Nations. . . . In other words, it is time to build up a complete case." Welles, like Early, tried to assure Roosevelt that Luce was being cooperative, but to little avail.[25]

Luce was enough of a realist to understand that a public fight with the president in wartime was not in his own or his company's interest. But like the president, his hatred continued to burst to the surface time and again, even though, also like the president, he faced constant efforts by his staff to keep him calm. "A session in Larsen's office . . . on Luce's anti-Roosevelt attitude," Billings wrote early in 1942. "You can't fight the Prex. Of the U.S. in wartime and expect to win." But Luce would not be deterred. Although he grudgingly permitted favorable coverage of Roosevelt by reporters and editors who admired the president, he pushed continually for more negative portrayals: "Do you realize what it means to have the President of the U.S. treated as a 'battleship' . . . ?" he told his editors in 1943. "Nothing is doing more to create a misunderstanding between the U.S. and other peoples than the exported adulation of F.D.R. The notion that F.D.R. is adored by all Americans (except a few evil millionaires) is not only a dangerous lie; it is also just a plain lie." He did not restrict his complaints to his own staff. He wrote testily to other journalists about their attitude toward the president. "Has Ray Clapper bowed down to the doctrine of the Indispensable Man or Men?" he asked the prominent columnist. "Are we hereafter helpless without Fuhrers singular or plural?"[26]

But Luce's hatred of Roosevelt was not just political. It was also intensely personal, and nothing stoked his resentment more effectively than the president's decision to bar him from traveling abroad during wartime. Roosevelt was careful to announce the ban as a matter of general principle: "On account of the extreme stringency of transportation, credentials at present are not being issued . . . to publishers, editors, and executives who wish to make visits to combat areas." Roosevelt's dislike of publishers was long-standing and well founded, and the new policy had the advantage of barring many people he disliked from traveling and finding new ways to criticize him. He was certainly as eager to keep the rabidly anti-Roosevelt publisher of the *Chicago Tribune*, Col. Robert R. McCormick, from traveling to the war zones as he was to bar Luce. But the ban, which was announced just as Luce was applying for permission to travel to China, was primarily directed at him—as Secretary of War Henry Stimson, unhappily saddled with the job of explaining the ban to him, privately confirmed in his diary: "It arose apparently out of the White House's rumpus with Luce." For almost three years he battled to have the restrictions lifted. "I am not, to be sure, a regular correspondent," Luce wrote Army Chief of Staff Marshall, whom Roosevelt had asked to enforce the ban. "But I take personal responsibility for reporting the war to upward of 20,000,000 Americans. . . . Surely it should not seem odd or unreasonable that I should have an occasional opportunity to visit the fighting fronts." The relatively reasonable tone of his imploring letters to Washington only occasionally revealed how distraught and angry he was. "It is, I am sure, unnecessary to point out to you how painful this situation has been for me personally," he wrote Marshall at one low moment. To others he spoke privately about what he considered a "deliberate insult," an act of "petty retribution," and an example of "vindictive and arbitrary power." Eventually the White House gave him permission to visit England, using the pretext that Britain was not technically a theater of war. But the ban on traveling elsewhere remained in place until after Roosevelt's death.[27]

If Roosevelt believed that barring Luce from the war zones would limit his ability to attack the administration, he was badly mistaken. Had Luce been allowed to travel, he would likely have spent much of his time visiting battlefields, writing enthusiastically about the American military, and serving as a cheerleader for the war. But stuck in New York, he was led by his anger at Roosevelt and his own frustration at being isolated from the most important event of his lifetime into a sullen period of hard-edged partisanship.

He insisted that the president had "fumbled the crisis." He expressed contempt for "the idea that Roosevelt alone did his job with anything more than average courage or average efficiency." The president's consistent "deceit" was something that "even my tin-lined stomach can't quite digest." The administration was "tired and stale in seventeen symptoms." Roosevelt exhibited a "capacity for cheapening the finer traditions of America." Luce wrote particularly harshly about the emerging consensus that Roosevelt had been a skillful steward of foreign policy leading up to the war. On the contrary, Luce charged, the president "was in the 1930's the high priest of the isolationist-pacifism of that decade." Claims to the contrary were the result of "successful, almost completely untruthful propaganda." Roosevelt, he wrote toward the end of the war, "has so confused war and peace that it is doubtful at this point whether we will ever unscramble the two. This Rooseveltian achievement is, of course, wholly in character, being simply a part of the 12-year-old Roosevelt technique of maintaining perpetual crisis."[28]

More visible to readers was Luce's increasing identification with the Republican Party. His full-throttled support of Willkie in 1940 had exposed him to considerable criticism; but in that campaign Luce had been less a Republican loyalist than an insurgent supporting a maverick candidate promising (however unconvincingly) a new kind of postpartisan politics. Luce's 1940 position had in many ways been a critique of the Republican Party's hidebound conservatism and an effort to move it toward a more moderate course. As the 1944 election approached, Luce once again supported Willkie's candidacy, although with far less emotional engagement than he had in 1940; but Willkie himself withdrew from the race early in April after coming in last in the Wisconsin primary. ("I had been encouraged to believe that the Republican party could live up to the standards of its founders," he explained bitterly, "but I am discouraged to believe that it may be the party of negation.") Luce responded equally glumly to the prospect of Thomas E. Dewey, the governor of New York, as the Republican nominee. "In the past few weeks," Luce told Willkie in June, "what I have been doing, as relates to politics, comes about as close as possible to zero." A month before the election, Willkie died of a heart attack following a strep infection. There had been much speculation in late summer 1944 that Willkie would have ultimately supported Roosevelt, with whom he had worked closely during much of the war and with whom—unknown to the public (and to Luce)—he had begun discussions about the possibility of a new party that they might form together.

Luce hardly paused before throwing his support to the front-runner, Dewey, a man he had previously viewed with considerable contempt. *Life* openly endorsed Dewey not long before the election. *Time* was more restrained. But Luce instructed his staff that the magazines should "render not merely passing judgments, but, practically, verdicts on candidates for and occupants of offices other than President of the United States."[29]

"What has been going on in TIME in the last several years," Luce explained, when he began to receive criticism from some of his colleagues, "has not been the sudden acquisition of prejudice or conviction but the attempt to make our implicit convictions explicitely [*sic*] coherent and rational." With that cursory justification, he began talking and writing about the Republican party with almost the same breathless enthusiasm and confidence with which four years earlier he had written of Willkie. "The nation is today actually Republican," he announced in 1942. "Taking into account Conservative Democrats, the New Deal (what remains) is a distinctly minority party." By 1944 he had convinced himself that the nation was as weary of Roosevelt as he was, that supporting the Republicans was almost as obvious a position for his magazine to take as supporting the war. "If we want the 'better side' to win in November," he wrote in 1943, "what we do now may be no less important than what we do (or don't do) on election eve. . . . It seems to me that we may as well agree that our disposition is definitely in favor of the Republican Party." So certain was he that the tide was turning toward Dewey that he asked Billings in early August "to throw out the monthly Roper survey [in *Fortune*] because it showed gains for Roosevelt." Billings protested, and Luce compromised by running a Gallup Poll showing Dewey ahead alongside the Roper. Not until shortly before election day did he finally acknowledge that Roosevelt would likely win. Even so, Billings noted, he was "deeply wounded" when some of his most intimate colleagues decided to "desert him politically" by voting for Roosevelt. Some prominent readers were also deeply alienated. *Time* had become a "Republican magazine," he heard increasingly from Democratic politicians and other public figures. And while Luce denied the charge, he could not honestly refute it. Shortly after the election he even began to consider working with the Republican National Committee on a reorganization of the party. "I am in no mood to perform an 'act of leadership,'" he explained. "But maybe we have got some moral obligation to give expression to some words of helpful wisdom to the Republican party . . . the whole to be scanned and evaluated by some top writer [from *Time*] . . . and the chief points assayed by [a] LIFE editorial. All this might really ring a bell."[30]

For a time in 1942 and 1943, there was speculation—some of it fueled by Luce's friends and colleagues—that he would run for the U.S. Senate in Connecticut or become secretary of state or otherwise thrust himself into public life. Luce himself publicly repudiated that idea and insisted (unpersuasively) that he would not only not run for office but that he would "retire completely from politics or personal leadership in public affairs." But in the fall of 1942 he rallied behind another political proposal—that Clare run for a seat in the House of Representatives in a district that had until recently been occupied by her stepfather, Elmer Austin.[31]

Clare's decision to run—a decision over which she publicly agonized for several months before entering the race—was not due just to ambition. It was also a result of her declining fortunes as a writer. Her effort to transform herself from playwright into political and war reporter, which began so promisingly in 1939 with her successful publication of *Europe in the Spring*, had by 1942 become something of an embarrassment. Her articles for *Life*, once eagerly published, became a source of awkwardness for editors who found them glib and superficial but feared the consequences of turning them down. Billings described them in his diary as "just a jumble of words . . . a mess." Colleagues from Time Inc. and from other publications began to balk at the number and the triviality of her articles in *Life*. "On all sides," Billings noted, "we are running too much 'Clare Boothe,' and her pieces are becoming a general joke."[32]

Both Harry and Clare almost certainly (if not openly) considered the state of their marriage as much as her career as they pondered whether or not she should run. By early 1942 the coolness that had begun to envelop their marriage only a few years after their wedding was rapidly increasing. They were already spending much of their time apart; and Clare, at least, was becoming increasingly morose about what she sometimes considered her complete isolation. "Such a mess," she wrote in her diary of a lonely trip to Greenwich not long after their marriage. "Such a place—God! It has a wild look to it. . . . No greetings are here for *me* . . . a twist of pain . . . So hurt here." Things had only gotten worse in the following years.

Their sexual relationship, troubled from the beginning, had come to a virtual end in 1939—a source of pain and frustration to them both. Harry blamed his inactivity on stress and exhaustion, but repeated efforts at escape and relaxation failed to restore his sexual appetite. After a while he began to claim that he had become impotent, which he may actually have believed for a time. But by late 1942 he had found himself with a healthy sexual appetite for other women, which suggests that his problem was not physical but psychological and probably specific to Clare—perhaps a product of their increasingly intense, and often bitter, competitiveness with each other. They fought constantly during their 1941 visit to China and were, Clare wrote, "not very happy." Guests in their homes sometimes sat in mute astonishment as Harry and Clare engaged in furious arguments from opposite ends of the dinner table. It seemed at times in 1942 that she was running against her husband almost as much as against her Democratic opponent. However partisan Harry became, Clare became more so. She openly rejected the muscular idealism of Harry's "American Century" vision for a tough, pragmatic, power-driven stance in the world. "I believe *any* means justify the patriotic end of helping our country to survive," she wrote Harry early in 1942. "If it should prove necessary in our lifetime and our children's to scrap 'our American way of life,' our free enterprise system, our two-party system of government, and our constitution to get it, I am for that." In her campaign in the fall of 1942 she expressed none of Harry's hopeful visions of the future and focused instead on what she described as the negligence and incompetence of the Roosevelt administration. "If we permit another year of bungling and muddling we will be a very long and bloody time winning it."[33]

Harry loyally supported Clare's congressional race. He partially funded it. He recruited Time Inc. employees to help her campaign. And he expressed great pride, both publicly and privately, when she won the election in November by a modest but comfortable margin. But they both understood that the move to Congress was not just an impressive new chapter in Clare's career but a way of distancing themselves from each other. Harry had long expressed his disappointment with the marriage through barbed self-criticism: "Others find me in excellent health and spirits. Only to you does it matter that my hair is falling out, that my teeth are decaying and that chances of my ever becoming a moderately respectable example of Nordic strength are rapidly vanishing." Clare had complained that "we have had so many arguments about the war in the past three or four years." Both spoke in almost identical language of the stress their marriage was creating. Harry wrote of "living through rather long periods of nervous strain," and Clare of "a strain on our nervous systems. . . . Bitter arguments still flourish like an evil tangleweed." Her move to Congress relieved some of the tension, but it left unanswered the question of their future. "We paused, and parted, perhaps forever?" Clare wrote Harry shortly before she left for Washington, just at the moment that he was beginning a new romance.[34]

A little more than eight years after his fateful meeting with Clare in 1934 at a party given by Elsa Maxwell at the Waldorf-Astoria Hotel, Harry attended another Elsa Maxwell event in 1943, also at the Waldorf. Clare was in Washington that evening, and Harry found himself in the company of Jean Dalrymple, an attractive forty-one-year-old theatrical agent and publicist to whom he was immediately drawn. He had had brief relationships with other women in recent years, none of them serious. But he soon began courting Jean in the same aggressive and slightly awkward way in which he had pursued Clare. Dalrymple responded at first to Harry's obvious loneliness. "He looked so unhappy, as if he needed somebody to talk to," she later recalled. But gradually their relationship became more serious, socially and sexually. It also became more public. Unlike during his secretive pursuit of Clare, he dined openly with Dalrymple and even accompanied her to occasional social events. He spoke often with her of his unhappiness with Clare. "The marriage was terrible for him," Dalrymple remembered. From time to time Luce tried to persuade Dalrymple to marry him, but she brushed the offers aside. While she insisted years later that she was never deeply in love with him, her real concern was her conviction that, however bad their relationship might be, he would never leave Clare. But that did not stop her from continuing the relationship for several years.[35]

For a while Harry seemed content with his double life—a public marriage to Clare and a quasi-private romance with Jean. He continued to live with his wife on the relatively rare occasions when they were in New York or Connecticut at the same time. But despite Clare's intermittent efforts to salvage their marriage, she too began a long and not particularly secret relationship, also more serious than the numerous and usually brief affairs in the earlier years of her marriage. She became involved with the American general Lucian Truscott, Jr., whom she met on a trip to England and for whom she briefly considered divorcing Harry until it became clear that Truscott would not leave his wife. Harry wrote Clare gloomily of "the dreary landscape of our two lives." He spent as much time with Jean as he could. He even stayed away from the office in a way he had not done since his early infatuation with Clare.[36]

Under other circumstances their blighted marriage might have come to an end in the early 1940s had it not been for a tragedy that changed both their lives. Clare embarked on a national speaking tour during the congressional recess in late 1943, and she spent the Christmas holidays in Palm Springs, California, with her daughter Ann and, briefly, Harry. He was very fond of his stepdaughter, perhaps in part because Ann's long absences from her mother and her deep loneliness mirrored some aspects of his own childhood. He wrote her often, and lovingly, signing his letters "Dad."

After the New Year the three of them traveled together to San Francisco for a few more days. On January 11 Harry flew back to New York, and Ann accepted a ride with a friend back to Stanford, where she was a senior. As the two young women drove through Palo Alto, their open convertible was struck by a car entering the road from a side street. Ann was thrown from the car and killed instantly. (Her companion suffered minor injuries.) When Clare called Harry with the news, his first grief-stricken words were, "Not that beautiful girl. Not that beautiful girl." He returned immediately to San Francisco, wiring Clare along the way: "Well west of Chicago proceeding and thoughts ever with you and our darling." In the meantime Clare—never before a religious woman—visited a Catholic church and summoned a priest to comfort her. The

notice in *Time* of Ann's death identified her as the daughter of Mr. and
Mrs. Henry Luce. The *Time* editors pointed this inaccuracy out to Luce.
But Harry insisted, and the magazine complied. Clare chose Mepkin as
Ann's burial site (a place they then infrequently used and that Ann had
rarely visited). After the burial, she could not bear to stay in the house
she had occasionally shared with Ann, and moved instead to Bernard
Baruch's nearby estate. Harry remained with her there for weeks. When
he tried to return to work in New York, Harry's secretary reported that
Clare "was throwing fits in South Carolina and thus keeping Luce from
coming back here." Clare later described her reaction to Ann's death as a
"nervous breakdown." Their shared grief brought them briefly closer
together than they had been in several years. Harry loyally supported
her successful reelection to Congress in 1944, again pressured his magazines to cover her more favorably, and briefly suspended his affair with
Jean Dalrymple. But it was not a lasting reconciliation.[37]

Despite the turbulence of his personal life, Luce's wartime missionary
zeal remained undiminished. Barred from the war zones, he continued
to focus on the postwar world as a major project of his magazines. As
with other issues, the role of the Time Inc. publications was not to
chronicle the many postwar visions being debated in American life.
Instead, Luce insisted, the company must itself present its own vision of
the future—a vision to be determined ultimately by Luce himself.

Little came of the "Postwar Department" he established early in the
war, until 1943, when Luce began to prod and dominate the project. He
did so in part because of his contempt for what he considered the Roosevelt administration's failure to take postwar planning seriously. But
even without that incentive, he surely would have been drawn to the
great task of imagining a new world. As was often the case with Luce's
enthusiasms, they took their most advanced form in the internal memos
he wrote to his staff—hoping, expecting that they would be translated
into copy for the magazines, and then raging when he discovered that
they did not. "If there is any gospel around here it is the Post-War
Memos," Luce wrote testily in May 1943 after sensing that his editors
were taking them lightly. "If any 'gospels' contrary to or inconsistent
with the Post-War Memos are to be uttered or implied in Time—then
the Editor of Time has a right to be given notice and to consider said
contrary-gospel before publication. . . . or has all my yammer to Senior
Editors for four years been so much crap? And how much longer do I
have to say that in order to be understood?"[38]

Luce's thinking about the postwar era was not entirely coherent. He wrote almost maniacally, memo after memo, with idea after idea, trying to come up with a philosophy that would explain the importance of American influence in the coming years while also imagining major transformations in other parts of the world. At one point he wrote ardently about the ascendancy of the middle class, as if that were the solution to the world's problems. "What you left-wingers have scornfully called 'middle-class ideals' built America, which, with all its faults, marked 'a decisive step in the ascent of the human race.' " Middle-class "leadership," he insisted, would "achieve the salvation of society." At times he dismissed the increasingly popular idea of a new League of Nations. "We are not currently in favor of any World Organization," he wrote in 1943. But less than two years later he enthusiastically endorsed the idea of a postwar United Nations and complained that Roosevelt and his international partners were not making it strong and effective enough. Not surprisingly he put enormous emphasis on the future of Asia: "We believe that the long range happiness of the U.S. depends more upon the salutary relations between Asia and the 'white man' than upon any other factor. That is, the inter-relationship between Asia and 'The West' is the greatest new factor in human life." Overflowing with ideas, enthusiasms, and frustrations, he drove his editors to distraction. In the end, he failed to goad them into publishing very much of what he wanted to say.[39]

Perhaps the most revealing statement of his beliefs came not in a memo to his colleagues but in a miserable letter to Clare in the midst of their marital difficulties in 1943. He seemed to believe somehow that their political disagreements were as much of a problem in their relationship as their personal ones, and he set out to establish his views in response to her claim that Time Inc. was guilty of "inconsistent shilly shallying." He presented her with what he called Time Inc.'s "Fourteen Points," even though they were his alone, never shared with his editors. He was "for the United Nations in prosecution of the war," "anti-administration in nearly everything," "pro-Chinese," "pro-Indian freedom," "pro Civil Rights including for Negroes," "pro, if not the Republican party, at least many Republicans," "pro air power," "pro free enterprise," "pro-collective bargaining and labor's just rights," "pro Henry Kaiser" (the progressive and widely admired aluminum executive), "pro art," "pro Free French and anti-Vichy," and "against the Imperial House of Japan." Taken together these positions represented the views of many moderately liberal Americans and suggested that at heart his vision of the postwar world was not very different from an emerging consensus among American elites. But it was also clear that Luce's hopes for the postwar world had no coherent structure.[40]

That became particularly clear a few months later when he was asked by a colleague how he would like the postwar world to look. Luce took the challenge and responded characteristically with an elaborately crafted document that was in some places prescient and at others dreamily utopian. He titled it "The Reorganization of the World." It would be composed of "six major Federations." Among them would be a "United States of Europe," a system that would preserve "national entities" but oversee them with "many pan-European institutions and policies . . . which will set a dynamic bias towards European Union." Luce was not, of course, alone in voicing this hope, but his outline came remarkably close to what eventually became the actual European Union. He was less foresighted in his view of the Soviet Union as a second great federation, which he hoped would "develop a prosperous and noble society." China, of course, would be the key to Asia: The West, he argued, should "encourage by every means the renaissance of a great Chinese civilization." India, should it achieve its "painful transition into modernity" and should it free itself from being "dominated by Europe," would be another stabilizing force in the world. And of course the United States (which would be "a stronger industrial and hence military power than any other two nations combined") and Great Britain (whose "ex-colonial domination" would be "a kind of binder for the world") would continue to play their now-established roles as the true leaders of the globe. (Luce gave only passing attention to the less powerful areas of the world of the time: among them the Middle East, Africa, and Latin America).[41]

As was his custom, Luce reached out to important thinkers around the country to help him with his great task. He asked the vice president of the University of Chicago, William Benton, to organize a group of faculty who might propose a "Statement of Principles" on economic development; but the scholars who joined the project became bogged down on "the monopoly question," something in which Luce had little interest. He corresponded frequently with Walter Lippmann, whose views of the postwar world were much more pragmatic than his own. In 1943 Lippmann was promoting the idea of a British-American alliance to oversee the postwar world. Luce tried to draw him into the headier and more idealistic conversations he and his colleagues were organizing, and Lippmann happily agreed to join. But despite their friendship and mutual admiration, they did not reach a meeting of the minds. ("I hope

I didn't seem to be an objector or an opponent to the general plan," Lippmann wrote Luce shortly after a brainstorming dinner.)[42]

Instead of building a coherent vision of the future, Luce moved toward a set of ideas that created an obvious, uncontroversial view of the postwar world that almost no one could oppose. It began with two simple questions. The first: "Does the American nation exist for any particular purpose?" The answer, he argued, "rises in your hearts" and makes clear that "the American nation does exist for a specific purpose—in the words of the Battle Hymn: 'To make men free.'" The second, more prosaic but equally important to Luce: "What, then, is the post-war TIME?" His answer was more complex but essentially the same. Time Inc.'s mission was "to explain about American journalism and in doing that we have to explain about America." Explaining America, Luce came to believe, was remarkably simple.

> If we had to choose one word out of the whole vocabulary of human experience to associate with America—surely it would not be hard to choose the word. For surely the word is Freedom. . . . Without Freedom, America is untranslatable. . . . And therefore it seems to me that we can sum up the whole of editorial attitudes and principles in the one word Freedom.

He had reached the end of his long and complicated effort to define America by avoiding the difficult questions:

> Despite all confusions by which we have been confused and may have confused others, I think we have achieved some intellectual right to say that we of Time Inc. have fought, are fighting and will fight . . . 'For the Freedom of All Peoples.' . . . We believe that the relation of the people of the U.S. with the other peoples of the world must be based on the principles of Freedom. (This can be endlessly celebrated.)[43]

XI

Losing China

A Soldier Died Today," *Time* announced solemnly in its first issue after Franklin Roosevelt's death on April 12, 1945. "Everywhere, to almost everyone, the news came with the force of a personal shock. The realization was expressed in the message of the eminent; it was expressed in the stammering and wordlessness of the humble." Roosevelt was "history's man . . . no public figure had ever seemed so close to so many citizens." In *Time*, in *Life*, in *Fortune*, the coverage of the president's death was reverent, emotional, and—as one editor wrote—"awe-struck." "In his time, no abler politician lived," *Time* noted. Roosevelt had displayed the "greatness" that his era demanded, and he had brought his nation "triumphantly through a great war and started it on the road to peace."[1]

Although Luce remained uncharacteristically aloof from the coverage of the president's death, he passively supported his editors' decision to provide admiring and respectful tributes. He himself wrote a gracious letter to Eleanor Roosevelt praising her husband's leadership. But privately he remained obdurate in his hatred. He described the fallen president bitterly as the man who "kept me, wholly without moral justification, physically isolated from the global war." It was his "duty," Luce once remarked, "to go on hating him." As for Harry Truman, Luce was initially hopeful, if only because the new president was not Roosevelt. "I know of no better way to communicate to you my profound good wishes for your Presidency," he wrote, "than to tell you of the confidence which, among themselves, a great number of your fellow citizens already feel in your character and ability." Even more gratifying than Truman's demeanor was the new president's decision to allow Luce to travel into the war zones, at last revoking Roosevelt's spiteful suspension of his passport. Barely a month after Roosevelt's death, Luce was en route to the Pacific.[2]

As excited as he was finally to be in a war zone, his trip was on the whole unremarkable. He spent most of his time on the aircraft carrier *Yorktown*, from which planes were bombing Japanese targets almost with impunity now that the Japanese air defenses had been almost completely destroyed. He saw little action, other than the multiple and occasionally fatal accidents committed by American sailors themselves. He spent much of his time sitting on the flight deck with a taciturn gunner's mate, watching the planes come and go. "A Quiet Cruise of a Task Force Group," he titled his notes on the trip for his editors, only half ironically; but he was energized nevertheless by his first experience with an American war front. As he gazed out upon vast stretches of ocean he envisioned a new "American frontier" between Okinawa and Manila that "will never be moved back from there. All this is extraordinarily in line with the genius of the American people."[3]

As always, Luce tried to arrange to see the most important figures he could find. (A much-sought-after meeting with Douglas MacArthur did not materialize, although Luce did manage a brief visit with his twenty-year-old son Hank, serving on a destroyer near the *Yorktown*.) As for men of power, he had to settle for the fleet commander, Adm. Arthur Radford. At one point Radford whispered privately: "Luce, don't you think the war is over?" Luce replied that Radford would know better than he did. But on his return to the United States he went immediately to Washington to report to Secretary of the Navy James Forrestal that the end of the war was in sight. Forrestal sent him to the State Department, where he told Undersecretary Joseph Grew—with considerable certainty but with no solid evidence—"that Japanese surrender could be obtained almost immediately—on one condition, which was that Japan should be allowed to retain the emperor, an idea he had heard often during his Pacific trip."[4]

Luce had high hopes for a meeting he managed to arrange with Truman, but the president either misunderstood the purpose of his visit or chose not to discuss the war with him. They had a cordial, perfunctory conversation that ended before Luce had a chance to make any recommendations. He heard later that Truman did not want to discuss an end of the Pacific war until after his meeting with Churchill and Stalin in Potsdam in July—a meeting that turned out to be especially notable because it coincided with a momentous event in New Mexico: the first successful detonation of an atomic bomb. Luce apparently had no knowledge of the successful outcome of the Manhattan Project and very likely had known nothing of the project at all. Through the remainder of the summer he continued to promote a negotiated peace with Tokyo: retaining the emperor in exchange for ending the war.[5]

His argument became largely moot on August 6, 1945, when the United States detonated an atomic bomb over Hiroshima. But Luce did not give up the fight. He and Joseph Kennedy called on Francis Cardinal Spellman of New York and implored him to urge the president to delay further bombings—arguing again that Japan could be made to surrender without more destruction. Nothing came of this effort. The second atomic bomb fell on Nagasaki on August 9, and the Japanese government surrendered less than a week later, but not before getting an agreement from the United States that Japan could retain its emperor. Most Americans celebrated the end of the war with little concern about the unleashing of this terrible new weapon. But Luce was deeply troubled both by the moral and the geopolitical implications of the atomic bomb. "The greatest and most terrible of wars ended this week, in the echoes of an enormous event," James Agee wrote in the August 20 *Time*, at Luce's behest, "—an event so much more enormous that, relative to it, the war itself shrank to minor significance. . . . In an instant, without warning, the present had become the unthinkable future."[6]

Luce's opposition to the use of atomic weapons was based on a complex, and never clearly articulated, set of concerns. He had religious qualms: Would this new capacity for destruction make faith obsolete? "In the atomic world," he wrote, "who shall rule and how?" What would happen to "the proposition of the Christian faith that there is ultimate sovereignty in the universe and that this sovereignty was uniquely revealed to man in Christ"? He was concerned as well about how the existence of the bomb might threaten America's ability to shape the postwar world once other nations—most notably the Soviet Union—acquired the weapon. "The idea of 'sharing' the atomic bomb with the Russians is crazy," he insisted in response to hopeful suggestions from scientists that peace could be ensured by providing nuclear technology to other great nations. The atomic scientists, he wrote contemptuously, "feel a sudden profound evangelical and wholly unnatural concern of conscience about their business." He was concerned as well about how the use of the bomb would allow the Japanese to redefine themselves as victims rather than aggressors. "I don't think the atomic bomb was handled right," he wrote to Billings in late August. "If the Japs have any good 'alibi,' it's the bomb."[7]

Solicitousness for the fate of the Japanese people had certainly not been evident in his magazines' coverage of the Pacific war. *Time* had expressed no concern about the Japanese-American relocation in 1942 and had reported sunnily on the "decent treatment" that these interned American citizens received. *Time, Life,* and even *Fortune* had joined eagerly in the extraordinarily racist depictions of the Japanese that pervaded most of the American media throughout the war—depictions that many contemporaries and some scholars have argued were significant factors in justifying the use of the bomb. Portraying the Japanese as savage, even barely human, made it easier to authorize unusually harsh assaults. One of *Time*'s first covers after the attack on Pearl Harbor had presented an almost simian portrait of Admiral Yamamoto, the commander of the Japanese Pacific fleet, in which both the background and the admiral's face were colored entirely in a vivid and lurid yellow. Another cover in early 1942, at the time the Dutch East Indies fell to the Japanese, had portrayed a Dutch naval officer, with a small picture behind him of a monkey wearing a Japanese helmet and carrying a gun swinging by his tail from a tree. "What would the [American] people say in response to Pearl Harbor?" *Time* asked shortly after the Pearl Harbor attack. "What they said was . . . 'Why the yellow bastards!' " *Life* lightheartedly captioned a photograph of American soldiers in a Pacific jungle: "Like many of their comrades they were hunting for Japs, just as they used to go after small game in the woods back home." There is no evidence that Luce personally encouraged these racist stereotypes, but—like almost all American editors during the war—he did little to stop them (although he did publish an anguished letter to *Time* from Pearl Buck reminding him that using "yellow" pejoratively would offend many non-Japanese Asians). Nor had Luce raised objections to the horrendous firebombings of Tokyo and other cities, which had produced more carnage than either of the atomic bombs.[8]

Whatever his views at the time, Luce's ultimate concern about the atomic bombings had less to do with Japan than with China. The demonization of the Japanese in the Time Inc. magazines was, in part, an effort to distinguish them from their portrayal of America's valiant Chinese allies. *Life* once ran a notorious photo essay, "How to Tell Japs from Chinese," concluding that the Japanese—"squat . . . massively boned head [had] aboriginal antecedents," as compared to the more refined and cultured features of the Chinese. But most of all, the atomic bomb contributed to what Luce considered the "massive failure" of the United States to stabilize China. "If the bomb had not been dropped," he wrote years later in an unfinished memoir, "and if the well-laid plans for the MacArthur invasion had been carried out—then, almost certainly, . . . there would have been a major Chinese offensive, with American-trained Chinese divisions. . . . It would have been success-ful. . . . Chiang Kai-shek would have been in a position to move armies up to Peking and Manchuria." As a result "Chiang would have had a chance." But the abrupt end of the war against Japan led instead to the introduction of Soviet troops into Manchuria, the rapid disengagement of American troops in China, and the ability of Mao's Communist forces to conserve their strength for the battle against the Nationalists. His views in 1945 never changed. Even in the year before his death, Luce continued to insist that sustained American support would have pro-vided China with the "great chance" to create a democratic nation.[9]

In October 1945 Luce was able to visit China for the first time in more than four years. Now that the war with Japan was over, he was eager to see how the Chiang regime was faring against the remaining challenges from its internal Communist enemies. In part Luce saw the trip as an antidote to his long, bitter conflict with Teddy White, whom Luce had come to believe was "an ardent sympathizer with the Chinese Commu-nists." He would be able to counter White's gloomy predictions and offer a more reassuring image of postwar China. He made sure to bring with him sympathetic editorial colleagues from Time Inc., among them Roy Alexander and Charles V. Murphy, firm anti-Communists and, like Luce, strongly committed to Chiang. He would hear no discordant voices from his traveling companions, and, almost needless to say, none as well from his Kuomintang hosts. Not surprisingly, perhaps, he was again encouraged by almost everything he saw.[10]

As usual Luce kept up a grueling pace during his visit, moving from city to city and province to province gathering impressions that he eagerly and voluminously recorded and sent back to New York. Every-where he went he found reasons for optimism. "Chiang Kai-shek, by a dramatically successful show of superior force, completed the political conquest of the vast hinterland of west China," he wrote triumphantly from Yunnan early in his trip. When told by an American general that Chiang had unwisely ousted a provincial governor, Luce insisted that, on the contrary, the "Gissimo did an important job very neatly." Arriving in Chungking, he was showered with invitations from Kuomintang leaders, culminating in a dinner with Chiang and "a wonderful conversation . . . of a philosophical nature." Late in the evening, after Chiang retired, Mme. Chiang continued the conversation, assuring Luce that "the Government now has a terrible responsibility not to disappoint the hopes of the people." In Shanghai, later in the month, he wrote enthusiastically of the Kuomintang's successes in restoring government authority. "This week," he said, "the historically unparalleled drama of the reoccupation of East, South, and North China moved toward its climax." He told Western journalists that he was "happily impressed," and he praised Chiang's "invincible effort." The great question he had brought with him, Luce said, "was whether it would be reasonable to be optimistic about the future of China. So far it seems to me that the answer is definitely in the affirmative."[11]

He was equally positive about the role U.S. forces were playing in China in helping the country recover from Japanese occupation. "American troops here have behaved excellently," he wrote, and "should continue to be a credit to their country. . . . The Chinese . . . welcome the Americans as a sign of a new day and examples of a better way to live." Other journalists wrote emphatically about the impatience of American soldiers to return home and the G.I.s' lack of respect for or confidence in the Chinese forces. One of the American soldiers who traveled with Luce, he wrote, recited "facts unflattering to China." Another "loud-mouthed wise-cracker," while passing a battalion of Chinese soldiers, shouted "the war's over; so now you're going to fight?" But Luce mostly ignored these comments. He continued to praise the high morale of the American troops and their commanders. "The desire of local Chinese officials to show their appreciation of Americans and to . . . make a good impression on them cannot be exaggerated," he wrote from Tientsin.[12]

It seemed at times that Luce was almost willfully blind to the power of the Communist insurgency around him. Virtually none of his cables back to New York took notice of the growing strength of Mao's forces in Manchuria and northern China; nor was there any significant mention of the corruption and bureaucratic incompetence of the Kuomintang that White had tried so adamantly to convey. And yet the Communists were far from invisible, even in Chungking. Luce attended a banquet there at which Mao himself was the guest of honor. The two men had a brief private conversation afterward. Luce wrote that Mao "was surprised to see me there and gazed at me with an intense but not unfriendly curiosity. His remarks: polite grunts." A few days later, after walking through "many a back-ally," he met briefly with Zhou Enlai. "We had a nice talk—and completely frank." But he drew no other conclusions from the meeting, and he expressed little interest in the hopeful but ultimately futile negotiations that were attempting to create a coalition government in which the Communists could participate. Nor did Luce express any doubts about the ability of Chiang and his government to prevail alone. "The biggest surprise, and the happiest," he wrote to Mme. Chiang as he prepared to return to America, "was to find that the spirit of the people in North and East China is so strong and healthy. The people do not seem to be cowed or corrupted by eight years of life under enemy and puppet patrol. Their sense of patriotism is high and is closely related to their admiration for the Generalissimo."[13]

Early in November, at a dinner Clare organized for his return to New York, Luce gave a long, rambling talk about his visit. He spoke hopefully about a new "understanding between the 'West' . . . and the 'East,' " and about a strengthened relationship between the United States and China. He urged a "restoration of business activity," and he spoke optimistically about the Kuomintang's ability to fend off the challenge from the Communists. But to many in his audience, some of them followers of the much different assessments of the plight of China that were coming from the *New York Times* (and that had come recently from *Time* itself in Theodore White's last dispatches), Luce's optimism seemed unrealistic. "He seemed to be spending his time modifying his sentences to make sure that all of them contributed to the utmost to make the Generalissimo a hero," Henry Wallace, one of the guests, recorded in his diary. Luce remained undeterred by the skeptics around him. He continued busily to press policy recommendations on officials in Washington. After a meeting with Assistant Secretary of War John McCloy, he wrote smugly of the praise he had received from McCloy for a recent *Life* editorial lauding the progress of Chiang and his regime and encouraging continued American aid. China, he insisted, was now the test of the Truman administration's ability to prove its strength and competence, "the opportunity for clear, forthright policy . . . and . . . for effective leadership at home."[14]

The first years after the war were dark ones for Luce—and not just because of the great issues facing the world. It was also a time of turmoil in his marriage. In the aftermath of Ann Brokaw's death, it was impossible for either Harry or Clare to live their once blithely separate lives, maintaining a public relationship when useful while enjoying romantic escapes with others during their long periods apart. But Harry, who had never wholly reconciled himself to the end of his first marriage, also now found it difficult to end his second, despite its bleakness and despite his continuing relationship with Jean Dalrymple. Clare tried to bury herself in work—her reelection to Congress in 1944 and her busy life in Washington. But politics no longer interested her very much, and she found herself spending more and more time away from it, including an ill-fated stint as an actress in summer stock in Connecticut. Her aide, Albert Morano, took over the running of the office. (A local newspaper, noting Clare's frequent absences from Washington, ran an acid story under a picture of Morano with a headline "Our Real Congressman," which he eventually became.) Well before the expiration of her second term, she made it clear that she would not be a candidate again. But her departure from politics, combined with her continuing estrangement from Harry, drove her deeper into depression, what she described as a sense of worthlessness, mixed with a yearning for death. Twice, according to Harry, she attempted suicide—although he did not consider the attempts serious. As always, he was incapable of responding effectively to her obvious calls for attention and comfort. On some days she simply sat alone in a darkened room. On others she tried to resume her once-active social life, but never for very long. She referred to her depression as "Mr. Screwtape" (a demonic figure in a C. S. Lewis novel) with whom she was in continuous struggle.[15]

Clare's depression and restlessness led her to a search for spiritual comfort—something else she realized she could not expect from Harry. Having tried and failed to right herself through intensive psychoanalysis, she turned instead to the Catholic Church and, at first unknown to her husband, began considering conversion. (She had previously been religiously inactive, although as a child she had occasionally been thrust into Episcopalian institutions.) She quickly attracted the attention of Monsignor Fulton Sheen, who had a renowned (and militantly conservative) radio program and who later became the archbishop of Rochester, New York. Sheen spent more time teaching Clare the precepts of the church than he had ever spent on any other convert, he later said. He stayed with her in part because she was an intelligent and inquisitive student, but also because he knew that capturing so eminent a woman for the church would enhance his own reputation. On February 16, 1946, before a handful of people (Harry not among them) at St. Patrick's Cathedral, she was baptized a Catholic. The editors at *Time* struggled to find a way to record the event—which was receiving wide attention across the country—and finally settled on a small political notice: "Congresswoman Clare Boothe Luce's 'good and sufficient reason' for deciding not to run for re-election in Connecticut suddenly became clear: she was received into the Roman Catholic Church." Billings, who managed the sensitive story, wrote privately that the conversion was "logical for a half-crazy woman who must always be doing the bizarre to attract notice." Harry, however, did not discourage her (despite his own lifelong commitment to the Presbyterian Church and despite his mother's appalled reaction to Clare's repudiation of the "glorious faith which is life to me"). On the contrary, he provided what Clare called the essential "aid and sympathy" that gave her the courage to take this step, and that "in the end . . . has saved my reason—and probably my life."[16]

Clare's conversion may have reduced her despair and what she called her intermittent "death wish." But it did not bring her real peace. Looking back over her marriage, she began to see herself as the victim of Harry's inability to express or even feel genuine love. "I have been cheated of my womanly inheritance, thru no fault of mine," she wrote Harry in 1947. "The cheaters appear to me as a crew of selfish, cruel . . . usurpers, of whom you are seen to be the callous leader. . . . For it is not your desire to love any woman—least of all now, me, with your body, mind, and soul." But Clare was less concerned about their shared past than about their cloudy future. She came to believe that Harry had supported her conversion because it would allow him to divorce her so that he could marry Jean Dalrymple. Clare wrote him: "You realized (I know now) that [the conversion] meant the end of any real husband and wife relationship. . . . You believed my conversion would mean *your* legal freedom. . . . You *assumed* a divorce would certainly follow . . . in a manner which left you on high moral grounds ('Ah! The Catholic Church broke up our marriage!')." Jean Dalrymple later recounted Harry's claim to her that "in [Clare's] religion, we are no longer married, because in her religion I'm still married to Lila. She cannot live with me as my wife." But Clare's lawyers, and the Catholic Church, argued otherwise—and Clare's friends (most notably Bernard Baruch) urged her to fight Harry on the ground of what he cared about most, Time Inc. She demanded 51 percent of the company's stock and $4 million. Harry unsurprisingly refused, and the prospect of a divorce—and remarriage—rapidly dimmed. The relationship with Jean sputtered along for a short while longer and then ended.[17]

For someone as remote and aloof as Harry, he was often surprisingly open about his marital problems in conversations with members of his senior staff, several of whom—eager to reveal their intimacy with Luce—promptly began circulating rumors about his private life, many of them false. Harry, they whispered, was considering suicide. He was being blackmailed by a woman. C. D. Jackson (the principal source of the rumors) claimed to have experienced a scene of "Clare on knees, holding Harry's legs, big melodramatic tears and crying 'It's all because I couldn't give you a baby that you don't love me any more.' " (In reality it had been Harry who had not wanted her to have a baby.) Despite the falsehood of most of these rumors, Harry was almost as miserable as Clare. According to Billings, Luce wondered "why he doesn't get any sympathy from his friends!" Billings was ready with his own answer:

> I was pretty depressed, just by the vague outlines of Luce's mess, and yet I wasn't really sorry for him because he is so cross and bad mannered and inconsiderate that I like to see him suffer. Yet I hope his private dirt doesn't splatter on the company and therefore on me. . . . I'm just tired of being disappointed in people—of having them collapse morally right before me.

And yet Billings also retained a shred of sympathy for his colleague of decades. "Poor lonely soul," he wrote. "Unable to get any normal wholesome fun out of life and when he does try, it all goes rotten. . . . A tragic spectacle!"[18]

It was not just the legal and financial obstacles that kept Luce in his marriage. His bond with Clare—tattered and bruised as it was— remained significant even in the midst of some of their bitterest battles. Clare, at the end of a long, morose, and angry letter, nevertheless wrote that "I would with the utmost joy die for you this or any other night. For I never loved another, except my Ann, so deeply." And Harry replied with, for him, remarkable warmth:

> I suppose what you are trying to make out . . . is what my heart says 1) about you and 2) about me. . . . Well, I can tell you quite simply about the first. You are the incomparable person in my life. I loved you without reservation in the dearest hope of happiness for us both. I failed in my love before and yet I deeply believe I would not fail again, because if there is an "again," it would be a most precious gift.

But these warm and loving sentiments seemed to be possible only in writing, and when they were apart. Harry was usually reserved and inarticulate in his actual conversations with his wife. And Clare wrote him that "I shall fail miserably, within a week if I permit myself any discussions with you on personal matters.... It is better, then, for quite a while ... to confine ourselves to only such matters as interest you or me [except] our ... ruined relations." Their marriage continued—but for the most part because of a chilly loyalty, with occasional clumsy efforts at reconciliation, and with little warmth or intimacy. "With Clare no longer in Washington," Billings wondered, "what does their private life together here become?" The answer was that they continued to remain apart more often than not; and that when they were together the only real passion came from Clare's occasional eruptions of anger and misery. "Grover came in," Billings wrote in the fall of 1947, "to confide that Clare was again on the rampage, and giving Harry hellish trouble."[19]

Shortly before the end of World War II, Harry sent Clare a long, sprawling, handwritten letter outlining his hopes for his own future. He wrote of a vague hope to be secretary of state, but dismissed it as unrealistic. Instead "I would like to be and be recognized as a great and good Editor," and "I would like to achieve that degree of personal integrity which I believe it is possible for me to achieve, but which to date I am far from having achieved." He said almost nothing in his letter about his relationship with his wife, but the specter of his failed marriages certainly loomed large in his sense that he had not yet achieved a position of real integrity. "I have too much fragmentation in my life. I am not all in one place—or, as it seems all in one piece." Since childhood he had dreamed of being both a great man and a good man. Now, and not for the first time, he was questioning both. Was his publishing empire helping to better the world as much as he had hoped? Was he conducting his personal life with the integrity and honesty he expected of himself? The answer to both questions, he feared, was no. The magazines, he believed, had yet to reach the importance and influence that Luce believed they could. They had not yet focused clearly enough on the great "human questions" that would define the next generation. And his personal life was, by almost any standard, in ruins: without love, without real friends, without the ability to experience what he called "enjoyment"—a lonely man whose only solace was work, but a man struggling still with the missionary fervor that had shaped his life. Unlike Clare however he could live stoically with his disappointments. His life was not what he had imagined it would be, but it had rewards enough—his fame, his power, and most of all his company and his magazines, always his indispensable refuge from other, less controllable, aspects of his life. "I *am* happy," he wrote Clare during a vacation in New Hampshire, ". . . because of all that life has given me," and perhaps most of all because of what he considered the opportunity to "be of service to the world," to help shape "the first global era in history."[20]

The magazines, and the company that contained them, had always been his first priority, more important to him than anything else in his adult life, including his marriages. When he began to tire of his life with Lila, he compensated by spending more time at the office. When things were going badly with Clare, which was much of the time, he often became especially engaged in his work. This was nowhere more true than in the dark days of his crisis with Clare and his thwarted romance. The end of the war was, for him, not a period of triumph but a call to new goals. Even before Japan's surrender in August 1945, Luce was launching what he called a "rethinking" of his magazines—all of them. For Luce, whose day-to-day connection with the magazines had long been intermittent, a major editorial rethinking was a way to reacquaint himself with his publications. To his editors, who were frantically working to publish their magazines every week or month, it was a considerable additional burden—but one they had no choice but to shoulder. As always when Luce tried to reassert his control, he kept everyone busy. He called frequent meetings, sometimes over dinner at his home or in restaurants, sometimes during working hours in the office, and sometimes through telephone calls at any time of the day or night. But most of all, as always, he wrote memos—long, rambling meditations that, as one of his editors later recalled, "landed on the desk with an unwelcome thud."[21]

T. S. Matthews, the managing editor of *Time*, responded to Luce's invitation to rethink by claiming that the magazine was becoming stale, was running too smoothly, was losing some of its best writers, and was in short "not as good as it should be . . . [not] as dull as the N.Y. *Times*; but . . . dull in a way all its own." He proposed making the magazine smaller, consolidating its sections, streamlining the staff, and ridding the magazine of "our flinty, our malicious but not altogether insane tone." Luce, even while pushing the rethinking, was at the same time defensive, especially of *Time*. "TIME *is* good enough!" he wrote in response to Matthews. It "needed no deep changes, just some polishing." Uninterested in Matthews's large, structural suggestions, he offered instead a list of small tweaks—better headlines, more coverage of Congress and the

Supreme Court, and more attention to religion and business. (He also hotly denied that *Time's* prose was still "flinty" or "malicious.") Matthews pointed to the many criticisms of *Time* as "opinion disguised as fact." But Luce dismissed such comments. He considered them attacks on the whole "newsmagazine idea." *Time* was supposed to be opinionated, he always insisted.[22]

Even so the self-criticisms continued. Henry A. Grunwald, then a rising editor on the magazine (and years later editor in chief), also wrote a long memo in 1949 on "the things that disturb me about TIME." They included "the magazine's weekly sameness," "signs of threatening shallowness," "morale (its weakness) and enthusiasm (its lack)." But Luce still continued to defend *Time*, even three years after he had launched the "rethinking" project, while at the same time pushing (and thus confusing) his editors to make it "more interesting." Just as Luce had rejected the suggestions of his editors, the editors strongly resisted many of his proposed changes. At one point he suggested a new section to be called "Punditry & Prophesy," an idea that Billings considered "pretty trashy" and that Luce soon abandoned. Mostly he simply evaluated the existing departments and nudged them to be "better." His work on *Time* after the war was, in short, less an effort truly to reshape the magazine than to assert his continued authority, which he often felt he was losing. At one point he wrote Matthews a snide memo about the leftist labor leader Harry Bridges, who Luce insisted was planning

> to conquer Hawaii. . . . He pretty nearly did it in November 1946 and you will recall that *Time* endeavored to be of the greatest possible assistance to him. This is to state as a matter of policy that, for the purposes of the 1947–48 battle, Time Inc. is 100% in favor of the property owners, capitalists and corporations of Hawaii and 100% against Harry Bridges and anyone who is in any way allied with him. . . . I hope—but without real hope—that Time Inc. led by *Time* will give some dynamic reflection on the above stated policy. I realize that is unlikely—if for no other reason than that I have laid it down as categorical policy.

Billings reproached him for his "wild exaggeration" and "bitter sarcasm," and Luce grudgingly apologized to Matthews. But he remained aggrieved and irritable, continued to argue with Matthews, and finally ordered him to take a year's leave to think about how to improve the magazine—the penultimate step in Matthews's movement out of the job, and the company. Matthews was a victim of his assertion of independence, not of poor editing.[23]

Luce was less happy with, and far less protective of, *Fortune* in the late 1940s. That was in part because *Fortune* was, for the first time in years, losing money. He spent months conferring quietly with a few senior colleagues on *Fortune*'s finances and on what could be done to strengthen them, and he pressured its managing editor, Ralph Paine, to explain why things were going so poorly. Luce dispatched Billings to investigate, and Billings came back with a blunt report, which he summarized: "the edit budget $10,000 over; Paine's memo on why he needs 25 writers; 17 people in art dept . . . the high-priced writers, my doubts as to the value of the Survey, a lack of 'liveliness' which may be due to sound but aging and unlively writers and editors." Planning for the future was, Billings noted after a meeting with Luce, "pretty discouraging because the editorial people were so mediocre. . . . [Luce] held his head in his hands in deep despair. . . . 'What's the use of my giving orders for a new *Fortune* if there isn't anybody to carry them out?' "[24]

But despite his discouragement, Luce announced in February 1948 that he was " 'rethinking FORTUNE' . . . 'radical thinking' . . . that takes little for granted, re-examines suppositions and habits." A month later he produced a twenty-five-page memo describing the "new" *Fortune*—a memo hastily written and only slightly affected by the many suggestions he received from Billings and others. ("An irritating document," Billings wrote in his diary after sneaking a look at a late draft, "philosophically involved, dark and murky, as Luce groped for new ideas. Why does he have to overcomplicate everything?") *Fortune*, Luce grandiosely announced, would become "a magazine with a mission. That mission is to assist in the successful development of American Business Enterprise at home and abroad." Although *Fortune* had long ago abandoned its reputation as a magazine that wrote from many different political and ideological perspectives, it had never openly committed itself to taking the side of business as an editorial policy. What Luce was proposing was a magazine devoted to highlighting the success stories of American capitalism—"great stories" providing "wonderful accounts of vitally interesting segments of the whole business scene."[25]

At the center of the "new *Fortune*" would be a long report in each issue on "Thirty Days of American Business Enterprise . . . a story full of active verbs . . . written by a super-journalist." Despite Luce's ebullience about his proposed innovations, the message to *Fortune* was at bottom a harsh and censorious one. "*Fortune* [would] no longer [be] concerned, uniquely, with Civilization-as-a-whole. . . . *Fortune* will not be making itself responsible for everything everywhere." (Or as Billings put it in his own recommendations to Luce, "El Greco ain't business.") Instead *Fortune* would focus almost entirely and almost always positively on "American Business Enterprise," aided by advisory boards composed of prominent business leaders. (Paine opposed the advisory-board proposal and threatened to resign until Luce backed away from it.) An unstated but critical part of this plan was that the new *Fortune* would have a smaller and less expensive staff. It was, Billings wrote, "a notice of dismissal" for most of the *Fortune* writers and editors.[26]

Within a year *Fortune* was a fundamentally different magazine—narrower in focus, more strongly committed ideologically to what some called the "March of Business," much reduced in personnel, and considerably more successful in attracting advertising and new subscribers from the business world. But despite Luce's directives, it did not become a business mouthpiece, in part because his eagerness to attract talent and celebrity to his magazines was as strong as his desire to promote his own views. Over the next decade *Fortune* welcomed serious and not always affirmative commentary on capitalism from major intellectuals: Daniel Bell, John Kenneth Galbraith, Lawrence Lessing, William H. Whyte, and other eminent social scientists with academic backgrounds and, in some cases, academic futures. They continued to publish articles in *Fortune* that represented some of the most challenging and often contrarian views of capitalism to be found in journalism.[27]

The overhaul of *Fortune* was the most radical change to come out of the "rethinking" project, but to Luce the most important target was *Life*. He had many concerns. The magazine was still immensely profitable, but there were signs of softening in both circulation and advertising. The most obvious explanation for these problems was the unstable economy of the postwar years. But Luce chose to blame the content of the magazine itself—and not entirely without reason. Daniel Longwell, the pioneering creative force behind the founding of *Life*, had at long last succeeded Billings as editor of the magazine. Longwell himself had insisted long ago that he would not be a good managing editor, and his actual job performance proved him right. More than once he told Luce he felt he should step down. For all his talent, he was weak and insecure as a leader and frightened of almost everyone. His always-visible tendency to stammer and mutter became much more frequent once he was promoted. Luce, despite his own history of stammering, ungenerously called it "the way a deaf man does to avoid unpleasant topics."[28]

But Luce was not just concerned about Longwell, or even about the quality of the editing. He had a larger goal in mind. He wanted *Life* to become less a picture magazine and more a vehicle for confronting what he considered the great challenges facing the world. *Life* had often contained serious material in the past, both textual and visual, especially during the war; but it had always considered itself at least as much entertainment as journalism. That was one of the secrets of its great success, even though Luce never conceded that point, and his colleagues rarely dared to raise it. Just as *Fortune* was now to be the voice of American business, *Life* was to be the voice of the new postwar world—and to a large degree, the postwar world as Luce hoped the United States would reshape it. "My mind is literally overpowered, paralyzed, by the nightmare of a tidal wave of knowledge by which, it seems, *Life* can and will engulf me," Luce wrote in 1948. But he did not wish to turn back that tide. Instead he intruded more and more into the editing of the magazine to ensure that readers were exposed to the great ideas that Luce believed they must absorb. Robert Elson, a long-serving Time Inc. editor, wrote in his in-house history of the company (after Luce's death) that "what had once been a young, ebullient, free-wheeling staff seemed bowed down by responsibility for the education of its vast audience while too frequently forgetting that *Life* was also supposed to be entertaining."[29]

The rethinking of *Life* had actually begun not with Luce but with Longwell, who in 1944 wrote a memo complaining that the magazine had lost its youth—not just the youth of the magazine but of the people who ran it. *Life*, he argued, "should be a young man's magazine. . . . We've reached a high but dead level of competence. . . . Our first and primary duty as editors is to make the magazine reflect its title." This was in Longwell's first year as editor. By 1946, however, he had begun to bow out and turn the weekly editing over to his talented colleagues Joseph Thorndike and Ed Thompson, both of whom understood that they were in a competition to succeed him. By then the number of people trying to rethink *Life* was growing almost exponentially. The magazine had what Billings called "a jittery uncertainty" and lacked "a smooth even flow of purpose." But equally troubling to him was the parade of intruders trying to "fix" the magazine, people who were "directly, or indirectly, pulling and hauling at the . . . editor—Larsen, Heiskell, Longwell, Billings, Luce. . . . If one man were editing straight-away for the next couple of years, there would be less feeling of fuzzy command." But that was not to be. In October 1946, Luce made Thorndike the editor. Three years later Thorndike resigned, frustrated by Luce's continual intrusion and what he considered the undermining of his authority. He was succeeded by Ed Thompson, who also encountered frequent interventions by Luce and others but nevertheless remained in the job until 1961.[30]

In the fall of 1948 Luce sent a memo to the *Life* editors that was, among his many such memos, distinctive for its elaborate metaphors. He referred to an English film about the love affair between British bird lovers and a small bird known as the tawny pipit. That love affair—that elevation of an ordinary, unimportant bird into an object of extraordinary fascination—was, Luce argued, the key to a successful magazine. "As long as the English were on top of the world, their imaginations were on top of themselves. . . . Everything they saw, everything they learned, was absorbed in their imaginations." The moral of this strangely contrived parable was that "if you want to make . . . anything . . . interesting, it must be loved by the writer and the editor." In other, more conventional memos, he made his views much clearer—that the magazine should express its love of what Luce believed was America's great moment, its unprecedented opportunity to be the new Britain, to reshape the world. In 1948, in response to a proposal for a "Western Culture" project, Luce grandiosely insisted that the series should aspire "to add up to a coherent interpretation of history. . . . The drama of Western Culture culminates in the creation of the United States of America. And this interpretation invites all Americans to take stock of American civilization at the moment of history when the U.S. has become the heir and chief guardian against the whole body of Western Civilization against the forces of reactionary neo-barbarism."[31]

But Luce did not stop with Western civilization. *Life*, he soon argued, must become something like a textbook for men and women in need of instruction (whether they knew it or not). They should be presented with "convictions as to the nature of man and the purpose of human life." To support that goal, he proposed "a combination of an introduction to, and summary of, Freshman Psychology A." *Life* should also, he argued, take on the social sciences "and show, by encyclopedic selection, what is the basic material and method of each of the disciplines." It should develop a concern "for the Non-European world . . . getting Americans acquainted with the many, many, many different peoples and customs and politics." And the magazine would, he insisted, develop a higher level of taste: "There is in picture journalism a special peril of bad taste; we will have no bad taste in *Life*."[32]

Above all he had decided that the most important element of the kind of journalism he was advocating was "faith." Faith, Luce said, was "what a man does actually believe in as shown by what he does and how he lives. . . . Like democracy itself, and inescapably with democracy, journalism must fight its way through to a better and brighter world—or at least perish honorably in the attempt." *Life*—which had begun to show people interesting photographs, to revel in the curious and the entertaining, and to attract eager readers to such trivial but entertaining features as Life Goes to a Party—that lively, inventive, and never-too-serious magazine was now to become a chronicle of the West's (and America's) march to democratic greatness.[33]

As was usually the case, Luce did not entirely get his way. *Life* continued to publish photographs and essays that were pure entertainment, and the magazine moved through the late 1940s and 1950s with continued popularity and success. But if Luce did not transform *Life*, he did alter it. *Life* was increasingly devoted to more serious material—often long, sometimes tedious, always worthy. Luce could rarely resist contributions from major world figures, no matter how dull their writing. His editors shuddered when he returned from trips abroad, fearful that he had brought with him yet another ponderous article from a king or minister or celebrity.

The most famous example of *Life*'s new role—and almost certainly its most prominent—was its publication of excerpts from the writings of Winston Churchill. This was a large and important innovation for *Life*, which had rarely before published material from books and certainly never so massive a series of texts as Luce wanted from Churchill. The courtship was long and complicated. Churchill's chief, and perhaps only, interest in the relationship was financial. No longer prime minister, he had to maintain his lavish lifestyle on his own. The combination of his own modest fortune and high British taxes left him feeling insecure and impoverished. *Life*, to Churchill, was a great revenue stream. Luce's interest, by contrast, was only indirectly financial. His principal motive was his belief that capturing the work of such a great figure would elevate *Life* to an even higher level of eminence in American publishing. Churchill was one of the great figures of his time and, Luce, as always with great figures he admired, wanted to be associated with him.

The relationship between Churchill and Luce began in 1945, when Walter Graebner, the London bureau chief for Time Inc., heard from Randolph Churchill that his father was interested in having some of his paintings reproduced in *Life*. Longwell and Thorndike were not enthusiastic about the idea, but Luce saw an opportunity to draw Churchill into a deeper association with the magazine. He paid Churchill twenty thousand dollars to reproduce sixteen pictures in the magazine—pictures that were more pleasant curiosities than significant art. A few months later Graebner accepted an invitation to Churchill's home and was read a series of secret speeches Churchill had made to Parliament during the war. Perhaps, he suggested, *Life* would like to publish several of them—for seventy-five thousand dollars. Luce paid fifty thousand dollars, even though he was bored by the speeches. Churchill accepted the fee. "Let's hope a wide public feels differently," he confided to Billings of the speeches. "It can be worth the space plus the money if, in some sense, Churchill becomes 'our author.' " What Luce really wanted was to publish excerpts from Churchill's promised but still unwritten memoirs. And he spared no effort or expense to acquire them.[34]

Over the next several years *Life* showered favors and money on Churchill. When Churchill complained that he could not afford a vacation because he could not take British currency out of the country, *Life* paid for long visits to Morocco, Florida, and other warm climates where he could paint and, Luce hoped, write. Luce gave lavish and fawning dinners for Churchill when he was in New York, and he traveled to England periodically to flatter and encourage him. It did not take long for Churchill to sign a contract. In the spring of 1947 Luce agreed to allow *Life* and the *New York Times* to share publication of the memoirs for the then-staggering sum of $1.15 million—$750,000 from *Life* and $400,000 from the *Times*. "But," Billings wondered, "will Churchill really buckle down and write top-notch stuff or will he just string a lot of murky official papers together?"[35]

Luce assured his colleagues that he would not interfere with the delicate task of editing Churchill's work, but he could not help himself. He began bombarding Churchill with suggestions on how to tell the history of the war. In particular he tried to persuade Churchill to share and write about Luce's own contempt for Roosevelt. "He played a most two-faced and ineffective part in the efforts to prevent the so-unneccesary [*sic*] war," Luce wrote, and thus betrayed his country and the world. He also prodded Churchill about what he called the failure at Yalta, which he also blamed on Roosevelt. Churchill read Luce's letters but never replied.[36]

Churchill ultimately did write the book, and more quickly than he had once predicted, even if in a way that made Graebner and Luce nervous. "Churchill does most of his work in bed," Graebner reported. "He

keeps six secretaries busy. . . . One secretary drives with him to and from
the country, as Mr. Churchill uses this time to dictate. 'I can do about
1,000 words while motoring to Chartwell—never less than 800,' says
Churchill." Longwell and a young *Life* editor, Jay Gold, were dispatched
to help edit the first volume, which dealt with the prewar years. It was
voluminous, sprawling, and often turgid. Luce himself jumped into the
editing process and wrote Churchill about problems of the "architectural structure" of the book. Churchill insisted that the incoherence of
the manuscript reflected the incoherence of the policies pursued by
nations in those years. But he was not a stubborn writer, and he gradually allowed the two editors to reshape his material to fit the magazine.

Publication of the excerpts began in the spring of 1948. They were
not popular with *Life*'s readers and had what Andrew Heiskell called "a
devastating effect on newsstand sales." Churchill wrote at great length,
occasionally brilliantly, often tediously, and sometimes almost incoher-
ently. Even the most rigorous editing could not make the material
consistently interesting. He also padded the memoirs with official documents and produced six volumes, not just the five promised in the contract. (He asked for more money, and Luce—after scaling down his
extravagant demands—augmented his fee.) But despite the many ways in
which the publication of the memoirs proved disappointing, Luce was
not deterred. Not only did he continue to publish excerpts from the
memoirs into the mid-1950s, but he also bought the serial rights to
Churchill's next major work, *A History of the English-Speaking Peoples.* He
published as well a multipart memoir by the Duke of Windsor (the former king), which was even less interesting to the editors and to most
readers than the Churchill materials. But if *Life* was going to be the serious and influential magazine he wanted it to be, Luce reasoned, how
could he fail to publish the work, however dull, of such eminent figures
in history?[37]

The serialization of Churchill's work was in many ways the launching point for making magazine journalism a vehicle for book promotion.
Not long after *Life* published Churchill's books, other magazines began
working to excerpt books from many other prominent figures from the
war years: generals, monarchs, politicians, diplomats. Rarely did any
magazine attract large readerships for these pedigreed texts, but the
prestige of being able to boast of such distinguished authors soon
became as irresistible to other editors as it was to Luce—and an increasingly competitive venture.

. . .

Because the rethinking project stopped well short of Luce's hopes, he began to think of new vehicles to help him tackle the great ideas he yearned to express. Luce had long dreamed of publishing a magazine of opinion. Time Inc.'s decision to end its brief association with the *Saturday Review* in the 1920s had long been a source of regret to him. Almost thirty years later he was still in search of a way to be a more important player in the battle for ideas. The most influential opinion magazines in the 1940s—the *New Republic*, the *Nation*, and others—were mostly liberal periodicals dominated by people committed to the New Deal. Luce never said so, but it was clear that he hoped to create a magazine that would offer a different and more conservative view of the world. The most important force in driving the project, however, was a new figure in Luce's life—Willi Schlamm, an Austrian émigré and a disillusioned Communist moving rapidly to the Right. (He would eventually end up as a mainstay of *The National Review*.)[38]

The relationship between Luce and Schlamm baffled many of their colleagues. For a relatively new and quite junior member of the *Fortune* editorial board, he seemed to have unusual access to Luce and was often the influence behind some of Luce's raging explosions about questionable taste in the magazines. In the summer of 1947 the two men vacationed together in the White Mountains, behavior so uncharacteristic that it threw Luce's longtime and deeply loyal secretary into a "tizzy," worrying aloud that "There's something terribly wrong with Mr. Luce." Schlamm began to be invited to dinners and events that others considered inappropriate for a junior editor. Luce's influential deputy Allen Grover referred to Schlamm's "evil and disruptive influence over Harry—this little nobody who had inserted himself into the very heart of a domestic crisis in the life of America's most effective publishing enemy of communism." Billings referred to "Schlamm's Svengali influence over Luce." Early in the planning of the new magazine Luce asked Tom Matthews to lead the development of the project, with Schlamm as his deputy. But within weeks Schlamm had persuaded Luce that he should be co-editor. Matthews disliked Schlamm, was furious to be asked to share authority with him, and ultimately withdrew from the project altogether. But Schlamm continued to promote the project, and Luce continued to support it.

Schlamm's original prospectus for the magazine was both cocky and indistinct. He wrote at length about the competition and cited the "cumulative dissatisfaction with most of the existing magazines" as a reason to create a new one. But his vision of an alternative was self-righteously vague and fussily conservative The magazine would reflect "a civilized respect for fundamentals, and mellowing experience." It would have a "sense of urgency and an understanding of the 'new.' " It would be "constructive and readable." And like other Luce magazines, all of which claimed to have "convictions" at their heart, Schlamm offered ideas that he suspected Luce would find attractive: "Man has a choice between Right and Wrong. . . . The standards we have inherited from the Scriptures and the Declaration of Independence are pretty good guesses of what decent people will accept as self-evident truths." This would not be "a magazine where 'everything goes.' If we have an opinion on any subject we mean it, and we shall stick to it." It would not be a magazine for the many, not "caviar for the masses," but a publication that would appeal to the "never-dying community of individuals who manage to combine esthetic sensitivity with intellectual curiosity and moral concern." It would "not promote *avant garde*," but it would embrace "a desire for religious reorientation . . . what some people already call 'an American Church-in-Progress.' " Many of Luce's colleagues found both the tone and the content of the prospectus almost insufferable in its arrogance. Others compared it to some of the more pretentious claims Luce and Hadden had made when promoting *Time* in the early 1920s. There was little support for the project from anyone but Luce himself.

Work on the new magazine, which at times was called *Measure* and at other moments called *Quest*, continued for three years. Schlamm solicited articles, produced crude dummies, and recruited possible contributors from Europe and America. But the opposition within the company was too great, and Luce's commitment, in the end, too faint. Early in 1948 he pulled the plug. With a stilted formality that reflected his discomfort, he made clear that not only would Time Inc. not publish the magazine, but that Schlamm was not free to take it elsewhere. He left a faint hope that the company might return to the project in a year or so and try again. (It never did.) And he encouraged Schlamm to propose another role for himself at Time Inc., which Schlamm interpreted correctly as an offer of no job at all. After a few token assignments, he left the company for good in 1949. He was, Billings noted in his diary, one of Luce's "private problem children—'pieces of his conscience.' . . . [Schlamm] should have gone years ago."[39]

The failure of the opinion magazine did not, however, dampen Luce's enthusiasm for using his publishing influence to shape the thinking of the nation. Luce rejected the new magazine not only because his colleagues opposed it, but also because he was uncertain that it would reach a large enough audience to have the influence he felt he needed. He was left with relying on his existing magazines, with their large circulation and great popularity. But he was also left with their entrenched editors who did not always welcome his ideas.

Luce continued to believe in the enormous importance to the world, and to the United States, of a free and democratic China. The failure of that goal—the ultimate defeat of Chiang Kai-shek's regime, and the establishment of Communist China—was the greatest disappointment of Luce's life. But for nearly two years after the end of World War II, he remained optimistic about the future—confident that the Chinese people, now liberated from the Japanese invasion, would not support a revolution but would instead yearn for peace, comfort, and prosperity under the government they knew. "People are sick to death of war, profiteering, exile, bloodshed and malnutrition," *Time* declared in a 1945 story titled "Bright with Hope." It began with an uncharacteristically rapturous cable from Teddy White: "China's hopes of peace are brighter than they have been for 20 years." *Time* predicted, implausibly, that the Soviet Union's entry into the Pacific war in the summer of 1945, and its alliance of convenience with China against Japan in the last days of the war, would ensure Russian support for the established government of Chiang against the Communists; and that Stalin was "morally bound to withdraw his Red Army from conquered Jap forces." The Soviet army, the magazine reported, "gave the back of its hand to Manchurian communists, forbade them to attempt any organization.... This is an extraordinary and encouraging sign."[40]

In Washington confidence in the future of the Chiang Kai-shek regime was a great deal weaker than it was in the Time Inc. Building in New York. The new Truman administration was unwilling to allow American forces to become engaged in a civil war in China. But it nevertheless hoped to stabilize China by providing American aid and by promoting negotiations between the Nationalists and Communists that it hoped would lead to the creation of a coalition government. To advance this vision Truman appointed the former Army Chief of Staff, Gen. George C. Marshall, as his "personal representative" in December 1945. (Marshall replaced the truculently anti-Communist brigadier general Patrick Hurley, whom Roosevelt had sent to China in 1944 in the aftermath of Stilwell's bitter departure. Hurley had blamed the problems of the Chiang regime on "traitors" in the State Department.)[41]

The "Marshall Mission," as the general's efforts in China came to be called, took place against a backdrop of considerable division in Washington between the military and the State Department. Navy Secretary James Forrestal, Army Assistant Secretary John McCloy, the recently dismissed Patrick Hurley, and others believed with Luce that true peace and reform could not come through negotiation but only through the defeat of the Communists; and that the Chiang regime needed substantial American military and economic support. Secretary of State James Byrnes, John Carter Vincent, the assistant secretary of state for Far Eastern affairs, and others were skeptical of Chiang's ability to withstand the Communist challenge, with or without American support, and wanted most of all to prevent the United States from becoming ensnared in a new war in Asia only months after the old one had come to a close. Marshall at first avoided siding with either camp, but little by little he became convinced that the State Department view was correct.[42]

Luce wrote Marshall warmly in support of his mission and offered his help. Marshall politely ignored the offer, but Luce set out to influence the general nevertheless. He was particularly eager to mobilize the community of American missionaries and other clergy who had served in China, men Luce believed would have both the knowledge and the moral stature to influence policy. He urged Marshall to invite Leighton Stuart—the former president of Yenching University in Beijing, a staunch supporter of Chiang, and a former colleague and friend of Luce's father—to consult with the general in China. Marshall declined the request, but Stuart made his way to China anyway, called on Marshall himself, and soon became a close confidant of the general. At Marshall's request, and to Luce's great delight, Stuart became the first postwar American ambassador to China in 1946 (and its last until the 1980s). Luce showered him with letters and wires urging more vigorous help to China and more pressure on Marshall to stand up to the Communists. "Washington has given too little attention to the problem," he warned. Aware that the consensus in Washington was that Americans had no heart for a commitment to China, he wrote that "General Marshall and yourself may underestimate the willingness of the American public opinion to support a program of vigorous assistance to China through a constitutional national government." And he worked hard to counter what he considered a growing chorus of destructive voices: "Teddy White's *Thunder Out of China*, Henry Wallace, *The New Republic*, *The Nation* . . . [and] a recent speech by John Carter Vincent [that] seemed to me . . . to be a shocking disservice to the best interests of the United States and China."[43]

Luce also reached out to Henry Van Dusen, the new president of Union Theological Seminary (which Luce's father had attended) and a recent visitor to China. In an article Luce solicited for *Life*, Van Dusen flattered Marshall as a man of "integrity . . . and wisdom," but challenged his approach to the China problem. The "intractable bar to peace," he insisted, "lies in the fundamentally irreconcilable character of the conflict between China's two factions. . . . May it not be the part of far-visioned statesmanship to face that inescapable issue now, before Communist strength can be mobilized at its fullest potential and while the Nationalist forces are still organized and equipped?" In short, better a conflict with the Communists now than a false truce that would certainly fail later. "China in Communist hands," he warned, "would be the most probable . . . prelude to World War III. . . . Consequently the U.S. *must* lend every practicable support to the constituted government of China."[44]

Luce soon began a broader campaign of support for Chiang, a campaign aimed at both the officials he believed would be the most important decision makers—Marshall above all—and at the American public. It began with his own trip to China in the fall of 1946, a year after his previous visit. Luce was, as always, eager for a reason to go to China; and in the spring of 1946 he had instructed one of his reporters there to organize a summer vacation for him on Iltus Huk in Tsingtao, the resort community in which he had spent summers as a child and which he had visited again in the early 1930s. "I have no desire to be paltry," Luce wrote. "Three or four bedrooms, living room, dining room and something to serve as library or study. Plumbing must, of course, be in order. I presume there will be no difficulty in getting servants." In the end Luce never took the vacation. But he continued to look for another opportunity to visit China, and he seized on a presumed "invitation" from Chiang.[45]

In fact there was no formal invitation. Luce had mentioned casually and unspecifically to Chinese officials in America that he hoped to visit China soon. But because he said it in the presence of Wellington Koo, the Chinese ambassador to the United States, and T. V. Soong, the Kuomintang finance minister, word of this vague exchange found its way to Chiang Kai-shek. He then mentioned that Luce would be welcome should he decide to come. Chiang's own unspecific welcome quickly became, in Luce's mind, and soon in the minds of U.S. government officials, a formal invitation. By the time Luce left for China, Stuart Symington, an assistant secretary of war, provided him with a luxurious U.S. Air Force plane for the trip at government expense. Luce arrived in

Shanghai on October 26, greeted by the mayor and the city's ranking American military officials. As usual he was lavishly entertained by the Kuomintang elite. "Luce dominated the conversation after dinner as he has at all these Chinese functions I have attended with him," Marshall's aide John Beal (a former *Time* editor) wrote in his diary after one such event. Not surprisingly Luce heard what he wanted to hear. He asked why the press had not paid more attention to the government's military successes. He asked for confirmation of his own belief that the course of war had "changed things" and that it had essentially ensured the victory of the Nationalists. He heard few arguments against his views.[46]

He had dinner with his old friend Leighton Stuart, by now the American ambassador, where conversation focused, to Luce's dismay, on the success of Teddy White's *Thunder Out of China*. He spent an afternoon on a houseboat near Nanking with Chiang Kai-shek, Mme. Chiang, and General and Mrs. Marshall, celebrating the Generalissimo's birthday—"a beautiful and memorable day," he later recalled. When they returned to shore the entire population of the village (which had ignored the group on its arrival) had been mobilized as a belated welcoming party. A private meeting with Marshall did little to change Luce's view that the general was badly in error on America's policy toward China. Marshall continued to believe that the solution to the Chinese crisis was to "get the Communists and the government together." He resisted Luce's proposal that the United States dramatically increase aid to the Chiang regime; Marshall argued that doing so would only confirm Chiang's refusal to negotiate in good faith with the Communists. Even Stuart, who had less confidence than Marshall in the possibility of a coalition government, believed that aid to Chiang should be conditioned on reforms within the Nationalist government, a requirement Luce opposed.[47]

Despite Marshall's public optimism, Luce's visit coincided with the failing negotiations between the Nationalists and the Communists, the cornerstone of the Marshall mission. Luce managed to arrange a meeting with Zhou Enlai, the Communist representative at the talks. Fred Gruin, one of *Time*'s correspondents, drove Luce to the gray-brick compound where the Communist delegation was staying. "In a small sitting room, a charcoal brazier lit against the season's chill and the inevitable steaming cups of tea at hand," Gruin recalled, Luce and Zhou sat down for a conversation, conducted entirely in English. "All the Chinese Communists now wanted," Gruin wrote, "was a genuine cease-fire in the civil war." Only later, after Luce had rushed to inform Stuart of the offer, did he discover that Zhou's proposal included a pull-back of Nationalist forces from the areas in which they were fighting successfully. "I must record," Luce wrote years later, "the utter confidence as well as the good humor with which Chou En-lai spoke to me. While he didn't say so in so many words, I had the chilling feeling that he expected soon to be in control of all China." (Years later Luce wrote: "At the end of my stay, I figured he was right." Nothing suggests that he actually believed that at the time.)[48]

Luce ended his trip convinced that "the Marshall Mission had failed." But since he had long ago come to disagree with its central aim—a negotiated settlement with the Communists—he was not entirely discouraged. Marshall's failure, he believed, would give new momentum to providing military aid to the Kuomintang. Luce left China, he said, "hopeful and with good prospect."[49]

Back in New York, Luce encouraged his reliably loyal editor, Charles Murphy, to complete a massive four-part profile for *Life* of Chiang Kai-shek, which Murphy had begun several months earlier, undeterred by the fact that Chiang was already perhaps the most frequently profiled person ever to appear in his magazines. But Luce encountered staunch resistance from Billings and other senior editors to the gushing, uncritical article. They persuaded him first to reduce it to a two-part piece and then, after a year of indecision, to kill it altogether. Luce acquiesced, in part for fear of seeming too partisan in his treatment of Chiang, a decision he later regretted. But as if to make up for this failure, he aggressively recruited the former diplomat William Bullitt in 1947 to travel as a "special correspondent" to China to report on the state of the civil war. There was little enthusiasm for this project among Luce's senior editors, who considered Bullitt an ambitious blowhard. "We all deplore Bullitt's mission to China and expect nothing from it," Billings wrote in his diary. "If only Luce could resist such arrant rascals!" But Luce's eagerness for articles from this controversial figure, a newly ardent anti-Communist, was unstoppable—as was clearly evident in the almost unprecedented fee of thirteen thousand dollars Time Inc. paid for the effort, despite Bullitt's lack of experience in or expertise on Asia. When Bullitt submitted his manuscript, Billings called it "superficial and mediocre," but did not dare to kill it. C. D. Jackson bridled at running a summary of the piece in *Time*. The *Life* editors balked at its length (and eventually persuaded Luce, over Bullitt's "violent objection," to cut it down from two parts to one). Luce conceded that "some people think [Bullitt's] a shit," but he remained committed to the piece, which ran both in *Life* and (as excerpts) in *Time* in October 1947. Unsurprisingly Bullitt echoed Luce's own conviction that the loss of China to Communism was an unacceptable outcome to the conflict, no matter what the cost to the United States. Like Luce, he believed that virtually all of Chiang's problems— the corruption, the bureaucratic incompetence, the brutality—were products of the pressures of war, that it was unrealistic to expect improvement until the Communists were defeated. He recommended sending Douglas MacArthur to advise Chiang on the conduct of the war (an oft-floated proposal that MacArthur had consistently refused to consider). "They would work together as brothers for their common cause," Bullitt rapturously predicted. "The whole Far Eastern horizon would brighten with hope." But if China were to fall "into the hands of Stalin," his alarmist conclusion warned, "all Asia, including Japan, sooner or later will fall into his hands. . . . The independence of the U.S. will not live a generation longer than the independence of China." Luce was delighted with the piece and helped arrange radio addresses and an exhausting speaking tour for Bullitt shortly after the article appeared.[50]

Luce was growing increasingly impatient with his own writers and editors, who were not, he complained, "observing the Editor-in-Chief's China policy." (Evidence of the problem, he believed, was the sandbagging of Murphy's Chiang profile, even though Luce himself had been complicit in the killing of the piece.) He set out again to express his own views of the situation in China, which should, he insisted, become part of Time Inc.'s "policy." He spent part of his trip home from China writing by hand an outline of his central precepts. What were the "fundamental motivations of Chiang Kai-shek?" Luce asked. Chiang aspired to "establish a China which shall be 1) united, 2) free of foreign domination, 3) progressively modern, hence a) strong, b) democratic." What stood mostly in the way of this "double purpose," he concluded, was a single problem: the Communists. Hence the principal goal of the United States must be to stop them so as to give Chiang the opportunity to achieve his "life purpose—the 'unity' of China."[51]

Back in New York he continued to bombard his editors with the urgency of the task. "Luce came to my M. E. [managing editor] lunch and talked steadily about China—almost a repeat of yesterday's lunch," Billings wrote. Matthews also received a memo from Luce complaining that Time-Life International was "not paying enough attention to China. . . . Nearly all the correspondents in China are doing a poor job." Hardly a day went by without a chiding memo to his senior editors: "It seems to me *Time* has paid awful little attention to [Wellington] Koo," he complained on one day. On another he wrote that "we need to focus again . . . on the prospects for success or failure, progress or chaos in China." Editors frequently found Luce "in a huffy unhappy mood about some *Life* text on China," or "suffering visibly over China." So harried did the editorial staff feel under Luce's pressure that they began to compile evidence that they were in fact reflecting his own strong views. The *Time* editors sent Luce groveling proof of their loyalty in April 1947 by listing the ways in which they had followed the editor in chief's line:

> The former U.S. policy of mediation had been invalidated by Chiang's "brilliant military victories," the increased stubbornness of the Communists. . . . Adoption of the new Constitution proved Chiang's democratic intention and justified increased U.S. support. . . . China would find it difficult to solve her currency problem without U.S. Aid. . . . The crisis . . . has been brought on by the lack of a positive U.S. Policy and by Marshall's "stiff-necked insistence that the Nationalist Government must be purified before the U.S. would give it decisive help in putting down a Communist revolution."[52]

A little more than two months after Luce's return from China, Marshall moved from Nanking to Washington and became secretary of state. President Truman, members of Congress, and the majority of the public gave Marshall credit for attempting what turned out to be an impossible task, and most Americans slowly began to prepare themselves for the likely defeat of the Chiang regime and the triumph of the Communists. But to Luce, and to other strong supporters of the Nationalist cause, Marshall's failed effort was part of a great and tragic betrayal—the willful abandonment of China to Communism through incompetence at best and a traitorous conspiracy at worst. Even before China fell, the recriminations began—and continued for a generation. The last years before the fall of Nationalist China produced stores of ammunition for those who were coming to constitute what became known as the "China Lobby."

Luce was never as fevered a member of the China Lobby as were many others. He continued to admire George Marshall, despite his great disappointment with the general's actions in China. He did not often accuse those he opposed of traitorous motives, and he seldom associated himself with the more hysterical press lords of the pro-Chiang right—William Randolph Hearst, Col. Robert McCormick of the *Chicago Tribune,* and others. But beginning in the last years of Nationalist government on the mainland, and continuing for many years after, his bitterness toward those whom he believed had failed China in the greatest crisis of its history steadily increased. The folly of allowing China to fall, Luce believed, was so self-evident that only weakness, stupidity, or—worse—disloyalty could explain America's course. "The measure of degradation of American policy in the Pacific," he wrote bitterly in early 1948,

> is the fact that a few guys like [Minnesota representative Walter Judd] and me have to go about peddling a vital interest of the United States and a historic article of U. S. Foreign policy as if it were some sort of bottled chop suey that we were trying to sneak through the Pure Food Laws. . . . [T]oday an American Government, attempting to "lead" the world—seems not to be in the slightest degree embarrassed by its total neglect of Asia.[53]

Like many critics of the Truman administration far to Luce's right, he began to characterize his opponents not as people with legitimate disagreements but as dupes of the Communists or worse. "Where's the agrarian democracy in mainland China that 'experts' . . . attributed to the . . . Communists?" he said contemptuously in the early 1950s. "On what basis," he asked, did ". . . so many people on the left, and so many people in the State Department, come to believe that Mao and his allies were potential allies of the United States?"—repeating the long-standing canard that admiration for Mao was a principal cause of America's abandonment of Chiang. In the heat of his despair he at times lost his ability to express disagreement—even with the people he most admired—in a restrained and respectful way. "I cannot think of any utterance which ever hurt me so much as your recent statement about Chiang Kai-shek and China," he angrily wrote Henry Stimson, who had, like Marshall, expressed a lack of confidence in the Nationalist regime. "I would like to think that you found it painful to write what you did. But perhaps you only wrote carelessly and irresponsibly." Increasingly he built on his already intense hatred of Franklin Roosevelt by joining the escalating right-wing criticism of the Yalta accords. "Suspicious as I was of Yalta," he wrote in reference to what he considered the secret betrayal of China, "I couldn't imagine that it was such a new high in Rooseveltian deceit. . . . I wonder if *Time* has yet become as indignant about Yalta as perhaps it ought to be." And even while he continued trying to persuade the leaders of government, he also began to reach out to people who shared his views on China, including some with whom he had little else in common—socially or intellectually.[54]

Luce's slow, cautious, but steady movement into the world of conspiracy theories was reflected by, among other things, his souring relationship with an organization he had helped to create: the Institute for Pacific Relations (IPR), a quasi-academic foundation in New York dedicated to helping Americans understand Asia and the Pacific. Luce had been a founding member in 1930 and had considered it an organization that "always strove for objectivity and the presentation of different sides of a problem, [which] were useful as references to *Time* and *Fortune*." He had attended occasional conferences, offered modest financial support, and maintained a cordial and supportive relationship with the institute's director, Edward Carter. In the early 1940s Luce joined an effort to construct an imposing new building for the institution, Pacific House, which would give the IPR a more important public face and would draw more attention to issues relating to China. Luce organized a dinner in 1943 to promote the idea. He recruited Juan Trippe, the president of Pan American World Airways, to head the fund-raising drive. And he assigned one of Time Inc.'s staff to assist with the effort. Despite his help, the project failed. But his supportive relationship with the IPR, even if somewhat strained, continued.[55]

In the spring of 1946 Alfred Kohlberg, a wealthy textile manufacturer who had significant investments in Asia and now feared that they were in danger, began a campaign to discredit the people he believed were participating in a vast conspiracy to undermine the Kuomintang and ensure the victory of the Communists. Among his principal targets was the IPR, of which he was a longtime but seldom-seen member. Kohlberg was an aggressive ideologue, and to him the IPR's openness to multiple views, which included some sympathetic depictions of the Chinese Communists, seemed tantamount to treason. He began spending long days in the New York Public Library uncovering IPR documents that supported his view. The people who managed the IPR's publications and research, he charged, "showed their bias by affiliation with a host of Communist and Communist front organizations." In August, Carter invited Kohlberg to a meeting to "clear the air." It only increased the animosity between them.[56]

Kohlberg had not been the first to warn Luce about Communist influence in the IPR. In 1943 his *Fortune* colleague Eliot Janeway had claimed to have discovered that the institution was "really manipulated by a group of dubious Communists and near-Communists who are intriguing madly behind a good front of respectable research men." Carter, he said, was "a stooge for these gentry." Luce, who usually respected Janeway's opinions, had ignored him. Kohlberg, by contrast, was the kind of man—brash, crude, vindictive, impassioned almost to the point of fanaticism—with whom Luce under ordinary circumstances would never have associated. Kohlberg had once even implied that Luce himself was a Communist dupe. But by late 1946 Luce had become largely intolerant of divergent views on China and was thus more credulous of Kohlberg's accusations. A Time Inc. colleague prepared a report for Luce on the activities of the IPR and concluded that the organization did not take a "communist line" and was, at worst, not wholly vigilant in keeping Communists and fellow travelers from publishing left-leaning material.

But Luce took no comfort from this mild and qualified defense. When Carter asked him for help in discrediting Kohlberg, Luce replied coolly that Kohlberg was "not 'discredited' in my opinion. . . . I am afraid, I would find that the Institute of Pacific Relations output had been of very little help in informing us on those aspects of Soviet or Communist behavior which present real challenges both to American ideals and American interests." A shaken Carter quickly assembled evidence of the IPR's substantial studies of the dangers of Communism, but Luce brushed it aside. "The main trouble with this letter is that it should have been written several years ago . . . the so-called Kohlberg charges are perhaps far from being judicial, nevertheless I am convinced that the question he raises with regard to I.P.R. cannot be brushed off with easy strokes of whitewash. In so far as I.P.R. has taken a 'line,' it is a line with which I disagree considerably." He was, he concluded, resigning from the organization and cutting off his financial support.

Carter unwisely replied by warning him of "the loss that would accrue more to you than to IPR if you became identified in the public mind with such [far-right] critics of the IPR as Kohlberg, [the writer] Upton Close, and Hearst." Luce did not communicate with him again, and Carter's plaintive letters were thereafter answered by surrogates. Less than two years later Carter resigned from the IPR. "The sad story of the Institute of Pacific publications," Luce wrote ruefully in 1949, "is one that I know all too much about—but I learned it too late!" Luce's own repudiation of IPR was certainly part of what led Carter to resign.[57]

. . .

As the situation in China deteriorated, both Harry and Clare developed
an unlikely friendship with Gen. Albert Wedemeyer, who had served for
a time as Chiang Kai-shek's military chief of staff and had then succeeded Stilwell as commander of American forces in China. Wedemeyer
was a talented and respected officer of highly conservative views. He
shared Luce's conviction that a Communist victory in China would be
an unacceptable danger to America. One of the few high-ranking American officers with significant experience in China, he was repeatedly proposed for new missions there. But time and again, he believed, his hopes
were thwarted by officials in Washington who found him too hostile to
the Communists (with whom Marshall was continuing to negotiate) and
too committed as well to the increasingly discredited Chiang regime.
Out of Wedemeyer's experiences (and out of Luce's characterizations of
them) emerged some of the foundations of the conspiracy theory of the
Nationalists' fall.

In the spring of 1946 Secretary of State James Byrnes proposed
Wedemeyer as ambassador to China, a position that had remained
unfilled since 1941. To prepare himself the general began communicating with Luce, over dinners when he was in New York, through correspondence when he was away. "When I take over," he wrote Luce,

> I predict that the Communists will seize upon this opportunity
> to abrogate agreements and of course in the minds of the public,
> both in China and abroad, they will attribute dissensions and
> confusions to me. . . . Of course the degree of wholehearted and
> straightforward cooperation I receive from the State Depart-
> ment will strongly influence my ability to accomplish our
> objectives.

Months later Wedemeyer learned that he would not receive the ambassadorship, which would go instead to Leighton Stuart. Wedemeyer himself was "disappointed but not angry," one of Luce's deputies reported.
But he did show some bitterness, and he claimed that John Carter Vincent and others in the State Department had fought his appointment "to
the bitter end." Luce himself, of course, had been to a large degree
responsible for Stuart's appointment as ambassador. But that did not
stop him from being drawn into the group who saw Wedemeyer as a
martyr to the cause of China.[58]

A year later, at about the same time that Bullitt went to China for
Life, Luce learned from Wedemeyer that Marshall had asked him to

return to China and prepare a report on how "to salvage the rapidly deteriorating situation." It is difficult to understand why Marshall decided to entrust such a sensitive assignment to Wedemeyer, whose views were very different from his own. But the decision likely reflected Marshall's respect for Wedemeyer's military prowess. "It is obvious to you," Wedemeyer wrote to Luce, "that although our government has committed itself openly and firmly to counter the spread of communism through the Balkans and in Western Europe, paradoxically we are refusing to apply a similar policy in the Far East." He was, he said, "determined to submit recommendations [to Marshall] . . . that will embody ideas that have been evolved as the result of years of study of history."[59]

On his return from China Wedemeyer offered Luce a summary of his findings. Much of it, to Luce's dismay, was harshly critical of Chiang and his government: terrible relationships between officers and enlisted men in the Kuomintang army; "widespread corruption and incompetence" in the government; the blindness of Chiang and other Nationalist leaders to the dire condition of his regime. "I doubt seriously that [Chiang] realized the true conditions that prevail," he wrote. But Wedemeyer nevertheless strongly recommended the provision of up to ten thousand military "advisors" to the Chinese army, a United Nations guardianship of northeastern China (a stronghold of the Soviets and the Chinese Communists), and significant additional American aid to the Chiang regime unconnected to reforms in his government. The report—which Luce and others eagerly awaited as a last chance for moving American policy toward a stronger defense of Nationalist China— did not appear, despite Luce's strenuous efforts to persuade Marshall to release it. "Pressure from every facet is being placed upon me," Wedemeyer told Luce. His efforts, he said, were being "stultified by vacillatory or European-conscious State Department officials. . . . I have pointed out to [Marshall] the implications of delay concerning the implementation of my recommendations, but so far nothing has happened." Luce directed his editors to insert an ominous and incendiary note into *Time:*

> A fortnight ago, Lieut General Albert C. Wedemeyer returned from his mission to China as a factfinder for the U.S. To the State Department he submitted a report of China's political, military and economic situation. On this report, presumably would be based one of the most important lines of U.S. foreign policy—what to do about China. Lieut. General Wedemeyer has always been anti-Communist. . . . His report on the Chinese

could not be anything but anti-Communist, and probably favored U.S. aid to China. If so, it was big news to both countries. What (or who), Americans wondered last week, was holding up its publication?

The answer, as Luce obviously suspected, was the State Department. Unhappy with Wedemeyer's aggressive recommendations and, particularly, with his proposal to deploy American military advisers in China, Marshall and his colleagues first asked the general to amend his report, and then, when he refused, buried it.[60]

Not until two years later did the Wedemeyer report become public, deep in the annexes of a massive State Department white paper defending American policy. The white paper defended the "suppression" of the report in 1947 by claiming that Wedemeyer's criticisms of the Chiang regime would have demoralized the Chinese government. The heart of the white paper, however, was a sharp rebuke to Luce and others who continued to claim that American policy was responsible for the defeat of the Nationalists. The blame for the "fall of China" fell, it argued, squarely on the shoulders of the Kuomintang, which "had apparently lost the crusading spirit that won them the people's loyalty during the early years of the war." Nationalist China had "sunk into corruption ... and into reliance on the United States to win the war for them. ... The reasons for the failures of the Chinese National Government ... do not stem from any inadequacy of American aid. ... [The Kuomintang's] leaders proved incapable of meeting the crisis confronting them, its troops had lost the will to fight, and the Government had lost popular support." This assessment, not surprisingly, enraged Luce and many other supporters of Nationalist China and greatly increased the bitterness that the Communist victory had already created. The "suppression" of the Wedemeyer report in 1947 and its eventual replacement by the State Department's white paper became still more fodder for the belief that there had been a government-inspired conspiracy to undermine the survival of a non-Communist China.[61]

By early 1948 the situation in China was beginning to seem irretrievable; and while the Truman administration continued to insist that it was committed to the Nationalist government, material support from the United States was diminishing. Marshall had come to believe that defeating the Chinese Communists in the field was "an absolute military impossibility." (Hence his ultimately unsuccessful effort to defeat the

Communists politically, through a coalition.) He was also convinced that the Nationalist army would not fight and that providing them with weapons was the same as arming the Communists. "Thirty-three divisions laid down their arms without a battle," he told a group of reporters in a private meeting, "so their equipment—the stuff we supplied them out of our reserves—is now in communist hands without a struggle." But the grim military prospects were only part of the calculation. Marshall and Truman also believed that the stakes in China were not high enough to justify an American intervention that was certain to be costly and had no assurance of success. "There are only four great centers of resources outside the U.S. which concern me a whit," Marshall told the reporters. "These are in Japan, Germany, England, and Russia. China has no resources other than manpower, and there is a real question in my mind whether this great mass of manpower is an asset or liability."[62]

For Luce, however, and for many others, no price could have been too high to defeat the Communists in China and preserve the Nationalist government. The cost of failure would be not only the loss of what Luce considered a great ally that could become an important asset to the democratic West. It would also be the beginning of Soviet domination of China and, eventually, all of Asia—a fundamental shift in geopolitical power. The unraveling of Kuomintang China was an almost unbearable prospect for Luce, especially as he saw many of the people who shared his commitment to China begin to turn away from the great project of saving it. "*Time* itself has not always been right," the disillusioned Time Inc. reporter William Gray wrote from Shanghai, "and I hope your approach does not indicate any upcoming claim of omniscience on China. . . . In China even American businessmen accuse *Time* . . . of giving a 'distorted picture without ever telling a specific lie.' " Luce ignored Gray's evaluation in much the same way that he had rejected White's.[63]

In May, Luce persuaded the Truman administration to send Charles Stillman, the president of the recently created Henry Luce Foundation, to China to help distribute American aid. "Charlie Stillman is the greatest single contribution which we of Time Inc. could make to the cause of upbuilding China. . . . He is *not* a diplomat or a college professor or a parlor pink or a rabble rouser," he wrote. "He is a businessman." But like the many other military officers, diplomats, reporters, businessmen, and philanthropists who had tried to rationalize the funding of the Nationalist government, Stillman found himself an impotent witness to the corruption and incompetence of the Kuomintang regime.[64]

As one effort after another collapsed, Luce became increasingly desperate and bitter. He used his magazines to express his own more and more isolated views. "American behavior in and toward China has been the most completely disastrous failure of U.S. foreign policy since the war," he wrote in *Life*. He leaped at even the most implausible proposals—including a vague and quixotic plan to energize Christians in China ("a simple concrete idea which . . . might help to solve the vexing problem of America's relation to China"). He used memos to his staff to vent his frustration. "What happens next in China?" he wrote angrily in August 1948. "What, if anything, does the U.S.A. prefer to have happen? One answer, of course, might be that the U.S.A. doesn't and shouldn't give a bloody damn." As the end approached and all hope vanished, he began to make the case for what might have happened had the United States acted more forcefully. The Truman administration had made three mistakes, he later wrote: "not to take Communism seriously enough . . . not to take China seriously enough . . . [and] to permit a personal distaste for Chiang Kai-shek to influence U.S. policy toward his government." Had the United States not given up on the Kuomintang too early, if the Soviets had not been allowed to enter Manchuria, if American forces had remained in China after the war, everything might have been different. And perhaps most of all he sought, almost wistfully, to rehabilitate the now-widely discredited Chiang, whom Luce continued to revere as one of the great figures in history. Chiang, he insisted, had retained the support of the Chinese people until war (and ungenerous critics) undermined him:

> There were a lot of good men in the [Kuomintang] government at all levels trying to do a good job. . . . The idea of "progress" express[ed] itself in manifold forms before the war as well as during it. Not just economic ideas, but ideas like the "emancipation of women." . . . The Chiang government . . . was even so well regarded that it was made one of the "Big Five" in the postwar world.[65]

As the dark year of 1948 progressed, Luce clung to a single hope: a Republican administration that would surely, he thought, commit itself more effectively to the defense of China. He was a strong supporter of Senator Arthur Vandenberg of Michigan, a onetime isolationist who had converted to the new internationalism of the postwar era. But Vandenberg was never a serious contender, and Luce eventually had to place his hopes in a candidate he had never much liked: Governor Thomas E.

Dewey of New York, running for president in his second consecutive election. "We lack big men, leaders or potential leaders, men of talent and integrity," Luce had complained in 1946, clearly remembering the death of Willkie and his disappointment in Dewey in 1944. But he eagerly embraced the great opportunity he believed the Republicans had. Democratic unity, he said, was "coming apart at the seams." The country was "clearly in a more conservative mood." And Truman himself was so deeply unpopular that even Democrats were dismayed. (*Time* described the audience's reaction to a Truman speech at a Democratic fund-raiser as "polite, bored tolerance toward the man they are stuck with in 1948.")[66]

Luce began a speech in the spring of 1948 with an almost cocky certainty: "On January 20, 1949, the businessmen of the United States will celebrate the [Republican] party's return to power after sixteen years in the wilderness." His own certitude drove *Time*'s reporting, which also threw caution to the wind. With unusual rashness the magazine repeatedly presented Truman's candidacy as doomed to defeat. "Only a political miracle or extraordinary stupidity on the part of the Republicans," the magazine claimed in March, "could save the Democratic party, after 16 years of power, from a debacle in November." Dewey and his running mate, California governor Earl Warren, constituted "the kind of ticket that could not fail to sweep the Republican Party back into power." Occasional stories toward the end of the campaign noted reviving enthusiasm for Truman, but *Time* never wavered in its confidence in the outcome. As late as November 1, the magazine crowed that the day of the Republican return to power was "surely at hand." *Life* prepared a single photograph for its postelection cover: a smiling Dewey—but fortunately for the magazine, it was not ready in time for publication before the election. "*Time* was just as wrong as everybody else," the magazine sheepishly reported once it was clear that Truman had won.[67]

By then, however, the chances of reversing the course of events in China had already vanished. Not even a committed Republican administration would have been able to save Chiang Kai-shek and his regime. "Our Christmas skies are darkened this year by the disasters which have overtaken your country," Luce wrote Chiang on December 24. "Be assured that your friends here know, as history will surely make clear, that you have fought with integrity of purpose for a cause you have cherished more dearly than any personal fate." On the same day he told colleagues at Time Inc. more bluntly that China was "down the drain, and what can the U.S. do about it?" Someone suggested "gunboats," but

Luce said no, "that's 19th century British policy." And yet even then Luce could not abandon hope. Once again he made the lonely rounds in Washington, where all the officials he met continued to state the administration's official position: "There is no disposition on the part of the U.S. government to give up China as a lost cause." But it was obvious to almost everyone that these pronouncements meant nothing, that the United States was helpless to reverse the Communist victory. The government was continuing to support a non-Communist China only to defend itself from criticism.

Luce outlined a course for Chiang that he still believed might change the outcome. If there could be "massive evidence that there does in fact exist in China a wide-spread will and determination to resist Communist domination," the regime might still survive. For that to happen Chiang would need to "declare that the Yangtze will be defended under your personal leadership," that he should "give to the ablest man in China not counting yourself the task of forming an entirely new government whose primary requisite shall be a capacity to govern," that there should be "a mighty demonstration of loyalty to this government by governors of provinces, mayors of cities, leading intellectuals and other representative men." But even as he wrote this hopeful, hopeless proposal, the man he was attempting to persuade was preparing for his exodus to Formosa. Chiang's response to Luce was friendly but pointedly evasive: "Your implicit faith in the cause of China's prolonged struggle against world totalitarianism will not fail to cheer the bleeding hearts of my people." Meanwhile, at a managing editors' lunch that Luce did not attend, Max Ways, the *Time* foreign editor, said bluntly: "We have lost China. The Communists do provide 'law and order,' and hence temporary prosperity. I suspect Luce has led us into folly and dead-ends with his China ideas during [the] last fifteen years." No one contradicted him. Luce was now almost alone in his own company.[68]

XII

Cold Warriors

The twenty-fifth anniversary of *Time* magazine in 1948 coincided with Luce's fiftieth birthday. Despite the lavish celebratory dinners and the generally positive coverage of these landmarks, both events seemed to hit him hard. His marriage was in disarray. His company was beset by troubles. His beloved China was slipping from his grasp and into the hands of the Communists. To his colleagues he seemed even more restless and impatient than usual—frustrated by his inability to shape events as he wished, overwhelmed with ideas for which he could find no adequate outlet.

Allen Grover, one of Luce's closest associates, believed after spending several weeks traveling with him in Europe that Luce was "getting bored with his office job at Time," that he felt that he had "nobody to talk to in the U.S., nobody of his intellectual level." Grover continued:

> Luce is a good man on the great issues. . . . But on the small issues, the personal relationships, he is a very bad man, thoughtless and arbitrary. . . . He has such intellectual arrogance that he does not believe anybody can tell him anything. . . . [H]e has so lost the art of conversational give and take that he has become a colossal bore. . . . Pleasant social conversation is just not in him anymore.

Billings, Grover's partner in analyzing Luce's state of mind, wrote of "the depth of [Luce's] professional melancholy." His conversations were "practically impossible to transcribe. . . . So much of his communication is by gesture and expression . . . nobody would believe it. . . . He says that it is no use talking to stupid people and most people are stupid. He is utterly arrogant in his manners; his tempers are sharp and awful. . . . We wondered if, for all his brilliance, he was going crazy."[1]

Grover and Billings were not alone in their views. A *Business Week* reporter, interviewing Luce for a twenty-fifth-anniversary story on *Time*, recorded his impressions of their conversation:

> I have never in all of my reasonably gregarious life sustained a conversation with anyone so incoherent. . . . All of his sentences, many of his words are broken . . . put together in a nonlogical pattern. . . . His incoherence comes from the many ideas in his head racing to get out of his mouth and getting in each other's way.

Stories abounded of Luce's increasing distraction. Colleagues reported that at lunches and dinners, he would talk almost incessantly, shoveling food into his mouth as he did so, and then—at the end—having no memory of having eaten and asking indignantly why the meal had not yet been served. At one lunch he overlooked the meal he had ordered and unthinkingly ate only a platter of green beans that happened to be near his seat. When a soufflé was presented at Luce's table at an opulent meal in Paris, he took a forkful and waved it over the dish interminably while his dismayed guests (and the chef) watched the soufflé collapse. He dressed expensively, but it was not usually noticeable. His secretary frequently called Luce's home and had items delivered to his office because he so often wore unmatched shoes or socks.[2]

By 1950 Luce appeared to be considering alternative paths in life. Early that year Connecticut Republicans approached Clare to see if she would be a candidate for the U.S. Senate. She declined but suggested trying to recruit Harry. And for several weeks, despite his previous refusal in the 1940s, he thought seriously about running. He had a "definite interest," Luce told the *New York Times* in January. "Several Republican leaders who seemed very much to want me have asked me to think about it, and I am thinking about it." He discussed the possibility with his editorial staff, insisting that he was unlikely to run but talking at length about the attractions of doing so. He felt, he said, "like a Pentagon general of propaganda who had a chance to get up under fire on the front lines." How could he say no? But at other times he claimed to be miserable at the prospect of entering politics. "I shouldn't have gotten into this and it's going to take a lot of coping for me to get out," he complained. Part of what worried him was the prospect of running against his friend and Yale classmate, William Benton, who was up for reelection. But the real obstacle was his fear of giving up his magazines and the power they gave him—power that he rightly believed was greater than any he could wield in the Senate. Weary as he may have been with running the company, he could not give it up. Early in February he announced he would not enter the Senate race.[3]

In the late summer of 1950 he announced that he would take a year's leave from Time Inc. "to collect his thoughts and travel." Billings would run the company in his absence and would even move into Luce's own, palatial office as a symbol of his new, if temporary, authority. But as with the Senate race, Luce wavered, even after he had announced his decision. "He just sits in his office, doing nothing and staring off into space," Grover reported. "He seems in the depths of gloom: certainly the happy prospect of a year off hasn't lifted his spirits. . . . [He] hates New York because he has been a personal failure here, has not established himself and Clare socially among New Yorkers. True! True!!" (Luce even talked at times, probably not very seriously, of moving the company out of the city—to Indiana, or Texas, or Westchester.) His longtime secretary, alarmed at his pending departure (and the disruption of her own routine as a result) began telling Billings what had once been carefully guarded secrets about Luce's life and his marriage. "Clare has no friends, and neither does Harry," she confided. Ed Thompson, the editor of *Life*, said that Luce was "very lonely." Billings wrote that Luce's "nerves are shot. . . . He's in bad shape." Once his sabbatical formally began, Luce continued to find excuses to return to the building, many of them connected to the roller-coaster course of the Korean War. Early in 1951 he abandoned the sabbatical altogether, moved back into his office, and tried to pretend nothing had changed.[4]

But things had changed. More than ever Luce felt isolated in his own company, unable to control the magazines as he wished and unable fully to articulate his own aspirations for them. As was often the case, he responded to frustration with travel—serious, purposeful, almost obsessive travel that would, he believed, help him understand the new postwar world that he still hoped to shape. "He seems to feel happily useful," Billings told Grover, "only when he is on large tours of inquiry, shooting through the firmament like an inquisitive comet." Luce took exhausting trips around the United States, calling on mayors, governors, business leaders, and what he liked to call "characters": "my favorite College President . . . [a] rich, civilized land owner . . . a busy country doctor . . . the civic-leading Rotarian . . . three fine, salty female characters." In the space of a few weeks, he visited Los Angeles, San Francisco, Sacramento, Boise, Seattle, Portland. On a later trip he went to Cincinnati and to Dallas, Fort Worth, and Snyder, Texas, and then, on another, to Chicago, Anaconda, Butte, and (again) Seattle and Portland. These travels seemed at least temporarily to refresh him, and he wrote back to his editors with enthusiasm about the "new America" he was discovering. Even in the smallest, least lovely towns, he found inspiration: "The Americans of Butte, Montana . . . do a job—a whale of a job, and they seem to be doing their big job with a) a considerable amount of fair and friendly dealing with each other; and b) a belief in progress."[5]

His trips outside the United States were even more frequent and more frantic. He often claimed that he did not want to spend his time meeting with important people, but in fact he did almost nothing else. The hapless Time Inc. correspondents in the cities he visited often spent nervous weeks organizing his meetings and events before confronting the tornado of his presence. "Our Mr. Luce . . . came and went, leaving us, among other things, completely limp and worn out," one of his Time Inc. hosts wrote after a Luce sojourn in Brazil. It turned, she said, "into a mad whirl for all concerned and toward the end took on . . . gigantic proportions." In the course of only a few days, he met with the president, a cardinal, the American ambassador (for a state dinner), ministers, business leaders, and one of the country's biggest ranchers. In England he met with both Winston Churchill and Clement Attlee, the first Labour Party prime minister, and left encouraged that Britain was not in fact turning into a socialist society. After a trip to the Continent—where he visited Germany and Austria—he wrote ebulliently about the progress American reconstruction had made and noted that there was "more political vitality in Europe of a non-Communist or anti-Communist nature than I had supposed." Grover, after reading Luce's copious memos of his travels, warned his colleagues that "the Boss has rediscovered Europe." Having made the rediscovery, Luce made repeated return visits. After a 1949 trip his office compiled a list of the people he had met—more than a hundred, among them the pope, the presidents or prime ministers of Italy, Switzerland, Belgium, and France, princes and princesses, statesmen, writers, and artists, Charles de Gaulle, Jean Monnet, the Duke and Duchess of Windsor. After a trip around the "rim of Asia," he compiled another such list of those he had spoken with "at serious length": the presidents of South Korea, Nationalist China, and the Philippines, the emperor and prime minister of Vietnam, the prime minister of Japan, and more than a dozen other governors, ambassadors, and ministers. "After all these encounters," Luce noted proudly, "I flew in 33 hours, 8,000 miles from Singapore to London to dine at 10 Downing Street with Winston Churchill."[6]

When he journeyed to more remote places, in which the famous and powerful were rare, he became an avid travel writer, producing long personal accounts of the landscapes, the people, and the cultures he encountered. On a trip through the Middle East, during which he visited Iran and the lands along the southern border of the Soviet Union, he wrote of the exoticism of the region: the "endless void" of the Persian deserts, the crude construction techniques of railroads in Tabriz, the strange markets in Azerbaijan, the shapes of mountains, trees, orchards, the lives of border patrols, men riding donkeys. But when he arrived later in Beirut, he reverted to his usual tendency to admire what was most "American" about the rapidly changing world. He was dazzled by the modern, business-driven city and its "American-minded" people. Its Western universities (most prominent of them the American University in Beirut) were, he said, "wonderful advertisements of what we like to think of as the 'best' in American life."[7]

Luce almost always considered the places he visited of enormous interest and importance, but he had a particular and somewhat gloomy fascination with the Arab world. The creation of Israel, he wrote, "was a shocking surprise to the Arabs and produced a reaction of bewildered disillusionment and hostility to the U.S. The Arabs are unable to explain the U.S. intervention except on the theory that America is literally ruled by the Jews." U.S. support of Zionism had, Luce said, left "a trail of social injustice and the smell of injustice." But always the optimist, he felt certain that "this bleeding can be stopped" if America would choose to act. "A Theodore Roosevelt, I believe, could settle this matter in a week."[8]

Luce's travels proved to be only intermittent distractions from the growing troubles facing his company in the dawning years of the Cold War. On August 3, 1948, Whittaker Chambers—no longer *Time*'s foreign editor but still a "special writer" for the magazine—testified before the House Un-American Activities Committee (HUAC) and accused Alger Hiss, a former State Department official, of having been a member of the Communist Party in the 1930s. At first the accusation seemed wholly implausible. Hiss was a respected diplomat who had accompanied Franklin Roosevelt to Yalta, had helped draft the United Nations Charter, and was a friend and associate of Dean Acheson, soon to become secretary of state. Hiss heatedly denied the charges and insisted he had never met Chambers (although he later conceded that he might have known him under another name). Given the contrast between the smooth, sleek, well-dressed Hiss and the rumpled, overweight, agitated Chambers, many people doubted the charges. But dogged Republicans, chief among them the first-term representative Richard Nixon, continued to pursue the case and kept it alive. In October, Hiss sued Chambers for libel. Chambers responded by making a new and explosive accusation. Hiss, he said, had not just been a Communist but also a spy for the Soviet Union. To support his claim he presented several reels of microfilm, which he had hidden in a pumpkin in the garden of his Westminster, Maryland, farm. The "pumpkin papers" seemed to support Chambers's story, and Hiss—although not yet without influential supporters—began his long, lonely years of prosecution, imprisonment, disgrace, and struggle for vindication that continued, unsuccessfully, for the rest of his life. (Classified Soviet documents released in the 1990s seemed to confirm Chambers's claim that Hiss had participated in espionage.)[9]

The Hiss-Chambers controversy shook Time Inc. badly, but only after months of escalating pressure. The left-leaning writers and editors who had so despised Chambers a few years earlier were mostly gone, eased out by Luce's increasing intolerance of them. The remaining staff, including Luce, admired Chambers, believed his story, and for a while sought to defend him. When Chambers offered to resign at the time of the first HUAC hearings, Luce replied, "Nonsense. Testifying is a simple patriotic duty." He told his colleagues that "Chambers is an honest man and we must give him our faith." Others at *Time*, among them Roy Larsen, were "deeply disturbed" about the reputational damage that Chambers's continued presence might cost the company. Tom Matthews, who vacationed in Newport, Rhode Island, reported that people he met there were asking about Chambers: "Who's this Communist who runs *Time* that just got arrested?" Billings, despite his belief that "the weight of credibility is now in Chambers's favor," worried that the case would be "an ordeal for us. . . . Has Time suffered a moral slip?"[10]

The October revelations of the "pumpkin papers" changed Luce's view. In accusing Hiss of espionage, Chambers had implicated himself as well by admitting that he had been one of Hiss's handlers. Luce was already becoming uneasy about defending Chambers as a result of the many gleeful attacks from such longtime enemies as Walter Winchell, Westbrook Pegler, and the *Chicago Tribune*, who accused him of "harboring a communist." ("It's our No. 1 public relations problem," Billings wrote. "We are under constant, nagging attack for having Commnists in our midst.") The Chambers case had become a "pain and embarrassment," Luce complained. And so he seized on the unsurprising revelation of Chambers's own role in espionage and used it as his reason for dismissing him. "Goddam it Whit," he said during a brusque final meeting with Chambers in December, "you told me you had been a *Communist*, but Jesus, Whit, you didn't tell me you had been a *spy?*" Chambers, who considered Luce's astonishment to have been disingenuous, replied with characteristic melodrama: "You know, Harry, when you took me on, I began to have some hope for America. I despair for it now."[11]

But the ghost of Chambers continued to haunt Time Inc. for years. The Hiss trial, and the huge attention it attracted, dragged on through 1949, and the controversy went on much longer, creating continuing awkward publicity for Time Inc. In the spring of 1950 Chambers began to show around the manuscript of his new book on the case, which he titled *Witness*. Luce tried to buy the serialization rights for *Life*, convinced (correctly) that the book would create a sensation. Some of his colleagues had doubts. "Chambers writes like an angel," Billings said, "but I don't know whether I believe him or not." Luce offered Chambers sixty thousand dollars for the rights. But a few days later Chambers signed on with *Life*'s fading rival, the *Saturday Evening Post*, sparking speculation among the Time Inc. editors that an embittered Chambers was wreaking public revenge. Most damaging of all, however, was that the Chambers issue had raised accusations that Time Inc. had been weak in the then-raging battle against Communism.[12]

"Communism is the most monstrous cancer which ever attacked humanity," Luce wrote the *Time* Paris correspondent in 1949, "and we shall do our best, however feeble, to combat it at all times and all places." He was, like most other Americans, an adamant Cold Warrior in the battle against world Communism. But he was also a participant in the campaign to identify Communist influence within the United States. As early as 1946 Luce was berating his editors for being "such a bunch of softies that they aren't able to fire anybody, especially if he's a Communist sympathizer. . . . I don't want any Communist sympathizers working for Time Inc." And so Time Inc. began slowly (and mostly quietly) to purge at least a few employees who had, or seemed to have had, Communist connections or sympathies. Luce tried to prohibit using the word "leftist" in the magazines, because he considered it a respectable but misleading euphemism for Communism. He lashed out at his editors for not being tough enough in print on radicals. Paul Robeson, he complained in 1949, "has . . . displayed his full traitorous attitude to the U.S.," but the Time Inc. publications had "never spelled it out."[13]

Luce was particularly hostile to those responsible for what he considered the "great betrayal" of his time: the failure to prevent a Communist victory in China. Two of his principal targets were John Carter Vincent and Owen Lattimore, both of whom, Luce believed, had misled policy makers in ways that facilitated "China's tragic disaster." He stopped short (barely) of calling them Communists. But *Time*, reflecting Luce's determination to drive them both out of any role in making policy, attacked them with a steady drumbeat of denunciations and innuendos.

Vincent was a career diplomat and the director of the State Department's East Asia desk during the civil war in China. He was, *Time* said, in "a perfect position to exercise enormous influence over our policy in China," and he had used that influence disastrously to press Chiang "into a coalition with the Chinese Communists." While the magazine grudgingly conceded that Vincent might not have been a Communist, it insisted that he had been as damaging to the national interest as any Communist could be. He was, *Time* stated, "one of the chief architects of a policy that led to a triumph for Communism [in China] and a disaster for the U.S." Because he had been charged by Truman's own Loyalty Review Board with having expressed "studied praise of Chinese Communists and equally studied criticism of the Chiang Kai-shek government . . . there is reasonable doubt as to his loyalty." Vincent left the foreign service in 1953, and *Time* made certain to report that the new secretary of state, John Foster Dulles, had accused him of "a failure to meet the standard which is demanded of a Foreign Service officer."[14]

If anything, Luce had even more contempt for Owen Lattimore, an Asia scholar and a professor at Johns Hopkins University, whom Luce had once briefly recruited as an expert adviser to his magazines. His sense of personal betrayal may have intensified his hostility. In the aftermath of World War II, Lattimore, like Vincent, had advocated a coalition government of the Nationalists and Communists in China and had been harshly critical of Chiang Kai-shek and his regime. And so as with

Vincent, *Time* avoided few opportunities to discredit him. The magazine portrayed Lattimore as a man enmeshed in "a powerful Communist web of propaganda and persuasion" that had a significant influence on policy. When congressional committees called Lattimore in to testify, *Time* noted that the case against him was made up entirely of hearsay. But the magazine added that while Lattimore "had not been proved a Communist . . . he had not proved that he was not one." That characterization mirrored Luce's own private comments about Lattimore: "The important point it seems to me is that, whether or not Lattimore is a Communist, the damage which his ideas have done to our country's cause is very great."[15]

Even so, Luce's attitude toward Communist subversion in America was more nuanced than that of many hard-core anti-Communists, as his reaction to Senator Joseph McCarthy made clear. A World War II veteran who ran for election in 1946 by egregiously exaggerating his war record and distorting his opponents' positions, McCarthy neared the end of his first term in the Senate with no achievements of consequence. But in 1950, having rejected other strategies to bolster his reelection chances, he chose anti-Communism—an issue of relatively little interest to him in the past—and used it to create a personal crusade that made him for a time the most famous figure in the search for Communist influence within the United States. McCarthy attracted an enormous constituency of passionate supporters, who saw him as he liked to portray himself—a tough street fighter taking on a sinister and dangerous elite. But McCarthy's recklessness also generated strong opposition, even from people who might otherwise have supported him.[16]

Luce was not opposed to exposing Communist influence in America, as his purging of his own company and his attacks on IPR, and on Vincent and Lattimore, made clear. But his broader interest in Communist ideas in America was an intellectual one, and he devoted most of his anti-Communist efforts to countering the arguments of the Left and making the case for his own more conservative liberalism. "I think we have a definite obligation to help the anti-totalitarian liberals find their proper signals in this day of the confusion of liberalism," he wrote in 1947 in an admiring account of the anti-Stalinist magazine the *New Leader.* "How I cheer for [Sidney] Hook's use of the word 'muddleheads.' " At the same time, however, he developed an early and very strong distaste for McCarthy. His dislike was partly cultural. McCarthy, was a crude and coarse man who embraced the kind of simplistic populism that Luce had always disdained. But he also disliked McCarthy because Luce believed that his excesses threatened to discredit more legitimate anti-Communist activities. The search for Communist infiltration of America "has become too much the . . . scapegoat of everything that's wrong with us," he wrote in 1950, as if his own attempted purge of Communists within Time Inc. had never happened. "The fact is that Communism is no longer a real issue, even indirectly, in America." Just as Prohibition had taken the public's mind off more serious problems in the 1920s, Luce felt, the fear of domestic Communism was doing the same in the 1950s. McCarthy's focus on elite leaders and institutions threatened the world Luce himself inhabited. Luce also considered McCarthy a great distraction, drawing the public's attention toward a minor issue (domestic subversion) and away from the most important challenge of the era (the struggle against the Soviet Union and the spread of Communism in the world). What the nation needed, Luce argued, was a coherent strategy for combating global Communism, not a witch hunt for subversives in America.[17]

As the United States struggled to build a strategy for dealing with Soviet Communism in the late 1940s and early 1950s, three broad groups competed to define the new paradigms of American foreign policy. The weakest, and most maligned, of these groups was the coalition of left-leaning liberals and those who were known as "Communist sympathizers" or "fellow travelers," who continued to believe that a peaceful and cooperative relationship with the Soviet Union and the Communist world was possible and desirable. Their leader for a time was former vice president Henry A. Wallace, a harsh critic of the increasingly combative view that government leaders were taking toward the Soviet Union. In 1948 he helped create a new Progressive Party, whose principal goal was to defuse the Cold War. There were significant Communist influences in the party, but most of its supporters were what Arthur Schlesinger, Jr., called, in his 1948 book *The Vital Center*, "doughface liberals," people who were not Communists but whom Schlesinger considered too weak and gullible to take a stand against the enemies of democracy.[18]

A second group argued that the United States had no choice but to confront Communism aggressively and forcefully, by war if necessary, so as to ensure its ultimate defeat. This was the position of Joseph McCarthy, but it had much broader support than that, mostly in the conservative wings of the Republican Party. For almost two decades this coalition's view of the Cold War was best expressed in a phrase that became the title of a campaign tract used as late as Barry Goldwater's

1964 presidential campaign: "Why Not Victory?" Their goals were the "rollback" of Communism where it presently existed and a greater readiness to use nuclear weapons in battles with Communist nations. They were strongly opposed to the third, and dominant, American strategy of the Cold War era: "containment."[19]

"Containment" emerged in response to the bewildered uncertainty that gripped the foreign-policy community in the last months of World War II and the first years of the tense and fragile peace. Its principal creator was a previously obscure American diplomat, George F. Kennan, who was stationed in Moscow in the 1940s. Kennan had a brilliant, astringent intellect that enabled him to discern patterns and strategies few others could easily see, and he helped transform American policy with a cable—known famously as "the long telegram"—that he sent to the State Department in February 1946, and with a subsequent article published anonymously in *Foreign Affairs* magazine. Kennan offered a rebuke to the Wallace "progressives," who thought that the Soviet Union, if treated well, could become a "normal" nation capable of cooperating with the West. In contrast, Kennan saw the Soviet Union as a profoundly ideological nation fundamentally different from the United States. "At the bottom of the Kremlin's neurotic view of world affairs," he wrote in the abbreviated language of his telegram, "is traditional and instinctive Russian sense of insecurity. . . . Thus Soviet leaders are driven by necessities of their own past and present position to put forward a dogma which pictures the outside world as evil, hostile, and menacing." Hence the militarism of the Soviet state and its fear of internal subversion and opposition. The Soviet Union, Kennan believed, was, in effect, a "conspiracy," which sought to extend its power through duplicity and intrigue. It was

> a political force committed fanatically to the belief that with [the] US there can be no permanent modus vivendi, that it is desirable and necessary that the internal harmony of our society be disrupted, our traditional way of life be destroyed, the international authority of our state be broken, if Soviet power is to be secure.[20]

Kennan's assessment of the nature of the Soviet Union was largely consistent with that of the anti-Communist right. But his cautious, pragmatic prescription for how America should respond to Communism was very different. The Soviet Union, he argued, was opportunistic but also risk averse. When challenged by a superior power it was likely to retreat as long as its vital interests were not in danger. "In these circumstances," he wrote, "it is clear that the main element of any United States policy toward the Soviet Union must be that of a long-term, patient but firm and vigilant containment of Russian expansive tendencies." At the same time the United States, through its own "spiritual vitality" in the world, could slowly help shape the future behavior of the Soviet Union. Once Russia could be made to feel "sterile and quixotic" in contrast to America, the "hopes and enthusiasm of Moscow's supporters must wane" and "added strain" would be placed on Soviet foreign policy.[21]

Kennan's views had a dramatic influence on the Truman administration, by providing both an explanation of Soviet behavior and a strategy for confronting it. A year after the *Foreign Affairs* article appeared, the president endorsed at least some of its central findings. In the face of Communist threats to Greece and Turkey, the president announced the "Truman doctrine," which declared that the policy of the United States was "to support free peoples who are resisting attempted subjugation by armed minorities or by outside pressures"—not to confront the Soviet empire directly, not to attempt to liberate countries already within Moscow's orbit, but to prevent Communism from spreading beyond its present borders. Containment—a policy that rejected both the hopeful view of a Soviet-American partnership and the combative call for an aggressive effort to destroy Soviet power—became the framework for the next half century of American foreign policy. (Kennan had not, in fact, advised resisting Communist expansion everywhere, but only into areas of "strategic interest" to the United States, by which he meant the great industrial powers, primarily Western Europe and Japan. Truman and his successors had a broader view of where to draw the line.)[22]

Luce was enthusiastic at first about what he considered Truman's long-overdue commitment to a strategy to counter Soviet power, as illustrated by the president's support of the struggles of Greece and Turkey against Communist threats. The president had finally abandoned what Luce considered the "confused" and "soft-headed" policies that had characterized Truman's first years in office and had acknowledged the necessity to combat Soviet ambitions. Luce supported the Marshall Plan and its ambition to combat Communism in Europe by rebuilding the economies of Western Europe. And his magazines embraced the containment strategy with considerable zeal. "Communist imperialism must be contained," *Time* declared in 1947, not long after

Kennan's article had appeared. "U.S. influence must expand to contain it." Similar language emerged repeatedly in memos and meetings in the first years after the war. "The No. 1 issue: Soviet Communism," Billings wrote of an editorial meeting with Luce. "We all quickly agreed it must be contained." Luce began discussing tactics that would undermine Communism from within—exactly the kind of approach that Kennan had recommended. "The big new thing in U.S. policy," he wrote in 1950, "should be to reach the people behind the Iron Curtain, to keep in touch with them, to handle the refugee problem on a big scale, etc."[23]

But while Luce and his colleagues accepted some elements of the containment policy, they chafed at its restraints and more often than not sided with those who believed that the policy was too timid for the gravity of its time. Their dissent began with long-standing grievances: the failure to support Nationalist China adequately, the culpability of Marshall and Acheson in those decisions, and the absence of a "moral" basis for America's foreign policy. "Marshall is a senile dodo, too conservative in this crisis," Billings complained. "Acheson is the symbol of error and disaster," Luce wrote. "He has no conviction that Communism can be stopped and pushed out of most of Asia in the foreseeable future." And even more damningly, in 1948: "I charge Truman and Marshall with endangering the future of humanity by their incompetence." Luce was slowly moving toward a different approach to the Cold War: the growing demand from the right for a policy that would do more than contain, that would, rather, "liberate the captive nations" and "roll back" the Iron Curtain.[24]

The outbreak of the Korean War in June 1950 elevated Luce's anxiety about the global crisis. Would the conflict lead to an "all-out atomic" war, or "piece-meal?" he wondered. "Suppose they sink a U.S. carrier. What'll we do?" His prediction was the use of atomic weapons against Russia. But the war also renewed his hopes for a significant shift in American foreign policy. As with most of his other international positions, his response to this new conflict was largely shaped by his preoccupation with China. Less than forty-eight hours after the war began, Luce was proposing an editorial for *Life* that would advocate a "reversal of Truman's policy toward China," reflecting his own view that "the defense of Formosa" (now the headquarters of the exiled Chiang and his followers) was "far more significant than the U.S. military participation in Korea." On the whole, in the first months of the Korean conflict, Luce was uncharacteristically supportive of the Truman administration, admiring the president's quick and forceful decision to resist the North

Korean invasion, comforted by the presence of Douglas MacArthur as commander of the United Nations (in reality overwhelmingly American) forces there. "The reaction of the plain man seems to have been, 'At last! It was the only thing to do,'" an exuberant *Life* editorial proclaimed. "Both the President and the plain man are to be congratulated: the President for the courage of the decision and the plain man for . . . good judgment on a very complicated matter." In the first months of the war this confidence seemed fully rewarded by MacArthur's dramatic military successes: the rapid reconquest of South Korea and the expansion of the war to the North, which Luce believed would ensure a reunification of the divided land under its anti-Communist (but far from democratic) leader Syngman Rhee. Luce was so confident of victory that, having once postponed his planned sabbatical, he left for a trip to the Middle East. Even the Truman administration, intoxicated by the prospect of victory, anxiously convinced themselves that MacArthur could be trusted to advance into the North without risk of widening the war.[25]

Luce's return from his aborted sabbatical in November 1950 coincided with the sudden and mostly unpredicted invasion of North Korea by the Chinese army—an intervention that MacArthur had predicted could be easily thwarted and would result in a "bloodbath" that would destroy the enemy's forces. Instead the Chinese routed the Americans, drove them out of North Korea, and again moved deep into the South. Luce, like many others, was deeply shaken. His first, and continuing, reaction was once again to blame Truman and "that bastard Acheson," not MacArthur, who had badly miscalculated the strength of the Chinese. It was the "worst defeat the U.S. had ever suffered . . . the abyss of disaster," *Time* reported. "The United States," Luce wrote privately, had "made a complete fool of itself" in its failure to provide enough air support to permit MacArthur to stop the Chinese. He even reproached his friend, Deputy Secretary of Defense Robert Lovett, by asking him to respond to "a most serious charge concerning the inadequacy of the air build-up, for which you have a large measure of responsibility." Luce visited John Foster Dulles, then an assistant to Acheson and a man whose views of foreign policy he greatly respected; and he was shocked to hear the panicked (and misinformed) Dulles say that the American forces had been surrounded and that "it is the only army we have. And the question is: shall we ask for terms?" But the disaster only strengthened Luce's belief that the war must be won—and even expanded—no matter the cost. The alternative would be "the loss of Asia to Communism. . . . No Asian could evermore put any stock in the promise that had given him hope against Communism." This new war, *Time* wrote grimly, "would have to be begun in the knowledge that Russia might come in too, which would lead to the atomic horrors of World War III."[26]

Luce was grimly ebullient about this expanded war and saw in it, at last, the great opportunity to destroy the Chinese army and, eventually, the Mao regime. "The US should prepare the Nationalist Chinese to return to the Mainland," *Life* wrote exultantly in September. In a January 1951 editorial the magazine went further, proclaiming that there was "no choice but to acknowledge the existence of war with Red China and to set about its defeat." Undeterred by the possibility of war with the Soviet Union, Luce asked his editors: "Are we—the U.S.—in favor of the liberation of all peoples from the Communist yoke?" Speaking as if Time Inc. were itself a nation-state with its own foreign policy, Luce answered his own question with emphatic language. The company's goal was " 'to beat the bejesus out of Stalinism'—or, more pompously, to liquidate the Soviet Communist Power System." After a rambling editors' meeting, Billings wrote that "Luce wants the Big War. . . . He's good and belligerent. . . . I suspect he'd be glad to war on USSR tomorrow." At one point Luce speculated about the wisdom of "plastering Russia with 500 (or 1000) A bombs." And in a rebuke to the Realpolitik of the Truman administration, he argued that "the struggle between Freedom and Communism is, at bottom a moral issue . . . a religious issue." What no one has a right to say, he added, "is that we can live peaceably and happily *with* this prodigious evil."[27]

By early 1951 MacArthur had stabilized the line of battle and was beginning to push the Chinese forces north. By March his forces had once again retaken Seoul and were moving toward the southern border of North Korea. Luce quickly regained his earlier enthusiasm for the war. "The destruction anticipated the first week of December just did not occur," he said with relief. "MacArthur did not blunder in North Korea and his army did not suffer a great defeat." "Confusion" was no longer the "key word," he claimed. "We are now serious about rearming. Things are not as bad as the press says and never were!"[28]

Almost immediately, however, a global debate began on how aggressive the American strategy in Korea should now be. To Truman and Acheson and, at least equally important, to America's European allies, another expansion of the conflict into North Korea and the likely extension of fighting into China would risk a new world war that could engage not just the Chinese but the Soviets. "If we go it alone in Asia,"

Truman said at the time, "we may destroy the unity of the free nations against aggression. Our European allies are nearer to Russia than we are. They are in far greater danger. . . . I do not propose to strip this country of its allies in the face of Soviet danger." To MacArthur, however, all the concerns and reservations about an extended conflict with the Chinese seemed like the kind of political meddling that many military leaders throughout history have consistently resented. But unlike other unhappy generals, MacArthur could not help venting his frustrations in public—in press briefings, in conversations with civilians, and in public letters. As his frustrations grew, so did his indiscretions. When asked why South Koreans eager to fight were being turned away, MacArthur attributed it to "basic political decisions beyond my authority" (even though he himself was responsible for the policy). A Hong Kong news agency reported that the general had said that "United Nations forces were circumscribed by a web of artificial conditions . . . in a war without a definite objective." And in early April 1951, in response to a letter from House Republican Leader Joe Martin complaining about the "cheapness" of the war effort, MacArthur wrote back: "It seems strangely difficult for some to realize that here in Asia is where the Communist conspirators have elected to make their play for global conquest. . . . As you point out, we must win. There is no substitute for victory." Luce and MacArthur had no experience with and even less patience for the concept of "limited war," and neither had any inhibitions about saying so. "Either get out of Korea entirely or fight the Chinese Reds in their homeland where it would hurt them," Luce argued. A failure to pursue the enemy across the 54th parallel, he believed, would be a form of "appeasement."[29]

Truman, on the other hand, considered MacArthur's statements a form of insubordination. On April 11, 1951, to the dismay and contempt of millions, Truman recalled MacArthur from his command of the UN forces in Korea and effectively ended his long military career. Luce spared no effort to use the event as a club against the Truman administration and the State Department. "MacArthur as Commander had not only a right but a duty to express his convictions about military strategy," he argued. *Time* offered a scathing denunciation of the president's policy that well exceeded even the magazine's normal level of polemicism:

> The drama of MacArthur's removal and homecoming . . . has brought [Truman's] foreign policy into the open. This pol-

icy . . . denies to the U.S. the efficient use of its power, guaran-
tees to the enemy the initiative he now has, promises that the
U.S. will always fight on the enemy's terms. The policy invites
the enemy, World communism, to involve the U.S. in scores of
futile little wars. . . . Up to now, World War III has been prevented by the fact that the U.S. is stronger than Communism.
The new policy almost certainly brings World War III closer
because it throws away a large part of U.S. strength.

Not surprisingly *Time* laid the blame on Luce's most-hated bête noire:
"It was Secretary Acheson's view which prevailed with the President: do
nothing to widen the war; let the Communists keep the initiative."[30]

Two weeks after MacArthur's dismissal, Luce paid him a visit in the
suite the general was temporarily occupying in the Waldorf-Astoria.
Meeting the famous and powerful was by now a routine part of Luce's
life, and yet he was still susceptible to what he considered true greatness.
And in the spring of 1951 no one seemed greater to Luce than
MacArthur. "I stepped into the drawing room, and there was the Great
Man alone in the big room, sunlight streaming from windows on three
sides," he wrote in a "private" memo after the visit. "I was amazed at the
sight of the man. . . . He looked healthy . . . handsome . . . and more
vigorous than any public man I know." MacArthur naturally defended
himself, adamantly denied that he had been insubordinate, and talked of
his concerns about the army he had left behind. To Luce's obvious
delight MacArthur blamed his dismissal on the State Department,
which he believed was running the war "down almost to daily detail."
The secretary of state, he charged, "has taken over the function of a
Prime Minister." Luce noted that this dubious claim was "an example of
how MacArthur never fails to come up with an original and stimulating
notion, completely out of the commonplace mold of the tiresome editorial writers." MacArthur tried to appear aloof, with no cares about himself. The "great outpouring" of support ("more than human") was "not
primarily for anything I have done." But his anger was clearly visible.
The government's attempt to silence his dissent on the war was, he
insisted, a short step from a government effort to silence the press. "You
will be next," he warned Luce. "By insidious ways already beginning, the
Press will be put under wraps. You must fight, you must fight now for
your freedom."[31]

In the aftermath of this visit Luce added MacArthur to the pantheon
of those he considered truly great men: among them Theodore Roo-

sevelt (whom he had never met), Wendell Willkie, Chiang Kai-shek, and Winston Churchill. Almost immediately he began lobbying his editors to choose MacArthur as *Time*'s next Man of the Year, even though by late fall, the pendulum of public opinion was already swinging away from him. "He won the Korean War," Luce implausibly argued (at a moment when the war still had almost three years to go). MacArthur had made "one of the speeches which will 'go down' at least in American history." And, Luce added, the "Old Soldier has not 'faded away.'" On the contrary he was a leading candidate for president—and one of very few Americans "who have a big popular following." His editors eventually overruled him and chose instead Mohammed Mossadegh, the new prime minister of Iran, who was already beginning to nationalize the nation's oil reserves (an action that would lead to his CIA-assisted overthrow in 1953). MacArthur, Luce's editors argued, was no longer the big news. What they almost certainly also thought was that any MacArthur article would be shaped by what Billings called "his excitement and enthusiasm for the Great Man," an example of "Luce's boyish susceptibility to Greatness."[32]

But Luce's adulation of MacArthur, which continued intermittently through much of the rest of his life, was not simply a product of starstruck infatuation. It was also because he thought MacArthur represented the best and perhaps last chance for the fulfillment of Luce's great dream—a strong American commitment to a non-Communist Asia and to the liberation of China. He wrote of his hopes in a *Life* editorial even before his eventful meeting with the general. MacArthur

> has a great role—a role of greatness—to play in this country now. . . . He was ousted for no petty reason but because he chose to challenge the whole drift of events and the dominant attitudes of the Government of the United States and of the United Nations. . . . [He] is today the only man of the West who has in Asia not only immense prestige but also the devoted loyalty of millions and millions of Asians. . . . How do they think of him? As imperialist? Conqueror? No—as liberator and friend.

MacArthur would, Luce predicted, lead the United States out of "the passive, helpless and hopeless position" into which Truman and Acheson had maneuvered America. "Can any man rise to the greatness our perils demand?" he asked. "[In] the dreary landscape of our time," only MacArthur "seems to have been shaped by greatness."[33]

. . .

MacArthur did not become a serious presidential candidate in 1952 as Luce had once hoped. Instead, as he himself had publicly predicted in his speech to Congress but had probably not really expected, he began slowly to "fade away." Luce never lost his deep admiration for "the great man," but his principal goal—especially now that the Korean War had failed to produce the results in Asia he had hoped for—was to defeat the Democratic administration in the 1952 elections and bring back a Republican government for the first time in twenty years. "I felt that it was of paramount importance to the United States that a Republican should be put in the White House," he explained years later of his position in 1952. "It had been 20 years since there had been a Republican Administration." Americans, he argued, "should have the experience of living under a Republican Administration and discovering that they were not thereby reduced to selling apples on street corners." It did not take him long to switch his loyalty to another popular general: Dwight D. Eisenhower.[34]

Ever since Wendell Willkie's death, Luce had been searching for a candidate whom he could unreservedly admire. He had supported Dewey in 1944 and 1948, but he had never really liked the man or had any significant relationship with him. He was friendly with Robert Taft, senator from Ohio and son of a former president. But Taft was too conservative and too isolationist for Luce to feel comfortable with him. Eisenhower was different. He was famous, popular, and, even without being particularly articulate, charismatic. His policy views were largely unknown, which allowed Luce (and many others) to imagine whatever positions he liked. "Luce is dazzled by Eisenhower's glamour. . . . He is deeply in love with his candidacy," Billings wrote after a lunch with his boss. Luce was an early and generous contributor to Eisenhower's campaign. But much more important, he mobilized his editorial staff to support it, showing a partisanship that was at times greater even than the favoritism the Time Inc. publications had shown toward Willkie in 1940. In the first issue of 1952 Life ran an effusive story making "The Case for Ike," who had not yet agreed to run. Eisenhower later, flatteringly, told Luce that the article had been "one of the factors" that had persuaded him to announce his candidacy (an announcement that also included his first declaration of membership in the Republican Party). Life itself took credit for being the "starters' gun" for the campaign. Once Eisenhower's candidacy was official, Luce accelerated his strong public support for him. He actively recruited two of his most important writers and editors to take leaves to work for the campaign. Emmet John

Hughes and C. D. Jackson became Eisenhower speechwriters. (Luce was less encouraging to Eric Hodgins, who wanted to work for the Democratic candidate, Adlai Stevenson, but grudgingly agreed to let him go as well.)[35]

During the Republican convention, *Time* pointedly argued that Eisenhower had a better chance of winning the general election than did Taft. The magazine identified critical states whose votes were still in flux, where Eisenhower would be particularly helpful to local candidates. The *Time* reportage accused the Taft campaign of "stealing delegates" and actively supported an effort to award disputed seats to Eisenhower. Particularly helpful to the Republicans was the publication of *Time* a day early to allow the Eisenhower campaign to distribute it widely to the delegates. "You were a veritable tower of strength," Henry Cabot Lodge, Jr., Eisenhower's campaign manager, wrote to Luce after the convention, and "played a tremendous part in laying the basis of public opinion" for Eisenhower's victory. "One of the lasting satisfactions of this adventure," Lodge added, "has been the fact that you and I have worked so closely for this great cause." During the campaign Luce himself, for the first time since the Willkie campaign, began writing speeches and memos and funneling them to Eisenhower through Jackson and Hughes. Eisenhower seldom used them but always remembered to thank him, a flattery that spurred Luce onward to even greater efforts. He even occasionally sat on the platform during Eisenhower rallies and joined the candidate on his campaign train, things he had never done even when Willkie was running. It was not just his loyalty to the party that drove his efforts. It was his enthusiasm for Eisenhower and the prospect of a close relationship to a president of the United States for the first time.[36]

Luce's blatant partisanship triggered a significant backlash within his own company, greater than the one he had encountered during the Willkie campaign. Even some colleagues who shared his politics felt uncomfortable with how one-sided they believed the coverage of the election was, although only a few dared to say so publicly. "*Time*'s political bias for Eisenhower is bringing in a deluge of protest letters," Billings noted, and editors were "moaning and groaning" over the company's stance. "Is *Time* a Republican magazine?" T. S. Matthews, the pro-Stevenson editor of *Time*, asked. "Open partisanship would certainly be better than surreptitious. Though best of all, I think, would be to be openly non-partisan. . . . How can *Time* possibly hope to attain and maintain a real integrity if it's partisanly concerned with getting somebody elected?" At one point a group of Time Inc. researchers (all women) tried to raise money to run an advertisement denouncing the magazine's "Ike slant." After a few days of pressure (and perhaps threats from above), "cooler heads . . . prevailed among the Stevenson girls." But the bitterness among the many Stevenson supporters in Time Inc. continued to grow until Luce finally accepted Matthews's advice and invited the entire editorial staff to a large dinner at which Luce hoped to "introduce himself" to his employees. His speech—long, rambling, at times unintelligible—was nevertheless a revealing event for many members of the staff who had rarely if ever seen him. But it did nothing to placate the anger of those who resented *Time*'s political position. He made clear that he supported Eisenhower and said bluntly that as the leader of the company he had the right to present the news however he thought best. "I am your boss," he unrepentantly announced. "I guess that means I can fire any of you."[37]

Luce continued to insist that *Time* was not a "Republican" magazine and that the institution did not favor any particular candidate. But he barred Matthews from handling a cover story on Eisenhower shortly before the election and edited it himself. Eisenhower, Luce wrote, "has picked up more real political experience than many politicians . . . get in a lifetime. . . . Ike is in top form, with a new self-assurance and gusto." The rebuke, and the partisan character of the story, helped Matthews to decide to resign.[38]

Despite his enthusiastic public support of Eisenhower, Luce remained uneasy about the candidate's ability to pursue the policies Luce hoped he would advance. "I think Ike is a good man—an extraordinarily good man," he wrote before the Republican convention. "My difficulty as to Ike lies in the area of 'great issues.' " Those issues were, of course, "how to cope with Soviet Communism," how to discredit the Truman-Acheson foreign policy, and how to ensure that the new president would pay sufficient attention to Asia. "The question," he wrote his editors, "is whether there is any validity to my reservations about Ike, and whether, if so, then there is any editorial duty to utter them." Without expressing his doubts openly Luce tried to put indirect pressure on Eisenhower through his relationship with John Foster Dulles, who was widely believed to be Eisenhower's likely choice as secretary of state. Dulles eagerly responded with an article entitled, "A Policy of Boldness," which expressed the hard-line foreign-policy views that had become a hallmark of the campaign (and that would be largely ignored after the election). It was in this article that Dulles first outlined what became a famous and controversial set of policies that seemed to repudiate much of the restraint that the containment policy had ensured. He called for the "liberation of the captive nations," for striking back against enemies "where it hurts, by means of our own choosing," and for using atomic bombs as "effective political weapons." (Dulles also wrote the foreign-policy plank for the 1952 Republican convention, echoing many of the ideas he had expressed in *Life*.) Luce happily called it "the embryo of a united Republican foreign policy." But he was far from confident that Eisenhower himself would abide by these principles, and he was worried that the candidate would be discouraged from boldness by "timid advisors." "In my judgment," Luce wrote not long before the election, "Ike wins or loses the election in the next few days, depending upon what he says on this Foreign Policy issue." Would Eisenhower continue to embrace the "do-nothing" containment policy? he wondered. "The U.S. has to take the most out-and-out stand against Communism," whether or not it antagonized America's allies and whether or not it ran greater risks than the Truman administration believed were wise.[39]

Eisenhower did little to allay Luce's worries in the last weeks of his campaign. The candidate did not focus much on foreign policy. Instead he continued to rely on his sunny personality and his vague suggestions of undefined change. His most important campaign promise was his pledge to "go to Korea," as if a brief visit to the front would itself transform the character of the war. But the effectiveness of this tactic underscored the enormous advantage Eisenhower's military experience made in a campaign in which Cold War issues were in the forefront of public opinion. Voters seemed to trust him to handle foreign policy whether or not he gave them any clues as to what that foreign policy would be. Even Luce, who had badgered Eisenhower for weeks to take stronger positions, forgot about his concerns in the elation of the growing strength of the Republican campaign. And when Eisenhower finally won by a substantial margin, bringing a Republican Congress with him, Luce felt in some ways as though the triumph was his as well. "Victory, its wonderful," he wired to colleagues and friends.[40]

In many ways Eisenhower's presidency met, and at times even exceeded, Luce's expectations. Luce had never had much of a relationship with previous presidents. Eisenhower showered him with attention. Luce in turn lavished praise on the man he still called "Ike," both in his private communications with the president and in his magazines. Within weeks of the election he had lunch with Eisenhower to talk about Asia, exchanged friendly letters with him, boasted to colleagues about Ike's tips on golf, "marveled at [Ike's] knowledgeability." His one disappointment came when Eisenhower turned down an invitation to dinner at Luce's home, but Luce remained undeterred. And Eisenhower in turn made great efforts to keep Luce in his camp. Republican leaders courted him elaborately during his trip to Washington for the inauguration, and he received the first of many invitations to the Eisenhower White House only a few weeks later. "We must give a full presentation of Ike in color photos," the bedazzled Luce wrote the editors of *Life* late in 1953, "at least four pages of Ike, Ike, Ike, to make the point [of Eisenhower's extraordinary "physical vitality"] unmistakable and unforgettable." Eisenhower's first, unremarkable State of the Union address a few weeks after the inauguration was, Luce proclaimed, "brilliant." A rumor circulated that Eisenhower was considering appointing Luce secretary of state, a flattering gesture even though both men knew that Dulles was the president's choice. "Some discussion of the plain fact that we are now regarded as Eisenhower's mouthpiece," Billings worried a few weeks into the new presidency. "Perhaps we have cheered a little too loud this first month."[41]

Luce's elation at Eisenhower's election—"a pink cloud of delight," one colleague wrote; "a date to see Eisenhower affects him like strong liquor," another commented—helped mute his growing concerns about the new administration's foreign policy. He grumbled occasionally about Eisenhower's passivity. "What's wrong with Ike?" he asked in an editorial meeting in June 1953. "Things are certainly going badly and he doesn't seem able to pull them together into a 'favorable situation.' " But he mostly kept his concerns to himself, even as the war in Korea moved in a direction that deeply disappointed him. Luce had clearly hoped that the election of Eisenhower would reverse the Truman-Acheson decision to limit war aims in Korea and preserve the prewar status quo. But Eisenhower and Dulles did not change Truman's course, and the Korean War ended in July 1953 with the partition still intact and, more important to Luce, the " 'foot draggers' in the Pentagon" still in place. Luce was "all for making some ringing 'Wilsonian' declarations," Billings wrote after an editors' meeting. "The net of the lunch was to knock down most of Luce's hopeful and unrealistic notions about the Eisenhower Administration." But Luce did not abandon those notions. He told himself that Eisenhower had entered office too late to change the course of the Korean War, and that over time the administration's foreign policy would become more assertive and principled. He was encouraged in this hope by John Foster Dulles.[42]

Luce had a closer, and longer, relationship with Dulles than he had with Eisenhower. They were not intimate friends, but their relationship was pleasant and mutually useful. After a lunch with Dulles early in 1953, before Eisenhower's inauguration, he wrote that he "could hardly contain myself for excitement because Dulles was unfolding a policy of action which comported entirely with my own views," a policy that would take a more aggressive stand against Korea than the Truman administration had done and that would recognize the importance of "launching Chiang Kai-shek against the mainland." Dulles "would not settle Korea on the present terms" and would favor a line "north of Pyongyang," which would give South Korea 90 percent of the country. But these were not the views of Eisenhower, as both men soon realized.

In 1954 Luce launched a "reappraisal" of how the magazines should portray the world. A *Life* article, "Policy for Survival," would, he hoped, become a "Spur-to-Action" to the president. For weeks memos flowed from his office to the editors of all three magazines, followed by lunches and meetings and arguments without end. Few of Luce's colleagues would challenge him directly, but many of them were at least partially resistant to the dark and even brutal quality of his view of the world. "We estimate that the climactic crisis of the 20th Century is at hand," Luce wrote ominously. It would require fighting "throughout and beyond" any conflict, as opposed to settling for half a loaf as in Korea. It meant taking "the offensive in Asia, seeking and using every opportunity to limit, reduce, undermine and destroy Armed Communism in Asia." American leadership, he claimed, "is in a decline, neutralism and appeasement are growing among our allies, communism is gaining among the masses, and the Kremlin is coming daily closer to . . . the domination of the world." The only policy that "will not carry the big nuclear risk is a policy of constant appeasement, or slow surrender. . . . In short: Pacifism." The three pillars of a successful foreign policy, he argued, would be "the attainment of atomic supremacy," the "liberation of China" through a "rollback of the Iron Curtain with tactical atomic weapons," and a reaffirmation of "the historic American stand in world politics of being for governments of *free* people, for *free people*, by *free* people everywhere."[43]

Like many such impassioned interventions, Luce's muscular new policy found little support even within Time Inc., let alone in the administration he was trying to influence. He did not promote it for long. Instead he tried to persuade himself that Eisenhower and Dulles were following something close to his own course, even if quietly. Dulles, he wrote, "is the champion of the proposition that politics (including international politics) has something to do with morals and that morals have something to do with God. . . . We must surely support [him] as vigorously as we can in this effort to establish a moral basis for our world politics." Luce must certainly have recognized that Eisenhower had no such inclinations. The president was concerned more about the economic cost of an aggressive military posture than about its morality, and he—with Dulles's perhaps-grudging support—created a foreign policy that differed relatively little from that of Truman and Acheson. Eisenhower did not attempt to "liberate" the captive nations; he mostly resisted defending countries and regions that were not of high strategic interest to the United States; and he refused to take active steps to "liberate" China. Dulles tried to compensate for Eisenhower's restraint with a largely rhetorical policy of his own, which he announced in *Life* in January 1956: "brinkmanship"—the willingness to use nuclear weapons against Communist aggression rather than rely on the expensive and difficult ground wars that Eisenhower opposed. The article created a firestorm of criticism from those who saw Dulles's piece as a recipe for nuclear war. But *Time* eagerly supported the policy and offered a litany of foreign-policy successes that it claimed had been the result of Dulles's supposed strength: "The fears and feelings of U.S. allies . . . must be balanced [against] the necessity of keeping before the world's mind the central fact of the peace: Communist aggression has been deterred only by the willingness and the ability of the free world to go to war rather than cringe before the threats." In reality there was little evidence to suggest that the president had any real willingness to go to war, and even less evidence that the promise of "brinkmanship" (a promise never actually delivered) had any significant impact on policy or its results.[44]

Luce's effort to promote an alternative to containment found a new target not long after the cease-fire in Korea: a war in Vietnam that had begun almost as soon as World War II ended. The conflict pitted the former French colonial rulers against a strong independence movement led by Ho Chi Minh, a Communist educated in Paris and Moscow and a fervent Vietnamese nationalist. During and after World War II, Ho led a growing nationalist movement known as the Vietminh. The Vietminh had opposed the Japanese during World War II. (Most of the French evacuated when the war began, and the few who stayed mostly collaborated with the Japanese.) Only a little more than a year after the Japanese withdrawal, the French bureaucracy and military moved back into Vietnam and tried to regain control of the country, which the Vietminh had already declared an independent nation under their rule. By 1950 the French and the Vietminh were engaged in an open war, which dragged on for almost four years.

Watching this spectacle from afar, Luce was once again excited at the prospect of a confrontation with Communists in Asia. He hoped that with American help the war might drive out the Communists and reunite Vietnam. But he hoped even more that the conflict might also spread to Vietnam's northern neighbor, China, opening up another opportunity for Chiang Kai-shek's forces to resume their war against the Communists. As early as 1947 *Time* was describing Vietnam as "the sickest part of ailing Asia today," an observation accompanied by a strong warning from William Bullitt in *Life* of the danger of "Soviet control." Luce soon latched onto Gen. Jean de Lattre de Tassigny, the commander of French forces, whom he now saw as Vietnam's MacArthur, and whom he invited to New York in hopes of strengthening American support for Indochina. "It makes me proud to think that I have been of some service to you and to our common cause," he wrote de Lattre after one such visit. Luce himself visited Vietnam late in 1952 and, while critical of the French for their "lack of moral seriousness," remained convinced that "the war can be won." And if the Chinese were to intervene, he added provocatively, "it will be quite as convenient for us to destroy Chinese Communist armies in Indo-China as anywhere else."[45]

Vietnam was, to Luce, another test of the willingness and ability of the United States to protect Asia from Communism. "There must be no more talk of a 'hopeless war,' " he ordered his editors. When his star photographer-reporter David Douglas Duncan published an article in *Life* in August 1953 in which he correctly declared that the French had already effectively lost the war, Luce, as usual unaware of what appeared in his magazines until after it was published, put him on the "inactive list" and accused him of exercising a "seductive power over managing editors" and of having an "emotional attitude towards the French." He then began a campaign of damage control in response to strong criticism from the French and from many American supporters of Vietnam.[46]

But Duncan soon proved to be the prescient one. Six months after his reviled article in *Life* appeared, the French army in Vietnam was hopelessly surrounded in an indefensible corner of North Vietnam,

Dien Bien Phu. A frenzied debate began in Washington over what the United States should do. Hard-liners within the administration—among them Vice President Richard Nixon—advocated U.S. military intervention against the Vietminh and even considered the use of atomic weapons. Luce, of course, was not privy to these secret deliberations, although he would likely have sided with the "no substitute for victory" mentality that shaped such views. But Eisenhower was not persuaded. The French surrendered and abandoned Indochina, which left the United States now the principal Western benefactor of Vietnam. Eisenhower settled for a negotiated partition of the country that, as in Korea, established a Communist north and a non-Communist south. Part of the peace agreement, hammered out at an international conference in Geneva, included a provision for elections to reunify the country within a few years.

Luce was dismayed by the "loss" of North Vietnam. He began to cultivate politicians and scholars who were part of the American Friends of Vietnam, which others soon began to call the "Vietnam lobby." And unsurprisingly Luce began to encourage his magazines to portray North Vietnam as a grim and oppressive police state awash in propaganda. It was, in the words of a 1954 *Time* article, a "land of compulsory joy." *Time* gave particular attention to one such piece of propaganda: a Vietminh announcement that "the Viet Nam revolution is an integral part of the world revolution led by the Soviet Union." And it noted that the "articulate" among the nearly half a million refugees who moved from the north to the south after the partition claimed that "the Viet Minh has destroyed the customs and friendlinesses of the past, and has spat upon family ties and religion." What should be done? "In the Asia of victorious Ho Chi Minh and his big brother Mao, there are millions marooned upon desolate sandbars: the act of rescue, if these Asians this late are considered worth saving, will take power, humanity and a steely nerve."[47]

And yet despite all the presumed parallels between the "loss" of North Vietnam and the "loss" of China, Luce was on the whole surprisingly restrained in his response to what he considered the disaster of the Vietminh's victory. He retained a lifelong contempt for the men he believed had abandoned China—especially Dean Acheson and Harry Truman (whom Luce once called a "vulgar little babbitt"). But he continued to admire and support the men who effectively abandoned North Vietnam—Eisenhower and Dulles. That was partly because Vietnam was not China, not the land of his birth and of his continuing preoccupation. But it was also because his stake in the success of a Republican government, and in his personal relationship with Eisenhower, outweighed his disappointment with the outcome of the Vietnam conflict. Decisions he would have pilloried mercilessly under Truman he quietly accepted under Eisenhower. More than that, he gradually pulled back from his aggressive prescription for American foreign policy and turned instead toward a campaign that, on the surface at least, appeared to be an example of the kind of soft idealism that he might once have scorned.[48]

Throughout the 1950s, and indeed throughout the remainder of his life, Luce developed a strong and growing commitment to what he liked to call "the rule of law." His interest in the law was unusual among the great causes he had championed in the past in that it produced little controversy. Virtually no one could object to a defense of the law. But Luce's reasons for this commitment were not as simple as they sometimes sounded. They were, in fact, a reflection of some of his deepest and most contested convictions.[49]

Among the first visible clues to Luce's controversial view of the law was a speech he gave at a convocation at Southern Methodist University in Dallas in 1951 to mark the opening of a new legal center. At first Luce had been reluctant to participate. He had never studied law himself (with the exception of the summer when he was an undergraduate at Yale in which he took some law-school courses), and he had no particular expertise in any legal field. To prepare for the speech he browsed through some legal journals in search of inspiration, and he came across an article by a legal scholar, Harold MacKinnon. It attacked the jurisprudence of one of the giants of American law, Oliver Wendell Holmes, who had sat on the U.S. Supreme Court from 1902 to 1932. It might be too much to say that Luce's subsequent interest in the law was the result of the serendipitous discovery of MacKinnon's argument. But many of his activities on behalf of the law in the coming years reflected this first, powerful encounter with the legacy of Holmes.[50]

The problem with Holmes, Luce believed, was exactly what Holmes's admirers most valued: his unromantic pragmatism, his brusque rejection of fixed belief. To Luce, Holmes's legal philosophy was "agnostic, materialistic." What had Holmes believed? "He believed, most importantly, that there is no ultimate truth anywhere to be believed in." Luce, on the other hand, believed that the law—and most other areas of human existence—had no meaning without being rooted in some kind of universal truth. For Luce that truth was "natural law," and the belief that "we live in a moral universe," and that the law must "conform to a moral order which is universal in time and space." Without the "immutability and unity of truth," not only the law but all of society would be rudderless, would "stand for nothing." To Luce, although not to all critics of pragmatism, the only real alternative to materialism was faith. "Freedom is real because man is created by God in the 'image' of God. Man carries within him something that the merely animal does not have, the divine spark." And so when Luce talked of the "rule of law," he was not simply talking about statutes and precedents. He was evoking the long history of belief in God's active presence in the world, and the existence of a universal set of truths derived from that presence.[51]

Luce's new interest in the law was also intimately connected to his intense (and often thwarted) effort to combat Communism. Having failed to persuade three presidents to launch an aggressive military and political assault against Communism, he began to tie the great contest between America and the Soviet Union to the law. The Soviet Union, he argued, "stood for nothing" and honored no principles. Soviet laws were meaningless because, like Holmes's philosophy, they had no basis in morality or faith. But a true regime of laws, Luce believed, could transform the Communist world, or at least reveal its emptiness to other nations. "A great global inquiry into law would expose the evils of the Soviet system," he argued. American law, if it could "mean something which is written somewhere in the hearts of all men," could represent "the principles by which we exist as a nation" and could become a powerful tool in the battle against Communism. It could "harness together our vast military might and our political and ideal purposes."[52]

What had begun as some random browsing in legal texts turned quickly into a preoccupation and a crusade. Luce began to seek invitations to give speeches on the law almost anywhere he could find an audience—at meetings of the American Bar Association, the Connecticut Bar Association, the Indiana Bar Association, the Missouri Bar Association, the Shelby, Tennessee, Bar Association, St. Louis University. But even as the sites of his speeches appeared to become more and more provincial, the content of his thinking was becoming more and more global. International law, he came to believe, could be the great force that would spread democracy and capitalism into a benighted world. It would be the tool by which the goals of the "American Century" might still be realized, the vehicle that would allow the United States to achieve its great mission in the world.[53]

Luce was always eager to tap the knowledge of scholars and intellectuals, and his interest in the law helped him develop a long and rewarding relationship with the aging William Ernest Hocking, a philosopher who had taught for many years at Harvard before retiring in 1943. Hocking was attractive to Luce because of their shared belief in the role of faith in the laws of the world, and also because of Hocking's conviction that philosophy was not just an academic pursuit but also a tool for shaping public affairs. As a young man Hocking had been a disciple of William James, the great Harvard philosopher who helped build the concept of "pragmatism" into a robust theory that shaped the worldview of much of a generation. But Hocking gradually returned to a form of idealism. Although he never wholly repudiated pragmatism, he qualified his commitment to it, beginning with his influential 1912 book *The Meaning of God in Human Experience*. It argued for the importance of faith in human affairs—not a faith dictated by Scripture or theological institutions, and not a faith derived from revelation, but rather a faith rooted in human experience—and especially in those affirming aspects of human experience that he believed reflected God's invisible presence. Luce's faith was somewhat more formal, and certainly less examined, than Hocking's. But Hocking was, Luce believed, a valuable and confirming ally in the battle against materialism and in the struggle to draw faith into the public world. In the early 1950s Luce began requesting Hocking's "guidance" as he developed his new interest in the law. He was still somewhat insecure about his plunge into the field, and he uncharacteristically expressed doubt and vulnerability. "Perhaps even I have overrated The Law," he worried. He feared that he had been "guilty" of "not caring enough about 'the people.' " And he asked Hocking for suggestions of "a little reading on the law as the necessary basis of the good society . . . a 'refresher' on a course I never took!" Hocking responded with a rambling list of suggested readings, words of encouragement, and scattered observations on the relationship between law and theology. But Luce was not really asking for advice on how to educate himself. He was seeking for ammunition in his already settled view of the role the law must play. Hocking, in the end, served more as a cheerleader of Luce's efforts than as a true mentor. Rather than test Luce's beliefs, he offered such encouraging but unilluminating notes as "in your notable speech on law, you justly criticised our foreign policy for giving too little attention to Law." But Hocking's approval was important to Luce, and their relationship helped give him confidence in the course he was pursuing.[54]

But Luce's sights were set higher than Hocking, and higher than the various bar associations to which he presented his new commitment to the law. His real goal was to draw national and world leaders into his orbit and to persuade them to embrace his own emerging beliefs. He began a far-flung correspondence with university presidents, members of Congress, and foreign leaders. But most of all he set out to influence the Eisenhower administration. Having failed to persuade the president and the secretary of state to take a more aggressive military position in Asia, he sought to draw them into a commitment to law as the basis of foreign policy. It turned out to be a difficult task, particularly when he was dealing with Dulles. To Dulles the "rule of law" was a pleasant aspiration with no practical role in the struggle against Communism. He never explicitly rejected Luce's ideas. "You can't have security without law," Dulles said supportively (and vaguely) in a 1957 meeting. But he went on to remind Luce of how difficult extending law into international relations would be. "The World Court is unemployed," he noted. "There are lots of arbitration agreements lying around but they are never used. . . . Between us and the Communists is an unbridgeable gulf in the matter of Law." On another occasion he warned that "there is still a strong reluctance on the part of nations . . . to submit their disputes to abitrament [*sic*] of justice." And later still Dulles wrote discouragingly, "I am touching on the subject of international law in my address at the UN. But there are so many other matters of greater interest and greater urgency that I fear it will not make much impression."[55]

To promote his ideas more effectively, he helped organize a committee of "petitioners" that included Charles Rhyne, president of the American Bar Association, Ross Malone, its president-elect, and Erwin Griswold, the former dean of Harvard Law School and former solicitor general of the United States. Together they urged Dulles to deliver the "main address at the Annual Meeting of the American Bar Association" in August 1958, to appoint a "Presidential Commission" to "advance the cause of world peace through law," and most of all to embrace a "hopeful interest in the subject." The group met with Dulles in July and encountered a notable lack of enthusiasm. "Mr. Dulles's reaction, to begin with, was negative," Luce recorded. "He had been trying to do all this before his visitors were born." People would "think it was a shortcut to peace whereas actually implementing these world-law proposals could take 100 years."[56]

Luce continued to hope for Dulles's support, and Dulles periodically encouraged him. Every now and then Dulles included in a speech or a public document a reference to the importance of the law; and although

LIFE

NOVEMBER 23, 1936 **10** CENTS

The first cover of *Life* magazine, 1936, featuring a dramatic Margaret Bourke-White photograph of the Fort Peck Dam in Montana. The picture's monumentality drew immediate attention to the new magazine and helped make it an immediate, sensational success. Bourke-White was the first great celebrity among *Life* photographers, but she was soon accompanied by a large retinue of equally talented (and in some cases equally famous) colleagues.

Luce looks over possible photographs for *Life*, flanked on the left by John Shaw Billings, the first managing editor of *Life*, and on the right by Daniel Longwell, the most energetic champion of the new magazine and eventually Billings's successor as managing editor.

Harry and Clare became great celebrities—partly as a result of the marriage of these two famous people, and partly because their marriage coincided with the runaway success of *Life*. They are shown here debarking the *Queen Mary* after a trip to Europe in 1938.

Luce's fascination with Wendell Willkie exceeded all but a few of his many political infatuations. He used his magazines zealously (and perhaps recklessly) to promote Willkie's cause—including this *Life* cover a few weeks before the 1940 presidential election.

Harry and Clare walk with Madame Chiang Kai-shek through a reverent group of Chinese near Chungking, in a 1941 visit. The crowd was organized by Kuomintang leaders to impress Luce, whose influence was important to the regime. Their hosts were not disappointed by their treatment in Luce's magazines.

An important event of Luce's 1941 visit to China was his first meeting with Theodore H. White. The much younger "Teddy" and the famous and powerful "Harry" struck up a close friendship that cooled several years later when White turned against Chiang Kai-shek, a man whom Harry continued to revere.

One of the many covers *Time* devoted to Chiang Kai-shek. In this one, he is accompanied by Madame Chiang, as "Man & Woman of the Year" in 1938.

After a long and frustrating period during which Roosevelt forbade publishers from visiting the war zones, Luce finally made his way to the Pacific front in June 1945. Harry Truman, the new president, overruled Roosevelt's ban. Luce is shown here on the left, along with *Time*'s managing editor, Roy Alexander, a *Brooklyn Eagle* reporter, and General Henry Larsen.

During the war years, with Clare in Washington as a member of the House of Representatives from Connecticut, Harry began a serious and relatively public affair with Jean Dalrymple, a theatrical publicist and producer four years Luce's junior. For a time, Luce talked of divorcing Clare and marrying Jean. But after Ann Brokaw's death, he gradually broke off the relationship.

Ambassador and Mr. Luce on vacation with Joseph P. Kennedy in 1956. Harry's unusual costume suggests his general discomfort with leisure.

Whittaker Chambers joined Time Inc. as a book reviewer, and rose to be the controversial editor of Foreign News, in which he relentlessly denounced the Soviet Union and communism. The Alger Hiss case, which began in 1948 and revealed Chambers's past life as a Soviet spy, led to his departure from the company.

Luce took advantage of his connection to the American embassy in Rome by traveling widely in Europe and hosting distinguished visitors. He is shown here escorting Winston Churchill in a 1955 visit.

Luce's growing interest in the importance of leisure in American life led him to support the creation of a sports magazine, a project many of his colleagues at first disdained. But because of the energy, commitment, and talent of Sidney James (*left*), most of Luce's colleagues soon came to support the project. James, Luce, and *Sports Illustrated* publisher Harry Phillips pose in 1954 in front of a blown-up cover of the magazine's first issue, August 16, 1954— a photograph of a baseball game in Milwaukee.

Luce's warm relationship with Dwight D. Eisenhower was one of the most rewarding of his life, and the only time he had an intimate friendship with a sitting president. *Time* was so sympathetic to Eisenhower that both the magazine's editors and many of its readers sharply criticized the coverage, to no avail.

Luce was an ardent supporter of the Vietnam War, and in the 1950s a great admirer of Ngo Dinh Diem, president of South Vietnam. The American Friends of Vietnam, modeled in some ways on earlier organizations supporting Nationalist China, attracted the support of many prominent figures. Luce presides here in 1959 over a meeting of the organization, with Diem seated next to him, waiting to speak.

In the late 1950s, Luce began a passionate affair with Lord Beaverbrook's young granddaughter, Lady Jeanne Campbell, which drew him into another painful battle with Clare. Eventually, the affair—which Luce at one time had hoped would lead to marriage—ended.

Luce's warm relationship with Eisenhower left him with an intensified interest in other important politicians. He was particularly drawn to John Kennedy, whom he had known through John's father for years. Kennedy is seen here walking through the Time-Life building in 1960, during his presidential campaign, after an interview with the Time Inc. editors.

Forty-one years after Luce cofounded Time Inc., he finally handed control of the company over to Hedley Donovan, a former *Fortune* editor whom Luce himself chose to succeed him. They are shown here during a lavish celebration of the transition in 1964.

it was almost never accompanied by any concrete policy or action, it helped prevent any serious strains in the relationship. Eisenhower, who had only slightly more commitment to the value of international law than Dulles did, also made rhetorical gestures to Luce and his colleagues—gestures that Luce eagerly embraced no matter how modest they were. During the Hungarian Revolution in 1956 Eisenhower denounced the "lawlessness" of the Soviet Union's invasion of a theoretically sovereign nation. Luce was exultant. "You took this occasion to hold up the banner of Law as it has not been held up in a generation," he wrote the president. But Eisenhower's public embraces of the "rule of law" were rare; and although he was less inclined than Dulles to express his reservations, he too had doubts about the viability of Luce's cause. Everyone agreed, Eisenhower wrote, that "a great world-wide push to enthrone law over force" would help settle "the world's differences." But beyond this broad principle, the president continued (echoing Dulles), "I am most uncertain of the meaning you intend to convey. . . . [I]t is manifest that the world is not yet ready to adopt and observe the principles of international law." The promotion of law, Eisenhower added, should not be the task of government but should be "largely a private one carried on through the Bar Associations." And so he spurned a proposal from Luce and Rhyne to create a "presidential commission on the rule of law." Instead Eisenhower gave encouragement to an initiative that moved the issue of law out of the White House and into academia—an initiative sparked by the departure from the administration of one of Eisenhower's most influential aides, Arthur Larson.[57]

Larson was chief speechwriter to the president, a position he used to help articulate a moderate vision of public policy that came to be known as "modern Republicanism." But by 1958 the president's interest in moderation was fading, and Larson began looking for a position outside government. Rhyne, a trustee of Duke University, proposed (with Luce's eager support) the creation there of a center for international law, which Rhyne invited Larson to lead. Larson resigned from the White House (carrying with him the nominal position of "consultant" to the president on "the advancement of the rule of law"). Luce was pleased that the movement for what he now called "world peace through law" was represented by a significant institution, and he supported Larson's efforts to bring more publicity to the cause, which Larson did very effectively. During his directorship of the Duke center, Larson attracted an impressive array of public officials and international leaders to speak or participate in conferences (Luce among them); he published articles and books on international law; and he helped raise the profile of international law and its possible value to global politics. But the creation of Larson's center was also an excuse for the administration to marginalize this inconvenient movement, in which Eisenhower and Dulles had little real faith.[58]

Among the most important concrete proposals to emerge from Luce's efforts was the repeal of the so-called Connally Amendment, a provision in the 1945 treaty by which the United States had joined the International Court of Justice. The Democratic senator Tom Connally of Texas, chairman of the Senate Foreign Relations Committee, had opposed any transfer of sovereignty to an international organization, and as a result of his amendment, the treaty gave the court no jurisdiction over "domestic" issues within the United States. The American government would alone decide what was "domestic" and what was not. To Luce and other champions of international law, the amendment was a major obstacle to what Larson called the "world rule of law," and the Duke center worked strenuously on behalf of its repeal—but to no avail. In the end Luce's quixotic crusade produced no new laws and no new policy, although it did contribute to making international law more a part of the nation's public discourse. He continued to hope for a revolution through law for years. "The year 1965," he wrote fifteen years after he began his efforts, "could be the year the Rule of Law idea really surfaces into public consciousness."[59]

Luce's commitment to Eisenhower—and his willingness to overlook disagreements with him—was greatly strengthened by the president's decision to name Clare the American ambassador to Italy early in 1953. For Eisenhower the appointment was a way to repay a Republican stalwart (Clare) and an important supporter (Harry) and to cement his relationship with a powerful media empire. It undoubtedly helped Clare's case that she was a famous convert to Catholicism and thus an appropriate liaison with the Vatican.* For Harry the appointment made possible a richer and more direct engagement with affairs of state than he had ever had before, while at the same time allowing him to remain in control of his magazines. In the four years in which Clare was ambassador, Harry spent almost half of his time in Rome, working partly in a Time Inc. office he had created for himself in the city, and partly in the embassy, where he was an unofficial adviser to Clare and an active participant in almost all public events.[60]

Clare's appointment to Italy was not universally popular, in the

---

*The ambassadorship to Italy was also the ambassadorship to the Vatican until 1974.

United States or in Italy, and it encountered some resistance from the State Department. Clare believed that Dulles himself was opposed to her candidacy. Harry constantly reassured her that everything would work out, even as he was quietly battling the obstacles that still stood in her way. Clare, in the meantime, became more and more agitated, convinced that there was a conspiracy to deny her the job, and fearful of the humiliation if—after extensive press coverage—the nomination was withdrawn. At the same time, as she often was in times of stress, she became preoccupied with her age (fifty in 1953). "I feel so old these days," she wrote in her diary in a low moment in January. "I no longer feel that the clothes enhance my beauty, rather they conceal the fact it is—as it must—wasting away." But her despair did not last long. Early in February the president announced Clare's nomination. The Senate confirmed it in early March, and Clare—after a round of lavish farewell parties—arrived in Rome in late April, accompanied by Harry and a retinue of friends and relatives.[61]

Harry stayed with Clare in the embassy (in separate bedrooms as always) for her first seven weeks in Rome before he returned to New York. But he came back regularly for long periods of time—on average twenty weeks a year over the four years of her term. It was a rare period of peace and commitment in their marriage. "My deepest concern was always HRL's *togetherness* with me on this!" she wrote in February 1953. "I now feel the deepest faith in his loyalty, and his sympathy and aid!" The ambassadorship brought them into a genuine partnership, something that had eluded them during the first eighteen years of their marriage. It was Harry who had negotiated with the president and the State Department for Clare's assignment to Rome. He had declined on her behalf offers that she be appointed secretary of labor or ambassador to Mexico. He donated five thousand dollars a month to the embassy to facilitate Clare's entertaining, and paid for extensive renovations to the ambassador's elegant but decaying residence. He brought his assistant Kip Finch to Rome with his family to serve his and Clare's needs. When Harry was in Rome he was omnipresent in the life of the embassy—a constant prod to the foreign-service officers to show the deference they owed the ambassador, a stickler for protocol, and a host at lunches and meetings that Clare could not attend. He was, one colleague said, "an extraordinarily good 'ambassador's wife.' " While Clare entertained dinner guests before the huge living room fireplace in the ambassador's residence, "he circled the outer fringes of the party making sure everyone else had a drink, had seen the Rouaults and the Churchills" (paintings that had once hung in their apartment in New York). In no other setting in his life had he been so solicitous a host.[62]

But Luce was far more than an attentive and supportive husband. As always his personal reconciliation with Clare was closely tied up with the opportunities her new position offered them both to exercise power and influence, which were much enhanced by the somewhat exaggerated belief of Italian leaders that the Luces had an "intimate friendship" with President Eisenhower. Allen Grover, Harry's jaded and somewhat disillusioned deputy, described him as

> obsessed with the subject of foreign policy and his direct influence on it. Nothing else interests him. He regards his position as "unique" for exerting pressure—Clare in Rome, C. D. Jackson [his once and future employee] in the White House, and his magazines to press his points. He fancies he is molding the destiny of the U.S., in the world.

Luce and his Time Inc. staff handled much of the embassy's correspondence (including a large amount that was addressed to him almost as if he were himself the ambassador). And he wrote regularly to Eisenhower and Dulles with accounts of Clare's successes. Harry also had a quasi-diplomatic life of his own in Italy. He traveled extensively, had meetings with ministers and provincial officials and leading industrialists— meetings not unlike those he had always conducted while traveling abroad, but much enhanced by his connection to the American Embassy. He was, Billings noted, "on the top clouds of Rome."[63]

At the heart of Clare's ambassadorship was the inevitable preoccupation with Communism that she shared with her husband—and with the State Department. Italy was among the Western European nations with a strong Communist Party that had at least some prospect of winning control of the government. Clare, encouraged by the foreign-service officers in the embassy, ignored the tradition of ambassadors not intervening in the politics of the countries in which they served. Instead, she became a staunch, and often strident, critic of the Italian Left. She was also critical of the dominant Christian Democratic Party for the weakness of its leaders and for its failure to adopt "a vigorous anti-communist attitude." It was, as one historian noted, an "ambitious attempt . . . to drastically transform Italy's political landscape."[64]

In the several national elections during her time in Italy, she openly warned voters that the United States would withhold its financial aid to the country should the Communists win. "If the Italian people should fall unhappy victim to the wiles of totalitarianism . . . of the Right or the Left," she threatened during a 1953 parliamentary campaign, "there would follow, logically and tragically, grave consequences" for the "intimate and warm" friendship between America and Italy. Skeptical of what she considered the wobbly leadership of Alcide de Gasperi, who had served as prime minister since the end of World War II, she actively supported the right-wing Christian Democrat Giuseppe Pella, whose "political virility" she admired. (Pella defeated de Gasperi in August 1953 only to be defeated himself five months later.) Discouraged, she began trying on her own to mobilize anti-Communist leaders—not just politicians but also industrialists, intellectuals, journalists, and others. She exhorted companies to purge their work forces of Communists and threatened them with a freeze on American aid should they fail to do so. Fiat, Italy's largest industrial corporation and a significant recipient of U.S. support, responded by creating a blacklist of "undesirable employees" who were dismissed or suspended because of their leftist politics. There was frequent and often outraged criticism from many quarters of Italian politics and from the Italian press about what they considered Clare's inappropriate interference in the nation's affairs. But she was not, in fact, a renegade, although her great fame and visibility helped make it appear so. She was taking steps that were entirely consistent with the Eisenhower-Dulles foreign policy and its strong commitment to combating Communism through nonmilitary means in Europe. It was also a reflection of Harry's own aggressive internationalism, which contributed much to Clare's controversial initiatives.[65]

Clare's life in the American Embassy in Rome was even more intensely busy than it had been in New York and Washington. Most politically appointed ambassadors left the real work to the career foreign-service officials and spent their time largely on ceremonial duties. Clare, however, took the diplomatic work seriously, spending hours every day at her desk laboring through cables and correspondence and meeting constantly with starstruck and somewhat puzzled subordinates unaccustomed to direct contact with the ambassador.[66]

Clare was a healthy woman who lived an active life well into her eighties, but she was also something of a hypochondriac who retreated to her bed frequently with undiagnosable ailments. Such incidents occurred particularly frequently and severely in Rome. Her illnesses drew Harry closer to her for a time. On many evenings they would sit together in her bedroom reading to each other, playing highly competitive games of Scrabble, and enjoying a kind of domesticity they had rarely experienced in the United States. Clare later told her secretary that the "years in Rome were the happiest of their married life." Harry periodically rushed to Italy to take her on long, restorative cruises in the Mediterranean or to quiet resorts in France or Greece. Her recovery after these absences reinforced the belief of some of her doctors and friends that her ailments were in some way self-inflicted, products of stress and exhaustion. Late in 1954 she began to have serious dental problems that she and others feared might be the result of poisoning. Finally the embassy announced that staff members had discovered that Clare's bed lay below a ceiling whose flaking lead-based paint had gradually been exposing her to low levels of arsenic. This alleged discovery was widely publicized, including in the pages of *Time*, but there were claims at the time that the story was apocryphal, that Clare's real problem was a viral infection that coincided with age-related dental problems and that the lead-paint story was a cover for extensive cosmetic dentistry that required her to spend months in New York. As she moved into her mid-fifties, she had become ever more concerned about maintaining her beauty, which she correctly realized was one of her most important assets in the high-stakes, male-dominated world of politics and diplomacy.[67]

By late 1956 Clare was becoming restless with her life in Italy. She was discouraged by the continuing weakness of the anti-Communist Right in the nation's politics, bored with the daily routine of the embassy, and eager for a larger place on the public stage. She urged Eisenhower to let her leave Rome to campaign for him in 1956. When rumors began to spread that the president was planning to replace Nixon as his vice presidential running mate, Clare began lobbying implausibly to succeed him. She sent out feelers about running for a Senate seat in Connecticut, but there was little enthusiasm in the state Republican Party for the idea. She was also mentioned as a possible secretary of the Department of Health, Education, and Welfare, but nothing came of that either. She finally resigned her ambassadorship early in 1958.

But she remained a prominent candidate for another diplomatic post: She hoped for London, to no avail. Finally in 1959 Eisenhower asked her to serve as ambassador to Brazil—a post she found much less attractive than Italy but that she halfheartedly agreed to accept. There was considerable criticism of the appointment, some of it rooted in Latin American resentment of Time Inc.'s coverage of the region. She also inherited the anger of some Democratic members of Congress who had run afoul of Harry's strong support of Eisenhower. At one point

Senator Wayne Morse of Oregon, who had recently changed his party affiliation from Republican to Democrat to the great dismay of *Time*, gave a long and scathing speech opposing Clare's nomination. Nevertheless she was easily confirmed. Harry encouraged her to go and promised to spend as much time with her in Rio as he had in Rome. But she continued to waver—both because of her lukewarm interest in the position and because of her fear it would have required her to oversee the end of American aid to Brazil, which would inevitably lead to criticism and failure. Friends reported that Clare was looking for a way out, and deliberately or not, she soon found one. She released a statement to the press shortly after the confirmation (over the advice of her advisers and without consulting Harry) that "I am grateful for the overwhelming vote of confirmation in the Senate. We must now wait until the dust settles. My difficulties of course go some years back and began when Senator Wayne Morse was kicked in the head by a horse." After a small firestorm of criticism in the Senate, she turned down the appointment, citing the "extraordinarily ugly charges" made against her and the likelihood of "a continuing harassment of my mission."[68]

For Clare the Brazil fiasco marked the end of her political career. She returned to New York, tried to get back to writing, made occasional speeches, and remained a sought-after celebrity in the social world. But she never regained the prominence she had once had. For Luce, however, the late 1950s had a different meaning. The experience had reinvigorated him and given him new enthusiasm about the future. No longer wholly preoccupied with the Cold War, he began to focus on what he considered the great success of the United States and the transformation of American life. He also began seeking not just power, but happiness.

XIII

National Purpose

The eight Eisenhower years were great years for the Republic," Luce wrote in his unfinished memoir in the mid-1960s. "Largely by their own efforts, individually or in voluntary association, the American people made giant strides in nearly every field of endeavor under the benign laws of their Republic." For a man who had recoiled from the nation's leadership for more than twenty years, a man whose mission in life had often seemed to be railing against the failures of national will and imagination, a man who continuously exhorted the country to change course, this sense of political contentment might have seemed out of character. But Luce's optimism was not sentimental nostalgia. It was a result of his warm personal relationship with Eisenhower and the flattering attention he received from the president. It also arose out of his conviction that the United States was surmounting its most serious problems and embracing "another word [that] had been put into the language, namely, 'Excellence.' "[1]

Luce considered the mid- and late 1950s not only a good time for America but a good time for him. His sojourn in Italy had rejuvenated him and had at least briefly restored some relative calm to his troubled marriage. His company was prospering as never before, and his magazines continued to flourish. Luce gradually slowed down his restless efforts to remake the magazines and, uncharacteristically, deferred to his talented editors more often than in the past. That made it possible for him to enlarge his activities outside Time Inc. He became increasingly involved with philanthropic organizations, intellectual projects, and new

personal relationships that contributed to a growing, if precarious, satisfaction with his life.

But Luce could never be wholly content for long. By the end of the
1950s he was once again facing new crises in his personal life. And at the
same time he was also embarking on a new mission—one that combined
his new optimism with his old impatience. He set out to lead an inquiry
into what he called the "national purpose," a project he embraced with
both enthusiasm and urgency and one that preoccupied him for the rest
of his life.

Luce's happiness with the Eisenhower administration, and with the state
of the nation, did not soften the opinionated tone in his magazines. On
the contrary, the Eisenhower years produced even more energetic criticisms than Time Inc. had received during the 1952 campaign. In the
past complaints about *Time*'s bias had often focused on Luce's attacks on
Roosevelt and Truman. By the mid-1950s a major complaint was about
the magazine's excessive approval of Eisenhower. Luce had, of course,
gone to extraordinary lengths in the past to promote Republican candidates, most notably in his passionate commitment to Wendell Willkie in
1940. But Eisenhower was the first serving president whom Luce wholly
admired, and the coverage of the Republican administration was so positive that even Luce's own editors began to complain. Thomas Griffith,
the Foreign News editor of *Time*, warned Luce in 1956 that the magazine was in danger of "losing the esteem that you and I (and so many
others) . . . want *Time* to deserve and to have." In the past, Griffith
noted, *Time* "used to cheat a little" at the end of a campaign, but now, he
charged, "it's a four-year proposition."[2]

Griffith's accusations were hard to refute. In a July 4, 1955, story
(with a cover portrait of Eisenhower framed by the Liberty Bell), *Time*
celebrated the "clear and convincing evidence of patience, determination, optimism and faith among the people of the U.S. In the 29 months
since Dwight Eisenhower moved into the White House, a remarkable
change had come over the nation. The national blood pressure and tem-
perature had gone down; nerve endings had healed over." The "new
tone could be described," *Time* claimed, as "the return of confidence." A
year later, during Eisenhower's reelection campaign, *Time* exulted over
the president's "zest" and his newfound political skills. "Cheerleaders
bounded and bounced in a political harlequinade, and Republican dignitaries lined up with grins wide enough for tooth inspection," the magazine wrote of Eisenhower's arrival at a campaign stop in San Francisco.
"The military hero who walked so gingerly for so long in the political

world has become a zestful party leader who thoroughly likes that world and its political inhabitants. Last week, by his every word and act, he proved it." *Time* even reported gratuitously on other journalists who wrote approvingly of Eisenhower. At one point the magazine ran a story reporting that the usually Democratic columnists Joseph and Stewart Alsop described Eisenhower's legislative program as a "conspicuous success."[3]

Time's undeniable favoritism in its reporting on American politics generated increasing criticism of other areas of the magazine. The Philippine ambassador gave a speech to the American Society of Newspaper Editors in 1959 describing *Time*'s editorial philosophy as "All the news as we angle it." A few years later the left-leaning New York magazine *Fact* collected complaints about *Time* from prominent people and published their stories of "lies," "distortions," and "rampant inaccuracies." (The editors apologized for not having enough room in the magazine to publish all the comments they had solicited.) "Every music column I have read in *Time* has been distorted and inaccurate," Igor Stravinsky claimed. The actress Tallulah Bankhead went on the *Tonight Show* to warn the audience, "Don't believe a word you read in *Time*. . . . It is made up of fakery, calumny, and viciousness." The parade of accusations continued for more than twenty pages: "I regard *Time* as prejudiced and unfair in its reporting" (Senator John McClellan); "There is not a single word of truth in *Time* magazine" (Broadway producer David Merrick); "*Time* slants its news" (poet Conrad Aiken); "Totalitarianism . . . rather than insight or intelligibility is the object of all of *Time*'s technical brilliance" (media scholar Marshall McLuhan); " . . . about the most inaccurate magazine in existence" (novelist P. G. Wodehouse). *Time* was not nearly as biased as these critics claimed, but there was enough "slanted" reporting to give the accusations credibility. Luce alternated between defensiveness and distress in the face of such attacks, and he occasionally made efforts to defuse the criticisms. But for the most part he simply lived with the charges of bias. "TIME will remain pro-Eisenhower and therefore pro-Republican," he defiantly wrote a critical colleague in 1955. He remained convinced that pure "objectivity" was both impossible and undesirable, and he was convinced as well that these were *his* magazines and should reflect *his* view of the world.[4]

Through much of the 1950s and the early 1960s, Luce's view of the world was disproportionately driven by his vision of American abundance and American social and cultural progress. And those views in turn helped drive the contents of his magazines, especially *Life*. This was not a radical shift for *Life*, which had always devoted considerable energy to promoting wealth, progress, and American lifestyles. But the 1950s and the early 1960s intensified its fascination with the flourishing economy and with the way the middle class lived. Just as *Life* in the 1940s had been the great chronicler of the war, it became in the 1950s the great chronicler of prosperity and consensus. As early as December 1945, the magazine happily proclaimed the return of "normalcy." Prosperity, of course, had been far from a norm even for middle-class Americans for most of the past fifteen years, and it remained far from the norm for many Americans even in the 1950s and 1960s. Nearly a third of Americans lived below the government poverty line in the first decade after the war. But *Life* was insistent that Americans were putting "their minds and energies to work" and were going back to "football games, automobile trips, family reunions and all the pleasant trivia of the American way of life."[5]

By 1954 the idea of abundance was a consistent subject for *Life*. On the one hand the magazine expressed wonder at, and some concern about, the great bounty Americans had created. "How does one prepare for an Age of Plenty?" the magazine asked in its Thanksgiving issue. "How can one feel thankful for too much?" A year later *Life* was still worrying: "Is abundance a good enough thing by itself for Americans to take pride in?" Mostly, however, *Life* celebrated the nation's wealth. In the magazine's own assessment of the state of the union (published shortly before the president's annual message), it claimed that Eisenhower's "reports get better every year"; and it cited "three major economic blessings which had previously seemed politically incompatible: rising wages, lower taxes and stable prices." A *Life* cover story later in 1956, "Peak Year for Big Jobs," announced an unprecedented $33 billion investment that was "reshaping the continent. . . . Even on a continent accustomed to huge projects," it was "more than ever before" and was "providing for the future." *Life* regularly trumpeted new milestones in American prosperity. "History's biggest stock issue" (the first public offering of the Ford Motor Company); "a remarkable recovery" for the "U.S. construction industry," which was filling "skylines with a spectacular array of bold new building shapes"; an unprecedented $250 million investment by Chrysler in a redesign of its 1955 models ("longer, lower, sportier . . . with a lot of horsepower"). "Last week," the magazine reported in July 1955 in a story on houseware manufacturers, "at a time when the country had more money to spend than ever before; the trend seemed to be running toward two pots for every chicken, fish, egg and carrot . . . a dramatic example of overall U. S. prosperity."[6]

The Time Inc. magazines even began to celebrate labor unions. Luce had long been mostly critical of unions, and the company was fighting off efforts to unionize of some of its own employees during much of the 1950s. But Luce was impressed with Walter Reuther's leadership of the United Auto Workers (UAW), which he insisted marked a major turning point in labor history. Everything about the union movement, he decided, was suddenly "new." The UAW had reached a new agreement with the automobile industry on a new "guaranteed wage" for workers while abandoning some of the more radical proposals the CIO had once promoted. "New Affluence, Unity for Labor," *Life* announced in a 1955 cover story. A "new era of peace" had emerged out of the labor wars of the 1930s and 1940s with the reuniting of the AFL and CIO in 1955. *Life* even profiled men it had once reviled: the "new kind of unionists," labor's newly responsible "wealth of leadership."[7]

Abundance was the key not just to business and wages but also to technology; and because Luce was suddenly fascinated by technological progress, *Life* reveled in the achievements of American scientists and engineers. "The advances have come with an overwhelming rush," *Life* reported in a "major series on the frontiers of our achievement," momentously titled "Man's New World: How He Lives in It." Americans had "been learning at a phenomenal rate," benefiting from government subsidies and from research at university and corporate laboratories. Among the great discoveries was atomic power, "man's great hope of harnessing fusion." By 1955, *Life* announced, the atomic industry was "big business," having developed methods for powering submarines with nuclear energy and creating electricity for consumers in atomic-power plants—the foundation "for a new industrial age." Equally dazzling was the birth of what *Life* called "the jet age," with its promise of faster travel for citizens and its opportunities for improved military capacities in warfare. *Life* devoted an entire issue in 1955 to the "Air Age," which argued that "the need and the will to master the world's air has brought changes which are reshaping our economy, our cities and our global relationships." But the progress so far, *Life* predicted, was paltry compared with the "true wonders" of the air age "not yet at hand" but "imminent." *Life* reveled as well in the great medical discoveries of the 1950s: the discovery of the Salk and then the Sabin vaccines that effectively eliminated polio; an advance in the treatment of cancer that "seem[ed] close to bringing under control" this "dread enemy"; improvements in X-ray technology; new techniques in heart surgery; and new and more sophisticated weapons to fight bacterial infections and viruses.[8]

Life's fascination with technology reached its highest point in the late 1950s and early 1960s, when the magazine became, in effect, the "official" chronicler of the manned space program. To *Life*, as to many Americans, nothing personified the linkage between scientific progress and the greatness of America's mission more than the goal of exploring outer space; and nothing excited Americans more than the idea of humans themselves doing the exploration. Almost as soon as the first seven Mercury astronauts were named (and overnight became extraordinary celebrities), *Life* moved in to buy exclusive rights to their stories for a total of five hundred thousand dollars. In the two-page advertisement announcing *Life*'s significant coup, the editors could hardly contain their excitement. "The Astronauts' own stories will appear only in *Life*," they wrote. "The lives that these seven men—and their wives—will lead between now and the day that one of them becomes the first American to orbit into outer space will in itself be one of the most absorbing, dramatic human stories of our time." Luce himself played no direct role in his company's commitment to the astronauts, but over time he too was drawn into their extraordinary magnetism and even began referring to them as "my boys."[9]

But to Luce, and thus to *Life*, the best evidence of America in this new "age of abundance" was the middle-class home. One of the most important and most inspiring successes of the postwar years, he believed, was the rapid growth in home ownership, facilitated by the proliferation of suburbs and generous federal support. Partly in response to his enthusiasm, *Life* launched a series titled "Modern Living," which focused almost entirely on the character of American homes. There were lavish features on opulent or innovative houses—a "push-button paradise" in Palm Springs, built by a wealthy manufacturer who called it a "mechanical dream house," with swimming pool, tennis court, nine-hole putting green, and a "human Lazy Susan" of seven outdoor couches that revolved "slowly under the sun." In other articles *Life* showcased the great variety of American home designs—a "cross-country roundup" of homes that illustrated regional styles—"rough timber and Texas Cordova stone" in the Southwest, "Scandinavian flavor" in the Midwest, redwood furniture in California, all of them crossing over and becoming national in their reach. There were stories on "pretty underpinnings for modern furniture," a "bathroom built for two," "stylish mixing of decor," the "return of elegance" in home decor, "opulence in plain rooms," and a "buyer's guide for antiques." A three-part series on housing in 1958 illustrated suburban growth across the country and focused on "ideas for better houses." Later *Life* chose "six outstanding homes" as examples of "the country's most livable houses in varying price ranges." Perhaps the most bizarre article in "Modern Living" was a 1955 feature, "H-Bomb Hideaway," which showed a newly designed bomb shelter inhabited by a smiling middle-class family of five, surrounded by canned foods. They were photographed in the three-thousand-dollar "luxury model" and were playing games, reading books, and sewing—a vision of doomsday domesticity almost indistinguishable from *Life*'s many other portrayals of suburban living.[10]

"Nobody Is Mad with Nobody," *Life* happily reported in its July 4, 1955, issue. America was "up to its ears in domestic tranquility." The country was "embroiled in no war, impeded by no major strikes, blessed with almost full employment," and "delighted with itself." As if to provide evidence of this remarkable moment, there were photographs of "delighted Vermonters at the Rutland fairground," a field of high wheat in the Midwest captioned "Abundant Again," a Junior Chamber of Commerce parade in Atlanta, a suburban den with multiple televisions, a convertible painted with dots to match the owners' Dalmatian, and a taffy-pulling competition in Peabody, Massachusetts. "Spirits and Industry Are Expansive," *Life* announced in another article featuring photographs of new cars, a performance by a symphony orchestra, and an automobile plant expansion in Flint, Michigan. In the 1950s, even more than in the past, *Life* was promoting what historians and intellectuals were beginning to call the "consensus," the belief that almost all Americans shared a broad set of ideals and aspirations. Those shared aspirations, *Life* seemed to be saying, were affluence, consumerism, and middle-class values and lifestyles. The magazine celebrated overt—if mostly contentless—patriotism, stable nuclear families, and male "breadwinners." It made occasional gestures to women's work outside the home, as in the 1956 article "My Wife Works and I Like It," which noted the role working women played in improving the family's lifestyle. But much more common were celebrations of female domesticity. When *Life* veered away from the middle class, it often focused on affirmative stories of immigrants embracing the "American way of life," or on marginal Americans entering the middle-class mainstream through hard work or philanthropy.[11]

The change in American life that had the biggest material impact on Time Inc. was the rapid growth of leisure and entertainment. Working hours for many Americans had been reduced; family incomes had risen.

Fortune published an ambitious series in 1953–54 on "The Changing American Market," and among its conclusions was that there had been a dramatic growth in leisure since the end of World War II and a booming search for entertainment. Or, as *Fortune* put it, there was "$30 Billion for Fun." *Life* was an energetic chronicler of the growth of leisure activities, just as it was of other aspects of abundance. It gave lavish coverage to the opening of Disneyland in Anaheim, California, in 1955. It was fascinated by the emergence of Las Vegas as a magnet for gambling and sybaritic entertainment. But perhaps most of all, *Life* took note of the growing interest in sport and outdoor life. It began to run more major articles than in the past on skiing, duck hunting, Little League baseball, wilderness hiking and camping, horseracing, water sports, and even bowling. It celebrated the sports ordinary people played and the outdoor activities they pursued. But it also celebrated the sports people watched—in stadiums, in arenas, and on television.[12]

By the spring of 1953 Luce was once again in what Billings called "an empire-building mood," which usually meant launching a new magazine. And even though Luce had never been very much interested in sports or wilderness activities himself, he began to imagine a "sporting magazine" that would capture what he believed was a growing market for leisure, and thus for sports. There was brief talk of buying up such existing magazines as *Outdoor Life* or *Popular Science*. But what Luce really wanted was "our own Sports Weekly." Some of his colleagues were aghast at the idea, convinced that a sports magazine would degrade the Time Inc. brand by focusing on trivial and consumer-driven activities. Others worried that the costs would be prohibitive and that the audience would be too narrow. "Time Inc. is not a 'sporting' outfit," Billings wrote contemptuously in his diary, noting that he was "really against a Sports Magazine" and saw it "only as a Luce whim." (Luce's deputy, Allen Grover, rarely disagreed openly with his boss—and did not do so on this issue—but he quietly agreed with Billings.) Other colleagues were similarly dubious about the project, and many of them told Luce bluntly that he was making a dangerous error. He was not impervious to these criticisms, and at times he wavered in his commitment. "I still don't see any real deep conviction about the magazine among its sponsors," Billings noted several months into the planning. But Luce did not give up.[13]

He enlisted the *Life* reporter Ernest Havemann, an avid sports fan, to supervise the planning of what was tentatively named "Sport." But almost immediately the two men were at odds. In one of the first substantive meetings on the new magazine, Havemann proposed a magazine written mostly by Time Inc. staff, just like the company's other publications. Luce strongly disagreed and insisted that outside writers should be the principal source of stories. This was partly because he wanted serious writers, and not sports fans, to shape the magazine; he feared that full-time sports writers would simply replicate the language to which sports fans were accustomed—"a style of writing at once labyrinthine and rococo," one newspaper editor predicted. But Luce's preference for outside writers was also partly because of his belief that using freelancers would be less expensive than building a staff, and Luce hoped to produce this magazine relatively cheaply. A few weeks into the planning Havemann wrote a bombshell memo, distributed widely among those working on the new magazine, in which he announced that he now believed that the project "was wrong and impractical" and that "he wanted out right away as head of the experimental department." His undisclosed "research" had convinced him that there was no real market for a general magazine on sports. People interested in baseball would not want to read about golf. People who liked tennis would not want to read about football. The potential audience was too fragmented to create a large-enough base to support "Sport." In the absence of Luce (who was in Rome with Clare), Billings enlisted Larsen to help him find a way out of the impasse Havemann had created. Both men shared Havemann's skepticism, but they dared not give up until Luce himself did.[14]

Their solution was to enlist Sidney James, a *Life* editor with no particular background or knowledge of sports, to take over the project. He was a man of boundless energy and what Luce later described as vast "nerve and enthusiasm." James breezily rejected the knotty problems of what he called "semantics and theory" that had plagued the project in its first months: the debates over whether the magazine should be directed at a mass audience (1,000,000 circulation or more) or, as Larsen tentatively suggested, a relatively small audience (around 350,000) that would, like *The New Yorker*, attract the affluent and elite readership that advertisers valued; and the debates over whether the magazine should cover sports alone or make itself into a magazine devoted to a larger conception of leisure and entertainment. James decided instantly that he liked the idea of a "100% sports weekly, either mass or class," but he decided too that he should be elastic in what "sports" meant. More important, he started immediately to lay out pages and collect articles. He even coined what became one of the magazine's most important promotional slogans: "The wonderful world of sport!" In less than a month he was ready to show layouts and covers to Billings and Larsen, who became sudden converts to the project. "I was duly impressed and exuded [*sic*]," Billings wrote. "Considering he . . . got it all up in about three weeks, it seemed pretty wonderful."[15]

Luce returned from Italy a few weeks later. He looked at what James had produced with something close to incredulity. When *Life* was in development, there were many weeks, even months, of deep unhappiness with the project; Luce had not been entirely satisfied even when the first issue of *Life* went to press. But James, without even having produced a complete dummy, had made Luce an immediate and passionate supporter of the magazine. The best evidence of that was that Luce himself began to spend hours, even days, in the "experimental department" where the magazine was being developed. "Sometimes it seemed that we saw more of Luce than we did of our wives," one member of James's staff later said. "Some of us were assigned to escort him to sports events and explain the action and identify the players." Over long lunches, Billings recorded, Luce "got on the why and wherefore of such a magazine—what's its purpose? To make money? Sure. But here's a big segment of human activity, anti-intellectual if you will, which Luce proposes to report in the intelligent adult style, also because it's never been done before." Luce's most resonant and bewildering statement, at least to some of his colleagues, was, "I hope we can have a civilizing influence." All of this seemed familiar to the many editors and writers who had worked with Luce in creating *Fortune* and *Life*—his high sense of purpose, his search for meaning, his long philosophical speculations. But this time something was missing: the Lucean brilliance that had always justified his frustrating meanderings. Luce was no less enthusiastic than he had been in the past. But whether because the subject remained alien to him, or because he was too long removed from the work of magazine production, he was no longer the driving force behind the new project. "Luce looked at spreads—this in, this out," Billings described work on an early dummy. "But then he'd get stuck and go silent for five and ten minutes for lack of a good idea. His inspiration is running low and he is no longer the creative genius of magazine journalism." Luce gradually reduced the amount of time he spent with the magazine, which left James to continue on his pragmatic path. Uncharacteristically Luce declined to write the prospectus for the magazine. James wrote it instead, and Luce—without much editing or questioning—announced that "it's very good, all in the right direction."[16]

The movement from the conception of the new magazine in June

1953 to the final commitment to publish it in December, less than six months later, was, at least by Time Inc.'s deliberate standards, remarkably fast. Through the first half of 1954, James and his colleagues, with Luce's intermittent but gradually fading presence, created dummy after dummy, still trying to find the right balance between pictures and text, and between serious writing and the long tradition of colloquial sports reporting. But almost everyone working on the magazine believed that it was on the right track—that it had started out good and was getting steadily better. Throughout the development stage of the magazine, the working title was "Sport." There was, however, already a magazine using that name, which had offered to sell itself to Time Inc. for $250,000, more than Luce was willing to pay. In May, with the publication date approaching, Harry Phillips, the Time Inc. publisher of the as-yet unnamed magazine, ran into a friend in a restaurant who offered an alternative. The friend owned the title of a defunct magazine, *Sports Illustrated*. Everyone involved was immediately enthusiastic, and the company purchased the name for five thousand dollars.

There continued to be naysayers within the organization. Havemann was a consistent critic, always insisting that the project was doomed no matter how much work and creativity was poured into it. Journalists in other organizations looked at the dummies and were dismayed at what they considered the pretensions of the project, which they predicted would alienate sports fans. Advertisers were skeptical, convinced that only "mugs" would have enough interest in sports to buy the magazine. Others wondered how any sports magazine could sustain interest through the year, especially in winter months when sports activities contracted. Traditional sports journalism was in many ways incompatible with the style and culture of Time Inc. But that was both its burden and its great advantage. Luce had always expected his company's magazines to be pathbreaking, raising the bar of both quality and innovation. *Time* was the first "newsmagazine." *Fortune* had aspired to be the handsomest and most literate business magazine ever published, and in many ways it had achieved its goal. *Life* had set out to be the greatest picture magazine ever created, with the best photographers and the most lavish formats, and it too largely succeeded. From the start Luce expected *Sports Illustrated* to be equally unprecedented. It would not be a "fan" magazine, filled with gossip, adulation, and over-the-top language. It would not concentrate on any one area of sport. It would not be a quasi-trade magazine like *Sporting News*, which was, in effect, the official newspaper of the baseball industry. It would not compete with the daily newspaper coverage of sports. It would not focus too much on what had happened in the previous week. It would, rather, be a magazine compatible with the Time Inc. tradition, not the tradition of the sports world. It would have a handsome and dignified format. It would publish extraordinary pictures. It would look at sports not just as fun but, Luce wrote, as something that was "deeply inherent . . . in the human spirit." And it would bring what Time Inc. had brought to all its magazines: a set of opinions and prejudices that in fact worked much better for *Sports Illustrated* than it did for Luce's other publications.

The powerful advertising executive Leo Burnett asked Luce to explain the "raison d'être" of *Sports Illustrated*, which was struggling to generate interest from advertisers. Luce responded, at considerable length, with a rationale that bewildered most sports journalists. "We have the H-Bomb and we have SPORTS ILLUSTRATED," he wrote. Americans were living under a cloud of mortal danger, but they were also assuming "that peace is possible . . . that . . . you live and work as if it is, right now." Peace, he said, was defined in part by "leisure . . . the pursuit of happiness," and for most Americans that meant "something to do with Sport." Sports reflected "the hopes of the American people in a very simple human way—in a way universally understood and richly appreciated." But the magazine did not really aspire to universalism. *Sports Illustrated*, like all of Luce's magazines, wanted to attract educated and literate readers—people who could be attracted to sophisticated writing on "things beyond their own personal routine—the Miracle Mile, The Conquest of Everest, in Hunting and Fishing in their own domain and all over the world. . . . And so what we got excited about was creating a magazine for *those* people." In their dummies the *Sports Illustrated* editors cut out advertisements from *The New Yorker* (still the American magazine with the most affluent readership) to suggest something of the elevated tone of this new sports magazine.[17]

The first issue of *Sports Illustrated* was published on August 16, 1954, a few days after issues actually appeared on newsstands. It sold out quickly. And on the whole it was greeted warmly by the press and by its readers. On the cover was a dramatic picture of a nighttime baseball game in Milwaukee, with the Braves' Eddie Mathews in midswing, framed by a vast crowd in the steeply overhanging stadium. Inside the editors introduced themselves as "a happily recognizable member of the Time Inc. family." To make the connection even clearer, the opening page was framed by pictures of the inaugural issues of *Time*, *Fortune*, and *Life*:

Today the word "newsmagazine" is as generic as cellophane.
Today the name FORTUNE is the nationally accepted
    hallmark of business journalism.
Today LIFE's weekly millions of copies are an accepted fact of
    American life.
It is our hope and our promise that in some tomorrow you will
    no longer think of SPORTS ILLUSTRATED as Time Inc's
    newest baby, but as the accepted and essential weekly
    reporter of the Wonderful World of Sport.[18]

The first story in this first issue, "The Duel of the Four-Minute
Men," chronicled the classic rivalry between Roger Bannister and John
Landy, the first two men to run a four-minute mile. It also illustrated
how unconventional a sports magazine it intended to be. "The art of
running the mile consists, in essence, of reaching the threshold of
unconsciousness at the instant of breasting the tape," the *Sports Illustrated* writer Paul O'Neil began:

> It is not an easy process . . . for the body rebels against such ago-
> nizing usage and must be disciplined by the spirit and the
> mind. . . . Few events in sport offer so ultimate a test of human
> courage and human will and human ability to dare and endure
> for the simple sake of struggle.

This elegant and sophisticated language was a sign of what *Sports Illustrated* aspired to be, and often accomplished—a magazine that would
elevate the world of sports from being "just a game" to being a powerful
metaphor for the human condition.

The first issue ranged widely across the landscape of sports. It
reported the first ascent of K2, the second-highest mountain in the
world. It covered a dramatic prizefight. It offered a feature on baseball
cards (complete with instructions on how to blow bubble gum), a lavishly photographed story on fly-fishing, another on foxhunting, a primer
on poison ivy, and an essay on golf. But the most distinctive article in the
first issue (and also the most self-serving) was an essay on the world of
sport itself, with the trumpeting title, "The Golden Age Is Now." It was,
the staff writer Gerald Holland put it, "as if no other world existed. . . .
For world-wide interest, for widespread participation, for thrilling triumphs of the human spirit, this is the greatest sports era in history."[19]

Frank Deford, who began writing for *Sports Illustrated* in 1962 and became one of the magazine's star writers for decades, described his own first reaction to the first issues when he was an adolescent athlete and fan. "It was a struggle to cozy up to *Sports Illustrated*," he wrote years later:

> [The magazine] often seemed ashamed of sports—except those swell activities engaged in by dukes and earls. One year one SI writer wrote 36 stories on yachting, while the magazine left baseball, football and basketball languishing on the sideline. . . . And yet, and yet. . . . Always within each issue there was something absolutely, well, lovely, there were intriguing paintings, stunning photographs of game action, and stories that actually read like stories, clever and engaging and whole. . . . *Sports Illustrated* was creating something altogether new, which was respectable sports journalism.

In its first year the magazine's cover stories illustrated why it was so different from conventional sports reporting. Of the three most popular spectator sports, baseball received six covers, football three, and basketball only one. Horseracing, with seven covers, had the most. Mostly, the magazine ranged widely across its chosen fields: yachting, auto racing, bird-watching (twice), skiing, bullfighting, gymnastics, track and field, mountain climbing, ballooning, scuba diving, and dogs. And on February 21, 1955, the magazine ran a cover of a smiling young woman in an unrevealing swimsuit (part of a feature on sports fashion)—an augury of one of the magazine's most popular and sometimes controversial features of later decades. Little wonder that advertisers, and some readers, had a difficult time deciding what *Sports Illustrated* was, and who it was for. But little wonder too that many readers were dazzled by the range of its stories and the power of its photographs (which were laid out in formats very much like those in *Life*, not surprisingly since most of the founding editors had started there).[20]

Luce took particular pride in the quality of the writers he could attract to *Sports Illustrated*, including some who had never been willing to write for *Life* and *Fortune*. The revered *New Yorker* writer A. J. Liebling submitted an elegant essay on Stillman's Gymnasium in New York City, where many notable boxers were trained. Wallace Stegner wrote an elegy to Yosemite National Park. Budd Schulberg wrote a sympathetic story about an aging prizefighter who was finally making it big. John Steinbeck insisted he could not write for *Sports Illustrated* because "my interests are too scattered and too unorthodox." But he wrote a long letter on his eclectic interest in sports that the magazine published anyway. And William Faulkner wrote an extraordinary (and predictably unorthodox) account of the 1955 Kentucky Derby.[21]

Most articles in *Sports Illustrated* were written by less visible staff writers, but the richness of the prose remained one of the magazine's most distinctive features. Robert Creamer, for example, wrote a story on the magazine's second "Sportsman of the Year," the Brooklyn Dodgers pitcher Johnny Podres. The article set out not just to describe a great baseball achievement but also to reveal the universality of sport. It was as much about Podres's family of miners as about his achievement in pitching the Dodgers to victory over the Yankees in the 1955 World Series. The story profiled the grandfather, Barney, who "climbed out of the mines of czarist Russia and came to America," raised a family, went into the mines of the Adirondacks, and "now . . . sits in his weather-beaten house in the company village of Witherbee, N.Y. ailing from 'the silica,' the miner's disease, his great hands folded." It described the father, Joe, who also worked in the mines, but who, having benefited from improved working conditions, played semipro baseball on weekends for years because he had "more time that is his own." And then Johnny Podres, the son of this hardworking, inconspicuous family, "became the personification, the living realization of the forgotten ambitions of thousands and even millions of onlookers who had pitched curves against the sides of their own houses and evoked similar visions of glory, only to end up at the wheel of a truck or behind a desk in an office."[22]

Sports Illustrated was much like *Life* in the initial disparity between its popularity among its readers and its limited appeal to advertisers. Circulation exceeded five hundred thousand in every issue in 1954, rose to six hundred thousand the following year, and climbed steadily through most of its history (to more than three million a week in 2009). It quickly established itself as by far the most famous and influential sports magazine ever published in the United States. Advertising, however, was painfully slow to catch up—particularly in relation to the enormous costs of publishing the magazine, which far exceeded the original estimates. Luce's instinctive response to problems was to improve the editorial quality of his magazines, and there were constant reevaluations of both content and appearance. But he was also obliged to spend considerable time as well promoting the magazine and denying rumors that it might be shut down (something Luce never contemplated). Not until 1964, ten years after its first issue, did *Sports Illustrated* produce its first profit. By then, its identity was firmly established. Although its subjects were sports, the outdoors, and other forms of leisure, its readership was comparable to such general interest magazines as *Time* and *Life*. And for Luce, at least, it was a gratifying achievement. It signified his own sense of the extraordinary American success story of a nation of abundance, social unity, and the "pursuit of happiness"—a pursuit that he believed *Sports Illustrated* reflected.

As Luce neared his sixtieth birthday, all of his lifelong idiosyncrasies and habits grew, if anything, more pronounced. A friend who attended a dinner party with Luce in Paris in 1956 gave an account of his demeanor that mirrored descriptions of him from many other people: "Physically he does look like an old man—his head triangular, large high brow, bald on top with puffs of white hair at each side; heavy straight dark bushy eyebrows; blue eyes and plastic [-rimmed] glasses, narrow chin, a face concentrated, released occasionally into a rather elfish, quizzical expression." He was dressed expensively, but—as was usually the case—somewhat sloppily. He had, his chronicler noted, "a rambling, desultory manner of speaking on politics . . . it lacked magnetism though evidenced sincerity. . . . He often did not finish sentences or abandoned them with impatience and started over again." He was intimidatingly serious, without much humor, a difficult partner in conversation because "he does not let one escape with a frivolity or evasion." But he left no one unaware of his power, his status as a "great man."[23]

Other friends and colleagues, all of whom were fascinated by Luce, reveled in gossiping about this unusual man. High-ranking figures in Time Inc. devoted much—and often all—their time in serving his needs: arranging his travels, acting as intermediaries between him and Clare, buying the gifts for friends that Luce himself never remembered to get, and occasionally helping to facilitate his personal and romantic relationships. For someone who had managed his own life without help through much of his childhood and adolescence, he was often strangely helpless in managing his adulthood. Those who served him understood his preoccupation with ideas, projects, and missions, and his impatience with the quotidian affairs of life. They stepped in, often without his knowing it, to protect him from his own distractedness.[24]

Distraction was, in fact, among his most prominent characteristics (as his fragmented conversation suggested). He was often coldly silent around others, but he was also at times unstoppably garrulous, talking interminably about whatever was on his mind and rarely allowing others to interrupt his herky-jerky flow of words. He was inattentive to money, and in stores or restaurants often paid too little (which greatly embarrassed waiters and salesmen) or far too much. He was, and had been for years, fantastically rich, and it was not only the extravagant Clare who was determined to live in great luxury. When Luce traveled he almost always stayed in the largest suite in the most expensive hotel in whatever place he was visiting. But he did this as a mark of status, not really because he himself particularly enjoyed the elegance of his surroundings. Within hours of his arrival his suite was often in amazing disarray—with papers, books, clothes, and food scattered on tables, chairs, sofas, beds, and floors. Even in his own homes, in which he slept (as he had for years) apart from Clare, his bedroom in an otherwise lavishly decorated apartment or house was often almost monastically spartan.[25]

Like many famous and powerful people, Luce had many friends but few real friendships. Most of the people he encountered were intimidated by his presence, unable to interact with him as an equal. But Luce's relative friendlessness was also a product of his personality. He was brusque and impatient, uninterested in small talk or gossip, always pressing for serious conversations even with people who were in no mood for such intensity. Nor was he willing to reveal very much about himself to others. He once said that he did not have a very high regard for "feelings," that they were "secondary" to thought. "I actually don't think he let anyone—but anyone—know him," a longtime friend conceded after many years of conversation and correspondence. He was, she said, "the loneliest man I've ever known." Luce recognized the absence of intimacy in his life, and he tried to fill the void with a series of intense, if never wholly open, friendships with women. His affair with Jean Dalrymple in the late 1940s had been one such effort to achieve real intimacy, but the relationship did not last. He had a longer and more important friendship with a woman he met by chance in Switzerland in 1946.[26]

Mary Bancroft was an intelligent, witty, combative woman from a distinguished but broken family, who spent much of her life in failed relationships—two marriages that ended in divorce, and affairs with such celebrated figures as the psychiatrist Carl Jung and the future CIA director Allen Dulles. Unbeknownst to Luce and most others who knew her, she had also served as an effective American spy in Europe during World War II. She met Luce by chance in 1947 at a dinner for visiting publishers in Zurich, where she was then living. Bancroft was an avid Democrat and liberal, and when introduced to Luce, she said, "So there you are, Public Enemy Number One." ("I loathed 'Timese,' " she later explained, and "thought that reading *Time* was actually reading a form of advertising, rather than what I regarded as journalism.") But she was nevertheless fascinated by Luce, and only when learning of his likely presence had she agreed to come to the dinner. Luce was clearly intrigued by her as well. "Is that any way to talk to a man who invented the American century?" he flirtatiously asked that evening, and then insisted that she sit next to him at dinner. On "that very first evening," she recalled years later, "I know I felt that here at last was someone I could say anything to . . . and wouldn't be hurt in any way as a result." They met several times again before he returned to New York, and they sustained an intense intellectual and at times emotional relationship that lasted for more than thirteen years.[27]

Their friendship was not an easy one. During much of their relationship Bancroft was simultaneously involved in her affair with Dulles (who repeatedly asked her, "Have you turned your friendship with Henry Luce to any practical advantage yet?" and who frowned when she told him no). Bancroft and Luce communicated primarily through letters, and in them they bantered and sometimes fought—over issues of politics and over their own personal problems and crises. They disagreed furiously at times about public figures whom he admired and she loathed: Douglas MacArthur, Richard Nixon, and most of all Whittaker Chambers, whom Bancroft attacked almost obsessively in long, convoluted letters that Harry apparently chose not to answer (although his side of the correspondence has not survived except in a few fragments).* When they were actually together, which was not often at first since they were so frequently on opposite sides of the Atlantic, they met in restaurants or hotels (where Bancroft always insisted that Luce book a sitting room for their conversations). They had long conversations that were, on the whole, less searingly personal than their letters were. When Bancroft moved back to the United States, and eventually to New York, their meetings increased but remained intermittent.[28]

*Luce's contributions to their correspondence remained in Bancroft's possession into the 1970s, when she apparently lent them to the writer W. A. Swanberg, who was writing a biography of Luce at the time. Swanberg took notes from the letters, which survive in his papers at Columbia, but the original letters seem to have vanished. Elizabeth Bancroft may have destroyed them at some point, or directed Swanberg to do so, but there is no available evidence to support any theory of their disappearance.

It was never a sexual relationship. Luce was already involved with Jean Dalrymple when they met. After that relationship ended he carried on a series of other sexual affairs (most of them relatively casual and brief) while continuing his friendship with Bancroft. "I feel no physical attraction between us!" she wrote Luce in 1951. "Every single man with whom I have, or ever have had, a friendship has been, I know, attracted to me and I am convinced that you are not." But neither was their relationship a purely intellectual one. Luce wrote her with deep affection ("Bless you—and may you never die"; "à Dieu, dear heart"; "I am taking to the boat (via England) an immense treasure—your letters. . . . Some part of the boat trip . . . will be devoted to serious study of this course in . . . the wisdom of love.") Her letters to him, he told her, were "minor masterpieces," and he thanked her for being "a bringer of happiness without effort or price or art." He also taunted her at times: "I was . . . amused to find you lined up with the conventional goody-goodies. Mary Bancroft a part of the Eleanor Roosevelt claque—ha!" He once asked her "why you are so relaxed about communism" (and received no answer), and he reprimanded her for taking up the causes of "all my ill-wishers." And yet he reveled in her thoughts: "One thing you and I have in common is that we know the sheer wonder of human existence, the utter amazingness of it." And he wrote of her "spirit . . . so wonderfully compounded of the eager and the compassionate. . . . You see things wonderfully, and your heart beats like four giant motors."[29]

To Luce, Bancroft was an engaging, provocative sparring partner, and at times a warm and intimate friend. But the relationship looked different to her than it did to him. He wanted warmth and support, fused with intellectual excitement. She wanted more—including somehow the ability to "save" him. Most of all that meant saving him from Clare, who to Bancroft was a source of both fascination and loathing. "It is perfectly extraordinary," she wrote in 1957, "to see this man, who is so tough, so able, so powerful, absolutely shattered by that woman." She read obsessively about Clare, accumulated a large collection of newspaper and magazine clippings about her, and gossiped about her with the Time Inc. executives she came to know (most of whom disliked Clare as much as she did). She wrote to Luce more often than she wanted—she seemed unable to stop herself—urging him to end the marriage. "Harry told me that he didn't think anyone had any idea how destructive [Clare] was," she wrote in her diary. "How preoccupied with herself, how never a day goes by that he doesn't have to do some 'errand' for her." Her response to Harry's frequent complaints about the marriage was to try to persuade him that he did not understand Clare, that her threats and apparent dependence on him were attempts to keep her in the marriage, that she wanted to stay with him because of the wealth and visibility he provided her, not because she loved him. "She doesn't want to give this up and will fight like a tiger whenever it seems endangered," she argued. She wondered how Harry could "endure her innate vulgarity," how he failed to see that "she's a razor sharp knife." He was, she wrote, "absolutely insane if he for one second imagines that he is going to turn her into a wife or anything else except what she is. . . . It is beyond me to know why he thinks Clare is dependent on him." What was the "worst thing he could imagine happening,", she asked him once. Killing herself, he replied. "I told him I didn't think she would kill herself," but he should "even stop being afraid of that. If she was going to kill herself, he couldn't stop her."[30]

Although Bancroft insisted that her interest in Clare was for Harry's sake, not her own—that she wasn't trying to free him to love her—there were times when her motives were not so clear. Her feelings toward Harry were sometimes more intense than she let on, as a diary entry suggested when they were in Paris together in 1950. She came to drop off a letter at the Hotel Ritz, where he was staying. Rather than leave it with the desk, she went to his room and, noticing the door ajar, stood there watching him for a long time and "wondering as I stood before that door . . . why he even bothered with me at all. . . . And I decided then it had something to do with truth—that I would always tell him the truth." Several years later she wrote him that "I still love you very, very, very dearly—but I ain't in love with you any more." Some of Luce's friends and colleagues tried at times to find out whether Bancroft might marry him if he left his wife. "He's afraid to go to bed with me," she told Allen Grover. "If you order me to marry him—that I might be able to pull off someday. . . . But he's not going to bed with me." She was often exasperated with him for the same reason other people were. She bridled at the limits of their friendship, and the lack of explanation for it. "WHAT IS THERE ABOUT ME THAT YOU WISH YOU HAD?" she shouted in frustration in one of her letters. She was usually the driving force in their friendship, the one who wrote the most letters, the one who arranged most of their meetings (sometimes calling his office five or more times a day to try to schedule a dinner or a drink). She was frustrated by his reticence ("He just can't be simple and open and straight about what he means," she complained). But she never pushed him to reveal his secrets.

"I am in bad trouble—really bad trouble—inside myself, and you've got to help me," she wrote Harry in 1955, a point when her relationship with Luce had become more important to her than she had previously revealed. "I have *got* to demolish the overexaggerated idea of me and my perceptions. . . . I've been playing with dynamite and I want—by telling you all this—to take out the fuse. . . . It is a fact that I walk around in your unconscious." She reproached him for what she considered his aloofness. "We have a bank full of unused assets. You pay no attention. . . . But that account is overdrawn."[31]

The imbalance in the relationship—Luce's platonic and mostly passionless affection for Bancroft, her growing preoccupation with, and unrequited commitment to, him—gradually eroded their friendship. They continued to see each other, although less frequently after 1956. In 1959 he returned to her all the letters that had passed between them, which augured the break they both knew would come. She wrote him wistfully, "What a picture it all is, Harry—not only of our friendship—but of the times—our 'times.' " In 1960 they parted amicably for good. Bancroft, no longer with any illusions, told him that she had become interested in someone else. Luce was well ahead of her—already deep in what became one of the most important relationships of his life.[32]

"For four years," Allen Grover observed in 1957, Harry had "dodged the issue" of his marriage. He could see Clare in Rome, in an attractive and interesting setting, and could then escape to New York for however long he wished to be there. "But now she is home," Grover lamented, "he can't get away from her." What made Clare's presence so difficult for him was that Harry had his own new romance—not one of the many sexual flings that they both had frequently entered but a genuine love that he believed equaled, and perhaps surpassed, the few real passions of his earlier life.[33]

Luce had long been friendly with Lord Beaverbrook, the powerful and imposing press baron of England, who was also a significant British political figure (even though he was Canadian-born). Luce visited him periodically in London, in the English countryside, in New York, and in various Mediterranean resorts. For more than a decade he had seen but barely noticed Beaverbrook's young granddaughter, Jeanne Campbell, the child of Beaverbrook's daughter and the Duke of Argyll. Their marriage had dissolved not long after Jeanne was born, and both of her parents remarried. Jeanne followed neither of her parents and grew up in her grandfather's home. By the time she was in her late teens, after boarding school and a brief time studying acting, she was serving as her grandfather's secretary and assistant, and traveling with him wherever he went. Her relationship with him was stormy, largely because of what he considered her promiscuity, including a brief affair that especially infuriated Beaverbrook—with Oswald Mosley, who had been the leader of the British Union of Fascists (known as Blackshirts) before World War II. In 1956, when she was twenty-seven, she left her grandfather's home to try life on her own.[34]

With the help of her grandfather's money and influence, she found an apartment in New York and a clerical job at Time Inc. During a vacation on the French Riviera with her grandfather, she encountered Luce—who was visiting Beaverbrook—for the first time as an adult. Jeanne was by now a tall, striking woman with untamed curly hair. Luce, thirty-one years her senior, was secretly attracted to her immediately, as he confided to Mary Bancroft on his return to New York. A few weeks later he walked into Jeanne's office in the Time-Life Building and invited her to dinner. He invited her again the next night—both times alone in Luce's apartment. (Clare was still in Rome.) Campbell later recalled the strange magnetism of this "shy, distant, gruff" man, whom to her surprise she began to find both "handsome and magnetic." She was nervous at first, not sure why Luce was interested in her.[35]

But Harry was relentless, for a time sending her so many roses that she worried her apartment looked like a funeral home; writing letters that, at first, Jeanne was too scared to read or answer; inviting her again and again to dinner, during which they had increasingly intimate conversations. It was not long before he told her he was in love with her, and not long after that they began a sexual relationship. Luce arranged a better job for her at Time Inc., as a researcher for *Life*. But Jeanne's affair with Harry did not remain a secret for long within the company. Finding her position in the company awkward, she finally quit. She had never much liked the job in any case, and, as she herself later admitted, "wasn't very good at it."[36]

It was, for the most part, a secret relationship. They almost always met in Jeanne's apartment. Most of the time she would make dinner. (Having grown up with chefs and servants, she had to teach herself how to cook. "I became pretty good at it, especially French cuisine," she remembered later.) In many settings Luce was oblivious to what he ate. But with Jeanne, she recalled, he "loved food, liked to talk about it and hear how it was prepared." It was not just food he liked to talk about. Among her many attractions to Luce was her eagerness to listen as he talked "about everything—his family, his travels, his marriage, his ideas." Jeanne was less voluble than he was, but she had a talent that eluded most people Luce knew: She made him laugh. (Many people knew Harry for years and never heard laughter from him.)

Jeanne was restless sometimes, eager to go out to a restaurant or a movie. But Harry—who had shown no inhibitions about being seen in public with Jean Dalrymple—was now extremely cautious. Every now and then they would venture out together briefly, but Jeanne remembered how uncomfortable he was, "always worried about who would see him with me." Having been through a traumatic, emotional conflict with Clare a decade earlier, he was perhaps more aware of the potential costs of this new relationship. But slowly an understanding began to grow between them that this was not just an affair but a long-term, perhaps permanent, union. Luce stopped sending roses and began buying her jewelry, furs, and other expensive gifts. Jeanne told her grandfather about Harry. (She later gave radically conflicting accounts of his reaction, from "he gave us his blessing" to "he was outraged.") It was, she said, as if he "knew that we would eventually marry." Luce himself, she recalled, spoke frequently of "when you are my wife." Still, it was not an easy relationship. It was defined—as almost all his relationships were—by his desires and his needs. Jeanne rebelled at times and could be tart and wounding. She was impatient with his caution and "promises which weren't fulfilled" of ending his marriage. During a trip they took together to Paris (where he felt more comfortable being in public with her), she replied to a complaint about what Luce considered her provocative wardrobe, "Why not? I'm your mistress after all." But despite her occasional pressure on him to make a decision, Harry continued with his dual life, never allowing himself to be put in a position that would require him to choose.[37]

At the same time that Harry was building his relationship with Jeanne, he was—willingly or not—rebuilding his relationship with Clare. In 1957 they began thinking about selling their Connecticut house in Ridgefield, which they had largely abandoned during Clare's absence in Rome and Harry's secret romantic life in New York. (In fact they kept it for another five years, after an ill-fated attempt to turn it into a research center for the study of the history of Time Inc.) But at the same time they bought a sprawling modern house in Phoenix, near the famous Arizona Biltmore. Their new home had great expanses of glass overlooking the hotel's golf course. It was part of an enclave of homes of enormously wealthy people, many of them retired. Clare, restless and for the first time in many years without an active professional career, began spending more and more time there—with long breaks while she pursued her newest passion, scuba diving. Harry, in the meantime, saw Clare's life in Phoenix as an opportunity for him comparable to her life in Rome. He could insulate himself from the conflict between his relationships—free to see Jeanne in New York, able to spend time with Clare far away from her competition. Despite his frequent complaints about Clare—to Mary Bancroft, to Jeanne, even to some of his professional colleagues—he was not ready to leave her. They seemed to the many visitors they invited to their Arizona home to be happier together than they had been for some time.[38]

Early in 1958, en route to Phoenix from New York, a friend of Clare's who was flying in the same plane as Harry passed him in the aisle and was shocked by how ashen and slack faced he looked. He shook off her efforts to help and seemed quickly to recover. But a few days later he developed what he thought was a bad cold and spent much of the day in bed. The next morning, February 5, he awoke late. Clare brought him some soup and found him sitting up in bed. "I'm dying," he told her. A houseguest watched him being carried to the ambulance. "I can still remember being outside in the garden when the stretcher came out carrying Harry," she recalled later, "looking so ill, so unlike the powerful Henry Robinson Luce the whole world knew." As he was wheeled into the emergency room, he joked darkly to Clare, "Life goes to a party."[39]

Luce had suffered a heart attack, serious but not fatal. He spent three weeks in the hospital, refused most visitors other than family, and made sure that news of his illness did not become public, fearful that the truth would destabilize Time Inc.'s stock price. Clare and the family retainers told the press that Harry was recovering from pneumonia. With the help of rest and anticoagulant drugs (which he took for the rest of his life), he gradually regained his strength and passed the time of his recovery playing Scrabble and especially bridge, with the same ferocious intensity that he and Clare had always competed. Luce, characteristically, invited the famous bridge expert Charles Goren to join their games (an ordeal for Goren because Harry, terrified of making mistakes, was a very slow player). Goren's reward was his picture on the cover of *Time* later that year.[40]

The period of Luce's illness coincided with a moment of great anxiety in the United States. Only a few months before Luce's heart attack, the

Soviet Union had launched its first satellite, *Sputnik I*, followed by a series of other successful satellite launches through the first months of 1958. To many Americans, watching the stumbling, halting path of America's own space program, the Soviet achievement appeared to be a sign of Russia's growing power and America's relative decline. The "Sputnik crisis," as it was widely named, was followed by an almost equally traumatic event for many Americans: the 1959 visit of Soviet premier Nikita Khrushchev, whose truculent manner and swaggering personality was a chilling reminder of the stakes in the Cold War. *Time*, for example, wrote of Khrushchev as "the embodiment of the elemental challenge" of Soviet Communism, the "naked drive for world power no less sustained than that of the late Joseph Stalin." Six months later, in May 1960, an American U-2 spy plane was shot down over the Soviet Union, its pilot—Francis Gary Powers—captured by the Russians and put on display before the world, a planned Eisenhower-Khrushchev summit conference in Paris summarily and humiliatingly canceled by the Kremlin only days before it was to convene.[41]

For more than two years beginning in the late 1950s, there were widespread efforts to determine why America appeared to be "falling behind." In fact the United States, far from falling behind the Soviet Union, was still greatly surpassing it in wealth, science and technology, and military strength. The precipitants of the anxiety—*Sputnik*, Khrushchev's visit, the U-2—were, in reality, symbolic and ephemeral events, or, in the case of the "space race," the reflection of an inadequate investment in rocketry by the Eisenhower administration. But in the eyes of many Americans, Soviet achievements were by definition evidence of American failure; and the blame, many critics claimed, lay less with the government than with an insufficient commitment to the future of the nation by ordinary citizens. The "success" of the Soviet Union, Walter Lippmann wrote in late 1959, was a result of its ability to have created "a purposeful society in which all the main energies of the people are directed and dedicated to its purposes." Americans, in contrast, "do not have great purposes which they are united in wanting to achieve.... We talk about ourselves these days as if we were a completed society, one which has achieved its purposes and has no further great business to transact." Americans were becoming too soft and materialistic, other critics argued. What the country needed, they insisted, was a sense of "national purpose," a bold and widely shared vision of what the United States should be. Few people embraced this view more enthusiastically than Luce, who now joined and, as always, hoped to lead the earnest search for the country's new goals.[42]

Trying to change the world was nothing new for Luce. Like other sons and daughters of missionaries, he never stopped thinking about how to make the nation live up to the Providential righteousness of America's destiny (a vision embedded in generations of American Presbyterian history). For years he had tried to define and promote America's mission in his magazines and speeches (most notably, in his famous "American Century" essay) and in his occasional intrusions into politics. But Luce also exhorted (and often funded) others to study important national and international issues and provide answers to the endless questions with which he wrestled. He was a great champion of committees and commissions and believed that putting smart and eminent people together (he was drawn especially to what he called "philosophers and thinkers") was always a good way to solve a problem. In 1946 he recruited Robert Maynard Hutchins, president of the University of Chicago, to form a Commission on Freedom of the Press. Its report disappointed him ("philosophically uninteresting") but did not deter his interest in future inquiries. He eagerly joined (and helped to finance) the Fund for the Republic, another group of "eminent thinkers" gathered to answer big questions: "What is a truly free society? How can such a society be maintained?" He immersed himself in the work of the Rockefeller Brothers Study Group, which gathered "experts" to consider American defense policy. He helped organize an international Conference on Industrial Development in 1957, which focused on the relationship between economic growth and free labor. Luce pushed the group to consider "the responsibility of my country—America's responsibility for the economic well-being of the world."[43]

He was active as well in the Committee for Cultural Freedom, which proposed a "Free World Academy" (never created) to train people to "defend freedom." (Norman Thomas, head of the American Socialist Party and one of the founders of the committee, resigned when Luce began to exercise leadership of the group; Luce, he believed, was turning the inquiry into Cold War propaganda. His dismay would likely have been even greater had he known that the committee was secretly funded by the CIA, a fact probably unknown to Luce as well.) Despite Thomas's ill will, Luce developed an interest in socialism, noted its similarities to some of his own beliefs, and proposed an inquiry into "the notes of warning, still sounded by Thomas—specifically warnings against complacency over current U.S. prosperity." He unsuccessfully invited Senator Hubert Humphrey of Minnesota to form a committee to define what Humphrey liked to call "quantitative liberalism," which Luce said contained "both much meaning and a lot of befuddlement." Luce was often rightly accused of bias and dogmatism, but he was also an intellectual omnivore, who devoured ideas from many sources and who sought out "interesting thinkers" on issue after issue.[44]

The growing interest in a "national purpose" was a natural cause for Luce to embrace. He asked Max Ways, now *Time*'s London bureau chief and a man Luce considered a "serious thinker," to return to New York in 1958 to evaluate the magazines' role in this new mission. Ways went further and wrote a book of his own, *Beyond Survival*, arguing for a more robust national commitment to the great goals the United States must embrace. Luce wrote an introduction to it calling for "the government and people of the United States to arrive at some convictions . . . about what they are doing in the world." Luce had, he said, come to realize that the "most commonly shared opinion" in the nation was that the United States "lacks a clear sense of purpose in world activities."[45]

Ways's book, published in 1959, encouraged Luce to go further. He began summoning meetings in the Time-Life Building to discuss "an idea for bringing into sharper focus the current ground swell of interest in the National Purpose" and taking the lead in launching a "national conversation." He invited philosophers, historians, sociologists, theologians, and many others to attend lunches, dinners, and daylong meetings. He considered creating a "*Life* contest" for "uncovering big thoughts from humble minds." And he charged his own staff, and many others, to come up with " 'original' statements on new basic principles." Those principles might be few—"two, or three, or four," Luce told his somewhat puzzled staff—"but certainly principles we must stand for and must be involved in our judgment—and our judgment in turn, we hope, working always on knowledge and more knowledge and understanding of what goes on in this extraordinary world." The search for a national purpose, he said, would be an " 'adventure' on a colossal scale." It would be "dangerous," a "formidable task," for which the American people must be "nerved." That could be achieved only by strong leadership— not just from political figures but also intellectual leaders, like Luce himself and like the big thinkers and influential men who were his usual companions in his search for "answers." Americans, he complained, "had tried to escape from leadership. . . . Here we are at the beginning of a really possible golden age of western culture, and you still want to believe that tending to wealth alone will give culture and a decent standard of living to all men on earth."[46]

As the clamor for a definition of "national purpose" grew in Eisenhower's last years in office, the president attracted increasing criticism for what seemed his own inadequate embrace of the challenge. In response, early in 1960 he summoned a President's Commission on National Goals that he charged with sounding "a call for greatness to a resolute people." Its report, issued in November shortly after the 1960 presidential election and titled *Goals for Americans*, was a pale restatement of long-standing Cold War convictions: that Americans should "preserve and enlarge our own liberties, to meet a deadly menace, and to extend the area of freedom through the world." Americans should make democracy in the United States "more effective" and should make individual lives "freer and more rewarding." The public response was tepid, and at times scornful. It was, the historian Stephen Graubard wrote, a "dreary piece" with no real substance. Even *Life*, which seldom criticized Eisenhower, noted its "generally indifferent and partly hostile press."[47]

By early 1960 Luce had settled on a plan of his own that was in many ways strikingly similar to Eisenhower's. He too would assemble a group of "big thinkers," just as Eisenhower had tried to do. And he would commission a series of "big essays" on the national purpose to be published in *Life* (and copublished by the *New York Times*) over several months. The idea had emerged from a series of private meetings Luce had arranged with "brainy people" such as Dean Rusk, soon to be secretary of state, and James Conant, former president of Harvard. Their conclusion was "to get six or seven men of light and leading to state positively what the 'national purpose' of the U.S. is or ought to be." Here, Luce deviated sharply from Eisenhower. He did not attempt to create a consensual report, which he predicted would be as bland and uninteresting as the president's. But essays by individuals, he predicted, would lead to "various ways by which many thousands of people may participate in the discussion." The "six or seven" essayists soon grew to ten (all men), and they were indeed distinguished thinkers and leaders drawn from what was by then known as the establishment: John K. Jessup, chief editorial writer for *Life* and the overseer of the project; Adlai Stevenson, two-time Democratic candidate for president; Archibald MacLeish, poet, playwright, and former Luce employee; David Sarnoff, founder and chairman of NBC; Billy Graham, the most famous evangelist in America; John Gardner, philanthropist and educational leader; Clinton Rossiter, eminent political scientist; Albert Wohlstetter, project director at the Rand Corporation; James Reston, *New York Times* editorial writer; and the columnist Walter Lippmann.[48]

"More than anything else," Luce wrote in his foreword to the book that followed the magazine and newspaper publication of the essays, "the people of America are asking for a clear sense of National Purpose.... From all over the land, there is evidence that this is what Americans are worrying about." The ten earnest essays that emerged from Luce's "National Purpose" project were far more interesting than the Eisenhower-commissioned study of the same subject, if only because they were by individual authors whose views were not always the same.

Not surprisingly the most common definition of a "national purpose" in the Luce-inspired essays was "freedom"—freedom as defined by the Declaration of Independence ("the pursuit of Happiness") and freedom as defined by the past century of American experience ("the right of men to choose their own ideas and pursuits, to be free from the arbitrary intervention of governments, to 'do what they like with their own' "). The "National Purpose" writers struggled to find a more robust and communal vision of freedom, something that would not only ensure individual happiness but would also enlist the broad public behind urgent national goals. Some called for a greater sense of shared morality, based in the founding documents of the Republic or in religious faith. "We must recapture our moral strength and our faith in God," Billy Graham wrote. Others called for greater "discipline," "hard work," "seriousness," and "sacrifice." But what would such individual commitments mean? One answer was practical: paying higher taxes to fund the Cold War or to meet urgent social needs. Another was moral energy. To some of the writers there was something unattractively self-indulgent about rampant consumerism, or what Archibald MacLeish described as "the flatulence and fat of an overfed people whose children prepare at the milk-shake counter for coronary occlusions in middle age." The people, as much as the government, needed a far more serious commitment to "large goals." To Clinton Rossiter the great challenge was "the steadily widening gap between the richness of our private lives and the poverty of our public services," an idea likely inspired by the economist John Kenneth Galbraith's popular 1958 book, *The Affluent Society*.

Running through almost all the essays, however, was the question that had inspired the entire National Purpose project in the first place: Was America "winning" the Cold War? Few writers were as blunt as David Sarnoff, whose vision of a national purpose was "a Program for a Political Offensive Against World Communism." But almost all shared at least some part of Sarnoff's fearful vision. "For the first time in American experience," Walter Lippmann wrote, "we are confronted with a rival power which denies the theory and the practice of our society, and has forced upon us a competition for the leadership of the world." Stevenson called for "recovering the public image of a great America" and for the "certain knowledge all round the world" that challenging the allure of Communism "and nothing less had been for years the public policy of the United States." MacLeish urged an expansion of America's confrontation with Communism from Europe to Africa, Latin America, and Asia. "The most important implication of our great prosperity," Albert Wohlstetter argued, "is that we can afford larger efforts . . . for protecting the political independence and self-development of the non-communist world."

Only James Reston seriously challenged the premises of the National Purpose project. The solution to the nation's problems, he insisted, did not lie in the character or behavior of the people. "Most of the great political crises of the American past," he wrote, "have been resolved by the will power or obstinacy of their leaders." Americans had accepted the sacrifices their government had asked: high taxation, military conscription, policing the world. "These are not the acts of a slack and decadent people. There is nothing in the record of free peoples to compare with it."[49]

Judged by its impact on its own time, the National Purpose project would have to be considered a success. The essays had a broad readership, in *Life*, in the *New York Times*, and in the subsequent book. They attracted much comment and considerable critical praise. The National Education Association, the Brookings Institution, and dozens of other organizations embraced the project and helped disseminate it. The book was circulated widely in schools and universities and remained a prominent and respected text into at least the mid-1960s. After the 1960 political conventions, both candidates—Nixon and Kennedy—contributed essays to the project, which, although too late for inclusion in the book, were published in *Life* and other venues. But it would be hard to argue that the project achieved its ostensible purpose as "a summons, of some urgency, to national debate." Nor have the essays survived as texts important to later generations. Taken together they were more confirming than alarming—thoughtful and intelligent statements of a broadly accepted set of conventional assumptions about American life at a particular moment. But for Luce, at least, they served his purpose: challenging what he had come to consider the complacency of his age, helping to push others to think more boldly about, if not a national "purpose," at least a national agenda.[50]

Luce's own agenda was changing too. His personal loyalty to Eisenhower remained unaltered, and neither he nor his magazines ever expressed any significant disillusionment with what many critics considered the president's flaccid leadership. But by 1960 Luce was clearly envisioning a more dynamic future than the Eisenhower administration had ever pursued. He was quietly breaking with the policies of the 1950s while remaining supportive of the president himself.

Luce differed with Eisenhower perhaps most notably on the issue of race. Eisenhower was a reluctant and halfhearted supporter of civil rights for African Americans, convinced that the law was an inadequate tool for producing racial justice and that only a change in the "hearts of men" (by which he meant white people) would lead to true equality, which to him was a relatively long-term goal. Luce, on the other hand, had been an outspoken supporter of civil rights for decades—beginning with *Time*'s attacks on lynching in the South in the 1920s and 1930s, and continuing with *Life*'s growing effort to portray African–American life with sensitivity and respect in the 1940s and 1950s. For a 1938 photographic essay, "Negroes," *Life* commissioned dramatic pictures by some of the magazine's best photographers, pictures that challenged stereotypes of "the bale-heaving stevedore . . . or the crapshooter." Instead, *Life* announced, "the white man will . . . be surprised at the achievements of the Negro in America." Five years later Luce circulated a memo to his staff stating that "TIME is unshakably committed to a pro-Civil Rights policy and pro-square deal policy for Negroes as for every kind of American." He was particularly pleased by the gratitude he received from the Harlem community for *Life*'s 1949 story, "Life Goes to a Ball in Harlem."[51]

By the late 1950s Luce's views—and those of his magazines—had evolved into active support for desegregation, to the distress of the recently retired Billings, now living in South Carolina, who was much less sympathetic to the cause of civil rights. "It seems to me," Luce replied curtly to Billings's dismay, that "we have done a pretty good job on this most difficult of U.S. questions." Luce applauded the 1954 *Brown* decision; and in 1956, at his urging, *Life* ran a series of articles on African-American life that provided a tough and at times harrowing picture of the poverty and injustice facing black men and women. In 1957, when federal courts demanded that Central High School in Little Rock, Arkansas, admit its first black students, the attempts to enforce the ruling produced such violence that Eisenhower finally had no choice but to send federal troops into the city to restore calm. Luce personally oversaw an ominous cover photograph in *Life* of paratroopers in Little Rock, accompanied by a harsh editorial that questioned Eisenhower's commitment to his own action. There was, *Life* declared, "room for doubt as to whether [Eisenhower] himself believes in the law he is enforcing" and had "resisted all public and private cries for drastic action." The president's reluctant and legalistic explanation for intervention in the crisis created an "inference that the president equates the Fourteenth Amendment with the Eighteenth (Prohibition), a disagreeable thing which has to be done even though it may be unwise." What the president appeared not to recognize, the editorial claimed, was the great progress African Americans had made on their own since the passage of the Fourteenth Amendment. They now had every right to expect "a living and progressive law, adjusting itself to changed realities, [which] must now include desegregation as part of [their] citizenship." *Time* simultaneously ran a cover story on Little Rock with harrowing accounts of the "racists" and "goons" who were helping create violence. In the meantime, at a meeting with his editors, Luce took note of the many criticisms *Time* and *Life* were receiving from the South—including a not-insignificant number of canceled subscriptions. He said that the magazines should keep after the story and that they should do it "big and good." In response Edward Thompson, *Life*'s managing editor, began an ambitious effort to examine racial discrimination in the North. Over the next five years the resources devoted to covering the civil rights movement steadily grew. Reporters, photographers, and stringers were occasionally beaten and otherwise injured, as were journalists from the many other organizations working in the South. *Life* began commissioning articles from prominent African Americans—among them the black-power advocate Stokely Carmichael and the great if controversial scholar W. E. B. DuBois. Luce was occasionally distressed by what he considered the extremism of some civil rights activists, and he was not even always wholly admiring of Martin Luther King, Jr. But he almost always supported his more liberal editors as they pressed harder and harder against what Thompson called the "great moral issue of our time."[52]

Luce's commitment to the civil rights movement was, like his engagement with the "National Purpose" project, a sign of his increasing engagement with the liberal activism that was coming to be embodied by the image and rhetoric of John F. Kennedy. And it came as something of a surprise to many readers of his magazines, and many of his own friends, that Luce was an admirer, if not necessarily a supporter, of the young senator. Luce had urged his editors to put Kennedy on the cover of *Time* in 1957 as he began his ascent. The story his editors wrote was as gushing as anything the magazine had written since Wendell Willkie:

[Kennedy] is an authentic war hero and a Pulitzer-prizewinning author (for his best-selling *Profiles in Courage*). He is an athlete (during World War II his swimming skill saved his life and those of his PT-boat mates); yet his intellectual qualifications are such that his photographer wife Jacqueline remarks, in a symbolic manner of speaking: "If I were drawing him, I'd draw a tiny body and an enormous head." Kennedy is recognized as the Senate library's best customer, reads six to eight books a week, mostly on American history. No stem-winding orator ("Those guys who can make the rafters ring with hokum, well, I guess that's O.K., but it keeps me from being an effective political speaker"), Kennedy instead imparts a remarkable quality of shy, sensemaking sincerity. He is certainly the only member of the U.S. Congress who could—as he did—make a speech with his shirttail hanging out and get gallery ahs instead of aws.[53]

This was not the first evidence of Luce's admiration for Kennedy. In 1940 Luce had written an introduction to *Why England Slept*, a book drawn from Kennedy's recently completed senior thesis at Harvard in which he traced the failure of British leadership in the late 1930s to avert what became World War II. Joseph Kennedy, the future president's father and in 1940 the American ambassador to Great Britain, was a friendly acquaintance of Luce's, and it was he who had proposed that Luce write the introduction. Luce had asked to see the manuscript. He later recalled that "I was very impressed by it. I was impressed by the scholarly work." In the introduction itself Luce wrote: "I cannot recall a single man of my college generation who could have written such an *adult* book on such a vitally important subject during his Senior year at college.... If John Kennedy is characteristic of the younger generation—and I believe he is—many of us would be happy to have the destinies of this Republic handed over to his generation at once."[54]

By 1960 Luce was in something of a quandary. In every election since at least 1940, he had been an impassioned supporter of the Republican candidate for president, or a passionate opponent of the Democratic candidate, or both. But the Kennedy-Nixon race was a clear exception. Luce was certainly not opposed to Nixon. He entertained the Nixons at his home in Phoenix in 1958 and in his New York apartment in 1959. He wrote fan letters to the vice president, praising him for various speeches and articles that he claimed to have admired. And in the summer of 1960 Luce praised Nixon's acceptance speech at the Republican convention, beginning his letter with: "In a few short months it will be 'Dear Mr. President,' so we hope and pray." But Luce was clearly also attracted to Kennedy. He sent flowers and notes to the ailing senator during his periodic hospitalizations in the mid-1950s. The two men had occasional lunches together in Washington in 1959 and early 1960, and they carried on an intermittent but mutually admiring correspondence. Kennedy's visit to the Time-Life Building in August 1960 was a notable event in the company's history. Many candidates had paid visits to the Time-Life headquarters over the years, but none produced so remarkable a response. Inside the building, employees lined the hallways as he passed; outside, large throngs crowded the streets waiting for a glimpse of the candidate (whom Luce uncharacteristically escorted to the door and into the crowd). Like many people in 1960, Luce was impressed by Kennedy's glamour, sophistication, poise, and ability to engage with intellectual issues. He was particularly impressed with Kennedy's voracious reading, and once expressed astonishment that the candidate, in the midst of a campaign, had read a new biography of McKinley that Luce had also just finished. (Charming and impressing smart people was one of Kennedy's most notable talents; Nixon had few such skills.) Luce was also attracted by Kennedy's well-educated view of American foreign policy and his strong commitment to anti-Communism and the Cold War—a stance that Luce sometimes considered stronger than Nixon's. (Kennedy's seeming toughness was particularly important to Luce because he had never forgotten, or fully forgiven, what he considered Joseph Kennedy's weakness in giving up on England in 1940.)[55]

Luce's magazines swung back and forth in their enthusiasms, reflecting not only the long-standing political divisions among the editorial staffs, but also Luce's own uncertainty about whom he preferred. After the Democratic convention *Life* praised the party's platform for "urging us all to look forward again—instead of backward, upward or around." In the past it had gone without saying that the Luce magazines would endorse the Republican candidate. But in 1960 Luce was bombarded with questions about whether or not he would do so again—and for a time he was uncertain of his answer. When the *New York Times* wrote in early August that Luce had expressed a "personal preference" for Nixon, Luce denied the story the next day. The *Wall Street Journal* reported that Luce was toying with "the surprising notion of backing Kennedy." Luce did little to dampen the speculation, replying in *Life* that "we have applauded both candidates for saying that world policy—and U. S. purpose—makes up the paramount issue." The sudden illness of Otto

Fuerbringer, *Time*'s managing editor and a staunch Republican, led in late summer to the temporary editorship of Thomas Griffith, a Democrat who was committed to rigorously fair and nonpartisan coverage (a significant departure from earlier *Time* election years). That made it easier for the magazine to reflect Luce's own admiration for Kennedy as well as for Nixon.[56]

On July 15, 1960, the night of Kennedy's acceptance speech in Los Angeles, Luce was at home in New York when Joseph Kennedy called and asked to stop by to see him.* Luce eagerly agreed. Kennedy arrived at about seven o'clock at Luce's Waldorf apartment and joined Luce and his son Hank for a lobster dinner. Over coffee they began a conversation about the magazines' attitude toward Jack. Luce later recalled saying that "of course Jack will have to be left of center," since that was what the Democratic Party required. "We won't hold that against him." But, he added, if Jack were to show "any signs of weakness . . . toward the anti-Communist cause, or . . . any weakness in defending and advancing the cause of the free world, why then we'll certainly be against him." Joe replied, "Well, there's no chance of that; you know that." When they gathered in front of the television to watch Kennedy's speech, the candidate's father interrupted frequently, often with obscene remarks about politicians who had not supported his son. He was particularly vitriolic in his characterization of Adlai Stevenson. Luce remembered the acceptance speech without great enthusiasm, but with "no particular criticisms of it." (He kept his lukewarm response to himself.) When Joe Kennedy got up to leave, he stopped at the door and said, "I want to thank you for all that you've done for Jack." Luce was "a little taken aback" by the comment and wondered "did we do too much" since he had never openly supported Jack Kennedy. But they were both aware that the Luce publications had treated Kennedy well—much better than they had treated any Democrat in many decades. And Luce could not disguise his fascination with John Kennedy, whom—shortly after his dinner with Joe—he privately described as "one of America's great success stories . . . a stirring prospect . . . a tough fellow, but educated, with a good and even beautiful mind." Several years later Luce recalled the evening with Joe: "It was a memorable moment in my life."[57]

Luce did, in fact, consider endorsing Kennedy that fall. There were long conversations with his senior staff, whose opinions were divided;

---

*Joseph Kennedy had left Los Angeles early to avoid allowing his own controversial reputation to draw attention away from his son.

and there were some editors, occasionally including Luce, who believed that Kennedy was in fact the more reliable leader in confronting the Communist threat. Luce wrote a private memo about a month before the election in which he said that "a lot of good" would come from a Kennedy victory. "It will shake up the country and perhaps bring on a great new burst of the old American dynamism." But in the end, and perhaps inevitably, *Life* endorsed Nixon, although in a guarded way that seemed designed to reduce the impact on Kennedy. Luce was never fully satisfied that Nixon's positions on foreign policy were as strong as Kennedy's, and he suggested as much in the late and somewhat tepid *Life* endorsement of Nixon days before the election. It praised Nixon's domestic policy but was silent on his foreign-policy positions.

Having encouraged Billy Graham to write a piece for *Life* about his admiration for Nixon, Luce ultimately pulled the story after talking with Kennedy about it. (Graham was relieved, fearful that publication would have politicized him.) When Kennedy finally won the close presidential election, Luce wrote Nixon expressing deep disappointment at his defeat. But he wrote Kennedy as well, saying that "we didn't find it difficult to find respectful and complimentary things to say about the President-elect." And soon after, he wrote to a friend: "We find it difficult to do anything but cheer the 35th president of the U. S. . . . At the moment there is a kind of good excitement in the air—reminding some of us old fellows of our boyhood hero, T. R."[58]

Luce's enthusiasm for Kennedy did not diminish once the election was over. He and Clare traveled to Washington for the inauguration, sat in the president's box for the swearing in, and attended a private dinner that night at which the new president was a guest. When Kennedy's *Why England Slept* was republished in 1961, Luce wrote an update to his 1940 introduction:

> Imagine that as a young man in college you wrote a book of judgment on the behavior of a contemporary empire. . . . Imagine that 20 years later when you are still young, you become President of the United States at a time when America faces grim possibilities of destruction and surrender. . . . Imagine, then, that you re-read the book you wrote in college and find that you would not be embarrassed by having it exposed again; this surely would be an extraordinary experience. Perhaps nothing like it ever happened before in the lives of all the leaders of men.[59]

Luce's relationship with Kennedy was never as intimate or rewarding as his friendship with Eisenhower, who had been a regular correspondent and who included Luce frequently in the president's famous
"stag dinners" and other events. Kennedy was more aloof and, at times,
less conciliatory. His tough White House staff, sometimes known as the
"Irish mafia" (or what Luce once called "the whole blinking Clan—
including selected O'Learys, O'Briens, etc."), could react furiously and
even vindictively if they did not like the Luce magazines' coverage of the
president, as they frequently did not. Kennedy himself could be
waspishly critical as well. Luce in turn was not always happy with
Kennedy's policies. He opposed the president's tentative efforts to
improve relations with China (efforts that produced no significant
results). He was dismayed by the ill-begotten Bay of Pigs invasion of
Cuba in 1961, not because of the decision to invade but because it so
conspicuously failed. Gen. Maxwell Taylor, former Army Chief of Staff
and soon to be "military representative" to President Kennedy, came to
New York with a seventeen-point rebuttal to the *Time* account of the
Bay of Pigs; Luce disputed all his criticisms, and Taylor left without
rancor. But complaints from the White House did not stop, in part
because Kennedy himself was, as Luce put it, a "regular and careful"
reader of *Time*, convinced of its influence and importance, and thus
highly sensitive to even minor criticisms. Luce was particularly irritated
by a long critical analysis of *Time*'s coverage of Kennedy from Theodore Sorensen, the president's special assistant. It was, Luce said, as if
"some schoolboy . . . had written an analysis for the White House
which was cited by Mr. Sorensen." And he was annoyed as well by the
barbed and slightly condescending congratulatory message that the
president sent to the fortieth anniversary dinner of *Time* in the spring of
1963 (which, to Luce's great disappointment, Kennedy failed to attend).
After kind words about Luce the president's message turned to the magazine itself:

> *Time* . . . has instructed, entertained, confused, and infuriated its
> readers for nearly half a century. . . . I am bound to think that
> *Time* sometimes does its best to contract the political horizons
> of its audience. . . . I hope I am not wrong in occasionally
> detecting these days in *Time* those more mature qualities appro-
> priate to an institution entering its forties.[60]

Luce shrugged off his disputes with the Kennedy White House and
remained, on the whole, an admirer of the President, who—despite his

occasional testiness—continued to cultivate Luce through letters and occasional invitations to the White House. Kennedy, Luce believed, echoed his own long-standing commitment to a more energetic pursuit of America's mission and purpose. Kennedy, like Luce, wanted a more robust and flexible military capacity that would give the United States the ability to pursue its goals without relying on nuclear weapons. And Kennedy, like Luce, called constantly for "action," for "getting the country moving again," for setting great goals. Luce loved Kennedy's space program, as its avid coverage in *Life* made clear. He greatly admired the president's Berlin Wall speech, with its ringing denunciation of Communism. (He was less pleased by the conciliatory speech at American University a few weeks earlier, in which Kennedy called for better relations with the Soviet Union.) Luce was especially impressed by Kennedy's handling of the Cuban missile crisis (perhaps in part because of Kennedy's flattering summons to Luce, in the midst of the crisis, to come to the White House and offer advice, a meeting that was probably also designed to influence *Time*'s coverage). Kennedy asked Luce if he supported an invasion—the favored course for most of the president's military advisers, and at the time apparently the president's own inclination. Luce supported a blockade instead, which was the option Kennedy ultimately chose. The successful resolution of the crisis was, Luce later wrote, "a high point" in American foreign policy."[61]

Luce was leading an editorial meeting in a private dining room in the Time-Life Building on November 22, 1963, when he heard the news of the assassination of President Kennedy. The editors dispersed immediately, leaving Luce behind, slumped over the table, his head in his hands. But he soon joined the epic effort to cover this extraordinary and terrible event—which included *Life*'s discovery, purchase, and partial publication of the famous Abraham Zapruder film, the home movie shot by a bystander in Dallas that became the most important recording of the assassination and the basis of myriad conspiracy theories. There was a vigorous debate over whether *Time* should violate its consistent policy of never putting a dead person on the cover of the magazine. Luce ordered a picture of Lyndon Johnson instead, a decision that produced much criticism. Equally controversial was Luce's insistence that the publisher's letter in the front of *Time* take note of Kennedy's "special feeling" for the magazine, a decision that also angered some readers, one of whom accused the magazine of deciding "to eulogize itself rather than the late President." But on the whole the *Time* and *Life* coverage of the assassination was extraordinarily thorough, visually powerful, and sensationally popular—so much so that the company quickly sold out the post-assassination issues even after almost doubling the print run. A few weeks later *Life* issued a "special memorial edition" that combined two issues of *Life* coverage into one massive magazine (with no advertising). It sold nearly three million copies.[62]

On the day after Thanksgiving, Jacqueline Kennedy called Theodore White—Luce's old protégé, sometime antagonist, and once-again Time Inc. correspondent—and asked him to come see her in the Kennedy family compound in Hyannisport. White drove up from New York through a storm in a rented limousine (frantic because he was leaving behind his aging mother who had just suffered a heart attack) and sat late into the night listening to Mrs. Kennedy's concerns about how her husband would be remembered. She worried that "history was something that bitter old men wrote." She wanted to get her own story out first. After a long and emotional description of her experience in Dallas, she told White that she could not stop thinking about "this line from a musical comedy." At night in the White House, she said, she and her husband sometimes lay in bed listening to the melancholy Lerner and Loew song "Camelot." The line she remembered was "almost an obsession," she said: "Don't let it be forgot, that once there was a spot, for one brief shining moment that was known as Camelot." And she gave special emphasis to the sentence, "There will never be another Camelot again." White dictated a story to his *Life* editor from the Kennedys' kitchen telephone at 2:00 a.m., and the "Camelot" theme became an iconic one that suffuses the public memory of John Kennedy to this day.[63]

Luce was not an emotional man, and ordinarily he would have recoiled from the treacly sentiments that ran through the "Camelot" interview in *Life*. But he was not immune to the deep sense of loss that permeated American public culture in the weeks after Kennedy's death. His view of Kennedy was, in fact, mostly consistent with the image that Theodore White's article had unleashed. Luce's relationship with Kennedy had been intermittent and not always warm; but he found himself nevertheless deeply shaken by the death of what he called "this memorable figure, this young man . . . [this] great and courteous person" whom he had known and admired for more than twenty years. "For my part," he said later, "it was a great privilege to know him for himself and to have had the privilege of knowing him when he was President of the United States. . . . There is no question that he made a tremendous contribution to the intangible attitude of the American people—toward government, toward life, toward the things that mattered."[64]

XIV

Letting Go

Luce's professional life in the late 1950s and early 1960s remained one of ambition, purpose, and commitment. But for a time, his private life was in turmoil. In late summer 1959 Clare discovered Harry's affair with Jeanne Campbell, after overhearing a telephone conversation between them and then asking friends, who were surprised she did not already know. Not long after she confronted him, Harry asked her for a divorce. For almost a year they battled over their future—a period of misery and anxiety for them both.

Harry wanted a divorce only partly because of his infatuation with Jeanne. As he looked ahead to the remainder of his life, he saw a bleak picture. His marriage, he had concluded, was irreparably broken. For years now he and Clare had lived mostly separately, with occasional reconciliations and periods of chaste companionship, among them the aberrantly pleasant years in Rome. He complained of the emptiness of his life—that he had no real friends other than his colleagues at Time Inc., that he was "not getting enough out of life," a problem he attributed to a "regrettable and even serious flaw in my make-up." There was, he wrote, "literally nobody in this big town [New York] who ever asks me to a friendly dinner or slightly social dinner, not even my good Time Inc. friends ask me.... What I get asked to is banquets or group-meetings." The affair with Jeanne was, in short, an effort to bring some companionship and warmth into an otherwise lonely life.[1]

Clare was at least equally unhappy, deeply resentful of Harry's neglect and what she considered his betrayal; but she was also fearful of life without him. Both Harry and Clare had conducted multiple affairs during their years of sexual estrangement. There was a tacit understanding between them that they would ignore these relationships as long as they were casual and brief. But as the Jean Dalrymple episode had made clear years before, Clare became almost obsessively frightened and angry when there was a real threat to their marriage. Harry's request for a divorce therefore threw her into a psychological tailspin that made both their lives much more difficult. In many ways the battle over Jeanne Campbell raised the same issues that the battle over Jean Dalrymple had raised more than a decade before.

Clare, suddenly removed from the political world, had been working on a novel through much of 1959 in an effort to relaunch her now long-deferred literary career. She was, she later claimed, making good progress on the book, working mostly in Caribbean resorts and in Phoenix. But when Harry proposed divorce, her work on the novel abruptly stopped, never to be resumed. Instead Clare spent the better part of a year writing almost obsessively about the travails of her marriage, in dozens of letters to Harry (many of them unsent); in multiple and redundant accounts of conversations about their troubles (some of them based on real conversations and some of them fictional ones in which Clare tried to inhabit Harry's mind and imagine his own view of their relationship); and in long private memos, filling hundreds of pages, in which she poured out her fears, hopes, resentments and, at times, self-loathing. Her titles suggest the range of her emotions: "A Memorandum on Bitterness," " 'Go in Peace,' or 'Stay in Peace,' " "Suspicious of HRL's Motives," "A Questionnaire on Love and Warmth," "What Happens to Me Without You," "The Situation." Sometimes she reproached herself for her treatment of Harry: "I have too long deeply wounded your masculine pride and your self esteem," she wrote shortly after learning about the affair with Jeanne. "The wounds continue raw and bleeding." But she blamed Harry as well: "You also have wounded, quite as badly, my femininity." Late one night a few weeks later, very drunk, Harry poured out a self-pitying story of what he now described as his many years of agony and humiliation, in boyhood "and well into manhood," a story that, Clare perceptively concluded, "formed in him the habits of extreme sensitivity to criticism, humorlessness, and lack of self confidence, which in succes, have turned him into an aggressive, overly assertive and talkative man who *will* not be interrupted."* On another night she poured out her own self-loathing: "I was absolutely overcome by rage . . . rage with myself. . . . I suddenly *did* realize it—that out of cowardice, funk, despair, I had ruined my own life. For twenty years I had lived alone—alone as a woman—in a cage whose door was always, at all times, open." She was obsessed at times with money and possessions, even though she had always had significant resources of her own from her first marriage and her plays. "I do not own one acre or brick of any of our 'homes,' " she lamented. "The paintings [Harry] gave me for birthdays and Christmases . . . were not *really* gifts to me" but the property of Harry's estate.[2]

Despite all the anger, all the regrets, and all the recriminations, both Harry and Clare once again found it difficult to imagine ending their marriage. When Clare said she would not fight the divorce, Harry backed away from his initial demand and said he would do nothing unless Clare "made the divorce decision mutual." Eight months later, after "endless" discussions of their plight, Clare announced what she called a " 'unilateral decision' that I would not consent to a divorce 'now or ever.' " Harry—having now visited Jeanne in Paris to discuss the future of their relationship—returned to New York to tell Clare that, despite her ultimatum, he would continue the affair with Jeanne and that he "would still marry her if I were in a position to do so." In the meantime he proposed a "legal separation" to allow him to live with Jeanne, while Clare remained officially (and financially) his wife. But a few days later, when she acquiesced and offered to allow the divorce, Harry once again changed his mind and insisted that he wanted the marriage to continue. His reasons, he said, were the immorality of divorce, "our long involvement: 25 years of marriage," and "prudential" reasons: "my family is against it, business associates, the church, my age," and the "damage to my public image and public responsibilities."[3]

The struggle over their marriage was never private. As with almost every aspect of their lives during their long marriage, both Harry and Clare relied on others to smooth their way and facilitate their needs, even in the midst of emotional chaos. At the center of this group of retainers was Harry's sister Beth—as always his confidante and now his intermediary between both Clare and Jeanne. Beth was always working in what she believed were Harry's best interests (even if Harry himself sometimes disagreed with her). Her husband, Maurice "Tex" Moore, a

---

*It was eerily similar to a lament about his blighted life that he had written to Lila decades earlier.

partner in one of New York's leading law firms and the chairman of the Board of Trustees of Columbia University, protected Harry's legal and financial interests. Roswell Gilpatric, a lawyer in Tex Moore's firm (and soon to be deputy secretary of defense in the Kennedy administration) was assigned at one point to mediate their marital dispute. People whom Clare called "the Timeincers" also intruded occasionally: Allen Grover, Roy Larsen, C. D. Jackson. Clare considered all of them her enemies. ("Any other vitally interested parties in this line up, which is about 10-to-1 against you and me?" she asked Harry caustically.)[4]

There were, of course, other participants as well—most prominently the press, which began publishing speculations about Harry's affair with Jeanne in 1959. The rumors attracted little attention until early 1960, when the story appeared in a column by the nationally syndicated gossip columnist Leonard Lyons. Harry, Lyons said, had decided to marry Jeanne. Clare publicly brushed the rumors aside and joked that "if I divorced Harry, and married the Beaver [Lord Beaverbrook], I would become Harry's grandmother." Harry denied the rumors too, but damningly. "Clare and I are here together," he responded to a press inquiry when they were both in Ridgefield. "It is all very premature to say the least." The early signs of public scandal almost certainly helped them both to begin reconsidering divorce.[5]

After months of fruitless discussions, Harry proposed the use of a "qualified witness" to help them mediate their differences. Their choice was John Courtney Murray, a Jesuit priest and eminent theologian with whom Harry and, more important, Clare had spent much time together. Murray had been helpful to Clare during her conversion to Catholicism and had become a frequent fixture in the Luces' many houses—seeming, some friends said, "more at home there than the Luces were." He had been a spiritual and moral adviser to both of them. During the marital crisis he worked steadily to avert a divorce, to the frequent irritation of both parties. But Father Murray was the only person with whom Harry and Clare felt comfortable sharing their troubles. Both of them wrote lengthy accounts for Murray of their feelings, and they used him frequently to mediate conversations that might otherwise have become unbearable. Clare poured out her misery in many letters to Murray: "All of the experiences of my life, public and private, have convinced me we live in an age fraught with violence, hatred, futility, greed, lust—in which 'the great' are often uglier and meaner than the small . . . an apocalyptic age—the age of the aborted American Century—a century reflected in the very confusions, weaknesses, greeds of its author." Harry was less melodramatic but equally frank. "I have resigned myself to a 'marriage of convenience' and have given up on love."[6]

In the midst of this agony, yet another group of companions and facilitators entered their lives: Gerald Heard, a writer, self-proclaimed philosopher, and sometime mystic, and his secretary and partner Michael Barrie. Clare had met them originally during her short stay in Hollywood in the 1940s, and they had been frequent visitors to Clare since then in Connecticut and more recently in Phoenix. Heard, who liked to call himself a "historian of consciousness and its evolution," had been experimenting with various hallucinogens and other drugs that would, he hoped, help break down the barriers that separated people from their deepest feelings and instincts—a goal that predicted some of the popular literature of the later 1960s, among them Norman O. Brown's *Love's Body* and Theodore Roszak's *The Making of a Counter Culture*. In 1960 Heard was particularly interested in LSD, which some psychiatrists were beginning to consider a possibly useful method of treatment.[7]

Clare had first tried LSD when Heard introduced her to it in 1958 in Connecticut, around the time of her withdrawal from the ambassadorship to Brazil. LSD was, she later wrote, responsible for "the serenity with which I faced that ordeal" and also for the later "burst of creative vitality" that took her to the Caribbean to start her new novel. Heard and Barrie came to Phoenix again the next year, in the midst of the Luces' marital crisis. They were accompanied by Dr. Sidney Cohen, one of the most prominent psychiatrists studying LSD. Clare began taking frequent doses under the supervision of Cohen, who kept careful records of her behavior and her statements during her periods of hallucination. (Correspondence from the time also suggests that she became infatuated with him, although there is little evidence that the feelings were reciprocated. "I flirted with you," she later wrote, but "you had not the slightest wish to flirt back.") Once again she found in LSD a refuge from her misery and anxiety.[8]

Perhaps hoping that LSD would provide Harry with the same "serenity" that it had given her, Clare persuaded him to join the experiment during one of his trips to Phoenix. Dr. Cohen kept a meticulous record of Harry's reactions, which were something of a letdown for both the doctor and the "patient." After taking "100 Gamma of LSD" at 11:45, Harry sat at his desk, lit a cigarette, and began reading Lionel Trilling's biography of Matthew Arnold, interrupting himself occasionally to discuss the relationship between Arnold and Cardinal Newman with Gerald Heard. About an hour and a half later Dr. Cohen recorded the following exchange: "CBL enters. She puts flowers near HRL and asks if he sees color vividly. HRL: 'No.' Reads aloud from Trilling re the religious life." Half an hour later Harry no longer felt "in command of myself" and said he wished "this stage would pass." But he was alert enough to begin a new conversation: "Talks about visit to Oxford last summer.... Talks about Lord Halifax.... Talks of Chartres Cathedral." At 2:50 p.m., more than three hours after he had taken the drug, Harry finally noticed a change in his response to his surroundings. As Cohen recorded Luce's reactions: "Now things are getting sharper, ... I'm beginning to see what Clare said. The aliveness.... This perception is fantastic. Oh yes, quite wonderful. Not the visionary gleam, but quite wonderful." At 3:50, Cohen noted, Luce "goes off to think for a while." Luce never tried LSD again, although he retained an interest in hallucinogenics. When asked later about his reactions, he said he had "not particularly enjoyed it" but had found it "bio-chemically speaking interesting."[9]

Years later, when her experimentation with LSD became public, Clare insisted that her use of the hallucinogen had "saved our marriage." Nothing in her voluminous contemporary writings about her marital problems suggests that this was true. But the marriage did survive.

In the spring of 1960 Harry promised to break off his affair with Jeanne, although in fact he continued it intermittently for almost another year, until Jeanne herself ended it in favor of a relationship with—and ultimately a brief marriage to—Norman Mailer. (Clare speculated that one reason for his breakup with Jeanne was that a prostate operation in 1960 had affected his sexual performance, but by then the affair was already unraveling.) Once the decision was made to continue the marriage, however, recriminations continued for a time. Harry was intermittently bitter about the diminished prospect of what he liked to call a "free life." "Okay," he said with unhappy resignation during one of their many conversations about their reconciliation. "As usual, you get what you want, but I have to take the Castor Oil." During another tense discussion he said, "I can't win against you." Most of all he wearied of the "incessant scenes and quarrels with Clare." It "had to stop," he told Father Murray. "I can't get any work done." Clare—emotionally exhausted—continued to express distrust. She was, she said, nothing but a "resident housekeeper" to Harry. He had chosen to continue "a marriage with me, because for a variety of prudential reasons, having nothing to do with me, it seems best on the whole for you." In July 1960 she wrote melodramatically in her diary, "I am of this morning, faced with the total disintegration of my personality and the final, fatal collapse of my ego. . . . I don't know *who* I am in relation to anybody in this world." Harry, clearly, was not the only cause of her misery. After years of professional and social prominence, she was no longer a major celebrity. She was mourning not only the problems of her marriage (problems she had once compartmentalized and largely ignored) but also the end of her dazzling public life. That was in part what made the survival of her marriage so important to her. Being married to Harry was, she feared, the only distinction she would have in the years to come. And so she fought ever harder to keep the marriage going and to force Harry to commit to it.

Clare imposed conditions on her reconciliation. Harry would have to end the affair with Jeanne, "unequivocally and finally," to "tell Beth and Tex . . . in my presence that the affair is over for good and that you desire to stay married to me," that he "escort me personally through the new TIME and LIFE Building as though you were pleased and proud to show it to me," and that he "write me a letter telling me . . . that you hope we can make a good life together for the rest of our lives." "Why is that letter so important?" Harry asked when Clare complained that he had delayed writing it. It would, she said, make clear that "he was in it 'for keeps' "[10]

Little by little, as Clare put it, "the terrible storm . . . subsided." Harry wrote, without anger, that "we should go on for the rest of our lives together . . . after all the needless amount of words, quarrels, arguments. . . . The decision to do so should be by a simple yes from me and a simple yes from you." They had no illusions about a great romance. They would, Harry said, "live from day to day and from season to season," and enjoy "Christian fellowship" and "affectionate companionship." By the fall of 1960, while Clare was spending several weeks in Hawaii, he was able to write to her with something of the warmth that had once been a more common part of their marriage. "Darling, I do miss you so, but it seems so useless to cry about that—except just to keep telling you that there is still a dream of real companionship I cling to despite all the ravages of war and time. We *will* have our Peace in our time because we are making it in love." And Clare, too, gradually found her way to a calm affection. "Your voice on the telephone this morning, so full of warmth and strength and lovingness . . . made me very happy. . . . I seem to have some sort of vision—very akin to LSD really!—that all is as it *must* be, 'everything composes.'" Years later, making notes while looking back at her diaries on what she called their time of "sturm und drang," Clare wrote:

> Well, we didn't . . . get a divorce. Partly perhaps because we both saw it was not the right thing morally, spiritually, ethically—or even practically. But also a little—a wonderful little—because we both saw no real chance for happiness or growth for the *other* in divorce. If love is a concern for the well being of the other, there was that much love—when the smoke of battle blew away anyway.[11]

Sometime in 1960 Clare wrote a long, introspective memorandum, addressed to Harry but evidently never delivered to him, about what she called "diminishments." To Clare the diminishments were her loss of a serious career, her loss with age of much of her beauty, her loss of sexual fulfillment, and most of all—in this time of despair—her "loss of hope." Harry was never one to record his own feelings honestly. He rarely spoke openly about his own "diminishments," but he was certainly aware of them. Although he was only in his early sixties, he looked like a much older man—the result of many years of intense work, travel, and anxiety, and of a lifetime of heavy smoking. He was suffering from heart and prostate troubles. Perhaps most of all he was aware of his failure to grasp his last chance for true romantic love, a failure that he himself had decided to absorb.

Nor did he often have the comfort of family. His reconciliation with Clare was successful as far as it went. They learned to avoid rancor and to create a familiar and usually comfortable companionship, but they continued to spend much of their time apart. He remained close to Beth Moore, but he saw little of his other siblings (his sister Emmavail, who still lived in Philadelphia and who seldom saw Harry; and his much younger brother, Sheldon, who—after a brief career in Time Inc.—moved on to new business efforts far from New York). Harry had somewhat more contact with his two sons, Henry III (Hank) and Peter. He was closer to Hank, who aspired to follow in his father's journalistic footsteps. Hank worked for a time at the *Cleveland News* and later joined Time Inc., where he spent much of his professional life although never rising to a position of great prominence. Harry expressed pride in Hank's achievements, but also worried that he was too dependent on his father's support. (Hank later became the longtime president of the

Henry Luce Foundation, which Harry established before his death and to which he left the largest portion of his estate.) After attending MIT Peter joined the air force and then moved to the West to work in aviation. He saw his father relatively infrequently. Harry wrote letters occasionally to both his sons, letters that were meant to be affectionate but that revealed little intimacy. They sometimes read like essays on the state of the world. ("A wonderful old philosopher, Alfred North Whitehead, . . . was one of the first to point out that in the twentieth century, for the first time in human history, conditions of human life changed radically in *one* generation," he wrote Peter on his twenty-first birthday.) Harry ensured that both his sons were financially secure, and in the late 1950s and 1960s he began to spend more time with Hank in particular. But after decades of only occasional attention to his sons, whom he had left behind in 1935 to marry Clare when both boys were under ten, the relationship always remained somewhat distant. Harry did develop a special interest in his grandchildren, and particularly in Christopher (known as Kit), Hank's son. Kit traveled with his grandfather occasionally, visited him and Clare periodically in Phoenix and Connecticut, and saw him more often than most of Harry's other relatives did. Kit had a relationship with Harry that few others did—one of uncomplicated affection.[12]

As often in times of stress and uncertainty, Harry turned to religion. He was a regular congregant of the Madison Avenue Presbyterian Church when he was in New York, and developed a close relationship with his pastor, David H. C. Read. Beginning in the late 1950s he spent an inordinate amount of time helping to plan and raise funds for a National Presbyterian Church, which would be built in Washington and would help Presbyterianism to have a more prominent role in the nation's capital. Eisenhower, himself a convert to Presbyterianism, supported the effort, which made Luce all the more eager to help. After many false starts and frustrations the new church finally opened—two years after Luce's death. During those same years Luce funded and built a Presbyterian chapel at a university in Taiwan, in memory of his father.[13]

But despite Luce's institutional loyalty to the Presbyterian Church, his private religious life was in fact restless, complicated, and at times despairing. The simple unquestioned faith of his youth was long gone, replaced by a much more intellectual, and almost academic, interest in religion. He began searching for what he called a "New Religion, the search for God, without Christianity," although he could never articulate what such a religion would mean, except to describe it as part of "the great liberal tradition." He was fascinated by Christianity in the same way he was fascinated by politics, business, culture, and many other areas of life. He spurred his editors to pay more attention to religion as a significant force in society, worth examining, and his magazines did cover religion more consistently than most other major press organizations. He developed intellectual relationships with major theologians: Reinhold Niebuhr, Henry Sloane Coffin, Henry Van Dusen, Paul Tillich, and many others; and he argued with them, in letters and in print, not usually about matters of theology but about the connection between faith and politics. At the same time he developed a strong curiosity about evangelical Christianity. In part that was because he considered its followers primarily "less well-educated" people and hoped he might learn something about their faith. Characteristically he reached out to the most prominent (and respectable) figure in the evangelical community, Billy Graham, whom he often invited to write for *Life*, and with whom he met occasionally. They maintained a regular correspondence. Luce was attracted to Graham in part because of his "old-fashioned religion" and his "extremely conservative politics," which he saw as an antidote to what he called the "agnostic materialism" of the New Deal and the British Labour Party.[14]

In the early 1950s, after Clare's conversion, he had developed a strong interest in the Catholic Church and in 1952 even signed a "Declaration of Intent," in which he promised to convert to Catholicism if John Courtney Murray were ever assigned to "an area of China including Shantung Province." The unlikelihood of that event suggests that he was not entirely serious, but his flirtation with—and defense of—the Catholic Church continued for years, as his long relationship with Murray made clear.[15]

Mostly, however, Luce wrestled not with denominationalism but with the meaning of faith—and the difficulties of sustaining it. "We urgently need a 'restatement' of Christian faith," he wrote, "in terms of the new kind of universe which science has been revealing and which even the common man apprehends as reality." How, he asked, could science and religion coexist? Luce read widely on this subject, discussed it with Hocking and other religiously oriented philosophers, and came to agree with the liberal French theologian-scientist Pierre Lecomte du Noüy, who wrote that "men are 'Collaborators with God in charge of evolution.'" In conversations with Murray he became interested in "natural law and/or the moral law," which he saw as a primarily Catholic concept that was disappearing from Protestantism. "In a sense," he wrote approvingly, Murray "worships the goddess of reason." At the same time he began to express contempt for what he called the "shallowly pietistic attitudes of much of 'official' Protestantism," and for the difficulty Protestants had in accepting the tough military challenges of the Cold War. What Luce called "the eggheads" of the Protestant and Catholic communities often derided his attempts to popularize theology in his magazines. But Luce rarely responded to criticisms of his religious views, in part because he himself was constantly questioning them—so seriously that at times he confessed that he was suffering from "a loss of faith or belief in God." As early as 1955 he worried that "theology is failing us badly . . . [and] has not got anywhere near to real coping with the real *new* human situation." In 1959 he went even further: "What a man says to God is less important than that he should say something, an actual person to an Actual Person. . . . The doubt tyrannizing over all doubts of our time is whether any dialogue is possible."[16]

As during earlier personal crises, Luce turned to his company and his magazines as a refuge from the storms raging around him. But by now the distance between him and his editors had grown so great that he began considering other, noneditorial plans for the company.

By the early 1960s Time Inc. had grown considerably even from its formidable size in the early 1950s. *Sports Illustrated* was expanding rapidly. Its staff had grown significantly. As a result the company's headquarters in one of the original Rockefeller Center buildings had become inadequate. *Sports Illustrated* and *Fortune* were already mainly housed in other buildings, a development Luce disliked because it made it harder for him to stay in touch with his editors. Even the staffs of *Time* and *Life* were feeling crowded. And so a search began for new quarters.[17]

Luce had begun thinking about moving as early as 1945, and in 1951 he dabbled with the idea of moving the entire company to a twenty-seven-acre plot in Westchester County. Plans were secretly under way for a "$5,000,000 'campus type' building." The move, Billings noted, was "partly dictated by the threat of A-bomb destruction in mid-Manhattan," a reflection of the anxiety that the Korean War and the deterioration of American-Soviet relations had created. But a more important consideration for Luce was "the decentralization trend of the times." *Reader's Digest*, the only magazine with a larger circulation than *Life*, had been very successful on a large suburban campus, and Luce was briefly attracted to that example. But the staff rebelled. Billings noted that "The country is no place . . . to do a good high-pressure news job. You vegetate. You end up smoking a pipe." When Eero Saarinen, the renowned architect Luce had chosen for the project, reported that the site was inappropriate for its proposed purpose, the idea quietly died.[18]

Luce then, implausibly, began to look for a large area in Manhattan where he could build something like a campus in the city, with parks and a swimming pool and tennis courts and with low buildings scattered across the site. "The *ideal* headquarters," he argued, "cannot be in any skyscraper slab." He identified a space near the United Nations building on the East Side of Manhattan, but the plan proved to be much too expensive. Once again Luce began to look outside New York, to a small town in Pennsylvania midway between Philadelphia and Wilmington. Billings called it a "fool idea," and the opposition of the staff killed this plan as well.[19]

In the end Luce decided to move the company only a block away from its current site—an area just west of Sixth Avenue, between Fiftieth and Fifty-first Streets where Rockefeller Center, Inc., had decided to expand. He reached an agreement with the Rockefellers to jointly build and own the building. Although he was disappointed that his more visionary proposals had failed, he was resigned to erecting a conventional office building and was pleased that it would at least meet the need for additional space. Despite his distaste for large "office slabs," he insisted that the new headquarters should be functional and efficient and not excessively expensive. He conceded that what the company "was *not* buying was a building of which we can be especially proud." Eventually Luce did express pride in the new headquarters, but his first reaction was closer to the truth. The building, designed by the modernist architect Wallace Harrison, was large, efficient, and undistinguished. The company moved into it in 1960.[20]

By the time of the company's transition into the new building, Luce was planning a transition of his own. Early in 1959, only months after his recovery from his heart attack, Luce invited Hedley Donovan, then the managing editor of *Fortune*, to his home and told him that he was considering retirement. As Donovan later recalled the conversation: "He said in a somewhat apologetic way that he had to bring up something 'rather personal.' He wondered if I would be interested, 'not right away, in a few years or so,' in being the next Editor-in-Chief of Time Incorporated." Donovan was a tall, handsome, sandy-haired Minnesotan, a Rhodes scholar, and a mildly conservative man who shared most of Luce's political views but little of his intensity. He was a nineteen-year veteran of Time Inc., and was forty-five at the time of their meeting. There was no announcement of the transition, and Donovan was left uncertain when or even whether it would occur, perhaps with good reason. (Shortly after his heart attack Luce had told his longtime assistant that "I'll never retire. I'll die at my desk.") But not long after the meeting with Donovan, Luce announced a sweeping reorganization of the senior staff, followed several months later with Donovan's elevation to editorial director of all the magazines, the position Billings had occupied in his last years with the company until his retirement in 1955. (Had Billings not left, Luce once confided to Mary Bancroft, he, not Donovan, would have been Luce's successor—something he had never told Billings, who retired still believing that Luce had little interest in or respect for him.)[21]

Although Luce made no public announcement of his retirement until almost five years after he told Donovan of his plans, he began preparing for his departure well before he left. One way he did so was to organize a lavish celebration of *Time*'s (and thus of Time Inc.'s) fortieth anniversary in 1963. (Clare asked him why a fortieth anniversary party and not a fiftieth; he answered that he did not expect to "be around" ten years later.) After months of preparation that cost several hundred thousand dollars and occupied the time of dozens of Time Inc. employees for weeks, eighteen hundred people gathered in the Waldorf-Astoria ballroom. The *New York Times* wittily (and slightly acidly) described the audience as "tycoons, pundits, cinemactresses and political sachems." It was indeed a great event for people watching. Among the guests were Lyndon Johnson, Walter Reuther, John Dos Passos, Douglas MacArthur, Gene Tunney, Jack Dempsey, Joe Louis, Gina Lollobrigida, Rosalind Russell, Bob Hope, Henry Ford, Norman Thomas, Henry Wallace, Everett Dirksen, Adlai Stevenson, Francis Cardinal Spellman, Dean Rusk, and Paul Tillich—who gave a keynote address that proved a bit too serious for some members of the audience. Most of the guests were people who had appeared on the roughly two thousand covers of *Time* since 1923. Luce explained the event, and the guest list, as a reflection of *Time*'s history, which "has told its story in terms of people, whereas 40 or 50 years ago the journalistic emphasis was on social or economic forces."[22]

The glamorous celebration of the fortieth anniversary coincided with the first signs of serious erosion of Time Inc.'s profitability. *Life*, the great revenue driver of the company for two decades, was in trouble. In

1959 the magazine recorded its first deficit, the beginning of a long and rarely uninterrupted financial deterioriation. The problem was not circulation, which was approaching seven million, its all-time high. The problem was advertising. *Life* charged the highest advertising rates of any magazine of its kind, and many advertisers now found that they could reach larger audiences for not much more money by promoting their products on television. *Life* showed profits in only a few years after 1959. Luce watched this decline with concern but also, as always, with confidence that the answer lay in raising the quality of *Life*'s contents. Once again he set out to write a new prospectus for the magazine that he had helped create in 1936 and that had rewarded him so richly. "So what would be the purpose of *Life* in the Sixties?" he asked. "My answer: *Life* is and shall be designed to be the magazine of national purpose. In his first statement as President-Elect, Jack Kennedy called for 'A Supreme National effort.' Amen." More specifically Luce listed the issues he thought *Life* should address: "win the Cold War," "create a better America," help to "bring about a great humane civilization." The production of *Life* would be "magazine-making at its highest and most skill-demanding level."[23]

The declining profitability of *Life* after 1959 put pressure on the company to find new generators of revenue. *Time* continued to prosper, but it could not alone sustain the aspirations of the company. *Fortune* was healthy too, but had never produced large profits. *Sports Illustrated* was still running deficits and would not show a profit until the mid-1960s. Luce, who had never been very enthusiastic about diversifying the company's investments, was now ready to consider new ventures. But he did not stray far from Time Inc.'s traditional mission.

For years the magazines had published occasional books. *Fortune* produced anthologies of notable articles. *Life* published "picture histories" of great events such as World War II and turned the magazine's excerpts of Churchill's memoirs into a book. *Time* created *Three Hundred Years of American Painting*, and *Sports Illustrated* tried to market books on golf and bridge. None of these efforts was particularly successful until the company decided to create a book-club-like system for marketing the company's publications. It started as the Life World Library but early in 1961 became an independent department of the company: Time-Life Books. Luce was somewhat skeptical of the project, complaining occasionally that "these books are going out with my name on them, and I won't have time to read them." But the new unit proved profitable enough to banish his doubts. By 1964 it was producing profits of more than six million dollars a year.[24]

Luce placed considerable hope in the company's Time-Life International division. Launched shortly after World War II, it had grown steadily through the 1950s with editions of *Time* and *Life* tailored to various parts of the world. In some cases it was published in local languages—Spanish, Italian, Japanese—and was producing modest but growing profits. By the late 1960s it was generating about 10 percent of the company's substantial revenues, but the high costs of production and marketing ensured that it produced far less than 10 percent of its profits. A few overseas editions continued for decades, but Time-Life International was disbanded in 1968.[25]

Time Inc. could get only so much leverage from recycling its editorial products in various forms, and this limited diversification did little to compensate for the great loss of earnings created by the decline of *Life*. But Luce remained cautious about moving into wholly new fields, and few people in the upper echelons of the company were willing to challenge him. The company remained profitable, and the magazines remained popular, but for the first time in its history Time Inc. was on a downward arc. Only after his death did the company begin seriously to diversify.

Luce did not slow down during his last years as editor in chief. As always, he traveled frequently, around the United States, to Europe, to Asia. He continued actively to oversee his editors, not as obsessively as he had sometimes done in the past, but enough to send a steady flow of often-unwelcome memos to the desks of his employees. His 1960 appointment of Otto Fuerbringer as managing editor of *Time* was controversial among the staff, who considered him—correctly—to be more rigidly conservative and autocratic than his predecessor, Roy Alexander. (Among many of his editors—and especially among those who had lobbied furiously against his appointment—he was known as the "Iron Chancellor.") Luce was not much troubled by Fuerbringer's politics. He liked him most of all for his efficiency and his extraordinary editorial skills. He had much the same appeal to Luce as such earlier controversial editors as Laird Goldsborough and Whittaker Chambers, whose ideological enthusiasms sometimes exceeded his own but who created good copy quickly and effectively.[26]

Fuerbringer's semi-Teutonic rigidity was the source of many of the criticisms Luce received from the Kennedy administration. Lyndon Johnson, once he became president, seldom complained to Luce about his coverage in the magazines (although he sometimes complained bitterly to others, among them John Steele, the *Time* Washington correspondent). Instead Johnson used his trademark tool: shameless flattery. He sent Luce frequent notes of praise, called him periodically on the telephone, invited him to informal dinners and private meetings, and praised him for his speeches and essays. He quoted Luce's speeches to others (always making sure that someone informed Luce that he had done so). He lavished him with thanks—"deep appreciation," "delighted with your praise," "forever in your debt"—for even the most trivial communication. He solicited Luce's suggestions for the president's speeches. He issued a proclamation in 1965 declaring "World Law Day," and made sure to write Luce about his role in creating it. When Luce was unable to attend the ceremony, the president said very publicly, "Who will send Mr. Luce's pen to him?"[27]

Luce himself had admired Johnson since the 1950s, expressed delight when he became vice president, and gave unexpected praise to the president's Great Society legislation. "Ours is a secular society," Luce said in a speech in Washington in 1965. "We set our sights on the Great Society, where there will be even more good. . . . How to bring joy into the world? How to make the Great Society a thing of glory—to build as if to the glory of God—ad majorum dei gloriam? It seems impossible, but there are hints of this vision."[28]

The 1964 campaign was a difficult one for Luce, because it led him to question his loyalty to the Republican Party. In 1960 he had admired John Kennedy but had endorsed (even if somewhat tepidly) Richard Nixon, largely because he saw relatively little difference between the two contenders and because Nixon was a Republican. But in 1964 Luce was troubled by the anger and bitterness that Barry Goldwater's supporters showed at the party's convention in San Francisco. He tried to explain it by arguing that "the prime significance of the Goldwater candidacy is dissatisfaction with the Republican Party, and the main reason for that dissatisfaction was that the Republican Party had been a loser, not a winner." But he could not accept the party's current "theory that the Republicans would have a good chance to win if they nominated a 'real,' that is a conservative Republican." In this "moment of time," he said, the Republicans had "very little chance to win. . . . Johnson has, I think, touched the more responsive nerve." He confided to Donovan that "I haven't, for some time, felt that the Republicans had anything noteworthy to say." Periodically Luce read a Goldwater speech or watched a campaign event and tried to persuade himself that the candidate was getting "better." He praised Goldwater for a "good serious speech on foreign policy" and a call for party unity that Luce described as "completely satisfactory. . . . [He] has largely purged himself of his previous failure to conciliate the so-called 'moderate Republicans.'"

But Luce was never comfortable with Goldwater. "The trouble, of course, is not what Goldwater said or failed to say," Luce wrote of a speech the senator made in Hershey, Pennsylvania. "The trouble is what he had previously said, and the impression which he has given as to what manner of man he is by what he has said." Shortly before the election he explained to Leo Burnett that "[a]fter months, or perhaps more accurately a year, of patient listening to Senator Goldwater's case, we did not find it sufficiently convincing." By then Luce was no longer editor in chief. But his resistance to Goldwater was shared by Donovan, and for the first time in many years *Life* provided no endorsement. Not long after the Republican convention, Luce's son Hank and his wife joined Harry and Clare for a night at the theater. As their car traveled through Central Park, Clare—an active Goldwater supporter—asked Hank whom he was supporting. Hank replied that he was voting for Johnson and then asked, "Dad, who are you for?" Hank recalled later, "I never got an answer," just "a conspicuous silence." He always felt certain that his father either did not vote at all or voted for Johnson.[29]

Luce's political ambivalence in these years reflected his uncertainty and confusion about what he considered the new character of American society. He was both interested in and puzzled by the emergence of the New Left—and he turned, improbably, to Father Murray as his guide. The New Left was based on "selective pacifism," Murray argued, and "might not be against all wars. In fact they might support wars of liberation in other parts of the world." Luce had no fixed opinions of his own about the New Left and peppered those around him—Clare, his colleague Robert Elson, Murray, and others—with questions. Luce had many blind spots, certainly, but he was seldom afraid of change; and in the early years of the New Left, he remained more or less open-minded toward it—with one conspicuous exception: Vietnam.[30]

The struggle for Vietnam was the last great crusade of Luce's life. It did not consume him in the way that World War II or the Chinese Revolution had, to be sure. But he believed in a non-Communist South Vietnam, in peacetime and in war, with unflagging commitment; and he tried to make his magazines support his views despite roiling controversy—in the country and in Time Inc. itself—about the wisdom of the war.

Luce's interest in Vietnam stretched back to the early 1950s and his dismay at the collapse of the French effort to defeat the Communist forces of the Vietminh. Not only had he hoped that the French would stave off Communism in Vietnam; he had also once again dreamed of a larger war that might provide an opportunity to overthrow the Chinese Communists as well. The failure of these hopes only intensified his interest in South Vietnam once it became an independent nation as a result of the 1954 Geneva conference which partitioned the country into a Communist North Vietnam and a non-Communist South. In 1957 Luce joined the American Friends of Vietnam, which supported the South Vietnam government. Luce contributed a modest amount of Time Inc. stock to the organization. He promoted the leadership of Ngo Dinh Diem, the president of South Vietnam, and his brother Ngo Dinh Nhu and argued that they "have contributed notably to the fight of their people against both Colonialism and communism." That same year Luce presided over a dinner for Diem on behalf of the International Rescue Committee. In his letter of invitation he wrote that Diem "is one of the great statesmen of Asia and of the world. He has held back the flood of Communism which threatened to engulf his country. . . . In honoring him, we pay tribute to the eternal values which all free men everywhere are prepared to defend with their lives." Such sentiments were widely shared in the mid-1950s, after Diem was invited to address an enthusiastic joint session of Congress and began to be called "the Churchill of Southeast Asia."[31]

Luce felt especially comfortable supporting the Vietnam War because he was, for the first time, fully aligned with the views of a wartime administration. His experience in World War II had been blighted by the mutual hostility between himself and Roosevelt. The Truman administration had ignored his impassioned pleas to save China and had supported the Korean War far more cautiously than Luce had hoped. But he harbored no such grievances toward the government during the Vietnam War. Eisenhower had strongly supported the American Friends of Vietnam in the 1950s and had provided lavish financial support to the Diem regime. Kennedy, who may or may not have hoped to extricate the United States from Vietnam, nevertheless supported the struggle publicly, expanded the American military presence there, and solicited Luce's advice. And Johnson, who first introduced combat troops into South Vietnam and eventually created an army of well over five hundred thousand, saw in Luce an ally who could help justify his policies to the world. To ensure Luce's cooperation, Johnson urged Henry Cabot Lodge, then serving as U.S. ambassador to Vietnam, to invite Luce to Saigon. "I hope very much that you can come," Lodge wrote flatteringly. "I know you will find much here that will interest you, and I know that it would help me to get the benefit of your thinking." Luce did not accept Lodge's invitation; but his support for Johnson, Lodge, and the war remained undimmed. He ensured that his magazines continued to support—and even sometimes went beyond—Johnson's Vietnam policies. His aggressive vision of the war, rooted again in his hopes for overthrowing the Communist regime in China, was expressed in *Time:* "No one talks seriously about a full-scale land war on China's mainland. But there can be no doubt whatever that China is the real enemy in Asia, and the greatest threat anywhere to world peace. . . . And there is room for argument that a more positive U.S. military policy toward Viet Nam would be to risk a confrontation with China in the right place at the right time."[32]

Johnson continued to seek Luce's help until near the end of his presidency: "I'd like old HL to come out of retirement down there in Arizona," Johnson told the *Life* correspondent Hugh Sidey in early 1967. "I'd like him to get in there and fight for me." Johnson, Sidey recalled, "doubled up his fist and punched the air a couple of times. 'I'd like him to help carry the battle.'" Sidey's letter conveying Johnson's message was sitting on Luce's desk in Phoenix in February 1967 on the day before he died. Less than a year later Hedley Donovan began leading the magazines toward a more skeptical view of the war.[33]

But while Luce's positions may have pleased the government, they created another ugly battle within Time Inc. itself, one that raged for years and caused more rancor than at almost any previous moment in its history. The controversy centered at first on a brilliant young reporter whom Luce liked and admired: Charles Mohr, a *Time* correspondent who had served in Washington, India, and beginning in 1962, Vietnam. After less than a year in Indochina, Mohr was beginning to have doubts about the optimistic reports that the military was providing and about the ability of the Vietnamese army to resist the growing strength of the Communist National Liberation Front, which became known to Americans as the Viet Cong. But back in New York, Fuerbringer treated Mohr's memos from Vietnam the same way Chambers had treated Teddy White's from China. Mohr's dark and sometimes brooding dispatches became in *Time* optimistic reports on the great progress the Americans and South Vietnamese were making. In the summer of 1963 Mohr was asked to write an article on Madame Ngo Dinh Nhu, the wife of Diem's powerful brother. He used the occasion to reveal the corruption, incompetence, and insulation of the Ngo family and their inability to make progress against the Communists. But when the story appeared in *Time*, it bore little relation to what Mohr had written. "The history of Vietnam is full of heroines," *Time* said. "Today the most formidable and in some ways the bravest woman in South Viet Nam . . . is Mme. Ngo Dinh Nhu." The story did include some of Mohr's criticisms of the regime, but after Fuerbringer's intrusion, even the criticisms were muted and sometimes openly rejected.

Not content with reshaping Mohr's story, Fuerbringer commissioned a piece for *Time*'s Press section a few weeks later that attacked the journalistic culture in Saigon, which, of course, included *Time*'s own reporters. "Have they given their readers an unduly pessimistic view of the progress of the war and the quality of the Diem government?" the article asked. The reporters, it charged, "are in love with their work, so in love, in fact, that they talk about little else. They have a strong sense of mission." They were "such a tightly knit group that their dispatches tended to reinforce their own collective judgment, which was severely critical of practically everything." A battle broke out in New York with the publication of the article. Richard Clurman, chief of correspondents, demanded a retraction; otherwise, he predicted, Mohr and others would quit. Fuerbringer refused. Clurman, at Luce's request, flew to Saigon to evaluate the reporters on his own. He returned even more insistent on challenging Fuerbringer's characterization of the journalists. To his surprise Luce agreed and ordered a story "saying we were wrong." But at the last minute, without telling anyone, the imperious Fuerbringer changed the wording before publication and removed the statement of error. Luce was furious, but he took no action against his managing editor. Mohr promptly resigned in the fall of 1963 and moved to the *New York Times*.[34]

On April 16, 1964, Luce announced his retirement as editor in chief—at a moment when, as the *New York Times* reported, Time Inc. was "the largest magazine publishing business in the world." He offered no reason for his decision, other than "it just seemed like a good moment." He told reporters that he would continue to work more or less full-time, but on a wider range of projects, few of which he could yet identify other than a possible memoir. For the moment, however, he seemed to revel in the attention he received and the importance that the press attributed to his career and his departure. "The entire Time enterprise," the *Times* wrote, "might be regarded as reflecting the missionary zeal of its founder for informing and uplifting the human race."[35]

Hedley Donovan, Luce's successor, received relatively scant attention. "Would Luce really retire?" some of his colleagues asked. Luce had named himself editorial chairman, and there was much speculation about what the title meant. Had he simply promoted himself so he could continue to manage the company more remotely? The lavish dinner Time Inc. held in May to mark the transition provided no answers. It was designed to honor both Luce and Donovan. But most of the speeches passed over Donovan without much notice and focused on Luce's achievements and legacy. Even Donovan himself felt the need to make the event about Luce. "Harry Luce has worked a kind of managerial miracle in this company," he said in his own remarks. "These magazines are going to continue, in many important ways, to be Harry's magazines." But in the months that followed, and to the surprise of many of the editors, Luce did actually retire from the company. He corresponded frequently with Donovan and other editors, and he continued to write and report for the magazines occasionally. He did not, however, challenge Donovan's authority and rarely criticized his successor's decisions—although everyone continued to feel Luce's presence and almost certainly felt somewhat constrained from moving too far beyond the magazine's long-established norms.[36]

Luce's brief retirement was a relatively happy time for him. He was not much less active than he had been during his years as editor in chief. He traveled constantly, both in the United States and abroad, still facilitated at every point by Time Inc. employees. He even tried to arrange a trip to mainland China to meet with Mao and Zhou. Richard Clurman, his partner in this effort, wrote enthusiastically: "Your going to China and seeing Mao strikes me as perhaps the biggest potential coup in all of journalism today." But in the end the trip proved impossible to arrange. He made dozens of speeches on issues he cared about and accepted honorary degrees. He spent more of his time in Phoenix with Clare than he had in the past, and he even began to purchase and renovate a new home in Hawaii, where Clare had longed to live for years. He returned often to New York, where he began, for the first time in many years, to enjoy a social life with friends. His doctors warned him that he was jeopardizing his health—"smoking cigarettes, bounding around the world, etc."—and predicted that "these things would shorten his life." Luce responded cavalierly: "I am taking off six years for the abuse that I give myself, but I am adding three or four years for what modern science now knows."[37]

Luce's principal activity in the years after retirement was working on his memoir, which friends and publishers had been urging him to write for years. He spent many mornings in Phoenix working on it at a desk in his bedroom. Although he had been a writer all his life, he had never before tried to write a book and seemed to have trouble deciding how to organize so much material and express so many ideas. And so he wrote in discrete chunks, sometimes borrowing heavily from speeches he had made and articles he had written, presumably hoping that he would be able to integrate them at some later point. What he produced was a series of short and sometimes sketchy essays that reflected many of his lifelong interests and beliefs. (Not much in the manuscript was about himself, so calling it a memoir was a misnomer from the start.) He wrote about people he admired (Willkie, Eisenhower, Dulles, MacArthur, Churchill, but surprisingly little on Chiang Kai-shek), and he also discussed people he detested (Roosevelt, Truman, Acheson, McCarthy). He wrote about "prosperity marking a radical change in the human condition," the "rule of law," Communism and its inevitable exhaustion, and the "Providential nature of history." Most of all he tried to explain what America meant and what its role in the world should be.[38]

"The United States," he wrote, "was dedicated to a proposition. That was something unique in the history of nations. . . . The proposition, of which Lincoln spoke, was that 'all men are created equal.' . . . What is necessary to understand here is that the American Proposition contains, indeed is founded on, truths or hypotheses which are unqualifiedly universal. . . . It was and is the American task to take the lead in creating a new form of world order." These were ideas he had been struggling to express during much of his life: in his first political efforts during his years at Yale, in the famous essay in *Life*, "The American Century," and in his search for a "national purpose." In the last months of his life he was struggling with them still.[39]

Luce's casual attitude toward his health represented a denial of a number of dangerous events in his medical past: gall-bladder surgery; hypertension; his 1958 heart attack; prostate troubles; osteoarthritis in his shoulder, arm, and neck; and a brief attack of arrhythmia in 1964. Each illness produced fear and anxiety. Each recovery produced relief and increased confidence in his ability to outlive his problems.[40]

On February 23, 1967, Luce flew back to Phoenix from California with Clare, who had just made a highly critical speech about the United Nations, somewhat softened by Harry's last-minute intervention. The next morning he slept late, uncharacteristically, and could not hold his food down once he had eaten. He continued to vomit through the day. Doctors were in and out of the house, but Luce insisted he was not seriously ill. He remained at home that night. The following day he felt no better, and at noon he was taken by ambulance to the hospital. "I seem to be unusually sleepy," he told his doctor. Clare, in the meantime, went on with her day. "I had a dinner party to go to that night," she recalled a few years later, "but I grew very uneasy and left about 9 p.m., went home, and called the hospital. He got on the phone at once; he said not to worry—he was all right and watching television. ('Perry Mason'—which is why I go on watching the darn thing.)" He was up and down late into the night, and at about three o'clock in the morning he went into the bathroom. A nurse heard him yell, "Oh God!" By the time the doctors rushed to his room, he was unconscious. Fifteen minutes later, he was dead—the victim of a massive heart attack. It was February 28, 1967, thirty-eight years to the day from the death of Brit Hadden, and forty-four years almost to the day since he had sat in the shabby little office he shared with Brit in downtown New York, holding the first issue of *Time* magazine and having "this sort of surprising feeling that it was pretty good."

Epilogue

The news of Luce's death spread rapidly across the vast world of Time Inc. Requests flew out from New York for stories about him, and correspondents from all over the globe flooded the headquarters with anecdotes and remembrances. When Brit Hadden died in 1929, the grief-stricken staff could not even bring itself to write an obituary and inserted instead a small announcement in *Time*'s Milestones section. For Luce, the company violated a forty-four-year tradition of never putting the image of a deceased figure on the cover of *Time*. At the urging of his son Henry Luce III and spurred on by the company's new leaders who feared alienating the Luce loyalists still among them, Hedley Donovan agreed to put Luce's image on the cover—a simple pencil drawing (adapted from an Alfred Eisenstaedt photograph) on a plain white background. (*Newsweek* superimposed an image of a similar *Time* cover— using the actual Eisenstaedt photograph—on its own cover the same week.) His picture appeared in newspapers all over the country and much of the world (including in Rome, where one paper reported that "Clare Boothe Luce's Husband Has Died").[1]

Luce's funeral took place in the Madison Avenue Presbyterian Church, where he had attended services for many years. His pastor and friend, David H. C. Read, conducted the service for eight hundred people at the church—and an additional twelve hundred Time Inc. employees who gathered in the reception area and the auditorium of the Time-Life Building, where they watched the service on a closed-circuit broadcast. Later that week, at a private ceremony, he was buried on the grounds of his onetime and seldom-visited home in Mepkin, South Carolina, by then a Trappist monastery. His grave was next to that of Ann Brokaw, Clare's daughter.[2]

In his will, Luce left most of his personal property to Clare—the Phoenix and Hawaii houses, their apartment in New York, the paintings she once complained that she did not own. He left the rest to other family members: a property in Morris County, New Jersey, which went to his son, Hank; another in Haverford, Pennsylvania, that Luce had bought for his sister and brother-in-law, which was left to Emmavail. He forgave all debts owed to him by his children. The most important part of his estate, of course, was his more than one million shares of stock in Time Inc. He left 55,000 shares to the Henry Luce Foundation, to which he had already contributed a much larger amount that together totaled approximately half of his holdings. He left 180,000 shares to Clare, in trust. His two sons each received over 71,000 shares. At the time, each share was worth slightly over $100.[3]

On the day of Luce's funeral, Time Inc. reported its first-quarter performance. There were record earnings of over $3,000,000, but the officers and the board worried about the softening of the economy and the declining health of some of the company's magazines. Their greatest concern was *Life*, which had never recovered from the fall in advertising that had begun in the late 1950s. The magazine continued to flourish editorially, and its readership remained enormous—indeed, for a time, it grew. But things had changed. Luce's idea of turning *Life* into a magazine of "national purpose" in the mid- and late 1960s, a period of almost unprecedented conflict and polarization, proved to be futile. The unstated compact between *Life* and its readers—that the magazine would celebrate American prosperity and consensus—was impossible to preserve in a rapidly changing and increasingly diverse society. *Life* could have survived and even embraced the changing culture, which provided at least as many compelling images (and important writing) as in its earlier decades. The real problem was its finances, which continued to go slowly downhill. Despite its vast circulation, advertisers were finding *Life* too expensive, especially when compared with television, which attracted many more viewers than the magazine did at a not much greater price—part of a broad shift in publishing that doomed many general interest magazines. *Life* struggled on, with many great editorial moments and with continued hope (and denial) into the early 1970s. But on December 8, 1972, Time Inc. announced that it was terminating what had been perhaps the most popular magazine in American history.

"We persevered as long as we could see any realistic prospects," Hedley Donovan, Luce's beleaguered successor, said glumly of the decision. The *Time* story on *Life*'s demise cited a prescient statement by Luce in the heady first years of the magazine in the late 1930s: "The other magazines, like TIME and FORTUNE, are enduring; they have a permanence about them. LIFE might only last 20 years. . . . Every issue of LIFE is like bringing out a new show on Broadway." The *Time* editors added: "Even the long runs have to close some Saturday night." *Life*'s last issue was dated December 29. At the bottom of the cover, in small print, the magazine said "Good bye."[4]

Time Inc. soldiered on and, for the most part, flourished. Only two years after the demise of *Life*, the company launched *People*, its first new magazine in twenty years, inspired by the long-standing People section in *Time* and which became a tremendous financial success, the first of many new Time Inc. magazines (more than a hundred by the end of the twentieth century). Few of them reflected Luce's belief that quality, sophistication, and a broad general readership should be the hallmarks of his publications. Luce had resisted expansion and diversification during his lifetime, but no such inhibitions impeded the company's growth after his death. The 1990 merger with Warner entertainment created what became now Time Warner, one of the three largest media companies in the United States. It now included film, music, cable television, and many other areas. In late 2000 Time Warner was acquired by America Online, the enormously successful Internet access company. It proved to be an ill-fated merger, but Time Warner survived the fiasco and remained a powerful and successful company, although the magazine division that had launched the company was weakening fast in the digital world of the twenty-first century. Luce's remaining magazines— *Time*, *Fortune*, and *Sports Illustrated*—were all experiencing significant revenue declines and editorial cutbacks. The magazines that were flourishing were mostly newer, narrowly focused periodicals, no longer attempting to attract a broad middle-class readership, but trying instead to identify subjects that would attract smaller but more intensely committed interest groups.

Henry Luce, who once expressed doubts about the lucrative Time-Life Books series because he feared he would not be able to read and approve them all, would likely have been bewildered by the vastness of what

Time Inc. later became—a company that no single man could any longer control in the way Luce had attempted, and had often succeeded, in doing. But in his own time, Luce was certainly among the most powerful media figures in America, and perhaps the world. His influence was in part the result of the enormous popularity of his consistently entertaining magazines, although other media were equally profitable and at least equally popular, especially after the advent of television. But what made Luce truly different from most other major media barons was his willingness to control the contents of his magazines. "To a remarkable extent," Alden Whitman wrote in the *New York Times* obituary, "the judgments and opinions that were printed reflected the focus of Mr. Luce's own views." He was, the *Times* added, "a man of missionary zeal and limitless curiosity" who "deeply influenced American journalism."[5]

Luce's willingness to make political judgments, to support politicians he admired (almost always Republicans), and to denounce government policies he disliked contributed to the intensity of his critics. Many of the denunciations of the Luce magazines—from presidents, statesmen, and other media chieftains—were a result of ordinary political disagreement or aesthetic distaste. Some criticized the company's venality. "*Time*'s business is to promote Time Inc. as a corporate empire," Andrew Kopkind, the former *Time* correspondent turned radical journalist, wrote shortly after Luce's death. "Like all imperial systems, it is self-justifying; worlds must be conquered because they are there. . . . The basic urge is to its own expansion."[6]

But for others, most prominently the members of the liberal-left intelligentsia, Luce was someone not just to disdain, but also to fear. His magazine empire, many intellectuals came to believe, was a powerful vehicle of propaganda, capable of narrowing the horizons of readers while at the same time manipulating and mobilizing them. To many such intellectuals of the postwar era, the great danger facing democracy was the easily deluded middle class, which they believed could easily fall under the influence of a powerful and persuasive media. Ominous examples of this power, they argued, were the propaganda that fascist and Communist regimes used to delude and control their own populations; or the McCarthy-like American demagogues whose manipulation of the media had led Americans into believing in what McCarthy himself called the "conspiracy so immense" of Communist subversion. This was the fear that inspired the historian Richard Hofstadter to write his famous 1964 essay on "the paranoid style," in which he argued that demagoguery and propaganda directed at many narrowly informed people caused them to lose faith in democracy and to become convinced that they were victims of conspiracies. The social scientist Theodor Adorno warned of the specter of totalitarianism and denounced the tame middle class that embraced mass culture and rejected the skepticism and independence that a democratic society required. To such critics, Luce and his magazines were a kind of anesthesia, drawing readers into an imaginary world of consensus and homogeneity and numbing them to the active inquiry that citizens needed to understand their world.[7]

Fueling that fear was Luce's great success in reaching a broad middle-class constituency and in creating an intimate relationship with many of his readers. That was perhaps ironic, since Luce himself was a fundamentally shy, lonely, and somewhat awkward man with few true friends. And yet like many other hugely successful politicians, entertainers, and others who were privately reclusive, he had the ability to connect publicly with millions of strangers. Luce's critics, and occasionally Luce himself, believed that his access to a large public gave him real power to control public opinion.

But in fact, and often to his own great frustration, Luce was almost never able to exercise as much power as he wished and as his adversaries believed he had. He hated Franklin Roosevelt and opposed most of what he did. But his opposition to Roosevelt—most visible in his passionate and at times reckless support of the failed presidential candidacy of Wendell Willkie in 1940—had almost no impact on Roosevelt's policies or on his political successes. Luce railed for years about America's failure to support Chiang Kai-shek and Nationalist China, but he could never overcome America's public and political unwillingness to challenge the Communist regime. Luce had close relationships at times with Eisenhower, Kennedy, and Johnson, but rarely did any of them take his advice or adjust policies to avoid his magazines' criticism. On the contrary, Luce more often adjusted his own views to sustain his relationship with people he considered important. There was much in the Luce magazines that was irritating and even infuriating to many readers, but there was little in them that could manipulate readers into abandoning their own political or cultural independence. His magazines were mostly reflections of the middle-class world, not often shapers of it. And despite their claims of disgust, even many of Luce's most ardent critics continued to read the magazines, often with as much pleasure as annoyance. Some of them wrote for *Life* and *Fortune* even while denouncing Luce in other venues.

Where Luce was most influential was in promoting ideas that were already emerging among a broad segment of the American population—

most notably in the early 1940s, when Luce wrote his famous "American Century" essay and worked energetically to persuade Americans of what was already an indisputable truth—that the United States was now the most powerful and important nation in the world, that it no longer lived in the shadow of Europe. To Luce, that meant that America had a responsibility to reshape the world, a belief many other Americans shared. He may have articulated this vision more effectively (and more grandiosely) than most Americans, but the ideas he expressed were not new to him. Many of them reflected earlier essays in *Life* by Walter Lippmann, and even Roosevelt's recently enunciated Four Freedoms.

Luce's intellectual life may have been rigid and polemical on issues that were of great importance to him. But on other issues, he was as skeptical, inquiring, and independent as the most hostile of his critics. He bitterly opposed many liberal initiatives, but on the whole he supported the growth of government power and embraced many of the great changes of his time—the growth of the welfare state, civil rights for minorities, and, at least tentatively, the emergence of feminism and gender equality. He understood the broad transformation of the capitalist economy in the postwar years, supported unions to ensure that the profits were not reserved to a few, and applauded what he considered "modern" industrial leaders who believed in progressive corporate responsibility. He was a mostly loyal Republican, but not an uncritical supporter of the party's right wing—always a moderate or liberal trying to draw the party into the mainstream. When it failed to do so, as in 1964 when Barry Goldwater ran for president, he repudiated the party's ticket. Luce always described himself as a liberal—not a liberal of the Left, but a liberal in his openness to new ideas and his embrace of progressive change.

Luce did not change the world. His most important legacy remains his role in the creation of new forms of information and communications at a moment in history when media were rapidly expanding. His magazines were always the most important of his achievements. They reached unprecedented numbers of Americans in the 1920s and 1930s and helped transform the way many people experienced news and culture. His expansion into radio and film, even though relatively short-lived, helped legitimize these emerging media as serious sources of news themselves. Like all powerful media, Luce's innovations had their day and then slowly lost their centrality as newer forms of communication took their place. And while his company survives still, far larger and wealthier than it was in Luce's lifetime, little remains of the goals and principles he established for it.

Time magazine's cover story on the death of Luce was titled "End of a Pilgrimage." It began with one of Luce's most pompous statements: "As a journalist, I am in command of a small sector in the very front trenches of this battle for freedom."[8] But the great and almost always futile crusades that Luce embraced are not his principal legacy. A simpler and more appropriate remembrance of his formidable life appeared almost two decades after his death, when *Time* added a new line to its masthead:

FOUNDERS,
BRITON HADDEN 1898–1929
HENRY R. LUCE 1898–1967.

NOTES

A NOTE ON SOURCES

The most important sources for an understanding of the life and work of Henry R. Luce are the vast Time Inc. Archives, which combine many of Luce's personal papers with the archives of the company he founded and led. The archives also contain a small collection of the papers of Briton Hadden and oral histories of a number of other Time Inc. founders.

Another invaluable source is a collection of letters and other materials that were for many decades in the possession of Luce's first wife, Lila Luce Tyng. My own use of these papers preceded their transfer to Harvard University, where they are now in the possession of the Schlesinger Library at the Radcliffe Institute.

A third important source is the collections of John Shaw Billings, who was one of the most important editors in the first three decades of Time Inc.'s existence. They are held in the South Caroliniana Library at the University of South Carolina, Columbia. Billings joined the company in the 1920s, became managing editor of *Time* in the 1930s, then the first managing editor of *Life*, and after that the editorial director of all Time Inc. magazines. His meticulously recorded diary is one of the most revealing sources for an understanding of the day-to-day workings of the company and of his own relationship with Luce. His papers duplicate many documents in the Time Inc. Archives but contain some that are not available elsewhere.

Another important window into the internal workings of Time Inc. is the vast collection of *Time* dispatches sent to New York from correspondents around the country and the world and preserved by the longtime general manager of the company, Roy Larsen. They are now at the Houghton Library at Harvard University. Also at Harvard are the papers of Theodore H. White, an important Time Inc. journalist in the 1940s and again in the 1960s.

The Clare Boothe Luce Papers in the Manuscripts Division of the Library of Congress are of great value in understanding her long and difficult marriage to Henry Luce. Also in the Library of Congress is another collection of the papers of Henry Luce, much of it duplicative of material in the Time Inc. Archives, but also with some materials not available elsewhere.

An important published work for anyone interested in the history of Time Inc. (and of Henry Luce) is the internally produced three-volume history of the company.

The first two volumes are by Robert T. Elson: *Time Inc.: The Intimate History of a Publishing Enterprise, 1923–1941* (1968) and *The World of Time Inc.: The Intimate History of a Publishing Enterprise, 1941–1960* (1973). The third volume is by Curtis Prendergast: *The World of Time Inc.: The Intimate History of a Changing Enterprise, 1960–1980* (1986). In researching the first two volumes Elson did extensive interviews with Luce, transcripts of which are available in the Time Inc. Archives.

ABBREVIATIONS

BH	Briton Hadden
CBL	Clare Boothe Luce
COHP	Columbia Oral History Project
ERL	Elisabeth Root Luce
FDR	Franklin D. Roosevelt
FDRL	Franklin D. Roosevelt Library
HRL Elson	Robert T. Elson interviews with Henry R. Luce, 1965–66
HRL	Henry Robinson Luce
HWL	Henry Winters Luce
JFKL	John F. Kennedy Library
JSB	John Shaw Billings
JSBD	John Shaw Billings Diary
LC	Library of Congress
LH	Lila Hotz/Lila Hotz Luce
LT	Lila Luce Tyng
MBW	Margaret Bourke-White
PPF	President's Personal File
PSF	President's Secretary File
TD	Time Dispatches
THW	Theodore H. White
TIA	Time Inc. Archives

MANUSCRIPT COLLECTIONS

Carl Albert Papers, University of Oklahoma Library
Frank Altschul Papers, Rare Books and Manuscript Library, Columbia University
American Friends of Vietnam Papers, Rare Books and Manuscript Library, Columbia University
Mary Bancroft Papers, Schlesinger Library, Radcliffe Institute, Harvard University
John Shaw Billings Papers, South Caroliniana Library, University of South Carolina
Margaret Bourke-White Papers, George Arents Collection, Syracuse University Library
Thomas Corcoran Papers, Manuscripts Division, Library of Congress
Russell W. Davenport Papers, Manuscripts Division, Library of Congress
Stephen Early Papers, Franklin D. Roosevelt Library
John Foster Dulles Papers, Seely G. Mudd Library, Princeton University
B. A. Garside Papers, Hoover Institution Archives, Stanford University
Manfred Gottfried Oral History, Time Inc. Archives
Walter Graebner Papers, Time Inc. Archives
Frances Fineman Gunther Papers, Schlesinger Library, Radcliffe Institute, Harvard University
Briton Hadden Papers, Time Inc. Archives
David Halberstam Papers, Mugar Library, Boston University
Stanley Hornbeck Papers, Hoover Institution Archives, Stanford University
Hotchkiss School Archives, Hotchkiss School Library

Ralph Ingersoll Papers, Howard Gottlieb Archival Research Center, Boston University
Institute for Pacific Relations Papers, Rare Books and Manuscript Library, Columbia
    University
Roy Larsen Papers, Time Inc. Archives
Daniel Longwell Oral History, Columbia Oral History Project, Columbia University
Daniel Longwell Papers, Rare Books and Manuscript Library, Columbia University
Clare Boothe Luce Papers, Manuscripts Division, Library of Congress
Henry R. Luce Papers, Time Inc. Archives
Henry R. Luce Papers, Manuscripts Division, Library of Congress
Henry W. Luce Papers, Hartford Seminary Foundation
Dwight Macdonald Papers, Sterling Library, Yale University
Nettie McCormick Papers, Wisconsin State Historical Society
Franklin D. Roosevelt Papers, Franklin D. Roosevelt Library
Henry Stimson Papers, Manuscript Division, Library of Congress
W. A. Swanberg Papers, Rare Books and Manuscript Library, Columbia University
Time Dispatches, Houghton Library, Harvard University
Time Inc. Papers, Time Inc. Archives
Rexford Tugwell Papers, Manuscript Division, Library of Congress
Lila Luce Tyng Papers, Schlesinger Library, Radcliffe Institute, Harvard University
Henry A. Wallace Papers, University of Iowa Library
Albert C. Wedemeyer Papers, Hoover Institution Archives, Stanford University
Theodore H. White Papers, Houghton Library, Harvard University
Wendell Willkie Papers, Lilly Library, Indiana University

INTERVIEWS

Jeanne Campbell, New York, N.Y., 1997
Richard Clurman, New York, N.Y., 1993
Thomas Griffith, New York, N.Y., 1995
Henry Grunwald, New York, N.Y., 1997
David Halberstam, New York, N.Y., 2004
Andrew Heiskell, New York, N.Y., 1996
Christopher Luce, New York, N.Y., 1993
Henry Luce III, New York, N.Y., 1993–98
Peter Luce, Denver, Colo., 1997
Elisabeth Luce Moore, New York, N.Y., 1994
David H. C. Read, New York, N.Y., 1995
Leslie Severinghaus, Coconut Grove, Fla., 1992
Lila Luce Tyng, Gladstone, N.J., 1993

PREFACE

1. Henry Luce interviewed by Eric Goldman, May 8, 1966, video, *The Open Mind*,
    WNBC Television, "A Profile of Henry R. Luce," TIA.
2. Henry R. Luce, "The American Century," *Life*, February 17, 1941.
3. W. A. Swanberg, *Luce and His Empire* (New York: Charles Scribner's Sons,
    1972).

I   AMERICANS ABROAD

1. Charles E. Ronan and Bonnie B. C. Oh, eds., *East Meets West: The Jesuits in
    China, 1582–1773* (Chicago: Loyola University Press, 1988); George H. Dunne,

Generation of Giants: The Story of the Jesuits in China in the Last Decades of the Ming Dynasty (Notre Dame, Ind.: University of Notre Dame Press, 1962); John King Fairbank, *The United States and China*, 4th ed. (Cambridge, Mass.: Harvard University Press, 1983), pp. 152–55; William R. Hutchison, *Errand to the World: Protestant Thought and Foreign Missions* (Chicago: University of Chicago Press, 1987), pp. 21–22.

2. James C. Thompson, Jr., Peter W. Stanley, John Curtis Perry, *Sentimental Imperialists: The American Experience in East Asia* (New York: Harper & Row, 1981), pp. 44–60; John King Fairbank, "The Many Faces of Protestant Missions," in Fairbank, ed., *The Missionary Enterprise in China and America* (Cambridge, Mass.: Harvard University Press, 1974), pp. 1–10; Jonathan Spence, *To Change China: Western Advisers in China, 1620–1960* (Boston: Little, Brown, 1969), pp. 34–56; Michael H. Hunt, *The Making of a Special Relationship: The United States and China to 1914* (New York: Columbia University Press, 1983), pp. 26–28.

3. George Marsden, *Fundamentalism and American Culture: The Shaping of Twentieth-Century Evangelicalism* (New York: Oxford University Press, 1980), pp. 30–31, 48, 86–88, 162–69; Jon H. Roberts, *Darwinism and the Divine in America: Protestant Intellectuals and Organic Evolution, 1859–1900* (Madison: University of Wisconsin Press, 1988), pp. 213–31; Randall Balmer and Lauren Winner, *Protestantism in America* (New York: Columbia University Press, 2002), pp. 73–75, 85.

4. William R. Hutchinson, "Modernism and Missions: The Liberal Search for an Exportable Christianity, 1886–1920," in Fairbank, *The Missionary Enterprise in China and America*, pp. 110–31; Martin E. Marty, "Protestants and the Chinese Wall," *Reviews in American History* 14 (September 1986): 391; Roberts, *Darwinism and the Divine in America*, pp. 181–208; Balmer and Winner, *Protestantism in America*, pp. 57–58, 84–85.

5. Clifton J. Philips, "The Student Volunteer Movement and Its Role in China Missions, 1886–1920," in Fairbank, *The Missionary Enterprise in China and America*, pp. 91–109; Valentin H. Rabe, *The Home Base of American China Missions, 1880–1920* (Cambridge, Mass.: Harvard University Press, 1978), pp. 90–93; Hutchison, *Errand to the World*, pp. 130–32.

6. Arthur T. Pierson, *The Crisis of Missions* (New York: Robert Carter and Brothers, 1886), p. 27; Philips, "The Student Volunteer Movement," pp. 92–96.

7. Philips, "The Student Volunteer Movement," pp. 102–3.

8. Spence, *To Change China*, pp. 34–36; Akira Iriye, *Across the Pacific: An Inner History of American-East Asian Relations* (New York: Harcourt, Brace & World, 1967), pp. 17–20; Rabe, *The Home Base of American China Missions*, pp. 92–106.

9. B. A. Garside, *One Increasing Purpose: The Life of Henry Winters Luce* (New York: Fleming H. Revell Company, 1948), pp. 23–28.

10. Ibid., pp. 29–34.

11. Ibid., pp. 30–34; Robert E. Speer, *A Memorial to Horace Tracy Pitkin* (New York: Fleming H. Revell Company, 1903), pp. 62–80; W. A. Swanberg, *Luce and His Empire* (New York: Charles Scribner's Sons, 1972), pp. 15–17.

12. Garside, *One Increasing Purpose*, pp. 44–58, 82–83; HWL to Howard Thurman, February 12, 1936, HWL Mss.

13. ERL to HRL, February, n.d., 1942, May 26, 1946, TIA; Garside, *One Increasing Purpose*, pp. 58–72; Swanberg, *Luce and His Empire*, p. 17.

14. William R. Hutchison, "Modernism and Missions," pp. 111–20; Jessie Gregory Lutz, *China and the Christian Colleges, 1850–1950* (Ithaca, N.Y.: Cornell University Press, 1971), pp. 12–24.

15. Garside, *One Increasing Purpose*, pp. 78–87; Gladys Zehnpfennig, *Henry R. Luce: Tycoon of Journalism* (Minneapolis: T. S. Denison & Co., Inc., 1969), p. 14; Lutz, *China and the Christian Colleges*, pp. 28–29; Jane Hunter, *The Gospel of Gentility: American Women Missionaries in Turn-of-the-Century China* (New Haven, Conn.: Yale University Press, 1984), pp. 164–66.

16. S. Cecil-Smith to HWL, July 20, 1913, LT; Garside, *One Increasing Purpose*, pp. 88–94.

17. Arthur H. Smith, *Chinese Characteristics* (New York: Fleming H. Revell, 1894), pp. 313, 329–30; Charles W. Hayford, "Chinese and American Characteristics: Arthur H. Smith and His China Book," in Suzanne Wilson Barnett and John King Fairbank, eds., *Christianity in China: Early Protestant Missionary Writings* (Cambridge, Mass.: Harvard University Press, 1985), pp. 153–74; Lawrence D. Kessler, *The Jiangyin Mission Station: An American Missionary Community in China, 1895–1951* (Chapel Hill: University of North Carolina Press, 1996), pp. 43–66; Sidney A. Forsythe, *An American Missionary Community in China, 1895–1905* (Cambridge, Mass.: Harvard University Press, 1971), pp. 21–30; Marty, "Protestants and the Chinese Wall," pp. 388–89; Hunt, *The Making of a Special Relationship*, pp. 28–29.

18. Diana Preston, *The Boxer Rebellion* (New York: Walker & Company, 2000), p. 276; Henry Keown-Boyd, *The Fists of Righteous Harmony: A History of the Boxer Uprising in China in the Year 1900* (London: Leo Cooper, 1991), pp. 27–29, 214–15; Jonathan Spence, *The Gate of Heavenly Peace: The Chinese and Their Revolution, 1895–1980* (New York: Viking Penguin, 1981), pp. 58–62.

19. Frederic A. Sharf and Peter Harrington, *China 1900: The Eyewitnesses Speak* (London: Greenhill Books, 2000), pp. 26–28, 151–239; Preston, *The Boxer Rebellion*, pp. 275–82.

20. Stuart Creighton Miller, "Ends and Means: Missionary Justification of Force in Nineteenth-Century China," in Fairbank, *The Missionary Enterprise in China and America*, pp. 273–80.

21. Lutz, *China and the Christian Colleges*, pp. 108–9, 121; John J. Heeren, *On the Shantung Front: A History of the Presbyterian Church in the U.S.A., 1861–1940* (New York: Board of Foreign Missions of the Presbyterian Church, 1940), pp. 124, 137–39; B. A. Garside, *Within the Four Seas* (New York: Frederic C. Bell, 1985), pp. 58–59; Garside, *One Increasing Purpose*, p. 98.

22. Family birth record, TIA.

23. ERL notes, n.d., 1898, TIA.

24. HRL to HWL, June 12, 14, 1903, TIA.

25. Elisabeth Luce Moore interview.

26. Hunter, *The Gospel of Gentility*, pp. 128–73; Elisabeth Luce Moore interview.

27. Elisabeth Luce Moore interview; Elisabeth Luce Moore oral history, TIA.

28. HRL to parents, December 24, 1916, TIA; Elisabeth Luce Moore interview.

29. HRL to ERL, July 7, 1912, TIA; Elisabeth Luce Moore oral history, TIA; Elisabeth Luce Moore interview.

30. Elisabeth Luce Moore interview; Elisabeth Luce Moore oral history, TIA.

31. HRL to parents, n.d., TIA.

32. HRL to Mary Linen, n.d., 1903, TIA; Garside, *Within the Four Seas*, p. 58.

33. HRL Elson interview, 1965, TIA; ERL to HRL, August 6, 1918, LT.

34. HRL Elson interview, 1965, TIA; Elisabeth Luce Moore interview.

35. HRL Elson interview, 1965, TIA; HWL to HRL, n.d., 1913, TIA; Rabe, *The Home Base of American Missions*, pp. 109–71.

36. *St. Nicholas*, n.d., 1909, TIA.

37. E. Murray to HRL, October 1, 1913, LT; HRL speech, Nov. 17, 1932, LT; Richard H. Goldstone, *Thornton Wilder: An Intimate Portrait* (New York: E. P. Dutton, 1975), pp. 12–13.

38. HRL to ERL, September 3, 1911, HRL to parents, September 19, 20, 1908, TIA.

39. HRL to parents, October 13, 1909, February 20, 1910, September, n.d., 1908, May 22, September 4, 1910, TIA.

40. HRL to parents, May 16, 1909, September 17, 1911, February 11, July 21, 1912, TIA.

41. HRL to parents, April 3, July 25, 1909, May 8, 1910, n.d., 12, 1911, TIA.

42. HRL Elson interview, 1965, TIA; HRL speech, November 17, 1932, LT.

43. HRL to parents, October 29, 1911, March 10, 1912, HRL to Emmavail and Elisabeth, February 11, 1912, TIA; Spence, *The Gate of Heavenly Peace*, pp. 94–153.
44. HRL to Miss Dolph, March 4, 1912, HRL to Mrs. Linen, January, n.d., 1912; HRL speech at Saint Thomas Church, New York City, December 13, 1942, TIA.
45. HRL to parents, July 14, 21, 1912, TIA.
46. Elisabeth Luce Moore interview.
47. Ella Shields to ERL, November 7, 1912, Sheldon Luce to Henry Kobler, October 11, 1963, TIA.
48. HRL to ERL, October 31, November 13, multiple n.d., 1912, TIA.
49. HWL to HRL, February 3, n.d., 1912, LT.
50. Elisabeth Luce Moore interview.
51. HRL to ERL, November 6, 1912, HRL to parents, November 8, 1912, TIA.

II   THE STRIVER

1. HRL to parents, November 13, 14, 22, 1912, TIA.
2. HRL to parents, November 22, n.d., December 1, 7, 9, 12, 1912, HRL to Emmavail, December 10, 1912, TIA.
3. HWL to HRL, n.d., 1913, LT; HRL Elson interview, 1965, p. 43, TIA.
4. HRL to parents, December 11, 16, 24, 1912, January 12, 19, 1913, TIA; "Idolatry," a poem by HRL, n.d., 1913, LT.
5. ERL to HRL, January 8, 1913, HWL to HRL, January 10, 13, 1913, LT; HRL to parents, January 26, 1913, HRL to ERL, February 9, 1913, TIA.
6. HRL to HWL, March 14, 1913, LT; HRL to HWL, March 18, 23, 1913, April, n.d., 1913, HRL to ERL, April 7, 1913, TIA; HRL travel diary, n.d., 1913, LT.
7. HRL to ERL, April 14, 1913, TIA; HWL to HRL, May 2, 1913, LT.
8. HRL to ERL, April 14, 1913, TIA; railroad tickets and tour receipts, n.d., 1913, LT; HRL to HWL, April 25, 1913, TIA.
9. Miss Dolph to HWL, August 6, 1913, LT; HRL to parents, August 24, 30, 1913, TIA; Harold Burt to ERL, August 31, 1913, Harold Burt to HRL, September 4, 1913, LT.
10. HWL to HRL, n.d., 1913, ERL to HRL, January 12, 1914, LT.
11. HRL Elson interview, 1965, p. 46, TIA; HWL to HRL, December 11, 1913, ERL to HRL, December 7, 1912, LT.
12. HRL to ERL, n.d., 1913, TIA.
13. E. Digby Baltzell, *The Protestant Establishment: Aristocracy and Caste in America* (New York: Random House, 1965), pp. 109–42.
14. Lael Tucker Wertenbaker and Maude Basserman, *The Hotchkiss School: A Portrait* (Lakeville, Conn.: Hotchkiss School, 1966), pp. 1–12; James McLachlan, *American Boarding Schools: A Historical Study* (New York: Charles Scribner's Sons, 1970), pp. 189–97.
15. HRL to HWL, January 11, 1914, HRL to Emmavail, September 20, 1913, TIA; Wertenbaker and Basserman, *The Hotchkiss School*, pp. 54–55, 64.
16. HRL to HWL, January 18, 1914, HRL to ERL, November 22, 1913, HRL to HWL, December 4, 1913, January 18, 1914, TIA; Erdman Harris, "Harry Luce '16 at Hotchkiss,'" unpublished essay, Hotchkiss School Archives.
17. Paul Bergen to HRL, January 22, 1913, LT; HRL to HWL, October 20, 1913, TIA.
18. HRL to HWL, November 16, 1913, HRL to parents, November 18, 1913, TIA; "Lower Mid Year," *Hotchkiss Literary Monthly*, June 1916, Hotchkiss School Archives.
19. H. G. Buehler to HWL, December 29, 1913, HWL to HRL, n.d., 1913, LT; *Hotchkiss Record*, January 14, 1916, p. 3, Hotchkiss School Archives.
20. HRL to parents, August 27, November 17, 1915, n.d., 1917, TIA; HRL Elson

interview, 1965, TIA; Wertenbaker and Basserman, *The Hotchkiss School,* pp. 47–53.

21. HRL to HWL, September 28, 1913, TIA.
22. HRL to parents, May 16, 1914, HRL to ERL, November 22, 1913, January 15, 1915, TIA.
23. HWL to HRL, December 19, 1913, LT; HRL Elson interview, 1965, p. 38, TIA.
24. Nettie Fowler McCormick to HRL, June 12, August 9, December 13, 1913, HRL to HWL, December 19, 1913, HWL to HRL, December 11, 1913, LT; ERL to HWL, November 2, 1913, Uncle Charlie to HRL, December 13, 1913, ERL to HRL, n.d., 1913, LT.
25. HRL to ERL, December, n.d., 1913, TIA.
26. Nettie Fowler McCormick to HRL, January 14, n.d., 1914, LT.
27. ERL to HRL, January 17, 1914, LT; "Walking Chart," n.d., 1914, TIA.
28. HRL to HWL, October 18, December 27, 1914, HRL to ERL, January 1, 1915, HRL to parents, August, n.d., 1915, TIA; ERL to HRL, October 10, November 28, 1915, September 1, 1914, HWL to HRL, December 22, 1915, Elisabeth Luce to HRL, October 2, November 3, 1915, Emmavail Luce to HRL, November 22, 1915, LT; B. A. Garside, *Within the Four Seas* (New York: Frederic C. Bell, 1985), pp. 58–59; Jessie Gregory Lutz, *China and the Christian Colleges, 1850–1950* (Ithaca, N.Y.: Cornell University Press, 1971), pp. 122–23; HRL to parents, August 12, 1915, TIA.
29. HRL to parents, August 19, 1915, TIA.
30. HWL to HRL, April 17, 1914, LT.
31. HRL to HWL, January 8, December, n.d., 1914, HRL to parents, n.d., 1914, TIA.
32. HRL to parents, n.d., 1914, HRL to HWL, October 4, 1914, HRL to ERL, November 2, 1914, HRL to HWL, November 7, 1914, TIA; *Hotchkiss Record,* n.d., 1915, February 1, 1916, April, n.d., 1916, Hotchkiss School Archives.
33. *Hotchkiss Record,* October 1, 1915, January 14, 1916; St. Luke's Society Prayer Meeting announcement, n.d., 1916, LT; HRL to ERL, n.d., 1915, HRL to parents, May 23, 1915, TIA; *Hotchkiss Literary Monthly* ("the *Lit*"), November 1914, March 1915, April 1915, May 1915, March 1916, May 1916, June 1916.
34. HRL to ERL, February 23, 1915, TIA; Isaiah Wilner, *The Man Time Forgot: A Tale of Genius, Betrayal, and the Creation of Time Magazine* (New York: Harper-Collins, 2006), pp. 28–29.
35. *Daily Glonk,* n.d., May 12, 1913, Hadden Mss., TIA; Noel F. Busch, *Briton Hadden: A Biography of the Co-Founder of Time* (New York: Farrar Straus, 1949), pp. 3–17; Hans L. Wydler, " 'The Late Gargantuan Man': Briton Hadden, The Other Founder of Time" (senior essay, Yale College, 1988), in Hadden Mss., TIA; Wilner, *The Man Time Forgot,* pp. 10–16.
36. BH to E. G. Driscoll, June 20, 1914, BH to mother, n.d., 1913, Hadden Mss., TIA; Busch, *Briton Hadden,* pp. 19–22, 26–28.
37. Undated letters, BH to mother, 1913, 1914, 1915, in BH Mss., TIA; *Hotchkiss Literary Monthly,* June 1916, Hotchkiss School Archives; Robert T. Elson, *Time Inc.: The Intimate History of a Publishing Enterprise, 1923–1941* (New York: Atheneum, 1968), pp. 33–34.
38. Undated letters, BH to mother, 1913, 1914, 1915, in BH Mss., TIA.
39. HRL to HWL, September 9, 1915, TIA; Wilner, *The Man Time Forgot,* pp. 32–34.
40. HRL to ERL, October, n.d., 1915, TIA.
41. *Hothckiss Record,* October 1, 1915, March 31, April 18, 1916, and 1915–1916, passim, Hotchkiss School Archives; Busch, *Briton Hadden,* p. 31; Wydler, "The Late Gargantuan Man," pp. 7–9; Wilner, *The Man Time Forgot,* pp. 33–36; Elson, *Time Inc.,* p. 32.
42. HRL to parents, September 26, 1915, HRL to ERL, September 22, 1915, TIA.
43. HRL to HWL, October 14, 1914, TIA; *Hotchkiss Record,* October 12, 1915, LT; H. G. Buehler to HWL, March 9, 1916, March 9, 1914, TIA.

44. HRL to HWL, March, n.d., 1916, HWL to HRL, April 10, 1916, H. G. Buehler to HRL, with HRL notations, March 9, 1916, LT.
45. HRL to parents, January 12, March 29, May 29, 1916, TIA; *Hotchkiss Record*, January 18, 1916, Hotchkiss School Archives.
46. HRL to parents, June 7, 25, 1916, HRL 23-2, LC; Wilner, *The Man Time Forgot*, pp. 33–35, 38–39; John Kobler, *Luce: His Time, Life, and Fortune* (Garden City, N.Y.: Doubleday, 1968), pp. 36–37.

III   BIG MAN

1. HRL to parents, June 25, 1916, TIA; Erdman Harris to HRL, n.d., September 5, 1915, LT; John Kobler, *Luce: His Time, Life, and Fortune* (Garden City, NY: Doubleday, 1968), pp. 36–37.
2. William D. Judson, Jr., ed., *Hotchkiss Verse, 1917–1926* (Hotchkiss Literary Monthly, 1926), p. 3.
3. HWL to HRL, December 8, 1915, May 14, 1918, LT; B. A. Garside, *One Increasing Purpose: The Life of Henry Winters Luce* (New York: Fleming H. Revell Company, 1948), pp. 154–87.
4. HRL to HWL, January 7, 1914, May 13, 21, 1917, March 11, 1918, TIA; Jessie Gregory Lutz, *China and the Christian Colleges, 1850–1950* (Ithaca, N.Y.: Cornell University Press, 1971), p. 123; Garside, *One Increasing Purpose*, pp. 147–62, 173–88.
5. HRL to parents, April 23, May 29, 1916, TIA; George S. Merriam, *The Life and Times of Samuel Bowles* (New York: The Century Company, 1885, 2 vols.).
6. HRL to Elisabeth Luce, July 9, 1916, HRL to parents, July 31, n.d., 1916, TIA.
7. HRL to parents, August 7, 1916, TIA.
8. HRL to parents, August 31, 1916, TIA.
9. HRL to parents, October 1, 1916, TIA.
10. Owen Johnson, *Stover at Yale* (1912; repr., New York: Macmillan Company, 1968); pp. 20–21; Henry Seidel Canby, *Alma Mater: The Gothic Age of the American College* (New York: Farrar & Rinehart, 1936), pp. 36–40.
11. HRL to parents, January 12, April 8, August 13, 1916, TIA; Canby, *Alma Mater*, p. 41.
12. HRL to parents, September, n.d., 1916, TIA.
13. HRL to parents, November 5, December 3, 1916, January 4, 21, March 30, 1917, TIA; Isaiah Wilner, *The Man Time Forgot: A Tale of Genius, Betrayal, and the Creation of Time Magazine* (New York: HarperCollins, 2006), pp. 41–43.
14. HRL to parents, January 4, March 11, 12, 1917, TIA.
15. HRL to parents, October 1, 8, 1916, TIA.
16. HRL to parents, September, n.d., October 15, 1916, HWL to HRL, October 24, 1916, TIA.
17. HRL to parents, March 31, April, n.d., 14, 1917, TIA.
18. Commencement address, Hotchkiss School, June 13, 1964, Hotchkiss School Archives; HRL to parents, March 29, 1916, TIA.
19. HRL to HWL, September 11, 1918, HRL Elson interview, 1965, p. 48, TIA.
20. HRL to parents, April 14, May 13, 1917, TIA; HWL to HRL, March 21, 1918, Thomas Sammons to HWL, with HWL to HRL note, April 5, 1918, LT.
21. HRL to parents, June 4, 1917, TIA.
22. HRL to parents, April, n.d., June 4, August 12, 1917, TIA.
23. HRL to parents, October 19, 1917, TIA.
24. HRL to parents, October 22, November 22, 28, December 16, 1917, TIA.
25. HRL to ERL, March, n.d., April 21, 1918, TIA.
26. HRL to parents, January 10, 1918, TIA.
27. HRL to parents, January 10, n.d., 20, 1918, ERL to HRL, February 20, 1918, TIA; HWL to HRL, March 4, 1918, LT; Wilner, *The Man Time Forgot*, pp. 48–50.

28. HRL to ERL, March, n.d., 1919, TIA.
29. HRL to parents, January 10, 1918, TIA; David Ingalls interview, July 28, 1948, Lila Luce Tyng interview; Elisabeth Luce Moore interview.
30. *Yale Daily News*, January 28, 29, February 1, 1918; HRL speech, June 13, 1963, TIA; Wilner, *The Man Time Forgot*, pp. 59–60; Lila Luce Tyng interview.
31. *Yale Daily News*, January 28, 29, February 1, 28, March 9, April 6, 9, 1918.
32. ERL to HRL, September 3, 1918, LT.
33. HRL Elson interview, 1965, TIA.
34. HRL speech, n.d., 1963, TIA; Noel F. Busch, *Briton Hadden: A Biography of the Co-Founder of Time* (New York: Farrar Straus, 1949), pp. 35–36; Robert T. Elson, *Time Inc.: The Intimate History of a Publishing Enterprise, 1923–1941* (New York: Atheneum, 1968), pp. 40–42.
35. HRL to HWL, August, n.d., September 6, 18, 1918, TIA.
36. HRL to HWL, September 11, 1918, TIA.
37. HRL to ERL, September, n.d., October, n.d., 1918, HRL to parents, October 13, 1918, TIA.
38. HRL to ERL, November, n.d., 3, 14, 1918, TIA.
39. HRL to HWL, December 15, 18, 22, 1918, TIA.
40. Henry Seidel Canby, *College Sons and College Fathers* (New York: Harper & Brothers, 1915), pp. 102–10; Canby, *Alma Mater*, pp. 58–59.
41. HRL to ERL, February 24, March, n.d., 1919, TIA; Johnson, *Stover at Yale*, pp. 21–22.
42. HRL to HWL, March 1919, HRL to ERL, May, n.d., 1919, TIA.
43. HRL to HWL, May 16, 1919, HRL to ERL, May, n.d., 1919, TIA; Johnson, *Stover at Yale*, pp. 305–7; Wilner, *The Man Time Forgot*, pp. 58–59; LT interview.
44. HRL to parents, August 10, September 25, n.d., December, n.d., 1919, HRL to ERL, n.d., 1920, HRL to ERL, March, n.d., April, n.d., 1920, TIA.
45. HRL to parents, June 20, 1920, TIA; HRL to LH, December, n.d., 1921, LT; Elson, *Time Inc.*, pp. 44–45.
46. HRL to parents, June 20, 1920, TIA.
47. ERL to HRL, July 24, 1918, HWL to HRL, April 19, 21, May 24, July 20, 1918, HRL to HWL, July 8, 1918, LT.
48. HRL to parents, n.d., 1919, January, n.d., 1920, TIA.
49. HRL to parents, July 9, 1920, TIA.
50. Thornton Wilder to HRL, May 17, 1921, LT.
51. "Mr. Luce at lunch with Bob Elson," memo on interview, April 29, 1965, TIA.
52. HRL to parents, September 2, 16, 1920, HRL to Emmavail, September 14, 1920, TIA.
53. HRL to parents, November 4, 28, 1920, TIA.
54. HRL to LH, December 4, 1921, LT.
55. LH to HRL, January 3, February 13, 1921, HRL to LH, January 1, February 14, March 20, April 8, 16, May 3, 1921, Dance card, Magdalen College, June 20, 1921, HRL to LH, June 2, 7, 10, 24, 29, 1921, LT; HRL to parents, December 1, 16, 24, 1920, April 3, 1921, TIA.
56. HRL to parents, December 24, 1920, TIA; HRL to LH, January 30, March 30, April 6, 1921, LT.
57. HRL to parents, June 21, 1921, TIA.
58. Ibid.

IV   "THE PAPER"

1. Isaiah Wilner, *The Man Time Forgot: A Tale of Genius, Betrayal, and the Creation of Time Magazine* (New York: HarperCollins, 2006), pp. 63–65; HRL Elson interview, 1965, TIA; "Notes on tape," n.d., TIA.

2. Ben Hecht, "Bedtime Story," transcript of radio broadcast, September 23, 1958, TIA; HRL Elson interview, 1965, TIA; "Notes on tape," n.d., 1965, TIA.
3. Alex Groner to Bill Furth, September 30, 1958, summary of Luce's reaction to Hecht story, *Chicago Daily News*, July 13, 20, August 10, 30, 1921, clippings in TIA; HRL to parents, n.d., 1921, September 21, 1921, HRL to ERL, n.d., 1921, TIA; "Notes on Luce interview," 1965, TIA.
4. HRL to parents, n.d., 1921, November, n.d., 1921, HRL to ERL, n.d., 1921, TIA.
5. HRL Elson interview, 1965, TIA; Robert T. Elson, *Time Inc.: The Intimate History of a Publishing Enterprise, 1923–1941* (New York: Atheneum, 1968), pp. 54–55.
6. HRL to ERL, n.d., 1921, TIA.
7. HRL to LH, November 28, December 4, 1921, LT.
8. HRL to LH, November 28, 1921, LT.
9. HRL to Henry Justin Smith, editor, *Chicago Daily News*, n.d., 1921, TIA; HRL to parents, December, n.d., 1921, TIA; HRL to LT, December 1, 1921, LT; *New York World* clippings, July–August 1921, Hadden Mss., TIA; Matthew Schneirov, *The Dream of a New Social Order: Popular Magazines in America, 1893–1914* (New York: Columbia University Press, 1994), pp. 85–91.
10. HRL to Henry Justin Smith, n.d., 1921, TIA.
11. HRL to LH, n.d., 1921, December, n.d., 1921, LT; HRL to parents, n.d., 1921, TIA.
12. HRL to LH, December 4, 1921, LT.
13. HRL Elson interview, 1965, TIA; HRL to LH, December 4, n.d., 1921, LT.
14. HRL to ERL, January, n.d., 1922, HRL to LH, December 12, 1920, LT.
15. HRL to Lila, n.d., 1922, LT; Noel Busch, "Interview with HRL," June 20, 1939, Hadden to mother, n.d., 1922, Hadden Mss., TIA.
16. HRL to Nettie Fowler McCormick, December 6, 1921, McCormick Collections, Series 2B, Box 177; Noel F. Busch, *Briton Hadden: A Biography of the Co-Founder of Time* (New York: Farrar Straus, 1949), pp. 64–65; James L. Baughman, *Henry R. Luce and the Rise of the American News Media* (Boston: Twayne, 1987), p. 24.
17. "Plans and Specifications of the Newspaper Man," *Literary Digest*, April 15, 1922, pp. 64–67; Elson, *Time Inc.*, pp. 81–83; Baughman, *Henry R. Luce*, pp. 24–28.
18. Gay Talese, *The Kingdom and the Power* (New York: World Publishing Company, 1969), pp. 159–63; Richard Kluger, *The Paper: The Life and Death of the New York Herald Tribune* (New York: Knopf, 1986), pp. 164–65, 184–86; *Columbia Journalism Review* 18 (November–December 1980): 73; Baughman, *Henry R. Luce*, p. 29.
19. Schneirov, *The Dream of a New Social Order*, pp. 2–6.
20. Ray Stannard Baker, *American Chronicle* (New York: Charles Scribner's Sons, 1945), pp. 96–101; Frank Luther Mott, *A History of American Magazines, 1885–1905* (Cambridge, Mass.: Harvard University Press, 1957), pp. 453–505, 589–619; Schneirov, *The Dream of a New Social Order*, pp. 75–124.
21. *Literary Digest*, April 15, 1922, pp. 64–67, May 12, 1928, pp. 5–7, 9–11; Mott, *History of American Magazines, 1885–1905*, pp. 568–79; John Tebbel and Mary Ellen Zuckerman, *The Magazine in America, 1741–1990* (New York: Oxford University Press, 1991), pp. 160–61; David Reed, *The Popular Magazine in Britain and the United States, 1880–1960* (London: British Library, 1997), pp. 128–29; Theodore Peterson, *Magazines in the Twentieth Century* (Urbana: University of Illinois Press, 1964), pp. 154–56.
22. Mott, *History of American Magazines, 1885–1905*, pp. 575–77.
23. Peterson, *Magazines in the Twentieth Century*, p. 154.
24. HRL to LH, n.d., 1922, LT; HRL Elson interview, 1965, TIA.
25. HRL to LH, February, n.d., March 21, 1922, LT; Robert T. Elson, *The World of Time Inc.: The Intimate History of a Publishing Enterprise, 1941–1960* (New York: Atheneum, 1973), p. 57.

26. Samuel Everitt to HRL, February 10, 1922, LT; Elson, *Time Inc.*, p. 61.
27. HRL to LH, May, n.d., 1922, *Time* circular, 1922, LT.
28. HRL to LH, May 31, June 2, 1922, LT; "Preliminary Circular," July 24, 1922, Larsen Mss., TIA.
29. HRL to LH, June 7, 15, 19, n.d., 1922, LT.
30. HRL to LH, April 30, June 7, July 14, 20, 1922, LT; HRL to HWL, n.d., 1922, TIA; HRL Elson interview, 1965, TIA.
31. HRL to LH, August 1, 12, 1922, LT.
32. HRL to LH, July 20, August, n.d., November 8, 1922, LT; "Money Raising," Luce interview, June 20, 1939, TIA; Elson, *Time Inc.*, pp. 9–14.
33. *Time* prospectus, 1922, "Specimen Issue," February 17, 1923, TIA.
34. HRL to LH, n.d., March 4, November 3, 8, 1922, LT; "Early Days," Luce interview, June 20, 1939, TIA.
35. HRL to LH, March 11, n.d., 1922, TIA; HRL Elson interview, 1965, TIA.
36. Manfred Gottfried oral history, August 4–6, 1961, pp. 1–6, TIA; HRL Elson interview, 1964, TIA.
37. Roy E. Larsen to Celia Sugarman, November 26, 1962, TIA; Larsen oral history, pp. 10–19, TIA; Elson, *Time Inc.*, p. 60; HRL to LH, February, n.d., 1923, LT.
38. HRL to LH, January, n.d., 1923, January, n.d., 25, 29, 1923, LT; Gottfried diary, January 22, 1923, TIA.
39. *Time* prospectus, 1922, TIA.
40. Ibid.; *Time* advertising circular, May 1922, LT; Larsen oral history, TIA.
41. Gottfried diary, January 3, 5, 7, 1923, TIA; HRL to LH, n.d., 1922, LT; Notes on Luce-Larsen discussion, January 28, 1957, TIA.
42. HRL to LH, November 8, 1922, LT.
43. HRL to LH, December, n.d., 20, 1922, January, n.d., February, n.d., 1923, LT; Specimen issues, December 30, 1922, February 17, 1923, TIA.
44. HRL to LH, December, n.d., 1922, January, n.d., 29, 1923, LT.
45. HRL to LH, n.d., January 25, 1923, LT; Gottfried oral history, 1964, TIA.
46. Gottfried oral history, 1964, TIA; HRL Elson interview, 1965, TIA.
47. Gottfried oral history, 1961, TIA.
48. *Time*, March 3, 1923.
49. HRL Elson interview, 1965, TIA; HRL to LH, March, n.d., 1923, LT.

v "TIME: THE WEEKLY NEWS-MAGAZINE"

1. HRL to LH, n.d., 1923, LT.
2. HRL to LH, July 15, 1923, March, n.d., 1923, LT; *New York Times*, March 2, 1923.
3. HRL to LH, March, n.d., 1923, HRL to Nettie McCormick, July 1, 1923, HRL to parents, March, n.d., 1924, LT; Robert T. Elson, *Time Inc.: The Intimate History of a Publishing Enterprise, 1923–1941* (New York: Atheneum, 1968), pp. 70–71.
4. Notes on Luce-Larsen-Paine discussion at Paine 25th anniversary luncheon, January 28, 1957, HRL Elson interview, 1965, TIA; *Time* Annual Report, 1924, TIA; HRL to LH, May 5, 24, 1923, LT; Elson, *Time Inc.*, pp. 70–71.
5. HRL to LH, n.d., May 8, 1923, Yale, Commencement Week Program, 1923, HRL to LH, June 21, 1923, HWL to H. L. Banghart, September 14, 1923, LT.
6. HRL to LH, March, n.d., 1923, October 7, 1923, LT; Time Inc. President's Report, December 31, 1923, TIA.
7. HRL Elson interview, 1966, TIA.
8. HRL to Harry Davison, April 15, 1925, "Description of Capital Structure of Time Inc.," April 10, 1925, HRL Elson interview, 1965, Roy Larsen letter to *Saturday Review* subscribers, December 2, 1924, TIA; Elson, *Time Inc.*, pp. 77–79.
9. HRL to LH, July 4, 18, 1923, LT.

10. James L. Baughman, *Henry R. Luce and the Rise of the American News Media* (Boston: Twayne, 1987), p. 38; HRL to Nettie McCormick, n.d., McCormick papers, Series 2B, Box 182.

11. Baughman, *Henry R. Luce*, p. 38; HRL to Nettie McCormick, n.d., McCormick papers, Series 2B, Box 182.

12. HRL to LH, July 2, 1923, HRL to Lila,, n.d., 1923, LT.

13. HRL to LH, n.d., February, n.d., 1923, July 18, 1923, LT.

14. HRL to LH, January 27, n.d., 1923, March, multiple n.d., March 18, 1923, LT.

15. Lila Luce Tyng interview; HRL to LH, March, n.d., 1923, LT.

16. HRL to LH, March, n.d., June, n.d., 1923, October 10, 1923, LT.

17. HRL to LH, June, n.d., 1923, July, n.d., 1923, HRL to Nettie McCormick, July 1, 1923, HRL to LH, July 5, 12, 1923, LT.

18. HRL to LH, October 12, 1923, LT.

19. HRL to LH, October 12, 18, 1923, LT.

20. HRL to LH, July 29, October 15, 19, December, multiple n.d., 1923, LT; W. A. Swanberg, *Luce and His Empire* (New York: Charles Scribner's Sons, 1972), p. 59.

21. HRL to ERL, December 2, 1923, with undated notations by ERL, TIA; HRL to LH, December 18, 1923, LT.

22. LH to HRL, n.d., 1926, LT.

23. "The Move to Cleveland," internal memo, n.d, TIA.

24. HRL to LH, May 8, n.d., 1923, LT.

25. "Mr. Luce at lunch with Bob Elson," memo, April 29, 1965, TIA: HRL Elson interview, 1965, "Summary of Assets and Liabilities," December 31, 1925, TIA.

26. HRL Elson interview 1965, "The Move to Cleveland," internal memo, n.d., TIA.

27. HRL to LH, n.d., 1925, n.d., 1926, LT; HRL to parents, n.d., 1924, Beth to HRL, n.d., 1925, HRL Elson interview, 1965, TIA; *Cleveland Times*, July 29, 1925, August 28, 1925; *Cleveland Plain Dealer*, August 28, 1925; Samuel Mather to Guy Emerson, n.d., 1925, TIA.

28. Interview with Lila Luce Tyng; "The Move to Cleveland," memo, n.d., TIA; Larsen memoir, August 1956, TIA.

29. "*Time* Likes Cleveland," *Clevelander*, June 1926, clipping in TIA.

30. *Cleveland Plain Dealer*, n.d., 1926, *Cleveland Press*, n.d., 1926, clippings in TIA; "Time Quiz: Questions and Answers," Dayton, Ohio, April 20, 1926, LT; *New York World*, March 18, 1927; HRL Elson interview, 1965, TIA.

31. Time Inc. Treasurer's Report, January 2, 1926, "General Report to the Board of Directors of Time Inc.," April 1, 1926, Time Inc., President's Report, January 1, 1927, BH to Larsen, March, n.d., 1927, Larsen Mss.; Larsen, "First Estimate 1927 Budget," "The Move to Cleveland," memo, n.d., HRL Elson interview, 1965, TIA; Elson, *Time Inc.*, p. 97.

32. HRL to LH, BH to Harry Davison, July 11, 1957, Larsen memoir, 1956, TIA; HRL Elson interview, 1965, TIA.

33. "Treasurer's Report," January 31, 1928, "Facts for Directors," April 8, 1929, TIA.

34. President's Report, February 24, 1927, TIA.

35. Noel F. Busch, *Briton Hadden: A Biography of the Co-Founder of Time* (New York: Farrar Straus, 1949), pp. 134–38, 180–81; HRL Elson interview, 1966, TIA; "Copyright Protection," editorial in *The Chicago Tribune*, n.d., 1929, TIA.

36. Staff rosters, 1923, 1924, 1927, 1929, TIA; T. S. Matthews, *Name and Address: An Autobiography* (New York: Simon & Schuster, 1960), p. 221.

37. Subscription circular, n.d., 1926, TIA.

38. *Time*, August 3, 1925, August 25, 1930, March 2, 1931; John S. Martin, "Briton Hadden as Editor and Co-Founder of Time," speech, New Haven, April 27, 1932, TIA.

39. *Time*, August 10, 1925, October 6, 1924, August 25, 1930; BH memo, n.d., TIA; Robert Withington, "Some New 'Portmanteau' Words," *Philological Quarterly* 9 (April 1930): 158–64; BH memo, n.d., TIA; Busch, *Briton Hadden*, p. 114.

40. *Time,* July 23, May 17, 28, 1923, October 27, 1930, April 6, 1931; Busch, *Briton Hadden,* p. 144.

41. Matthews, *Name and Address,* pp. 217–18, 221; Busch, *Briton Hadden,* p. 133.

42. Joseph J. Firebaugh, "The Vocabulary of Time Magazine," *American Speech,* October 1940, pp. 232–42; Busch, *Briton Hadden,* pp. 110–13; "The Index of Time," November 1932, Hotchkiss School Archives; "The Log Takes a Lot of Time," U.S. Naval Academy, March 23, 1928, "Columns," University of Washington, February 1931, R. T. Johnson to HRL, May 5, 1934; "Time: But Not the Weekly Newsmagazine," White Company, May 1934, *Rochester Times-Union,* March 27, 1929, *Edmonton Journal,* n.d., TIA; ERL to HRL, September 10, 1926, LT.

43. HRL Elson interview, 1965, TIA; HRL speech in Rochester, NY, n.d., 1928, LT; Democratic National Committee receipt, October 29, 1928, LT; *Time* advertisement in *Christian Century,* November 13, 1924, TIA.

44. *Time,* February 4, 1929.

45. *Time,* March 3, 1923.

46. Dwight Macdonald, "'Time' and Henry Luce," *Nation,* May 1, 1937, p. 502; *Covering History: TIME Magazine Covers, 1923–1997* (New York: Time Inc., 1998); Frederick S. Voss, *Faces of Time: 75 Years of Time Magazine Cover Portraits* (New York: Little, Brown, 1998), pp. 12–16 and passim.

47. *Time,* September 14, 1925, March 2, 10, 1923, May 23, 1927.

48. *Time,* March 24, April 21, August 6, 1923, January 14, 1924, August 10, 1925, October 12, 1931; Richard Washburn Child, "Making of Mussolini," *Saturday Evening Post,* June 28, 1924; Child, "What Does Mussolini Mean," *Saturday Evening Post,* July 26, 1924; Child, "Mussolini Now," *Saturday Evening Post,* March 24, 1928; David Nasaw, *The Chief: The Life of William Randolph Hearst* (New York: Houghton Mifflin, 2000), pp. 323, 355–56, 380, 470–74; John Patrick Diggins, *Mussolini and Fascism: The View from America* (Princeton, N.J.: Princeton University Press, 1972), pp. 26–28, 42–57.

49. *Time,* December 10, 1923, June 9, 1930; Swanberg, *Luce and His Empire,* pp. 76–78.

50. Goldsborough to HRL, n.d., 1929, TIA.

51. *Time,* March 9, 1936; HRL Elson interviews, 1957, 1965, TIA; Swanberg, *Luce and His Empire,* pp. 129–30.

52. Busch, *Briton Hadden,* pp. 192–93; HRL Elson interview, 1966, TIA; *Time,* March 3, 1927.

53. *Time,* March 5, April 28, 1923, March 10, 1924, June 1, 1925, May 24, 1926, June 30, 1930.

54. HRL Elson interview, 1965, TIA.

55. Advertising flier, 1925, TIA.

56. Joan Shelly Rubin, "'Information, Please!' Culture and Expertise in the Interwar Period," *American Quarterly* 35 (1983): 499–517.

57. Sinclair Lewis, *Babbitt* (1922; repr., New York: Signet, 1950), p. 152; "A Tour Through Time Colony," advertising pamphlet, 1927, *Time* circulation map, 1924, *Time* advertisting circular, 1927, TIA.

58. Copy for *Time* circular, n.d., TIA; "This Class-Ridden Democracy," advertising pamphlet, 1928, TIA; "Success comes mysteriously . . . ," advertising pamphlet, 1929, TIA.

59. Elson, *Time Inc.,* p. 82; *Time* internal newsletter, January 7, 1929, "A Tour Through Time Colony," advertising pamphlet, 1928, TIA.

60. Busch, *Briton Hadden,* pp. 215–16; HRL to Lila, March, n.d., 1923, Lilian Rixey to Noel Busch, June 28, 1948, TIA.

61. HRL Elson interview, 1965, TIA.

62. *Tide: Dedicated to the Flow of Business,* April 1927, E. D. Kennedy to David Edwin Sanders, October 29, 1928, E. Robin Little memo, April 7, 1953, Lilian Rixey to Noel Busch, October 4, 1948, HRL Elson interview, 1957, Hadden diary, Hadden Mss., TIA.

63. HRL memo to staff, March 15, 1928, TIA; Gottfried oral history, TIA; Lila Luce Tyng interview.

64. "Hadden illness & death," *Time* memo, May 5, 1965, HRL Elson interview, 1965, Lilian Rixey to Noel Busch, June 28, 1948, BH to Harry Davison, October 26, 1926, TIA; Lila Luce Tyng interview.

65. Walter Buell to HRL, June 28, 1926, TIA; Lila Luce Tyng interview.

66. HRL to LH, n.d., 1927, LT; Lila Luce Tyng interview.

67. "Hadden Illness & Death," *Time* memo, May 5, 1965, TIA.

68. Ibid; "Bulletin on Mr. Hadden," January 30, 1929, February 5, 1929, TIA; Gottfried oral history, TIA.

69. Gottfried oral history, HRL to Daniel Winter, January 19, 1929, Lilian Rixey to Noel Busch, June 28, 1948, TIA.

70. *Time*, March 11, 18, 1929.

VI EMPIRE BUILDING

1. Lila Luce Tyng, Elisabeth Luce Moore interviews; HRL to HWL, n.d., 1929, HRL to Board of Directors, May 1929, TIA.

2. Hadden will, Hadden Mss., TIA; *Brooklyn Eagle*, March 8, 1929; Howard V. Luce to HRL, February 28, 1929, TIA.

3. HRL to Roy Larsen, September 3, 1929, Charles Stillman to Harry P. Davison, September 3, 1929, "Time Inc. Stock," memo, November 15, 1967, Robert Elson to Jim Linen, April 19, 1966, "Employees' Stock Purchase Plan," October 14, 1929, HRL to Davison, September 3, 1929, HRL to Board of Directors, September 4, 1929, TIA.

4. "Financial Prospectus and Plan of Operations," n.d., 1930, HRL Elson interview, 1965, HRL to Roy Larsen, n.d., 1928, HRL to Harry P. Davison, February 7, May 24, 1929, "Special Report to the Board of Directors," February 1929, "Report of the Experimental Department," May 24, 1929, HRL to Davison, May 24, 1929, TIA.

5. "Preface to Fortune," 1929, form letter, October 21, 1929, TIA.

6. *World's Work*, January 1929.

7. Eric Hodgins oral history, 1968, p. 49, COHP.

8. "The American Tycoon," HRL speech, March 27, 1929, TIA; Louis Galambos, *The Public Image of Big Business in America, 1880–1940: A Quantitative Study in Social Change* (Baltimore: Johns Hopkins University Press, 1975), pp. 191–21.

9. "The American Tycoon," HRL speech, March 27, 1929, TIA; Eric Hodgins oral history, 1968, p. 49, COHP; John K. Jessup, ed., *The Ideas of Henry Luce* (New York: Atheneum, 1969), pp. 221, 223–24, 385–86; James L. Baughman, *Henry R. Luce and the Rise of the American News Media* (Boston: Twayne, 1987), p. 64; Galambos, *The Public Image of Big Business in America*, pp. 222–49.

10. Lila Luce Tyng interview; HRL Elson interview, 1965, TIA.

11. HRL to Board of Directors, May 24, 1929, HRL, "Prospectus for a Monthly Magazine," draft, n.d., 1929, TIA; Announcement of *Fortune* (advertisement), *New York Times*, January 24, 1930 ("The First Number of the Most Beautiful Magazine in America"), "Preface to *Fortune*," 1930, TIA; *Brooklyn Eagle*, October 6, 1930; Robert T. Elson, *Time Inc.: The Intimate History of a Publishing Enterprise, 1923–1941* (New York: Atheneum, 1968), pp. 140–41; Milton St. John, "True Stories de Luxe," *Nation*, March 4, 1931, p. 239; John Huey, Daniel Okrent, *Fortune: The Art of Covering Business* (Layton, Utah: Gibbs, Smith, 1999).

12. HRL, "Topics for *Fortune*," n.d., HRL notes on *Fortune*, untitled, n.d., "Preface to *Fortune*," 1930, HRL, "Prospectus for a Monthly Magazine," draft, n.d., 1929, TIA.

13. "Preface to *Fortune*," 1930, "Announcing *Fortune*," form letters to subscribers,

July 8, October 21, 1929, "Directive for the Editorial Development of FOR-TUNE," n.d., 1947, TIA.

14. C. L. Stillman to Roy Larsen, "April Results," May 20, 1930, Stillman to HRL, Larsen, June 9, 1929, Larsen to Johnson, August 8, 1930, HRL to Board of Directors, May 24, 1929, TIA; Elson, *Time Inc.*, p. 141.

15. Scott Donaldson, *Archibald MacLeish: An American Life* (Boston: Houghton Mifflin, 1992), pp. 209–10.

16. HRL to Board of Directors, May 24, 1929, TIA; HRL to MBW, May 8, 1929, Parker Lloyd-Smith to MBW, May 22, June 10, 1929, MBW to Parker Lloyd-Smith, June 16, 1929, Box 49, MBW Mss.; Elson, *Time Inc.*, pp. 135–36; Vicki Goldberg, *Margaret Bourke-White: A Biography* (New York: Harper & Row, 1986), pp. 79–100, 105; John R. Stomberg, "Art and *Fortune*: Machine-Age Discourse and the Visual Culture of Industrial Modernity" (Ph.D. diss., Boston University, 1999), p. 117.

17. Tom Durrance to "Fill," December 9, 1944, Box 50, MBW Mss.; *New York Mirror*, September 22, 1930; Goldberg, *Margaret Bourke-White*, pp. 101–12.

18. *Fortune*, February 1930; Stephen Bennett Phillips, *Margaret Bourke-White: The Photography of Design, 1927–1936* (New York: Rizzoli, 2005), pp. 18–53; Susan Goldman Rubin, *Margaret Bourke-White* (New York: Harry N. Abrams, 1999), pp. 22–47; Ronald E. Osman and Harry Littell, *Margaret Bourke-White: The Early Work, 1922–1930* (Boston: Godine Paragon, 2005), pp. xxvii–xxxvi, 83–88.

19. *Fortune*, February 1930; Upton Sinclair, *The Jungle* (1906; repr., New York: Barnes & Noble Books, 2003), pp. 102–3, 140–41.

20. *Fortune*, December 1930, July 1930, May 1933, March 1931, August 1931; Terry Smith, *Making the Modern: Industry, Art, and Design in America* (Chicago: University of Chicago Press, 1993), pp. 159–98; Stomberg, "Art and *Fortune*," pp. 125–48; Michael Augspurger, *An Economy of Abundant Beauty:* Fortune *Magazine & Depression America* (Ithaca, N.Y.: Cornell University Press, 2004), pp. 80–85.

21. *Fortune*, March 1930.

22. HRL, "Aristocracy and Motives," 1930 speech, TIA; *Fortune*, September 1932.

23. *Fortune*, May 1930, April 1930, September 1930, January 1931; Augspurger, *An Economy of Abundant Beauty*, p. 35; Alfred Chandler, *Strategy and Structure: Chapters in the History of the Industrial Enterprise* (Cambridge, Mass.: MIT Press, 1962), pp. 114–62.

24. Milton St. John, "True Stories de Luxe," pp. 239–40; HRL memo to editors, May 18, 1944, HRL Elson interview, 1966, TIA.

25. HRL, "To members of FORTUNE's Research Staff," April 13, 1933, Ingersoll to HRL, April 26, 1933, TIA; Ingersoll to *Fortune* Researchers, April 27, 1933, HRL to Ingersoll, January, n.d., 1933, January 9, 1933, HRL to Archibald MacLeish, n.d., 1930, TIA; Ingersoll, "Answers to Time Inc. Questions," March 28, 1956, Ingersoll Mss.; Archibald MacLeish, "The First Nine Years," *Writing for Fortune* (New York: Time Inc., 1980), p. 8; Galambos, *The Public Image of Big Business in America*, pp. 246–49.

26. Robert Coughlan, "A Collection of Characters," in *Writing for Fortune*, p. 74; John Chamberlain, "How I Really Learned About Business," in ibid., p. 28; Dwight Macdonald, "Against the Grain," in ibid., p. 150; Michael Wreszin, *A Rebel in Defense of Tradition: The Life and Politics of Dwight Macdonald* (New York: Basic Books, 1994), pp. 22–23; Laurence Bergreen, *James Agee: A Life* (New York: E. P. Dutton, 1984), pp. 106–8; Roy Hoopes, *Ralph Ingersoll: A Biography* (New York: Atheneum, 1985), pp. 93–97.

27. Donaldson, *Archibald MacLeish*, pp. 242–44; Hoopes, *Ralph Ingersoll*, p. 97; Charles J. V. Murphy, "I Wish My Fortune Years Were Just Beginning," in *Writing for Fortune*, pp. 40–43; *Fortune*, September 1933; Ingersoll to HRL, March 7, 1934, TIA; *Fortune*, March, May, June, July 1934, February 1936, September 1934.

28. *Fortune*, July, October 1934.

29. Macdonald to Dinsmore Wheeler, March 8, 1935, Macdonald to Nicholas Macdonald, September 25, 1963, TIA; Michael Wreszin, ed., *A Moral Temper: The Letters of Dwight Macdonald* (Chicago: Ivan R. Dee, 2001), pp. 52, 352; Wreszin, *A Rebel in Defense of Tradition*, pp. 47–53; Bergreen, *James Agee*, pp. 158–77, 244–45, 257–61; William Stott, *Documentary Expression and Depression America* (Chicago: University of Illinois Press, 1973, 1986), pp. 259–314.

30. Macdonald to Nancy Rodman, July 20, 1934, TIA; Wreszin, *A Moral Temper*, p. 49; *Fortune*, June 1936; HRL Elson interview, 1965, TIA; Dwight Macdonald, " 'Fortune' Magazine," *Nation*, May 8, 1937, pp. 529–30.

31. Macdonald to HRL, n.d., 1936, TIA; Wreszin, *A Moral Temper*, pp. 67–71; HRL to Ingersoll, April 29, 1933, HRL to Alexander Legge, May 31, 1933, HRL to MacLeish, July 27, 1933, HRL to staff, May 13, 1937, MacLeish to HRL, May 5, 1937, July 18, 1938, Russell Davenport to HRL, February 14, 1951, TIA; *Fortune*, April 1934, December 1935; HRL Elson interview, 1965, TIA.

32. HRL to Louis Howe, Sept. 15, 1933, HRL to Stephen Early, September 22, 1933, Stephen Early to HRL, Sept. 21, 1933, MacLeish to HRL, n.d., 1937, Hodgins to HRL, November 11, 1936, HRL to Hodgins, November 11, 1936, January 21, 1937, TIA; Elson, *Time Inc.*, pp. 250, 261–64; HRL, "Respectus," May 10, 1937, HRL to staff, May 13, 1937, TIA.

33. John K. Jessup, "Comments (At Random) on the 'Respectus,' " n.d., 1937, E. D. Kennedy, "Decline of Fortune," November 29, 1937, Davenport to HRL, February 14, 1951, Research staff to Davenport, April 7, 1938, TIA.

34. *Fortune*, October 1936; HRL speech, "Calculability of Abundance," November 10, 1937, TIA.

35. HRL speech, Rochester, New York, March 1928, HRL speech, Scranton, Pennsylvania, April 19, 1934, TIA; Jessup, *The Ideas of Henry Luce*, pp. 219, 224–26.

36. *Fortune*, February, June 1938, February 1939; Joseph Thorndike, "The Liberal and Salutary Path: *Fortune* Magazine and the Search for a Business Liberalism" (thesis, University of Virginia, 1993), pp. 48–60.

37. *Fortune*, March 1939, March 1940.

VII   "TIME MARCHES ON"

1. HRL, "General Memorandum," September 3, 1931, "Time Incorporated: Who's Who and Where," internal office map, n.d., TIA; JSBD, August 3, 1931; HRL Elson interview, 1966, TIA.

2. HRL to HWL, May 7, 1932, HRL to ERL, n.d., 1932, LT; JSBD, April 22, 1932.

3. Leslie Severinghaus interview.

4. HRL to LH, n.d., 1932, May 12, 1932, HRL to Henry, May 19, 1932, LT; *Victoria Colonist*, May 9, 1932; Severinghaus journal, pp. 1–12, TIA.

5. HRL to LH, May 27, 1932, LT.

6. HRL to HWL, May 7, n.d., 1932, Severinghaus journal, pp. 12–26, TIA; Leslie Severinghaus interview; Eugene Barnett to Edward Haag, June 1, 1932, Courtland Van Deusen to HRL, May 30, 1932, Nelson Johnson to HRL, June 14, 1932, LT.

7. HRL to LH, June n.d., 1932, Severinghaus journal, pp. 26–31, TIA; W. A. Swanberg, *Luce and His Empire* (New York: Charles Scribner's Sons, 1972), p. 98.

8. HRL to HWL, May 7, 1932, HRL to LH, June 10, 1932, Severinghaus journal, p. 16, TIA; Leslie Severinghaus interview; Mme. Wellington Koo with Isabella Taves, *No Feast Lasts Forever* (New York: Quadrangle Books, 1975), p. 189; Sterling Seagrave, *The Soong Dynasty* (New York: Harper & Row, 1985), pp. 311–13.

9. Seagrave, *The Soong Dynasty*, pp. 307–8.

10. HRL, "Notes on U.S.S.R.," August 1932, Severinghaus journal, pp. 33–45, TIA; Leslie Severinghaus interview.

11. HRL memo to Time Editors, n.d., 1933 ("Salaries"), JSB Mss.

12. JSBD, May 15, 1930, May 1, 1931, January 28, October 14, 31, 1932, June 17, 1933; Robert T. Elson, *Time Inc.: The Intimate History of a Publishing Enterprise, 1923–1941* (New York: Atheneum, 1968), pp. 158–59.

13. JSBD, January 14, February 18, March 24, November 11, 1932, January 15, April 16, September 28, November 16, 24, 1933, March 22, 1934; HRL Elson interview, 1965, TIA.

14. Skyline dummy, 1931, TIA; *Architectural Forum*, June 1937; JSBD, March 3, 1932; HRL to MBW, May 10, 1932, Box 49, MBW Mss.; Robert T. Elson, *The World of Time Inc.: The Intimate History of a Publishing Enterprise, 1941–1960* (New York: Atheneum, 1973), pp. 186–94; Elson, *Time Inc.*, pp. 322–24.

15. JSBD, September 23, 1935, April 3, 1936; *Letters*, 1934–1937, TIA; Elson, *Time Inc.*, pp. 204–5.

16. Larsen to Richard Krolik, March 10, 1970, Larsen Mss., TIA; *Editor and Publisher*, November 3, 1928; David Alan Campbell, "The Origin and Early Developments of the Time Incorporated Radio Series the *March of Time*" (M.A. thesis, Central Missouri State College, 1969), pp. 26–41; Frank C. Tucker III, "A Critical Evaluation of the *March of Time*, 1931–1932" (M.A. thesis, Central Missouri State College, 1969), pp. 6–12.

17. HRL Elson interview, 1965, TIA.

18. *March of Time* script, March 27, 1931, TIA; Tucker, "A Critical Evaluation of the *March of Time*," pp. 27–28; Larsen to Richard Krolik, March 10, 1970, Larsen Mss., TIA; Raymond Fielding, *The March of Time, 1935–1951* (New York: Oxford University Press, 1978), pp. 16–18; Eric Barnouw, *Documentary* (New York: Oxford University Press, 1974), p. 1310; Elson, *Time Inc.*, pp. 177–80.

19. Larsen to HRL, June 20, 1932, Larsen Mss., TIA; Fielding, *The March of Time*, p. 19.

20. HRL memo, "The Opportunity," August 1934, TIA; *Christian Science Monitor Weekly Magazine*, October 30, 1935, p. 15; HRL to JSB, August 24, 1934, JSB Mss.; Forsyth Hardy, *Grierson on Documentary* (London: Faber & Faber, 1966), pp. 201–2; James L. Baughman, *Henry R. Luce and the Rise of the American News Media* (Boston: Twayne, 1987), pp. 77–79; Fielding, *The March of Time*, pp. 31–32.

21. HRL, "The Opportunity," August 1934, TIA; William P. Montague, "Public Opinion and the Newsreels," *Public Opinion Quarterly* 2 (January 1938): 51; Richard Mersan Barasm, " 'This Is America': Documentaries for Theaters, 1942–1951," *Cinema Journal* 12 (Spring 1973): 22–23; *Four Hours a Year* (New York: Time Inc., 1936), pp. 3, 21; Fielding, *The March of Time*, pp. 22–45; Elson, *Time Inc.*, pp. 227–40.

22. HRL to Ingersoll, n.d., 1938, HRL to Thomas J. White, January 31, 1935, TIA; David Nasaw, *The Chief: The Life of William Randolph Hearst* (New York: Houghton Mifflin, 2000), pp. 506–7.

23. HRL to Hearst, January 31, 1935, Hearst to HRL, February 1, 8, 1935, TIA; "Hearst," *Fortune*, October 1935; Ingersoll to Thomas J. White, May 13, 1936, Daniel Longwell to HRL, March 8, 1935, TIA; *Four Hours a Year*, p. 19; Nasaw, *The Chief*, pp. 507–8.

24. Dick Duncan to Bob Parker, memo, March 5, 1967, TIA; JSBD, March 15, 1935.

25. *Four Hours a Year*, pp. 44–47; Fielding, *The March of Time*, p. 6; "Summer Theaters," "Wild Ducks," "Dogs for Sale," "Pests in 1937," *March of Time*, 1935–1937.

26. "Lake Tana, Africa!", "East of the Suez!", "War in China," *March of Time*, 1936–1937; "Japan—Master of the Orient," *March of Time*, 1939.

27. "Inside Nazi Germany," *March of Time*, 1938; Fielding, *The March of Time*, pp. 187–95.

28. Otis Ferguson, "Time Steals a March," *New Republic*, February 9, 1938, p. 19;

George Dangerfield, "Time Muddles On," *New Republic*, August 19, 1936, pp. 43–45; Irving Lerner (using the pseudonym "Peter Ellis"), *New Masses*, July 9, 1935, p. 30, May 11, 1937, p. 29; Ralph Steiner and Leo T. Hurwitz, "A New Approach to Film Making," *New Theater*, September 1935, pp. 22–23; William Alexander, "The March of Time and the World Today," *American Quarterly* 29 (Summer 1977): 184–85, 188–92.

29. Raymond Fielding, "Mirror of Discontent: The *March of Time* and Its Politically Controversial Film Issues," *Western Political Quarterly* 12 (March 1959): 145–52; Fielding, *The March of Time*, p. 201.

30. Raymond Fielding, "Time Flickers Out: Notes on the Passing of the *March of Time*," *Quarterly of Film, Radio, and Television* 11 (Summer 1957): 354–61.

31. JSBD, November 12, 1931; Lila Luce Tyng interview; Elisabeth Luce Moore interview; HRL Elson interview, 1966, TIA.

32. Sylvia Morris, *Rage for Fame: The Ascent of Clare Boothe Luce* (New York: Random House, 1997), p. 30; CBL memoir, n.d., CBL Mss.; Alan Brinkley, "Clare Boothe Luce," *Notable American Women: A Biographical Dictionary—Completing the Twentieth Century* (Cambridge, Mass.: Harvard University Press, 2004), pp. 399–400; Ralph Martin, *Henry and Clare: An Intimate Portrait of the Luces* (New York: G. P. Putnam, 1991), pp. 27–39, 50–52.

33. Martin, *Henry and Clare*, pp. 52–56, 69–83; Morris, *Rage for Fame*, pp. 74–160.

34. Helen Lawrenson, *Stranger at the Party: A Memoir* (New York: Random House, 1975), pp. 102–5; Morris, *Rage for Fame*, pp. 161–238.

35. Lila to ERL, Emmavail, and Leslie Severinghaus, August 2, 1932, LT; Laura Z. Hobson, *Laura Z: A Life* (New York: Arbor House, 1983), pp. 136–38; Morris, *Rage for Fame*, pp. 240–41.

36. Lawrenson, *Stranger at the Party*, pp. 114–16; Roy Hoopes, *Ralph Ingersoll: A Biography* (New York: Atheneum, 1985), pp. 119–121; Morris, *Rage for Fame*, pp. 240–44.

37. HRL to CBL, December 23, 1934, CBL to HRL, August 15, 1935, CBL Mss.; Morris, *Rage for Fame*, pp. 242–48; Hoopes, *Ralph Ingersoll*, pp. 118–21; Martin, *Henry and Clare*, pp. 140–41.

38. HRL to CBL, January 3, 11, March 5, May 11, 13, July 21, n.d., 1935, November 22, 1937, CBL Mss. HRL to LH, February 7, March 26, 30, n.d., 1935, LT; HRL to Peter Paul Luce, n.d., 1935, LT; HRL to CBL, May 1, 12, 1935, CBL Mss.; HWL to LH, July 17, 1935, Mary Bradley to LH, n.d., 1935, LT Mss.; JSBD, November 9, 11, 23, 1935; Lila Luce Tyng interview; Elisabeth Luce Moore interview.

39. CBL to HRL, August 15, 1935, HRL to CBL, March 7, 1935, CBL Mss.; Morris, *Rage for Fame*, pp. 251–53.

40. JSBD, November 25, 1935; HRL to LH, n.d., 1935, TIA; Lawrenson, *Stranger at the Party*, pp. 117–18; *Time*, November 25, 1935; Morris, *Rage for Fame*, pp. 276–80.

41. JSBD, May 22, 1936.

42. HRL Elson interview, 1966, Preface to *Fortune*, August 1929, Larsen oral history, p. 23, TIA; Edmund Wilson, *Letters on Literature and Politics* (New York: Farrar Straus & Giroux, 1977), pp. 405–6; *The New Yorker*, September 26, 1926, pp. 13, 19; David Laskin, *Partisan: Marriage, Politics, and Betrayal Among the New York Intellectuals* (Chicago: University of Chicago Press, 2000), pp. 193–94; Michael Augspurger, *An Economy of Abundant Beauty: Fortune Magazine & Depression America* (Ithaca, N.Y.: Cornell University, 2004), pp. 55–62; Jacques Barzun, *The House of Intellect* (New York: Harper & Brothers, 1959), pp. 42–45.

43. Elson HRL interview, 1966, TIA; James Thurber, *The Years with Ross* (New York: Little, Brown, 1957), p. 16; Hoopes, *Ralph Ingersoll*, p. 76.

44. Ingersoll to Katherine Sergeant White, November 9, 1933, TIA; Ingersoll, "Answers to Time Inc. Questions," March 28, 1956, Ingersoll Mss.; *Fortune*, August 1934.

45. "Time . . . Fortune . . . Life . . . Luce," *The New Yorker,* November 28, 1936, pp. 20–25; Bernard DeVoto, "Distempers of the Press," *Harper's,* March 1937, p. 447.

46. HRL Elson interview, 1966, Harold Ross to HRL, November 23, 1936, HRL to Harold Ross, November 24, 1936, TIA; JSBD, November 19, 1937.

VIII   "LIFE BEGINS"

1. Clare Boothe Brokaw to Condé Nast, May 7, December 9, 1931; HRL to Edna Chase, January 25, 1954, Condé Nast to HRL, October 17, 1938, TIA; John R. Whiting and George R. Clark, "The Picture Magazines," *Harper's,* June 18, 1943, pp. 159–60.

2. Elisabeth Luce Moore interview; Sylvia Morris, *Rage for Fame: The Ascent of Clare Boothe Luce* (New York: Random House, 1997), pp. 281–84; Laura Z. Hobson, *Laura Z: A Life* (New York: Arbor House, 1983), pp. 184–85; Helen Lawrenson, *Stranger at the Party: A Memoir* (New York: Random House, 1975), pp. 65–66.

3. JSBD, August 24, 1936; Andrew Heiskell interview.

4. Elisabeth Luce Moore interview; Roy Hoopes, *Ralph Ingersoll: A Biography* (New York: Atheneum, 1985), pp. 146–48; Morris, *Rage for Fame,* p. 287; Wilfred Sheed, *Clare Boothe Luce* (New York: E. P. Dutton, 1982), pp. 78–79; Ralph G. Martin, *Henry and Clare: An Intimate Portrait of the Luces* (New York: G. P. Putnam, 1991), pp. 156–60.

5. Clare Boothe Luce, *The Women* (1937; repr., New York: Dramatists Play Service, 1966), pp. 89–90 and passim.

6. Andrew Heiskell interview; JSBD, September 6, December 29, 1939, October 18, 1941.

7. Elisabeth Luce Moore interview; Henry Luce III interview; Peter Luce interview; HRL to CBL, n.d., 1936, HRL to CBL, December 8, 9, 11, 18, 19, 1936, CBL Mss.

8. HRL to CBL, January 1, 1937, n.d., 1939, CBL Mss.; HRL to Peter Paul Luce, n.d., 1935, LT Mss.; Charles E. Clapp, Jr., to HRL, May, n.d., 1936, Corinne Thrasher to HRL, May 6, 1936, TIA; *Architectural Forum,* June 1937; Corinne Thrasher to Town of Stamford, February 16, 1939, Allen Grover to HRL, August 3, 1939, Alex Groner to Andrew Heiskell, November 3, 1961, Edward Durrell Stone to HRL, December 19, 1939, HRL to Stone, December 23, 1939, "The Henry R. Luce Estates' Disaster in the Swamps," research memo for *Time* cover story on Stone, TIA; Morris, *Rage for Fame,* pp. 286, 296–305; Elisabeth Luce Moore interview.

9. HRL to CBL, May 17, 18, November 22, n.d., 1937, June 13, 1939, CBL to HRL, June 1, 3, 1939, CBL Mss.

10. John Cowles to HRL, March 26, 1932, TIA; Isaiah Wilner, *The Man Time Forgot: A Tale of Genius, Betrayal, and the Creation of Time Magazine* (New York: HarperCollins, 2006), pp. 4, 223; *Four Hours a Year* (New York: Time Inc., 1936); HRL to Fayette Dow, August 10, 1936, TIA; interview with Daniel Longwell, January 31, 1956, COHP.

11. *Berliner Illustrierte Zeitung,* February 13, March 21, April 17, 1935; *Illustrated London News,* April 26, 1930, August 8, 1931, March 11, 1933, April 27, 1935; *Vu,* January, April 1935, March 1936; Dwight Macdonald to Henri Cartier-Bresson, December 27, 1933, January 22, 1934, TIA; Beaumont Newhall, *The History of Photography* (Garden City, N.Y.: Doubleday, 1964), pp. 180–86; HRL, "Organization of Editorial Staff of the Picture Magazine," n.d., 1936, TIA.

12. Martin Heidegger, "The Age of the World Picture," in William Lovitt, trans. and ed., *The Question Concerning Technology and Other Essays* (New York: Harper & Row, 1977), p. 133; Hanno Hardt, "Pictures for the Masses: Photography and

the Rise of Popular Magazines in Weimar Germany," *Journal of Communication Inquiry* 13 (1989): 7–30; Dwight Macdonald, "Kulturbolshevismus Is Here," *Partisan Review*, November 1941, pp. 449–50; Bernard Rosenberg, "Attitudes to Mass Culture," *Dissent*, Winter 1956, pp. 25–28; John P. Sis, "The Things That Pass," *Commonweal*, September 16, 1955, pp. 593–95.

13. HRL Elson interview, 1966, HRL to the Editorial Staffs of Time and Fortune, December 1, 1933, HRL to Collins, November, n.d., 1933, John S. Martin to W. A. Dwiggins, February 28, March 2, 9, 13, 30, 1934, Dwight Macdonald to David Hulburd, March, n.d., 1934, Dwight Macdonald to Jack Sussman, January 23, 1934, C. D. Jackson to HRL, April 9, 1934, Ralph Ingersoll to HRL, April 11, 1934, Roy Larsen to HRL, April 7, 1934, HRL, "Apology: To be read After reading Dummy No. 3," April, n.d., 1934, HRL, "Important Notice," June 12, 1934, TIA.

14. HRL Elson interview, 1966, TIA; Longwell to HRL, June 12, 1935, Longwell Mss.; Kurt Korff, "Essential Outline for a New Illustrated Magazine," n.d., 1936, Kurt Korff to HRL, July 31, 1936, TIA; HRL Elson interview, 1966, TIA; Robert T. Elson, *Time Inc.: The Intimate History of a Publishing Enterprise, 1923–1941* (New York: Atheneum, 1968), pp. 269–70; Ingersoll to Korff, April 14, 1936, Ingersoll to the Staff of TIME Inc., n.d., 1936, Ingersoll to Stillman et al., June 8, 1936, MacLeish to Ingersoll, June, n.d., 12, 1936, Ingersoll, "Notes on a Picture Magazine," May 15, 1936, MacLeish to HRL, June 17, 1936, Ingersoll to HRL, "The Earnings Capacity of *Time*: The Weekly Newsmagazine," October 28, 1938, TIA; Ingersoll, "Memorandum," January 27, 1969, Ingersoll Mss.

15. P. I. Prentice to H. P. Zimmerman, April 29, 1936, H. P. Zimmerman to Charles Stillman, July 21, 1944, TIA; Ingersoll to HRL, November 15, 1936, TIA; Elson, *Time Inc.*, pp. 283–84.

16. P. I. Prentice to HRL, February 24, 25, 27, March 2, 1936, "Operating Figures of The New Magazine," n.d., 1936, TIA; Ingersoll to Longwell, May 6, 1936, TIA; Elson, *Time Inc.*, p. 283.

17. "Prospectus for a New Weekly Magazine," n.d., 1936, "Preface to a New Magazine," n.d., 1936, HRL to Staff, June, n.d., 1936, HRL to H. P. Zimmerman, February 25, 1936, Longwell to Ingersoll, March 26, 1936, Ingersoll to Staff, June 8, 1936, HRL to Sheldon Luce, July 15, 1936, HRL to Dorothy Thompson, August 6, 1936, Dorothy Thompson to HRL, July 15, 1936, HRL, "Recording of a Decision of Major Importance," August 18, 1936, HRL to Harry Davison, August 12, 1936, HRL to William Griffin, August 19, 1936, "March of Time: The Weekly Picture Magazine," August, n.d., 1936, HRL to Archibald MacLeish, June 29, 1936, Howard Black to "All Life Representatives," April 13, 1937, HRL to Rooney Finkenstaedt, January 17, 1938, TIA; McGeorge Bundy, "These Picture Magazines," *Yale Daily News*, February 9, 1938, HRL to Bundy, February 28, 1938, Bundy to HRL, March 1, 1938, HRL to Hunt, June 20, 1963, TIA.

18. "Prospectus for a New Weekly Magazine," n.d., 1935, JSB Mss.; Ingersoll, "Notes on Picture Magazine," May 15, 1936, Ingersoll to Staff, "Prospectus No. 1," June 8, 1936, Archibald MacLeish to HRL, June 27, 1936, HRL to MacLeish, June 29, 1936, TIA; HRL, "A Prospectus for a New Magazine," n.d., 1936, JSB Mss.

19. Laura Hobson to Ingersoll, June 3, 1936, Hobson to HRL, October 19, 1936, Richard de Rochemont to C. D. Jackson, July 28, 1936, HRL to Allan Billingsley, February 25, 1936, Prentice to Ingersoll, May 12, 1936, "Possible Names for Picture Magazine," n.d., 1936, "Prospectus for a New Weekly Newsmagazine," n.d., 1936, Larsen to Prentice, August 22, 1936, Ingersoll to Prentice, August 22, 1936, Larsen, "March of Time: The Weekly Picture Magazine," August 20, 1936, TIA; Elson, *Time Inc.*, pp. 278, 290–91.

20. James A. Linen to HRL, August 7, 1936, HRL to Linen, August 19, 1936, Larsen to subscribers, November 18, 1936, Ingersoll to T. Harry Thompson,

October 12, 1936, TIA; *Time*, October 19, 1936; *News-Week*, November 28, 1936; *New York Herald Tribune*, October 8, 1936.

21. "Dummy," n.d., 1935, TIA; Loudon Wainwright, *The Great American Magazine: An Inside History of Life* (New York: Alfred A. Knopf, 1986), pp. 35–37; "Dummy," n.d., 1936, Robert Chambers to HRL, August 19, 1936, HRL to Harry Davison, August 12, 1936, William Griffin to HRL, August 18, 1936, Paul Hollister to HRL, August 9, 1936, HRL to Hollister, August 12, 1936, Hollister to HRL, August 25, 1936, TIA; Andrew Heiskell interview.

22. "Rehearsal," September 24, 1936, Ingersoll to Sadler, Longwell, HRL, September 19, 1936, Ingersoll to P. I. Prentice, October 3, 1936, Ingersoll to Laura Hobson, October 5, 1936, HRL to Ingersoll, November 2, 1935, Dorothy Thompson to HRL, October 7, 1936, HRL to Dorothy Thompson, November 19, 1936, Longwell to Kay Mills, October 5, 1936, Longwell to Egmont Arens, October 21, 1936, TIA; Wainwright, *The Great American Magazine*, pp. 37–40; Elson, *Time Inc.*, pp. 284–87.

23. HRL, "Organization of Editorial Staff of the Picture Magazine," n.d., 1936, JSB Mss.; HRL to John S. Martin, October 23, 26, 1936, HRL, untitled announcement, October 28, 1936, TIA.

24. JSBD, October 23, 1936; "Billings," in-house memo, June 30, 1939, TIA; Andrew Heiskell interview.

25. HRL, "To All 'Life' Writers," October 30, 1936, JSB, untitled notes on instructions from HRL, October, n.d., 1936, HRL to Larsen et al., October 19, 1936, HRL, "Editorial Responsibility and Initiative," November, n.d., 1936, TIA; "Life's editorial organization," November, n.d., 1936, JSB Mss.; Longwell, "The Getting of Pictures," November 16, 1936, TIA.

26. *Life*, November 23, 30, 1936; Wainwright, *The Great American Magazine*, pp. 69–79; Terry Smith, "Life-Style Modernity: Making Modern America," in Erika Doss, ed., *Looking at Life Magazine* (Washington, D.C.: Smithsonian Institution Press, 2001), pp. 33–35.

27. HRL letter to Time subscribers, n.d., 1936, P. I. Prentice to J. J. Crowley, November 20, 1936, Roy E. Larsen to subscribers, November 18, 1936, TIA; Wainwright, *The Great American Magazine*, pp. 62–63; "From the Publishers; Prospectus for the New Life," December 1936, TIA.

28. P. I. Prentice to Ingersoll et al., November 21, 1936, Misc. photos and photocopies, November–December 1936, Prentice to "All Employees," December 8, 1936, *Information Bulletin*, Time Inc., November 1936, American News Company Circular, December 28, 1936, TIA.

29. Prentice to J. J. Crowley, November 20, 1936, Prentice to "All Employees," December 8, 1936, Prentice to "Newsstand Men," December 20, 1936, John H. Amadon to editors, December 10, 1936, Prentice to Amadon, December 14, 1936, HRL Elson interview, 1966, TIA; Elson, *Time Inc.*, pp. 277, 297–303.

30. JSBD, February 2, March 22, 1937; Heiskell interview; HRL untitled memo, March 15, 1937, Larsen, "Review of Life as of July 28, 1937," JSB Mss.; Elson, *Time Inc.*, pp. 300–9.

31. "Report on Production," n.d., 1937, TIA; JSBD, January 16, 1937; Larsen, "Review of Life as of July 28, 1937," TIA; "The Current Fad for Picture Mags," *Literary Digest*, January 30, 1937; Elson, *Time Inc.*, pp. 301–9.

32. Elson, *Time Inc.*, p. 309.

33. HRL, "Redefinition of Life—Part I," July 6, 1938, JSB Mss.; Larsen, "Review of Life as of July 28, 1937," TIA; Larsen, "Life—August 1938," August 17, 1938, JSB Mss.; Elson, *Time Inc.*, pp. 340–42; Andrew Heiskell interview; Wainwright, *The Great American Magazine*, p. 98.

34. JSBD, April 15, 1938; HRL to Larsen, JSB, May 10, 1938, HRL to Staff, "Editorial Plan & Organization, May 16, 1938, HRL, "Redefinition of LIFE—Part I," July 6, 1938, JSB Mss.; HRL to Andrew Heiskell, July 30, 1938, TIA; Larsen to Ingersoll et al., August 22, 1938, JSB Mss.

35. *Life*, April 10, 1938; JSBD, March 25, 28, April 11, 1938, February 24, March 11,

July 8, 1939; Larsen memo to staff, n.d., 1938, TIA; Heiskell interview; Morris L. Ernst, *The Best is Yet . . . Reflections of an Irrepressible Man* (New York: Harper & Row, 1945), pp. 138–42; Elson *Time Inc.*, pp. 337–42.

36. JSBD, February 25, 26, March 28, April 15, April 16, 1938; Larsen to Ingersoll et al., August 22, 1938, Andrew Heiskell to Luce, July 29, 1938, TIA; Andrew Heiskell interview.

37. JSBD, August 11, 1937, February 11, 12, 1938, February 11, 1939; HRL, "Redefinition of the editorial contents and purpose of LIFE," March, n.d., 1937, TIA; HRL, untitled memo, March 15, 1937, JSB Mss.; HRL to Hunt et al., June 20, 1963, "LIFE and People," n.d., 1938, HRL, "Editorial Plan & Organization," May 16, 1938, HRL, "Redefinition of LIFE," July 6, 1938, TIA.

38. Andrew Heiskell interview; Thomas Griffith, *How True: A Skeptic's Guide to Believing the News* (Boston: Little, Brown, 1974), pp. 139–42; JSBD, October 22, 1937, August 25, 1939; HRL Elson interview, 1966, TIA; Elson, *Time Inc.*, p. 304; James L. Baughman, *Henry R. Luce and the Rise of the American News Media* (Boston: Twayne, 1987), pp. 95–98.

39. C. D. Jackson to HRL et al., n.d., 1936, TIA; HRL Elson interview, 1966, TIA; Elson, *Time Inc.*, p. 323–25.

40. HRL Elson interview, 1966, TIA.

41. HRL speech to Association of Advertising Agencies, April 30, 1937, TIA; John K. Jessup, ed., *The Ideas of Henry Luce* (New York: Atheneum, 1969), pp. 35–43.

42. Wainwright, *The Great American Magazine*, jacket copy; Douglas Waples, *People and Print: Social Aspects of Reading in the Depression* (Chicago: University of Chicago Press, 1937), pp. 5–6, 72.

43. Wilson Hicks, *Words and Pictures: An Introduction to Photojournalism* (New York: Harper & Brothers, 1952), p. 85; "W. Eugene Smith," interview in Paul Hill and Thomas Cooper, eds., *Dialogue with Photography* (New York: Dewi Lewis, 1979), pp. 203–5.

44. Susan Goldman Rubin, *Margaret Bourke-White* (New York: Harry N. Abrams, 1999), pp. 56–57; William Stott, *Documentary Expression and Thirties America* (New York: Oxford University Press, 1973), pp. 5–63; Michael Denning, *The Cultural Front: The Laboring of American Culture in the Twentieth Century* (London: Verso, 1996), pp. 158–59; Richard Pells, *Radical Visions and American Dreams: Culture and Social Thought in the Depression Years* (New York: Harper & Row, 1973), pp. 194–251.

45. Erika Doss, "Introduction," in Doss, ed., *Looking at* Life *Magazine*, pp. 11–12; Daniel Longwell interview, January 13, 1956, COHP.

46. *Life*, November 23, 1936.

47. *Life*, May 10, 1937.

48. *Life*, November 30, 1936, November 8, 1937, August 7, 1939, January 24, 1938, April 19, 1937, August 14, 1939, March 22, 1937.

49. *Life*, November 25, 1940, February 1, 1937, December 7, 1936, February 6, December 11, 1939.

50. *Life*, April 19, 1937, December 28, 1936.

51. *Life*, October 10, 1938; "LIFE and People," n.d., 1938, TIA; Wainwright, *The Great American Magazine*, pp. 100–1.

52. *Life*, April 19, May 24, 1937, July 25, September 5, 1938, January 1, 1940.

53. *Life*, July 18, 1938, February 15, April 12, 1937, November 14, December 26, September 5, 1938, January 13, 1941, October 10, 1938, January 4, 1937.

54. HRL to Longwell, August 12, 1944, Mary Fraser, "Women," n.d., 1949, TIA.

55. *Life*, April 11, August 7, 1938, February 6, 1939, May 31, 1937, December 11, 1939; Jeanne Perkins Harman, *Such Is Life: An Insider's View of America's Greatest Picture Magazine* (New York: Thomas Y. Crowell, 1956), pp. 19–23.

56. HRL to JSB, January 16, 1945, TIA; *Life*, n.d., 1945; Robert B. Westbrook, "I Want a Girl Just Like the Girl that Married Harry James," *American Quarterly* 42 (December 1990): 596–602, 610–11.

57. *Life*, April 24, 1939, December 12, 1938, December 13, October 25, 1937, Sep-

tember 12, 1938; Terry Smith, "Life-Style Modernity: Making Modern America" in Doss, ed., *Looking at Life Magazine*, pp. 26–28.

58. Alfred Politz Research Inc., AUDIENCE: *A Study of the Accumulative Audience of Life* (New York: Time Inc., 1950), pp. 20–21; Paul F. Lazarsfeld, Bernard Berelson, and Hazel Gaudet, *The People's Choice: How the Voter Makes Up His Mind in a Presidential Election* (New York: Columbia University Press, 1944), pp. 134–36; Carl F. Kaestle, *Literacy in the United States: Readers and Reading since 1880* (New Haven, Conn.: Yale University Press, 1991), pp. 263–66.

59. John Loengard, *Life Photographers: What They Saw* (Boston: Little, Brown, 1998), p. 20; William Brinkley, *The Fun House* (New York: Random House, 1961), p. 3; John G. Morris, *Get the Picture: A Personal History of Photojournalism* (New York: Random House, 1998), pp. 22–23; Carl Mydans, *More Than Meets the Eye* (New York: Harper Brothers, 1959), p. 11; Rudolf Janssens and Gertjan Kalff, "Time Incorporated Stink Club: The Influence of *Life* on the Founding of Magnum Photos," in David Nye and Mick Gidley, eds., *American Photographs in Europe* (Amsterdam: Vu University Press, 1994), pp. 223–42.

IX   MAN OF THE WORLD

1. JSBD, March 21, 1939, February 12, 1941.

2. HRL to Dorothy Thompson, January 13, 1939, TIA.

3. HRL to René Chambrun, October 12, 1939, HRL, "Time, War and Truth: When Men Take Sides," internal memo, n.d., 1939, TIA.

4. HRL to Ingersoll, n.d., 1938, HRL to TIME employees, January 30, 1939, TIA; JSBD, February 14, 1938, April 1, 1939.

5. Patricia Divver, "The Ideology of TIME," internal memo, July 21, 1953, JSB Mss.; Ingersoll to HRL, October 28, 1938, TIA; JSBD, November 18, 1938, January 25, 26, 1939, April 29, November 13, 1940; James L. Baughman, *Henry R. Luce and the Rise of the American News Media* (Boston: Twayne, 1987), p. 115.

6. HRL to Eric Hodgins, August 3, 1940, Richardson Wood to HRL, August 16, 1940, Manfred Gottfried to HRL, August 23, 1940, HRL to Managing Editors, November 20, 1939, William Benton to Harold Lasswell, October 3, 1939, HRL memo, "Time, War and Truth: When Men Take Sides," n.d., 1939, TIA; Charles Wertenbaker, *The Death of Kings* (New York: Random House, 1954), pp. 21–28; T. S. Matthews, *Name and Address: An Autobiography* (New York: Simon & Schuster, 1960), pp. 243–48.

7. "The Ideology of TIME," JSB Mss.

8. *Time*, May 4, July 20, September 21, November 2, 9, 1936, March 22, July 20, 1937, August 22, October 24, 1938; "The Ideology of TIME," JSB Mss.

9. *Life*, January 24, May 23, 1938, October 23, 1939; *Fortune*, March, May 1937, August 1938, February 1939.

10. *Time*, March 27, April 17, July 10, September 4, 11, 1938, August 28, 1939; "The Ideology of TIME," JSB Mss.

11. *Life*, September 25, 1939.

12. *Life*, June 10, 17, July 22, August 26, 1940, January 20, 31, 1941; *Time*, September 16, November 16, 1940, January 6, 1941; "The Ramparts We Watched," *March of Time*, 1939; Robert T. Elson, *Time Inc.: The Intimate History of a Publishing Enterprise, 1923–1941* (New York: Atheneum, 1968), pp. 381–85; "War and Peace," *Fortune*, December 1939.

13. *Life*, January 13, 1941; *The New Yorker*, October 25, 1941.

14. HRL to Roy Larsen, Russell Davenport, July 14, 1939, Paul Prentice to HRL, November 14, 1940, TIA.

15. HRL to FDR, June 11, 1940, HRL to Russell Davenport, October 15, 1940, HRL to Dorothy Thompson, January 13, 1939, HRL memo, "Time Inc.'s General Attitude Toward Foreign Policy," January 18, 1939, HRL to Manfred Gottfried, July 29, 1939, HRL, "Questions and Answers, n.d., 1939, TIA; HRL to Senior Group,

"WAR," July 26, 1940, Longwell Mss.; Clarence Streit, *Union Now: A Proposal for a Federation of the Democracies of the North Atlantic* (New York: Harper & Bros., 1939), pp. 1–3, 33–35; HRL to Roy Larsen, Russell Davenport, July 14, 1939, TIA.

16. HRL to Senior Group, "WAR," July 26, 1940, Longwell Mss.

17. "Memorandum for Mr. Luce," n.d., 1938, "Mr. Luce's European Trip," June 22, 1933, TIA; *Time*, June 17, 1938; HRL dispatch, "Germany," "Czechoslovakia," "Paris," n.d., 1938, TIA; Elson, *Time Inc.*, p. 354.

18. John Gunther to Frances Fineman Gunther, June 26, 1939, Frances Fineman Gunther Mss.

19. HRL to Lila, July 28, 1939, LT; HRL to Manfred Gottfried, July 29, 1939, TIA; *New York Times*, June 28, July 3, 1939; Alice B. Toklas, *What Is Remembered* (New York: Holt, Rinehart & Winston, 1963), p. 161; Richard H. Goldstone, *Thornton Wilder: An Intimate Portrait* (New York: E. P. Dutton, 1975), p. 148; *Time*, August 21, 1939; Elson, *Time Inc.*, pp. 409–12; JSBD, January 13, September 15, 1939.

20. HRL to Allen Grover, May 2, 1940, Grover to HRL, May 2, 1940, HRL to Grover, May 3, 1940, HRL to Larsen, May 9, 1940, TIA.

21. HRL dispatch, May 15, 1940, HRL to Roy Larsen, May 10, 1940, CBL to JSB, May 10, 1940, HRL to Roy Larsen, May 11, 1940, HRL to editors, May 11, 1940, George Jean Nathan to HRL, May 23, 1940, HRL to George Jean Nathan, telegram, May 25, 1940, TIA.

22. HRL to Larsen, April, n.d., 1940, HRL radio addresses, May 22, June 1, 1940, TIA.

23. HRL to David Hulburd, May 12, 1940, TIA.

24. Russell Davenport, *The Dignity of Man* (New York: Harper & Brothers, 1955), pp. 10–11; *Fortune*, April 1940; Warren Moscow, *Roosevelt & Willkie* (Englewood Cliffs, N.J.: Prentice-Hall, 1968), pp. 56–60; Ellsworth Barnard, *Wendell Willkie: Fighter for Freedom* (Marquette: Northern Michigan University Press, 1966), pp. 152–54; Bill Severn, *Toward One World: The Life of Wendell Willkie* (New York: Ives Washburn, 1967), pp. 114–17; *Life*, May 13, 1940.

25. Oren Root, *Persons and Persuasions* (New York: W. W. Norton, 1974), pp. 20–36; Donald Bruce Johnson, *The Republican Party and Wendell Willkie* (Urbana: University of Illinois Press, 1960), pp. 63–65; Davenport to Larsen, May 2, 1940; Larsen to HRL, May 2, 1940, TIA.

26. Interview with Corinne Thrasher, W. A. Swanberg Mss.; W. A. Swanberg, *Luce and His Empire* (New York: Charles Scribner's Sons, 1972), p. 177; Barnard, *Wendell Willkie*, p. 137.

27. HRL to Davenport, October 14, 1940, HRL to Willkie, October 18, 1940, HRL to Willkie, n.d., 1940, TIA.

28. HRL to Davenport, September 12, 1940 (unsent), HRL to Davenport, October 18, 31, 1940, C. D. Jackson to HRL, October 1, 1940, HRL to Jackson, n.d., 1940, TIA; Vasilia N. Getz to FDR, November 19, 1937, FDR to Homer Cummings, November 19, 1937, J. Edgar Hoover to FDR, December 11, 1937, Corcoran Mss., LC; Alan Brinkley, *The End of Reform: New Deal Liberalism in Recession and War* (New York: Alfred A. Knopf, 1995), pp. 56–57.

29. *Time*, May 6, June 10, 24, 1940; *Life*, May 6, 13, 1940.

30. *Life*, July 8, 1940; *Time*, July 8, 1940; Russell Davenport to Roy Larsen, July 8, 1940, TIA.

31. Don Parry to HRL, August 9, 1940, HRL to Gottfried, Norris, Matthews, Larsen, September 18, 1940, TIA.

32. Willkie to Davenport, n.d., 1940, TIA; *Time*, September 9, 1940; HRL, "Fairly Specific Points about the Willkie Campaign," August, n.d., 1940, TIA.

33. HRL to Davenport, September 16, 1940, HRL to Willkie, September 30, 1940, TIA.

34. HRL to Davenport, September 13, 30, October 11, n.d., 1940, HRL, "Fairly Specific Points about the Willkie Campaign," August, n.d., 1940, TIA.

35. *New York Times*, September 11, October 10, 27, 1940; HRL to Davenport, October 21, 27, 1940, October 28, 1940, HRL to multiple recipients, November 8, 1940, TIA.

36. Willkie to HRL, December 3, 1940, TIA; *New York Times*, December 3, 1940; HRL to Willkie, March 28, 1941, Willkie to HRL, June 17, 1941, November 17, 1943, March 17, 1944, HRL to Willkie, March 8, June 8, 1944, HRL, "Personal Memo," July 31, 1944, TIA; Johnson, *The Republican Party and Wendell Willkie*, pp. 278–80, 300–5; *New York Times*, October 10, 1944; HRL to Joseph Ball, October 21, 1944, TIA.

37. Stephen Early to HRL, September 5, 1940 (unsent), Early to FDR, January 13, 1942, FDR to Early, January 17, 1942, PSF 132, FDRL; FDR to Early, December 3, 1940, Lowell Mellett to HRL, December 7, 1940, HRL to Mellett, December 11, 1940, FDR to Mellett, December 31, 1940, PPF 3338, FDRL; *Time*, November 11, 1940.

38. "Meeting at Columbia Club," minutes, July 11, 1940, Francis P. Miller to HRL, July 19, 1940, HRL to Miller, July 20, 1940, Ward Cheney to HRL, September 23, 1940, HRL to Walter Lippmann, July 29, 1940, TIA.

39. "Memorandum of Meeting," July 25, 1940, Joseph Alsop to HRL, July 23, 1940, Francis Miller to HRL, July 23, 1940, HRL to Francis Miller, July 25, 1940, HRL, "Memorandum," July, n.d., 1940, TIA.

40. HRL to Lew Douglas, July 15, 1940, HRL, "War Diary," July 28, 1940, TIA; Elson, *Time Inc.*, p. 435.

41. HRL, "War Diary, July 27, 1940, TIA.

42. Ibid.; *Time*, July 29, September 9, 16, 30, 1940; Robert E. Herzstein, *Henry R. Luce: A Political Portrait of the Man Who Created the American Century* (New York: Scribner's, 1994), pp. 17–20.

43. HRL to Ward Cheney, November 18, 1940, Cheney to HRL, November 26, 1940, HRL to Cheney, November 27, 1940, TIA.

44. JSBD, December 24, 1940, January 2, 21, February 1, 1941; HRL to Robert McCormick Adams, October 25, 1941, HRL speech to Association of American Colleges, January 9, 1941, HRL speech to Mid-Continent Oil and Gas Association, Tulsa, January 11, 1941, HRL speech to National Automobile Dealers Association, Pittsburgh, January 22, 1941, TIA; Herzstein, *Henry R. Luce*, pp. 171–74; Elson, *Time Inc.*, pp. 461–64.

45. JSBD, June 1, 1940; Swanberg, *Luce and His Empire*, pp. 170–71.

46. *Life*, June 3, July 22, October 28, 1940, June 5, 1939.

47. MacLeish, "Draft of a Statement of Belief," July 25, 1940, HRL to MacLeish, July 10, 1940, HRL to Leighton Stuart, January 6, 1940, TIA.

48. "When We Say 'America,'" in John K. Jessup, ed., *The Ideas of Henry Luce* (New York: Atheneum, 1969), pp. 89–90.

49. "War," HRL to Senior Group, July 26, 1940, TIA; Elson, *Time Inc.*, pp. 412–13, 461–64; Herzstein, *Henry R. Luce*, p. 179; Daniel Longwell to HRL, August 5, 1940, Longwell Mss.

50. *Life*, February 17, 1941; Henry R. Luce, *The American Century* (New York: Farrar & Rinehart, 1941).

51. "Response to Mr. Luce's THE AMERICAN CENTURY," March 14, 1941, TIA; Gail Goodin to The Editor of LIFE, February 22, 1941, Russell B. Coover to HRL, February 18, 1941, H. L. Burton to "Life Inc.," February 15, 1941, A. Taltosh to HRL, February 16, 1941, J. Frederick Emanuel to "LIFE," February 17, 1941, Robert E. Duffy to HRL, n.d., 1941, HRL Mss. Boxes 107–108, LC.

52. Freda Kirchwey, "Luce Thinking," *Nation*, March 1, 1941; W. A. Swanberg, *Norman Thomas: The Last Idealist* (New York: Scribner's, 1976), pp. 250–51; Ronald Radosh, *Prophets on the Right: Profiles of Conservative Critics of American Globalism* (New York: Simon & Schuster, 1975), pp. 217–18.

53. HRL to Robert A. Taft, May 26, 1943, HRL to William Ernest Hocking, March 23, 1944, HRL to Bartley Crum, October 29, 1957, TIA.

54. Baughman, *Henry R. Luce*, p. 135.

55. John C. Culver and John Hyde, *American Dreamer: A Life of Henry Wallace* (New York: W. W. Norton, 2000), pp. 275–80; Edward L. and Frederick H.

Schapsmeier, *Prophet in Politics: Henry A. Wallace and the War Years, 1940–1945* (Ames: Iowa State University Press, 1970), pp. 29–33.

56. Henry A. Wallace, "The Price of Free World Victory," in *Prefaces to Peace* (New York: Simon & Schuster et al., 1943), pp. 369–75.

57. Ibid., pp. 373, 375; Henry A. Wallace to HRL, May 16, 1942, Wallace Diaries, vol. 10, p. 1575, Wallace Mss.; Richard J. Walton, *Henry Wallace, Harry Truman, and the Cold War* (New York: Viking Press, 1976), pp. 10–14; Jessup, *The Ideas of Henry Luce*, pp. 121–22; Dwight Macdonald, "The (American) People's Century," *Partisan Review* 9 (July–August 1942): 294–301; Eric Foner, *The Story of American Freedom* (New York: Norton, 1998), pp. 232–33.

58. Wallace, "The Price of Free World Victory," pp. 374–75.

59. HRL to Stanley K. Hornbeck, November 13, 1939, Hornbeck to HRL, November 18, 1939, HRL to Ambassador Hu, February 14, 1941, Box 281, Hornbeck Mss.; "Five Years of United China Relief," n.d., 1945, Lauchlin Currie to HRL, April 12, 1941, HRL to Thomas W. Lamont, April 15, 1941, United China Relief financial statement, April 19, 1941, HRL to James G. Blaine, March 22, 1941, HRL to Bernard Baruch, April 19, 1941,TIA; HRL to Frank Altschul, Altschul Mss.; Theodore Roosevelt, Jr., to HRL, April 2, 1941, TIA.

60. Jonathan D. Spence, *The Gate of Heavenly Peace: The Chinese and Their Revolution* (New York: Viking, 1981), pp. 275–352; Takashi Yoshida, *The Making of the "Rape of Nanking": History and Memory in Japan, China, and the United States* (New York: Oxford University Press, 2006), pp. 11–42; HRL, "China: To the Mountains," June 4, 1941, Helen Meyer to HWL and ERL, May 16, 1941, "Mr. Luce Comes Back From China," compilation of HRL cables, n.d., 1941, HRL to Thomas W. Lamont, April 22, 1941, TIA.

61. HRL, "China: To the Mountains," June 4, 1941, TIA.

62. Ibid.

63. Ibid.; "Mr. Luce Comes Back From China," unsigned Time Inc. Memo, n.d., 1941, TIA; *New York Times*, June 18, 19, November 30, 1941; Helen Meyer to HWL and ERL, May 16, 1941, HRL CBS radio speech, June 11, 1941, HRL speech at United China Relief dinner, June 18, 1941, HRL speech to Rochester Chamber of Commerce, April 22, 1942, HRL to Gottfried, November 3, December 26, 1941, TIA; HRL to Larsen et al., June 16, 1941, JSB Mss.

64. Theodore H. White, *In Search of History: A Personal Adventure* (New York: Harper & Row, 1978), pp. 13–55; Thomas Griffith, *Harry & Teddy* (New York: Random House, 1995), pp. 8–14.

65. THW to David Hulburd, June 9, 1939, TD; "Ploughshares Into Swords," unpublished manuscript, 1939, THW to Gerson Herzel, October 4, 1940, THW Mss.; Theodore H. White, "China the Ally," *Fortune*, September 1941.

66. *Time*, May 19, June 2, 9, 1941; *Life*, May 26, 1941; Elson, *Time Inc.*, p. 467.

67. *Time*, November 17, December 8, 1941; *New York Times*, November 26, 27, 1941; *Washington Post*, November 27, 1941.

68. *Time*, December 8, 1941; *Life*, December 8, 1941.

69. Elson, *Time Inc.*, p. 484; Swanberg, *Luce and His Empire*, p. 189; *Time*, December 15, 1941; *Life*, December 15, 1941; JSBD, December 17, 1941; Elisabeth Luce Moore interview.

70. Swanberg, *Luce and His Empire*, p. 189; HRL to Ursula Vossvon Wehren, June 25, 1948, TIA; Elisabeth Luce Moore interview; Leslie Severinghaus interview.

71. HRL to FDR, December 16, 17, 1941, FDR to HRL, December 22, 1941, PPF 3338, FDRL.

X   TIME INC. GOES TO WAR

1. JSBD, February 25, 1942, December 29, 1944; Time Inc., "Memorandum for U.S. Employment Service: The News Publishing Activities of TIME Incorpo-

rated," September 24, 1942, JSB Mss.; "News for the Gulf," *Business Week*, September 25, 1943.

2. "Analysis of Roper Survey, June 1942," n.d., TIA; THW to David Hulburd, June 14, October 11, 1942, THW Mss.; Time Inc., "Memorandum for U.S. Employment Service: The News Publishing Activities of TIME Incorporated," September 24, 1942, JSB Mss.; Robert E. Herzstein, *Henry R. Luce: A Political Portrait of the Man Who Created the American Century* (New York: Scribner's, 1994), pp. 397–99; Robert T. Elson, *The World of Time Inc.: An Intimate History of a Publishing Enterprise, 1941–1960* (New York: Atheneum, 1973), pp. 37–42.

3. *Life*, December 15, 22, 1941; HRL speech before a *Life* dinner meeting, July 17, 1942, TIA; HRL, "Basis for an Editorial Program for all Publications in 1943," JSB Mss.

4. P. I. Prentice to HRL, September 7, 1945, H. R. Hodgins to C. B. Yorke, "Time Inc.—Influence and Responsibility, Report No. 2," March 31, 1944, HRL to Jessup, JSB, Longwell, August 23, 1944, Thurman Arnold to HRL, September 9, 1943, HRL to Arnold, September 13, 1943, Arnold to HRL, October 23, 1943, TIA; T. S Matthews to HRL et al., September 17, 1944, JSB Mss.; *Princeton University Library Chronicle*, February 1944; Michael G. Carew, *The Power to Persuade: FDR, the Newsmagazines, and Going to War, 1939–1941* (Lanham, Md.: University Press of America, 2005), pp. 66–71.

5. HRL to Managing Editors et al., June 7, 1944, JSB Mss.; HRL to All Members of TIME INC., June 23, 1944, TIA; HRL, "Basis of an Editorial Program for all Publications in 1943," January 1943, JSB Mss.; HRL to The Senior Editors of TIME, December 18, 1943, John Hersey to HRL, July 27, 1944, TIA; HRL to JSB et al., June 16, 1944, HRL to Gottfried, November 13, 1944, JSB Mss.

6. HRL to Eric Hodgins et al., March 6, 1944, HRL to T. S. Matthews et al., October 5, 1944, HRL to staff, February 11, 1944, TIA; Elson, *World of Time Inc.*, pp. 60–61.

7. *Life*, October 12, 1942; HRL to "some of my friends in Great Britain," November 11, 1942, C. D. Jackson to HRL et al., October 17, 1942, T. S. Matthews to David Hulburd, London Cable 5250, October 12, 1942, TIA; HRL to Ed Lockett, July 22, 1943, HRL statement "to members of the British Press," October 15, 1942, JSB Mss.; Andrew Heiskell oral history, COHP; Andrew Heiskell interview.

8. Whittaker Chambers, *Witness* (New York: Random House, 1952), pp. 86–87, 193–96; Sam Tanenhaus, *Whittaker Chambers* (New York: Random House, 1997), pp. 3–163.

9. Whittaker Chambers, n.d., internal memo, TIA; *Time*, February 12, 1940; HRL to Chambers, May 6, 1942, TIA; Tanenhaus, *Whittaker Chambers*, pp. 166–67.

10. *Time*, January 6, 1941, February 16, 1942; Tanenhaus, *Whittaker Chambers*, pp. 172–73.

11. Manfred Gottfried oral history, Time Inc., 1961, pp. 161–62, TIA; *Time*, July 17, August 7, 14, 1944; Chambers, *Witness*, pp. 496–500; Elson, *World of Time Inc.*, pp. 104–5.

12. Fillmore Calhoun to Allen Grover, February 6, 1945, John Hersey to HRL, February 1945, Chambers to HRL, September 18, November 10, 1944, "Excerpt from Billings Monthly Editorial Report," January 17, 1945, TIA; Chambers, *Witness*, pp. 497–98; HRL to JSB, January 6, 1945, JSB Mss.; Chambers to HRL, January, n.d., 1945, TIA; JSB to Charles Wertenbaker, January 15, 1945, Wertenbaker to JSB, January 15, 1945, JSB Mss.; HRL to Chambers, January 17, 1945, TIA.

13. *Time*, March 5, 1945; JSBD, February 19, 22, 1945.

14. JSBD, November 20, 22, 1944; Chambers, *Witness*, pp. 501–4; Chambers to HRL, November 4, 1945, TIA; Tanenhaus, *Whittaker Chambers*, pp. 194–96.

15. *Time*, March 22, 1943; JSBD, April 19, 21, 1944; Elson, *World of Time Inc.*, pp. 118–19.

16. Pearl Buck to HRL, n.d., 1943, HRL, "Private Memorandum on Pearl Buck's Article on China," n.d., 1943, TIA; *Life*, May 10, 1943, May 1, 1944; THW to David Hulburd, March 13, May 15, June 22, 1943, "Cable from T. H. White," n.d., 1943, HRL to JSB, March 24, 1944, HRL to THW, April 3, 1944, THW to HRL, April 12, 1944, TIA; Theodore H. White, *In Search of History: A Personal Adventure* (New York: Harper & Row, 1978), pp. 207–8; Peter Conn, *Pearl S. Buck: A Cultural Biography* (Cambridge: Cambridge University Press, 1996), pp. 272–73; Patricia Nels, *China Images in the Life and Times of Henry Luce* (Savage, Md.: Rowman & Littlefield, 1990), pp. 104–6; THW to HRL, May, n.d., 1944, THW Mss.

17. HRL to THW, July 19, 1943, TIA; HRL to JSB, March 24, 1944, HRL to THW, April 3, 1944, HRL to Managing Editors, June 12, 1944, THW to HRL, July 21, 1944, JSB Mss.; Elson, *World of Time Inc.*, p. 121.

18. Barbara Tuchman, *Stilwell and the American Experience in China*, 1911–1945 (New York: Macmillan, 1971), chaps. 9–20, and pp. 340, 354–57; White, *In Search of History*, pp. 176–79; Thomas Griffith, *Harry & Teddy* (New York: Random House, 1995), pp. 80–81; THW to HRL, October 19, 1944, TIA.

19. *Time*, November 13, 1944; HRL to Brooks Atkinson, November 21, 1944, TIA.

20. THW, "Chungking Cable No. 23," November 21, 1944, TD; HRL to THW, December 13, 1944, THW to Matthews, January, n.d., 1945, TIA; *Time*, March 1, 1943, December 18, 1944, January 1, 1945; *Life*, March 1, 1943.

21. William Palmer Taylor to James Linen, December 9, 1944, Mary Johnson Tweedy to HRL, February 26, 1945, TIA; Richard Watts, "Reading Luce in China," *New Republic*, December 3, 1945, pp. 740–42; HRL to Management Executive Committee, March 12, 1945, TIA.

22. JSBD, August 13, 1945; HRL to THW, August 14, 1945, JSB Mss.; THW, "Chungking Cable No. 250," August 14, 1945, TD; THW to HRL, August 15, 1945, JSB Mss.; HRL radio address, November 14, 1943, TIA; White, *In Search of History*, pp. 209–13.

23. THW to HRL, June 26, 1946, HRL to JSB, August 13, 1945, TIA; HRL to Charles Wertenbaker et al., July 1, 1946, JSB Mss.; Corinne Thrasher to Allen Grover, July 3, 1946, HRL to THW, June 29, 1946, TIA; THW to HRL, August 1, 1946, THW Mss.; JSB to HRL, July 15, 1946, THW to HRL, August 1, 1946, JSB Mss.; JSBD, February 26, 1945; CBL to Patricia Neils, January 22, 1985, CBL Mss.; Theodore H. White and Annalee Jacoby, *Thunder Over China* (New York: A. M. Sloane Assocs, 1946); White, *In Search of History*, pp. 246–49; Griffith, *Harry & Teddy*, pp. 152–60; Joyce Hoffmann, *Theodore H. White and Journalism as Illusion* (Columbia: University of Missouri Press, 1995), pp. 72–74.

24. FDR to Stephen Early, January 17, 1942, TIA; HRL to Early, January 10, 1942, Early to FDR, January 13, 1942, HRL to Early, January 19, 1942, Early Mss.; *Life*, December 15, 1941; *Time*, January 12, 1942; Felix Belair to HRL, January 19, 1943, TIA.

25. JSBD, January 21, 1942; FDR to Sumner Welles, February 28, 1942, Welles to FDR, March 7, 1942, PSF Welles 2-42, FDRL.

26. JSBD, January 8, 1942; HRL to Managing Editors, November 1, 1943, JSB Mss.; HRL to T. S. Matthews, February 11, 1943, HRL to Raymond Clapper, December 4, 1943, Clapper to HRL, December 6, 1943, TIA.

27. Richard Norton Smith, *The Colonel: The Life and Legend of Robert R. McCormick* (Boston: Houghton Mifflin, 1997), pp. 432–40; Henry Stimson Diary, vol. 41, September 27, 1943, Stimson Mss., LC; HRL to George C. Marshall, March 27, 1943, HRL to John J. McCloy, August 26, 1943, PPF 3338, FDRL; HRL to FDR, October 23, 1943, PPF 2442, FDRL; JSBD, August 30, 1944; HRL to George C. Marshall, April 27, 1944, George C. Marshall to HRL, June 7, 1944, TIA; Elisabeth Luce Moore interview.

28. HRL to Gottfried, July 28, 1944, HRL to JSB, July 14, 1944, JSB Mss.

29. HRL to Larsen, August 23, 1943, TIA; Jessup to HRL, August 30, 1944, JSB

Mss.; Richard Watts, Jr., "Reading Luce in China," pp. 741–42; Warren Breed, "Social Control in the Newsroom," *Social Forces* 33 (May 1955), 326–35.

30. HRL, Memo to staff, February 11, 1944, TIA; HRL to Gottfried, November 5, 1942, HRL to The Policy Committee, July 12, 1944, HRL Confidential Memo, February 10, 1944, JSB Mss.; Culbert Olson to HRL, November 11, 1942, HRL to Olson, January 29, 1943, TIA; R. L. Buell, "Republican Reorganization," November 29, 1944, HRL to Jessup, November 30, 1944, JSB Mss.; Herzstein, *Henry R. Luce*, p. 377.

31. HRL to CBL, May 5, 1943, October 19, 1943, CBL Mss.; JSBD, January 31, 1945.

32. CBL Diary, April 19, n.d., CBL Mss.; JSBD, October 18, 1941, July 1, 1942; Sylvia Morris, *Rage for Fame: The Ascent of Clare Boothe Luce* (New York: Random House, 1997), pp. 460–61.

33. CBL to HRL, November 23, 1941, November 23, 1942, CBL Mss.; Morris, *Rage for Fame*, pp. 442–44; CBL speech to Connecticut State Republican Convention, September 10, 1942, CBL Mss.; *New York Times*, September 11, 1942.

34. Morris, *Rage for Fame*, pp. 360, 442; CBL to HRL, November 23, 1942, CBL Mss.

35. JSBD, June 22, 1943; Ralph G. Martin, *Henry and Clare: An Intimate Portrait of the Luces* (New York: G. P. Putnam, 1991), pp. 246–50.

36. HRL to CBL, n.d., 1943, CBL Mss.; HRL to JSB et al., August 12, 1944, JSB Mss.

37. HRL to Ann Brokaw, February 16, 1939, April 13, 1940, n.d., Helen Meyer to Ann Brokaw, May 16, 1941, CBL Mss.; *Stanford Magazine*, July–August 2003; *Time*, January 24, 1944; HRL to CBL, January 11, 1944, CBL Mss.; W. A. Swanberg, *Luce and His Empire* (New York: Charles Scribner's Sons, 1972), p. 232; JSBD, January 22, September 6, November 8, 1944; Elisabeth Luce Moore interview.

38. HRL to JSB et al., May 12, 1943, HRL to Gottfried, May 27, 1943, TIA.

39. HRL to Editors, February 15, August 17, 1943, TIA; *Fortune*, May 1945; Elson, *World of Time Inc.*, pp. 128–30.

40. HRL to CBL, n.d., 1943, CBL Mss.

41. HRL to Managing Editors, August 17, 1943, HRL to Policy Committee, October 30, November 3, 1940, TIA.

42. HRL to William Ernest Hocking, July 30, 1943, March 23, 1944, William Benton to HRL, November 1, 1943, TIA; HRL to Lippmann, January 3, 1943, Lippmann memo, January, n.d., 1943, HRL to Lippmann, January 5, 1943, Lippmann to HRL, January 6, 1943, HRL to Lippmann, February 25, 1943, Lippmann to HRL, March 8, 1943, Lippmann Mss., Yale.

43. HRL address, Ohio State University Commencement, June 11, 1943, JSB Mss.; HRL, "The Practice of Freedom: A Memorandum on the Fundamental 'Attitudes and Convictions' of TIME INC.," August 1943, TIA; HRL, "Articles of Faith," September 6, 1943, JSB Mss.

XI   LOSING CHINA

1. *Time*, April 23, 30, 1945; *Life*, April 30, 1945; *Fortune*, May 1945; JSB to editors, August 14, 1945, JSB Mss.

2. HRL to Eleanor Roosevelt, April 13, 1945, TIA; JSBD, April 12, 1945; HRL unpublished memoir, n.d., TIA; JSBD, May 14, 1948; HRL to T. S. Matthews et al. January 16, 1947, JSB Mss.; John K. Jessup, ed., *The Ideas of Henry Luce* (New York: Atheneum, 1969), p. 18; Robert E. Herzstein, *Henry R. Luce: A Political Portrait of the Man Who Created the American Century* (New York: Scribner's, 1994), p. 377; HRL to Truman, April 17, 1945, TIA.

3. HRL to JSB, May 27, 1945, JSB Mss.; Robert T. Elson, *The World of Time Inc.: The Intimate History of a Publishing Enterprise, 1941–1960* (New York: Atheneum, 1973), pp. 131–33.

4. HRL, unpublished memoir, 1966, TIA; David Hulburd to HRL, May 18, 1945, "Memo to Mr. Luce from Mr. Mayer," May, n.d., 1945, JSB Mss.; Bill Gray to Eleanor Welch, May 20, 1945, TIA; Bill Gray Cable #122, May 21, 1945, Shelly Mydans cable to David Hulburd, May 26, 1945, JSB Mss.

5. Bill Gray to Eleanor Welch, May 20, 1945, JSB Mss.; Elson, *World of Time Inc.*, p. 133.

6. *Time*, August 20, 1945.

7. HRL to Daniel Longwell, August 27, 1945, HRL to T. S. Matthews, November 12, 16, 1945, HRL to JSB, August 23, 1945, TIA.

8. *Time*, December 15, 22, 1941, January 26, 1942, August 7, 1944; *Life*, December 22, 1941, September 6, 1943; *Fortune*, February 1942, April 1944; *Time*, November 30, 1942, June 21, August 9, 1943; Pearl S. Buck to HRL, December 18, 1941, HRL to Pearl S. Buck, December 19, 1941, Pearl S. Buck to HRL, December 19, 1941, TIA; John W. Dower, *War Without Mercy: Race and Power in the Pacific War* (New York: Pantheon, 1986), pp. 37, 58, 65–67, 161, 181, 189, 224, 330.

9. HRL, unpublished memoir, 1966, JSB to Tasker et al., "The Chinese Communists," August 24, 1945, TIA; Elisabeth Luce Moore interview; Christina Klein, *Cold War Orientalism: Asia in the Middlebrow Imagination, 1945–1961* (Berkeley: University of California Press, 2003), pp. 176–77.

10. HRL to Leighton Stuart, September 24, 1945, TIA; THW, Chungking Cable 242, Part II, August 13, 1945, HRL to Tasker, August 13, 1945, HRL to THW, August 14, 1945, THW, Chungking Cable 250, August 14, 1945, Eleanor Welch to THW, August 14, 1945, THW, Chungking Cable 251, August 14, 1945, Chungking Cable 253, August 15, 1945, JSB Mss.; Eleanor Welch to THW, August 15, 1945, HRL to Mme. Chiang Kai-shek, October 28, 1943, TIA; JSBD, April 27, August 28, 1945.

11. HRL Cable 1, October 7, 1945, HRL cable, "Tsingtao: Fastest Growing City in China," October 21, 1945, TIA; HRL and Charles Murphy Cable, October 27, 1945, JSB Mss.; HRL to Chiang Kai-shek, April 21, July 7, 1945, TIA.

12. HRL cables to JSB, October 19, 20, 1945, JSB Mss.; "Mr. Luce's Chungking Diary," October 1945, TIA.

13. "Mr. Luce's Chungking Diary," HRL to Mme. Chiang Kai-shek, October 29, 1945, TIA.

14. HRL to Mme. Chiang Kai-shek, October 28, 1943, TIA; Henry A. Wallace diary, vol. 23, November 1, 1945, Wallace Mss.; HRL to Jessup, November 13, 1945, JSB Mss.

15. CBL diary, April 9, 1937, n.d., 1944, CBL Mss.; JSBD, August 7, 1945; CBL to HRL, n.d., 1947, CBL Mss.

16. *Time*, February 25, 1946; JSBD, February 13, 17, 1946; CBL to HRL, n.d., 1947, ERL to CBL, February 20, 1946, CBL Mss.; Elisabeth Luce Moore interview.

17. CBL to HRL, n.d., 1947, CBL memo, "Suffering Excruciating Emotional and Mental Misery," August 10, 1947, CBL Mss.; Ralph G. Martin, *Henry and Clare: An Intimate Portrait of the Luces* (New York: G. P. Putnam, 1991), pp. 258–62; JSBD, August 27, 1947.

18. JSBD, August 11, 17, 1947.

19. CBL to HRL, n.d., 1947, HRL to CBL, July, n.d., 1947, HRL to CBL, n.d., 1947, HRL to CBL, February, n.d., 1948, CBL Mss.; JSBD, August 17, 1946, September 25, 1947.

20. CBL to HRL, n.d., 1946, HRL to CBL, n.d., 1946, HRL to CBL, n.d., 1947, CBL Mss.

21. Andrew Heiskell interview; Gore Vidal, "The Woman Behind the Women," *The New Yorker*, May 26, 1997, p. 74.

22. JSBD, March 5, 1946; Matthews to HRL, February, n.d., 1946, HRL, "Editorial Program for TIME in 1946," March 6, 1946, Margaret McConnell to Roy Alexander, November 5, 1946, TIA.

23. T. S. Matthews to HRL, August 30, 1948, HRL, "Editorial Program for TIME in 1946," March 6, 1946, HRL, "Agenda for Discussion," November, n.d., 1949, Henry Grunwald to T. S. Matthews, June 10, 1949, TIA; Elson, *World of Time Inc.*, pp. 207–9.

24. JSBD, January 6, 16, 25, December 10, 20, 1946, May 27, June 4, July 21, 22, 1947, February 9, 12, 17, March 11, 1948.

25. HRL to JSB et al., February 13, 1948, HRL, "Directive for the Editorial Development of *Fortune*," March 23, 1948, JSB Mss.

26. HRL, "Directive for the Editorial Development of *Fortune*," March 23, 1948, JSB Mss.; JSBD, March 22, 1948.

27. JSBD, July 20, 1948; Elson, *World of Time Inc.*, pp. 201–3.

28. JSBD, May 20, 1946; Elson, *World of Time Inc.*, pp. 187–89.

29. Elson, *World of Time Inc.*, p. 192; HRL to Joseph Thorndike, n.d., 1948, TIA.

30. JSBD, October 20, 1948, August 5, 1949; Elson, *World of Time Inc.*, pp. 187–88.

31. HRL to Editors, October, n.d., 1948, TIA; Elson, *World of Time Inc.*, pp. 192–93; JSBD, October 21, 1948; HRL to Thorndike, March 1, 1948, TIA.

32. HRL to Thorndike et al., October 20, 1948, HRL to JSB et al., August 9, 1949, JSB Mss.; HRL to Thorndike et al., October 28, 1948, TIA.

33. HRL to Thorndike, March 1, October 20, 1948, TIA; HRL, "Notes on *Life*," August 9, 1949, JSB Mss.

34. HRL to JSB et al., January 23, 1946, JSB Mss.; JSBD, January 23, 1946; *Life*, January 7, 1946; Elson, *World of Time Inc.*, pp. 155–56.

35. JSBD, January 19, 23, March 5, November 12, 27, 1946; HRL to Churchill, January 14, 1948, TIA; John Osborne, "Recollections of Winston Churchill at Dinner at the Union Club, New York," April 5, 1949, JSB Mss.; JSB, "Churchill Dinner, Ritz Carlton March 25, 1949," JSB Scrapbook #49, transcripts of March 25, 1949, dinner for Churchill, JSB Mss.

36. Churchill to HRL, November 22, 1947, Graebner Mss.; HRL to Churchill, January 14, 1948, JSB Mss.

37. Walter Graebner to HRL, January 23, 1947, JSB Mss.; Elson, *World of Time Inc.*, pp. 216–20; JSBD, December 2, 1947, February 10, 1948; *Life*, December 8, 1947; Walter Graebner to Ed Thompson, November 26, 1953, Graebner Mss.

38. *New Republic*, July 21, 1945.

39. HRL to Schlamm, January 26, 1948, JSB Mss.; JSBD, January 16, 19, March 1, 1948, February 16, 17, 23, July 5, 1949.

40. *Time*, September 24, 31, 1945.

41. John Robinson Beal, *Marshall in China* (Garden City, N.Y.: Doubleday, 1970), pp. 1–8; HRL to Henry Stimson, November 21, 1946, HRL Memo, November 17, 1945, TIA.

42. John J. McCloy to HRL, November 15, 1946, TIA; Beal, *Marshall in China*, pp. 113, 283, 341; Robert E. Herzstein, "Henry Luce, George Marshall, and China: The Parting of the Ways in 1946," in Larry Bland, ed., *George C. Marshall's Mission to China, December 1945–January 1947* (Lexington, Va.: George C. Marshall Foundation, 1998), pp. 115–45; HRL to D'Orsay Hurst, July 4, 1947, TIA.

43. HRL to George C. Marshall, November 29, 1945, HRL to James Forrestal, August 12, 1946, HRL to Leighton Stuart, October 7, December 7, 1946, May 17, 1947, TIA; Leighton Stuart, *Fifty Years in China: The Memoirs of John Leighton Stuart* (New York: Random House, 1954), pp. 179–85; *Time*, October 28, December 30, 1946.

44. JSBD, August 22, 23, 1946; *Life*, September 2, 1946.

45. HRL to Wes Bailey, March 16, 1946, TIA.

46. Beal, *Marshall in China*, pp. 243–44, 260–62, 264; HRL unpublished memoir, 1966, TIA; Sterling Seagrave, *The Soong Dynasty* (New York: Harper & Row, 1985), pp. 430–34.

47. Beal, *Marshall in China*, pp. 260–62, 264; HRL unpublished memoir, 1966, TIA.

48. HRL unpublished memoir, 1966, Fred Gruin, "Reminiscence," March 2, 1967, Fred Gruin memo, March 7, 1985, TIA.
49. Beal, *Marshall in China*, pp. 264–66; HRL unpublished memoir, 1966, pp. 20–21, 21, 22; Robert E. Herzstein, *Henry R. Luce, Time, and the American Crusade in Asia* (New York: Cambridge University Press, 2005), pp. 73–74.
50. *Life* edit memo, n.d., 1946, TIA; JSBD, August 8, October 7, 1946, September 25, October 7, December 16, 1947; HRL to William C. Bullitt, July 3, 1947, TIA; *Life*, October 13, 1947; *Time*, October 13, 1947; Charles Edison to HRL, October 14, 1947, TIA.
51. HRL notes on China trip, October, n.d., 1946, TIA.
52. JSBD, November 14, 15, 1946, February 13, 21, 1947, HRL to Wertenbaker et al., May 21, 1946, HRL to Matthews et al., September 27, October 7, 1946, TIA; HRL to William Gray, December 9, 1946, JSB Mss.; Boyce Price to HRL, April 8, 1947, TIA.
53. HRL to Arthur Vandenberg, January 12, 1948, HRL to Robert Lovett, January 22, 1948, TIA; HRL to Max Ways and John Osborne, August 12, 1948, JSB Mss.
54. HRL to Henry Stimson, January 15, 1948, Stimson to HRL, March 31, 1948, HRL to Stimson, April 20, 1948, Stimson to HRL April 28, 1948, HRL to JSB et al., February 27, 1946, Charles Edison to HRL, October 14, 1947, Fred Gruin memo, May 18, 1984, TIA; Elisabeth Luce Moore interview.
55. Allen Grover to HRL, April 3, 1951, TIA; Edward C. Carter to HRL, May 23, 1933, August 11, 1934, HRL to Edward Carter, August 16, 1941, Institute for Pacific Relations Mss.; HRL to Juan Trippe, September 22, 1943, TIA; HRL to Edward Carter, May 26, 1941, Institute for Pacific Relations Mss.
56. Edward C. Carter to HRL, May 23, 1933, Kohlberg to Philip C. Jessup, March 15, 1946, Kohlberg to HRL, August 8, 1946, Institute for Pacific Relations Mss.
57. Allen Grover to HRL, April 3, 1951, TIA; Douglas Auchincloss to HRL, January 7, 1943, Boyce P. Price to HRL, August 30, 1946, HRL to Edward Carter, August 9, September 4, 1946, Institute for Pacific Relations Mss.; HRL to Alfred Kohlberg, August 9, 1946, Edward Carter to HRL, September 18, 22, 1946, Bernard Barnes to Edward Carter, November 26, 1947, HRL to Griffith, December 5, 1949, TIA.
58. Albert Wedemeyer to HRL, July 2, 1946, Wedemeyer Mss.; Jim Shepley to Allen Grover, transcript of telephone conversation, July 26, 1946, TIA.
59. Wedemeyer to HRL, October 10, 1947, Wedemeyer Mss.
60. HRL to General Chang Chun, September 21, 1946, TIA; Keith Eiles, "The Man Who Planned the Victory," *Hoover Digest*, 2001, Hoover Institute On-line Publications; Wedemeyer to HRL, October 10, 1947, HRL to George C. Marshall, October 7, 1947, Wedemeyer Mss.; *Time*, October 6, 1947; Department of State, *United States Relations with China* (Washington, D.C.: U.S. Government Printing Office, 1949), pp. 758–814.
61. *United States Relations with China*, pp. vii–xiv.
62. Eddie Jones to Dave Hulburd, November 26, 1948, TIA; Paris Dispatch 7126, John Osborne, November 16, 1948, TD.
63. Shanghai Dispatch 592, William Gray, January 29, 1948, TD; HRL to JSB, March 8, 1948, TIA.
64. HRL to Leighton Stuart, May 25, 1948, Mme. Chiang Kai-shek to HRL, June 15, 1948, TIA; JSBD, September 16, 1948.
65. *Life*, April 5, 1948; HRL to Robert Lovett, January 22, 1948, HRL to Leighton Stuart, January 27, 1948, HRL to Max Ways and John Osborne, August 12, 1948, "Truman, China and History," Time Inc. internal report, n.d., 1961, HRL to Osborne and Ways, November 27, 1948, TIA.
66. HRL to Larsen, June 17, 1946, TIA; *Time*, March 1, 15, 1948; Rexford Tugwell diary, June 10, 1944, Tugwell Mss., LC.
67. HRL speech, June, n.d., 1948, TIA; *Time*, March 1, 15, July 5, November 1, 8, 15, 1948.

68. JSBD, December 24, 1928, May 20, 1949; HRL to Chiang Kai-shek, December 24, 30, 1948, Chiang Kai-shek to HRL, January 17, 1949, TIA.

XII   COLD WARRIORS

1. HRL to Roy Larsen, February 6, 1948, TIA; HRL to Max Ways, January 29, 1948, HRL to T. S. Matthews, February 4, 1948, JSB Mss.; JSBD, March 5, 1948, May 31, 1949, January 25, 1954; JSB, "Luce Talk," June 29, 1950, "Random Luce Notes," January 5, June, n.d., 1949, JSB Scrapbook #49, JSB Mss.
2. Merlyn Pitzele to HRL, December 28, 1948, TIA; *Business Week*, March 6, 1948; Elisabeth Luce Moore interview; Henry Luce III interview; Andrew Heiskell interview.
3. Herbert Bayard Swope to HRL, January 9, 1950, TIA; *New Republic*, January 30, 1950; *New York Times*, January 4, 15, 16, February 1, 1950; JSBD, January 4, 5, 6 10, 12, 13, 16, 20, 24.
4. HRL, "Memo to Staff," September 8, 1950, "Luce to Take Sabbatical," FYI, September 15, 1950, JSB Mss.; JSBD, September 1, 7, 11, 18, 1950, January 22, 26, 1951, January 26, 1952, April 6, 1953.
5. JSB to Grover, n.d., 1950, JSB Mss.; Robert T. Elson, *The World of Time Inc.: The Intimate History of a Publishing Enterprise, 1941–1960* (New York: Atheneum, 1973), p. 252; HRL to JSB, March 3, 1946, "Random Notes on some people in the West," February 14–23, 1946, "Notes on a Trip to Portland, Seattle, Butte, Anaconda & Chicago," June, n.d., 1948, "Notes on a journey to Cincinnati, St. Louis, Fort Worth and Snyder, Texas," October 31, 1949, TIA.
6. Connie White to family, June 15, 1946, CJBW and WWW to "Our Parents," June 12, 1947, HRL, "Notes on conversation with Mr. Attlee," March 8, 1948, HRL to John Osborne, August 16, 1947, "Western Civilization," May 1949, Allen Grover to JSB, May 1, 1946, "Notes on Trip to Germany and Austria," n.d., 1946, "Mr. Luce's Trip to Europe—1949: List of People," JSB Mss.; HRL memo, n.d., December 1952, HRL, "1953 in Asia," n.d., 1952, TIA; *Life*, February 23, 1953.
7. HRL, "Five Day Voyage of Max Thornburgh and Henry Luce Through the Northern Provinces of Persia," November 1950, HRL to Roy Alexander, "Policy Memorandum on Iran," December 5, 1950, TIA.
8. HRL, "Five Day Voyage of Max Thornburgh and Henry Luce Through the Northern Provinces of Persia," November 1950, HRL to Roy Alexander, "Policy Memorandum on Iran," December 5, 1950, HRL to JSB, November, n.d., 1950, TIA.
9. Allen Weinstein, *Perjury: The Hiss-Chambers Case* (New York: Alfred A. Knopf, 1978), pp. 161–65, 174–76, 184–95; William Allen White, Jr., to HRL, January 31, 1950, TIA; John Early Haynes and Harvey Klehr, *Venona: Decoding Soviet Espionage in America* (New Havenk Conn.: Yale University Press, 1999), pp. 167–73.
10. JSBD, August 17, 20, 1948, February 25, 1949; Elson, *World of Time Inc.*, p. 238.
11. JSBD, December 9, 18, 1948, March 9, 10, 1950; James A. Linen to Staff, December 10, 1948, TIA; Weinstein, *Perjury*, pp. 276–77.
12. JSBD, April 21, 24, 26, 1950.
13. HRL to André Laguerre, "A Letter on General Policy," February 14, 1949, TIA; HRL to JSB et al., September 14, 1946, JSB Mss.; HRL to Matthews and Alexander, May 10, 1946, HRL to Thorndike, June 9, 1949, TIA.
14. *Time*, June 12, 1950, January 8, May 21, October 1, 1951, February 11, March 3, December 29, 1952, January 12, March 16, 1953; Elizabeth Carter Vincent to HRL, February 20, 1953, HRL to Elizabeth Carter Vincent, March 5, 1953, TIA.
15. *Time*, May 1, 1950, October 1, May 21, 1951, February 11, March 10, 1952;

HRL to Albert Dick, April 22, 1950, TIA; Robert P. Newman, *Owen Lattimore and the "Loss" of China* (Berkeley: University of California Press, 1992), pp. 200–1, 396–97.

16. David M. Oshinksy, *A Conspiracy So Immense* (New York: Free Press, 1983), pp. 72–114; Thomas C. Reeves, *The Life and Times of Joe McCarthy* (New York: Stein & Day, 1982), pp. 161–234.

17. HRL to Philip Jessup, February 4, 1947, n.d., 1950, HRL to JSB, March 6, 1946, HRL to Matthews, April 9, 1946, TIA; JSBD, September 21, 1950; Elson, *World of Time Inc.*, p. 276.

18. Arthur M. Schlesinger, Jr., *The Vital Center* (Boston: Houghton Mifflin, 1948), pp. 35–50, 159–60.

19. Oshinsky, *A Conspiracy So Immense*, pp. 191–97; Barry Goldwater, *Why Not Victory* (New York: Macfadden-Bartel, 1962).

20. George F. Kennan, *Memoirs, 1925–1950* (Boston: Little, Brown, 1967), pp. 547–57.

21. "X" [George F. Kennan], "The Sources of Soviet Conduct," *Foreign Affairs* 25 (July 1947): 566–82.

22. John Lewis Gaddis, *Strategies of Containment* (New York: Oxford University Press, 1982), pp. 55–65.

23. *Time*, February 24, March 24, 1947; JSBD, February 3, September 23 1949; HRL to JSB, January 2, 1946, HRL to Robert Elson, March 7, 1947, TIA; HRL to JSB, July 20, 1950, JSB Mss.

24. HRL, "Dulles," n.d., 1946, TIA; HRL to Matthews et al., February 27, 1948, JSB Mss.; JSBD, January 4, 1951.

25. JSBD, July 14, 21, 1950; Elson, *World of Time Inc.*, p. 282.

26. JSBD, December 8, 1950, January 10, February 16, 1951; Elson, *World of Time Inc.*, p. 290; *Life*, December 11, 1950, January 8, 1951.

27. HRL to Alexander et al., April 5, 1950, March 7, 1951, TIA; *Life*, January 8, 1951; JSBD, February 14, August 11, December 5, 1950.

28. JSBD, January 19, 1951.

29. John W. Spanier, *The Truman-MacArthur Controversy and the Korean War* (Cambridge, Mass.: Harvard University Press, 1959), pp. 191–92; William Stueck, "The March to the Yalu: The Perspective from Washington," in Bruce Cumings, ed., *Child of Conflict: The Korean American Relationship, 1943–1953* (Seattle: University of Washington Press, 1983), pp. 219–37; William Manchester, *American Caesar: Douglas MacArthur, 1880–1964* (Boston: Little, Brown, 1978), pp. 638–40; JSBD, April 11, 13, 1951.

30. HRL, "Notes," April 24, 1951, TIA; *Time*, April 23, 1951.

31. HRL, "Private Notes," April 25, 1951, TIA.

32. JSBD, April 24, 1951; HRL to Matthews et al., December 10, 1951, HRL to Matthews, December 15, 1951, TIA; *Time*, January 7, 1952.

33. *Life*, April 23, 1951; HRL, "Memo to Myself," July 11, 1955, TIA.

34. Elson, *World of Time Inc.*, pp. 301–9; HRL unpublished memoir, pp. 46–54, TIA.

35. Allen Grover to Harold E. Talbott, January 31, 1952, Talbott to Grover, February 1, 1952, Eisenhower to HRL, January 8, 1952, TIA; *Life*, January 7, 21, 1952; *Time*, January 7, 14, 1952; Andrew Heiskell interview; Elisabeth Luce Moore interview; Elson, *World of Time Inc.*, pp. 301–9; HRL unpublished memoir, pp. 46–54, TIA.

36. JSBD, June 16, 19, September 3, 12, 16, 18, 22, October 23, 1952; HRL, "Notes on the Convention," n.d., 1952, TIA; *Time*, July 7, 14, 1952; Henry Cabot Lodge to HRL, July, n.d., 1952, Bob Elson to Miss Thrasher, September, n.d., 1952, "Mr. Luce's Schedule for Joining the Eisenhower Train," September 17, 1952, TIA; Elson, *World of Time Inc.*, p. 308.

37. HRL to T. S. Matthews, October 25, 1952, HRL to C. D. Jackson, September 17, October 23, 1952, HRL to Eisenhower, September 3, 1952, Eisenhower to HRL, September 17, 1952, HRL, "Illinois," n.d., 1952, TIA; JSBD, October 23,

27, November 6, 1952; Elson, *World of Time Inc.*, pp. 315–20; Robert Manning, *The Swamp Root Chronicle: Adventures in the Word Trade* (New York: Norton, 1992), pp. 150–52.

38. *Time*, November 3, 1952.
39. "Memo from Henry R. Luce," June 25, 1952, TIA; *Life*, May 19, 1952; HRL, "Concerning the World Struggle," n.d., 1952, TIA; Robert E. Herzstein, *Henry R. Luce,* Time *and the American Crusade in Asia* (New York: Cambridge University Press, 2005), pp. 162–63.
40. HRL to Andrew Heiskell et al., November 5, 1952, TIA.
41. HRL to Eisenhower, January 5, 1953, Eisenhower to HRL, January 5, 1953, HRL to Alexander et al., December 17, 1953, TIA; JSBD, December 22, 1952, January 7, 8, 9, 19, February 2, 27, 1953.
42. JSBD, March 20, June 19, 1953; HRL to Editors, August, n.d., 1953, TIA; Elisabeth Luce Moore interview; Richard Challener, interview with HRL, July 28, 1965, John Foster Dulles Mss.
43. HRL to Editors, "Foreign Policy—Time Inc.," July 9, 1954, HRL to Editors, "Mistakes of the Last Ten Years (Pre-Eisenhower)," August 10, 1954, HRL, "Elaboration of preceding summary of Policy for Survival," August 12, 1954, C. D. Jackson to Editors, August 26, 1954, "Preface," n.d., 1954, TIA.
44. HRL, "Dulles," n.d., 1953, HRL to Thompson et al., January 17, 1955, "Reverberation Over Dulles Statement," n.d., 1956, Jim Pitt to Bernard Barnes, January 18, 1956, TIA; *Life*, January 16, 1956; *New York Times*, January 22, 1956; *Time*, January 23, 1956.
45. HRL to Jean de Lattre, May 17, 1949, de Lattre to HRL, October 10, 1951, HRL to de Lattre, October 26, 1951, comment of HRL on Laguerre Memo on Talk with De Lattre, n.d., 1950, HRL, "1953 in Asia," n.d., 1952, HRL, "America and Asia," n.d., 1952, TIA; *Life*, February 23, 1953.
46. HRL, "1953 in Asia," n.d., 1952, TIA; JSBD, August 4, 1953; JSB to HRL, August 4, 1953, JSB Mss.; HRL to JSB, August 5, 1953, W. A. Swanberg Mss.; Dowling to HRL, July 11, August 5, 1953, JSB Mss.
47. *Time*, November 22, 1954; William H. Hunter, "The War in Vietnam, Luce Version," *New Republic*, March 23, 1963, pp. 15–17.
48. HRL to Jessup, September 10, 1951, TIA.
49. HRL to Gottfried, April 4, 1944, TIA.
50. John K. Jessup, ed., *The Ideas of Henry Luce* (New York: Atheneum, 1969), pp. 179–90; Elisabeth Luce Moore interview; JSBD, April 6, 1951; HRL to William Ernest Hocking, March 21, 1952, TIA.
51. Harold R. MacKinnon, *The Secret of Mr. Justice Holmes* (Berkeley: University of California Press, 1950); Jessup, *The Ideas of Henry Luce*, pp. 154–59; JSBD, June 10, 11, 1952.
52. HRL, "Peace is the Work of Justice," *Connecticut Bar Journal* 30 (December 1956): 340–53; HRL, "Peace is the Work of Justice," (revised) October 23, 1956, Carl Albert Mss., University of Oklahoma; HRL memo, February 15, 1943, TIA; JSBD, February 14, 20, 1950.
53. JSBD, July 3, November 6, 1953.
54. William Ernest Hocking, *The Meaning of God in Human Experience* (New Haven, Conn.: Yale University Press, 1916), pp. 3–6, 68–70; HRL to Hocking, March 21, 23, 28, 1952, June 29, 1956, May 24, 1957, October 16, 1965, Hocking to HRL, June 22, 1956, May 13, 1957, September 27, October 31, 1965, TIA.
55. Richard Challener, "Transcript of a Recorded Interview with Henry Luce," John Foster Dulles Oral History Project, Princeton University Library, pp. 10–13; HRL to J. E. Wallace Sterling, April 7, 1955, Oscar Hammerstein to HRL, December 26, 1958, Robert Menzies to HRL, March 25, 1957, Dulles to HRL, May 10, 1957, HRL to Dulles, May 24, August 8, September 7, 16, 1957, HRL, "Talk with Secretary Dulles at D.O.S.," August 22, 1957, Philip K. Crowe to HRL, June 3, 1958, HRL to Thomas J. Watson, May 2, 1959, TIA.

56. Rhyne, Malone, Griswold, HRL, "Aide-Memoire for the Secretary of State," July 1, 1958, Malone, "Memorandum re Meeting with John Foster Dulles," July 1, 1958, Malone to Earl Osborn, July 4, 1958, HRL to Charles Rhyne, May 11, 1959, TIA.

57. HRL speech, St. Louis University, November 16, 1955, Jim Shepley to Fred Gruin, July 2, 1958, HRL to Eisenhower, July 17, 1958, Eisenhower to HRL, July 18, 1958, HRL to Eisenhower, July 22, 1958, Ann Whitman to C. D. Jackson, n.d., Eisenhower to HRL, December 20, 1958, TIA.

58. David Stebenne, *Modern Republican: Arthur Larson and the Eisenhower Years* (Bloomington: Indiana University Press, 2006), pp. 224–25, 232–34; HRL to Arthur Larson, July 23, 1958, "A Presidential Commission on the Rule of Law," n.d., 1958, Arthur Larson to HRL, August 1, 6, 1958, HRL to Arthur Larson, August 4, 1958, HRL to Eisenhower, August 4, 1958, Eisenhower to Arthur Larson, August 11, 1958, Arthur Larson to HRL, May 15, 1959, HRL to Charles S. Rhyne, May 11, 1959, TIA.

59. HRL to Arthur Larson, December 15, 1958, Arthur Larson to HRL, December 14, 1959, HRL to John Jessup, February 19, 1960, TIA; *Time*, September 7, 1959, November 22, 1963; HRL to Eustace Seligman, February 3, 1960, Barry Goldwater to HRL, February 1, 1962, HRL to Barry Goldwater, February 5, 1962, HRL to William O. Douglas, February 8, 1965, HRL to Tom Clark, February 8, 1965, TIA; *Arizona Republic*, January 22, 1965; Challener, "Transcript of a Recorded Interview with Henry Luce," pp. 14–15; Stebenne, *Modern Republican*, pp. 228–34.

60. "HRL Travel Schedules," April 1953–December 1956, TIA; Elisabeth Luce Moore interview.

61. "Chronology of Events," 1953, CBL diary, January 6, 9, 10, 25, 1953, CBL Mss.

62. CBL diary, February 3, 1953, CBL Mss.; HRL to CBL, January 17, April 5, n.d., 1954, Jim Bell to *Time* desk, February 28, 1967, TIA; JSBD, June 9, 1953; Luigi Barzini to HRL, June 12, 1956, TIA; JSBD, April 4, 1953; "The Reminiscences of William Morrow Fechteler" (1962), pp. 139–40, 172, COHP.

63. JSBD, September 10, 22, 1953, January 23, 1954; HRL to Eisenhower, April 27, 1953, HRL to C. D. Jackson, December 1, 1954, Charles Auchincloss to HRL, April 25, 1953, HRL to Charles Auchincloss, April 30, 1953, HRL to Bernard Berenson, May 18, 1955, HRL to Enrico Minola, December 2, 1953, HRL to Giuseppe Medici, March 13, 1954, HRL, "Conversation of Malgodi," August 31, 1956, TIA.

64. Mario del Pero, "Containing Containment: Rethinking Italy's Experience During the Cold War," *Journal of Modern Italian Studies* 8 (2003): 532–55; Mario del Pero, "American Pressures and Their Containment in Italy during the Ambassadorship of Clare Boothe Luce, 1953–1956," *Diplomatic History* 28 (2004): 407–39.

65. Del Pero, "American Pressures," pp. 421–27.

66. Letitia Baldrige, "My Life with Mrs. Luce," *Town and Country*, n.d., pp. 78–82, TIA.

67. Ibid., p. 82; Elisabeth Luce Moore interview; Ralph G. Martin, *Henry and Clare: An Intimate Portrait of the Luces* (New York: G. P. Putnam, 1991), pp. 330–32.

68. Elisabeth Luce Moore interview; Henry Luce III interview; Richard Clurman interview; Martin, *Henry and Clare*, pp. 352–54.

XIII NATIONAL PURPOSE

1. HRL unfinished memoir, pp. 46–48, TIA.

2. Robert T. Elson, *The World of Time Inc.: The Intimate History of a Publishing Enterprise, 1941–1960* (New York: Atheneum, 1973), pp. 394–95; Thomas Griffith, *The Waist-High Culture* (New York: Harper & Brothers, 1959), pp. 100–3.

3. *Time*, July 4, 1955, September 3, 1956, February 22, 1954; HRL, "Republican Nominations," July 27, 1965, HRL Mss., LC.

4. Carlos Romulo speech to American Society of Newspaper Editors, April 16, 1959, TIA; *Fact*, January–February 1964; "The *Time* Version," *Commonweal*, November 15, 1957; HRL to William V. Griffin, August 12, 1955, TIA.

5. *Life*, December 3, 1945; Wendy Kozol, *Life's America: Family and Nation in Postwar Photo-Journalism* (Philadelphia: Temple University Press, 1994), pp. 19–21.

6. *Life*, November 15, 29, 1954, June 13, July 25, 1955, January 16, 30, April 9, September 10, 1956, August 25, 1958.

7. *Life*, February 14, December 12, 1955.

8. *Life*, December 6, 1954, January 31, April 11, May 2, August 8, 1955, June 18, October 29, 1956, July 29, October 7, 1957.

9. René Carpenter to Edward Thompson, September 25, 1959, Edward Thompson to René Carpenter, October 1, 1959, Carmichael to Graves, memorandum, February 20, 1959, TIA; *New Yorker*, October 15, 1960; *Esquire*, July 1960; Edward Thompson to John Glenn, January 13, 1962, HRL to C. D. Jackson, March 2, 1962, TIA; Walter Cunningham, *The All-American Boys* (New York: Macmillan, 1978), pp. 167–68; *Life*, August 17, 1959; Loudon Wainwright, *The Great American Magazine: An Inside History of Life* (New York: Alfred A. Knopf, 1986), pp. 251–79; Tom Wolfe, *The Right Stuff* (New York: Farrar, Straus & Giroux, 1979), pp. 140–42.

10. Andrew Heiskell interview; *Life*, February 21, May 23, 1955, May 7, 1956, October 14, 1957, September 29, October 6, 20, November 3, December 8, 1958, June 20, October 19, 1959.

11. *Life*, November 22, 1954, July 4, 1955, December 24, 1956; Kozol, *Life's America*, pp. 69–75.

12. Editors of Fortune, *The Changing American Market* (Garden City, N.Y.: Hanover House, 1955), pp. 7–12, 197–229; *Fortune*, August 1953; *Life*, September 6, 1954, June 20, August 15, 1955, January 23, June 18, 1956, February 18, September 23, 1957, March 17, 1958.

13. JSBD, June 9, 16, July 27, 28, 1953.

14. JSBD, July 7, 9, 27, 28, August 6, 13, 1953; Elson, *World of Time Inc.*, pp. 342–43, 348.

15. JSBD, August 18, 19, 21, 25, September 3, 14, 18, 25, 1953; HRL speech to *Sports Illustrated* staff, n.d., 1965, TIA; Elson, *World of Time Inc.*, pp. 343–45.

16. JSBD, September 25, November 17, December 14, 15, 18, 1953, January 27, 1954.

17. JSBD, March 16, 30, 31, 1954; Andrew Heiskell interview; HRL to Leo Burnett, October 13, 1955, TIA.

18. *Sports Illustrated*, August 16, 1954.

19. Ibid.

20. Frank Deford, "Introduction," in *Sports Illustrated: The Anniversary Book* (New York: Time Inc., 2004), pp. 10–11; *Sports Illustrated*, August 16, 1954–August 9, 1955.

21. *Sports Illustrated*, August 23, 1954, May 16, June 13, December 5, 1955, December 20, 1965; Rob Fleder, ed., *Sports Illustrated: Fifty Years of Great Writing, 1954–2004* (New York: Time Inc., 2004).

22. *Sports Illustrated*, January 2, 1956.

23. Audrey Foote, Journal Entry, Paris 1956, Timothy Foote to Henry Luce III, n.d., 2000, Henry Luce III to Timothy Foote, February 14, 2000, privately held; Corinne Thrasher to Grace Cunningham, January 28, 1959, TIA.

24. Andrew Heiskell interview, Elisabeth Luce Moore interview; Mary Bancroft to HRL, May 13, 1950, Bancroft diary, February 9, 1957, January 17, 1960, Bancroft Mss.

25. Andrew Heiskell interview; Elisabeth Luce Moore interview; Henry Graff interview; JSBD, January 12, 1953; Richard Clurman interview; Mary Bancroft diary, December 10, 1950, Bancroft Mss.

26. Mary Bancroft to HRL, April 22, 1958, Bancroft to W. A. Swanberg, July 31, 1971, Bancroft Mss.

27. Mary Bancroft to HRL, September 7, 28, 1947, Bancroft to Allen Dulles, September 27, 1947, Bancroft memo, January 22, 1971, Bancroft Mss.

28. Mary Bancroft to HRL, September 7, 1947, February 18, 1948, n.d., 1951, Bancroft memo, January 22, 1971, Bancroft Mss.

29. Mary Bancroft to HRL, July 10, 1951, April 22, 1958, Bancroft Mss.; HRL to Bancroft, August 10, December, n.d., 1948, May 11, 13, 19, 1949, November 26, 1949, February 22, May 7, 1950, Bancroft to W. A. Swanberg, March 15, 1971, W. A. Swanberg Mss.

30. Mary Bancroft diary, February 9, May 3, 1957, January 17, 1960, Bancroft to HRL, January 1, 1948, February 25, 1952, July 17, 1955, Allen Grover to Bancroft, June 10, 1954, Bancroft Mss.

31. HRL to Mary Bancroft, June 10, 1950, Swanberg Mss.; Bancroft to HRL, February 25, 1952, July 17, 1955, February 19, 1956, Bancroft diary entry, January 17, 1960, Bancroft Mss.; Corinne Thrasher to HRL, July 10, 1947, TIA.

32. Mary Bancroft to HRL, August 20, 1959, Bancroft Memo, December 1, 1970, Bancroft Mss.

33. Mary Bancroft diary, February 9, 1957, Bancroft Mss.

34. Jeanne Campbell interview; transcript of Jeanne Campbell interview with W. A. Swanberg, September 16, 1972, W. A. Swanberg Mss.; *Daily Telegraph* (London), November 29, 1996; Wilfred Sheed, *Clare Boothe Luce* (New York: E. P. Dutton, 1982), pp. 125–26; Ralph G. Martin, *Henry and Clare: An Intimate Portrait of the Luces* (New York: G. P. Putnam, 1991), pp. 335–37.

35. Jeanne Campbell interview; Campbell-Swanberg interview, n.d., Swanberg Mss.

36. Jeanne Campbell interview; *Daily Telegraph* (London), September 23, 2007; Martin, *Henry and Clare*, pp. 344–46.

37. Jeanne Campbell interview; Campbell-Swanberg interview, Swanberg Mss.; W. A. Swanberg, *Luce and His Empire* (New York: Charles Scribner's Sons, 1972), pp. 403–4; Martin, *Henry and Clare*, pp. 344–48.

38. *New York Times*, March 25, 1966; Alex Groner to Andrew Heiskell, November 3, 1961, Bill Furth to Heiskell, November 30, 1961, Ralph Paine to HRL, October 30, 1961, HRL to Paine, November 13, 1961, "Notes of phone call from HRL in Honolulu," August 2, 1965, TIA; *New York Times*, March 25, 1966.

39. Mary Bancroft to W. A. Swanberg, May 1, 1971, Bancroft Mss.; Jeanne Campbell interview; Elson, *World of Time Inc.*, pp. 428–29; Martin, *Henry and Clare*, pp. 346–48.

40. Elisabeth Luce Moore interview; Elson, *World of Time Inc.*, pp. 428–29; Martin, *Henry and Clare*, pp. 346–48; *Time*, September 29, 1958.

41. *Time*, September 8, 1959, May 16, 1960.

42. "Let There be *Life!*" *Nation*, November 23, 1957, p. 378; *New York Herald-Tribune*, September 17, 1959; John W. Jeffries, "The 'Quest for National Purpose' of 1960," *American Quarterly* 30 (Autumn 1978): 453–55.

43. "The Reminiscences of Robert Hutchins," 1967, pp. 77–78, COHP; HRL to Hutchins, December 15, 1946, TIA; *New York Times*, June 14, October 19, 1957, July 14, 1958.

44. W. A. Swanberg, *Norman Thomas: The Last Idealist* (New York: Charles Scribner's Sons, 1976), p. 377; Norman Thomas to HRL, June 20, 1956, HRL to Thomas, June 25, 1956, Bill Furth to Hedley Donovan, June 25, 1956, HRL to Marshall Berger, June 23, 1958, HRL to Hubert Humphrey, August 20, 1959, TIA.

45. Elson, *World of Time Inc.*, pp. 464–65; Max Ways, *Beyond Survival* (New York: Harper Bros., 1959).

46. HRL to John Courtney Murray, January 6, 9, 1960, HRL to Archibald MacLeish, February 16, 1960, HRL, "The Age We Enter," January 1958, HRL, "The Future of the American Proposition," n.d., 1962, TIA.

47. *New York Times*, February 7, 8, 1960; President's Commission on National

Goals, *Goals for Americans* (Englewood Cliffs, N.J.: Prentice-Hall, 1960); Stephen R. Graubard, "The Nation's Goals," *Commonweal* 73 (1961): 379–81.

48. John K. Jessup et al., *The National Purpose* (New York: Holt, Rinehart & Winston, 1960).

49. Adlai Stevenson, " 'Extend Our Vision . . . to All Mankind,' " pp. 22–23, 34–35, Archibald MacLeish, " ' We have Purpose . . . We All Know It,' " pp. 41–42, Clinton Rossiter, "We Must Show the Way to Enduring Peace," pp. 87–88, David Sarnoff, " 'Turn Cold War Tide in America's Favor,' " pp, 49–50, Walter Lippmann, "National Purpose," pp. 131–32, Albert Wohlstetter, "No Highway to High Purpose," pp. 106–7, James Reston, "Our History Suggests a Remedy," pp. 116–17, all in Jessup et al., *The National Purpose.*

50. Jeffries, "The 'Quest for National Purpose' of 1960," pp. 467–70; Joe David Brown to HRL, August 19, 1952, HRL, "The Future of the American Proposition," n.d., 1962, TIA; Elson, *World of Time Inc.*, p. 464.

51. *Life*, July 19, August 30, 1937, October 3, 1938, March 21, 1949; "*Life* and Negroes," memo, n.d., 1939, Edward S. Lewis to HRL, March 23, 1949, J. G. Coughlin to HRL, May 23, 1949, Peter Prentice to HRL, October 13, 1943, HRL to editors, October 14, 1943, TIA.

52. HRL to JSB, March 25, 1956, Edward K. Thompson memo, March 21, 1956, Moffett to Thompson, November 16, 1956, Dick Stolley to Edward K. Thompson et al., October 4, 5, 6, 8, 1956, Edward K. Thompson to Bob Wallace et al., December 4, 1956, TIA; *Life*, February 20, 1956, September 16, 23, 30, October 7, 1957; *Time*, October 7, 1957; Long to Rowen et al., April 27, 1961, Edward K. Thompson to Sam G. Sanders, February 22, 1963, TIA; Andrew Heiskell interview.

53. *Time*, December 2, 1957.

54. John F. Kennedy, *Why England Slept* (New York: W. Funk, Inc., 1940); HRL, "Foreword to John Kennedy's book *Why England Slept*," July 1940, TIA; John Steele, interview with Henry R. Luce, November 11, 1965, pp. 1–3, JFKL; John F. Kennedy to HRL, July 9, 1940, TIA.

55. HRL to Nixon, April 28, 1959, Nixon to HRL, February 24, 1958, February 13, 1959, HRL to Nixon, July 29, 1960, William Benton to HRL, August 1, 1960, HRL to William Benton, August 2, 1960, Jacqueline Kennedy to HRL, n.d., 1954, Time Inc. Newsletter, August 12, 1960, TIA; Steele, interview with Luce, November 11, 1965, pp. 8, 13–18, JFKL; Henry Luce III interview.

56. Richard Clurman interview; Andrew Heiskell interview; *Life*, August 15, 1960; Elson, *World of Time Inc.*, pp. 472–75; *New York Times*, August 5, 6, 1960.

57. Steele, interview with Luce, November 11, 1965, pp. 9–12, 18, JFKL; Albert Furth to Bela Kornitzer, June 15, 1962, TIA; Henry Luce III interview.

58. Steele, interview with Luce, November 11, 1965, pp. 18–20, JFKL; HRL to Nixon, November 14, 1960, HRL memo, July, n.d., 1960, TIA; John Pollack, *Billy Graham: Evangelist to the World* (San Francisco: Harper & Row, 1979); John Pollack memo, n.d., HRL to William Dwight Whitney, January 26, 1961, TIA; *Life*, August 15, 1960; Elson, *World of Time Inc.*, pp. 475–76.

59. Philip L. Graham to HRL, December 29, 1960, "Inauguration Schedule," Emeline Nollen to Mrs. William Scarlett, June 6, 1961, "Foreword to . . . *Why England Slept*," 1961, TIA.

60. HRL to Joe David Brown, September 29, 1962, TIA; Steele interview with HRL, November 11, 1965, pp. 22–31, JFKL; John F. Kennedy, "Message to *Time*'s Fortieth Anniversary Dinner," May 6, 1963, TIA; David Halberstam, *The Powers That Be* (New York: Alfred A. Knopf, 1979), pp. 351–67.

61. John F. Kennedy to HRL, June 12, August 9, 1962, HRL to John F. Kennedy, June 23, August 10, 1962, TIA; Steele interview with HRL, pp. 34–37, JFKL; Otto Fuerbringer to John Steele, December 1, 1962, HRL, "Meeting with JFK on Monday, October 24, 1962," Fuerbringer to HRL, December 1, 1962, TIA.

62. *Time*, November 29, 1963; *Life*, November 29, 1963; Curtis Prendergast, *The*

World of Time Inc.: The Intimate History of a Changing Enterprise, 1960–1980 (New York: Atheneum, 1986), pp. 120–33.

63. *Time*, November 29, 1963; *Life*, December 9, 1963; Theodore H. White, *In Search of History: A Personal Adventure* (New York: Harper & Row, 1978), pp. 518–26.

64. Steele interview with HRL, pp. 41–42, JFKL; Elisabeth Luce Moore interview; Henry Luce III interview.

XIV   LETTING GO

1. HRL to CBL, n.d., 1960, CBL Mss.; Jeanne Campbell interview; Elisabeth Luce Moore interview.

2. CBL to John Courtney Murray, October 25, 1959, CBL to HRL, n.d., 1959, CBL untitled, undated memo, 1959, CBL to HRL, n.d., 1959, CBL Mss.

3. HRL to John Courtney Murray, n.d., 1960, CBL Mss.

4. CBL to HRL, n.d., 1959, CBL untitled, undated memo, n.d., 1960 CBL Mss.; Elisabeth Luce Moore interview.

5. Ralph G. Martin, *Henry and Clare: An Intimate Portrait of the Luces* (New York: G. P. Putnam, 1991), pp. 367–72.

6. CBL to John Courtney Murray, October 25, 1959, n.d., 1960, CBL, "Memo for John Courtney Murray," n.d., 1960, HRL to John Courtney Murray, n.d., 1960; CBL Mss., Elisabeth Luce Moore interview.

7. CBL to Gerald Heard, June 26, 1951, CBL to Sidney Cohen, n.d., 1961, CBL memo, n.d., 1960, Gerald Heard to CBL, February 15, 1966, CBL Mss.; *New York Times*, March 2, 1968; Norman O. Brown, *Love's Body* (New York: Random House, 1966); Theodore Roszak, *The Making of a Counter Culture: Reflections on the Technocratic Society and its Youthful Opposition* (Garden City, N.Y.: Doubleday, 1969).

8. CBL to Sidney Cohen, n.d., 1961, "Report to Dr. Sidney Cohen," April 30, 1962, CBL Mss.; *Financial Times*, August 7, 1982; *Washington Post*, October 22, 1996.

9. HRL to Michael Barrie, July 21, 1959, TIA; "HRL took 100 Gamma of L.S.D.," n.d., 1960, CBL to Sidney Cohen, March 12, 1960, HRL to Gerald Heard, April 21, 1960, CBL diary, "LSD experiments," n.d., 1960, September 11, 1963, CBL to HRL, April 20, 1960, Gerald Heard to HRL, February 9, 1960, March 1, 1961, January 28, September 7, 1963, CBL Mss.; *New York Post*, March 2, 1968; Michael Barrie to HRL, July 27, 1961, Albert Furth to Ken Froslid, September 18, 1961, TIA.

10. HRL to CBL, n.d., 1960, CBL memo, n.d., 1960, HRL to John Courtney Murray, n.d., 1960, CBL to John Courtney Murray, October 25, 1959, CBL Memo to John Courtney Murray, " 'Go in Peace' or 'Stay in Peace,' " n.d., 1960, CBL, "Imaginary Interview," June 10, 1960, CBL Mss.

11. CBL to HRL, February 29, 1960, CBL, "Pulling for the Horizon," March 18, 1960, CBL, "What happens to me without you," n.d., 1960, HRL to CBL, July 20, 1960, n.d., 1960, CBL, "A Memo to Harry about Diminishments," n.d., 1960 (annotated later), CBL to HRL, November 26, 1961, HRL to CBL, n.d., 1962, August 8, 1962, May 6, 1966, CBL Mss.

12. HRL to Peter Luce, May 17, 1950, February 18, 1953, TIA; JSBD, December 28, 1949; HRL to CBL, July, n.d., 1959, CBL diary, n.d., 1960, CBL Mss.; Henry Luce III interview; Peter Luce interview; Elisabeth Luce Moore interview; Christopher Luce interview.

13. Elisabeth Luce Moore interview; Henry Luce III interview; HRL to Chiang Kai-shek, October 23, 1957, April 26, 1958, "The National Presbyterian Church," May 23, 1972, Emmie Nollen to Gloria Conn, July 8, 1965, HRL, "Two Assurances of Faith" (New York: Henry Luce Foundation, 1964), TIA.

14. JSBD, October 7, 1950, August 20, 1951; HRL to James A. Pike, December 23, 1961, Pike to HRL, December 29, 1961, HRL to André Laguerre, February 23, 1954, HRL to Claude E. Forkner, June 30, 1956, HRL to Henry Van Dusen, June 28, 1962, Van Dusen to HRL, n.d., 1964, HRL to Van Dusen, September 10, 1964, TIA; *New York Times*, January 10, 1946.

15. "Declaration of Intent of Henry Robinson Luce," April 7, 1952, CBL Mss.; HRL to Bishop G. Bromley Oxnam, n.d., 1949, Oxnam to HRL, January 3, 1950, Harold Matson to Robert Coughlan, August 11, 1948, HRL to Evelyn Waugh, August 18, 1949, HRL to Matthew Cavell, March 4, 1946, HRL to Editors, "The Catholic Faith," n.d., 1960, TIA; "The Time of Henry Luce's Life," *Christian Century*, May 22, 1963.

16. HRL, "A Speculation about A. D. 1980," December 1955, TIA; "Random Notes on HRL's random remarks about Courtney-Murray," n.d., 1960, CBL to HRL, n.d., 1960, CBL Mss.; HRL to Henry Sloane Coffin, October 21, 1948, Coffin to HRL, October 22, 1948, HRL to Archibald MacLeish, May 16, 1959, HRL to Bishop James A. Pike, December 23, 1961, TIA.

17. Andrew Heiskell interview; Henry Luce III interview; Robert T. Elson, *The World of Time Inc.: The Intimate History of a Publishing Enterprise* (New York: Atheneum, 1973), pp. 331–34.

18. JSBD, July 16, 1947, January 3, 1951, March 20, 1952.

19. Elson, *World of Time Inc.*, pp. 331–34; JSBD, January 5, 1951; Andrew Heiskell interview; Henry Luce III interview.

20. Henry Luce III interview; CBL memo, n.d., 1960, CBL Mss.; Elson, *World of Time Inc.*, pp. 331–34; Curtis Prendergast, *The World of Time Inc.: The Intimate History of a Changing Enterprise, 1960–1980* (New York: Atheneum, 1986), p. 8.

21. HRL to Staff, April 21, 1960; *New York Times*, April 22, 1960, April 17, 1964; Prendergast, *World of Time Inc.*, pp. 11–12; W. A. Swanberg, *Luce and His Empire* (New York: Charles Scribner's Sons, 1972), pp. 442–43; Henry Luce III interview.

22. *New York Times*, May 7, 1963; *Advertising Age*, March 25, 1963; Murray Gart to HRL, May 8, 1963, HRL to Paul Tillich, May 14, 1963, TIA; Andrew Heiskell interview.

23. HRL, "*Life*: A New Prospectus for the Sixties," n.d., 1962, TIA; Prendergast, *World of Time Inc.*, pp. 37–48; Loudon Wainwright, *The Great American Magazine: An Inside History of Life* (New York: Alfred A. Knopf, 1986), pp. 336–39.

24. Andrew Heiskell interview; Henry Luce III interview; Prendergast, *World of Time Inc.*, pp. 65–80.

25. Andrew Heiskell interview; Richard Clurman interview; HRL memo to staff, n.d., 1964, "Books," TIA; Prendergast, *World of Time Inc.*, pp. 87–100.

26. Henry Grunwald interview; Andrew Heiskell interview; HRL, "The Rim of Asia, 1964," n.d., 1964, TIA.

27. John Steele to Otto Fuerbringer and R. Clurman, December 12, 1964, Lyndon B. Johnson to HRL, December 5, 1963, November 10, 1964, Fischer to HRL, July 16, 1964, John Steele to HRL, February 6, 1965, Lyndon B. Johnson to HRL, March 24, September 8, 1965, HRL to Lyndon B. Johnson, August 16, 1965, Robert Storey to HRL, July 9, 1965, HRL to Harry McPherson, September 3, 1965, TIA.

28. HRL to Lyndon B. Johnson, July 16, 1960, Lyndon B. Johnson to HRL, July 26, 1960, HRL to Lyndon B. Johnson, November 17, 1960, November 27, 1963, May 13, 1964, HRL speech, Washington, D.C., January 26, 1965, TIA.

29. HRL, "The Significance of the Goldwater Nomination," n.d., 1964, HRL to Arthur Goodhart, July 28, 1964, HRL to Hedley Donovan, August 13, 1964, HRL to Leo Burnett, October 26, 1964, HRL to Thomas Griffith, September 4, 1964, TIA; *Time*, October 30, 1964; *Life*, October 30, 1964; Henry Luce III interview.

30. Robert Elson to John Courtney Murray, April 28, 1966, Murray to Elson, May 4, 1966, "Notes on a Conversation," April 28, 1966, TIA.

31. John W. O'Daniel to HRL and CBL, March 29, 1957, O'Daniel to HRL, May 15, 20, 31, 1957, HRL to O'Daniel, May 24, June 10, December 18, 1957, American Friends of Vietnam Mss.; Leo Cherne to HRL, April 12, 1957, HRL to Cherne, April 15, 1957, press release, May 2, 1957, TIA; cable to LIFE, April 23, 1957, TD; *Time*, February 11, October 21, 1957, February 8, 1959, May 7, 1960.

32. Dwight D. Eisenhower to HRL, May 12, 1957, HRL to Henry Cabot Lodge, April 14, 1961, Lodge to HRL, April 19, 1961, December 13, 1965, HRL to Lodge, September 15, 1966, Lodge to HRL, September 20, 1966, TIA; *Time*, February 26, 1965; Elisabeth Luce Moore interview; Richard Clurman interview.

33. Hugh Sidey to HRL, February 16, 1967, TIA; Andrew Heiskell interview.

34. *Time*, November 30, 1962, August 9, October 11, 1963; Richard Clurman interview; David Halberstam interview; David Halberstam, *The Powers That Be* (New York: Alfred A. Knopf, 1979), pp. 459–67.

35. *New York Times*, April 17, 1964.

36. *Time*, April 24, 1964; "The Luce-Donovan Dinner," May 25, 1964, TIA; Henry Grunwald interview.

37. HRL to G. D. Birla, March 8, 1966, HRL to Norman Chandler, August 25, 1965, "Notes of phone call from HRL in Honolulu," August 2, 1965, TIA; CBL, "Notes on HRL's health," May 25, 1972, CBL Mss.

38. Cass Canfield to HRL, July 18, 1959, Michael Bessie to HRL, January 5, 1965, April 16, 1966, HRL to Michael Bessie, January 8, 1965, April 19, 1966, HRL unpublished memoir, n.d., 1966–67, TIA.

39. HRL unpublished memoir, n.d., 1966–67, TIA.

40. Dr. Milton Benjamin Rosenbluth, Medical Summary, November 30, 1942, Rosenbluth to HRL, April 20, 1951, Julius Ochs Sulzberger, October 31, 1947, TIA; "The Practical Management of Hypertension," *Bulletin of the New York Academy of Medicine* XX (November 1944): 557–74; CBL, untitled memo on HRL's health, May 25, 1972, CBL Mss.

EPILOGUE

1. *Time*, May 10, 1967; *Newsweek*, May 13, 1967; *New York Times*, March 1, 1967; Curtis Prendergast, *The World of Time Inc.: The Intimate History of a Changing Enterprise, 1960–1980* (New York: Atheneum, 1986), pp. 203–7.

2. *New York Times*, March 1, 2, 4, 1967.

3. CBL, untitled memo on HRL's health, May 25, 1972, CBL Mss.; HRL Elson interview, 1964, TIA; HRL to LH, March, n.d., 1932, LT Mss.; HRL will, April 15, 1964, TIA; *New York Times*, March 1, 2, 4, 1967.

4. Andrew Heiskell interview; *Time*, December 19, 1972; *Life*, December 29, 1972; Loudon Wainwright, *The Great American Magazine: An Inside History of Life* (New York: Alfred A. Knopf, 1986), pp, 340–45, 412–31.

5. *New York Times*, March 1, 1967.

6. Andrew Kopkind, "Serving Time," *New York Review of Books*, September 12, 1968.

7. Richard Hofstadter, "The Paranoid Style in American Politics," *Harper's*, November 1964, pp. 77–86; Hofstadter, *The Paranoid Style in American Politics* (New York: Alfred A. Knopf, 1966); Theodor W. Adorno, *Culture Industry* (London: Routledge, 1991); T. W. Adorno, Else Frenkel-Brunswik, Daniel J. Levinson, and R. Nevitt Sanford, *The Authoritarian Personality*, ed. Max Horkheimer and Samuel Flowerman (New York: Harper and Brothers, 1950).

8. *New York Times*, March 1, 1967.

ACKNOWLEDGMENTS

I owe more than usual thanks to the many people who helped me during my prolonged work on this book. I begin with my editor and friend of thirty years, Ash Green. Our long and happy relationship has meant a great deal to me, as has his help on all my books—not least on this one. I am grateful as well to the many people at Knopf who have helped this project through production—among them Sarah Sherbill, Andrew Carlson, and Soonyoung Kwon. My agent, Peter Matson, has provided support, advice, and friendship for many years.

I was fortunate to receive support in the early stages of my work from the Media Studies Center at Columbia University and the Russell Sage Foundation, and I want to thank their directors, Ev Dennis and Eric Wanner, as well as the colleagues I met at both institutions.

I have been particularly fortunate in the assistance I have received from talented research assistants, many of them graduate students at Columbia. They include, among others, Dustin Abnet, Chris Cappozola, David Ekbladh, Robert Fleegler, Charles Forcey, Lisa Jarvinen, David Kaden, Jon Kasparek, Robert Lifset, Kevin Murphy, Sharon Musher, Nathan Perl-Rosenthal, Kevin Powers, Russell Rickford, Elizabeth Robeson, Jesse Salazar, Moshik Temkin, Benjamin Waterhouse, and Tim White. I am deeply grateful to them all. I thank as well Bill Hooper and the rest of the staff of the Time Inc. Archives, the Manuscript Division of the Library of Congress, and the Franklin D. Roosevelt Library. Martin Baldessari was of great help in identifying and acquiring photographs.

I am grateful to Henry Luce III and Jason McManus for their help in gaining me access to the Time Inc. Archives; and Peter Luce, who provided me with material privately held by the family. I am also grateful to the many people who generously shared with me their memories of Henry R. Luce: among them his sons Peter Luce and Henry Luce III; his sister, Elisabeth Luce Moore; his brother-in-law Leslie Severinghaus; his first wife, Lila Luce Tyng; his grandson Christopher Luce; his Time Inc. colleagues Andrew Heiskell, Richard Clurman, Thomas Griffith, Robert Manning, and Henry Grunwald; his pastor David H. Read; and Jeanne Campbell, Sander Vanocur, and Henry Graff. David Halberstam provided me with his own memories of reporting in Vietnam and the experience of Time Inc. correspondents there. Arthur Schlesinger was, as always, a generous friend and was enormously helpful in guiding me to people who could be helpful to me.

I owe a very special debt to the friends and colleagues who read and commented on the manuscript: among them Eric Foner, Nicholas Lemann, David Nasaw, and Frank Rich. I was able to present parts of my work to many people over the years, and the responses of those who attended these events helped me immeasurably: in the United States, the Twentieth-Century Politics and Society Workshop at Columbia (with special thanks to Ira Katznelson and Bob Shapiro), the Russell Sage Foundation, Vassar College, Columbia Journalism School, New York University, and the University of Colorado at Boulder; in Britain, the Rothermere American Institute at Oxford University, the Work in Progress Seminar of the Oxford History Faculty, Nuffield College, Oxford, the University of Reading, Cambridge University, the University of Essex, University College, London, and King's College, London; in Paris, L'École des Haute Études en Sciences Sociale and Sciences Po; and in Italy, the University of Florence and the University of Torino. Most of all, I am grateful to Columbia University and to my friends and colleagues in the Columbia Department of History from whom I have learned so much.

This book is dedicated to my wife, Evangeline Morphos, for her constant interest in this project, for her invaluable help with it, and for her love and support. This is also for my daughter, Elly, the light of both our lives.

INDEX

A NOTE ABOUT THE AUTHOR

Alan Brinkley is the Allan Nevins Professor of History at Columbia University. His previous books include *Voices of Protest: Huey Long, Father Coughlin, and the Great Depression*, which won the National Book Award for History; *The End of Reform: New Deal Liberalism in Recession and War*; and *Liberalism and Its Discontents*. His essays, articles, and reviews have appeared in *The American Historical Review*, *The New York Times Book Review*, *The New York Review of Books*, the *London Review of Books*, *The Times Literary Supplement*, and *The New Republic*, among other publications. He lives in New York City.

A NOTE ON THE TYPE

This book was set in Janson, a typeface long thought to have been made by the Dutchman Anton Janson, who was a practicing typefounder in Leipzig during the years 1668–1687. However, it has been conclusively demonstrated that these types are actually the work of Nicholas Kis (1650–1702), a Hungarian, who most probably learned his trade from the master Dutch typefounder Dirk Voskens. The type is an excellent example of the influential and sturdy Dutch types that prevailed in England up to the time William Caslon (1692–1766) developed his own incomparable designs from them.

Composed by North Market Street Graphics,
Lancaster, Pennsylvania

Printed and bound by Berryville Graphics,
Berryville, Virginia